Operations Management

McGraw-Hill Series in Management

Consulting Editors:
Fred Luthans and Keith Davis

Operations Management

SECOND EDITION

James B. Dilworth

University of Alabama at Birmingham

The McGraw-Hill Companies, Inc.

New York   St. Louis   San Francisco   Auckland
Bogotá   Caracas   Lisbon   London   Madrid
Mexico City   Milan   Montreal   New Delhi
San Juan   Singapore   Sydney   Tokyo   Toronto

Dedicated with love to Ginger, Jimmy, Caroline, Jessica Leigh, and Michael, and to the memory of my father, my mother, and Andrew

McGraw-Hill

*A Division of The **McGraw-Hill** Companies*

This book was set in ITC New Baskerville by The Clarinda Company.
The editors were Lynn Richardson, Dan Alpert, and Curt Berkowitz;
the design was done by Keithley and Associates, Inc.;
the production supervisor was Denise L. Puryear.
The photo editor was Kathy Bendo;
the photo researcher was Mia Galison.
R. R. Donnelley & Sons Company was printer and binder.
Cover photo: © Color Box, FPG International

Library of Congress Cataloging-in-Publication Data

Dilworth, James B., (date).
    Operations management / James B. Dilworth. — 2d ed.
        p.   cm.
    Includes bibliographical references and index.
    ISBN 0-07-017021-5
    1. Production management.   I. Title
TS155.D544   1996
658.5—dc20   95—39692

Chapter 1: Burger King® Corporation. Chapter 2: Lonnie Duka/Tony Stone Images. Chapter 3: Jerry Swanson. Chapter 4: Lawrence Migdale/Stock, Boston. Chapter 5: Micheal Simpson/FPG. Chapter 6: Frank Siteman/Tony Stone Images. Chapter 7: Motorola. Chapter 8: Ed Lallo/Gamma-Liaison. Chapter 9: Bob Grieser, San Diego, California. Chapter 10: Ted Horowitz/Stock Market. Chapter 11: © Tim Redel, New York City. Chapter 12: Daemmrich/Stock, Boston. Chapter 13: Peter Miller/Image Bank. Chapter 14: Billy E. Barnes/Jeroboam. Chapter 15: Alex Bartel/Picture Cube. Chapter 16: Lawrence S. Burr, Fairfax, California. Chapter 17: J. Sohm/Chromosohm/Image Works. Chapter 18: Barros & Barros/Image Bank.

About the Author

JAMES B. DILWORTH is Professor of Management at the University of Alabama at Birmingham. He received his B.S. at the University of Alabama and his M.S. at Oklahoma State University. Before obtaining his Ph.D. in Industrial Engineering and Management at Oklahoma State University, he worked for eight years in industry, first as an industrial engineer, and later as a manager of production control, an internal consultant, and a manager of the office of public systems. A specialist in production and operations management, Professor Dilworth has published many articles and is certified at the Fellow level by the American Production and Inventory Control Society. He is the author of *Production and Operations Management,* Fifth Edition (McGraw-Hill, 1993) and *Production Observations from Japan* (American Production and Inventory Control Society, 1985) and is the editor of *Strategic and Tactical Issues in Just-in-Time Manufacturing* (Proceedings of the 1985 Conference of the Association for Manufacturing Excellence). Professor Dilworth received the Dean's Teaching Award for the 1984–85 academic year from the University of Alabama in Birmingham. In 1987, he prepared a research report for the Association for Manufacturing Excellence titled *Information Systems for JIT Manufacturing.*

CONTENTS IN BRIEF

CONTENTS

PREFACE

THE IMPORTANCE OF STUDYING OPERATIONS MANAGEMENT

As a primary business function, along with marketing and finance, the operations function plays a vital role in achieving a company's strategic plans. Since the operations function produces the goods and provides the services, it typically involves the greatest portion of the company's employees and is responsible for a large portion of the firm's capital assets. It has a major impact on quality and is often the visible face of the company with which the customer must deal. Customer service, product/service delivery, quality issues, and the effectiveness of many customer interactions are all operations activities.

In the face of increased international competition, U.S. firms have lost market share and have responded by working to improve both their operating efficiencies and the quality of their goods and services. With this renewed emphasis on operations, it has become increasingly important that students have an understanding of operations management's significance to the success of the companies where they will work.

Most business schools offer at least one course that provides students with a basic knowledge of the issues and methods involved in the production of goods and/or services. This book provides material for such a course, and it includes material on production of both goods and services because both are important segments of the economies in developed and developing nations.

In the United States, for example, manufacturing still contributes greatly to the GDP and services provide many of the jobs. An operations management course is an important opportunity for students to gain a basic understanding of issues in both manufacturing and services. If we are to prosper economically, managers must be knowledgeable regarding ways in which they can efficiently improve the internal and external service aspects of their business and the quality of their products. Knowledge of both manufacturing and services is valuable for students in various disciplines. For example, marketing majors may become involved in selling products of a manufacturer or in selling to manufacturers. Finance majors may work in banking and may make loans to manufacturers or service companies. Therefore I have tried to include a discussion of issues that operations managers face and have presented them in the contexts of manufacturing and services where it seemed appropriate.

MAJOR THEMES IN *OPERATIONS MANAGEMENT,* SECOND EDITION

As I prepared this book I tried to keep in mind several major forces that are helping to reshape operations management. I've devoted a significant amount of time to integrating these forces into *Operations Management,* 2nd Edition, and they have become themes that are woven into the text. They are outlined below:

- QUALITY—More material on quality and continuous improvement has been added. A chapter on total quality management has been updated and moved to the foundation material in the front part of the book and related more closely to strategy considerations.

- GLOBALIZATION—This book provides more recognition of the global extent of business, competition, the creation of goods and services, and the scope of operations.

- TECHNOLOGY—This book provides more discussion of the use of computers and other technology in operations. In addition, more problems have been added for which computer solutions are recommended.

- SERVICES—This book reflects the growing importance of services. It recognizes and integrates the applicability of many of the operations management issues and methods to service businesses as well as to manufacturing.

BRIDGING THE GAP BETWEEN THEORY AND PRACTICE

Students are more interested and motivated to learn a subject if they can see that actual companies in the "real world" are using the ideas and methods that they study. This edition includes *more examples*, both in boxed inserts and throughout the main text.

In addition, the new four-color design incorporates a number of photographs (many featuring real companies) that enhance interest and exemplify important text concepts.

ORGANIZED FOR FLEXIBILITY

The material within each chapter is structured to provide flexibility. Generally, the first part of each chapter introduces a topic, discusses why it is important, and relates it to the field of operations management. The application of tools, methods, and techniques is generally discussed in the latter part of a chapter or in a chapter supplement. This structure enables a professor to teach a descriptive course by omitting, or not emphasizing, the latter parts of the chapters and the quantitative supplements and using mostly discussion questions and cases, instead of problems. For a more quantitative course, one may devote more class time to the tools and problems and let the students read the chapters' introductory discussion material outside of class.

Additional revisions have been made to this edition to further maximize flexibility. The material on work measurement and time standards has been de-emphasized by making it a supplement. Since this material can be used in estimating capacity and facility size requirements it is placed where location and layout are discussed. Additionally, since readers who use linear programming will probably employ computers to perform the calculations, the supplement that reviewed the detailed steps of the simplex method has been deleted.

KEY CHANGES IN *OPERATIONS MANAGEMENT,* SECOND EDITION

Following are some of the significant content changes you may notice:

- Information on global competition and the importance of a customer focus has been integrated into Chapter 1.
- The historical perspective has been updated and placed in Supplement A.
- Information on the cost of quality and some competitive advantages of quality has been included in Chapter 2 on strategy.
- Total quality management, with the addition of quality function deployment (QDF) to help incorporate the voice of the customer into the design of goods and services, has been moved to Chapter 3.
- Chapter 5 on location now includes a discussion on determining the size and capacity needed in a facility.
- The discussion of information technology has been expanded in Chapter 7.
- Material on compensation has been combined with material on job design in Chapter 8.
- Tools for improvement have been compiled into a new Chapter 9 titled "Review and Redesign for Continuous Improvement."
- Statistical process control has been moved to Chapter 10 as the first chapter in Part Three on planning and controlling operations.
- Chapter 11, "Planning for Operations and Capacity," has been resequenced and simplified.
- Examples of period order quantity and minimum feasible lot size have been added.
- The supplement on maintenance has been revised to address total productive maintenance.
- The end-of-chapter bibliographies have been updated to add some more-recent references.

PEDAGOGICALLY SOUND

The text also includes numerous pedagogical devices to facilitate student learning. These devices include:

1. Chapter outlines
2. Key terms
3. Numerous figures
4. Application boxes to illustrate concepts with simplified example cases
5. Operations Management in Action boxes to provide examples from actual companies
6. Value boxes describe how the subject of each chapter can help add value for customers and help companies achieve competitive excellence
7. Chapter summaries

8. Solved demonstration problems

9. Numerous, quality, end-of-chapter exercises and problems

10. Computer-based problems in selected chapters

All materials have been updated, and the solved demonstration problems and end-of-chapter materials have been expanded in number.

ANCILLARY MATERIALS

For the convenience of professors and students, a number of ancillary materials are available to supplement this book:

For the Instructor

- The SOLUTIONS MANUAL, which is available to professors, provides detailed solutions to all end-of-chapter questions and problems. It also contains solutions to unsolved problems and suggested responses to discussion questions.

- The INSTRUCTOR'S MANUAL AND TEST BANK helps the instructor use the text effectively. It provides a wealth of supplementary information for enriching lectures such as, learning objectives, lecture outlines and notes, and transparency masters. Transparency masters include solutions to solved problems and other visual aids to enhance lecture material. The Instructor's Manual includes over 1,000 test items and features a range of problems to test students' knowledge, as well as containing separate answer sections for test-making facility. The test items include true/false, multiple-choice, essay questions, and problems.

- The COMPUTERIZED TEST BANK also facilitates test construction. It contains all questions from the Test File and is available to all adopters.

- The TRANSPARENCY ACETATES include 75 color overheads and include both text illustrations and original material.

- VIDEO CASSETTES. Contact your local sales representative for information regarding our Production/Operations Video Cassette Library.

For the Student

- MANAGING SERVICES: IMPROVING SERVICES THROUGH OPERATIONS MANAGEMENT by D. Keith Denton of Southwest Missouri State provides the information needed to become more knowledgeable about how to manage services and also provides a source for handling "real-life" service situations. It can be assigned as an outside reading or it can be used as a game or simulation.

Software

Software packages that can be used with this text are available from McGraw-Hill. They include two free-standing packages and two packages that require lotus or compatible spreadsheet software. Both of the Lotus template programs are available with extensive macro programs to perform operations management calculations. These templates run on IBM PC/PC-XT or true compatibles. They are available separately or packaged with the text.

- SOFTWARE TOOLS FOR OPERATIONS MANAGEMENT by Willbann D. Terpening of Gonzaga University. The primary purpose of this software is to allow the student to explore many of the techniques in operations management more productively through the use of personal computers. It is available in both 5 1/4 inch and 3 1/2 inch versions for IBM PC/PC-XT or true compatibles.

- OM EXPERT by Hamid Noori of Wilfrid Laurier University is stand-alone software consisting of thirty-two separate programs grouped into twelve modules. The software has exceptional graphics capability, is easy to use, and is available in 3 1/2 inch and 5 1/4 inch formats for IBM PC AT and compatible equipment.

- PRODUCTION/OPERATIONS MANAGEMENT TOOLS FOR SPREAD-SHEETS by Sam L. Savage of the University of Chicago and Stanford University is Lotus template software that includes add-ins like WHAT'S BEST! The software focuses on improving students' model-building skills and is available in both 5 1/4 inch and 3 1/2 inch versions.

- SPREADSHEETS FOR OPERATIONS MANAGEMENT by Everette S. Gardner, Jr., of the University of Houston is Lotus template software. These templates are industrial-strength computational engines and are available in both 5 1/4 inch and 3 1/2 inch versions.

ACKNOWLEDGMENTS

This book has drawn on the talents, advice, and encouragement of more people than I can possibly acknowledge. I would, however, like to recognize the contributions of many who have helped. First, I want to thank my wife and children, who also have experienced the hefty time demands of this project and have understood and helped me in numerous ways. I want to thank our dean, Gene Newport, my department Chair, Kris McAlister, and my other colleagues at UAB for their support, interest, and encouragement.

I am grateful to my editor Lynn Richardson, and to Dan Alpert and Curt Berkowitz, whose talents and cooperation have been essential in making this book. Working with them helped add pleasure to the task while keeping the project moving. I have not worked as directly with others, but many at McGraw-Hill, including Joe Piliero, Design Manager, and Denise Puryear, Production Supervisor, have applied great talents and hard work to make this book a success. I am sincerely grateful for their efforts. I also appreciate the contributions of Valerie Raymond for her excellent work in selecting photographs and preparing captions for them.

I want to thank Larry Ettkin, a friend at the University of Tennessee at Chattanooga, who has provided much assistance through the years and helped shape much of the material that has evolved into the book.

I greatly appreciate the comments and splendid advice of my colleagues who have reviewed and made recommendations for various editions of *Operations Manage-*

ment and who helped to establish a sound base from which we could work to develop this text:

Ben Abramowitz, University of Central Florida

Leland Ash, Oregon State University

Frank Barnes, University of North Carolina at Charlotte

Charles Bimmerle, North Texas State University

Alfred Bird, University of Houston

Roy Clinton, Northeastern Louisiana University

C.W. Dane, Oregon State University

Steve De Lurgio, University of Missouri, Kansas City

Keith Denton, Southwest Missouri State University

Lawrence P. Ettkin, University of Tennessee at Chattanooga

Jatinder Gupta, Ball State University

Basheer Khumawala, University of Houston

Thomas MacFarland, Westfield State College

Graham K. Morby, University of Massachusetts, Amherst

Emre Veral, Baruch College

Chiang Wang, California State University, Sacramento

I am also greatly indebted to the following reviewers who provided valuable input into planning the revisions that shaped *Operations Management,* Second Edition: Sal Agnihothri, SUNY—Binghamton; Eugene Fliedner, Texas A&M University; Mark Hanna, Miami University; Dan Reid, University of New Hampshire.

I again want to express my gratitude to Betty Smith, our department's secretary, who has helped in many ways as these materials have been developed. Her assistance to me and the department is greatly appreciated.

James B. Dilworth

FOUNDATION MATERIAL

Part I of this book contains four chapters and five informational supplements. Together they provide a foundation for the further study of production and operations management. Chapter 1 introduces the operations function in manufacturing and in service settings and briefly reviews some of the activities of operations managers. Three types of manufacturing operations introduced in the first chapter are job shop, batch, and repetitive production plants. Following Chapter 1, Supplement A presents some significant events in the evolution of operations management to provide historical perspective on the field; Supplement B provides a verbal tour of a plant engaged in repetitive production; Supplement C provides a tour of a plant engaged in job shop production; Supplement D outlines many of the work activities in a distribution system for a retail chain.

The operations function is a vital component of a business, making major contributions to achievement of the company's strategic plans. Chapter 2 discusses how operations relate to the long-range, strategic decisions that managers make to guide a company. Supplement E, which follows Chapter 2, provides an overview of the decision-making process and the use of models in decision making.

An important goal of strategy is to gain competitive advantage or keep from yielding competitors the opportunity to gain competitive advantage. Today, many companies are competing on the basis of quality. Chapter 3 discusses capabilities companies use to gain competitive excellence with an emphasis on quality management.

Managers must make decisions based on inferences about the future. They must attempt to answer such difficult questions as, What are the future developments for which we need to be planning and reaching decisions? What will be the expected outcome of each possible course of action we may take? Forecasting, the basis for much of management's planning and control activities, is the subject of Chapter 4.

Forecasts may reveal a need for decisions in either of the two major categories that constitute Parts II and III of the book. Forecasts are the basis for decisions pertaining to the *design* of the production system—issues that are discussed in Part II. Forecasts also help managers make decisions relating to the *operation* of the production system—issues that are discussed in Part III.

ZEROING IN
ON OPERATIONS

CHAPTER 1

THE OPERATIONS FUNCTION

The subject of our discussion in this book is the *operations function* (also called the *production function*) in business, which is the activities and people who are directly and many who are indirectly responsible for providing the goods and services the business sells to its customers. We will often refer to the operations function as simply "operations" and treat it as a singular noun since it refers to a single function. The scope of operations is broader than some readers may initially have in mind. In a manufacturing company, for example, operations is much broader than just the activities that occur in the factory. In order to provide goods, products must be developed, materials and components must be purchased from suppliers, facilities and processes must be developed and maintained, the product must be distributed, customer support and other activities must occur to help create the value that customers are willing to pay for. Likewise, in a service company, there must be such activities as development of a product (service package), provision of any necessary facilities and equipment, training and other activities that support the frontline service provider. We consider the operations function an integrated system that obtains the necessary inputs, transforms them to make them desirable to the customer ("adds value to

Figure 1.1
Conceptual Diagram
of a Production System

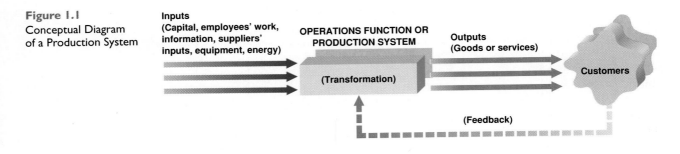

them") so the customer wishes to purchase them, and gets the product (goods or services) to the customer. Figure 1.1 is a schematic that summarizes this view of the operations function.

If a company is to survive and prosper, its operations function must not only perform its work well, but also make certain its work is well integrated and coordinated with all other parts of the business. Operations is one of the three primary, or core, functions within a business, with the other two being the marketing function and the finance function. Since a business must have customers if it is to survive, there is a *marketing function* which works to find and create demand for the company's offerings, represents the customer's viewpoint to the company, and represents the company to customers. Also, a company needs financial resources so it can pay for its facilities and pay its employees, suppliers, and so forth. The third primary function is the *finance function,* which performs activities to obtain financial resources for the company and guide the organization in the wise use of those resources. In some instances, the work of the three primary functions overlaps as depicted in Figure 1.2, but these functions and all other parts of a company must work together if a company is to achieve its full potential. Other parts of a company perform important activities such as legal work and public relations to help the organization carry out its mission. Activities associated with managing human resources are a vital part of every function within an organization, so we do not treat human resources as a separate function. The role of top managers or general managers is to plan, direct, and coordinate the work of all the many parts of a large organization so they work in mutual support of common goals.

Having businesses perform operations for us certainly contributes to our quality of life. For a few moments imagine what life would be like if there were no organized

Figure 1.2
Core Functions
within Organizations

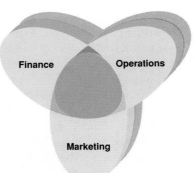

groups other than the family unit to provide goods or services. Each family would have to build its own home. Most family members would have to work to raise food with whatever crude implements they could fashion for themselves. Transportation would be limited; people would have to travel by horseback or in horse-drawn carts, on rafts or simple boats, or on foot. Communication would be limited to word of mouth or letters carried by someone who happened to be going to the desired destination. Heating the home and cooking would require many hours of cutting wood or obtaining other fuel. The activities required to obtain the necessities of life would consume so much time that great composers, artists, surgeons, and inventors would have little opportunity to develop. None of the advances in medicine, communications, law, and transportation that we have today would exist. There would be no cities, and rural life would be very different from what it is today.

Fortunately, the world today is quite unlike the one described above. Many organizations produce goods and provide services for us to use. The skills, efficiency, and productivity that are achieved within these organizations are much greater than individuals could achieve by working alone. Even though we sometimes think the things they produce are not as well made as we would like them to be, we must admit that they are better than we could make for ourselves in the time required to earn the money we pay for them. We not only have more and better goods and services than we could produce ourselves, but we also have more leisure time to enjoy books, television programs, concerts, travel, ball games, and so on. We profit from exposure to broader expanses of the world, have better health care, and enjoy more material wealth because there are businesses that provide us with goods and services. Both manufacturing and nonmanufacturing operations make important contributions to increasing our standard of living.

All functions within a business must be performed well if the company is to succeed. The operations function plays a major role in producing or providing what the customer receives from a company. Hence, it has a major influence on customer satisfaction, which is a vital determinant of market share, current and future revenue, and business success. In many companies operations retains the greatest percentage of the employees and is responsible for the largest part of the controllable budget. Therefore, operations plays a significant role in the success of an individual business. If a nation's economy is to prosper, the collective business enterprises within the nation must function well. You can see that operations plays a major role in building the competitive success of businesses and certainly is a topic worthy of further study.

THE RACE FOR COMPETITIVE EXCELLENCE

The past few decades have highlighted the vital power and importance of operations to businesses and to entire national economies. Global competition has intensified companies' competitive struggles to survive and prosper. Developed and developing nations seek to add to their wealth by supplying goods and services in this expanding global market. Goods and services (but more often it is goods because they are more exportable) cross national boundaries and money flows in the reverse direction to pay for them. If a nation is to avoid trade deficits, its businesses must be sufficiently competitive to export a value equal to the value of its imports. That is, a sufficient number of its businesses must be "world-class" competitors.

The United States, with relatively free-spending consumers and borders that are relatively open to trade, has been a major market for much of the global trade. U.S.

companies are painfully aware of the heightened competition for a share of the U.S. market and for shares of the world market. The number of competitors in the customer attraction contest has increased, and the level of competition has become more intense. In many industries such as steel, automobiles, semiconductors, cameras, televisions, video recorders, and facsimile machines, U.S. manufacturers have lost or failed to gain large percentages of the domestic market. The Japanese have been particularly effective at gaining markets in the United States.

Numerous factors have been mentioned as parts of the reason why domestic producers failed to hold market shares they once had or to introduce new products that would compete successfully in some of these fields. A few of the factors that can have serious impact on competitiveness will be discussed briefly.

In the United States, where both consumers and the government operate on borrowed money to a great extent, the demand for funds is high relative to the supply, causing interest rates to be higher than in many other countries. Factors such as a higher cost of capital, a focus on rates of return, and fear of company takeovers have resulted in a lower rate of capital investment in research and development and other investments that would support improvements in long-term competitiveness. Failure to invest in improvements can have grave consequences for a business. Companies are more likely to gain market share when they invest in product and process development and equipment that would raise competitiveness. When companies or nations experience growth in market share, there is a need for additional capacity, which permits companies to select what appears to be the best available (not necessarily the *latest*) technology at that time. Therefore, the firms can become even more competitive and gain yet more market share. Thus, companies and nations that are gaining market share have a potential to sustain, and even improve, their competitive advantage. They can achieve an *improvement spiral* as shown in Figure 1.3.

Conversely, companies or nations that have a higher cost of capital are less likely to make as many investments of capital and human effort to help them become competitively equal or superior. There is greater risk that a profitable rate of return will not be achieved. These firms are likely to experience declining sales, so they will seldom need to add new capacity, which would give them more opportunities to improve their processes. As a result, they fall further behind in competitiveness.

Figure 1.3
Improvement Spiral
or Competitive Tailspin

And so forth

Increased market share

Better competitive performance

Better plant & equipment

Need for more capacity

Gain in market share

Successful competitive maneuvers

Loss of market share

No need for expansion

Operate with older plant & equipment

Poorer relative performance

Further loss of market share

Business disaster

There is a real danger that a company or nation that allows itself to become under-competitive to a sufficient degree will fall into a *competitive tailspin,* or self-aggravating spiral of decline, which could become a death spiral, as shown in Figure 1.3.

The process of more frequent stages of healthy growth—such as adding new locations, improving facilities and capital equipment, and adding new people with fresh ideas and other experience—can lead to beneficial human resource development in addition to simply improving the physical assets. Of course, there often is a temporary decline in productivity when a company makes changes in its process technology. However, a study of productivity indicated that new investment, when managed well, supports cumulative long-term productivity growth and learning.[1] The addition of capacity and new equipment often causes companies to engage in more training and retraining that help develop a more skilled work force. Employees in such companies are more likely to be receptive to change, more prone to seek improvement opportunities, and more capable of accomplishing the intended improvements. Companies that are not growing or are declining are more likely to have employees who become stuck in the same old work methods. Employees may not be stretched to find better ways to work if the company is not using as much capacity as it did in the recent past. One would therefore expect to find a more capable work force where lower capital costs stimulate or facilitate investments and growth. The capabilities of all employees are one of the important internal factors that companies must nurture as they become world-class and stay in the global race. Other internal factors are discussed in the following section.

Faced with opportunities either to enter an improvement spiral or sink into the disaster of a competitive tailspin, both manufacturing and service companies are making serious efforts to improve their competitiveness. As more companies enter the global market, the number of competitors that a company must match will increase. A company may have to match the capabilities of the best companies in its field, just to keep the market share it has.

In a free-market economy, customers determine how successful a business will be. Customers evaluate a company's offerings in comparison to its competitors' offerings and decide which to purchase, based on the customers' perceptions and their own needs, desires, and budgets. Advertising and good sales effort help make customers aware of the company's goods and services and their desirable features. At the most basic level, evaluations and buying decisions made by customers add up to overall sales volume and market share.

Adding What Customers Value Is an Important Key

A company serves its customers by adding *value* to the goods and services its customers obtain from it. The company's work transforms inputs so they have more of the features, attributes, or characteristics the customer needs or finds desirable; that is, they make the goods and services have more worth or value to the customer. It should be stressed that value is based on the customers' perception of the worth or desirability of a good or service. Therefore, if a company seeks to build competitive excellence it must strive to understand its target market and provide customers with more of what they value than they would receive from the company's competitors, and for the amount they intend to spend.

[1] Robert H. Hayes and Kim B. Clark, "Why Some Factories Are More Productive than Others," *Harvard Business Review,* September–October 1989, p. 68.

HOW COMPANIES ADD VALUE

An information box like this is included near the front of each of the following chapters. It indicates how the subject of that chapter can help add value to a company's output or reduce the resources required to provide the value so that the company's value ratio can be improved. Adding value for customers in an efficient or cost-effective way helps a company achieve competitive excellence.

Since their funds are limited, most customers perform some evaluation to determine which company's product seems to be the best deal. Generally, they conceive of some ratio of the benefits of buying compared to the burdens that buying will impose, and we will call this a value ratio. The customer's *value ratio* can be thought of as a general ratio of the amount of desirable features or value in a good or service (a general assessment of quality as broadly interpreted) divided by the cost of the good or service. Some customers may take a short-term view and consider only the initial purchase price, while others may consider the total cost over the long term for making a purchase. Therefore, companies may try to enhance the customer's value ratio by improving their products and/or reducing the cost or inconvenience of purchasing them. Cadillac, for example, offers free roadside service. As an example of the impact of a better value ratio one might consider the German camera manufacturer Voigtlander, which went out of business when Japanese companies such as Canon offered cameras with 90 percent of the features for only 50 percent of the cost.

Working to achieve high quality and desirability of its outputs while trying to achieve low costs through efficient use of all inputs places a company in the position of trying to enhance its own form of value ratio. The company's value ratio can be thought of as the desirability of its goods and services to the customer divided by the cost to provide the goods and services. To achieve a high value ratio a company must be very effective at producing what the customer desires and very efficient in using all the resources required to provide it. That is, the company must achieve high *total factor productivity,* which is the ratio of the market value of its output to the cost of all the resources required to produce the output. In general, productivity is a measure of efficiency expressed as a ratio of output to input. Often we see productivity reported as output per hour worked, which measures only labor productivity. As more companies are engaged in services and knowledge work and as more companies automate, labor productivity is too narrow a measure of how efficient a company or an economy is. Total factor productivity includes the cost of such factors as labor, materials, capital, energy, and any other major inputs required to provide the output.

Companies that are successful in keeping their costs low have the potential to reduce the price of their goods and services to provide customers with a better value ratio. Alternatively, the company could use its extra income to fund product improvements, which might also improve its customers' value ratio. Of course, extra income might be used to provide higher employee compensation, improve the company's financial position, or for other purposes.

The customer's value ratio can be improved without a reduction in the price of a good or service. A company can improve its quality or provide more convenience or service at the same or even a somewhat higher price. A good objective for a company is to look for ways to provide the greatest amount of customer satisfaction per dollar spent. Sometimes a small increase in cost can result in a much greater increase in customer value and customer satisfaction.

What Do We Mean by Excellence?

There is no single quantifiable measure by which to judge excellence. To be excellent in a sport or subject means we must excel in it or be outstandingly good at it. A dictionary will say that being excellent means "being significantly better than average, better than most, or being superior." So an *excellent* company is one that is better than most or near the top in its industry at providing customer satisfaction and will probably be gaining market share or will retain a strong market share. We must qualify this definition to some degree. First, not every customer will perceive the company's work in exactly the same way. Some customers may evaluate a company's product or service on a very short-term basis and others may use long-term measures to judge satisfaction, but an excellent company should achieve good results over the long term. If a company is to be around to provide satisfaction on a long-term basis it must remain financially healthy. Not every company that does whatever it takes to make the customer happy will always be financially healthy. A company could make many customers happy for a short time by selling below cost or providing more services than are financially feasible. In such a case, the company might not be around to serve its customers and those who would like to be customers in the future. A company that seeks to be excellent should do an outstanding job of understanding and serving its customers' needs while preserving, or even improving, its long-term financial health. Therefore, a company must operate efficiently while it seeks to provide customer satisfaction so that it has a high value ratio and can provide a high value ratio to its customers.

Florida Power & Light

Recognized internationally for quality management, Florida Power & Light was severely tested during Hurricane Andrew. Its lean, flexible organization allowed for rapid mobilization, winning high acclaim. But an excellent company doesn't rest on its laurels; Florida Power & Light continues to use its capabilities to prepare for deregulation and competition.

Even an excellent company could have financial problems beyond its control. Competition could erode prices below that necessary to provide reasonable returns or even below cost. The costs of some of its inputs could become excessive, or other challenges may occur. These realities make it even more important that companies operate efficiently. As we study ways to manage operations to help a company become excellent we will discuss ways that companies can improve such characteristics as responsiveness and quality and also ways they can operate more efficiently. Throughout much of this book we will discuss issues that operations managers face and how managers can deal with these issues, improve their operations, and strive for excellence. Before we get to the specific issues we will overview some general types of operations and their characteristics.

TYPES OF OPERATIONS

The U.S. Department of Commerce classifies businesses according to Standard Industrial Classification (SIC) codes. Table 1.1 lists these codes, which have been grouped into those that deal primarily in goods and those that deal primarily in services. By subdividing the field of operations into manufacturing operations and service operations, we will be able to focus from time to time on some of their unique characteristics and activities. Sometimes the dividing line between these types of operations may seem fuzzy. All businesses are in the service business, to some degree. They are in the business of doing something for the customer—of performing activities that have value to the customer—if they want to survive in the competitive world of business. The primary unique capability that customers purchase from some companies is the companies' ability to manufacture tangible products. When we discuss these companies, we use the term *manufacturing companies* or *manufacturing operations*. The others are referred to as *service companies, services,* or generally as *nonmanufacturing operations*. Let's look in more detail at the difference between these two types of operations.

Manufacturing Operations

Manufacturing operations generally transform tangible input or raw materials into tangible output. Other inputs, such as labor skills, management skills, capital, and sales revenue, are used as well. Manufacturing operations perform some chemical or physical processes such as weaving, sewing, sawing, welding, grinding, blending, refining, or assembling to transform their raw materials into tangible products.

Service Operations

Customers deal with some nonmanufacturing companies to obtain purely intangible services, such as advice or instruction; customers may seek help in completing tax forms, for example. Customers deal with other nonmanufacturing companies, such as wholesalers or retailers, to obtain goods—but these companies do not make the goods. They serve their customers primarily by transporting, packaging, storing, and so on, rather than by performing manufacturing processes. Thus, our major criterion for classifying operations is whether these operations manufacture goods or provide some type of service operation, even though they may provide tangible goods or some less tangible services to customers.

Table 1.1
PRODUCERS OF GOODS AND SERVICES

PRIMARILY GOODS PRODUCERS	PRIMARILY SERVICE PRODUCERS
Agriculture, forestry, and fishing Crops, livestock, agriculture services, forestry, fishing, hunting, and trapping	**Transportation and public utilities** Railroads, local passenger transit, trucking, warehousing, U.S. Postal Service, water transportation, airlines, pipelines, communication, electricity, gas, and sanitation
Mining Metal mining, coal mining, oil and gas extraction, and nonmetallic minerals	**Wholesale trade** Durable goods and nondurable goods
Construction General building contractors, heavy-construction contractors, and special trade contractors	**Retail trade** Building materials, general merchandise stores, food stores, automotive dealers and service stations, apparel and accessory stores, furniture and home furnishing stores, and eating and drinking places
Manufacturing Food, tobacco, textile mills, apparel, lumber, furniture, paper, printing, chemicals, petroleum, coal products, rubber, plastic, leather, stone, clay, glass, primary metal, fabricated metal products, machinery, electric and electronic equipment, transportation equipment, instruments, and miscellaneous manufacturing industries	**Finance, insurance, and real estate** Banking, credit agencies, security brokers, insurance carriers, and real estate
	Services Hotels, personal services, business services, auto repair, motion pictures, amusement, health, legal, education, social services, museums, zoological gardens, and membership organizations
	Public administration

Industries listed are based on the U.S. Department of Commerce Standard Industrial Classification System.

Service operations also transform a set of inputs into a set of outputs. A restaurant uses such inputs as meat, potatoes, lettuce, the chef's skills, servers' skills, and many others. Some of the transformation processes involve storing supplies, blending ingredients into desirable combinations, and altering the form of the inputs by cooking, freezing, heating, and transporting them to the proper tables at the proper time. Less tangible transformations involve the provision of a pleasant atmosphere, perhaps even entertainment. The outputs include, one hopes, a satisfied patron. Other outputs include wages and purchase payments sent into the economy and refuse sent into the refuse collection system (which is yet another service system).

Educational institutions use such inputs as books, students, and instructional skills to produce knowledgeable and skilled individuals as their output. Hospitals use scientific equipment, professional skills, and tender loving care to transform sick people into well ones. Repair shops use repair parts, equipment, and worker skills to

Cunard Cruises is a service operation with inputs that include great food, the skills of a talented crew, and the environment of the QE2. Cunard uses these inputs to create an environment where customers can themselves be transformed into happy world travelers.

transform malfunctioning inputs into properly functioning outputs. All types of operations, then, transform inputs into outputs.

The proportions of the U.S. work force that are employed in various kinds of businesses have changed over the years. As production technology has changed, the percentages of the work force in agriculture and in manufacturing have declined during this century. Figure 1.4 shows the percentages of the work force employed in several types of business since 1900. Notice the large increase in the percentage of the work force employed in services. Manufacturing and agriculture are still important to the nation. Manufacturing still makes up about the same percentage of the gross domestic product (GDP) that it did in 1950. With the increase in productivity that follows the application of new technology, though, fewer people are needed to manufacture products. Operations will continue to employ new technology and strive for improved productivity to remain competitive. We now turn our attention to some of the subdivisions within manufacturing and service operations.

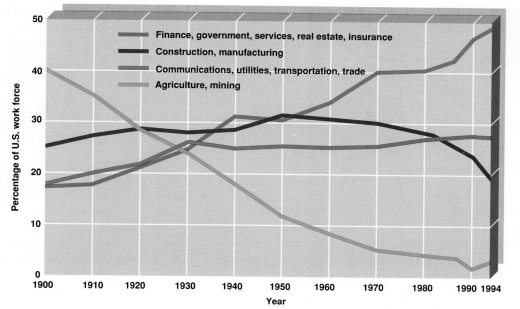

Source: Employment and Earnings, U.S. Department of Labor, Bureau of Labor Statistics, January 1982; January 1985; January 1991; and January 1995; *Long-Term Economic Growth, 1860–1970,* U.S. Department of Commerce, Bureau of Economic Analysis, June 1973; and *People and Jobs,* U.S. Department of Labor, Bureau of Labor Statistics, April 1975.

TYPES OF MANUFACTURING OPERATIONS

Manufacturing companies and plants are referred to by a variety of terms that describe something about their manner of operation. The facility, equipment, and operating methods (sometimes called the production system) that a company uses depend on the type of product it offers and the strategy it employs to serve its customers. Some of the terms refer to the stage at which the company holds inventory.

Some companies are *make-to-stock producers;* that is, they make items that are completed and placed in stock before the customer's order is received. The end item is shipped "off the shelf" from finished-goods inventory after receipt of a customer's order. In contrast, some companies make to order. A *make-to-order producer* completes the end item after receipt of the customer's order for the item. If the item is a unique, custom-designed item, the customer will probably have to wait for many of the materials to be purchased and for the production work to be performed, because the producer cannot anticipate what each customer might want and have the necessary raw materials and components on hand to shorten the production lead time. If components or materials are frequently used by the business, however, the producer may keep some of them in stock—particularly if the lead time to purchase or produce these items is long. When the company produces standard-design, optional modules ahead of time and assembles a particular combination of these modules after the customer orders it, the business is said to be an *assemble-to-order producer.*[2] An

[2]Terms from James F. Cox, III, John H. Blackstone, Jr., and Michael S. Spencer, *APICS Dictionary,* 7th ed. (Falls Church, Va.: American Production and Inventory Control Society, 1992).

example of an assemble-to-order producer is an automobile factory that, in response to a dealer's order, provides an automatic or manual transmission, air conditioner, sound system, interior options, and specific engine options as well as the specified body style and color. Many of the components would already have been purchased and started into production when the dealer placed the order. Otherwise the lead time to deliver the automobile would be much longer.

Other terms are used to distinguish the characteristics of factories and the ways that products are manufactured. The extent to which a factory (or a smaller production area within a facility) has the flexibility to produce a variety of products is one characteristic often used to distinguish between types of factories. Factories or production areas encompass a wide range in regard to this characteristic. At one extreme is a factory that makes custom products in low volume or in single units and probably will never repeat production of one of them later. At the other extreme is a factory that makes only one standard product in very high volume. Although several types of factories could be described within this range, we primarily use only three in our further study. The job shop, batch, and repetitive production factories are described and used to present some of the general characteristics and management methods that we will study with regard to manufacturing.

Job Shops

A *job shop* manufacturing business contracts to make to order custom products in accordance with designs supplied by the customer. Some of these businesses engineer and build items based on performance requirements specified by the customer. Typically, the volume of each product is low, so these companies must contract to make a wide variety of products in order to achieve a sufficient level of sales. To increase the chances of making sales and to maintain a volume of business, these factories need general-purpose production equipment that can perform a broad range of operations and employees who have a broad range of skills. Job shops are generally classified as high-variety, low-volume manufacturers.

Each job may be unique, requiring a special set of production steps performed in a particular sequence (a "routing") to convert the raw material into the desired finished item. The next item may require a totally different sequence of production steps from the previous one. Consequently, there is no standard path of material flow through this type of facility. The production equipment must be general-purpose, and materials-handling equipment should be flexible, with the capability to move various sizes and shapes of objects along widely varying paths. Flexibility is important in this business. These companies face a big challenge in planning, scheduling, and coordinating the production of numerous components of a wide variety of unfamiliar products. Job shops may carry an inventory of some raw materials they use frequently, but often the largest percentage of their inventory is work in process (WIP) that accumulates between process stages because of the sporadic material flow.

Examples of job shops might be a drapery shop that makes custom draperies, a woodworking shop that makes custom kitchen cabinets, or a metal fabrication shop that makes special machinery.

Repetitive Manufacturing

Repetitive manufacturing, repetitive production, and *production lines* are terms used for mass production facilities that produce a high volume of the same or similar units of product that follow the same path, that is, have a common "flow path" through the production steps. An example would be an automobile assembly line. There may be two-door and four-door models in different colors; some get automatic transmissions, and others get manual-shift transmissions; but all have a fixed flow path (routing) through the same sequence of work stations to convert the raw material into the finished product. This is also an illustration of mixed-model assembly on an assembly line.

Typically, material is moved along the path in small lots, often one part at a time. The products are usually made to stock, and the items are not identified as belonging to a particular order during their production. The production equipment in this type of facility performs the same operation repeatedly and may be specifically designed to do a particular operation rapidly and reliably with little variation in its results from cycle to cycle. Materials-handling equipment can also be specifically designed to transport a specific shape of product through a fixed path. Frequently, automated equipment is used. Schedules usually are expressed as rates, such as a specified number of units per hour or per day. Inventories of raw materials may be held to ensure a supply, so the factory can operate and finished goods may be accumulated to smooth fluctuations in demand. Work in process is low since items move quickly through production. Typical products of this type of production might be televisions, telephones, refrigerators, microwave ovens, and roller skates.

Batch Manufacturing

A vast number of possible combinations of product variety and average volume per product are depicted by Figure 1.5. The region at the upper left (high variety and low volume) generally describes job shops. The region at the lower right (low variety and high volume) generally describes repetitive manufacturing. Many manufacturing operations fall somewhere between these two regions on the figure and are often called batch manufacturers. A *batch manufacturing* facility makes some intermediate variety of products and produces an intermediate volume of each. The volume of any one item is not sufficient to justify dedicating a set of equipment to its production, so a few or several products share the production resources. The company will make a batch (a production run), maybe less than a hundred or up to a few thousand of one product, then switch over the equipment and make a batch of another item. Eventually it will repeat production of the items.

Production equipment in batch manufacturing must be capable of performing some variety of tasks, but the range of possible operations is much narrower than in a

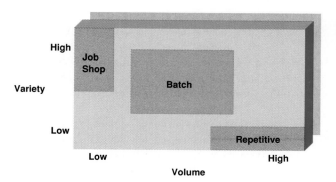

Figure 1.5
Classification of Manufacturing Types

Figure 1.6
Degree of Flexibility
of Production Systems

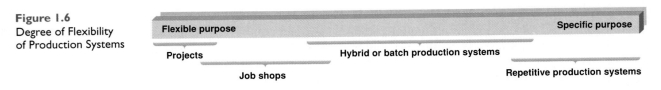

job shop. Attachments and tooling may be installed (that is, the equipment is "set up") to run one type of item. After a batch is completed, the equipment may be set up anew to run some other item. The ability to change back and forth quickly is important in this type of production system. A company may achieve a high degree of focus (that is, reduced range of changes it must make) if it runs families of items that require the same or nearly the same processing steps. The paths of material flow may vary if the company does not have a high degree of focus. If there is focus, however, the flow paths may be identical and the materials-handling equipment can be more specialized, perhaps automated.

An example of a batch manufacturer might be a company that makes small hand tools. It might make ¼-inch drills, then electric screw drivers, hand mixers, ½-inch drills, then ⅜-inch drills, and so on.

The three major types of manufacturing introduced above differ greatly in the degree of flexibility they have to produce a variety of products. They can be thought of as falling along points on a continuum, with the very flexible job shop at the left and the specific-product, repetitive factory at the right. Figure 1.6 shows such a continuum.

Process and *project* are two other terms that sometimes are used to describe types of manufacturing operations. Some repetitive production operations produce a product that blends together in bulk rather than being in discrete units. The industries that produce these types of products are sometimes called *process industries,* particularly if some physical or chemical reaction is used. Examples of process industries include petroleum refineries, flour mills, cement factories, and chemical processing plants. (Chemical processing can also take place with batches of material, in what is sometimes called "batch-process" production.)

Lying at the high-flexibility end of the continuum is the low-volume type of operation often referred to as a *project.* Most projects are of relatively long duration, and the same personnel are often assigned to a project for a significant part of this time. In the manufacturing category, projects include such items as ships, bridges, buildings, and large, special machines. Project teams can be formed for a variety of undertakings in manufacturing operations and in services.

TYPES OF SERVICE OPERATIONS

We will refer to operations that do not produce tangible outputs as *services* or *service operations.* Like manufacturing operations, services can be subdivided according to the degree of standardization of their outputs—that is, whether they are *standard services* or *custom services*—and/or the processes they perform. Some service activities might be thought of as projects because they involve the activities of a team of people over a period of time. In the service category, a project might be a software package or a training program. Table 1.2 displays a comparison of manufacturing and services based on their flexibility and the degree of standardization of their output.

Table 1.2
EXAMPLES OF TYPES OF MANUFACTURING AND SIMILAR SERVICES

CHARACTERISTIC OF OPERATION	MANUFACTURING OPERATION AND EXAMPLES	SIMILAR SERVICE AND EXAMPLE
Long-duration activities of a team for low-volume goods or services	**Project:** Building a bridge, dam, house, or special machine	**Project:** Developing software, preparing for a banquet, translating a foreign-language book for a publisher
Short-duration activities to provide custom goods or services	**Job shop:** Making custom industrial hardware, printing personalized stationery, making drapes	**Custom service:** Charter air or bus travel, repairing autos, providing health care, providing special-delivery mail service
Processing of groups of similar standard items	**Batch manufacturing:** Similar standard items made periodically in batches: hand tools, complements that feed an assembly line	**Standard service in groups:** Schedule air or bus travel, audience entertainment
High-volume processing of standard goods or services that are in discrete units	**Repetitive manufacturing:** Light bulbs, refrigerators, televisions, automobiles	**Standard service:** Providing fast food, standard insurance policies, dry cleaning, personal checking accounts, distribution and wholesaling of standard products
High-volume processing of unit goods that flow together in bulk (nondiscrete units)	**Process industries:** Chemicals, refining oil, milling flour, making paper	(No apparent service equivalent)

Service operations can be divided into categories according to another classification scheme that provides useful insights into the management issues they face. Some service operations deal primarily with tangible outputs, even though these operations do not manufacture the items. These types of operations include whole-sale distributors and freight transportation companies, and they can use many of the materials management principles and techniques that a manufacturing operation might use. The ideas of materials handling are also important in some operations that deal with tangible items.

Other service operations deal primarily in intangible products or pure services, such as advice or counseling, as their outputs. One should recognize that an operation does not necessarily provide *only* services or *only* goods. Facilitating goods may be provided with services, and facilitating services may be provided with goods. For example, we can obtain the same goods (although in a different form) from a grocery store or from a restaurant. We think of a grocery store as primarily providing goods. We trade with a restaurant especially for the services it provides in selecting, preparing, and serving food, which is actually a tangible good. When we have a car "serviced," the process may include the installation of some parts. The service is provided by someone who knows which parts to replace and how to replace them and who spends the time to perform this service.

Table 1.3
A CLASSIFICATION OF SERVICE OPERATIONS

Service (Non-Goods-Producing) Operations		
PROVIDERS OF TANGIBLE PRODUCTS	**PROVIDERS OF SERVICES**	
Mail service	Services in which the customer often is not present as a participant	Services in which the customer often is present
Library service		
Wholesale and retail distributors		Examples:
Examples:	Examples:	Health care
Television sets	Preparing tax forms	Hair care
Radios	Architectural design	Travel
Watches	Landscaping	Legal advice
Refrigerators	Repairing watches, automobiles, appliances	Financial advice
Air conditioners	Rating and issuing insurance	Marriage counseling

Operations that deal mainly in services can be further divided according to the degree to which the customer is a participant in the process. Many services are custom services, so the customer often has some contact with the service provider. The customer, however, does not have to be present during the process for some types of service, such as having clothes laundered or a watch repaired. Table 1.3 shows a classification of some types of services based on the extent to which the customer is normally present as a participant when the service is provided. The table shows an additional breakdown depending on whether the customer deals with the provider to obtain a service package which primarily consists of making available some tangible item (that the service company did not manufacture, of course) or less tangible services such as analysis, repair, or advice. Supplement D, which follows this chapter, discusses a service operation whose primary function is to make tangible products available to customers.

UNIQUE CHARACTERISTICS OF SERVICE OPERATIONS

Each type of operation has its unique characteristics. When they are viewed in sufficient detail, the problems of any operations system are found to be unique and dynamic, that is, changing through time.

At a general level, however, four differences between manufacturing and service operations can be recognized:

1. Generally, productivity is more easily measured in manufacturing operations than in service operations because the former provides tangible products, whereas the products of service operations are usually intangible. A factory that produces automobile tires can readily count the number of tires produced in a day. Repair service operations may repair or replace portions of a tangible product, but their major service is the application of knowledge and skilled labor. Advisory services may provide only spoken words, an entirely intangible product and one very difficult to measure.

2. Quality standards are more difficult to establish and product quality is more difficult to evaluate in service operations. This difference is directly related to the previous one. Intangible products are more difficult to evaluate because they cannot be held, weighed, or measured. We can evaluate a repair to a tangible product by comparing the product's performance after the repair with its performance before the repair. It is more difficult to know the worth of a service such as legal defense. No one knows for certain how the judge would have ruled had the attorney performed in some different manner.

3. Persons who provide services generally have contact with customers, whereas persons who perform manufacturing operations seldom see the consumer of the product. The marketing and customer relations aspects of a service often overlap the operations function. The doctor-patient relationship, for example, is often considered to be a very important component of the physician's services. In the service of hair care, the hairdresser-patron contact is necessary. The impact of discourteous salespersons or restaurant employees is of great concern in many establishments.

4. Manufacturing operations can accumulate or decrease inventory of finished products, particularly in standard product, repetitive production operations. A barber, in contrast, cannot store up haircuts during slack times so that he or she can provide service at an extremely high rate during peak demand time. Providers of services often try to overcome this limitation by leveling out the demand process. Telephone systems, for example, offer discount rates during certain hours to encourage a shift in the timing of calls that can be delayed.

There are several other general differences between manufacturing and service operations. Normally, the proportion of expenses required for materials handling is smaller for services than for manufacturing operations. Exceptions are such organizations as wholesale distributors and mail delivery services, which are primarily materials-handling operations. The transformation they perform is one of place rather than of physical form, so handling represents their major cost. Usually a manufacturing operation has a greater percentage of its assets invested in facilities, equipment, and inventory than a service organization. Since they have more equipment, manufacturing operations generally depend more heavily on maintenance and repair work. Health care institutions are probably an exception to this generality because their equipment must perform satisfactorily. We discuss and compare various aspects of managing services and manufacturing operations throughout the text.

MANAGERS' ROLES IN OPERATIONS

Some companies have an executive with a title such as operations manager, production manager, vice president of operations, or director of operations. In a sizable company, many persons serve in managerial roles within the operations function, even though they may not have one of these titles. Many managers, from the top executive to the supervisors of direct workers, play vital roles in planning the right things for operations to do and in seeing that these things are done well. These people include line managers and others in such activities as planning, quality control, scheduling, and maintenance. We discuss some of the decisions and activities of these persons in a later section; but, first, we should mention some important skills these persons should have.

Skills Needed by Operations Managers

In trying to work through others to accomplish the objectives of operations, managers must possess and employ a variety of skills. Two major categories of management skills are discussed below.

TECHNICAL COMPETENCE   Since managers make decisions about the tasks that other people are to perform, they must understand two major aspects of an organization: They need a basic understanding of the technology with which the production system works, and they need adequate knowledge of the work they are to manage. *Technical competence* can be obtained through training and experience or through the use of staff specialists and consultants. Today's highly technical processes and the trend toward conglomerates have brought with them an increase in the use of staff organizations specializing in various aspects of operations.

BEHAVIORAL COMPETENCE   Many group activities exist because people find that they can achieve more, both in work accomplished and in rewards achieved, by working as a group than by working alone. Generally, humans are gregarious animals and fulfill some of their needs in social interaction. Management must therefore consider the social as well as the physical aspects of work and workers. Since managers work through others, their work necessarily involves a great deal of interpersonal contact. A good manager should have *behavioral competence*—the ability to work with other people.

Throughout the book we review ways that managers work to help their organizations provide high quality at reasonable cost within lead times that customers find satisfactory. Often, the decisions and actions of managers are grouped into categories referred to as the functions of managers. Some of the functions of managers often presented in introductory management courses are listed in Table 1.4. Presented below each major function or category are several of the decisions or activities that managers in operations might perform in discharging the specific management function. The table provides some information about the types of decisions and activities discussed in this book. Table 1.4 also relates the activities we will be discussing to the functions of management with which you may already be familiar.

OVERVIEW OF THE BOOK AND ISSUES DISCUSSED

A basic theme of the book is that the operations function must be managed well if a business is to provide high value to its customers and be competitive. Each chapter discusses a type of issue with which operations managers typically must deal. Figure 1.7, which should be read from the bottom up because it builds from the foundation, provides an overview of the book and the types of issues discussed. This information, intended as an alternative to the table of contents, provides the reader with a schematic representation of the book's contents.

Table 1.4
DECISIONS AND ACTIVITIES OF MANAGERS IN OPERATIONS
(Grouped According to Familiar Management Functions)

Planning

Establish the mix of goods and services to be provided	Arrange facilities and equipment
Plan the locations of facilities	Decide on the number of shifts and work hours
Plan the capacities of plants and work centers	Set the master schedule of what products to make when
Decide what production methods to use for each item	Establish improvement projects or other projects
Plan acquisitions of equipment	Organize changes in new processes or procedures

Organizing

Centralize or decentralize operations	Assign responsibility for every activity
Organize by functions, products, or hybrid arrangement	Arrange supplier and subcontractor networks
Establish work center assignments	Establish maintenance policies

Controlling

Encourage pride in performing as expected	Establish systems to ensure that quality is controlled
Compare costs to budgets	Compare work progress to schedule
Compare actual labor hours to standards	Compare inventory level to targets

Directing

Establish provisions of union contracts	Issue job assignments and instructions
Establish personnel policies	Issue routings and move tickets
Establish employment contracts	Issue dispatch lists

Motivating

Challenge through leadership examples, specific objectives, and expectations	Motivate through tangible reward system
Encourage through praise, recognition, and other intangibles	Motivate through enriched jobs and challenging assignments

Coordinating

Coordinate through use of common forecasts and master schedules	Report, inform, communicate
Coordinate through common, standardized data bases	Coordinate purchases, deliveries, design changes, maintenance activities, tooling
Observe actual performance and recommend needed performance	Respond to customer inquiries about status of orders

Training and Developing Personnel

Show a better way	Give more advanced job assignments
Encourage employees to seek a better way	Support employees in training programs

The book is divided into three major parts, each of which is represented by a rectangular block in the figure. For each chapter, one or more questions are presented to give an indication of the types of issues that are addressed in the chapter. The lower block, titled "Foundation Material," represents the material in Part I (the first four chapters), which provides general background material. The first chapter intro-

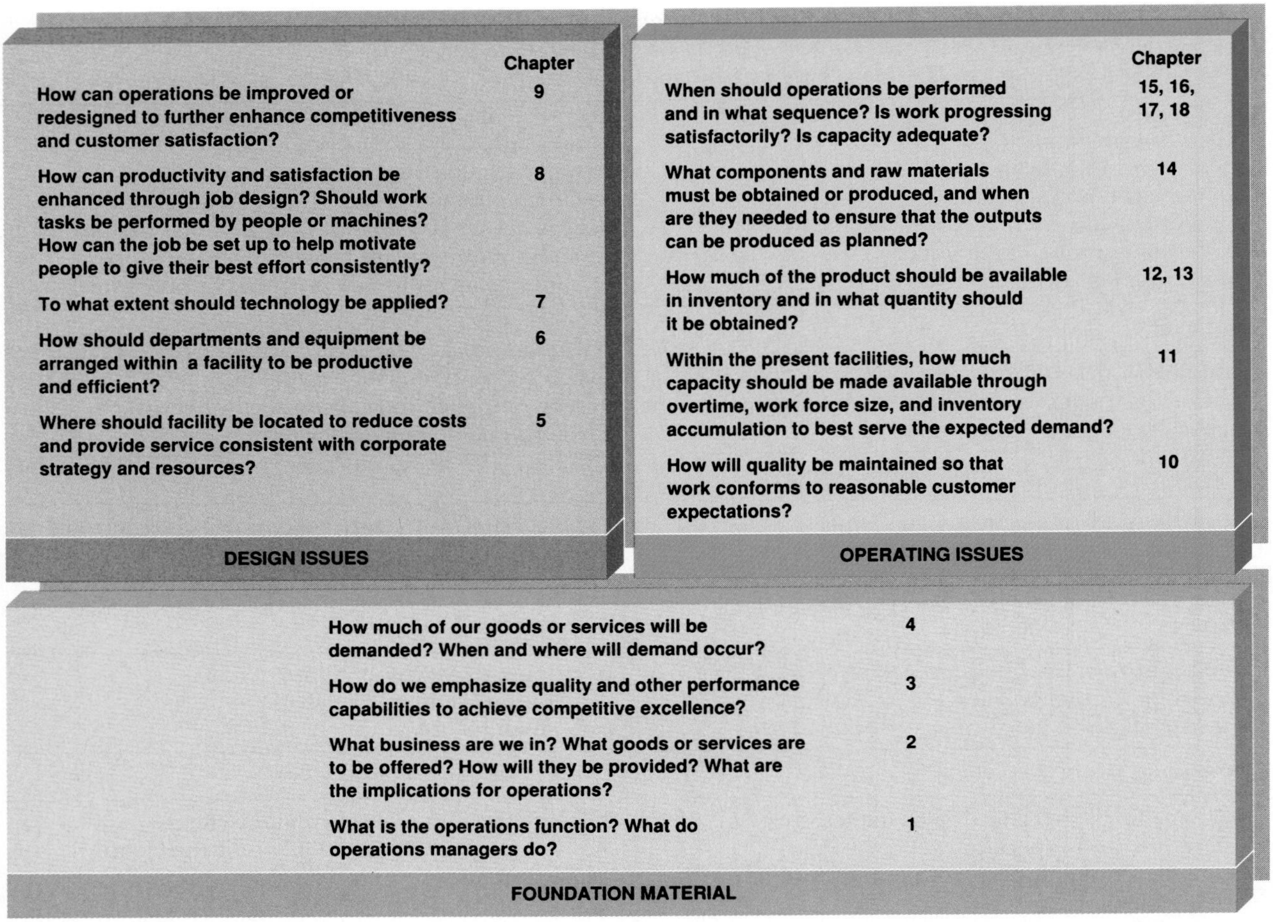

	Chapter
How can operations be improved or redesigned to further enhance competitiveness and customer satisfaction?	9
How can productivity and satisfaction be enhanced through job design? Should work tasks be performed by people or machines? How can the job be set up to help motivate people to give their best effort consistently?	8
To what extent should technology be applied?	7
How should departments and equipment be arranged within a facility to be productive and efficient?	6
Where should facility be located to reduce costs and provide service consistent with corporate strategy and resources?	5

DESIGN ISSUES

	Chapter
When should operations be performed and in what sequence? Is work progressing satisfactorily? Is capacity adequate?	15, 16, 17, 18
What components and raw materials must be obtained or produced, and when are they needed to ensure that the outputs can be produced as planned?	14
How much of the product should be available in inventory and in what quantity should it be obtained?	12, 13
Within the present facilities, how much capacity should be made available through overtime, work force size, and inventory accumulation to best serve the expected demand?	11
How will quality be maintained so that work conforms to reasonable customer expectations?	10

OPERATING ISSUES

	Chapter
How much of our goods or services will be demanded? When and where will demand occur?	4
How do we emphasize quality and other performance capabilities to achieve competitive excellence?	3
What business are we in? What goods or services are to be offered? How will they be provided? What are the implications for operations?	2
What is the operations function? What do operations managers do?	1

FOUNDATION MATERIAL

Figure 1.7
Types of Issues
Discussed in the Parts
of the Book

duces what the operations function is and some of the different operations one may find. The second chapter discusses how the operations function fits into the overall planning of a company and identifies some of the things operations must do well to support the company's overall strategy. The third chapter presents the importance of quality and other competitive capabilities in designing and running all aspects of the company. Chapter 4 presents some tools used in forecasting the level of demand operations is expected to serve. The forecast is a basis for both major categories of decisions that constitute the other two parts of the book. The forecast level of demand is an important input into designing an operations system that can successfully carry out the company's strategy. The forecast is also important in indicating the amount of inputs that should be obtained and the work activities that should be conducted in running the system once it has been designed and established.

Part II discusses issues that relate to the design of the operations system. Decisions related to design often must be made with a long lead time because of the lengthy studies and work involved in locating, designing, and establishing a facility that will properly support the company's strategy. The types of facilities and technology selected and the jobs that are assigned to employees are directly related to the design issues.

Part III presents material about running the operation system. The demand forecast provides estimates of what type of products (goods or services) will be required during each period of a planning horizon. Plans can be made for how much capacity should be made available in each period. Any necessary materials must be made available and managed wisely. Specific work activities must occur as the schedule requires, and quality must be achieved as the work is performed.

SUMMARY

Businesses and other organizations have three core functions (marketing, finance, and operations) and several other functions that perform the work. The operations function is that part of an organization responsible for producing the goods and providing much of the services the organization provides it customers. The operations function obtains the appropriate inputs and transforms them in such a way that they become more usable and desirable so they have value to the customer. Therefore, operations plays a major role in achieving quality and customer satisfaction.

Operations often contains the greatest percentage of a company's employees and is responsible for the greatest portion of its controllable budget. Therefore, operations plays a major role in helping a company achieve an improvement spiral and seek excellence instead of falling into a competitive tailspin.

Operations can be divided at a very general level into manufacturing and service operations. Manufacturing operations may range from repetitive producers of standard products sold in relatively high volume to job shops that produce highly customized items. Much of the general area between these categories is referred to as batch manufacturers. Services can range from highly custom operations such as health care to standardized operations such as fast food taco stands. Generally, it is easier to measure productivity and quality in manufacturing operations than in services. Services often are "produced" as they are received by the customer so they cannot be inventoried like tangible products; consequently, services generally have more contact with the customer.

Operations managers, like other managers, work through others to establish and achieve the objectives of their organizational units. Important activities of managers include planning, organizing, directing, motivating, coordinating, and controlling activities plus training and developing subordinates. To be successful in these activities, a manager should possess both technical and behavioral skills. Operations managers must apply these skills to achieve productivity and quality while providing goods or services on time.

KEY TERMS

Operations function	Excellent	Batch manufacturing
Production function	Manufacturing operations	Process industries
Marketing function	Service operations	Project
Finance function	Make-to-stock producer	Services
Improvement spiral	Make-to-order producer	Standard services
Competitive tailspin	Assemble-to-order	Custom services
Value	producer	Technical competence
Value ratio	Job shop	Behavioral competence
Total factor productivity	Repetitive manufacturing	

DISCUSSION QUESTIONS

1. What are the three primary functions that must be performed in all organizations? Define each one and explain how they are interrelated.
2. Define *repetitive production* and *job shop*. How are the two terms related?
3. Briefly discuss *standardized* and *custom service* as they relate to service operations. In what ways are these two types of service operations similar to repetitive production and job shop manufacturing operations?
4. List and briefly describe the four major differences between manufacturing operations and service operations.
5. Find a recent magazine or newspaper article that discusses one or more of the problems facing U.S. manufacturing operations today. What is being done about the problem(s)? Be prepared to discuss the problem(s) and attempted solution(s) in class.
6. Briefly describe some of the ways you have observed nonmanufacturing operations try to improve productivity.
7. Why are quality and productivity generally more difficult to measure in service operations than in manufacturing?
8. What are two major goals operations managers must achieve in the operations function in order to keep their companies competitive?
9. What is the central theme of the book?

BIBLIOGRAPHY

Albrecht, Karl, and Ron Zemke. *Service America: Doing Business in the New Economy.* Homewood, Ill.: Dow Jones-Irwin, 1985.

Cohen, Stephen S., and John Zysman. *Manufacturing Matters: The Myth of the Post-Industrial Economy.* New York: Basic Books, 1987.

Dertouzos, Michael L., et al. *Made in America: Regaining the Productive Edge.* Cambridge, Mass.: MIT Press, 1989.

Drucker, Peter F. *The Frontiers of Management.* New York: Truman Talley/Dutton, 1986.

Fitzsimmons, James A., and Mona Fitzsimmons. *Service Management for Competitive Advantage.* New York: McGraw-Hill, 1994.

Haas, Elizabeth A. "Breakthrough Manufacturing." *Harvard Business Review,* March–April 1987, pp. 75–81.

Hall, Robert W. *Attaining Manufacturing Excellence.* Homewood, Ill.: Dow Jones-Irwin, 1987.

Heskett, James L. *Managing in the Service Economy.* Boston: Harvard Business School Press, 1986.

Huge, Earnest C., with Alan D. Anderson. *The Spirit of Manufacturing Excellence.* Homewood, Ill.: Dow Jones-Irwin, 1988.

Jacob, Rahul. "Beyond Quality and Value." *Fortune,* Autumn–Winter 1993, pp. 8–11.

Skinner, Wickham. *Manufacturing: The Formidable Competitive Weapon,* New York: Wiley, 1985.

Stalk, George, Jr., and Thomas M. Hout. *Competing against Time: How Time-Based Competition Is Reshaping Global Markets.* New York: Free Press, 1990.

Waterman, Robert H., Jr. *The Renewal Factor: How to Get and Keep the Competitive Edge.* Toronto: Bantam, 1987.

People who lived two centuries ago were more closely tied to agriculture than most people are today. Rural households—and most of them were rural—had to be more self-sufficient than families typically are today. A large percentage of people's time was required just to produce their food. In the towns, there were small stores that sold products and small shops that made them. The assortment of goods would be considered narrow by today's standards, and they were expensive in terms of the amount of work required to earn their price.

Production methods also were different during this era. For one thing, parts were not interchangeable. Each component of a product was fashioned to fit that particular item and might not fit any other. One person might make the entire product,

custom-making each part to fit with the others. Any replacement parts had to be custom-made. A typical workshop was small, as was the typical work force, which might have consisted of an artisan and a few helpers or apprentices. The artisan was the equivalent of today's manager and could observe the entire work force during most of its activities. The tasks involved relatively low levels of technology and were not complicated to direct. Verbal instructions could be provided through direct, face-to-face communication but probably were not often necessary. The apprentice would learn simply by observing the master artisan.

The evolution of production from the small workshops of that era to the vast factories of today is often referred to as the *Industrial Revolution*. It was this movement that brought about the need for more formal and sophisticated methods of management. During the Renaissance, such men as Galileo, Kepler, and Newton had helped to further the understanding of the principles of science and mechanics. The printing press had been developed and put to use so that the dissemination of knowledge was much broader than at any previous time. Master mechanics and skilled artisans working in small shops learned of useful new methods and materials. Many small inventions and improvements to existing inventions were made possible and, in turn, gave birth to the machine age and the Industrial Revolution.

THE INDUSTRIAL REVOLUTION

The Industrial Revolution began in England in the late eighteenth century and spread to other parts of Europe and to the United States. In 1776, Adam Smith's *The Wealth of Nations* praised the advantages of the *division of labor,* or *specialization,* (1) because the reduced scope of one person's operations allowed the worker to develop dexterity quickly, (2) because it saved time otherwise required to shift from one operation to another, and (3) because specialists were more likely to find or develop specialized mechanical devices to assist their operations. Smith early recognized the increased productivity offered by *mechanization,* or the use of machines.

It is significant that the development of the United States as a nation coincided with the development of the factory system of production. Smith's ideas on industry and the division of labor were of interest to early U.S. political leaders. Alexander Hamilton stressed the importance of establishing manufacturing in the newly founded nation.

THE FIRST U.S. FACTORY

During the years before the American Revolution, England had prohibited the export of such items as textile manufacturing machinery or plans from which such machines could be made. However, Samuel Slater, who served an apprenticeship in an English textile mill, came to the United States with the necessary plans for a mill stored in his phenomenal memory. In December 1790, near Providence, Rhode Island, Slater produced the first cotton yard made automatically in the United States. The superiority of the process he introduced was recognized and was applied so rapidly that, by the end of the War of 1812, there were 165 mills in Massachusetts, Connecticut, and Rhode Island alone.[1] The factory system flourished in New England and the U.S. textile industry was well under way.

SPECIALIZED LABOR AND STANDARDIZED PARTS

In 1790, Eli Whitney made a phenomenal proposal: Within 2 years he would supply the army with 10,000 muskets at $13.40 each. He proposed to accomplish this feat by the use of specialized labor producing *interchangeable parts.* To fulfill the contract given him by the Congress, Whitney established a factory near New Haven, Connecticut. He had to improve the existing metalworking machines and develop new ones to achieve the required dimensional accuracy. Through these efforts, Whitney did much to establish the U.S. metalworking

industry. Manufacturers began to use standardized parts in their products. A worker could install any properly made part of the appropriate type in a product, rather than having to custom-make a part to fit a specific assembly. Specialized labor, or workers who made only a particular item, could become very skilled and efficient at that specific job. Thus, the factory system of production was born.

GROWTH OF THE FACTORY SYSTEM IN THE UNITED STATES

Conditions in the United States were well-suited to the development and spread of the factory system. Capital was available to provide the investments necessary to form large production companies, and those who controlled the capital—wealthy merchants, bankers, and landowners—were willing to invest in business. The lack of tariff barriers between the new states and the development of canals and turnpikes facilitated mass marketing of mass-produced goods. Raw materials for the developing manufacturing system were abundant. The development of the steel plow and the reaper opened the Great Plains to agricultural production, and the factories that produced these and other machines provided jobs that enabled large numbers of people to live in industrial cities rather than being tied to the land for survival.

The spread of industry led to mass employment, which provided incomes that made mass consumption possible. Mass consumption provided the demand that enabled mass production to prosper.

THE NEED FOR NEW MANAGEMENT SKILLS

The Industrial Revolution was characterized by a shift of the production process to large factories, which were a significant departure from the small shops of earlier periods. Larger groups of people were employed, each working on only a small portion of the total product and having little contact with those who were making other parts of the same product. Specialization of labor brought about new requirements for management, since coordination was crucial and much more difficult to achieve. In view of this increased need for management skills, it is surprising that few management studies were produced. The first hundred years of the Industrial

[1]Edward C. Bursk, Donald T. Clark, and Ralph W. Hidy, *The World of Business* (New York: Simon & Schuster, 1962), vol. 2, p. 1085.

Revolution, however, were almost devoid of recorded management developments.

THE MANAGEMENT MOVEMENT

The second hundred years of the Industrial Revolution might be called the century of the management movement. In 1886, Henry R. Towne presented a classic paper, "The Engineer as an Economist," before the American Society of Mechanical Engineers (ASME). "The matter of shop management," he said, "is of equal importance with that of engineering." Towne stimulated interest in management and began the management movement. Five significant components of that movement are outlined below.

The Scientific Management Era

Frederick W. Taylor, a young member of the ASME, was stimulated by Towne's statement to become involved in changing the concepts and practices of management. In his work at the Midvale Steel Company in Philadelphia, Taylor had observed that workers were left relatively free to carry out their job assignments at their own pace by their own methods. He used the scientific method of logical inquiry and idea testing to experiment with work methods in search of the best way to perform a job. In 1906 he presented a paper, "On the Art of Cutting Metals," in which he stated that management had four major duties:

1. To develop a science of management for each element of a job to replace the old rule-of-thumb methods.
2. To select the best worker for each job and to provide workers with training in order to develop their skills.
3. To develop a hearty cooperation between management and the people who carried out the work.
4. To divide work between managers and workers in almost equal shares, each doing what he was best suited to do, instead of placing most of the responsibility on the worker, as was customary.[2]

[2] Frederick W. Taylor, *The Principles of Scientific Management* (Norwood, Mass.: Plimpton Press, 1911; reprinted New York: Norton, 1967); also reprinted in *Scientific Management* (New York: Harper, 1947), p. 36.

Although not all the ideas that came to be known collectively as *scientific management* originated with Taylor, he synthesized them, made them operational, verified that they worked, and publicized them in a book called *The Principles of Scientific Management* and in other works. He remained active in the movement until his death in 1915. Taylor stressed that his concepts were not merely a set of tools but a philosophy of the sharing of responsibility and cooperation between labor and management. Despite these efforts, scientific management was widely misunderstood, and some "efficiency experts" exploited and increased this misunderstanding.

Taylor is called the father of scientific management, but he was not alone in his pioneering efforts. Among others, Frank and Lillian Gilbreth shared in the search for the "one best way" to perform a job and developed the principles of motion study. Henry L. Gantt worked with Taylor and invented the "Gantt chart" for scheduling work and for checking actual progress against a plan.

Not all the management pioneers were in the United States. Similar activities were taking place in Poland, Russia, France, and England. Henri Fayol, a French executive, studied management from the top down, with emphasis on overall administration. In 1916 he published a book on general and industrial administration, and other works followed.

The Human Relations Era

The pioneers of scientific management recognized the human element in management and addressed its psychological aspects in some of their writings. Most of their emphasis, however, was on efficiency. The most noted recognition of workers' social needs occurred with the investigations at the Hawthorne plant of the Western Electric Company (1927–1932), under the direction of Elton Mayo of Harvard. The experiments emphasized the need to take workers' attitudes and sentiments into account and give workers a sense of being contributing members of the company. Since the Hawthorne studies, management theorists have done much to incorporate the findings of psychologists and anthropologists into management studies.

The new emphasis of this *human relations era* did not exclude the earlier interest in work efficiency; it simply added a new consideration: that managers should also be interested in the people who do the work. Later studies in *sociotechnical systems* have delineated a technical system for performing work and a social system of interactions among the persons involved.

The Management Science Era

Management science had its beginnings during World War II under the labels *operational research* and *operations research*. Today the terms are used interchangeably. During World War II mathematical analysis of military data led to new decisions that improved the effectiveness of the military effort. Soon after the war these analytical methods were applied to problems of government and industry, with promising results. *Management science* is concerned with the application of mathematical and statistical theory to business situations. It involves the use of models (often equations or formulas) to describe and provide an understanding of a problem and its alternative solutions. Usually, the objective is to achieve the best, or optimum, solution. Management science is not a redirection in management but a change in the approach to solving management problems and an addition to the tools that are available for solving management problems.

The Information Age

Advances in information and communications technology have had a major impact on the way business is done and on the management process. Capabilities such as satellite communication, facsimile transmission, and electronic data interchange (EDI) have made global operations easier and more common. Electronic data interchange makes it possible for a company to better coordinate with its suppliers and customers by sharing more information faster. The entire supply chain can be more responsive to the ultimate consumer of the product while having lower inventory and less risk.

Rapid improvements in computers and information technology have resulted in changes in operations. Computers have become more powerful, compact, rugged, faster, and less costly. In many instances mainframes and minicomputers have been replaced, or their need reduced, by use of powerful microcomputers. Applications that previously could not be cost-justified are now feasible and provide significant savings. Software is more widely available and more persons are computer lit-

erate. Many establishments, banks for example, conduct most of their transactions through computers.

The broad availability of computers and development of technology have led to networking groups of machines so they can share software, data, printers, plotters, and so forth. Companies can update on-line catalogs, price lists, or technical data at all of their sites rapidly and simultaneously. Networks can be used to advantage in numerous other ways. Multifunctional design teams, for example, do not have to be at the same site. Computer-generated designs and other data can be transmitted to dispersed participants who can communicate through E-mail, telephone, and so on. "Groupware," or software to support group activities, allows the exchange of ideas and data so that groups such as improvement teams can "meet" and have productive interactions without having to travel to a common site.

Telecommuting allows some employees to work at remote locations. Data communications allows companies that have large amounts of data entry work to have this work done away from their data center, even in other countries, and transmitted by phone line or satellite back to the data center. Also, software development and maintenance can be performed at remote sites, even imported from other countries. Such developments as these, along with reduced trade barriers, have made possible competition from all parts of the globe so that management must deal with new challenges.

The Trend toward Management by Empowerment

Some of the changes mentioned above have affected the ways that companies are organized and managed. Global competition makes it necessary for firms to effectively employ all of the capabilities of the entire work force. Information technology can now add great power and speed to analyses and it can distribute information to all appropriate action centers. Coupled with these forces and capabilities, we now have a better-educated and more-informed work force than existed during the time many traditional management principles were developed. Also, there is a broader management understanding that many workers want a role in decision making, rather than just selling hours to the company and performing as directed during those hours.

The business environment is changing too rapidly to allow all decisions to be passed through many layers of management, and cost pressures have encouraged companies to "delayer" or down-size their structures. There is a trend away from the use of numerous layers of a chain of command through which managers perform all the evaluation, analysis, planning, and directing while expecting the other employees simply to execute the detailed plans. Today, workers play broader roles in many organizations. They work in temporary assignments in ad hoc teams and in more-permanent assignments on self-directed work teams. In these teams, and as individuals, they apply their firsthand knowledge to help interpret situations and shape responses in their workplaces and also help develop improvements to other parts of the company. These changes—along with more high-technology products that have relatively short lives—have increased the pace of business. There have been other changes in the technology available for production.

GROWTH OF TECHNOLOGY

Early production tasks relied on human effort both to control the process and provide the energy to make it go. Next, machines were used to power the processes, but the processes were still manually controlled. Then, automation provided automatic control so that a machine could sense its output, compare it to some preset target value, and adjust its settings if necessary. Today, computers make it possible to send various instructions to machines so that the machines can change the target measurements or the types of items they are making.

Computers have changed both the way businesses are run and the way processes are controlled. Computers perform such functions as keeping accounting records, scheduling work, tracking job progress, and keeping personnel data. Computers are used also in the processes performed by service businesses—automatic airline ticket reservations and automatic bank teller machines, for example.

Automated manufacturing continues to become more flexible and versatile. Today materials-handling systems can move objects to various locations in response to the computer signals they receive. Computer-controlled robots can execute various manipulations of work objects or tools. Production machines can execute various commands without human assistance and can operate as unstaffed machining centers. Combinations of automatic materials-handling systems and automatic machines, coordinated under the control of a computer, are being operated as unstaffed factories during part of the day. Designers can use computer graphics and powerful simulation programs to develop and test designs. These designs can then be translated into instructions to operate automatic equipment in the type of factory just described. Much remains to be done to make this type of processing broadly available, but the technology is at hand.

JAPANESE INFLUENCE ON OPERATIONS MANAGEMENT

While technology can be used to some extent to improve efficiency and productivity, much can be gained from new management practices and operating methods. The concepts of *just-in-time (JIT) production,* which originally were practiced in Japan, are continuing to be employed more broadly in other parts of the world. These concepts rely on employing only a minimum of inventories or other resources to make products. Companies operating under this philosophy coordinate their operations so that one work center produces only what is required by subsequent work centers, and this production occurs just when the necessary components are needed. The method characteristically produces items in small lots, which means setup costs must be low and workers must have multiple skills so that they can shift back and forth between various items. Successful implementation of JIT production also requires that companies develop reliable supplier networks, sound preventive maintenance programs, and excellent quality control programs to avoid defective components.

THE RISE OF THE SERVICE SECTOR

Advances in the technology available to perform work and in work efficiency have changed the percentages of the work force required to perform some types of work. Advances in agricultural technology have resulted in the movement of many persons from agricultural work. The United States underwent a change from an agricultural nation to an industrial nation. More recently, the country has changed further and is now said to be a postindustrial economy or a service economy. Figure 1.4 in Chapter 1 shows the changes that have occurred in the composition of the U.S. work force during the twentieth century, as agricultural employment has declined and service employment has risen. Blue-collar manufacturing jobs are projected to decline still further as companies continue to automate in order to remain competitive. Other manufacturing jobs will be lost as companies that are no longer competitive discontinue operation or move offshore. Agriculture and manufacturing will remain vital to the nation's economy and will contribute greatly to the GNP, but fewer people will be required to perform the direct labor of production.

Many of the changes that have affected and will continue to affect operations managers are summarized in these conditions:

1. Operations have become dispersed over wider geographical areas.

2. Operations have come to use more and increasingly varied technology.
3. Operations have become increasingly diversified.
4. The aggregate mix of operations has changed, with service operations accounting for an increased proportion of employment.
5. The trend in management style is toward management by empowerment.

Global competition continues to grow. Companies have reduced direct-labor, administrative, and middle-management jobs. There are fewer layers between top management and the direct workers so that companies have become leaner and more responsive to change.

Competitive pressures and advances in technology will continue to force successful businesses to seek improvements and to change. Operations managers and persons in all business functions will be called upon to seek new challenges and to meet them.

KEY TERMS

Industrial Revolution
Division of labor, or
   specialization
Mechanization

Interchangeable parts
Scientific management
Human relations era
Sociotechnical systems

Management science
Just-in-time (JIT)
   production

Most people are familiar with standardized manufactured items that are made in high volume—examples are televisions, refrigerators, and bicycles, in addition to automobiles. When we are in the market for a particular item of this type, we decide whether we want to buy the item, and often we may select a particular set of standard-design options that we want with the product. The Nissan plant is an excellent example of a facility producing this type of product. However, needs also exist for manufactured goods that are not standard items and that are required in only small volume. Facilities that are used to make these types of products require versatile equipment and plant arrangements, and they need people who can perform a variety of tasks in the course of a week's work. Teledyne Brown Engineering provides an outstanding example of such an operation.

Teledyne Brown Engineering (TBE) has a job shop manufacturing operation that produces small-volume, unique items for aerospace companies and government agencies, primarily in support of the U.S. space program. TBE's predecessor was moved to Huntsville, Alabama, in the early 1950s to provide manufacturing support for the fledgling rocket and space program, which was being developed around a group of German space scientists and engineers whom the U.S. government had located there. The company grew as the National Aeronautics and Space Administration (NASA) developed programs at the nearby Marshall Space Flight Center and as other space efforts advanced, with TBE performing such work as research and engineering support in addition to manufacturing. During the 1960s, TBE employed several hundred persons in manufacturing, many of whom worked in support of the manned lunar landing. A number of subsidiaries or separate companies have been spawned from this manufacturing operation. The original manufacturing operation, now called Fabrication and Assembly Plant 1 (Figure C.1), has about 60 employees involved in mechanical manufacturing. Another part of the company also produces custom electronic components and systems that may be used separately or may sometimes be incorporated into systems produced in mechanical manufacturing.

COMPANY PRODUCTS

The company bids on "design-and-build" work and prototype production from other designs; therefore, the volume is low. Many of the products are flight hardware, launch-support equipment, and handling equipment for space items. NASA and the U.S. Air Force are two major customers. Work comes to the manufacturing operation as a set of blueprints and specifications prepared by TBE's engineers or those from other companies. For some jobs, the company submits a fixed-price bid for the work. Design-and-build work may be done on a cost-plus–fixed-fee basis, because it is difficult to estimate the cost to produce something that has not yet been fully designed. The hourly rate is bid, and the hours may be audited to see that they were actually spent on the authorized project. Some products may have unusual shapes that are complex to produce, particularly for flight items. To lighten these items, any unnecessary material is removed from the places where stress is low. Some parts, such as a telescope

Figure C.1 General Layout—TBE

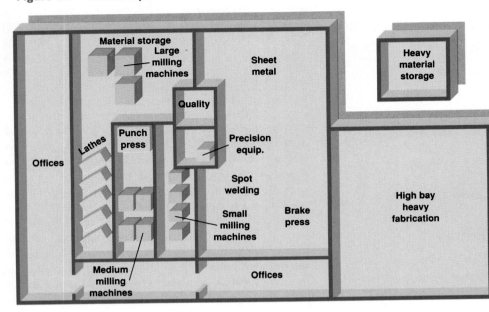

mount, are very delicate and require close-tolerance work; that is, the size must be within a few thousandths of an inch, or less, of the desired dimensions. Other parts may be large structural members that are machined from a block of aluminum originally weighing almost a ton; the material is machined away until only the final item, weighing about 120 pounds, is left. Figure C.2 shows an example of small parts in an assembly made by Teledyne Brown. Figure C.3 shows a more extensive project—a crystal growth furnace built for NASA to fly in the first U.S. microgravity laboratory.

Figure C.2 An Assembly of Small Items Made by Teledyne Brown

Teledyne Brown Engineering

Figure C.3 A Crystal Growth Furnace Built for NASA to Fly in the First U.S. Microgravity Laboratory

Teledyne Brown Engineering

TRENDS IN OPERATIONS

With the decline in space defense spending, TBE has made some changes in its operations. The trend is to refrain from capital spending and try to increase output with the same level of resources. The company is producing some commercial products that still have relatively low demand volume. For example, it is producing some electronic devices for use in the medical field and an automatic meter reader for utility companies. With good potential export markets for some of its products, the company is working to become registered to the international quality standards, ISO 9000.

The uncertainty in space and defense funding and a shift toward commercial manufacturing have encouraged the shift to more use of teams and a reduction of one layer of management in the shop. Each team has a team leader who helps coordinate the team's work and is responsible for quality on commercial work. The company is developing more flexibility by cross-training workers so they can work as electronics assemblers or as machine operators in the mechanical production processes. This also helps provide more employment security for the workers. The following discussion describes the company's work on low-volume, custom work.

INDIVIDUALIZED JOB PLANNING

The set of blueprints for a job is studied by a planner, who determines the sequence of operations required to convert a standard available mill shape, a special ingot, or a special casting into the desired final product. These operations are specified on a route sheet to tell the shop what work to do. The route sheet, blueprint, and any special instructions accompany the material through the shop to instruct workers about what work is to be done at each location and where the part should be moved next. Work that is performed in support of design often has several engineering change orders (ECOs) during fabrication. That is, the design is changed before the part is completed. This condition makes it difficult to plan the amount of work to be done in a particular week or to schedule a definite completion date for some jobs.

Although the space industry is relatively young, changing technology has had an effect on TBE's manufacturing operations and on other parts of the business as well. For instance, 10 or more years ago, a large portion of the mechanical manufacturing work was in fabricating sheet metal into chassis, control panels, and cabinets to hold electronic devices. But microminiaturization has advanced to the point where a function previously performed by equipment housed in three large cabinets can now be performed by a few chips contained in a device that can be held in one's hand. Today, a small portion of TBE's business involves electronics cabinets or other sheet-metal work. In an enterprise such as this, it is important that the company have versatile equipment and personnel so that most of the required operations can be performed and the company can adapt to the requirements of its market.

MATERIALS HANDLING

There is no need for automatic material movement between operations because the production volume is so low that little movement is required and because there is no set path through which items move. Small parts can be carried by hand, and some larger parts can be rolled manually on wheeled carts. Occasionally a crane or forklift may be required to move large parts in the machine shop. Heavy fabrication and structural steel weldments often must be moved with a forklift and an overhead crane, which are available in the heavy fabrication area.

GENERAL-PURPOSE EQUIPMENT

A wide variety of operations can be performed at various locations in the plant. The equipment must be of adequate size and must work to sufficiently close tolerances to perform to various levels of required accuracy. Operations might consist of drilling, tapping (cutting threads in a hole into which a bolt can then be screwed), milling a flat surface, turning a cylindrical shape, shearing or bending flat sheets of metal, bending material to various angles, welding machined or formed parts into more complex shapes, and assembling parts or subassemblies into custom items or major subassemblies. Each section of the plant is equipped and staffed to perform a particular type of operation. Figure C.4 shows an overview of some equipment in the machine shop with numeric control (NC) lathes to the left side and large NC milling machines to

Figure C.4 View of Machine Shop Showing NC Lathes (left) and Large NC Milling Machines (right)

Teledyne Brown Engineering

Figure C.5 Manually Controlled Lathes for Production of Parts with Cylindrical Shapes

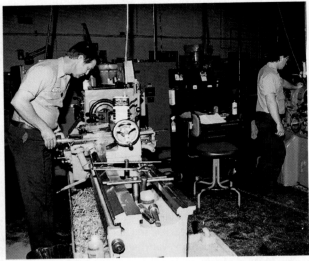

Teledyne Brown Engineering

the right. Figure C.5 shows lathes for turning cylinders so that the outer surface can be cut away to produce an object that has a round cross section. Figure C.6 shows larger NC milling machines with computer controls to locate the cutting tool accurately with respect to the work item. With this type of machine, a parts programmer studies the blueprint and programs a few key coordinates and instructions concerning the size of the block of metal from which the part is to be made, the depth of each cut to be made in the metal, and the size of the cutter to be used. A computer develops the detailed instructions, which are then transferred to the machine. The machine's small computer controls every movement of the machine. Some machines of this type have automatic tool changers, but they are useful primarily in higher-volume operations in which one operator tends multiple machines that are making identical parts.

You can see that the type of manufacturing business pursued by Teledyne Brown Engineering requires a versatile plant arrangement and types of equipment that can accurately perform a wide variety of operations. Also important are skilled workers who can operate the sophisticated equipment. All critical operations are carefully inspected to ensure that quality is controlled to meet the necessary standards.

Figure C.6 Numeric Control (NC) Milling Machine for Production of Parts with Flat Surfaces

Teledyne Brown Engineering

DISCUSSION QUESTIONS

Compare some of the characteristics of a repetitive manufacturing factory and a job shop by referring to Supplement B and Supplement C. Compare and contrast the characteristics suggested by the questions listed below. You can make two columns of answers, one for Nissan Motor Manufacturing Corporation's factory and the second column for Teledyne Brown's fabrication plant. Try to identify primary differences between the two companies.

	NISSAN MOTOR	TELEDYNE BROWN
1. What does the facility offer for sale?		
2. What entity designs the items produced?		
3. To what degree can the company control potential disruptions caused by design changes, and how would it do so?		
4. How would each company probably forecast demand so it could plan employment levels, budgetary needs, etc.?		
5. Compare the degree to which employees will need a variety of skills.		
6. What type of production equipment is used?		
7. What type of materials-handling equipment is used?		
8. How are products scheduled and tracked through the facility?		
9. What methods can be used to ensure that the product conforms to the design specifications?		
10. How does the company deal with suppliers?		
11. How would product cost information be collected?		

TOUR OF A SERVICE OPERATION

A View of Wal-Mart's Distribution System

During the 1980s Wal-Mart grew at a compound rate of about 25 percent per year. In the last three of those years Wal-Mart's sales doubled to $32.6 billion, to make the company number one in retail sales in the United States.[1] This rapid growth is made possible by many factors, including the relentless efforts of Wal-Mart's outstanding employees. The company's sales associates achieve a very high level of sales per employee. Another factor is the rapid increase in the number of Wal-Mart and Sam's Wholesale stores—and there are still several areas where the company has yet to expand. Other important factors in the company's amazing success are the everyday low prices made possible by everyday low operating expenses and an inventory and distribution system that makes sure very few items are out of stock, so very few sales are missed. The distribution system has kept pace with the rapid growth in the number of stores it must serve, and yet it is so efficient that the low operating costs shown in Table D.1 have been achieved.

It might seem that it would be less expensive just to have the suppliers ship merchandise directly to the stores, but this is not the case. Wal-Mart stocks approximately 1,500 stores through 18 distribution centers strategically located throughout the country. A typical distribution center (DC) may serve as many as 150 stores. The largest DC is seven football fields long and has 27.6 acres under the roof. To move merchandise efficiently, this DC is equipped with over 7 miles of conveyor that, in some sections, moves items as fast as 370 feet per minute. The conveyor network provides the DC with the capability to handle, sort, and load for shipment as many as 15,000 cases of goods per hour. Approximately $1.5 billion worth of merchandise flows through one DC in a year.

The company purchases merchandise from over 9,000 suppliers through its central purchasing offices at the Wal-Mart headquarters in Bentonville,

Table D.1
COMPARISON OF MAJOR RETAILERS IN THE UNITED STATES

COMPANY	U.S. SALES ($ BILLIONS)	OVERHEAD (% OF SALES)
Wal-Mart	32.6	16
Sears	32	29
K Mart	30	23

Source: "Mr. Sam Stuns Goliath," *Time,* February 25, 1991, p. 62.

Arkansas. Purchasing maintains close, long-term relationships with the company's suppliers. These relationships enable Wal-Mart to buy large quantities of goods at low prices and to ensure that the merchandise will be delivered to the DCs when needed, without delay.

Electronic data interchange (EDI) is used to link with suppliers for rapid, accurate communication of order information. EDI is a linking of the buyer's and seller's computers through a data communication link, such as a telephone line or satellite link. Purchase orders can be transmitted directly without incurring the delay of mail delivery. Low prices and quick delivery give Wal-Mart the ability to maintain high sales and rapid inventory turnover. An example of Wal-Mart's close supplier relationship is seen with one of its main vendors, Procter and Gamble. Procter and Gamble has an office in Fayetteville, Arkansas, that is dedicated to serving the needs of Wal-Mart. Twelve Procter and Gamble executives who work full time on the Wal-Mart account are assigned to this office.[2]

Wal-Mart's use of satellite communications is a key factor in its success in distributing goods to their stores. In 1987 Wal-Mart installed the nation's largest private satellite communication network which linked all retail stores and distribution centers to the company's data processing and computer

---

[1] "Mr. Sam Stuns Goliath," *Time,* February 25, 1991, p. 62.

[2] *Discount Store News,* December 18, 1989, p. 109.

communication center (which is the size of a football field) in Bentonville, Arkansas. Every night a store sends an order via satellite to the main office in Bentonville. These orders are, in turn, downloaded to the appropriate distribution centers, where the orders are filled and delivered. Satellite communication is cheaper, faster, and more accurate than a dedicated telephone network.[3] This advanced communication system allows every store to have a merchandise assortment tailored to its specific market.

The main office maintains records of the current stock levels at each distribution center. Consequently, they can determine when a center will need a certain item and, within a preestablished lead time, will issue a purchase order to the supplier for a specified delivery date. The distribution center is given a 3-month projection of shipping volume, so that each distribution center's management can plan staffing requirements in the various functions.

For the most part, a supplier will deliver the merchandise to the distribution center. When a truck

[3]Ibid., p. 203.

arrives, but before it is cleared to enter an unloading dock, a trucking manifest must be provided by the driver. A trucking manifest is a list of items on the truck and the purchase order number for that shipment. If the two documents match, the delivery truck is sent to a specific unloading dock.

The awaiting associates in the receiving department check each carton in the shipment against the original purchase order. This verification is facilitated by a bar code scanner. Each item on the purchase order has a bar code, and the associate scans the bar code on the purchase order as the goods are being unloaded. The computer verifies that the item was ordered, and the associate counts and enters the number delivered. If the merchandise is accepted, then it is placed on pallets. A computer-generated label, with the pallet's bar code, is attached to each pallet. This pallet label includes the location in a reserve storage rack where the pallet is to be placed. For items not suitable to be placed on pallets, labels are attached to the cartons.

After items are received, they will follow one of two general flow paths through the center, as shown in Figure D.1. One path is for "predistributed mer-

Figure D.1   Conceptual View of Stock Flow (Not Actual Layout and Not to Scale)

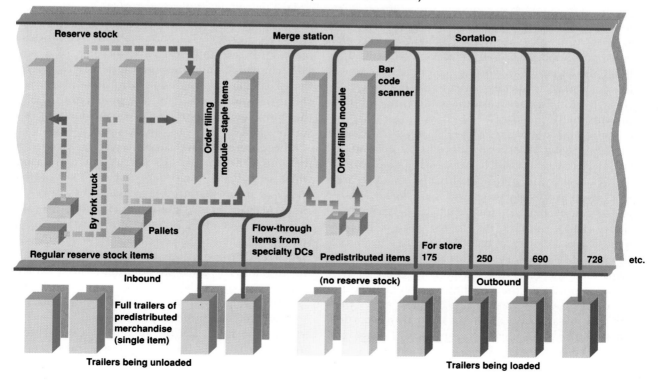

Figure D.2   Satellite Dish at Each DC and Each Store Links Them to the Communications Network

James B. Dilworth

Figure D.3   Trailers Being Loaded, Unloaded, or Waiting at a Wal-Mart

James B. Dilworth

chandise" and another is for "reserve or staple stock." Predistributed (or flow-through) stock follows a fairly direct path. One type of this flow-through stock is tabloid merchandise, or "TAB"—high-volume items that are taken from the inbound delivery trucks, put directly on the conveyor system, and diverted to trucks as they are being loaded to go to the stores served by the DC. A second type of flow-through stock is containers from other DCs that are to be distributed to stores served by this DC. For some specialty items, such as shoes, soft goods, and hobby and craft items, one DC will supply all the others. Flow-through merchandise goes directly from the unloading area to the merging station, after which it flows on the same conveyor system with the reserve stock.

The reserve stock takes a less direct path through the center. Once reserve stock has been received, it is transported by forklift to the reserve stock area. The associates who transport this merchandise are given the title "reserve stockers." The stocker operates a forklift that is equipped with a radio frequency (RF) terminal. This employee scans the bar code on the pallet tag, and the computer terminal displays the reserve location that the pallet has been assigned in the reserve stock area. The goods are then transported to the slot shown on the RF terminal display. Once at the designated area, the employee scans the location bar code at that particular slot. The computer then signals to the stocker whether he or she is at the appropriate place; if so,

the stocker scans the pallet tag so that the exact location of that merchandise will be recorded.

Items in the reserve stock area are subsequently moved to an order-filling module, when inventory there needs to be replenished. The order-filling module is a conveyor surrounded by merchandise so the associates at that station can "pick" the appropriate items in the requested amounts to fill the orders placed by individual stores. These workers pull items from the shelves around the module, attach a preprinted bar code label to each unit, and place it on the conveyor. This label has a bar code number which indicates the store that requested that particular item, along with other information about the case. Once items are pulled and labeled, the conveyor transports them to the merging and sorting stations.

The different flows are brought together in the merging station. In this station, a "batch" is formed which contains all the orders destined for a particular set of stores that are being loaded at a specified time. Management determines which stores are included in each batch based on the distance to the stores, the potential to combine store loads, the customized delivery program to which the store belongs, and the backhaul potential. The first batch pulled each day is the items that go on the twenty-four trucks that have to travel the greatest distance or have high volume requirements. The second batch is the items for the next-most-distant stores, and so forth. A batch is then sent to a sortation con-

Figure D.4   An Associate Scanning the Bar Code on an Incoming Carton

Mark Perlstein

Figure D.5   Slotter Lift Truck Removing a Carton from the Reserve Stock Area to Go to the Order-Picking Module

Mark Perlstein

veyor line, where it is sorted. In the sortation area, a laser scanner reads the store number from the bar code labels on each item. This scanner activates diverters on the conveyor line which channel the merchandise to one of twenty-four outlets. Each of these conveyor branches leads to a loading door. At each loading door is a trailer being loaded to deliver goods to a particular store. Twenty-four trailers can be loaded every 1.5 hours. Each day, every store will receive a shipment of goods from its supplying distribution center. Sometimes one trailer might contain the orders for more than one store, and the driver will go to multiple stores on a delivery route. Usually, however, one trailer contains a shipment for only one store.

Wal-Mart's success in maintaining its world-class distribution system can be largely attributed to teamwork fostered by a supportive management. The middle managers at the centers realize that the hourly associates are the ones who are actually responsible for the distribution of goods to the stores. With this knowledge, management tries to establish an atmosphere of teamwork. As one manager indicated, "My role is to set priorities, establish boundaries, and remove obstacles in order to help the associates accomplish their work."

STRATEGIC GUIDANCE FOR OPERATIONS

Companies spend a great percentage of their income and employee hours carrying out activities that stem from plans and decisions in various parts of the company. As these activities continue, they help to shape the destiny of the entire company. The accomplishments of a company can be astounding if all its parts work together toward the same carefully established, appropriate goals. But if different parts work toward different goals or if the entire company cooperates toward inappropriate goals, efforts are wasted. The results may even spell disaster for the company.

Top managers are responsible for making the vital decisions that set the company's overall goals and keep all parts of the company pulling together toward these goals. Decisions that have a long-range impact on the general direction and basic character of a company are called *strategic decisions*. Through strategic planning, managers evaluate the company's relationship with its external environment and establish the basic directions for the company.

One view of strategy is that, regardless of what is recorded on planning documents, the implicit strategy or achieved strategy of an organization is revealed by the pattern of decisions made over time. Strategic decisions that shape the future of units within an enterprise are made at several levels in the enterprise and not all of them are expressly identified as strategic plans. At the highest or most general level is an institutional strategy that provides very general long-range guidance for the total enterprise. Through statements and/or actions, top decision makers express the basic values and principles of the organization that shape the basic character and culture of the organization.

The broadest expression of the direction in which a company will apply its efforts is a statement of its *mission*, which explains the fundamental purpose of the enterprise. The company's mission statement describes in general terms what key decision makers want the company to accomplish and what kind of company they want it to become. A company's mission is its very long-range purpose and, consequently, is changed infrequently. A specific mission focuses the scope of the company's search for opportunities in the marketplace, further defines the types of organizations with which it must compete, and helps the company identify its competition and other threats it must guard against. That is, the company's intended mission will identify the parts of the total environment that are most relevant to the company's decisions. Consider, for example, Apple Computer's mission statement:

> It is Apple's mission to help transform the way customers work, learn and communicate by providing exceptional personal computing products and innovative customer service.
>
> We will pioneer new directions and approaches, finding innovative ways to use computing technology to extend the bounds of human potential.
>
> Apple will make a difference: our products, services and insights will help people around the world shape the ways business and education will be done in the 21st century.

A large diversified company may consist of multiple business units, either individual companies or *strategic business units (SBUs)*. An SBU is a part of a company with its own distinctive market and set of competitors and can be run almost as a separate business. In some cases an SBU might become a separate company, such as Saturn Corporation established by General Motors to compete more effectively in the compact automobile market. The strategic planning and actions that determine the business or set of businesses that a company will be in are referred to as corporate strategy. Corporate strategy in a multiple business company involves managing a portfolio of businesses and business units and directs such actions as mergers, acquisitions, joint ventures, and divestitures to shape the overall business to its best advantage and to maintain a strong, successful company. General Electric provides an outstanding example of corporate strategy in its maneuvers to move the company into more technology-based businesses and global markets. Some highlights of these changes are described in the accompanying box.

Each business unit or a single business company has a *business strategy* that guides business practices and directs how it will deal with its customers, competitors, and conditions. Major questions that should be addressed at this level are, Who are our customers? and What are their needs, desires, and expectations of the business? The business-level strategy can be based on this information to plan how the business can provide what the customers will perceive as the best way to satisfy their needs. If a company is to survive and prosper it must consistently provide customer satisfaction.

GE'S GLOBALIZATION STRATEGY

General Electric (GE) started the 1980s with a widely diverse set of businesses and about 350 product lines. It was felt that diversity would be a strength if each business were number one or number two globally in its market. If not, the objective was to fix it, sell it, or close it. Only two GE businesses, plastics and aircraft engines, were truly global in 1980. The company sold businesses that made up 25 percent of its 1980 sales, and it spent $17 billion on acquisitions during the 1980s. Many of the changes during the 1980s are outlined here:

1980—Acquired portions of Thorn EMI medical equipment sales and service operation

1981—Expanded Bergen op Zoom plastics plant in the Netherlands
Acquired air pollution business from Envirotech Corp.

1982—Dedicated $130 million expansion of R&D center
Invested $300 million in automating locomotive plant in Erie, Pennsylvania
Sold central air-conditioning business

1983—Opened dishwasher plant in Louisville, Kentucky, as first phase of $1 billion investment in major appliances
Introduced Signa magnetic resonance for diagnostic imaging
Expanded mortgage business by acquiring AMIC

1984—Sold Utah International mining operations to BHP of Australia
Sold housewares business to Black and Decker
Acquired Employers Reinsurance Corp.
Sold Family Financial Services, a second-mortgage subsidiary

1985—Revised management structure to eliminate sector level, creating a leaner, flatter, more market-driven business structure

1986—Acquired RCA Corporation including the National Broadcasting Company
Acquired 80 percent of Kidder, Peabody Group, Inc.

Formed factory automation joint venture with FANUC Ltd. of Japan
Opened $325 million plastics manufacturing facility in Burkville, Alabama

1987—Acquired CGR medical equipment business from Thomson S.A. of France in exchange for consumer electronics business
Expanded financial services business by acquiring Navistar Financial Corporation Canada, Gelco Corporation, and D & K Financial Corp.

1988—Expanded plastics business by acquiring Borg-Warner's chemicals business
Expanded appliance business by acquiring Roper Corporation
Acquired Montgomery Ward Credit Corporation
Sold semiconductor business to Harris Corporation
Initiated joint venture in motors with Robert Bosch of Germany

1989—Established joint ventures in appliances, power generation, and electrical equipment with GEC of the United Kingdom
Agreed to acquire a majority interest in Tungsram Company (lighting) in Hungary
Formed mobile communications joint venture with Ericsson of Sweden

In 1980 two-thirds of the revenues came from slow-growth businesses like core manufacturing and natural resources. After the changes outlined above, two-thirds of the revenues are from high-growth technology and services. The company entered the 1990s with thirteen businesses, each near the top in its market. All thirteen report directly to the three executive officers. In 1980 some of the companies had as many as nine layers of management. All companies have reduced layers, and now some have as few as four to make the corporation respond much faster. Operating profits from outside the United States were about 40 percent of the total in 1989. This overview shows some of the broad strategic changes a company can make to define the types of goods and services the company will offer, the geographical area it will serve, the way it will be organized, and other issues.

Each function within a business has a *functional strategy* that is a long-range plan of how that function will support the accomplishment of the business strategy. Since the operations function is responsible for producing the goods or providing much of the service the customer buys, it has a major responsibility to carry out much of the business strategy. Part of the operations strategy involves planning how to develop, maintain, and apply the capabilities required to satisfy customer needs better than any of its competitors. Much of the discussion in this chapter will deal with business and operations strategy. It is assumed that the company has already selected the business(es) it is in. Most of our considerations will address how the company seeks to gain competitive advantage or achieve competitive excellence and how the operations function helps the company compete.

STRATEGY PROVIDES FOCUS

Top managers formulate strategy to provide more definitive direction and guidance to the organization. Strategy is a long-term master plan of how the company will pursue its mission; it establishes the general direction in which the company will move. In formulating strategy, top managers establish corporate objectives and make broad-reaching decisions on such matters as the breadth of the product line the company will choose to offer, the geographical scope it will try to serve, the types of competitive actions it will employ and to what extent it will use them, the types of social involvement in which the company will engage, the amount of resources that will be committed to various company endeavors, and performance objectives for such matters as the company's market share, growth, and profitability.

General policies and subunit objectives guide and coordinate decisions at the lower levels of an organization. *Policies* are official statements, expressed or implied, that guide decisions and actions of company members in a consistent general direction. Sometimes a company's overall strategy is explicitly defined and circulated to lower-level managers to provide unified direction for decisions on short-term matters or on problems of more limited scope. Each subunit of the company, such as operations, develops strategies to accomplish the objectives assigned to that particular unit. It is logical that decisions and actions within a company will be better coordinated and will be more consistently directed toward the company's strategic goals if the company's strategy is explicitly recognized. Objectives and policies that are consistent with the overall strategy should therefore be formulated, communicated, and recognized throughout the organization. Each part of the organization then translates these objectives and policies into actions appropriate for it to take. Each unit then develops its tactics, which are shorter-range plans that focus primarily on the smaller part of the organization. When each unit's tactics are based on the company's strategic goals, operating decisions in each part of the organization are likely to be coordinated with those of other parts of the organization and lead to accomplishment of the overall strategy.

After clearly defining its strategy, a company or an SBU is better able to establish policies and objectives that will guide all its subunits of the organization. The efforts of each part of the company operating under the guidance of these policies and objectives can be more effectively and efficiently channeled toward the common strategy. Figure 2.1 outlines the relationships among the elements and activities involved in formulating and implementing corporate strategy. It shows that various external and internal conditions influence the selection of the company's mission. A

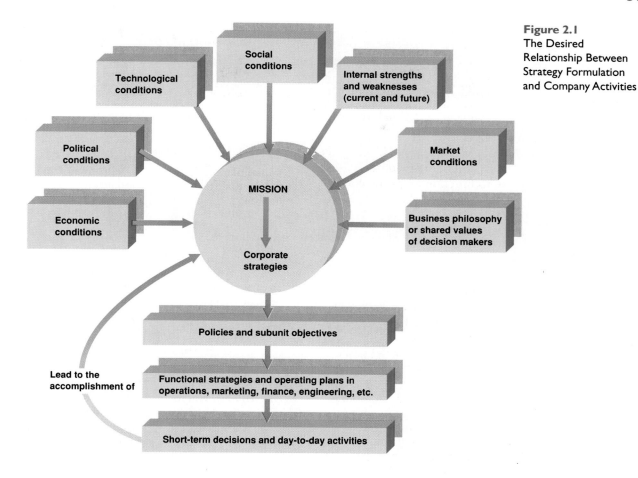

Figure 2.1
The Desired
Relationship Between
Strategy Formulation
and Company Activities

company's mission would seldom be changed; but if it were, it would then become another factor to be considered in formulation of the company's strategy. Since activities in any part of the company can change internal conditions over time, and since external conditions continuously change, the company's strategy must be reevaluated regularly. Strategic changes can also change the objectives and activities of various components of the organization and affect development of strategies within functions such as operations.

DIFFERENT OPERATIONS, DIFFERENT STRATEGIES

A company's overall strategy addresses many broad issues and can even include plans for social involvement, stockholder relations, and employee relations. One important aspect of the overall direction of a firm is its *competitive strategy* for marketing. At a very general level, one can identify some characteristics of marketing strategies often associated with the types of operations introduced in Chapter 1. Primarily, strategies of companies with a custom product will tend to differ from those of companies with a more standardized product. Table 2.1 shows some general features of

Table 2.1

MARKETING STRATEGIES ASSOCIATED WITH VARIOUS TYPES OF OPERATIONS

TYPE OF OPERATION	TYPE OF PRODUCT	TYPICAL PROCESS CHARACTERISTICS	TYPICAL CHARACTERISTICS OF MARKET STRATEGY
Service Project Job shop manufacturing	Make to order as customer needs or specifies	Use of broadly skilled workers and general-purpose equipment; emphasis on good initial planning of work, quality, flexibility	Selling diversity of capabilities and ability to provide features customers desire, ability to perform a quality job, ability to achieve reasonable delivery times
Mass service	Standard service	Special-purpose facility	Selling desirable characteristics of the service
Repetitive manufacturing	Make for inventory product designed to have features desired by many potential customers	Use of workers with narrower skills, specialized equipment, perhaps automation; emphasis on efficiency and cost control; good distribution system to make items readily available	Selling the desirability of features that are already designed into the product plus the desirability of the price, availability, service. Market research is important to ensure that product features are appropriate for the market

marketing strategy for various types of operations. In addition to different approaches to marketing there must be different approaches to operations in different business strategies. We shall discuss this idea further in several following sections.

OPERATIONS: A VITAL ELEMENT IN STRATEGY

The operations function has great value as a competitive weapon in a company's strategy. Because it is the part of the firm that must produce the goods or provide the services that the consumer buys, the operations function plays an important role in implementing strategy. The operations function establishes the level of quality as a product is manufactured or as a service is provided. The operations function often is responsible for the largest part of a company's human and capital assets. Thus, much of a product's cost is incurred within operations, and this cost affects the price that must be charged and the profit margin that can be achieved. Finally, the ability of the operations function to perform determines to a great extent the ability of the company to deliver goods and services within lead times that enhance customer service.

It is clear, then, that the operations function has an important influence on the cost, quality, and availability of the company's goods or services. Operations' strengths and weaknesses can have a great impact on the success of the company's

Table 2.2

OPERATIONS STRATEGY FACTORS TO BE CONSIDERED

Degree of vertical integration and procurement policy—make-or-buy decisions, use of long-term supplier partners, or frequent competitive bidding

Centralization versus decentralization of facilities—the number, type, and location of operations facilities to be used (pattern of warehouse support and transportation methods)

Organizational structure—centralization versus local planning, spans of authority, use of teams, management style

Human resource issues—skills planning, training, selection criteria, employment security, compensation (skill-based pay, salaried work force, profit sharing, team incentives)

Types of process technology and equipment to be used—special-purpose, focused equipment for high-volume, standard work or general-purpose equipment; the degree to which automation versus manual operation will be used

The information system that will be used to collect, analyze, and distribute information on work progress, purchasing, inventory, quality, personnel, etc.

The quality control and improvement methods to be used—quality at the source versus inspection, degree of prevention to be stressed

The strengths that are to be developed and stressed in order to gain competitive advantage and seek excellence

overall strategy. Therefore, the capabilities of operations must be fully evaluated when corporate strategy is formulated. One way companies obtain realistic input on the capabilities of the functional areas is to involve line managers in the strategic planning process. A planning staff may collect and interpret information on economic conditions, technological developments, competitors' actions, and the like. Line managers, however, usually determine the actions that the company can and should take in response to those conditions.

One reason for long-range planning is the need to develop appropriate capabilities as conditions change. Operations decisions in such areas as staffing, training, equipment selection, plant capacity, and layout must be consistent with corporate strategy. These decisions cannot be reversed rapidly, so long-term directions must be recognized and changed gradually if operations' resources are to be used to their full potential in pursuit of the company's goals. The capabilities of operations must be developed and aimed over time so that they contribute to the type of competitive strength the company wishes to emphasize. The operations function contributes to the company's distinctive competence, that is, the area in which the company tries to excel, so it stands out from its competitors and attracts customers.

Numerous issues must be considered in development of the operations strategy. Long-range plans must be made regarding many aspects of the operations function to develop a function that fits with the remainder of the business and is consistent with its other parts. Several issues that must be planned in the development of operations strategy are mentioned in Table 2.2. Various aspects of many of these issues will be discussed throughout the book. We will next discuss some considerations that are part of the strategy formulation process.

HOW STRATEGY CAN HELP ADD VALUE FOR CUSTOMERS

Definition of a mission and strategic guidance help focus a company's resources and efforts on common goals so they support one another. This focus and coordination can better serve the target markets at lower cost than if a company's elements are not well coordinated and mutually supporting. This chapter discusses how companies evaluate conditions to determine the best opportunities for the company or sepa-

rate business units and to identify the customer group(s) on which they will focus. Identification of the target customers allows the company to define the values that are important to customers and to establish the degree to which various performance characteristics, such as flexibility, quality, cost, and dependability, should be emphasized to represent the maximum value to the target customers.

STRATEGY FORMULATION

Because strategy deals with broad issues and long-range plans, strategy formulation is a multifaceted activity requiring diverse information from a variety of sources. Managers must continuously monitor information from outside the company to look for indications of new opportunities or threats. They also must constantly evaluate internal conditions to realistically evaluate the capabilities and limitations of subunits down through the organization. Effective and appropriate strategy can be developed if the organization has an accurate assessment of the conditions it faces and the capabilities it has to carry out the plans it makes. Strategy formulation does not always follow a prescribed sequence. Since apparent strategy is a pattern of decisions, it is played out over time. Strategic decisions occur as external evaluations reveal new competitive challenges and new opportunities or as the internal evaluations reveal that the company is weak relative to its competitors in some area. Internal evaluation may also reveal a strength that could be used to advantage or should be further developed to provide a competitive advantage. We will discuss some of the conditions that are often considered in formulating strategy and, then, some effects these matters have on operations.

External Conditions

The following are some of the major *external conditions* that might influence a company's strategy:

1. *Economic conditions.* Levels of consumer and capital spending; GNP; number of households and growth patterns in the target markets; current stage of the business cycle; interest rates; and employment levels.

2. *Political conditions.* War or peace; tariffs; foreign trade restrictions; monetary exchange rates; political stability in nations of interest and in neighboring countries; national, state, and local government spending in various budget categories; labor policies; environmental policies; and fiscal and monetary actions.

3. *Social conditions.* Trends toward more leisure time and casual life-styles; trends away from conspicuous consumption to more efficient living; greater awareness of physical fitness; increase in number of single parents; changes in status

of women and minorities; appearance of more breadwinners per family; trends toward more dining out.

4. *Technological conditions.* New products to offer or compete against, such as word processors and storage through shared logic, digital watches and clocks, calculators, home computers, office computers, electronic controls for automobile engines; new formulations of plastics, metals, fabrics, and chemicals; new processes to use or to compete against, such as automated process control, robots, continuous casting of basic metals, long-wall mining equipment, computerized medical diagnostic equipment, satellite transmission of information, laser printing, synfuels, nuclear power, solar energy, and electron beam welding.

5. *Market conditions.* Functions of a potential product, needs and desires of customers, primary concentrations of present and potential customers, possible distribution methods; potential competitors, their location, their strategies, their vulnerable points; barriers to entering the market, for either the company or its competitors; cost structure of product (high fixed cost or variable cost), availability and cost of necessary materials and equipment; price structure of product, sensitivity of market to price, potential volume of sales and profitability over the product's life cycle.

Information about such topics as those listed above keeps managers aware of conditions that might represent opportunities to the organization. Opportunities include, for example, situations in which the company might gain market share, introduce a new product, or provide leadership in community affairs. Environmental information also makes managers aware of any threats or new challenges. For example, competitors' moves might reduce a company's market share unless new plans are implemented, or new expectations in the labor market might call for the provision of day care for employees' children. Evaluation of external conditions proceeds along with an evaluation of internal conditions.

Internal Conditions

There must be an adequate match between the key requirements of the market within which a company competes and the capabilities of the company. The purpose of internal reviews is to assess the company's capabilities to move forward when opportunities exist and to identify any weaknesses early enough to correct them, particularly if external conditions represent a threat in that area. The idea then is to identify *internal strengths* and *internal weaknesses* in relation to those of competitors and in relation to the capabilities the company must have to execute its strategy. Internal conditions that should be evaluated include:

Market understanding and appropriate marketing capabilities

Existing products (goods and/or services)

Existing customers and relationships

Existing distribution or delivery systems

Existing supplier networks and relationships

Human resources:
    Management capabilities
    Current worker skills and motivation
    Access to necessary worker skills

Ownership of or access to natural resources

Current facilities, equipment, processes, and locations

Mastery of special technology

Patent protection for products or processes

Available capital and financial strength

A basic objective of evaluating internal conditions is to determine how the company's resources can be best used to capitalize on the opportunities or to counteract the threats revealed by the external evaluation. In evaluating the match between its capabilities and the demands imposed by potential opportunities or threats, a company will consider such questions as What advantages do we have in serving present and future customer needs? What are our weaknesses? How can we strengthen those weaknesses? Can we attract and train sufficient workers and develop managers fast enough to grow at the desired rate? Can our available capital be better invested in different programs or projects? What are the internal limitations for improving any of those weaknesses or capitalizing on any of those strengths?

Identification of opportunities can trigger research and product development programs. Discovery of areas in which the company has insufficient strength may lead to new initiatives in hiring or training employees. Mergers and acquisitions are sometimes used as a way to strengthen internal capabilities, to implement growth strategies, and to reduce competition.

In considering internal strengths and weaknesses, the business might also determine which areas of the business to strengthen and the types of strengths to build so that it will stand out as distinctively superior to its competitors. Some of the factors mentioned above will probably be more important to the customers the company tries to attract. A point that we will mention a few times is that if a company wishes to strengthen some area in order to gain competitive advantage it should be in an area that is important to the customer. If it is not important to the customer it will provide little or no competitive advantage. It is always important for a business to know its market and to listen to the voice of the customer.

In planning the strengths it should build, a business should also consider four general performance characteristics that describe major classes of capabilities a company might choose to emphasize to make the company more capable than its competitors of satisfying the group it seeks as customers. Special strength in one or more of these might give the company a distinctive competence and make the company stand out from its competitors. The four major performance characteristics are described below.

Cost efficiency. A company that emphasizes cost efficiency will see that its capital, labor, and other operating costs are kept low in relation to other, similar companies. Wal-Mart (discussed in Supplement D) is an example of a company that emphasizes cost efficiency.

Quality. A company that emphasizes quality will consistently strive to provide a level of quality that is significantly superior to that of its competitors, even if it has to pay extra to do so. Rolex is a company that stresses quality.

Dependability/Service. A company that stresses dependability can be relied on to have its goods available for customers or to deliver its goods and provide services on schedule if it is at all possible. Nordstrom's is recognized as providing excellent service in its department stores.

Maytag's "lonely repairman" ads emphasize dependability and, because Maytag owners don't have to call the repairman, imply cost efficiency.

Maytag Company

Flexibility. A company that develops flexibility can quickly respond to changes in product design, product mix, or production volume. The 3M company uses flexibility to advantage by developing, adapting, and providing new products quickly and frequently.

Each of the major performance capabilities includes a cluster of subdimensions, each of which might be given different amounts of emphasis in a company's strategy. We will develop this idea in more detail later. Each major capability can be thought of as a corner of the pyramid or tetrahedron shown in Figure 2.2.

A business might like to occupy as much space in the pyramid as possible so it would appeal to many customers. Also this would not leave any space where its com-

Figure 2.2
Possible Positions of
an Operations Function

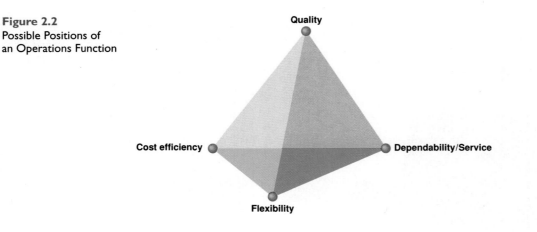

petitors can establish a distinctive competence that might attract customers. However, a company usually cannot be all things to all customers—regardless of how appealing that may seem. If a company maintains inventory at many convenient locations and provides great service during and after the sale, some other company can probably have lower cost. Likewise, a company that is the low-cost operator will probably not spend as much as its competitors on cross-training workers and maintaining extra capacity, so it probably will not be the most flexible business in its market. Some trade-offs usually have to be made, and they are expressed when the company decides which performance characteristics have the higher relative priority. Businesses can work to broaden the capabilities they have. In some instances flexible automation can be used to reduce labor costs, increase flexibility, and reduce human variability and error, thus broadening the capabilities of an operation and improving quality. Just-in-time manufacturing is being used successfully in many nations to broaden the capabilities of companies and make them more competitive, often without automation. Operating with low inventory reduces holding costs and space requirements so that total costs are lower. Production in small amounts allows the company to detect problems before many defective items have been made, so quality is improved. Efficient, flexible equipment and cross-trained workers provide flexibility. These ideas are discussed further in this book. Consider, for example, Porsche's strategy to move toward more cost efficiency while retaining its quality image (see accompanying box).

Each of these performance capabilities will be discussed further in the remainder of the chapter. Quality is the most basic or fundamental of the performance capabilities. Broadly considered, quality is the ability to serve the customer's needs. If a good or service does not meet the customer's needs and the customer does not want it, then it makes little difference how reliably or cost efficiently the company can deliver it. We discuss quality first and in much greater detail than the other three performance capabilities because it justifiably receives great amounts of attention in outstanding and excellent companies. Almost any company needs to have an effective quality system in place and must consistently work at quality just to maintain an acceptable level. Companies that seek to be excellent or world-class competitors, however, must make a concerted effort to achieve quality levels significantly beyond the average or merely acceptable level. We will begin our discussion of quality with a more-detailed consideration of what it is.

OPERATIONS MANAGEMENT IN ACTION

PORSCHE'S STRATEGY FOR COST EFFICIENCY

Recent changes in direction at the German auto manufacturer Porsche AG provide an example of a strategic response to external and internal conditions. Other European manufacturers of higher-priced autos, such as Jaguar and Ferrari ended up being acquired by larger companies that had profits elsewhere and wanted to add high-end products to their product lines. Porsche, with losses of about $150 million in 1992 and $95 million in 1993, took a different road to become leaner and healthier and stay independent. Some of the relevant conditions are outlined below.

- *Technological conditions:* Porsche's production methods involved considerable hand labor by highly paid craftspeople. Production methods also were relatively inefficient and inventories were excessive.

- *Economic conditions:* The decline in value of the U.S. dollar made imported autos more expensive in the United States, which was Porsche's major market.

- *Market conditions:* Porsche sells a rather expensive sports car. Japanese manufacturers have introduced cars that compete in the luxury market and have earned respect in the higher-priced market. Other, lower-priced Japanese cars entered the sports car market. For example, Toyota produces a midengine sports car and the Mazda Miata was introduced. In the United States, once Porsche's biggest market, sales fell from 30,000 cars in 1986 to less than 4,000 in 1993.

In response to these and other conditions, the company made a full-scale attack on bloated costs. The work force was reduced from 9,000 to about 6,300 and fringe benefits were pruned. About 40 percent of the managers were released. Two former Toyota production engineers were hired to improve efficiency while preserving the company's quality standards. Production time for the Carrera 911 was reduced from 120 hours to 80 hours and quality was improved. Inventory has been reduced by about $63 million and the factory now hums to a just-in-time tune. The company began operating in the black in May of 1994.

Porsche has doubled the size of its marketing department and new managers were brought in (six of them were from BMW). The goal is to capitalize on the Porsche image, improve customer service, and increase sales volume—even if it means moving into a lower-priced market. A new, lower-priced model, the Boxster, which will have 36 percent common components with other models will be introduced in 1996. The company plans to expand sales and service outlets to Brazil and other markets outside Europe and the United States. It is apparent that the company is working to cover more of the space in the pyramid of competitive capabilities and that its customers are being presented with an improved value ratio.

Source: "Porsche, Once Near Collapse, Now Purrs," *The Wall Street Journal,* December 15, 1994, p. A10.

JUST WHAT IS QUALITY?

Since quality is important to a company, let us examine further what we mean by quality, because it sometimes means different things. In fact, the term "quality" is sometimes used when the more appropriate term "grade" should be used. For example, a Lincoln Town Car is a higher grade of automobile than a Ford Escort. The Lincoln has more features, space, and comfort. Both may be high-quality cars, built to give trouble-free performance and to conform well to the consumer expectations that are appropriate for their respective market niches and price ranges.

Armand Feigenbaum, a noted authority on the subject, defines quality as "the total composite product and service characteristics of marketing, engineering, manufacturing and maintenance through which the product or service in use will meet the expectations of the customer."[1] From this definition we see that the customer's

[1] Armand V. Feigenbaum, *Total Quality Control,* 3d ed. (New York: McGraw-Hill, 1983), p. 7.

intended use of a product can affect its quality. A product must be adequate for the application the customer has in mind. A company might sell an outdoorsman a sleek, deluxe-model pickup truck with high-traction tires by leading him to believe that it will perform as well off the highway as a four-wheel-drive vehicle. It may be an extremely well-made two-wheel-drive vehicle, and beautiful. But if the customer becomes mired down at a sandy beach or desert or in a muddy swamp, he will be just as dissatisfied with it as he would have been with a poorly made four-wheel-drive vehicle. You can see that advertising and sales personnel, and many persons in the company besides those who actually build a product, have a responsibility for quality.

Several important implications of the definition and example above should be noted.

1. Satisfaction, hence quality, depends upon the evaluations of persons external to the company that produces the goods or services. It is not determined by some internal standard—unless that standard has been carefully established on the basis of accurate interpretations of customer information and feedback about their needs and expectations.

2. All parts of the company play a role in seeing that the customer's needs and expectations are met.

3. Customer satisfaction usually relates to long-term use of goods or results of a service, so its evaluation is based on comparison, over considerable time, with the customer's perception of competitive offerings.

4. Quality is a dynamic, moving target. Goods or services must be improved over time as competitors improve. What was a quality product yesterday may not be one tomorrow.

5. Quality requires a composite of attributes to satisfy a range of expectations of numerous customers or potential customers. Quality often means different things to different people. A company or other organization tries to serve a variety of persons, many of whom possibly expect a different set of attributes or emphasize different attributes to different degrees. A company that wants to provide quality to a particular market segment must learn what attributes are important to that particular market. Let us look further at some attributes or dimensions that may affect a person's perception of quality.

A person may evaluate at least eight aspects of a product or service to see if it satisfies her or his needs.[2] *Performance,* such as the color and clarity of the picture on a television set, is one characteristic of quality. *Features,* such as whether the TV has remote control, are another. *Reliability* (how likely is it to need repair?), *serviceability* (how difficult and expensive is it to repair, and how long will it take?), and *durability* (how long will it last?) are also characteristics by which we judge quality. *Conformance* measures how well the product meets the specifications or target set by its designers. *Aesthetic characteristics* (such as how an item looks, feels, tastes, or smells) are more subjective and sometimes more difficult to measure objectively. So far, we have mentioned seven characteristics, and customers really can't measure all of them. The eighth characteristic is *perceived quality,* which is a feeling of confidence in the level of quality that consumers develop on the basis of what they do see, their prior experiences, and the reputation of the company.

[2]David A. Garvin, "Competing on the Eight Dimensions of Quality," *Harvard Business Review,* November–December 1987, pp. 101–109.

The attributes mentioned above are suitable for describing manufactured products, and many are also appropriate for describing services. Service quality is difficult to describe in quantifiable measures that can be used within a company to determine consistent and correct work practices. When quality is viewed as customer satisfaction, however, customer surveys provide a way to measure service quality. Researchers have sought attributes that are important in measuring the quality of various types of services. Five major attributes found to be important in describing service quality are listed below.[3]

1. *Reliability,* the ability to perform the promised service dependably and accurately

2. *Responsiveness,* the willingness to help customers and provide prompt service

3. *Tangibles,* physical facilities, equipment, and the appearance of personnel

4. *Assurance,* the knowledge and courtesy of employees and their ability to convey trust and confidence

5. *Empathy,* the caring, individual attention provided to customers

Since customers are provided with both goods and services in many instances, a company must meet the needs listed in both sets of attributes mentioned above. Later we shall discuss the importance of identifying more specifically which attributes are important to customers and how to build strengths in these areas. Knowing what is important to customers provides guidance for the development of operations strategy as well as marketing strategy. It also is important for employees in all parts of a company to know what is of primary importance to customers if they are to provide customer satisfaction and help build business success.

THE STRATEGIC SIGNIFICANCE OF QUALITY

Quality is a powerful competitive weapon. Consumers of goods and services generally seek the greatest value, that is, the maximum amount of quality they can obtain per dollar, in the price range they plan to spend. Other things being equal, a company that can provide its goods or services with superior quality can often gain market share from competitors who do not provide equal levels of quality. This increased volume can enable a company to operate with economies of scale and make more profit.

The point made above is supported by an analysis of PIMS (profit impact of market strategy) data from over 2,000 business units in some 200 companies.[4] A business unit is a component of a company that has a distinct set of products, customers, and competitors. An estimate of quality relative to that of the business unit's competitors showed a strong positive correlation to relative market share. The business unit's return on investment (ROI) and return on sales (ROS) also had a high positive correlation with relative quality. Basically, customers elect to purchase the best-quality goods or services in the competing price range. Over time this is reflected in the business unit's market share. See Figure 2.3.

[3]Valerie A. Zeithamal, A. Parasuraman, and Leonard L. Berry, *Delivering Service Quality: Balancing Customer Perceptions and Expectations* (New York: Free Press, 1990), p. 26.
[4]Bradley T. Gale and Richard Klavans, "Formulating a Quality Improvement Strategy," *Journal of Business Strategy,* Winter 1985, pp. 21–32.

Figure 2.3
Relative Quality Boosts
Rates of Return

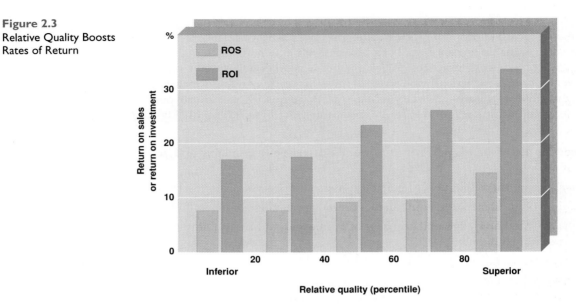

Improved quality is often advantageous even if it does not increase a company's market share. There are some niches and markets where high-quality items can command higher prices than other products. The PIMS data showed that the units with the highest relative quality rankings obtained a price that was about 8 percent higher than the units with the lowest relative quality rankings. If a higher perceived level of quality can be achieved at a cost that is less than the increase in price, quality has a favorable impact on profit, even without generating an increase in market share. Happily for the companies in the PIMS data base, achieving high customer-perceived quality did not result in higher direct cost.

In addition to the information above, there is support in the operations management literature for the idea that efficient quality control and improvement can actually reduce costs.[5] This point is not obvious or intuitively clear. However, in manufacturing, a great deal of labor and material can be wasted by making scrap and by performing rework. Much capacity and labor can be wasted in making items incorrectly, then screening the bad items from the good, and reworking those that are defective. It is less expensive to make things right the first time than to make them over and do it right on the final try. It is less costly to provide satisfactory service to a customer the first time than to do it the second time after providing the service once and having to deal with a dissatisfied customer.

THE COST OF QUALITY

The costs that a company expends because of poor quality or to prevent the costs of poor quality are referred to as quality costs, or the *cost of quality.* These costs exist in both manufacturing and service businesses, but they vary from industry to industry. Quality costs can be divided into four major categories; the first two include the costs to try to control quality, and the second two include the costs that result from

[5]Jeffrey G. Miller and Thomas E. Vollmann, "The Hidden Factory," *Harvard Business Review,* September–October 1985, pp. 142–150.

failure to control quality. A review of some of the costs in each of these categories provides further understanding of quality costs.

1. *Prevention costs.* The cost of preventing defective work is usually expended before the product is made or the service is rendered. These costs include quality planning, activities to prevent defects in design, design reviews, education, training, process control, process improvements, and working with suppliers before items are manufactured or services are performed.

2. *Appraisal costs.* The costs of appraisal are incurred for auditing service procedures to make sure they conform to prescribed work practices. In manufacturing they include inspection, tests, gauges and test equipment, and other expenses necessary to determine the condition of a product after it has been made but before it is released to the customer. These costs include checking material furnished by suppliers, in-process and final inspections and tests, maintenance of the associated equipment, and the cost of materials used in destructive tests.

3. *Internal failure costs.* Internal failure costs would include correcting or repeating any service activities before a service customer leaves an establishment. In manufacturing, these costs pertain to failures or defects found before the item is shipped to the user. These costs include expenses for producing items that are scrapped, reworking and retesting defective items, the lost value for items sold as seconds, and the costs of delays and administrative time to review nonconforming materials for disposition.

4. *External failure costs.* External failure costs are associated with defects found after items are shipped to the customer. Warranty costs, product liability suits, allowances for defects, returned items, and costs associated with handling complaints fall in this category. In a service business this category would include the costs of errors and delays. The loss of future business caused by external failures is more difficult to measure, but can be a sizable cost in this category.

It is estimated that the costs of correcting their own mistakes—that is, the cost of failing to control quality—may be as high as 40 percent of sales for some companies and that the industry average is about 25 percent. Companies are finding that money spent on a good program to control quality can be more than repaid by reductions in their costs of internal and external failure. It has been said that the cost of bad quality is, in essence, infinite to a company that goes out of business because its customers demand high quality and can obtain it elsewhere. Quality can be strategically important and a company may save money by providing it through a sound program. The best way to keep quality costs low is to make items correctly the first time and avoid the costs associated with poor quality.

Tennant Co. in Minneapolis is the world's number one manufacturer of power floor sweepers and scrubbing equipment for both domestic and industrial applications.[6] The company established a steering committee of six top executives to redirect corporate culture toward improving quality and productivity. Figure 2.4 shows a significant improvement in quality cost as a percentage of sales, and it indicates a redistribution of costs that reflect operating in a preventive mode rather than in a corrective mode, which frequently results in a reduction of the total quality cost.

[6]Brad Gador, "Quest for Quality—Tennant Company, Minneapolis, MN," *Target*, Fall 1989, pp. 27–29.

Figure 2.4
Cost of Quality
at Tennant Company

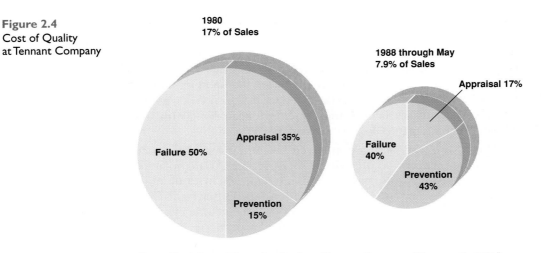

Source: Brad Gator, "Quest for Quality—Tennant Company, Minneapolis, MN,"
Target, Fall 1989, p. 25. Courtesy of The Association for Manufacturing Excellence.

Imagine the strategic advantage a company can achieve through quality! The company may actually have lower costs, but it may be able to sell its products at a higher price than its competitor. A company with this advantage occupies a greater percentage of the space in the strategic pyramid and leaves less space for its competitors to establish distinctive positions. Such a company can earn higher profit even in the face of serious price competition. It might gain market share, which often leads to economies of scale and higher profit. Since quality can have such a serious impact on a company's costs and competitive position, it is not surprising that many U.S. companies are working to improve many facets of their companies and trying to improve their quality relative to that of international competitors. But the challenge is serious because all companies involved in global competition are working to improve quality at the same time.

We will now consider some of the strategic advantages a business might achieve by developing strength in the other three major performance capabilities. As these are presented, some of the attributes or subdimensions of these performance capabilities are pointed out along with some competitive advantages each might help achieve.

COST EFFICIENCY

Some companies stress cost efficiency as a capability that allows them to stand out from their competitors and appeal to customers. All successful businesses must achieve at least a sufficient amount of cost efficiency to stay solvent. We saw that improved quality, when achieved wisely, can reduce some costs such as the cost of rework and scrap. Costs can also be reduced through such means as wise selection of suppliers, shipping methods, processing technology, materials handling methods, appropriate work force size and skills, and in other ways.

Cost efficiency can be used directly as an advantage by reducing the customers' cost to buy from the company. Charles Schwab, other discount brokers, discount department stores, Drugs for Less, and many other companies use this performance characteristic for competitive advantage. For some businesses customers may take either of two perspectives with regard to cost, so the company must present the proper one for its market. Some customers take a short-term perspective and consider only the initial cost or purchase price. These customers, for example, might accept a credit card that is free or has a low first-year fee. Other customers take a longer-term view and consider the cost of owning, such as the interest rate and renewal fees for the credit card example. For most businesses low initial cost to the customer requires efficiency in producing the goods and services. A company that stresses low long-term cost to the customer over the life of a manufactured product usually must do more testing and design work to add robustness and durability. This expense usually necessitates a higher initial price, so customers must be educated to the product's advantages. A long-term perspective may also require the company to provide more maintenance support and customer service for its goods or services.

Cost efficiency can help a company achieve competitive advantage without passing savings directly to the customer in lower prices. Cost efficiency could enable the company to have higher retained earnings that could be used strategically to fund such actions as research and development (R&D) programs to develop better goods and services or better processes. Improved financial strength might be used in other ways, such as to fund acquisitions that would help build other competitive strengths.

FLEXIBILITY

Companies need some degree of general flexibility so they can adapt and respond to change. Most companies must develop new products and respond to changing demand patterns. A company must strive for continuous improvement so it will not fall too far behind its competitors. And continuous improvement requires continuous change. A company that refuses to change will probably be left behind. Companies that improve (change) the fastest will probably move to the lead in their industries.

Managers that seek to build leading companies will need to attract employees that tolerate change, and even seek it. These managers should also provide and nurture a culture that seeks change. Processes must be upgraded, employees must

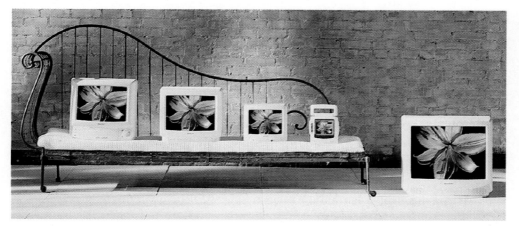

Wanting the flexibility to respond quickly to customer needs, Sony built a state-of-the-art television factory in the United States to be close to its U.S. customers. As a result, Sony has been able to constantly innovate, without sacrificing quality.

Sony

develop and apply new skills and accept new work methods, and so forth. A flexible, adaptive organization is essential in most business arenas today. Other than the general ability to change and adapt, there are more-specific types of flexibility that can help companies gain competitive advantage.

A second form of flexibility is the ability to develop and bring new products to market quickly. Companies that sell standard goods and services and have a "quick-to-market" ability can gain competitive strength by providing rapid, effective product innovation. If they are first to offer a new product they can have 100 percent of the market until a competitor introduces something comparable. Chrysler Corp., for example, had its Neon on the market only 3 years after the project was approved, which is at least a year faster than usual for U.S. companies. Companies that are flexible enough to be rapid followers can enter new markets before the market must be shared with many others and without the expense of extensive research and development. Flexibility to quickly modify products in response to customer requests, complaints, or market opportunities that are discovered will allow a company to stay ahead of its competitors and achieve high levels of customer satisfaction.

A third form of flexibility that helps some companies compete is "mix flexibility." Mix flexibility allows a company to quickly and easily change products or the mix of products it makes. A batch manufacturer that makes a variety of standard products needs mix flexibility so it can phase in new products or change from the production of one to production of another in little time and with little expense.

Mix flexibility is the mainstay of companies that offer custom services or custom goods, such as the Teledyne Brown fabrication shop discussed in Supplement C. Increasing the breadth of capabilities the company has will increase the likelihood that the company can successfully bid on the customer's work. Also, the ability to perform work profitably and with customer satisfaction depends on the range of capabilities the company has and the ease with which it can adapt to the needs of different customers.

A manufacturing company might develop mix flexibility by purchasing general-purpose equipment or flexible automation equipment, cross-training workers, and developing quick setup capabilities. Mix flexibility allows a company to change product mix as consumer preferences change or as seasonal demand shifts the relative demands of a mix of goods or services. As a service example, consider a lawn care firm that shifts from weed treatment and fertilization in the spring, to pruning shrubs and cutting grass in the summer, leaf raking in the fall, and then breaks out the snow blowers in the winter.

A fourth form of flexibility is "volume flexibility" or the ability to scale up or down the level of sales the company can profitably serve. A company that develops this characteristic can respond to seasonal demand patterns, growth trends, or erratic changes in demand without the expense and risk of carrying large amounts of finished goods inventory. Allen-Bradley's computer-integrated manufacturing factory (presented in a box in Chapter 7) that produces motor contractors is an example of both volume flexibility and mix flexibility.

DEPENDABILITY/SERVICE

McDonalds, which certainly has been successful in its industry, prides itself on providing consistent food flavor and quality. It, and most fast food restaurants, must also provide dependable, consistent service. Fewer patrons would continue to eat

"The best service in the business" is something Southwest Airlines has a right to tout. Winning consecutive Triple Crown Awards is a tribute to their dependability.

Southwest Air

there if it took three or four times as long to receive their orders even when there were no crowds at the counter (i.e., a "*sometimes fast* food restaurant").

Dependability for a make-to-stock manufacturer, or for a wholesaler or retailer, means that the company can be depended on to have items in stock almost always. Another way of saying this is that the company has a high service level. If a company is out of stock it may miss the sale of that particular item. There is an added danger that the customer who has to go to the competitor to get the item may continue to do business there. A make-to-order company demonstrates dependability by meeting the delivery commitments it makes to customers. Sometimes customers make elaborate work schedules based on delivery commitments provided by their suppliers. Obviously, companies that want to achieve customer satisfaction have to make realistic delivery commitments and be committed to meeting them.

There are aspects of dependability and service other than deliveries. Companies that excel at service go out of their way to help the customer. They may provide advice, training, installation, periodic maintenance, and many other services to assure customer satisfaction beyond that provided by competitors.

OPERATIONS MANAGEMENT IN ACTION

"MADE IN USA" CLOTHING HEADS FOR UPSWING

Tonight, after you trade in your suit for more comfortable duds, twist the collar around and check the label. Increasingly these days, what you'll find is a "Made in the USA" tag.

That's because big-name retailers and manufacturers of trend-sensitive apparel are shifting some production to the United States from overseas plants to keep up with clothing fads, restock empty racks and maintain greater control over quality.

Esprit de Corps has shifted production of such items as leggings, crop tops, and sleeveless shirts from Asia to the San Francisco area in the last 18 months, for example. Liz Claiborne Inc. has moved production of 1 million sweaters a year from Asia to a Brooklyn factory.

"We needed to be responsive to the consumer, we needed quicker turnaround time and we needed to be close to the fashions," said Jack Listanowsky, executive vice president for manufacturing and operations for New York–based Liz Claiborne.

Most of the clothing companies returning to the United States make juniors' and trendy women's clothing. While domestic production of such apparel as women's suits and dresses has plunged in recent years, production of trendier and more casual apparel for women has increased, according to Census Bureau data.

The number of knit T-shirts and tank tops made domestically, for example, climbed 74.8 percent, to 132.9 million units in 1993, after falling to 76 million units in 1988. Domestically produced women's sweaters climbed 11.5 percent, to 40.7 million units in 1993, after falling to a low of 36.5 million units in 1991.

For the domestic garment industry, which has lost 500,000 jobs in the past decade, this shift back to domestic production for some clothing items is good news.

Clothiers making the shift say their "turnaround time," or the time it takes from placing an order to receiving the manufactured goods, has been cut by as much as 5 months. The shorter cycle, they say, lets them decide on colors and styles closer to the fashion season.

Priestland said that shift back to domestic production is manufacturers' response to savvy consumers who demand a wider range of merchandise and retailers that must fill orders before a trend fades.

Also, since many retailers were glutted with inventory during the recession, store owners are keeping stocks low and must be able to replenish them quickly, according to industry experts.

"In more recent years, retailers in general have increasingly been pushing the inventory risk back to the vendors," said Donald Trott, retail apparel analyst at Dean Witter Reynolds Inc.

Keeping up with teenage fads that change faster than MTV videos has been easier for Esprit de Corps, the San Francisco–based children's and juniors' clothing manufacturer, since it has moved 50 percent of its contract work to the United States, according to company executives.

During the past 18 months, Esprit has shifted production of leggings and novelty knits, which include crop tops and sleeveless shirts, from Asia to the San Francisco area. It also has increased the volume of T-shirts it buys from U.S. manufacturers. Although Esprit won't reveal exact numbers, its juniors' division had a reported $110 million in sales in 1993.

Liz Claiborne Inc., which purchased a Brooklyn sweater factory that was under Chapter 11 bankruptcy protection 2 years ago, produces about 1 million sweaters a year there for its clothing divisions, such as Lizsport, Lizwear and Elizabeth.

Listanowsky said manufacturing in the United States has cut turnaround time in half for fill-in orders—rush orders made during a season to replenish sold-out items.

"We could do a fill-in order in 20 to 25 days," he said. "In the Orient, it would take 60 days and then you would still have to fly them out."

Manufacturers still producing offshore because it is cheaper are missing the bottom line, according to Bruce Herman, president of the Garment Industry Development Corp. Clothing makers willing to dole out more for domestic production will make gains in sales because they can respond faster to trends, Herman said. "Even a $12 skirt is subject to fashion," he said.

Source: From Melissa Lee, "'Made in USA' Clothing Heads For Upswing." Copyright © 1994 *The Washington Post.* Reprinted with permission.

BECOMING EXCELLENT AT THE RIGHT THINGS

We have discussed some of the attributes or subdimensions of the four major performance capabilities a company might choose to emphasize and some competitive advantages they might provide. The true measure of competitive excellence is providing what the customer needs, desires, and expects (and perhaps a little more). It seems humanly or organizationally impossible to be the strongest company in its industry with regard to all the attributes and subdimensions we have discussed. A company must identify who its customers are and what their needs are. Then it can develop the appropriate strengths to be better than its competitors.

To be excellent a company must develop exceptional strength in the winning combination of attributes that are most relevant to the market they serve. You might say they must identify and excel at their most important critical success factors. The accompanying box illustrates the strategic significance of flexibility that allows rapid introduction of new products and quick response to customer orders through such efforts as supplier linkages and support, location, and effective materials management. If, however, a business can determine some of the specific subdimensions of the major performance capabilities customers prefer, it can more-precisely focus the types of strengths or capabilities the business needs.

One author refers to the key capabilities as "order winners" because they have the potential to attract customers to the company over its competitors. Some level of the other capabilities may be "qualifiers" that are necessary to even be considered in the market.[7] One empirical study showed that companies rank-order the four or just list the ones that are to be stressed.[8] In defining the relative importance given to the four performance criteria, a business unit or company defines its position; that is, the space that it will occupy in the pyramid shown in Figure 2.2.

A company can often identify what it takes to be outstanding in the customer's eyes through competitive comparisons, surveys of internal and external customers, benchmarking, focus groups, or other means. Metropolitan Life Insurance Company (see accompanying box) found that its customers desired reliability, responsiveness,

---

[7]Terry Hill, *Manufacturing Strategy: Text and Cases* (Homewood, Ill., Irwin, 1989), p. 44.
[8]Ann Marucheck, Ronald Pannesi, and Carl Anderson, "An Exploratory Study of the Manufacturing Strategy Process in Practice," *Journal of Operations Management 9*, no. 1 (January 1990):101–123.

APPLICATION

ATTRIBUTES THAT SHOULD BE EMPHASIZED FOR QUALITY

Metropolitan Life Insurance Company used a set of attributes to more fully describe the types of services that were important to different sets of its customers. Customers can be internal, such as users of services from its data processing department, or external, such as customers who purchase life insurance policies. Surveys were used to determine customer expectations and their perceptions of the performance that was provided for the five major attributes of service quality mentioned in the text. By identifying what is important to its customers the company can establish performance standards so its employees know what they are to do. Occasional customer surveys are used to pinpoint specific problems or opportunities to improve customer satisfaction.

Source: John J. Falzon, "Measuring the Quality of Services," *Total Quality Performance* (New York: Conference Board, 1988), pp. 54–58.

Table 2.3
OPERATIONS STRENGTHS NEEDED TO ACHIEVE BUSINESS ADVANTAGES

CUSTOMER DESIRES TO BE STRESSED OR ADVANTAGE TO BE SOUGHT	CAPABILITIES OR STRENGTHS TO BE DEVELOPED AND USED
Features, durability, reliability, serviceability performance, aesthetics	Knowledge of the "voice of the customer," very capable R&D, capable service innovators or product designers
Conformance	Commitment to total quality management, standardized procedures, consistent equipment
Promptness, responsiveness	Sufficient capacity and/or inventory, commitment of employees, quick-response suppliers, smooth working relations internally and with suppliers, elimination of bottlenecks
Assurance	No hassle service, consistency, warranties
Empathy, care, concern	Personnel selection, training, and placement; policies; a supportive culture
Service reliability and dependability	Empowerment and training of employees to adjust and correct performance
Volume flexibility	Low breakeven point, reserve capacity, flexible suppliers
Mix flexibility	Multiskilled workers, multipurpose equipment, quick setups (change-overs), flexible suppliers, good communication and coordination
Cost efficiency for initial price	Low cost of capital, little reserve capacity, in-house ability to adapt equipment with low investment, equipment maintained for long life, low work-inventory cost, low unit-labor cost (i.e., high output/wage or salary cost)
Cost efficiency for life-cycle cost	Design of goods and services with long-term cost to user in mind; plus the items listed in the cell above
Service/dependability	Accurate scheduling and control system, committed employees, accurate inventory system, responsive supplier partners, reserve capacity, preventive maintenance

tangibles, assurance, and empathy discussed above as attributes of service quality. After identifying what it takes to achieve customer satisfaction, the next step is to build strengths and strategies that exploit this knowledge. Since operations produces the goods and provides much of the service that the customer receives, many of the strengths that achieve customer satisfaction must exist there. Operations must be considered when a company examines its internal strengths and weaknesses before establishing realistic strategies.

Operations strategies, just like other functional strategies, should include building the right strengths to support the overall business strategy and achieve competitive excellence. The right efforts must be stressed throughout the company in all dealings with both internal and external customers. Operations and other parts of the business must be capable and committed to doing their best in their part of all activities. Table 2.3 lists several attributes of the major performance capabilities a company might stress as part of its strategy. The table also outlines strengths for each attribute that might be stressed in an operations strategy to support the company's emphasis and help achieve excellence. From this table and the previous discussion you can see that operations can play a major role in helping a company execute its competitive strategy. The next chapter and much of the rest of the book will address many of the issues to consider and the methods to use in seeking excellence in operations.

SUMMARY

Strategy can be considered a pattern of decisions that determines the basic direction and character of a company over the long term. Strategic planning attempts to guide the pattern of decisions in what is considered the best direction to carry out the company's mission. Planning should be based on a careful assessment of external conditions and internal capabilities. The external assessment seeks to identify opportunities or threats to the company while the internal review seeks to identify the company's strengths and weaknesses. A company desires to develop strengths where threats are likely and where it intends to exploit opportunities. Strengths can be developed through a variety of methods such as research and development, training and education to develop or improve skills, mergers, joint ventures, and so forth.

Strategic goals and plans of a company or business unit will affect decisions regarding many issues. Some of the areas that are influenced are the degree of vertical integration, the degree of centralization and type of organization structure, human resource policies, technology selection, the approach to quality, and the strengths that will be stressed to appeal to customers and gain competitive advantage.

A company may contain multiple business units and may plan a different strategy for each. The operations function within a business or business unit often includes a large percentage of the employees, spends a large percentage of the budget, and produces much of what the customer receives in goods and services. Therefore, operations plays a major role in helping a strategy succeed.

It is important that all the company's resources be coordinated and directed toward the company's strategic objectives. Each function must develop the appropriate strengths to carry out its part of the strategy. Four general types of competitive strengths that operations can use to gain competitive advantage are quality, flexibility, dependability and service, and cost efficiency. Each of these general characteristics represents a cluster of more-specific capabilities a company may use to gain advantage over its competitors. A company and its operations function must be reasonably good at many of these performance capabilities, but it cannot be the best in its industry at everything. Logically, the measures in which the company strives to excel should depend upon the needs, desires, and expectations of its customers. It is important for the company to carefully study and stay close to the customers in each market segment in which it competes.

Quality is an important dimension that many companies emphasize and a basis upon which many companies compete. When considered from a broad definition, quality represents the desirable features of goods or services that make the company's output have value to the customer. Quality is a major part of the numerator of the value ratio introduced in Chapter 1. Quality can sometimes allow a company to earn a higher margin and, if achieved wisely, it can even reduce costs. The cost of quality includes prevention, assessment, internal failure cost, and external failure cost. Sometimes an expenditure on prevention can reduce failure cost by an amount much greater than the expenditure. The next chapter discusses the use of quality as a means of seeking competitive excellence and improvement.

KEY TERMS

Strategic decisions	Cost efficiency	Perceived quality
Mission	Quality	Responsiveness
Strategic business units (SBUs)	Dependability	Tangibles
Business strategy	Flexibility	Assurance
Functional strategy	Performance	Empathy
Policies	Features	Cost of quality
Competitive strategy	Reliability	Prevention cost
External conditions	Serviceability	Appraisal cost
Internal strengths	Durability	Internal failure cost
Internal weaknesses	Conformance	External failure cost
	Aesthetic characteristics	

DISCUSSION QUESTIONS

1. What does the term *corporate strategy* refer to?
2. What level of management is responsible for development of a company's overall strategy?
3. List five external conditions that might exert an important influence on the process of shaping the strategic plans of a company.
4. How does the operations function play a significant role in ensuring the success of a company's strategy?
5. List four major performance characteristics that a company can elect to emphasize to give it a distinctive strategy.
6. Explain what is meant by a target position with regard to four performance criteria. Why would a company not want to keep changing so its competition would always be confused?
7. Other than the positioning decision, list at least six categories of strategy decisions for a manufacturing company.
8. What are some of the capabilities that are desirable for the operations function to have in a manufacturing company that elects to emphasize cost efficiency?
9. What are some of the capabilities that are desirable for the operations function to have in a manufacturing company that elects to emphasize quality?
10. What are some of the capabilities that are desirable for the operations function to have in a service company that elects to emphasize dependability of delivery?
11. What are some of the capabilities that are desirable for the operations function to have in a service company that elects to have flexibility in its volume of work?
12. **a.** In your opinion, where are most hospitals positioned within the pyramid discussed in the chapter and presented in Figure 2.2 (see page 58)? What is the reason for your answer?

    b. If you know of any hospitals that are positioned differently, discuss these differences.
13. Compare an automobile shop near your school or the repair shop you use with the service department of a local Mercedes dealer, in terms of where they are positioned within the pyramid shown in Figure 2.2.
14. Visit a fast food establishment. Do any items on the menu appear to be inconsistent with the degree of quality, flexibility, and service that you typically would expect to be offered? If so, and if the staff are not busy, ask how they prepare this item quickly with high quality and low cost.

BIBLIOGRAPHY

Albrecht, Karl, and Ron Zemke. *Service America: Doing Business in the New Economy.* New York: Warner Books, 1990.

Bowen, David E., Richard B. Chase, Thomas G. Cummings, and Associates. *Service Management Effectiveness: Balancing Strategy, Organization and Human Resources, Operations, and Marketing.* San Francisco: Jossey-Bass, 1990.

Chase, Richard B., and David A. Garvin. "The Service Factory." *Harvard Business Review,* July–August 1989, pp. 61–69.

David, Fred R. *Concepts of Strategic Management.* 5th ed. Englewood Cliffs, N.J.: Prentice-Hall, 1995.

Davidow, William H., and Bro Uttal. "Service Companies: Focus or Falter." *Harvard Business Review,* July–August 1989, pp. 77–85.

Engledow, Jack L., and R. T. Lentz. "What Ever Happened to Environmental Analysis?" *Long Range Planning 18,* no. 2 (April 1985):93–103.

Garvin, David A. *Operations Strategy: Text and Cases.* Englewood Cliffs, N.J.: Prentice-Hall, 1992.

Hayes, Robert H. "Strategic Planning—Forward in Reverse?" *Harvard Business Review,* November–December 1985, pp. 111–119.

————, **and Steven C. Wheelwright.** *Restoring Our Competitive Edge.* New York: Wiley, 1984. Chap. 2.

Heskett, James L. *Managing in the Service Economy.* Boston: Harvard Business School Press, 1986.

Hill, Terry. *Manufacturing Strategy: Text and Cases.* Homewood, Ill.: Irwin, 1989.

Huff, Anne S., and Rhonda Kay Reger. "A Review of Strategic Process Research." *Journal of Management 13,* no. 2 (Summer 1987):211–236.

Marucheck, Ann, Ronald Pannesi, and Carl Anderson. "An Exploratory Study of the Manufacturing Strategy Process in Practice." *Journal of Operations Management 9,* no. 1 (January 1990):101–123.

McConkey, Dale D. "Planning in a Changing Environment." *Business Horizons,* September–October 1988, pp. 64–72.

Moody, Patricia E., ed. *Strategic Manufacturing: Dynamic New Directions for the 1990's.* Homewood, Ill.: Irwin, 1990.

Pearce, John A., II, and Fred David. "Corporate Mission Statements: The Bottom Line," *Academy of Management Executive 1,* no. 2 (May 1987):109–116.

Porter, Michael E. *Competitive Advantage: Creating and Sustaining Superior Performance.* New York: Free Press, 1985.

Scarpello, Vida, William R. Bolton, and Charles R. Hofer. "Reintegrating R&D into Business Strategy." *Journal of Business Strategy 6,* no. 4 (Spring 1986):49–56.

Skinner, Wickham. *Manufacturing: The Formidable Competitive Weapon.* New York: Wiley, 1985.

————. "The Productivity Paradox." *Harvard Business Review,* July–August 1986, pp. 55–59.

Stalk, George, Jr., and Thomas M. Hout. *Competing against Time: How Time-Based Competition Is Reshaping Global Markets.* New York: Free Press, 1990.

Stonebraker, Peter W., and G. Keong Leong, *Operations Strategy: Focusing Competitive Excellence.* Boston: Allyn and Bacon, 1994.

Thompson, Arthur A., Jr., and A. J. Strickland, III. *Strategy and Policy: Concepts and Cases.* 6th ed. Homewood, Ill.: Irwin, 1992.

Wheelwright, Steven C. "Reflecting Corporate Strategy in Manufacturing Decisions." *Business Horizons,* February 1979, pp. 57–66.

DECISION MAKING

ecision making is the act of selecting a preferred course of action among alternatives. The act of decision making enters into almost all of a manager's activities. Managers must reach decisions about objectives and plans for their organizational units. They must decide how to direct, how to organize, how to control. They must not only make many decisions, but also guide subordinates in reaching decisions of their own. Much of a manager's time is spent in gathering and evaluating information so that he or she will know if a decision is needed and the necessary background information will be available if it is.

Since decisions are so frequently made in all areas of life, one may wonder why so much has been written about decision making in management. The answer is very simple, though it may appear harsh: Businesses and other organizations survive by making and implementing enough of the right decisions; they fail either because they make the right decisions but are unsuccessful in implementing them or because they make the wrong decisions and succeed in implementing them. The success of business and nonprofit organizations hinges on their ability to make good decisions and to implement their decisions well.

Implementation may involve the manager's competence in working with others. Depending on the particular decision, implementation may range from very simple to impossible. It may merely require communicating the decision to one individual who recognizes its wisdom (that is, finds it consistent with her or his view of the world) and performs the required acts. Or it may require long-term programs that will revise the organization's complete method of operation. New people, equipment, responsibilities, organization components, and/or communications patterns may be necessary.

Making and implementing decisions are crucial parts of management. The making of decisions is the major focus of the mathematical and statistical tools of the management sciences. Implementation involves influence, leadership, gaining acceptance of ideas, and other important capabilities dealt with in the behavioral school of management thought. Management sciences attempt to improve the decision-making process. One should understand that management does not consist of mathematical models; the models are tools to aid management in reaching decisions. The management science school and the behavioral school are two sides of the same coin; both help to improve management's chances of success. Much of the material written on operations management deals with methods of making good decisions in planning and controlling the use of resources.

Usually it is not possible to recognize and investigate every strand in the complex web of interrelationships that can be affected by a decision. Humans operate within the limits of what has been referred to as "bounded rationality"; that is, limitations to their ability, time, money, and information usually keep them from reaching totally optimum decisions. This is one reason that persons are assigned to manage only part of a total system. When a decision is designed to optimize some criterion for a part of a business, it still may not optimize (that is, it suboptimizes) the broader goal of the total business. In reaching a decision, one should try to maintain a perspective that is broad enough that the decision does not seriously suboptimize the goals of the overall organization. For example, a local goal to minimize the maintenance department's costs could seriously impair the operating effectiveness of the total company. These matters should be considered in the phases of decision making, which we discuss next.

PHASES OF DECISION MAKING

Decisions are made by many methods. No doubt some successful decisions have been made by illogical processes, and some poor decisions have been made by very sophisticated logic. Psychological, emotional, and nonrational factors influence the process. The predominant factor in many decisions is probably experience: "We've done it this way in the past and it worked, so we'll go on doing it this way." In a rapidly changing world, organizations must guard against this mind-set. Some decisions are based on a follow-the-leader approach: "If they can do it, so can we." Ego may be involved in a decision: "I'll never buy from him again." A manager who walks into a workplace and has a feeling of being crowded, or almost trips over a large object protruding from a small space, may immediately decide to enlarge or rearrange the workplace.

A detailed study of decisions based on some of the preceding factors might be interesting and perhaps amusing, but it would teach us little about improving the process of reaching decisions. Study of an approach that can be identified, learned, and improved is a much better investment of time for a potential manager. Such an approach requires a structured, organized, and logical view of decision making. The processes of discovery, analysis, and exploration involved in decision making have been divided into a series of phases to provide this desired expository structure. The actual mental processes and behavior are quite complex. Decision making is a series of interrelated, often overlapping phases, each representing a different point of emphasis rather than a distinctly separate step. The major phases of decision making are discussed in the following sections.

Recognition of the Need for a Decision

Recognizing the need for a decision is not so simple as it may seem. The need arises when actions do not meet objectives and/or objectives need to be reestablished. Frequently either of these situations is termed a problem. The objective of the first phase of decision making can be interpreted as recognizing that there is a problem and defining it. *Problem* in this context can mean an opportunity to change or improve as well as a failure to achieve some intended objective.

Good managers should always be searching for problems and potential problems. Their technical and behavioral competence will provide valuable insights into the operations under their supervision. A manager who understands the situation is in a better position to spot potential problems before they develop into more serious problems requiring more difficult decisions. One purpose of the reporting and control systems in a company is to make managers aware of problems that need management attention.

It is imperative that the problem be properly defined once its symptoms have been recognized. Obviously, solving the wrong problem is unlikely to give the desired result. The problem-definition phase requires a look behind the scenes. To solve a problem, one needs to look beyond the symptoms to discover the basic underlying causes.

Identification of Objectives

Obviously, one cannot make the right decision unless one knows what "right" is. Some criterion or criteria for judging alternatives should be developed in the decision-making process. Sometimes two people facing the same situation reach totally different decisions. It would appear that they have different value systems; that is, they wish to accomplish different objectives. Organizations are more likely to be successful—at least, they will require less coordination effort—if the members agree on what they are seeking to accomplish. Managers can reduce wasted time and uncertainty for their subordinates by keeping them informed about objectives.

An understanding of objectives is desirable in searching for and identifying solutions to a problem. This understanding is by no means essential, however; some managers (and other persons as well) do not want to be very explicit in setting objectives. They may not be able to describe what they are looking for, but if they look at enough alternatives, they can tell you which they like best. They identify the desirable features in alternatives as they study the alternatives.

Subordinates are often frustrated when they are expected to aid in decision making or to seek alternatives under these conditions. It is desirable to have at least general guidelines or objectives to assist associates. Obviously, the final choice must be based on some criterion, explicit or implicit. Subordinates often learn their boss's desires by inferring them from past decisions. Small, informal organizations typically operate in this manner.

Search for Reasonable Alternatives

It is seldom possible to identify and explore all possible alternatives because of limitations of time and money. Talent may also be limited. Certainly creative thinking is a valuable asset in the search for alternatives. The search for alternative solutions is sometimes stopped if the incremental gain from developing an additional alternative is not expected to be greater than the incremental cost of further search. Sometimes, however, major improvements or breakthroughs can be achieved through radical creative efforts. Groups sometimes begin with a "clean slate" to totally redesign a process or perhaps eliminate the need for it and thus solve a problem.

Use of highly skilled or expert people in the decision-making process can provide insights into the technical limitations and the feasibility of some alternatives. However, they would seldom have all the possible alternatives already in mind. Rank-and-file employees also may participate in multidisciplinary teams and provide insights into the problems and implementation challenges for proposed solutions. The search process is usually exceedingly complex and is probably a heuristic process. Examination of alternatives may lead to a change in the direction of search for other alternatives. As one identifies alternatives with desirable characteristics, the search is directed toward finding other alternatives with these types of characteristics. If weak points are found in some alternatives, then the search will seek alternatives that lack these shortcomings.

Evaluation of Alternatives

The objective of the fourth phase, evaluation of alternatives, is to compare the expected consequences of selecting particular alternatives. A formal, explicit computation of the expected consequences considers both the possible outcomes and the likelihood that they will occur. Such an approach is taken in decision theory (to be discussed later in this supplement). Some preliminary evaluation should have occurred in the preceding phase of decision making as unreasonable alternatives were discarded. Those alternatives that were retained should now be subjected to further scrutiny.

Because each alternative may have several possible outcomes to be evaluated, determining the outcomes and estimating the likelihood of their occurrence can be a time-consuming process. Considerable data collection may be a necessary part of the process. Dealing with a large number of alternatives, each with several possible outcomes, and large amounts of data on each possible outcome is a challenging task. For this reason formal, well-organized approaches to evaluation are of great assistance. Some people find models and quantitative techniques the most valuable tools to use in approaching this task.

Evaluation of alternatives should include consideration of factors other than the possible outcomes. Often there are differences in the methods and costs necessary to undertake alternatives. Therefore, consideration must also be given to the cost of implementation, the time required to put each alternative into effect, and the likelihood that one can obtain the necessary resources to attempt a particular alternative.

The objective is to select the "best alternative," that is, the one whose expected consequences are most consistent with the objective. If at any stage of evaluation we find that an alternative could not be the best, that alternative requires no further evaluation. For example, one alternative may cause us to lose $200,000, although this outcome is very unlikely. If one of our criteria is that we are willing to risk losing no more than $100,000, this alternative is rejected without further examination. Decision making does not consist of distinctly separable steps but is really a process, during which emphasis is placed on various parts of the whole. The phase of evaluating alternatives overlaps selection (which is discussed next) because in some instances alternatives are "selected out" (eliminated from further consideration) before the final decision is reached.

Selection of the Best Alternative

This phase of the decision process is sometimes confused with decision making per se. Granted, one can make a decision by randomly selecting any possible alternative, but only by chance would such a procedure arrive at the best alternative. One may not always reach the best decision even after expending all available effort on the preceding phases, but the greater the effort in the previous phases, the more satisfactory the decision is likely to be.

Selection may be based on the degree to which an alternative appears to achieve the objective. Sometimes, however, the objective may be simply to surpass some minimum threshold—that is, to find a satisficing solution—and several alternatives may meet this criterion. In such cases a person or a group may establish further criteria to select the acceptable alternative with the minimum cost or the minimum time to accomplish or meet some other objective. Perhaps no alternative meets the criterion. The selection may then be based on how near the alternative comes to achieving the objective sought. A potential scheme may be completely abandoned because no alternative is found to achieve the objective. The decision in this case is to select the alternative not to act. This, of course, is often a feasible alternative.

Implementation

Decision making is often considered a primarily mental process. But if we include all the phases preceding resolution or selection, the process may also involve much physical action in data collection and analysis. The point was made earlier that merely making a decision seldom accomplishes the intended goal. A decision usually must be implemented before it becomes effective—unless the objective of the decision is to determine one's attitude toward a particular subject. When such a decision is made, uncertainty is removed and the objective is accomplished. Management decisions, however, usually involve actions to be taken or discontinued.

Part of the evaluation phase involves preliminary consideration of procedures necessary to implement possible decisions. The implementation phase involves the many subdecisions required to plan and carry out the selected alternative. Who must do what, at what time, in what manner, at what place? Decisions and plans must be made and communicated to everyone who must contribute to the implementation. Further, anyone who, by being uninformed, could interfere with the implementation should be informed of the plans.

Planning the implementation of a selected alternative should also be included in the development of control procedures. In this phase a broad outlook might include developing control procedures for the decision being implemented. Managers frequently plan to have periodic reporting and performance reviews. Determining the types and amount of data to be reported is another subdecision to be made about the selected alternative. Control procedures help keep the alternative performing properly until its preplanned discontinuance or until a decision is made to change it.

MODELING

Decision making involves extensive mental processing. The analysis and comparison of alternatives involve suppositions. Only very rarely will all possible alternatives actually be tried. Often the alternatives will be considered abstractly, in thought or imagination. The decision maker may visualize them in operation and visualize the possible outcomes. Sometimes these concepts can be expressed in words so they can be communicated to others. Often other forms of expression, called *models,* are useful in depicting alternatives and in analyzing their performance.

A model is an abstract representation of some real-world process, system, or subsystem. Models are used in all aspects of life. We think and speak with models rather than with actual tangible objects. Accountants do not collect actual dollars in different containers to keep track of various accounts. Instead they write numbers in various locations to represent amounts in the accounts. Words and numbers are symbols that stand for something else; that is, they are abstractions of reality, or models. We carry in our memories a vast array of useful models. When we construct a paragraph to describe something, we are producing a model of the aspects or features that we feel are pertinent and wish to convey. We are accustomed to dealing in abstractions, so the *modeling* process is certainly not a new, incomprehensible mystery.

Types of Models

Beyond our basic representations of reality such as words, numbers, and symbols, there are three general categories of complex models that are useful in analyzing and understanding real-world situations.

SCHEMATIC MODELS A schematic model is a representation in the form of lines and colors, usually on some flat surface, that provides an image of a real-world situation. Graphs, maps, and charts are all schematic models.

PHYSICAL MODELS Physical models are usually three-dimensional representations of other objects. They are tangible objects made to look and perform like some aspects of the system being modeled. A globe is a simple physical model of the planet earth. Small model airplanes are tested in wind tunnels to determine the expected aerodynamic characteristics of larger aircraft.

MATHEMATICAL MODELS Mathematical models use arrangements of symbols to depict the process or system being modeled. These symbols are arranged to form equations or mathematical expressions in the same way as the more familiar word symbols are arranged to form sentences to express concepts. This kind of model is the least familiar to most people, but it can provide a high degree of abstraction and it serves as a powerful analytic tool. The equation $A = B + C$ is a mathematical model stating that the object we symbolize by A is the simple sum of the thing we are calling B and the thing we are calling C.

The Modeling Process

Models are developed when the need for a decision is recognized and when one seeks to understand how the real world works. When real-world situations are exceedingly complex, models are necessarily incomplete. Time limitations, expense, and com-

plexity usually preclude the development of a model of every aspect of the real world. Consequently, a model is usually a simplification of the real-world situation; otherwise, it would be just as easy to work with the real world as with the model.

Several procedures may be used in simplifying a real-world situation and developing a model. Often the model developer attempts to include in the model only those aspects of the real world that are relevant to the decision at hand. Other simplifying measures may also be taken to reduce the complex real-world situation to a manageable form. Higher-degree mathematical relationships may be simplified to linear (straight-line) relationships. Some components of a complex system may be grouped into larger subsystems to reduce the number of items that must be manipulated. Conditions of certainty may be assumed even though the actual conditions may be probabilistic.

When a simple model has been developed, it is then tested to see if it is adequate for the intended use. If it is not, it may be improved by the abstraction of additional features of the real world until the model is considered valid. *Validation of a model* means gaining confidence that the information it provides about the real world is accurate for its intended purposes. The iterative nature of modeling is indicated by the loop in the left-hand portion of Figure E.1. The model can be put to use once it appears to be a valid representation of the real world. Application of the model is shown in the right-hand section of the figure.

The Value of Models

The results of the modeling process can sometimes be very useful to decision makers. As an analogy, consider the testing of a small model airplane in a wind tunnel. Such a test provides information with much less expenditure of time and money than a test of a full-scale plane would require. Further, the test can be made with much less risk. Very little property damage or human injury would result from a failure of the test model. Similarly, management can use models to reduce the time, cost, and risk involved in decision making. Any attempt to operate a real business by every reasonable alternative in an attempt to find the best method would be extremely risky, expensive, and time-consuming. Such erratic changes in procedure would frustrate

Figure E.1   The Modeling Process and Use of Modeling in Decision Making

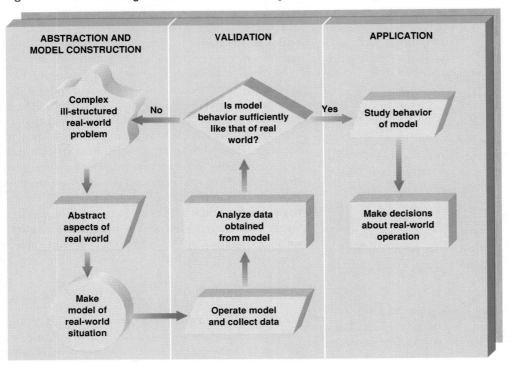

employees and reduce their confidence in management. After one alterna tive had been tried, it would be difficult or impossible to restore the identical conditions so that the second alternative could be tried. Once an alternative leading to failure had been attempted, further experimentation would be impossible. Models provide managers with some understanding of a system so that they may manage it with reasonable expectation of success.

MODELS OF DECISION MAKING

Models of real-world systems assist decision makers by identifying some of the feasible alternatives and displaying their estimated consequences. Having obtained information, the decision maker still must select the preferred alternative. The final selection is a perplexing challenge and often is the most crucial phase of decision making. Models of the decision process are of great assistance in displaying known data. Two of the models used by managers are decision matrices and decision trees.

Statistical Decision Theory

Statistical decision theory has become recognized as a model of rational selection from alternative courses of action. This model is intended to represent a process of decision making that will lead to the best selection in accordance with an established criterion. Like any other model or process, it does not guarantee the wisdom of the criterion; it merely leads to the alternative that meets the criterion.

GENERAL FEATURES   Certain basic elements are common to decision making in all situations:

1. Alternative courses of action, sometimes called *alternative acts* or *alternative strategies*. As mentioned previously, the objective is to select the best of these alternatives from the total set.
2. Conditions outside the control of the decision maker that will determine the consequences of a particular act. These conditions, sometimes termed *events* or *states of nature*, must be mutually exclusive, and all possible conditions

must be listed (that is, they must be collectively exhaustive).

3. *Payoff or loss*, as a measure of the benefit to the decision maker of a particular state of nature resulting from a particular course of action.

4. Some criterion or measure of what constitutes the objective being sought by the decision maker.

5. An *environment* representing the extent of knowledge about the state of nature that will occur.

THE DECISION MATRIX The first three elements listed above are often displayed in a *decision matrix* to organize some of the features of a situation into an orderly format. The alternatives A_i are listed as row headings, and the events E_j are listed as column headings, or vice versa. The consequences C_{ij} (payoffs or losses) are then displayed within the body of the matrix at the intersection of the appropriate alternative and the appropriate event. Table E.2 illustrates a decision matrix (sometimes called a *payoff matrix*, payoff table, or loss table).

DECISION ENVIRONMENTS The environment within which a decision is to be made arises from the degree of certainty about the state of nature that may occur. The environments can be:

1. *Certainty:* The decision maker knows which state of nature will occur.

2. *Risk:* The decision maker does not know which state of nature will occur but can estimate the probability that any one state will occur.

3. *Uncertainty:* The decision maker lacks sufficient information even to estimate the probabilities of the possible states of nature.

Under conditions of certainty, the decision maker needs only one column of the matrix—the one corresponding to the state of nature that will occur. The highest payoff or the smallest loss in this column leads to the best decision—if the best alternative is in the set being examined and if the forecast of consequences is correct. The most common environment for decision making is that of risk. The decision maker may have past data from similar circumstances or subjective estimates of the probabilities.

Table E.2
ILLUSTRATIVE DECISION MATRIX

ALTERNATIVE ACTS OR STRATEGIES	States of Nature (Events)			
	E_1	E_2	. . .	E_N
A_1	C_{11}	C_{12}	. . .	C_{1N}
A_2	C_{21}	C_{22}	. . .	C_{2N}
A_3	C_{31}	C_{32}	. . .	.
.	.	.	. . .	.
.	.	.	. . .	.
.	.	.	. . .	.
A_M	C_{M1}	C_{M2}	. . .	C_{MN}

DECISIONS UNDER UNCERTAINTY When the decision maker has no estimates of the probability of events or does not wish to use expected monetary value as a decision criterion, some other selection guide must be used. The *maximax* criterion selects the alternative with the maximum possible return. Under such a criterion the decision maker would examine the payoff matrix, find the largest payoff, and select the alternative associated with it. This is a criterion of extreme optimism. The *maximin* is a more pessimistic criterion, under which the decision maker examines only the worst possible outcome of each act and selects the act that will give the largest payoff if the worst circumstances occur.

There are other possible reasons for choosing an alternative. For further discussion of this subject the reader should consult a text on decision theory or statistics.

A decision matrix may be considered a mathematical model of the decision situation. It seems appropriate to consider it in this way when the calculations of *expected monetary value (EMV)* are used to represent a measure of an alternative's desirability. The EMV for an act is found by summing for every state that can occur the products obtained when the probability that the state will occur is multiplied by the amount that is expected to be received if the act is taken and the state occurs.

Decision Trees

Decision trees also use calculations of EMV to measure the attractiveness of alternatives. Decision trees, however, use graphical models as well to display several relevant aspects of a decision situation. These graphical models consist of treelike structures (hence the name) with branches to represent the possible action-event combinations. The conditional payoff is written at the end of each branch. A tree gives much the same information as a matrix, but, in addition, it can be used to depict multiple-stage decisions—a series of decisions over time.

The conventions used to represent a situation by a decision tree are shown in Figure E.2. Decision points usually are represented by square blocks with branches representing all alternative decisions emanating from the square. A triangle and a negative number on a branch from a decision point repre-

---

APPLICATION

EXAMPLE OF A DECISION MATRIX

Larry Locke has been in business, in a city that shall remain nameless, for the past 2 years. He and his partner, Kirk Key (the mayor's son-in-law), have a sideline business selling used road machinery and paving equipment, which they buy at very good prices from a city agency. The mayor has received some uncomplimentary publicity, and his chances of being reelected are rather slim.

Larry and Kirk are considering an opportunity to sell all or part of their business. The potential buyer has made three offers: to pay $60,000 for the entire business, to pay Larry $30,000 for his half of the business, or to pay Larry and Kirk $10,000 each so that each of them would own one-third of the company. A matter of risk pertains to the chances that the mayor will be reelected. Larry estimates that the odds are 2 to 1 that the mayor will be defeated in the upcoming mayoral race (that is, the probability is two-thirds that he will lose). Larry constructed the payoff table shown in Table E.1. The numbers in the table represent the present worth of the money he will receive if a particular event-act combination occurs.[*]

The EMV was calculated for each alternative. The EMV for an alternative is calculated by multiplying each payoff that the alternative can yield by the probability that the payoff will occur and summing these probability-weighted payoffs. Larry calculated the EMV for the first alternative A_1 by multiplying $50,000 by $\frac{1}{3}$

and adding to it $12,000 times $\frac{2}{3}$. If there had been more than two possible events, this summation would have been continued until all events had been included. The expression for the expected monetary value is

$$EMV_i = \sum_{j=1}^{n} C_{ij} \cdot P(S_j) \qquad \text{[E.1]}$$

where EMV_i = expected monetary value of ith alternative act

C_{ij} = payoff or loss for ith alternative and jth event or state of nature

$P(S_j)$ = probability that jth event or state of nature will occur

Larry used equation E.1 to calculate the expected monetary value of each alternative, as shown in Table E.2. He showed the result to his partner, Kirk Key. They agreed that the expected monetary value was the criterion they should use as a basis for the decision. After considerable discussion, they decided to sell the Locke and Key Machinery Company, lock, stock, and barrel.

[*]Income that will be received in the future has been discounted to its present value. That is, it has been converted to an equivalent amount of money at the present time so we can compare amounts at the same time. This conversion allows for the fact that if we have money, it can earn interest for the use of it.

Table E.1
POSSIBLE PAYOFFS FOR LARRY LOCKE

ALTERNATIVE ACTS	States of Nature (Events)		
	S_1, MAYOR REELECTED $P(S_1) = \frac{1}{3}$	S_2, MAYOR DEFEATED $P(S_2) = \frac{2}{3}$	EXPECTED MONETARY VALUE (EMV)
A_1, keep a $\frac{1}{2}$ interest	$50,000	$12,000	$24,667
A_2, keep a $\frac{1}{3}$ interest	40,000	10,000	20,000
A_3, sell all his interest	30,000	30,000	30,000

Figure E.2 Symbolic Example of a Decision Tree

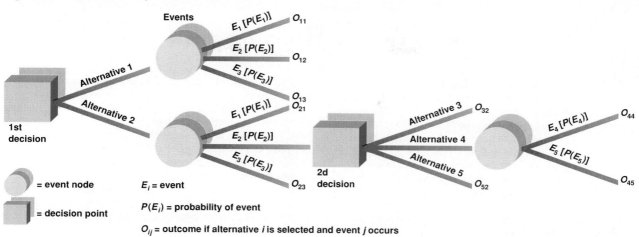

sent the cost if that alternative is selected. This amount is deducted in calculating the expected value for the branch. When a decision has been made not to follow one of the branches, that branch can be "sawed off" the tree by two short lines marked across it. Actions not under the control of the decision maker are represented by circular-event nodes. Branches from the circles represent the possible states of nature or events that may occur. The probability of each event branch, represented by $P(E_i)$, is shown on each branch. The sum of the probabilities on all branches emanating from an event node must be 1.

It is useful to visualize that the decision maker is going to progress in time from left to right and will end up at one end of one branch of the tree. At some points (squares) the decision maker can select the branch to take. At other junctions, chance will determine the direction in which he or she must go.

One solves the problem represented by a decision tree by working from right to left. Each outcome at the end of an event branch is multiplied by the probability that it will occur, and these products are summed to obtain the EMV at the event node. This EMV represents the expected gain (or loss) if the sequence of decisions and events results in the decision maker's reaching this point in the tree.

At any decision point immediately prior to an event node, it is assumed that the decision maker will proceed along the branch with the highest EMV, so the other branches to the right of the decision point can be sawed off. The EMV of the remaining branch from the decision point is transferred to the decision point. This process is continued until the amounts at the right-hand ends of all event branches have been multiplied by their probabilities and summed to the event nodes, and until all the event nodes have been either sawed off or transferred to the left. Eventually the leftmost decision block is reached, and the preferred decision is considered to be the one indicated by the branch with the highest EMV.

EXAMPLE OF A DECISION TREE

Carl Bright has operated Bright Cleaners ("Service with a Bright Smile") for 10 years. He purchased a small cleaning plant when he was discharged from the army and has subsequently added a second location. The business has grown until both plants are being used to their full capacity and there is no room for enlargement. Bright does not want to relocate either business because he feels a major reason for his success is the convenient locations he has acquired.

Bright recognizes that his cleaning operations are very crowded, and he would like to improve the way items are moved between the various stages of processing (sorting, cleaning, pressing, and so on). He is considering having an overhead conveyor system installed to free some floor space currently occupied by dollies used to roll the material between processes. An out-of-town company has proposed to come in and install the conveyor, but Bright is undecided about the work he wants done. The company will equip either location and replace the dollies at the other location for $25,000. If it equips both locations while its work crew and equipment are in town, the cost will be only $45,000. If a conveyor is not installed, Bright must spend $1,000 to replace the dollies that are now used to move material.

Bright feels that the conveyor will save time for his employees, resulting in a present worth (PW) of savings that he estimates at $16,000 per plant. The real potential economic gain resulting from the conveyor is the possibility of increased business resulting from faster service and increased usable work space. There is no absolute guarantee, however, that any new business will materialize. If the conveyor is slower than Bright has estimated or if it breaks down often, Bright Cleaners may lose its reputation for service. Bright has estimated the present worths (PWs) of increased profits at each location and the probabilities that they will be achieved, shown in Table E.3.

The town is small enough that advertising and a reputation for prompt service are assumed to affect the success of both locations in the same way. So, for simplicity, the same probabilities are used for single and joint results at the two locations. Actually, Bright could consider the probabilities of a large increase in business at one location and no increase, a moderate increase, or a large increase in business at the other. The decision tree could also be used to consider revising the probability estimates for the level of business at the second location after Bright sees how things turn out at the first installation. (These features are not considered because our objective is to illustrate the features of a decision tree without adding complications that may obscure the basic method.)

Bright constructed the decision tree in Figure E.3. His analysis showed the expected values of the three alternative decisions that could be made, shown in Table E.4.

Bright considered the expected values and decided he is definitely interested in the conveyors, but he is still not sure that he wants to risk an extra $20,000 on the initial installation when the increase in expected value for initially installing two conveyors instead of one is only $2,300. Carl Bright is not from Missouri, but his favorite uncle lived there for 6 years. Carl has decided he will spend $50 or $60 on long-distance calls to talk with other people who have installed conveyors. He wants to recalculate the expected values after he gets more information on the reliability of conveyors, the probability of increases in business, and so on. If Carl buys new dollies, he will have a $1,000 out-of-pocket expense. He may also have an opportunity cost between $0 and $55,000, depending on the amount of future business he would forgo. The uncertainty of the future prevents his being sure that there is any opportunity loss.

Table E.3
PRESENT WORTHS AND PROBABILITIES OF INCREASED PROFITS FOR BRIGHT CLEANERS

INCREASE IN BUSINESS (PERCENT)	PRESENT WORTH OF ALL FUTURE PROFITS PER LOCATION	PROBABILITY OF OCCURRENCE
0	$16,000	0.30
3	30,000	0.50
6	50,000	0.20

Figure E.3   Decision Tree for Bright Cleaners (Dollar amounts in thousands)

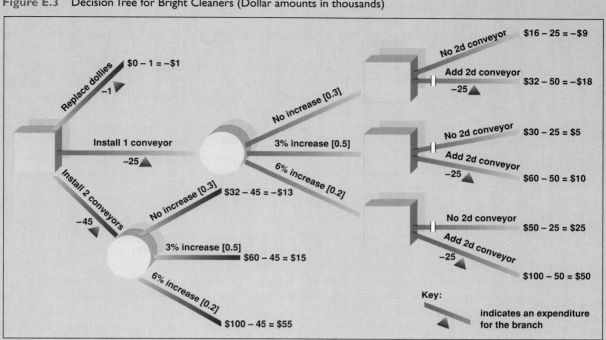

If Bright buys one conveyor, he may have a net out-of-pocket cost of $9,000 or a gain of $10,000 or $50,000 if his estimates of cost and volume are correct. His estimates are based on 0, 3, and 6 percent increases in business. Actually the percentage increase in business is a continuous variable. The discrete case is a simplification of the actual situation.

Table E.4
EVALUATION OF ALTERNATIVE DECISIONS FOR BRIGHT CLEANERS (In Dollars)

ALTERNATIVE STRATEGIES OR ACTS	State of Nature			EXPECTED MONETARY VALUE OF EACH STRATEGY (Σ PAYOFF $\times$ PROBABILITY OF PAYOFF)
	NO INCREASE IN BUSINESS (PROBABILITY 0.3)	3% INCREASE IN BUSINESS (PROBABILITY 0.5)	6% INCREASE IN BUSINESS (PROBABILITY 0.2)	
Replaces dollies				
Payoff	−1,000	−1,000	−1,000	
Payoff times probability	−300	−500	−200	−1,000
Install one conveyor initially, evaluate, and install 2d conveyor if indicated				
Payoff	−9,000	10,000	50,000	
Payoff times probability	−2,700	5,000	10,000	12,300
Install two conveyors initially				
Payoff	−13,000	15,000	55,000	
Payoff times probability	−3,900	7,500	11,000	14,600

SUMMARY

Operations managers are required to make decisions as they plan, organize, direct, and control operations activities. Many techniques discussed in this supplement can be used in the course of decision making, even though the decision maker may not consciously develop each step of the process in some formal procedure. Certainly, not all operations management problems can be reduced to models, but many models have been developed and applied in operations management. Two general types of models—the decision matrix and the decision tree—were presented. They were selected for presentation because they depict the decision process itself. They show that one must identify alternatives, forecast the outcome for each alternative, and determine which alternatives seem most appropriate for the objectives. When conditions are not certain, probability can be used to guide the decision maker, who must identify his or her objective or criterion. The decision maker who does not identify an objective is unlikely to find the best way to accomplish it. Even though a decision tree or decision matrix may not be used, decision makers try to estimate the results of various alternatives and make some adjustments according to the likelihood that those results will occur.

Models other than decision trees or decision matrices are presented in future chapters. Some of these models also evaluate alternatives and include probabilities that various outcomes or states of nature will occur. Forecasts frequently are the means by which managers become aware that decisions about the future should be made. Forecasts also help to determine the conditions under which alternative solutions to problems will be implemented and the outcomes expected. Chapter 4 discusses forecasting and some tools for forecasting.

KEY TERMS

Decision making	States of nature	Maximax
Models	Decision matrix	Maximin
Modeling	Payoff matrix	Expected monetary value
Validation of a model	Certainty	(EMV)
Statistical decision theory	Risk	Decision trees
Alternative acts	Uncertainty	

DISCUSSION QUESTIONS

1. Why is delaying a decision a form of making a decision? Can managers today avoid the decision-making process?
2. Is making the right decision sufficient to ensure success for a manager? Why, or why not?
3. Why is it popular today to allow subordinates to participate in the decision-making process?
4. The idea of optimization implies that we can identify all possible alternatives and evaluate them from the viewpoint of the total system. *Suboptimization* refers to the fact that we can optimize only a subset of a total system. Discuss some reasons that suboptimization is a fact of life.
5. Name the six phases of the decision process.

6. Explain the role of models in the decision process. Name and describe the three types of model used.
7. On what strength would the accuracy of statistical decision theory rely?
8. What is the most common environment for decision making?

PROBLEMS

1. A local radio station (WGIV; Giveaway 93) currently has a giveaway contest under way. Once a contestant is selected, he or she is given two choices: take $93 in cash or pick one of three envelopes. The contents are $500, $100, or merchandise which is estimated to be worth $20.
   a. Draw the decision tree for this decision.
   b. What decision should be made to achieve the highest expected monetary value?
2. The Luckyshoe Company, manufacturers of horseshoes, needs to construct a new manufacturing facility. (The last one was lost due to a fire.) They have two choices, a small facility or a large facility. If demand for horseshoes is favorable, the large facility will generate a net present worth (PW) of $11 million; the small, $7 million. The small facility could be expanded if demand remained high, resulting in a net PW of $10 million. If demand is unfavorable, the large facility will have a net PW of $3 million; the small, $5 million. The probability of favorable demand is 0.60; unfavorable, 0.40.
   a. Draw the decision tree for this decision.
   b. Decide what Luckyshoe should do to achieve the highest EMV.
3. A young company has been successful in its first two years of operation and is planning to open a second location. Its management is trying to decide whether to build a small, medium, or large facility. The level of demand at the new facility can be described as poor, moderate, or good, with the probability for poor of 0.20, for moderate of 0.55, and for good of 0.25.

   If a large facility is built and business is good, the net present worth of the after-tax earnings is estimated to be $175,000. If business is moderate for the large facility, the PW will be $100,000; and if business is poor, the facility will lose a PW of $50,000.

   A medium-sized facility will lose a PW of $20,000 if business is poor and will make a PW of $110,000 if business is moderate. If business is good, the medium-sized facility is expected to earn a PW of $120,000, or it can be enlarged at a cost of $50,000 to earn a PW of $165,000 before the cost of the expansion is deducted.

   A small facility is estimated to earn a PW of $15,000 if business is poor. If business is moderate, the small facility is expected to earn a net PW of $60,000, or it can be enlarged moderately at a cost of $40,000 to earn a PW of $90,000 before the cost of the enlargement is deducted. If business is good, the small facility will earn a PW of $60,000, or it can be enlarged moderately at a cost of $40,000 to earn $90,000 (as above) or greatly at a cost of $60,000 to earn a PW of $160,000 before the cost of the expansion is deducted.
   a. Draw the decision tree for this decision.
   b. Decide what the company should do to achieve the highest EMV.
4. Demand for electric power in a region appears to be growing at a rate of 6 percent per year, and a new generating plant is being designed to serve this demand. The company feels that there is 0.70 probability that the demand will continue to grow at this rate and a probability of 0.30 that the demand growth may slow to about 5 percent. A smaller plant costing $290 million and a larger plant costing $340 million are being considered. If the smaller plant is built and demand remains high, the generating capacity can be expanded.

The net present worth of all future annual operating revenues minus disbursements other than those for recovery of the plant investment is $485 million if the larger plant is built and demand is high. If demand is low, the company will have used valuable capital in excess capacity and will have to follow uneconomical alternatives in other operating decisions within the company, so that the PW will be only $375 million.

Should the company elect to build a smaller plant and the demand be low, the PW will be $410 million. If the demand is high under this condition, the company has the option of purchasing power so that the PW will be $370 million, or it can expand the plant's generating capacity for $90 million. With expansion programs there will be some inefficiencies and lost revenues so that the PW will be $480 million.

a. Draw the decision tree for this analysis.

b. Which decision should the company make to maximize the expected present worth after the cost of the plant is deducted?

5. The Flying Turkey Airline runs a gambling junket flight from a Midwestern city to Las Vegas. Passengers are charged $100 in advance. This amount is refunded if the passenger does not show for the flight. The airline thus loses $100 in revenue for each empty seat. If the flight is overbooked, however, the airline has to pay $160 (a loss of $60) for a commercial flight for each passenger it cannot accommodate. The probabilities of no-shows are shown in the decision matrix below. How many passengers should the airline overbook for each flight?

ALTERNATIVE STRATEGIES	States of Nature (Number of No-Shows)			
	0	**1**	**2**	**3**
Probability	0.5	0.25	0.15	0.10
Overbook 0				
Overbook 1				
Overbook 2				
Overbook 3				

6. Widget, Inc., has just developed a new product. Since all available production capacity is being utilized and the introduction of this product will not affect sales of the current product line, a new manufacturing facility is needed. Widget has three choices: a small, medium, or large facility.

If a large facility is built and sales are good, the PW of after-tax revenues is $25 million. If sales are moderate, the PW will be $15 million. A PW of $5 million is expected if sales are poor. Two additional options exist when sales are poor. They can sell the facility for an after-tax price of $8 million, or they can subcontract the extra capacity to another company for an after-tax PW of $10 million.

Alternatively, the construction of the medium facility would result in the following PW of revenues: good sales, $20 million; moderate sales, $18 million; and poor sales, $12 million.

A small facility is estimated to generate the following PW of after-tax revenues: good sales, $15 million; moderate sales, $14 million; and poor sales, $12 million. This facility can be expanded for an additional cost of $7 million if sales are good. The new PW of revenue would be $20 million.

Alternatively, the construction costs (in PW) are: large, $10 million; medium, $8 million; and small, $5 million.

The probability of good sales is 0.3, moderate sales 0.3, and poor sales 0.4.

a. Draw the decision tree for this decision.

b. What decision should Widget make in view of the above information?

7. Expando manufacturing company is expanding its product line. To meet this increase in production requirements, three strategies are considered feasible: overtime, subcontracting, or expansion. The use of overtime should produce a PW of $2,000 if demand is high or $3,000 if demand is low. If subcontracting is used, it should result in a PW of $3,000 when demand is high or $2,000 when demand is low. Expansion would probably contribute $6,000 for high demand or only $1,000 for low demand. The probabilities of demand are 0.4 for high and 0.6 for low. Construct a decision matrix and use EMV to determine the best decision for Expando.

BIBLIOGRAPHY

Bierman, Harold, et al. *Quantitative Analysis for Business Decisions.* 8th ed. Homewood, Ill.: Irwin, 1991.

Eppen, G. D., F. J. Gould, and C. P. Schmidt. 4th ed. *Introductory Management Science.* Englewood Cliffs, N.J.: Prentice-Hall, 1992.

Lee, Sang M., Laurence J. Moore, and Bernard W. Taylor. *Management Science.* 3d ed. Boston: Allyn and Bacon, 1989.

Levin, Richard I., David S. Rubin, and Joel P. Stinson. *Quantitative Approaches to Management.* 6th ed. New York: McGraw-Hill, 1986. Chaps. 4 and 5.

Render, Barry, and Ralph M. Stair, Jr. *Quantitative Analysis for Management.* 5th ed. Boston: Allyn and Bacon, 1993.

Simon, Herbert A., et al. "Decision Making and Problem Solving." *Interfaces 17,* no. 5 (September–October 1987):11–31.

SEEKING EXCELLENCE THROUGH QUALITY MANAGEMENT

The preceding chapter discussed the relationship between operations and the overall strategy of a business. It was mentioned that the broadest level of long-range guidance for the total business is an institutional strategy or culture that establishes the values and beliefs of the business. A belief in and a deep commitment to quality is a part of the culture of excellent companies. Quality was mentioned as one of the four major performance capabilities that a company can emphasize to various degrees in its strategy to distinguish itself from competitors in a way that will appeal to its target market. In our study of operations, quality is stressed as the most fundamental of those performance capabilities because very few customers will consider doing business with a company if the level of quality is not at least adequate. Further, many companies have found that high quality provides a very effective advantage over their competitors, and they have achieved significant cost and profit benefits from this strategy.

In this chapter we discuss total quality management as a means of integrating quality values into the culture and work systems of a company. *Total quality manage-*

HOW TOTAL QUALITY MANAGEMENT CAN HELP ADD VALUE FOR CUSTOMERS

Since TQM focuses all parts of the company on quality it helps provide the customer with much higher quality. Prudent expenditures for the cost of preventing errors can often lead to larger reductions in the cost of failure and thereby reduce total cost. Companies strive for continuous improvement so that better value can be offered to customers through better quality and lower cost. Companies that get things right the first time use their capacity more efficiently because they do not have to use capacity to do things over. This is one of the ways that costs are reduced and it also makes the company's schedules and quality more dependable.

ment (TQM) is a philosophy and approach to managing an organization so that high quality, as perceived by the customer, is a primary common value *throughout* the organization, and *all parts of the organization* work to achieve outstanding quality and to improve quality. A basic philosophy of quality management is presented early in the book because it should be an underlying principle that helps guide decisions in regard to the issues discussed in the remainder of the book.

Quality is not the responsibility of any one department—it is the responsibility of all parts of a company and involves the dynamic interaction of many entities within a company. Obviously, then, quality does not happen without a great deal of intentional effort to make it occur. There must be an organized system or framework that directs and coordinates all parts of an organization in identifying and performing all the work necessary for high customer satisfaction. A TQM process can be different for each company depending on such factors as its customers' needs, employee capabilities, supplier support, and the company's current state of development in its quest to continuously improve. This chapter, therefore, is intended to give an overview of some of the general elements in a quality management process and emphasize the need for a quality orientation in all the subjects in this book regarding the design and operation of the operations function.

A good overall framework for presenting the general parts that are important in achieving high quality is provided in the criteria for the Malcolm Baldrige National Quality Award (MBNQA). These awards are made annually to recognize U.S. companies for business excellence and quality achievement. Awards may be given in any of the three categories of manufacturing, service, and small business—so the criteria provide a general view of what nationally recognized experts have established as important elements of an outstanding quality process. The framework for the criteria, shown in Figure 3.1, identifies four major elements that are important in achieving excellent quality.[1]

A fundamental element in achieving excellent quality (shown in the upper right corner of the framework) is establishment of definite goals for such important matters as customer satisfaction, customer retention, and market share gain. The first part of this chapter addresses the establishment of fundamental goals of high quality

---

[1]Shown in the framework are seven blocks that represent seven major criteria or aspects of a company's quality process that are evaluated as a basis for awarding the MBNQA. The kinds of information used to evaluate a company on each of these criteria are included in an Application box at the end of this chapter.

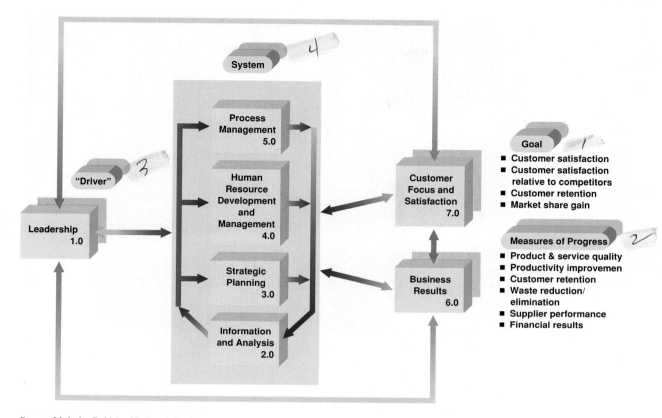

Source: Malcolm Baldrige National Quality Award: 1995 Award Criteria, U.S. Department of Commerce, p. 5.

Figure 3.1
The Malcolm Baldrige
National Quality Award
Criteria Framework

and discusses methods of focusing on customer needs and satisfaction in designing the goods and services that will be provided to customers.

A second element is to establish objective ways, where practical, to measure progress toward the company's goals. In its attempts to change its performance, a company should verify that it is changing the right things. One of the precepts of total quality management is to base decisions on facts and hard data rather than on just opinions and intuition. Some of the performance results that a company might measure are also indicated in Figure 3.1. It is assumed that if a company has established goals to work toward, it will measure its performance in comparison to those goals. In the discussion of various issues throughout the book, references are made to some of the types of information and measurements that are relevant to the decisions at hand. Information flow related to quality is discussed briefly in this chapter.

A third element (shown at the left side of the framework) is leadership that demonstrates a commitment to high quality and establishes a climate of high-performance expectations for providing customer satisfaction. Plans, strategies, objectives, and budgets must be established to encourage and facilitate progress. Employees must be stimulated, motivated, guided, and recognized for high-quality work. Company leaders must ensure that their decisions, behavior, and communications are supportive of the established goals. Management issues, decisions, and decision tools are the primary topic of the entire book. Some aspects of management that specifically relate to quality are discussed in this chapter and in Chapter 10.

When George M.C. Fisher moved from Motorola to Kodak, he brought with him a leadership style committed to quality. He has refocused the company on its core business, photography, and has set goals for reaching new markets. He has also placed a new emphasis on digital technology. Breaking up a rigid hierarchy, Fisher has stressed accountability. Employees with questions can E-mail Fisher and get a response, or they can catch him at breakfast in the company cafeteria.

Kodak

The fourth element necessary to achieve high quality is the system that performs the work-related processes in a company. Since operations performs much of the work to provide goods and services to customers, it is a major part of this system. Part II of the book (Chapters 5–9) examines many aspects of designing an operations system that is capable of performing with outstanding customer satisfaction and competitiveness. Also, a company's quality philosophy will influence the way the company and the operations function are run. Part III of the book (Chapters 10–18) discusses many of the management issues that are involved in running the operations system so that its work conforms with the established design and with company objectives.

A GOAL OF EXCELLENT QUALITY

Outstanding quality will not happen by accident. If a company is to achieve total quality then quality must be a key goal for the operations function and all the other parts of a company. It is important that customers perceive quality in their contacts with all aspects of the company from the first sales brochure or sales call through the billing cycle and throughout the life cycle of the good or service purchased. If a company is to be competitive, quality work is also important in all support activities that the customer does not see, such as scheduling and materials management. A major aspect of TQM is the degree of emphasis that is placed on quality, as perceived by the customer, as a common unifying force in the organization. Management leadership and motivation at all levels of the organization are important factors in achieving exceptional quality.

How does an organization unite and mobilize its resources to achieve superior levels of quality and strive to improve it still further? A basic ingredient is that managers must make quality a key part of the organization's culture (that is, one of the values shared by members of the organization and believed to be important). For all parts of an organization to coordinate toward some common goal, the goal must be communicated, recognized, and reinforced by the policies, decisions, and actions throughout the organization. Some of the early seminars that were held in Japan to help improve its industrial management and quality capabilities started with this point. They quoted a philosophy statement from Newport News Shipyard:

> We shall build good ships here,
> At a profit if we can,
> At a loss if we must,
> But, Always good ships.[2]

This was and still is a good example of making quality a primary company goal.

Ford Motor Company says, "Quality is job one," meaning it is the first priority.

IBM at Research Triangle Park says, "We will deliver defect-free competitive products and services on time to our customers."

These statements must not be just phrases for advertisements or hollow slogans. They must be genuine beliefs of the group. A clear message from top management and actions proving its sincerity are vital to instill quality values throughout the organization. Such a goal can become the bedrock criterion that guides actions of all members of a company. So a key ingredient is for a company to commit sincerely to make quality happen and to do the work that it requires. W. Edwards Deming (mentioned in box below) has said that the failure to achieve quality in the United States can be blamed 80 percent on the system, which can be changed only by management, and 20 percent on the workers. Wayne Brunetti (executive vice president of Florida Power and Light Company, which was awarded the Japanese national prize for quality in 1989) stated that there are four major barriers to the implementation of a successful quality program; top management, middle management, first-line supervision, and technical staff who think they are the only experts and have all the relevant knowledge.[3] Pride in one's work and careful attention on the part of the worker are necessary but not sufficient to achieve quality. Management must also do its part and see that other requirements are met. Managers can allow work to become routine and fail to provide the environment and impetus for continuous improvement. Managers may feel threatened by giving workers the power and authority to improve quality or to stop a process if it is not operating properly.

Managers must establish quality improvement goals as part of the recurring planning cycle for each organizational unit and should show genuine interest in support for progress toward these goals. Recognition, even celebration, of progress helps to encourage this work and to show the sincerity of upper management's commitment. Managers must consistently show their commitment to quality. The priority of quality will show in policies, budgets, and other decisions.

Quality must be facilitated in the budgets for various departments or other units. The phrase "Quality is free" does not mean you can ignore quality in the budget. It means that quality will repay its costs. Initial funding must be provided, and it should

---

[2]David A. Garvin, *Managing Quality: The Strategic and Competitive Edge* (New York: Free Press, 1988), p. 181.
[3]Wayne Brunetti, *"Reaching for the Prize: A Lesson in Quality,"* Public Uti;lity Fortnightly, April 12, 1990, pp. 12-14.

be recognized that the repayment may appear as reduced costs in some other department. For example, the efforts to develop an improved product design may be recovered much later through reduced warranty cards. A superordinate goal of high quality may not require any change in the permanent organization if the company is already organized to carry out the day-to-day work effectively and efficiently. Quality will require that all employees work together smoothly as a team to see that the customer's needs are served without mistakes and within reasonable cost.

Three Types of Activities Are Important to Quality

A company must apply its goal of high quality in the following three major areas if it is to achieve outstanding results: *quality of design, quality of conformance,* and *quality of service.*

QUALITY OF DESIGN   A company must identify who its customers are and what attributes are important to them. Then it must design each good or service (that is, establish its specifications) so that it meets the customer's needs. This is an important basic step. Perfect production that meets an inferior product design will not satisfy the customer. The best time to solve many problems is before processing begins and before the customer sees any defective goods or services.

QUALITY OF CONFORMANCE   The next challenge is to develop and correctly use the production technology (processes and skills) to produce every good or service so that it conforms to the design (that is, it meets the specifications). Obviously, accomplishing this economically is a challenge also. The key is usually economical prevention of errors rather than having to do the work over.

QUALITY OF SERVICE   Customer-perceived quality is affected by what customers receive and the way they are treated when they deal with any part of the company. "Moments of truth" are those short periods when customers are in contact with representatives of a company and are influenced to remain loyal customers or not.[4] Beyond the previous steps, the company must see that its goods and services are sold with the proper expectations on the customer's part. The customer should be instructed how to use and service the product properly so that it safely meets the customer's needs for an appropriate time.

A Customer Focus Is Important

Since quality means satisfying customer needs, a necessary part of quality is understanding who the customers are and what their needs are. Peters and Waterman reported in *In Search of Excellence* that the excellent companies stayed close to the customer. Products and services should be designed and delivered with the customer's viewpoint in mind. It makes good marketing sense—an item or a service is easier to sell if the final customer thinks it will serve his or her needs. The item will do just that if genuine quality has been achieved.

Performance is sometimes improved by considering that there are two types of customers and everybody in a company has a customer to serve. The *external customer* is an individual or company who purchases the company's product and provides the income to pay for the operation of the company and hopefully some profit. *Internal*

---

[4] Jan Carlzon, *Moments of Truth: New Strategies for Today's Customer-Driven Economy* (New York: Ballinger, 1987), p. 3.

OPERATIONS MANAGEMENT IN ACTION

IDEAS FROM DR. DEMING

Dr. W. Edwards Deming, a statistician and proponent of statistical quality control, was one of the Americans who went to Japan after World War II to help reindustrialize that war-torn country. Deming is given much of the credit for the great improvement in the quality of Japanese goods. In fact, the highest award given in Japan each year for industrial quality is named the Deming Award. Deming has been a critic of quality efforts in the United States, attributing most of the problem to the system and saying that managers are responsible for it. Deming has evolved fourteen major points for improving quality, which are summarized below.

Deming's 14 Points

1. Establish the objective of constant innovation and improvement.
2. Adopt a new philosophy, we cannot accept the old mistakes and defects.
3. Cease dependence on mass inspection, require statistical evidence that quality is built in.
4. End the practice of awarding business on the basis of price.
5. Use statistical methods to find the trouble spots.
6. Institute modern methods of training on the job.
7. Improve supervision—do what is right for the company, don't just turn out the required quantity.
8. Drive out fear, so people will feel secure to point out problems and ask for information.
9. Break down barriers between departments and with suppliers and customers so there will be open, effective communication.
10. Eliminate posters and slogans, they don't help people solve problems. Go to work and show people how.
11. Eliminate work standards that prescribe a numerical quota, they disregard quality and put a ceiling on production.
12. Remove barriers between workers and their right to pride in workmanship.
13. Institute a vigorous retraining program to keep up with changes and new developments.
14. Create a top management structure that will push every day for these points.

Source: W. Edwards Deming, *Quality, Productivity, and Competitive Position* (Cambridge, Mass.: MIT Press, 1982), pp. 16–17.

customers are employees or units within a company, such as the worker who performs the next production task on the item that another worker is processing. An internal customer may be the person who receives the memorandum one is typing or a market study that one is preparing. The worker who is to operate a machine that another worker is repairing is an internal customer. If each employee works to understand the needs of the next customer and to provide that customer with only good items and service, it will result in high quality to the external customers. This chain of working to serve the next customer leads to better cooperation and teamwork.

It is important to consider the needs of both internal and external customers. However, it is the external customer's needs that drive the needs of internal customers. For example, the external customer is the customer of the shipping department at a wholesaler. The shipping department is the customer of the warehousing department, which is the customer of the purchasing department. The purchasing department can be considered the customer of the supplier from which the merchandise came. For one step to do a high-quality job for its customer the preceding steps must have done a good job. It is also the needs of the external customer that drive much of the design of goods and services. We will discuss design in considerable depth because it has a large impact on what the external customer perceives as quality and affects what internal customers need to do. Additionally it affects cost, speed of improvement and innovation, and many other aspects of customer service.

PRODUCT DEVELOPMENT AND DESIGN FOR EXCELLENCE

Innovation! Innovation is an often used method of gaining competitive advantage. Having the right product for sale and having a very effective method of providing it are some of the greatest strategic advantages a company can have. Of course, new products or processes do not remain unique to a company for long. Many companies introduce innovative products or new processes to provide their goods or services. If they bring these to market quickly, they may gain competitive advantage and market share. New products provide great opportunities for profit before there are close alternatives and before price competition reduces the company's margin. Competitors will follow quickly to keep from yielding competitive advantage and losing market share. Companies require flexibility if they are to be able to introduce new products rapidly and change their product mixes often.

The exterior appearance of a manufactured product affects the initial attention of potential buyers and the pride of ownership for those who do buy. The internal components of a product affect its performance, reliability, and durability—hence, the customers' long-term satisfaction. The number, type, and complexity of a product's components also affect the type of suppliers with which a company must deal and the amount of work and operating costs a company will have. The types of components used in a product can also affect the production processes required to make them and hence the capital investment and personnel skills which are important to the company. You can see that design affects many aspects of operations in addition to the company's pricing, sales, revenues, and costs.

A product innovation for a service company might be something like a new type of checking account for a bank or a new set of features for a life insurance policy offered by an insurance company. Drawings may not be the appropriate medium to express the "design" of such intangibles. Instead, the design may be a list that describes in some level of detail what the customer is to receive and the work activities to be performed. This lets the customer know what to expect, and it lets the service employees know what is expected of them. Definition of the steps to be performed in providing a service helps in planning the facility and equipment that will

At Chrysler, the Neon design team strives to innovate in the subcompact market. Designed to be sporty, the Neon features "best-in-class" horsepower and aerodynamic design. Its cab-forward structure gives the interior extra roominess and improves visibility. Cost was also a consideration during the design process, and the Neon is among the lowest priced in its class, a definite competitive advantage!

Chrysler Corporation

best support good performance. A clear service definition facilitates training of employees so they are more skilled, leading to more efficiency and consistency among employees. A definition of what the company provides can also help determine what it is important to measure, and this helps in determining information system needs and ways to check quality.

Consider the following example of an innovation in service design to serve a particular market segment. A bank in a Midwestern college town offered free checking if the customer maintained a balance that was several hundred dollars higher than the typical student maintains. A sizable fee per transaction was charged to customers who did not maintain the minimum balance. The bank did not have many student customers even though there were automatic teller machines (ATMs) near the campus.

The bank's price structure was based on the costs to serve the typical customers, many of whom were business persons who used teller transactions to deposit business checks and cash receipts. The cost of a teller transaction was about 2.5 times the cost of an ATM transaction (mid-1980s). Students did not want to go to the branch bank and wait in line to be served by a teller. They wanted to be able to mail in a deposit (or, better yet, have a parent do it), to write a few checks for books, fees, and so on, and to be able to withdraw spending money. In addition to its other types of accounts, the bank introduced a new type of account with a low fee for nonteller transactions and a higher fee for teller transactions, to discourage the use of this more costly service. The new account served the needs of both the bank and the new customer segment it attracted.

This example shows that there are multiple goals to pursue in the design of a service, and this is true for a manufactured product. Both must have market appeal and be reasonably easy to produce with quality and economy. It has been estimated that 70 percent or more of a manufactured product's cost is fixed by its design, because this establishes the number of parts that must be made or purchased, the types of material and equipment that will be used, and the amount of labor that will be needed. Designers must be careful to consider many ramifications of design as they work. A general guideline often used by designers of manufactured items is to reduce the number of parts a company must make through standardization and simplification. *Standardization* involves having fewer choices of components and products that must be produced, so there is more focus to the production operations. The use of common components in multiple models of a product is an example of standardization. *Simplification* involves having no more parts than are necessary to perform the product's intended function and trying to reduce the complexity of those parts. Table 3.1 shows some of the advantages that can result from these efforts.

Reliability is one aspect of quality that should be considered in the design phase. Reliability engineering may be used to improve the *mean time between failures (MTBF)*, which is the average time that an item will operate between repairs. One method sometimes used to increase reliability is product simplification, to reduce the number of components in the product and to simplify those that remain. When there are fewer parts, there are fewer opportunities for something to fail. Parts reduction can pay other dividends by reducing such things as purchasing, storing, production, handling, and assembly costs.

Traditional Approach to Manufactured-Product Design

The traditional approach to product development involves a series of fairly discrete steps, each performed by a different unit of a company. First a concept may be

Table 3.1
POSSIBLE ADVANTAGES OF REDUCING THE NUMBER OF PARTS IN A COMPANY'S PRODUCTS

Shorter design time is often possible

Lower cost to make and maintain drawings or design files

Easier to fabricate and test prototype

Less tooling and fewer fixtures to design

Fewer items requiring purchasing activity

Less materials handling

Less storage of production parts and service or repair parts

Fewer inspections or tests

Shorter parts lists, price lists, or catalogs to print and update

Fewer machines required so investment in space and equipment can be lower

Lower labor and materials costs

Less planning, scheduling, and coordinating effort required

Shorter assembly time

Fewer parts to fail often gives greater product reliability

Lower cost means a company can be more profitable or more flexible in its pricing

developed by marketing to express the general type of product or features which are believed to appeal to a particular market niche. Product development engineers then develop preliminary designs, and perhaps prototype units are fabricated and tested. After a product design is selected, decisions are made regarding which parts will be purchased and which will be made in-house. Process engineers then develop production methods, select the necessary equipment, and design the tooling, fixtures, or other devices that will be needed to manufacture the parts. Meanwhile the purchasing department seeks qualified suppliers for components that will be purchased and for raw materials that will be used for in-house production parts. In many cases this involves negotiation for the lowest price, so very rigid designs and specifications for the items must be developed. There is little room for suppliers (who probably know a great deal about that type of item) to recommend improvements or cost-saving ideas. Persons from quality control examine the design to determine if weaknesses are evident and to design the test devices and procedures to check the product when production starts. Late in the game, packaging specialists develop ways to package the item for its protection in distribution and perhaps to make an attractive display of the item. At some point field service people must figure out how to service it.

This series of steps has a great potential to consume excessive time, to perhaps overlook some product enhancements, and even to accept knowingly some minor product shortcomings. Participants at any stage of the process have to study considerable documentation to understand the project up to the stage at which they participate. If they have a suggestion for an improvement at some prior step, it might even be necessary to ignore it and press on to get the product on the market within a reasonable time.

Today's competitive pressures have forced many companies to change from the procedures just described. "Time-based competition" makes companies try to be very fast in introducing new products and to have very short production lead times to make and deliver products to customers.[5] A company that is a rapid innovator can put several trial products on the market during the time it takes a slower company to develop something new. If a trial product is a hit, a flexible company can gear up rapidly and capture a great share of the market. If not, the company can evaluate customer reaction, modify the product accordingly, and move on.

Improving the Design Process

Team design is a method to improve the design process and to help achieve rapid innovation and product development. Team design, also called *concurrent engineering* or *early manufacturing involvement,* seeks to bring many of the relevant skills to bear early in the design process, and these skills work in parallel to develop new product. Participants from such functions as marketing, engineering, production, purchasing, and quality work together as a design team. They look for ways to develop a product that serves the customer's needs, draws on the greatest contributions that suppliers can make, is easier or less costly to manufacture, and will have desirable quality levels.

Ford Motor Co. used Team Taurus to bring together representatives from design, engineering, manufacturing, sales, marketing, and service in the earliest stages of the car's design. The result was the Taurus, the automobile that played a large part in turning the company around in the 1980s. Ford and others, as we shall see, are incorporating technology to further improve the design process.

The previous discussion has shown that there are multiple goals in developing a new tangible good or service product and several parts of a company often play a role in its design. The product must be something the business is capable of providing and hopefully selling at a profit. The product also must be something that serves the needs of the customer. As stated earlier, it is much easier to sell an item if it is designed to be something the customer desires rather than just whatever the business might want to provide. The "voice of the customer" must be sought and listened to throughout the entire cycle of developing new goods or services. Quality function deployment is a methodology that helps focus product design or redesign efforts on the needs and desires of the customer.

Quality Function Deployment (QFD)

Quality function deployment (QFD) seems to have been first applied in the Kobe Shipyards by Mitsubishi Heavy Industries in constructing large tankers that were custom-designed to meet the needs of each individual customer. When translated directly from Japanese it is not clearly apparent what the term means but it refers to a methodology for development or evolution (deployment) of the features, attributes, or characteristics (functions) that give an item high quality. This methodology can be used in the design or redesign of a tangible good or a service. QFD can assist in strategic planning because it helps identify the strengths or capabilities that a company must have or should develop in order to fulfill the needs of a target market. It focuses on the customer's needs and desires as the primary drivers of the remaining analysis.

The QFD methodology uses a series of matrix tables to summarize and communicate a great deal of information that is developed in the process. QFD is sometimes referred to as "the house of quality" because the tables that are developed have a gable roof–shaped peak on top of a box and resemble the outline of a house.

[5]George Stalk, Jr., and Thomas M. Hout, *Competing Against Time: How Time-Based Competition Is Reshaping Global Markets* (New York: Free Press, 1990).

A simple example will show how this type of table is used in the QFD process. Suppose that a manufacturer of plastic tableware is interested in developing a plastic coffee mug for use by mobile coffee fans—those persons who transport a mug of coffee as they travel in an automobile. The first step is to gather information about the needs and desires of this target market group. Customer surveys, benchmarking, focus groups, and other forms of customer input such as complaints or praise for existing similar products can be used to help identify customer desires. The customer desires or needs (which we will call "needs") are listed along the left side of the matrix. It is helpful if the priorities or relative importance of these needs are identified. An actual application might reveal 20, 40, or more needs.

For our example, suppose a thorough investigation of customer desires reveals that they would like a mug that is difficult to turn over, will not splash coffee out when they hit bumps in the street, is easy to grasp, will not block vision while it is held to the mouth, will hold at least a cup (8 ounces) of coffee, and will keep the coffee warm for an extended time. This set of needs lists what the customers desire. Often, in applying QFD, a multidisciplined team of people work to develop a list of possible "methods," or ways the company might satisfy the customer needs. For our example we might choose people from marketing, product design, process engineering, production, and packaging. A product concept might be developed to include such features as a no-splash lid with a small hole in it through which one can drink, a wide base with a non-slip rubber surface on the bottom, and a large mug-type handle. Marketing might recommend preferable colors. Engineers would recommend the type and thickness of the plastic. Packaging representatives might recommend that the

Figure 3.2
The House of Quality
Matrix for the Mobile
Mug

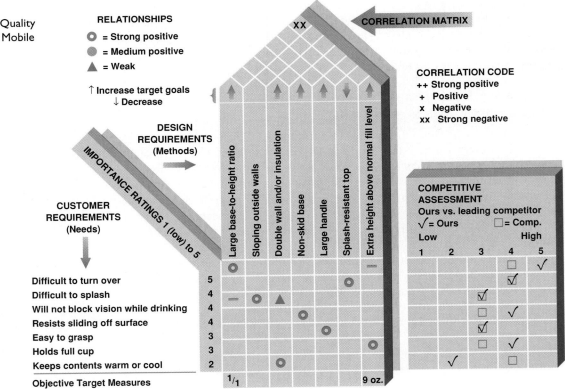

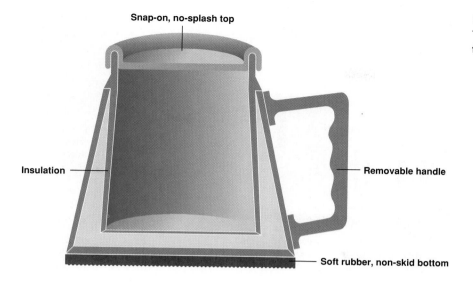

Snap-on, no-splash top

Insulation

Removable handle

Soft rubber, non-skid bottom

Figure 3.3
The Design Concept for the Mobile Mug

handle be removable for shipment inside the mug to make a smaller package and to decrease the likelihood of damage. These methods of meeting the needs, along with the original customer requirements and other information from a QFD analysis, are shown in Figure 3.2 as an example of a house of quality matrix. A design concept for a coffee mug that would meet the customer requirements is shown in Figure 3.3. Additional phases of analysis would probably have been conducted and other matrices developed between the initial definition of customer requirements and the final design.

The QFD process for development of a more-complicated product might involve a series of four phases of analysis, with a matrix or set of matrices developed at each phase. As an example of a more-complicated application, suppose an automobile manufacturer found that some customers needed more electrical power to recharge their auto batteries quicker because they frequently used their vehicles on short drives while the air conditioners, headlights, and other electrical accessories were on. Quicker recharge would be listed as a need in the matrix for the first round of analysis. The method of meeting this need might be listed as a larger-capacity alternator.

In the second round of analysis the methods from the previous matrix become needs and the analysis focuses on how these needs will be met. In the second round of analysis the larger-capacity alternator would be listed on the left side of the matrix as a need, which is one of the design objectives. The methods of providing a larger-capacity alternator might include larger rotating wiring, a larger shaft, and a larger case to contain these parts.

A third round of analysis would then focus on how the new larger case would be produced. One method that would be needed to produce the larger case is larger casting dies or molds. Other analyses would be performed in the third phase for all the other new parts that will be needed in the new alternator.

The fourth round of analysis would consider such matters as the equipment, operator training, and maintenance required to make the new processes serve the customer requirements. For our example, casting with larger dies would be a need that must be met. One of the methods of meeting this need would be to use new casting procedures. The revised casting procedure might require such changes as more metal in the furnace charge, different pouring temperatures, a new flow rate of

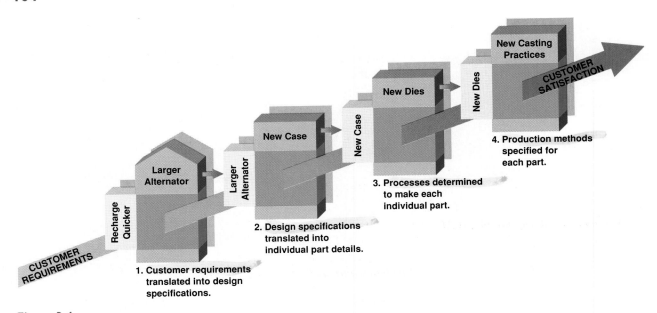

Figure 3.4
The Four Phases of
Quality Function
Deployment (QFD)

coolant to the casting dies, and so forth. A schematic showing the four phases of the QFD process for this example is presented in Figure 3.4.

An important benefit of the QFD process is that it originates with the customer requirements, and each level of analysis and the matrices that are developed are all linked back to the original customer requirements. Each phase of analysis just goes deeper into the details of how those requirements are going to be served.

This planning and communicating routine leads to the development of the product and the process at the same time. It has been shown to uncover and solve problems before the production phase begins, thus reducing engineering changes. Changes that occur after production begins are disruptive and may require the redesign of tooling or other equipment, which can be very expensive. Therefore, QFD can reduce the time and cost of getting a product on the market and can result in a product that provides greater customer satisfaction and gains higher market acceptance. One can readily see that QFD can contribute to achieving quality in design and other strategic advantages. Another strategic advantage is to get new product concepts to market long before competitors have anything similar on the market. We will now discuss some means that are used to complete the development and design process more quickly.

Technology Improves the Design Process and Deployment of Results

Working at a computer or work station with a high-resolution screen, a designer can apply *computer-aided design (CAD)* to generate various views of components and assemblies. Designs can be developed, analyzed, and modified with this technology faster than by drawing lines on paper with conventional drafting procedures. The computer can rotate images, construct various views, zoom in and magnify parts, and check for possible interference between parts. Computer-generated designs also have other advantages. They can be stored in a computer data base that is accessible to other programs and other parts of the company. A common data base facilitates coordination (with very little paperwork) of the efforts of other parts of the company,

Table 3.2
MAKING MORE WITH LESS (Results of Using DFA to Analyze a Gun-sight Component)

	BEFORE	AFTER	REDUCTION, %
Assembly time (minutes)	129	20	85
Number of parts	47	12	75
Number of assembly steps	56	13	78
Metal fabrication (minutes)	757	219	71

such as tool design, quality control, and purchasing, which often need accurate descriptions of the latest product design.

Computer-aided engineering (CAE) can use the product's description to analyze some aspects of its performance and estimate the deflection of its parts under various loads. Several designs can be subjected to preliminary tests and compared without taking time to make prototypes of all. *Computer-aided manufacturing (CAM)* software can use stored data about the parts to generate commands that operate automated machines, so much of the paperwork and human programming can be reduced. When CAD and CAM are combined, it is called *computer-aided design and manufacturing (CAD/CAM)*.

ARTIFICIAL INTELLIGENCE IN DESIGN   Many of the suggestions and guidelines for good design, such as those that would be made by members of a multifunction design team, have been incorporated into rules for artificial intelligence software that will review a design and recommend improvements. These packages try to reduce the number of components, make the components simple and inexpensive to fabricate, make all the parts so they fit together easily, and reduce the assembly task. Such programs have been used by General Electric, Westinghouse, Xerox, IBM, New York Air Brake, and Texas Instruments. Table 3.2 shows some of the results achieved by Texas Instruments from running a design-for-assembly (DFA) program on a sighting device that it makes for the Pentagon. A program of this type, called design for manufacturability and assembly (DFMA), was credited with reducing manufacturing costs by over $1.2 billion in 1 year at Ford Motor Co. Ford used this program from bumper to bumper for its 1993 model. In the future this technology may be combined with artificial intelligence and CAE to serve as a real-time design adviser. The program would run while the designer worked and offer suggestions on how to improve the product's design.[6]

It is evident that companies are using technology to design products that are better and more easily produced and to develop and introduce the products more quickly. These capabilities can be used to gain competitive advantage. Thus, strategic planning should address the methods of design and applications of technology, in addition to considering the items that are designed for the company to offer in the market.

There is much more to achieving exceptional quality than having a good product design or service concept definition. The design is the goal to be achieved—but the company must also achieve conformance to the design in its work and it must provide outstanding support service to provide high quality as perceived by the customer. It was shown that teamwork is helpful in developing a good design. Teamwork

[6]"Pssst! Want a Secret for Making Superproducts?" *Business Week,* October 2, 1989, pp. 106, 110

and coordination also are essential in carrying out the other activities that are necessary to achieve quality.

EFFECTIVE ORGANIZATION AND TEAMWORK

Quality is a team sport. Definitely quality is not the responsibility of a single department with a title like "quality control" or "quality assurance." Quality must be designed and built into the goods or services step by step as they are produced and provided. All the inspection and all the testing after the product is made do not add value. They just verify that the quality is there or reveal the sad news that much of the effort was wasted. Numerous parts of the company, and its suppliers, must be involved to achieve the common goal of providing the external customer with high perceived quality. Consequently, a great deal of coordination and communication are necessary to achieve maximum effectiveness of these resources. (See the box on Deming's principles, particularly point number 9.) One of management's challenges is to establish the necessary communication linkages and to see that various parts of a company are coordinated.

Some of the interrelationships that occur between parts of a manufacturing firm can be viewed by referring to an expanded diagram, such as Figure 3.5, showing some inputs, transformations, and outputs that occur and the flow of some information related to quality. The flow of materials is shown as blue arrows, and the flow of information is shown as red arrows. At or between each stage of processing there may be monitoring of the work item and/or critical parameters of the work-processing equipment to determine how each stage of the process is operating. This information

Figure 3.5
The Flow of Product Material and Quality Information

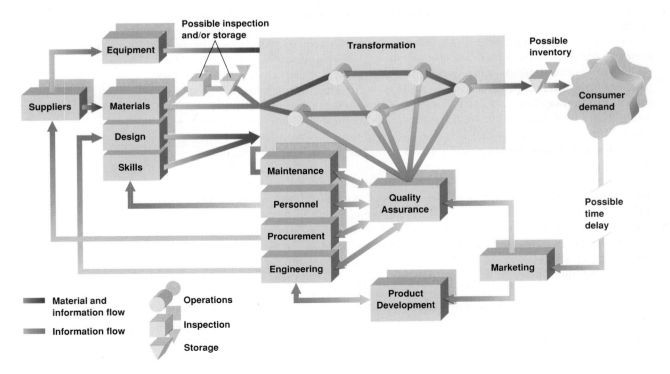

can be used to adjust a particular stage of the process or stop the entire process if something is wrong. This information also can be transmitted, compiled, and interpreted in a central quality assurance unit as shown in Figure 3.5.

The goal is prevention of defects rather than correction by sorting defective items from the good ones and reworking or scrapping the defective items. This means the inputs must consistently conform to the specifications for good quality and the transformation processes must be controlled so they consistently operate properly and conform to their specifications. The result should be output that consistently conforms to the specifications.

Consider some of the communication and coordination that assists in achieving quality. Marketing provides information from customer interviews, market surveys, and consumer evaluation magazines, which may lead to the development of new products or modifications to existing ones. Customer service personnel provide data from warranty claims and from field repairs after warranty, which may be used to identify weaknesses in the design of existing products. Suppliers and potential suppliers may suggest new materials for products or new production processes.

Employees may suggest design revisions to make components easier to produce or assemble. They may also suggest improved production methods. Product development personnel experiment to find product improvements while process engineers or industrial engineers seek improved production methods. Feedback from inspections performed by production workers or by quality control personnel and product testing reports may indicate a need for revision of the product or the production processes.

Initially, process engineers develop equipment or perhaps purchase equipment and modify it so that it is technically feasible to produce all the necessary components of a product. Subsequent operation may reveal better ways to make some items. Feedback from quality checks may show that equipment is not operating satisfactorily to make quality consistently high, so maintenance procedures may be improved. Suppliers may suggest improved processing equipment or supplies. Equipment selection criteria may be revised, and finance personnel may become involved to revise capital investment plans.

Persons in human resources work to select and hire employees with the proper aptitudes and skills to perform high-quality work. They also may develop and coordinate training programs to improve certain skills. Data on incoming material may lead purchasing or quality engineering to work with suppliers to improve their performance.

Sales and repair personnel must receive training and information from other parts of the company so they can suggest where the product should or should not be used, how to use it effectively, and how to maintain it to prolong its service. These front office contacts with customers need communication links and support from other parts of the organization to achieve the prompt, accurate service that leads to customer satisfaction.

It is apparent that many parts of the company play important parts in achieving quality (that is, serving the needs of external customers), and their work is often interrelated. Teamwork is vital in day-to-day operations, and it is important in achieving improvements. The idea of making each person or group responsible for seeing that their internal customers are provided with quality service has often been found to be effective in fostering teamwork. Persons meet with their customers and discuss ways to improve the work performed for the customers. This is one way to overcome the "functional silo" effect in which persons specialize in performing a particular type of work and do not develop interest in the big picture of which their work is a part. Employees who stay inside the "silo" do not explore such matters as who is served by the work, why the work is done this way, and how the work might better serve the purpose.

Employee Participation for Quality Improvement

In addition to fostering teamwork among the persons operating in the company's normal organizational structure, managers may use other teams. The use of teams allows employees to participate in problem solving and decision making. These experiences often build morale and motivation, as well as leading to growth and development of employee skills and bringing valuable experience and insight to bear on the issues they deal with.

QUALITY CIRCLES   One form of teamwork that has been used to help improve quality is the quality circle. *Quality circles,* or *quality control circles,* represent an organized effort to make constructive use of workers' intimate familiarity with their own work problems by focusing the workers' creative capabilities on finding solutions to those problems. A quality circle is a group, usually made up of five to twelve workers from the same work area, that meets regularly (in many instances, once a week) and voluntarily solves problems related to the work in their part of the company. Often the employees are paid for the time they spend in these meetings, which may last an hour or more. A few points are basic to the success of a quality circle program:

- The quality circle must work on the right problems. This means that communications should be open and the circle should have access to data pertaining to its work.

- Employees should be motivated to contribute their talents. All levels of management should openly and actively support the quality circle program. Circle members should be given recognition for their developments, and the circle should be given financial support, making it possible to implement worthwhile solutions developed by the group. If bonuses are paid to the workers, they are usually small and represent recognition rather than pay for any savings that result. (Participants in the quality circles with which the author is familiar seem highly favorable, even excited, about the circle activities.)

- The participants must have the necessary problem-solving skills. This means that training in certain basic problem-solving techniques is a major part of instituting a quality circle program. They also must have any necessary support from technical specialists.

Specific techniques that may be used by members of quality circles or other persons to identify problems and solve them are discussed in Chapter 9.

EMPLOYEE SUGGESTION PROGRAMS   Typically, suggestion programs have not been emphasized and have not been as effective as they might have been. Some companies are making their suggestion programs more effective by focusing more attention on them. Programs have a better chance of working where there is a unifying goal to improve quality and employees feel that their ideas will be reviewed and responded to in a reasonable time. Naturally there must be employment security before employees are motivated to develop ideas that reduce the amount of work required. There must be some form of recognition for contributions, even if there is

OPERATIONS MANAGEMENT IN ACTION

AT MOTOROLA, QUALITY IS A TEAM SPORT

In an article by this title, the January 21, 1993 *New York Times* reported on the championship presentations that culminated a year-long Total Customer Satisfaction Team Competition among quality improvement teams in Motorola, Inc. The competition, an Olympics of sorts, highlights the quality improvement accomplishments of Motorola employee teams from around the world. The company has almost 4,000 teams involving about 40,000 of the company's approximately 100,000 employees.

The twenty-four finalist teams were treated to a trip to Chicago where each presented its accomplishments to a panel of judges composed of the company's top managers. Teams were judged not just on their results, but also on how they accomplished the results and how well the team shared its results with other parts of the company.

The stories of the teams help explain Motorola's early win of the Malcolm Baldrige National Quality Award (1988) and its continuous progress since then. The contest is only one of several ways the company encourages and acknowledges achievements in quality. The company estimates that it is saving about $2.2 billion annually through quality programs that have increasingly emphasized teamwork. Not every company is large enough to have its own worldwide competition each year. But any company should benefit from friendly competition among teams to see which can accomplish the most improvement.

no monetary reward or only a small one. Companies may award points that are good toward catalog purchases, sponsor recognition banquets for groups of employees, or provide dinner at a nice restaurant for the family of each employee who made a valuable suggestion. Other benefits to employees come from having a more competitive company that is more likely to provide employment and raises in the future.

AD HOC TEAMS   Special-purpose teams may be formed from time to time to solve problems or to seek ways to improve quality. Usually these are *multifunctional teams,* which means they bring together persons from a variety of departments with different skills to investigate multiple aspects of a problem and find a solution. These teams are different from a standing committee in that they disband when the particular issue for which they were formed is resolved. Use of these teams allows various functions to present their views on the subject, which helps prevent the overlooking of some important points. It also builds a broader understanding of company operations by exposing members to the challenges that other departments face.

Suppliers Are Part of the Team: Long-Term Partnerships

Wholesale and retail service organizations are dependent on suppliers for their entire product and may spend over two-thirds of their sales income for items from suppliers. Many manufacturers spend more than half their sales dollar on purchased raw materials and subassemblies that become a part of their products. These companies must be provided with high-quality inputs from their suppliers if they are to provide outstanding quality to their customers. Both the supplier and the company that later passes the item to another customer must provide customer satisfaction (i.e., good quality) if they want to continue selling to that account. Recognizing this mutual interest, many suppliers and purchasers are forming long-term partnerships and working together to improve costs, quality, and service. Suppliers who have great

By the time Harley-Davidson riders celebrated 90 years of motorcycle making at a rally in 1993, Harley-Davidson had put its rocky past behind. In the past, engineers and managers dictated to employees. Workers are now encouraged to speak up and be part of the process. Their input is recognized as essential to maintaining the emphasis on quality.

Patti McConville/The Image Bank

experience in making a particular type of item have a great amount of expertise to offer in design and production problems. The information gathered by the user is also valuable in pointing out areas that might need improvement and changes in customer preferences.

A company must not have an excessive number of suppliers if it is going to work closely with them. Many companies have only one or two suppliers for a particular item or group of items. A company may begin by identifying its critical items and working to select qualified suppliers who are willing to partner and share information. Over time the companies develop effective working relationships and improve quality.

Standards Facilitate Inter-Firm Quality: ISO 9000

In dealing with its suppliers a company will often specify certain requirements or quality standards that a supplier must meet in order to qualify. A company may be a supplier to many customers. For example, Intel is a supplier of computer chips to many computer manufacturers. It would be very complicated and time-consuming to study and comply with dozens of different standards and they might not all be compatible. It is very useful, particularly in global trade, to have one common, internationally recognized standard for any supplier. ISO 9000 provides such a standard.

The term ISO 9000 is becoming more widely used in discussions of quality and competitiveness. Managers in the United States and many other parts of the world are recognizing that ISO 9000 is important in their efforts to improve quality and gain global competitiveness.

ISO 9000 is a series of standards for quality management and assurance developed under the direction of the International Organization for Standardization

(ISO) in Geneva, Switzerland. The series of standards has five major subsections which apply to certain situations.

ISO 9000 provides the guidelines for the use of the other four standards in the series.

ISO 9001 is the standard with the broadest scope. It applies where the supplier is responsible for the development, design, production, installation, and servicing of the product.

ISO 9002 applies if the supplier is responsible for production and installation, but not for design, development, and servicing of the product.

ISO 9003 applies to final inspection and testing of products. It has no standards for production, so it is more applicable for distribution companies.

ISO 9004 provides guidelines for managers of organizations to help them develop their quality systems. It gives suggestions to help organizations meet the requirements of the previous four standards.

Most industrialized nations (about 100) have adopted ISO 9000 or "harmonized" versions that are virtually the same. The standard is general enough to apply to almost any good, service, or facility. It is the specific facility, however, that is registered or certified to the standard.

To become "registered to the standard" a facility must document what its procedures are for every element in the standard. These procedures must be consistent with the recommendations and requirements of the standard. Then an approved third-party registrar audits to verify that, indeed, the work at that facility is performed in accordance with the documented procedure. Follow-up audits are made later. In other words, the facility is checked to see if it says what it does and does what it says. Being registered to the standard does not guarantee quality or make it better. It does mean that work evidently follows a documented procedure and, therefore, should be consistent. Use of the standard can facilitate quality improvement because errors that are made consistently are easier to find and correct. We will now discuss the idea of consistent performance further.

MONITORING PERFORMANCE FOR QUALITY AND IMPROVEMENT

One of the guiding principles for achieving quality performance is to base decisions on factual data rather than on assumptions and intuition. Companies must gather and interpret significant amounts of data from a variety of sources to guide their activities so that high quality and continuous improvement are achieved. Generally, information from both external and internal sources is relevant. We will briefly overview some of the types of data that may be used, beginning with external data.

In our discussion of the design of goods and services, it was mentioned that companies must obtain information about customers and from customers as a basis for the design. Even after goods and services are initially designed, companies should continue to monitor current levels and trends in customer needs and expectations. This information might reveal needs for improvements or opportunities for new product offerings. Companies also should continue to monitor customer satisfaction as a means of discovering problems early or detecting other opportunities to improve.

Other external information may monitor existing supplier partners. As mentioned earlier, there must be a two-way flow of information to make this relationship most productive and beneficial to both parties. Suppliers often can contribute many suggestions that improve quality. It is important to always take a positive approach in monitoring internal and supplier performance. When problems or opportunities to improve are discovered all the relevant parts of the company and the relevant suppliers should not be made to feel threatened and should work together in a spirit of teamwork. Negative treatment is counter productive: people might try to hide problems, making it difficult to find the underlying causes in the system and, therefore, to solve the problem.

Additional external information can be very helpful. Outstanding companies also monitor the activities, methods, goods, and services of competing companies to compare their performance and learn of possible improvements. Companies also seek information about admirable performance of other companies that might provide insight into improvements in some part of the company or better ways to manage.

One means of monitoring how the company's products and services compare with those of other companies is *benchmarking*. Benchmarking may reveal that some aspects of the design, processing, or service should be improved. Benchmarking is the process of using as standards for comparison the products, services, and practices of competitors or companies that are exceptionally good at some particular function. A company may purchase and disassemble competitors' products to determine how functions are accomplished, what materials are used, probable production methods, tolerances, and estimated costs.

Alternatively a company may compare some part of its operation to those of some outstanding company to gain ideas for improvement. Often companies that are not competitors are willing to share data. For example, Xerox used L. L. Bean as a model of how to pick items from a warehouse and package orders for shipment. Bean was almost three times as fast as Xerox.[7] Companies can learn and improve if they are willing to seek and study. When companies feel that they already know the best way, continuous improvement is dead.

The company will also need to gather and interpret much internal data to monitor and ensure proper operation of all internal processes that serve the external customer and the other processes that support this work. The flow of internal information to monitor and control the flow of work and to ensure quality was discussed briefly in the earlier section "Effective Organization and Teamwork" and was indicated in Figure 3.5. Data that is collected on repeated performance of any step in a process or on the final result of a process will no doubt contain variation. This inherent variation can sometimes mislead decision makers into mistaken interpretations of a situation.

Visualize the following situation. Suppose we had a control knob for a process that had inherent variation in its result (and all processes have some variability). If we turned the adjustment higher every time we got a low measurement and turned it down every time we got a high one, we would cause a more erratic process. The likelihood of getting results outside some specifications would be increased. Sometimes the first inclination does not solve the problem.

Care should be taken to obtain enough factual data as the basis for decisions. The condition of a process, such as that mentioned above, probably should be inferred on the basis of a sample of several observations—so that random variation

[7]Robert C. Camp, "Competitive Benchmarking: Xerox's Powerful Quality Tool," *Making Total Quality Happen* (New York: Conference Board, 1990), p. 42.

would be averaged out. Some understanding of statistical theory can help prevent decisions being made solely on the basis of opinion or on an insufficient number of observations from a process.

Companies are training personnel in statistical concepts such as sampling and statistical process control so they better understand random variables and distributions. Some companies are also studying a field called design of experiments (DOE). This knowledge can help them collect and interpret data that result from combinations of several variables in their processing steps. With these principles they can gain insights into the complex combinations of processes they operate. Companies can learn which steps in their systems must be controlled most carefully and which are less critical. Data collection and statistical analyses provide a more factual basis for decisions.

In regard to statistical concepts, it is important that companies reduce the variance in the results of their processes if they want to improve quality. We will elaborate on this concept in the following section.

Consistent, On-Target Performance

Consistency in producing goods or services in accordance with the design is important to providing quality. Probably you would not take your friends to a restaurant where the food usually is excellent but sometimes is horrible. Champion golfers need consistent results from their swings. Imagine the problems if the ball unpredictably went anywhere from 10 degrees to the left to 10 degrees to the right but on average went straight for the hole. Uncontrolled variability is the enemy of quality. The reason for a defect is that something varied from the target value.

For a tangible product, the design will probably specify several characteristics to be controlled and the *tolerance limits* within which they should be held. The characteristic might be the weight of a frisbee, the thickness of paint on the hood of an automobile, the percentage of some vitamin in a capsule, and so forth. Suppose that metal parts are to be cut from flat metal plates and that the dimensions (length and width), location of the center of a hole, and the diameter of the hole are specified. The design calls for a length of 6.750 centimeters, and the tolerance is ±0.010 centimeter. This means that the *lower specification limit (LSL)* is 6.740 centimeters and the *upper specification limit (USL)* is 6.760 centimeters.

If several of these parts were made by the same worker, using the same procedure and equipment, and only acceptable materials were used, not all the parts would be exactly the same length. There would be some part-to-part variation, even though it might not be noticeable without careful measurement. (Some characteristics require rather sophisticated technology to measure.) This dispersion is due to *chance causes,* that is, random variations that are inherent in the process due to the cumulative effect of small variations in conditions such as temperature, friction, vibration, and so on. If we had run some of the parts and then changed machines or operators, or if we had changed the production procedures, we would have introduced *assignable causes* of variation. A company must take care not to have assignable causes such as equipment malfunctions, inconsistent work practices, and so on, that might cause excessive dispersion in the product. Even then there will be a certain amount of *inherent variation,* or chance-cause variation, in any series of processing steps. This inherent variation must be less than the range between the upper and lower specification limits if we want to have the capability to produce 100 percent acceptable parts. Care should be taken to see that the process is aimed at the target value in addition to keeping the dispersion very low, just as the golfer with a consistent swing must aim for the hole. A process with low dispersion may be capable of holding the tolerance if it is centered at the proper dimension.

The concept of *process capability* has a specific meaning in the field of quality, as do many other terms. We will discuss it further. Suppose we had produced a few dozen of the parts mentioned above. We can measure the lengths of the parts and construct a histogram of the data. We would probably find a bell-shaped distribution of values because most of the measurements usually are near the target value and relatively few are farther from the target. Let's assume that a normal curve represents the distribution of lengths produced by this process. From the length measurements we can calculate *s*, an estimate of the standard deviation of the population of lengths for parts made by this process.[8] We use the standard deviation as a measure of dispersion, but there are others. The spread of the process caused by its variability is approximately 6 times the standard deviation. If the spread of the process is too wide, not all items produced by the process will fall within the specification limits. That is, the process does not have the capability to meet the tolerances. The capability of the process can be expressed quantitatively as a process capability index.

The *process capability index C_p* basically is the ratio of the allowable process spread to the actual process spread.[9] Equation 3.1 can be used to calculate a numerical expression of a process capability:

$$C_p = \frac{USL - LSL}{6s}$$ [3.1]

where USL = upper specification limit
LSL = lower specification limit
 s = standard deviation of the process

A variety of relationships between the tolerance range or specification limits and the process dispersion might be found. Three of these are illustrated in Figure 3.6 as situations A, B, and C. In situation A the process is just capable of "holding the tolerances," or operating within the tolerance limits. We could make about 100 percent acceptable parts if the process is centered exactly on the target value. The capability index for this situation is 1.0.

Situation B is not desirable. We cannot make 100 percent defect-free products even if the worker is careful to see that the process is centered exactly on the desired measurement. The process capability index for situation B is less than 1.0, say, about 0.6.

Situation C is the most desirable. The process can be centered slightly off the target and still not make any defective product. The process capability index for situation C is about 2.0. It is desirable to have the capability index above 1.0 to allow some margin in where the process is centered. (As the process dispersion gets lower, the index increases.) You can see that it is desirable to keep the process dispersion low and to work to make it even lower. Some U.S. companies are operating with process capability indices of 3 or higher.

One way to make processes more consistent is to develop *standard practices* that all workers follow. The practice should be viewed as the best method known thus far, but probably not the best one possible. Employee participation should encourage sugges-

[8] $s = \sqrt{\dfrac{\Sigma(X - \bar{X})^2}{n - 1}}$

[9] Victor E. Kane, "Process Capability Indices," *Journal of Quality Technology*, January 1986, pp. 41–52.

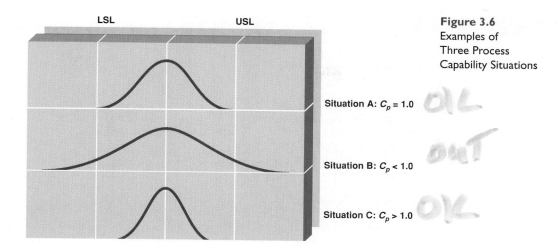

Figure 3.6
Examples of
Three Process
Capability Situations

tions for improvements. Suggestions that have merit should be tried, and if they are improvements, they should become the new standard practice. These practices facilitate worker training and provide refresher references if workers rotate jobs or fill in for a coworker who is absent.

Preventive maintenance on machines and tooling helps to keep the operation consistent. Tooling and fixtures often can be designed to be more error proof. For example, consider a flat part that has a hole in only one end. The fixture that holds the item for further processing might be made with a pin located so that it protrudes through the hole. The part could not be placed in the fixture the wrong way because there would be no hole to fit over the pin. (Errorproofing is sometimes referred to as "pokayoke," which is the Japanese term for the technique.) In some cases companies have moved to automated processes to overcome human variation. Numerous other methods should be sought to reduce variation and the chances of error.[10]

INSTILL ONGOING IMPROVEMENT

The point is made several times in this book that there is no finish line in business. Companies that do not get knocked out of the race just win the opportunity to run in the next year's race. Companies have to see how they compare with the competitors and try to stay in front or near the front. But the competition does not stop.

A company must improve its quality and then look for ways to improve some more. It may seem a paradox that a company is supposed to reduce its variance and become more consistent while at the same time it is to be ever changing to improve customer service and satisfaction. The concept refers to reducing the variability between the actual results and the target value that was intended. This is one part of continuous improvement. Another important part of improvement is to move the target value in a direction that will better serve the customers' needs. When viewed in this way the two goals do not appear to be in conflict. All parts of a company must work together toward both of these goals if the company is to be its best. To further elaborate on some characteristics that are important in a company that seeks to pro-

[10]L. P. Sullivan, "Reducing Variability: A New Approach to Quality," *Quality Progress,* July 1984, p. 16.

THE MALCOLM BALDRIGE NATIONAL QUALITY AWARD

This award was established in 1987 to promote awareness of quality as an increasingly important competitive element, promote understanding of the requirements for excellence, and share information on successful strategies. The criteria for the award are divided into seven major categories and are expressed rather broadly so they can be applied to both manufacturing and service companies. The seven criteria are outlined below along with general guidelines for the type of information that should be submitted in applying for the award. Evaluators award points in each category, depending upon their assessment of the company's programs and performance in that category. The maximum points that can be awarded in each category are shown to indicate the relative weights given to the categories. Some statements of the types of information that should be submitted to describe the company's performance in each category are provided in the description and give some indication of the factors that are considered important. The total points possible are 1,000.

1.0 Leadership (90 points)

Describe the senior executives' leadership and personal involvement in setting directions and in developing and maintaining a leadership system for performance excellence. (45)

Describe how the company's customer focus and performance expectations are integrated into the company's leadership system and organization. (25)

Describe how the company includes its responsibility to the public in its performance improvement practices. (20)

2.0 Information and Analysis (75 points)

Describe the company's selection and management of information and data used for planning, management, and evaluation of overall performance. (20)

Describe the use of competitive comparisons and benchmarking to support improvement of overall performance. (15)

Describe how data related to quality, customers, and operational performance, together with relevant financial data are analyzed to support company-level review, action, and planning. (40)

3.0 Strategic Planning (55 points)

Describe the strategic planning process for overall performance and competitive leadership for the short term and the longer term. (35)

Summarize the company's key business drivers and how they are translated into action plans. (20)

4.0 Human Resource Development and Management (140 points)

Describe how human resource planning and evaluation are aligned with the strategic and business plans and address the development and well-being of the entire work force. (20)

Describe how work and job design and compensation and recognition approaches enable and encourage all employees to contribute effectively to achieving high-performance objectives. (45)

Describe how education and training address company plans, including building company capabilities and contributing to employee motivation, progression, and development. (50)

Describe how the company maintains a work environment and a work climate conducive to the well-being and development of all employees. (25)

5.0 Process Management (140 points)

Describe how new and/or modified products and services are designed and introduced and how key production/delivery processes are designed to meet both key product and service quality requirements and company operational requirements. (40)

Describe how the key product and service production/delivery processes are managed to ensure that design requirements are met and that both quality and operational performance are continuously improved. (40)

Describe how key support service processes are designed and managed so that the current requirements are met and operational performance is continuously improved. (30)

Describe how the company assures that materials, components, and services furnished by other businesses meet the company's performance requirements and how supplier relations and performance are improved. (30)

6.0 Business Results (250 points)

Summarize the results of improvement efforts using key measures and/or indicators of product and service quality. (75)

Summarize results of improvement efforts using key measures and/or indicators of company operational and financial performance. (130)

Summarize results of supplier performance improvement efforts using key measures and/or indicators of such performance. (45)

7.0 Customer Focus and Satisfaction (250 points)

Describe how the company determines near-term and longer-term requirements and expectations of customers and markets, and develops listening and learning strategies to understand and anticipate needs. (30)

Describe how the company provides effective management of its responses and follow-ups with customers to preserve and build relationships and to increase knowledge about specific customers and about general customer expectations. (30)

Describe how the company determines customer satisfaction, customer repurchase intentions, and customer satisfaction relative to competitors and describe how these determination processes are evaluated and improved. (30)

Describe the company's customer satisfaction and customer dissatisfaction results using key measures and/or indicators of these results. (100)

Compare the company's customer satisfaction results with those of competitors. (60)

Source: Malcolm Baldrige National Quality Award—1995 Award Criteria (Gaithersburg, Md.: National Institute of Standards and Technology, 1995).

vide outstanding quality, the accompanying box shows the types of information that must be submitted by companies that apply for the Malcolm Baldrige National Quality Award. Many companies that do not intend to apply for the award use these criteria as guidance for their quality efforts. This overview of the award serves as an overview of important concepts and provides a suitable closing for a chapter that is an overview of quality management. Later, in Chapters 9 and 10, we will look in more detail at tools and methods for monitoring and improving quality.

Companies interested in ongoing improvement can use the Malcolm Baldrige criteria as guidelines. The Ritz-Carlton Company ranked high in all seven catagories when it won the Malcolm Baldrige National Quality Award in 1992.

Richard Dunoff/The Stock Market

SUMMARY

Numerous factors must be managed well to compete in today's global economy. Quality offers strategic advantages and is one vital area in which a company must excel. Companies may also choose to emphasize cost efficiency, dependability and service, and flexibility to various degrees. From a strategic standpoint, quality is the satisfaction of customer needs and expectations. It can be divided into several dimensions or aspects that may be emphasized to differing degrees depending on what is important to a particular target market. To achieve quality a company must understand its market and work to achieve quality of design, quality of conformance, and quality of service.

Quality function deployment (QFD) is a methodology used to make certain the voice of the customer is well represented in the development of a design for a good or service. It helps to identify and focus efforts on *what* the customer wants. The design process then develops *how* the customer needs will be met. Often multidisciplined teams are involved to share different perspectives during the design process and improve the end result. Technology such as CAD and CAE can be employed to speed the design process.

To excel, a company must make quality a key goal that is part of the culture of the company, and all parts of the company must pursue that goal. Managers must instill in all workers the importance of quality and continuous improvement. The parts of a company must work together as a well-coordinated team because quality is a total company effort. In working to achieve quality, the company may also

Maintain a customer focus

Use employee participation

Design quality into goods and services

Collect and apply factual data for decisions

Monitor and control performance internally and in respect to selected benchmarks

Make a commitment to continuous improvement

ISO 9000 is a series of international quality standards that establish more-uniform expectations about quality practices so that companies can better deal with their customers and suppliers. These standards require that companies document their quality practices and follow them consistently.

In attempting to reduce variability and improve process capabilities, companies work to improve processes and standardize practices. As companies work to improve quality all their competitors might also work to improve quality in order to maintain their relative competitiveness. The result is a general improvement in quality levels.

KEY TERMS

Total quality management (TQM)	External customers	Mean time between failures (MTBF)
Quality of design	Internal customers	Team design
Quality of conformance	Standardization	Quality function deployment (QFD)
Quality of service	Simplification	
	Reliability	

Computer-aided design (CAD)

Computer-aided engineering (CAE)

Computer-aided manufacturing (CAM)

Computer-aided design and manufacturing (CAD/CAM)

Quality circles

Multifunctional teams

ISO 9000

Benchmarking

Tolerance limits

Lower specification limit (LSL)

Upper specification limit (USL)

Chance causes

Assignable causes

Inherent variation

Process capability

Process capability index, C_p,

Standard practices

DEMONSTRATION PROBLEM

Problem

The specifications for one characteristic of a part call for its width to be 3.000 ± 0.008 centimeters. The process has been run under controlled conditions so that no assignable causes of variation have been introduced, and samples have been taken. The standard deviation of the process was estimated to be 0.003 centimeter.

(a) What is C_p for this process? What does this value say about the process capability?

(b) What percentage of the units would be outside the specifications for the width of the part if the process were operated and centered at 3.000 centimeters? Assume a normal distribution of measurements.

Solution

(a) $C_p = \dfrac{USL - LSL}{6s} = \dfrac{3.008 - 2.992}{6(0.003)} = \dfrac{0.016}{0.018} = 0.889$

Since this index is less than 1, the process is not capable of producing all the items within the specifications, even if the process is operated so that its mean is centered exactly between the specification limits.

(b) Since the normal distribution is symmetrical and centered between the specification limits, the portion outside the upper and lower limits will be twice the portion outside one limit. The portion outside the upper limit can be found by converting the upper limit to a Z value and referring to Appendix I:

$Z = \dfrac{x - \mu}{\sigma} = \dfrac{3.008 - 3.000}{0.003} = \dfrac{0.008}{0.003} = 2.667$ or 2.67

Appendix I shows that the area to the left of a Z of 2.67 is 0.9962. The area to the right of this value is $1 - 0.9962$, or 0.0038. Since the curve is symmetrical, an equal amount will be to the left of the lower specification limit. The total portion outside the specifications will be $2(0.0038) = 0.0076$, which is 0.76 percent.

Question

What will happen to the percentage of defectives if the process mean is not kept halfway between the specification limits?

DISCUSSION QUESTIONS

1. In the discussion of strategy in Chapter 2, quality was mentioned as one of the performance characteristics that a company may choose to emphasize. Describe three means by which higher quality might lead to greater profits for the company.
2. How can additional efforts to improve quality result in reduced cost?
3. What are some of the possible advantages of standardization that allows the use of common components in multiple products offered by a company?
4. It is said that everyone in a company has a customer. Explain this, and relate it to total quality management.
5. It has been said by some that companies just need more pride in their work and careful attention to detail in order to achieve very high quality. Yet, Deming and others have said that workers are responsible for only about 20 percent of the quality problems. What else is needed, and who is responsible for these factors?
6. What is the "functional silo" effect? Why is this effect detrimental to the achievement of high quality?
7. Describe three organized means that companies can use to facilitate employee participation in quality improvement.
8. Why is it often necessary to establish tolerance limits or specification limits on each side of the target value (i.e., a range of acceptable values) for a quality characteristic?
9. The specifications for the weight of bags of hard candy are 8.00 ± 0.02 ounces. Each piece of hard candy weighs 0.20 ± 0.01 ounce. Do these specifications seem reasonable for the bag-filling process? Why?
10. **a.** What is the general meaning of process capability?
    b. Describe in general terms what ratio a process capability index compares.
11. List some ways that can be used in manufacturing to reduce the variability of processes. Indicate if these or very similar ideas can also be used in services.
12. The criteria for the Malcolm Baldrige National Quality Award address many aspects of a company that are not in the quality control department and that are beyond the activities of the persons who produce the goods or provide the services to customers. Does it matter what the other parts of a company do, as long as the parts just mentioned are working to provide quality? Why?

PROBLEMS

1. The specifications from the manufacturer of a particular type of metal coating call for the temperature of the drying oven to be 370 ± 10°F. The company that is considering using this coating has run tests by taking a large number of temperature readings from various parts of its oven at random times. The standard deviation of the readings about the mean temperature setting was found to be 2.06°F. What is the capability index?
2. The manufacturer of a carbonated drink mix recommends that its drink concentrate be 6 ± 1 percent of each drink so the drinks will have the intended flavor. A manufacturer of drink dispensers is testing its mixer valves to determine the percentage of concentrate dispensed. What would the standard deviation of the distribution of concentrations have to be for the dispensing equipment to meet the recommendations with a capability index of 1.25?
3. The specifications for a critical characteristic of an electric resistor call for it to have a resistance of 500 ± 25 ohms. The process for making the resistors produces a normal distribution of measurements of resistance with a standard deviation of 5 ohms.
    a. Calculate C_p for this situation.
    b. Is the process capable of performing the operation successfully?
    c. How far can the process mean deviate from the target value before the process will begin making 1 percent defectives with regard to this characteristic?

4. The specifications for one dimension of a part are 1.750 ± 0.003 centimeters. When parts of this general size are made, the process has a standard deviation of measurements of 0.0015 centimeter.
   a. Calculate the process capability index.
   b. Is the process capable of meeting these specifications?
   c. If the process is used and is kept centered at 1.750 centimeters, what percentage of the parts will be outside the specifications for this dimension?

5. Suppose that the company in problem 4 wishes to produce 10,000 parts that are within the specs (specifications) and that it operates the process centered at 1.750 centimeters. All parts that are outside the specs are scrapped, and the company will receive only $1.00 for each of them. It costs the company $36 to produce each part.
   a. How many parts should the company start so that it can expect 10,000 good parts to be completed?
   b. What would be the cost of internal failure in this situation?

6. Suppose that in problem 5 all parts that are too large can be reworked to be within the specs at a cost of $9.00. All parts that are too small will still be scrap, as stated in problem 5.
   a. Under these conditions, how many parts should be started to complete 10,000 good parts?
   b. What will be the cost of scrap and rework?

7. Care was taken to operate a metal casting process so that no assignable causes of variation were introduced, and randomly selected castings were weighed. The target weight of the castings was 28 pounds. The following weights came from 30 random observations.

28.00	28.04
28.04	28.01
28.03	27.94
28.01	28.01
27.99	27.98
27.96	28.00
28.03	28.02
27.98	27.99
28.03	28.03
27.98	28.03
28.02	28.01
28.00	27.99
27.98	28.02
28.02	27.96
28.05	27.96

   a. Estimate the standard deviation of the process.
   b. What is C_p if the specifications are 28.0 ± 0.1 pounds?

BIBLIOGRAPHY

Banks, Jerry. *Principles of Quality Control.* New York: Wiley, 1989.

Baum, Herbert M. "White-Collar Quality Comes of Age." *Journal of Business Strategy,* March–April 1990, pp. 34–37.

Bounds, Greg, Lyle Yorks, Mel Adams, and Gipsie Ranney. *Beyond Total Quality Management: Toward the Emerging Paradigm.* New York: McGraw-Hill, 1994.

Brunetti, Wayne. "Reaching for the Prize: A Lesson in Quality." *Public Utilities Fortnightly,* April 12, 1990, pp. 9–16.

Buzzell, Robert D., and Bradley T. Gale. *The PIMS Principles: Linking Strategy to Performance.* New York: Free Press, 1987.

Caropreso, Frank, ed. *Making Total Quality Happen.* New York: Conference Board, 1990.

Ciampa, Dan. *Total Quality: A User's Guide to Implementation.* Reading, Mass.: Addison-Wesley, 1992.

Denton, D. Keith. *Quality Service.* Houston: Gulf Publishing Co., 1989.

DeSouza, Glenn. "Now Service Businesses Must Manage Quality." *Journal of Business Strategy,* May–June 1989, pp. 21–25.

Gabor, Andrea. *The Man Who Discovered Quality: How W. Edwards Deming Brought the Quality Revolution to America.* New York: Penguin, 1990.

Garvin, David A. "Competing on the Eight Dimensions of Quality." *Harvard Business Review,* November–December 1987, pp. 101–109.

———. *Managing Quality: The Strategic and Competitive Edge.* New York: Free Press, 1988.

Hunt, V. Daniel. *Quality in America: How to Implement a Competitive Quality Program.* Homewood, Ill.: Business One Irwin, 1992.

Juran, Joseph M. *Juran on Planning for Quality.* New York: Free Press, 1988.

Kane, Victor E. "Process Capability Indices." *Journal of Quality Technology,* January 1986, pp. 41–52.

Larson, Carl E., and Frank M. J. LaFasto. *Teamwork: What Must Go Right/What Can Go Wrong.* Newbury Park, Calif.: Sage, 1989.

Ryan, Thomas P. *Statistical Methods for Quality Improvement.* New York: Wiley, 1989.

Schein, Lawrence, and Melissa A. Berman. *Total Quality Performance.* New York: Conference Board, 1988.

Van Matre, Joseph G. *Foundations of TQM: A Readings Book.* Fort Worth: Dryden Press, 1995.

Zeithaml, Valarie A., A. Parasuraman, and Leonard L. Berry. *Delivering Quality Service: Balancing Customer Perceptions and Expectations.* New York: Free Press, 1990.

FORECASTING
DEMAND

CHAPTER 4

INTRODUCTION

The previous two chapters discussed some of the broad, strategic options that a company or division must evaluate. Managers must decide whether to offer standard or custom goods or services, what features the goods or services will have, in what territories they will be offered, what mix of performance characteristics the organization will work to develop and emphasize, and many other matters. To a large degree, the desirability of an option depends on the expected impact of the decision on future demand, that is, a forecast of market acceptance.

A *forecast* is an inference of what is likely to happen in the future. It is not an absolutely certain prophesy. Even very carefully prepared forecasts can be wrong. In fact, it is extremely rare for a forecast to be exactly right. Even though forecasting efforts are not 100 percent accurate, they should not be neglected, because forecasting is very important.

In addition to being an important input for long-range, strategic decisions, forecasts are an important basis for shorter-range decisions in day-to-day operations. Businesses must develop forecasts of the level of demand the company should prepare to meet. Since service operations generally cannot store their outputs as inventory, they must try to estimate the level of future demand so they can have the proper amount of service capacity. If they overstaff, they waste resources; if they understaff, they may lose business, time, customers, and their overworked employees.

The forecast provides a basis for coordination of plans for activities in various parts of a company. When all parts of the company base their work on the same forecast, they prepare for the same future and their efforts are mutually supportive. In a manufacturing company, for example, the personnel department can work to obtain the right number of employees with the right mix of skills. Purchasing can contract for the proper amounts of raw materials and purchased components. Finance can estimate the income that will be generated by sales and can determine the capital required, so the company can arrange to obtain any necessary funds at the appropriate times and at reasonable rates. The forecast is therefore a vital basis for the coordination of the plans of various elements within a company. It is important that a forecast be made and that all parts of the company work from the same assumptions about the future.

Various considerations in regard to forecasting are presented in this chapter, along with a discussion of several methods and models commonly used in forecasting. The primary focus is on demand forecasts, because demand directly affects the plans and decisions within the operations function. Before going into the details of demand forecasting, we consider a few areas in which managers may use forecasts.

Businesses May Use Forecasts in Several Subject Areas

In making decisions that guide company actions, managers need to make inferences about the future in several subject areas. Three relevant subject areas are technological developments, business conditions, and the expected level of demand.

TECHNOLOGICAL FORECASTS A *technological forecast* is an estimate of rates of technological progress. Certainly electric utilities are interested in the rates of technological advancement in solar and nuclear power. Chemical and petroleum companies want to know about the development of processes to make usable fuel from oil shale. Technological changes will provide many companies with new products and materials to offer for sale, while other businesses will be faced with competition from those companies. Even if the product remains unchanged, a new process for producing it can be developed, thus rendering large capital investments obsolete. Technological forecasting is probably best performed by specialists in the particular technology. Although technological developments affect operations management, the forecasting of these developments is not within the focus of managing operations and will not be considered specifically.

ECONOMIC FORECASTS Government agencies and other organizations publish *economic forecasts,* or statements of expected future business conditions. Expectations of the general business climate are of interest to government agencies in anticipating tax revenues, levels of employment, needs of the economy for money, and other matters. Business can obtain ideas about long- and intermediate-range business growth from this type of forecast. The details of general business or economic forecasting, however, are outside the scope of our study.

DEMAND FORECASTS The *demand forecast* gives the expected level of demand for the company's goods or services throughout some future period and is usually an instrument in the company's planning and control decisions. Since the operations function is responsible for providing the company's goods and services, operations decisions are greatly influenced by demand forecasts. We assume in this chapter that the company intends to make—and is successful in making—the level of sales equal to the demand. Thus, for simplicity, it is assumed that the demand forecast can be developed from past sales data without adjusting for any missed sales.

Numerous Factors Affect Demand

The portion of total demand that actually flows to a particular company is a result of many forces in the market. Basically, it depends on the size of the total market for the particular good or service and the share of the market that the company captures. A number of forces that are beyond the company's control, as well as others that the company can at least influence, act to determine the level of demand that the company receives.

THE BUSINESS CYCLE Sales are influenced by demand, and demand is influenced by a large number of factors. One factor that influences demand is the status of the economy as the *business cycle* goes through the phases of recovery, inflation, recession, and depression. Government actions and reactions are intended to mitigate the severity of these variations, but they are still a fact of life in much of the business world.

HOW FORECASTING CAN HELP ADD VALUE FOR CUSTOMERS

Forecasts help a company anticipate changes in customer demand so the company can be responsive with the types of features customers desire. Forecasts provide an estimate of future levels of demand so that companies can have the necessary capacity and materials available to quickly and reliably respond to customers. The forecast helps prevent underproduction that would cause poor customer service. It also helps prevent excess production that would result in higher costs and also reduce the flexibility of a company. Accurate long-range forecasts of capacity needs help to prevent excessive capital investments that would raise costs so that companies cannot offer low prices to improve value.

Figure 4.1
Stages of Product Life
Cycle

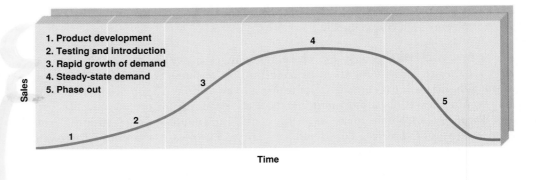

1. Product development
2. Testing and introduction
3. Rapid growth of demand
4. Steady-state demand
5. Phase out

Sales

Time

PRODUCT LIFE CYCLE A product, whether goods or services, is not sold to the same percentage of the population or target market every day of its existence. Normally, each successful product may be considered to pass through five stages in its *product life cycle*, as shown in Figure 4.1.

If a product has market appeal and enters the rapid-growth stage, competitors will usually introduce similar products in an attempt to capture part of the market. The result is changing competitive pressures, which may slow the growth rate. A product that has a long life eventually reaches a point where almost everyone who desires to own it and can purchase it has already done so. At such a point demand diminishes. Consumable items (toothpaste, clothes) and some services (haircuts, car washes) do not reach such a point in the life cycle, because they are "consumed" and repurchased. Market research and product improvement efforts are undertaken to modify nonconsumable products so that their appeal in the marketplace lasts longer than it otherwise would. In the meantime, research and product development activities should be under way so that new goods or services can be introduced to keep the company going when other offerings are phased out.

Even though the product life cycle of classic toys like teddy bears and Barbie dolls seems endless, in fact, it's modification that keeps these products fresh. Teddy bears are softer, bigger, more brightly colored, or just about any other appealing variation. Barbie now can be "outfitted" to do the many activities young girls do today, from sports to scholarship. Regardless of the length of the individual PLC, all toys sell better in December.

Marvin E. Newan/The Image Bank

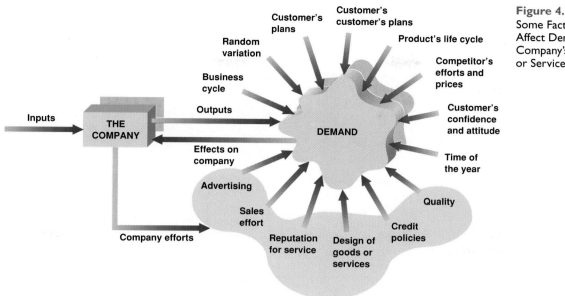

Figure 4.2
Some Factors That Affect Demand for a Company's Product or Service

It is probably rare for a product to experience several years of steady-state (or unchanging) conditions that affect demand for it. One can readily see that there is a danger in extrapolating trends very far.

OTHER FACTORS   A large number of other factors influence demand (see Figure 4.2), particularly when one considers secondary influences, that is, factors that affect the customer's demand for goods and services, which in turn affects demand for the company's product or service. Figure 4.2 shows schematically some of the factors that affect demand.

Forecast Horizons and Update Frequencies

At designated time periods, usually each month, the new sales records are compiled, and actual demand is compared with forecasted demand for that period. This comparison indicates whether the forecasting method is working satisfactorily and helps management decide if any plans need to be revised because of unanticipated levels of demand. Sometimes an evaluation of forecast accuracy is done by a subjective review. Alternatively, an objective calculation such as a tracking signal (to be discussed later) is used. New sales data are periodically used to develop an updated forecast, usually on a monthly or quarterly basis. These frequent forecasts estimate demand, usually for a horizon (that is, the number of future periods it is used to project) of up to 1 year. In addition to a 1-year forecast, many companies will annually develop a longer-range (often 5-year horizon) forecast to be used as the basis for long-range planning. A company may have multiple forecasts, each of which focuses on a different horizon, to facilitate decisions that involve different lead times. Some of the characteristics of forecasts with different horizons and some decisions based on these types of forecasts are shown in Table 4.1. It is important that these decisions and forecasts be consistent. That is, short-range decisions should be leading toward the objectives established by the longer-range decisions.

Table 4.1
TYPES AND CHARACTERISTICS OF FORECASTS

RANGE OF FORECAST	REPRESENTATIVE HORIZON, OR TIME SPAN	APPLICATIONS	CHARACTERISTICS	FORECAST METHODS
Long	Generally up to 5 years or more	Business planning: Product planning Research programming Capital planning Plant location and expansion	Broad, general Often only qualitative	Technological Economic Demographic Marketing studies Judgment
Intermediate	Generally up to 1 season to 2 years	Aggregate planning: Capital and cash budgets Sales planning Production planning Production and inventory budgeting	Numerical Not necessarily at the item level Estimate of reliability needed	Collective opinion Time series Regression Economic index correlation or combination Judgment
Short	Generally less than 1 season; 1 day to 1 year	Short-run control: Adjustment of production and employment levels Purchasing Job scheduling Project assignment Overtime decisions	May be at item level for planning of activity level Should be at item level for adjustment of purchases and inventory	Trend extrapolation Graphical Explosion of short-term product or product family forecasts Judgment Exponential smoothing

The time span appropriate for one decision may be inappropriate for another. Forecasting methods therefore vary with the plans to be formulated. Some decisions are oriented primarily toward short time spans. The current level of demand places short-term requirements on the operations function and on other parts of an organization as well. For example, the current level of demand influences decisions about the number of hours to be worked and the use of overtime or part-time work in the operations function. It also influences the activities of procurement, shipping, and receiving subunits.

The general trend of demand is equally important. Projection of the trend may stimulate such long-range planning as the expansion of capacity, the opening of a new plant, or the closing of an existing facility or its conversion to a new purpose. A new facility may require a rather long planning horizon to allow time to evaluate and select the site, design the facility, raise the necessary capital, construct the building, recruit and train personnel, and purchase the equipment and supplies necessary to begin operation. Construction of a nuclear power plant may require 10 years or more from initial plans to actual power production. Obviously a power company must know well in advance that it will need additional generating capacity.

Judgment Needed in Forecasting

Forecasting is an art or a special skill rather than an exact science. The key inputs in a science are constant laws of nature, whereas the key inputs of forecasting are information, analysis, experience, and informed judgment. There are no natural laws that make the relationships between demand and other variables continue to behave as in the past. Economic conditions, competitors' actions, consumers' preferences, and other social phenomena often are whimsical. Judgment must be exercised to see that appropriate forecasting methods are developed and properly applied.

A company does not always develop an independent forecast for each specific item. Some companies have 40,000 or 50,000 items or more. Items may be collected into groups whose demands are influenced by the same factors so that they tend to move together. Decisions must be made about which items to group for an aggregate forecast and what percentage of the total should then be represented by each specific item. Judgment is used to determine what data to collect for possible evaluation and use in forecasting. A forecaster must exercise judgment in evaluating tabulated data and graphs to discern whether there is some pattern to demand or whether changes in demand appear to be related to factor(s) that can be identified and used to forecast future changes in demand.

A choice must be made to use mathematical equations to express the relationship of demand to other variables or to use a purely subjective approach to develop the forecast. When a purely subjective approach is used, the forecaster forms an opinion of the relative influence of many factors on demand and estimates the resulting demand. If a mathematical model is used, one must still decide which variables to evaluate in developing it and which of many possible equations to use. Suppose that demand data are available for several years. One must decide whether to use the data for only the most recent few years or for a longer period. If a quantitative measure of forecast accuracy is used to evaluate possible models, judgment must be used to select the appropriate measure among several, because often they point to different models as being the best.

For as long as the model is used, someone should continue to judge whether the model that was developed because it fit the demand data in past periods is still appropriate to use for current and expected future conditions—that is, whether the same forces are still acting on demand, whether they are exerting the same relative influence, and whether they can be expected to continue to do so. In some cases, forecasters may develop versatile models that will adapt to changing conditions. No matter how routine or automated forecasting is made, one should never conclude that careful attention and thought can be abandoned. Often a good approach is to use two or more complementary methods of forecasting to see how closely they agree. If different forecast methods give divergent estimates, judgment is again needed to determine why and to develop an estimate that is considered to be the best forecast.

As you see, significant evaluation and judgment may be required to choose the model that is considered best in predicting the demand for a product or product family.

OVERVIEW OF FORECASTING METHODS

As mentioned earlier, a forecast can be developed through either a subjective approach or an objective, quantitative approach. We group forecasts into two major categories, depending on whether the demand estimate is developed solely on the basis of subjective opinion or through the use of some mathematical formula—a quantitative approach. Methods in the first group are called subjective, qualitative, opinion-based, or judgmental forecasts and are discussed in the next section.

Figure 4.3
Breakdown of Forecast
Methods or Models

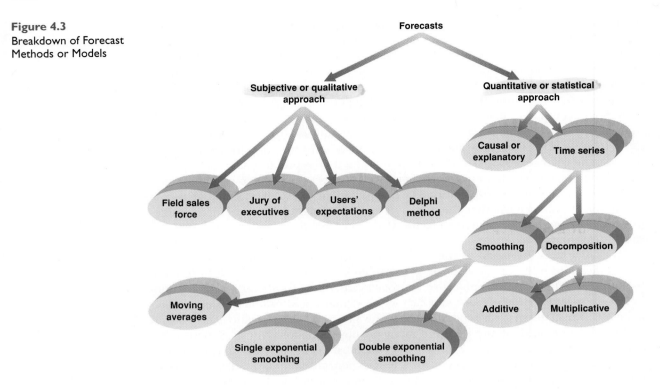

Figure 4.3
Breakdown of Forecast
Methods or Models

Following the section on subjective forecasting methods is a discussion of several methods that are developed through a quantitative or mathematical approach. These are called quantitative or statistical forecast methods or models. (Often a quantitative forecast that is expressed as a formula or equation is referred to as a model, instead of using the more general term *method*.) Statistical forecast methods can be further subdivided on the basis of the variable or variables that are considered to be related to demand and used to predict future levels of demand. In one subgroup, called time series models, time is the only independent variable used to forecast demand. The other subgroup consists of causal or explanatory models that use one or more other variables instead of, or in addition to, time as a basis for forecasting demand. A further breakdown of this group into specific models is shown in Figure 4.3. The methods and models shown in this figure are discussed in the material that follows.

SUBJECTIVE FORECASTING METHODS

Certainly the simplest and sometimes the fastest methods involve only subjective opinion, without expressing the forecast in mathematical formulas. Of the many possible subjective methods, we consider four. Each method uses a different source for the subjective opinion.

Field Sales Force

The first subjective forecasting method is that of having each sales representative estimate the sales within his or her territory. The estimates are combined and reviewed at successive levels of the management hierarchy so that the opinions of the district managers and the sales managers are also incorporated.

Forecasts of this nature have several advantages. One is that they are easily divided by territory, branch, sales representative, or product. The sales representatives may be more highly motivated when they have a feeling of participating in the planning process. This method provides input from persons in direct contact with the customer. A method such as this is more suitable for a new product.

Since this is a subjective method, it has the disadvantage of being subject to individual biases. Sales representatives may be unduly influenced by recent market responses. If the sales performance goals are based on the forecast, sales representatives may be tempted to underestimate. If the forecast is a basis for the allocation of some scarce products, sales representatives may overestimate.

Jury of Executives

The second subjective forecasting method involves the averaging of independent estimates or a discussion by a group of executives that results in a single estimate. Sometimes one senior officer reviews estimates from sales, production, and finance executives and applies his or her judgment to arrive at a single estimate.

An advantage of this method is that it can provide a forecast in a relatively short time. It also brings a variety of viewpoints to bear on the subject and can foster team spirit.

This method, however, requires the time of highly paid executives. It is more difficult to develop breakdowns by territory, district, sales representative, and product. It is also subject to biases due to individual attitudes and situations.

Users' Expectations

A company may seek subjective opinions from people outside the organization. One such method is the users' expectations method. Sales representatives may poll their customers or potential customers about their purchasing plans for the future. Mail questionnaires or telephone surveys may be used to obtain the opinions of existing or potential customers.

An advantage of this method is that it provides the forecaster with an opportunity to learn some of the thinking behind the customer's intentions. The forecaster may obtain users' views of the product's advantages and weaknesses as well as insight into the reasons why some consumers are failing to buy the product. Such information makes this method useful in planning product improvements or product developments.

One potential disadvantage of the users' expectation method is that it may annoy some highly valued customers. This method commands more confidence than it may warrant because customers' buying expectations are based on their forecasts, which are also subject to change and error. This method of forecasting often requires considerable time and a large staff.

Delphi Method

When several knowledgeable persons are asked to provide subjective estimates of demand or forecasts of probable advances in technology, several opinions are likely to emerge. In such circumstances, one has to determine which opinion to accept or how to bring the group to a consensus. The *Delphi method* is a systematic means to obtain consensus from a group or panel of experts. The panel does not meet as a committee to discuss, debate, or persuade. Panel members usually are kept separate and asked not to confer. Preferably, the membership is not revealed to the panel. This measure is intended to evoke each member's unbiased opinion by preventing the influences of group dynamics. Otherwise, members may feel pressured to yield to a socially dominant individual or may fear loss of face if they back away from a publicly stated opinion. A panel coordinator contacts each participant, usually by a mail questionnaire.

Care should be taken so that the initial questionnaire avoids ambiguity and fully explains the matter about which an opinion is being sought. Otherwise, a diverse group of people who never meet to discuss the issue may reach divergent conclusions as to just what the issue is. The experts send their opinions to the panel coordinator, who tallies the results. If opinions differ significantly, another round of responses is solicited. The coordinator reveals the results of the previous tally to the panel members without identifying the holders of the opinions. Members whose opinions differed from, say, the middle 50 percent of the estimates are asked to reconsider their opinions and offer a written rationale if they feel that an estimate outside this range is still appropriate. Additional rounds of estimates can be obtained until the panel closes in on a value or a range that is narrow enough to be useful as a forecast or consensus on the matter under consideration.

The Delphi method is the last subjective forecasting technique we will discuss. We now move into an overview of the quantitative forecasting methods, after which we will discuss specific quantitative models in considerable detail.

QUANTITATIVE FORECASTING METHODS

Quantitative forecasting methods use a mathematical expression or model to show the relationship between demand and some independent variable or variables. There are two major types of quantitative forecasting models: time series models and causal models. *Time series models* use time as the independent variable and project the "demand pattern" (that is, the past relationship between demand and time) to estimate demand in the future. *Causal models*, sometimes called "associative models" or "explanatory models," use some independent variable or variables instead of, or in addition to, time, with which demand has tended to show a consistent relationship in the past. Values of the independent variable(s) are used to calculate the future value of demand that the model predicts. Of course, for the model to be useful as a forecasting tool, changes in the independent variables must take place with sufficient lead time before the associated changes in demand. (These variables are also called *leading indicators*.)

Use of either of the two types of quantitative models (time series or causal) as a forecasting tool rests on an assumption of continuity. That is, one assumes that the type and degree of relationship between demand and the independent variable(s) that existed in the past will continue in the future. We do not have to understand why the relationship exists, but for the model to work, the relationship must continue to follow the model if the model is to be a useful forecasting tool. As we begin to consider relationships that might exist in the demand data we should first mention some preliminary steps in analysis of demand data.

Preliminary Analysis

A first step in development of a quantitative forecasting model is to collect sufficient data on past levels of demand. Data for as far back in time as the conditions are considered to be indicative of the conditions expected in the future may be appropriate. Data for 2 or 3 years are desirable for some models such as time series decomposition. If sales data are to be used they must be adjusted for any occasions when demand exceeded sales because of the lack of product, capacity, and so forth. Each of the demand values should represent approximately equal blocks of time and should be in chronological order.

The effects of any unusual or irregular event that caused a change in demand and is not expected to recur at regular times in the future should be removed from the data. Examples of this type of event are the effect on motel and restaurant sales near the sites of the Olympics or World Series or an unusually high demand of a product or service as a result of a strike or natural disaster at a competitor's business. Irregular events of this nature distort the demand pattern that would normally exist.

Often it is helpful to make a graphical display of the data to see if a pattern is present that may help to predict future values. The components of a pattern that the forecaster may look for in the data are discussed in the next section.

Components of a Time Series

Time series models often are adequate forecasting tools if demand has shown a fairly consistent pattern over time and the conditions under which the pattern has occurred are expected to continue. A *time series* is a sequence of data collected for equal intervals of time and arranged in the order of their occurrence. A chain of

The annual Macy's Thanksgiving Day parade may mean one thing to a New York City police officer: overtime. Forecasting seasonal events helps the police plan when they'll need extra people on the job.

Thomas Craig/Picture Cube

Figure 4.4
A Four-Year Time Series and Its Components

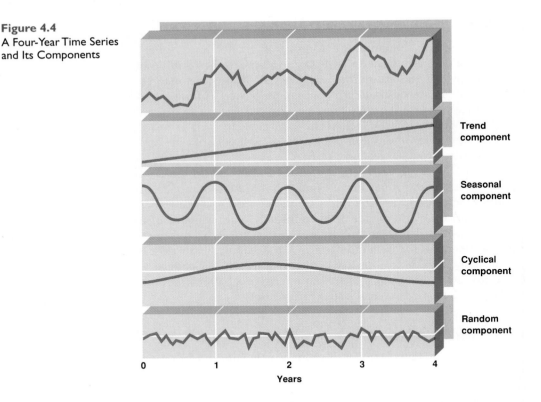

daily, weekly, or monthly sales data is an example of a time series. Such a series may have a fairly consistent pattern that repeats over time. Sometimes a pattern is not apparent in the raw data, but the data can be decomposed into components that show a pattern which is helpful in projecting the data. Four commonly recognized components of a time series are its trend, seasonal, cyclical, and random components, which are briefly described below and are shown in Figure 4.4.

1. The *trend component* is the general upward or downward movement of the average level of demand over time.

2. The *seasonal component* is a recurring fluctuation of demand above and below the trend value that repeats with a fairly consistent interval. Demand for many products or services is weather-related and repeats a general pattern each year. Seasonal patterns, however, can repeat weekly, monthly, or with some other interval.

3. The *cyclical component* is a recurrent upward and downward movement that repeats with a frequency that is longer than 1 year. This movement is usually attributed to business cycles (inflation, recession, etc.), so it may not have a consistent period of repetition. As many as 15 or 20 years of data may be required to determine and describe the cyclical component.

4. The *random component* is a series of short, erratic movements that follow no discernible pattern.

Of the four components in a time series, only the trend and seasonal components are identified in the models discussed in this chapter. Random variations, by definition, are unpredictable, so they are not identified. Cyclical variation requires many years of data to determine its degree and repetitiveness. Demand data for the same product are seldom available for sufficient years to permit the effects of cyclical variation on demand to be identified. Fortunately, most operations decisions do not require enough lead time for cyclical variations to have serious impact. Long-range decisions for distant time periods are usually general plans that will be revised and refined as those time periods draw closer. Consequently, the cyclical component will not be isolated. One should recognize that a trend estimate may be somewhat high if it is estimated from data that were collected during a rising business cycle and somewhat low if estimated from data collected during a decreasing cycle. Even without this possibility, a large element of uncertainty is associated with a trend projected very far into the future.

When Various Models Are Appropriate

The model that is appropriate for forecasting a demand pattern depends on the demand pattern to be projected and the forecaster's objectives for the model. We briefly discuss the situations in which each model may be used before we go into the details of how to calculate a forecast with the model.

TIME SERIES SMOOTHING   When the random component of a time series has fluctuations that deviate substantially from the average level of demand, it is often useful to smooth out the data by averaging several observations to make the basic pattern more apparent. Four averaging techniques—the simple moving average, weighted moving average, single exponential smoothing, and double exponential smoothing—are discussed in this chapter. In general, the first three techniques are appropriate to produce final forecasts only if the data exhibit no trend, that is, if the slope is horizontal. Double exponential smoothing is an averaging technique that can be used to identify and project a trend when the general level of demand is changing over time.

TIME SERIES DECOMPOSITION   Time series decomposition is more appropriate if seasonal variation is evident in the demand pattern and the effect of seasonality is to be included in the forecast. Time series decomposition can be used when the general trend in the demand pattern is horizontal and when it is not. The concepts of both additive and multiplicative seasonal variation are discussed after the smoothing models are presented.

CAUSAL MODELS   Sometimes demand does not exhibit a consistent pattern over time because the level of one or more other variables that have an effect on demand has changed during the period when the demand series was collected. If a forecast is to be made for periods during which the levels of some of these variables may be changed, the effect of these variables must be identified and used to predict future demand. Causal or explanatory models are useful for this purpose. A very extensive search may be required to identify variables, or combinations of variables, whose change precedes changes in demand and with which demand tends to be correlated consistently. If such variables can be found, one can use values of the variables to predict future levels of demand. Models that may be used to determine and project the relationship among the causal variables and subsequent levels of demand include linear regression, curvilinear regression, and multiple regression. Use of linear regression as a causal model is briefly introduced near the end of the chapter.

The above discussion has presented some general characteristics of time series and causal models and when each may be used appropriately. By looking at the demand pattern, a forecaster has some idea of the types of quantitative models to try to see which fits the demand data better. In evaluating and comparing forecast models it is desirable to use some quantitative measure of forecast accuracy. The next section discusses some quantitative measures that can be used to measure the accuracy of forecast models to see which appears to do the best job of fitting the demand data.

MEASURES OF FORECAST ACCURACY

Since demand is influenced by many factors whose future values are not known, it is unrealistic to expect a demand forecast to be exactly right every time. In fact, in most forecast situations, it is rare for a forecast to be exactly right in any time period. A forecast error is a difference between the forecast value and the actual demand. We can expect a forecasting model to make errors, but an unbiased model will overestimate about as much as it underestimates. A calculation of the average error made by a forecast model over time provides a measure of how well the forecast matches the pattern of past data. This measure is often used as an estimate of how well the model will fit the demand pattern one is trying to predict. Such a measure for alternative forecast models provides a basis for comparison to see which model seems to do the best job. Four useful measures of forecast accuracy, often referred to as measures of forecast error, are discussed below.

Mean Absolute Deviation (MAD)

A common measure of forecast error that is fairly easy to compute is the *mean absolute deviation (MAD)*. It is the one we will use primarily in this chapter. The MAD is the mean of the errors made by the forecast model over a series of time periods, without regard to whether an error was an overestimate or an underestimate. The MAD is sometimes called the mean absolute error (MAE). To calculate the MAD, one subtracts the forecast value from the actual value for each time period of interest, changes all the signs to positive, adds, and divides by the number of values that were used to obtain the sum. The expression for these operations is given in equation 4.1.

$$\text{MAD} = \frac{\sum_{t=1}^{n} |A_t - F_t|}{n} \qquad [4.1]$$

where A_t = actual demand in period t
F_t = forecast demand in period t
n = number of periods being used
$| \ |$ means: use the absolute value, that is, ignore the direction of the deviation
Σ means: sum all n values

Suppose that a forecast of 125 units had been made for the demand in every period for the data given in Table 4.2. The MAD could then be calculated as shown in Table 4.2. Spreadsheet programs are very helpful in developing tables such as Table 4.2 and often can be used to compute the forecasts. Spreadsheet programs are particularly valuable when large amounts of data are to be used.

The MAD is similar to a standard deviation, but it is easier to calculate because it does not require squaring numbers or taking square roots. If the forecast errors are normally distributed, the MAD will be about 0.8 times the standard deviation of the

Table 4.2
CALCULATION OF MAD, MSE, AND MAPE

(1) DEMAND A	(2) FORECAST F	(3) DEVIATION A − F	(4) ABSOLUTE DEVIATION |A − F|	(5) SQUARED ERROR (A − F)^2	(6) PERCENTAGE ERROR $\left(\dfrac{A - F}{A}\right)100$	(7) ABSOLUTE PERCENTAGE ERROR $\left\|\dfrac{A - F}{A}\right\|100$
120	125	−5	5	25	−4.17	4.17
130	125	+5	5	25	3.85	3.85
110	125	−15	15	225	−13.64	13.64
140	125	+15	15	225	10.71	10.71
110	125	−15	15	225	−13.64	13.64
130	125	+5	5	25	3.85	3.85
		−10	60	750		49.86

$$MAD = \frac{60}{6} = 10$$

$$MSE = \frac{750}{6} = 125$$

$$MAPE = \frac{49.86}{6} = 8.31\%$$

$$MFE = \frac{-10}{6} = -1.67$$

forecast errors. About 58 percent of the errors will be less than 1 times the MAD, 89 percent of the forecast errors will be less than 2 times the MAD, and 98 percent will be less than 3 times the MAD.

Mean Square Error (MSE)

Numerous small forecast errors, above and below the actual demand, that average one another out are about the best one can expect in forecasting. Usually, the effects on operations of small errors are not serious. These errors may be smoothed out by inventory or overtime work. Large errors may, however, be difficult or impossible to correct for—even if a few large errors average to the same amount as more-numerous small errors. Consequently, a method of measuring errors that penalizes large errors more than small errors is sometimes desired. The *mean square error (MSE)* provides this type measure of forecast error. Multiplying each forecast error by itself (squaring the errors) gives a large weight to large errors and a small weight to small errors. The MSE is found by squaring each of a series of errors made by the forecast model, summing these squared errors, and dividing by the number of errors used in the calculation. Given the symbols defined above for the MAD, the equation for the MSE is

$$MSE = \frac{\sum_{t=1}^{n} (A_t - F_t)^2}{n} \qquad \text{[4.2]}$$

If, for example, we had forecast three periods and the errors were 22.8, −26.2, and 29.3, the MSE would be $\frac{1}{3}(22.8^2 + 26.2^2 + 29.3^2) = 688.3$.

Mean Forecast Error (MFE)

A good forecast model should not only have a small average error, it should also be unbiased. An unbiased model is as likely to make a positive error as a negative error. That is, it does not have a tendency to overforecast more than it underforecasts, or vice versa. For an unbiased model the positive errors over a series of forecasts should add to about the same amount as the negative errors so that the running sum is close to zero. The sum of the signed forecast errors over a series of forecast periods is called the *running sum of forecast errors (RSFE)*. If the RSFE generally moves away from zero over time it means that the forecast is biased. The RSFE is used to compute the *mean forecast error (MFE)* which also provides a measure of forecast biasedness since it is based on signed errors.

The MFE is calculated by summing the forecast errors over a series of periods (as in column 3 of Table 4.2) and dividing this sum by the number of errors used to compute the sum. Again using the same symbols, we can express the equation for the mean forecast error as

$$\text{MFE} = \frac{\sum_{t=1}^{n}(A_t - F_t)}{n} = \frac{\text{RSFE}}{n} \qquad [4.3]$$

Ideally, the MFE should be zero. If the MFE departs from zero over time it indicates that the model may be biased and tells the average amount per period by which the forecast has departed from the actual demands. For example, a MFE of -5 means that the forecast exceeds the actual demand by an average of 5 units per period. If the MFE is based on a series of the last ten periods then there is a cumulative over-forecast of 50 units during this time span. Such data must be interpreted in view of how large the MFE is relative to the average level of demand. The MFE or the RSFE can be used to test for consideration for use or to monitor models to see if they have become biased. Near the end of the chapter we discuss use of the RSFE to monitor forecast models.

Mean Absolute Percentage Error (MAPE)

Instead of knowing that a forecast model has a mean error of 26.1 or a mean square error of 688.3, it is sometimes more informative to know the relative error. An error of 26.1 in predicting a series that has an average value of about 500 will probably be considered pretty good. An error of 26.1 in predicting a series that averages 50 may be another matter. The relative error that a forecasting model makes can be measured by the *mean absolute percentage error (MAPE)*. Equation 4.4 provides an expression for calculating a MAPE in terms of the symbols used above.

$$\text{MAPE} = \left(\frac{100}{n}\right)\sum_{t=1}^{n}\left|\frac{A_t - F_t}{A_t}\right| \qquad [4.4]$$

Calculation of the MAPE is illustrated in columns 6 and 7 of Table 4.2.

The above discussion provides ways that forecast models can be tested to see which does the best job of fitting a series of demand data. Now that we have a means of testing and comparing models, we will discuss some specific quantitative models that might be tried. The following material presents more-detailed characteristics of some models and how to calculate forecasts with them.

TIME SERIES SMOOTHING

We begin our discussion with the simple moving average. Other smoothing models discussed in this section are the weighted moving average, single exponential smoothing, and double exponential smoothing. After this section, time series decomposition is discussed, followed by causal models.

Simple Moving Average

A *simple moving average (SMA)* is a method of computing the mean of only a specified number of the most recent data values in a series. Assume, for example, that we were keeping records of monthly sales. We might compute a 3-month moving average at the end of each month to smooth out random fluctuations and get an estimate of the average sales per month. This number would be useful to see if the average had increased or decreased since some prior period. A moving average is also useful for other reasons. If there is no noticeable trend or seasonality in the data, the moving average gives a forecast of the mean value of sales in future periods. A moving average can be used to average out seasonality if the number of periods included in the average is equal to the time required for the seasonal pattern to start to repeat itself—that is, 12 months of monthly data, four quarters of quarterly data, and so on, if the seasonal pattern repeats each year.

To compute a 3-month moving average, at the end of each month we add sales for the latest 3 months and divide by 3. If we want a 4-month moving average, at the end of each month we sum sales for the latest 4 months and divide by 4. At the end of a period t, the n-period SMA, which might be used as a forecast for period $t + 1$ if the mean is changing very little or very slowly over time, is given by equation 4.5.

$$SMA_{t+1} = \left(\frac{1}{n}\right) \sum_{i=t+1-n}^{t} A_i \qquad \text{[4.5]}$$

where SMA_{t+1} = simple moving average at end of period t (It might be used as a
             forecast for period $t + 1$.)
      A_i = actual demand in period i
      n = number of periods included in each average

An example of the computations for a 3-month simple moving average is shown in Table 4.3. At the end of month 22, the demands for months 20, 21, and 22 are

Table 4.3
EXAMPLE OF 3-MONTH SIMPLE MOVING AVERAGE

MONTH	DEMAND FOR MONTH (UNITS)	TOTAL DEMAND DURING PAST 3 MONTHS (UNITS)	3-MONTH AVERAGE DEMAND UNITS/MONTHS)
20	120		
21	130	------- 360 ------- ÷ 3 ----▶	120
22	110	380	126.67
23	140	360	120
24	110	380	126.67
25	130		

added and divided by 3, to give a value of 120. At the end of month 23, the demands for months 21, 22, and 23 are added and divided by 3, to give a value of 126.67, and so on.

Averaging multiple periods helps smooth out random fluctuations so that the forecast or average has more stability. *Stability* is the property of not fluctuating erratically so that the forecast moves in a way consistent with the basic demand pattern. Gaining stability is an advantage if the degree of random fluctuation in the demand data is high. A moving average will gain stability if a greater number of periods are used in the average. Gaining stability is desirable only to the extent that it provides sufficient smoothing of random fluctuations. If the number of periods in the average is too great, the average will be so stable that it will be slow to respond to nonrandom changes in the demand data.

Responsiveness is the ability of a forecast to adjust quickly to true changes in the base level of demand. Both stability and responsiveness are desirable in a forecast. Unfortunately, these two characteristics are in conflict. Several demand periods are required to determine whether the new level of demand is persisting or whether a change has been just a random fluctuation. If a forecast is changed in immediate response to each change in actual demand, it will also respond to random fluctuation. If a demand pattern is known to have relatively small random fluctuations about some fairly stable level, then a responsive forecasting method should be used to smooth these erratic ups and downs. If a demand pattern is known to have large random fluctuations, then a stable forecasting method should be used. Both responsiveness and stability are difficult to achieve with a forecasting method that looks only at the series of past demands without considering factors that may have caused a change in that pattern. Naive forecasting methods alone do not take into consideration the external causative factors.

The responsiveness of a four-period moving average to a shift in a stable level of demand is illustrated in Figure 4.5. Random variations have been omitted but would be expected to cancel out one another fairly well, so that the average would be close to the values depicted in the figure. Notice that the four-period moving average took four periods to adjust to the new level of demand. A ten-period moving average would have required ten periods to adjust. An *n*-period moving average would require *n* periods to adjust. We see that the responsiveness of a moving average forecast is inversely related to the number of periods in the average.

Stability is illustrated in Figure 4.6. Notice that a single random fluctuation above the stable average will be reflected in the average, causing it to increase by $1/n$ times the random fluctuation, where n is the number of periods in the average. Thus the more periods included in a moving average, the more stable the forecast will be. Since a moving average is an average of a group of past demand values, it does not

Figure 4.5

Responsiveness of a Moving Average to a True Shift in the Average Level of Demand

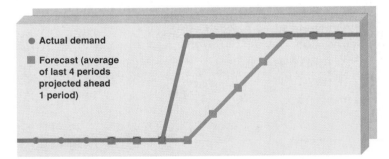

● Actual demand

■ Forecast (average of last 4 periods projected ahead 1 period)

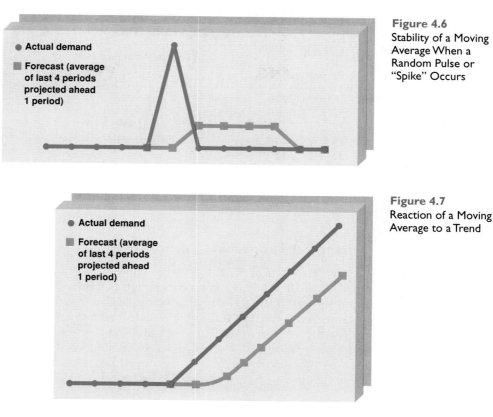

Figure 4.6
Stability of a Moving Average When a Random Pulse or "Spike" Occurs

Figure 4.7
Reaction of a Moving Average to a Trend

anticipate future trends. In the presence of a consistent trend in demand, the simple moving average will lag $(n + 1)/2$ periods behind the next value that will occur. If it were plotted on the time period corresponding to the center of the time periods being averaged, it would be close to the trend line. When it is used as a tool to forecast (meaning to "throw ahead"), however, the actual demand values will already have moved to a level that is different from the average. This property of the simple moving average is illustrated in Figure 4.7. If the up trend continues, the forecast average will always be below the actual values.

Weighted Moving Average

Equal weights were assigned to all periods in the computation of the simple moving average. The *weighted moving average* assigns more weight to some demand values (usually the more recent ones) than to others. Table 4.4 shows the computations for a 3-month weighted moving average with a weight of 0.50 assigned to the most recent demand value, a weight of 0.30 assigned to the next most recent value, and a weight of 0.20 assigned to the oldest of the demand values included in the average. The rationale for varying the weights is usually to allow recent data to influence the forecast more than older data. If there is a long-run trend in demand, a weighted average with heavier emphasis on recent data is an improvement over a simple average, but it will still lag behind demand. We cannot average the past sales values and get a higher value than any past sales value, which is what we desire when we are trying to project the next value in a continuing upward trend. A method of adjusting for the presence of a trend in demand data is discussed later.

Table 4.4
EXAMPLE OF A 3-MONTH WEIGHTED MOVING AVERAGE

| MONTH | DEMAND | Weighted Values for Month | | | | WEIGHTED MOVING AVERAGE |
		MONTH 22	MONTH 23	MONTH 24	MONTH 25	
20	120	0.2×120				
21	130	0.3×130	0.2×130			118
22	110	0.5×110	0.3×110	0.2×140		129
23	140		0.5×140	0.3×140	0.2×140	119
24	110			0.5×110	0.3×110	126
25	130				0.5×130	

Single Exponential Smoothing

Another form of weighted moving average is the exponentially smoothed average. This method keeps a running average of demand and adjusts it for each period in proportion to the difference between the latest actual demand figure and the latest value of the average. If the single smoothed average at period t is used as the forecast for the next period, SF_{t+1}, equation 4.6a or 4.6b can be used to calculate the forecast. Equation 4.6b is often preferred if one wishes to calculate a measure of forecast error because the error is shown in parentheses for each period.

$$SF_{t+1} = \alpha A_t + (1 - \alpha)SF_t \qquad \text{[4.6a]}$$

$$SF_{t+1} = SF_t + \alpha(A_t - SF_t) \qquad \text{[4.6b]}$$

where SF_{t+1} = simple smoothed forecast for time period following period t
SF_t = smoothed average forecast for period t
α = smoothing constant that determines weight given to previous data $(0 \leq \alpha \leq 1)$
A_t = actual demand in period t

The smoothing constant α is a decimal value between 0 and 1. Often it is set at a value that produces forecasts that fit past data better than forecasts computed with any other value of α. It also influences the stability and responsiveness of the forecast. Examination will show that if α were set to equal 0, the old forecast would not be adjusted in any way, regardless of the actual demand that occurred. This would result in a perfectly stable forecast, but it would not respond in any way to changes. If α were set to equal 1, the latest forecast would equal the last actual value—very responsive but not stable if there is any random fluctuation in the data. Values of α between 0.1 and 0.3 are often used in practice.

Since each single smoothed forecast depends on the previous forecast, a series of forecasts must be started with an initial forecast made by some other method. One might use a simple average for a few demands, a judgment forecast, or just the first actual demand as a forecast for the second period. It may take several periods for the forecasts to reflect the ability of the model rather than the accuracy of the initial forecast. If a small value of α is used, little weight is given to the actual demand, so it will take longer for the effect of the actual demand to "wash out" the effect of the initial forecast. If several values of α are tried to see which makes the model fit the demand data best, the comparison should exclude the first several forecasts made with each value of α. The first several values of demand that are forecast are influenced by the

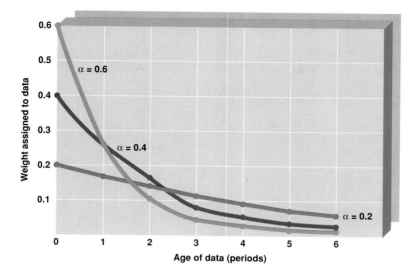

Figure 4.8
Weights Assigned
to Past Data by
Exponential Smoothing
with Various Values of α

initial forecast more than by the model being evaluated. Exclusion of the first several periods is illustrated in the next application box which shows a comparison of forecasts made using $\alpha = 0.1$ and $\alpha = 0.2$.

Exponential smoothing gets its name because a series of weights that decay exponentially are assigned to past data as the data get older. Our latest forecast, SF_{t+1}, depends on the latest actual value, A_t and the previous forecast, SF_t. But SF_t depended on A_{t-1} and SF_{t-1}; SF_{t-1} was determined by A_{t-2} and SF_{t-2}; and so on. One can see that many periods are included in the average even though they do not appear explicitly in equation 4.6. The weights given to data will be a function of α, as shown in Figure 4.8.

Figure 4.9 shows a series of data ranging randomly from −30 to +30 units about a mean of 196. The line in the figure represents the single exponentially smoothed average computed with $\alpha = 0.2$. Notice that the model smooths much of the erratic variation in the data. Single exponential smoothing is appropriate to estimate the mean if the mean remains fairly stable over time.

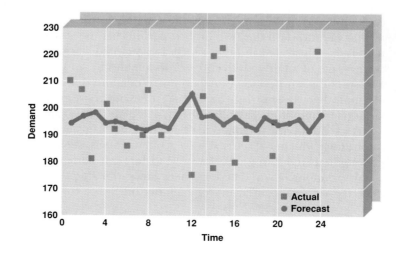

Figure 4.9
Single Exponential
Smoothing to Smooth
Random Fluctuation
about a Horizontal
Mean

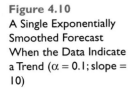

Figure 4.10
A Single Exponentially Smoothed Forecast When the Data Indicate a Trend ($\alpha = 0.1$; slope = 10)

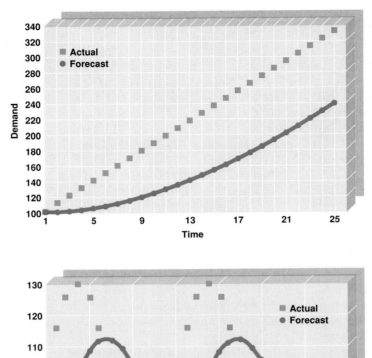

Figure 4.11
A Single Exponentially Smoothed Forecast with Seasonal Data ($\alpha = 0.2$)

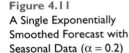

Single smoothed forecasts are a form of moving average, so they also have the limitation of lagging behind a trend in actual demand. Since single smoothed forecasts adjust to deviations by only the fraction α, these forecasts will fall farther and farther behind until they will be $1/\alpha$ periods behind if the trend persists. These limitations are illustrated in Figure 4.10. Exponential smoothing is intended to estimate the average of a fairly uniform level of demand by smoothing out the fluctuations. It also smooths out periodic fluctuations in demand due to seasonal variation. The single smoothed forecast lags behind the demand movements and does not swing with so large an amplitude as does the actual demand. This can be seen in Figure 4.11.

A trend in the demand pattern can be adjusted for by double exponential smoothing, which is discussed next. Other models, such as Winters' model for triple exponential smoothing, can be used to forecast demand when both trend and seasonal variations occur. These models add a third type of smoothed average to estimate the seasonal coefficient for each period.[1]

[1]See, for example, Spyros G. Makridakis, Steven C. Wheelwright, and Victor E. McGee, *Forecasting Methods and Applications,* 2d ed. (New York: Wiley, 1983), pp. 103–109.

EXAMPLE OF SINGLE EXPONENTIAL SMOOTHING AND MAD

The regional distribution center for the Kumfort King Company has been developing models to forecast demand for some replacement parts it stocks. Several sizes of blower motors are used in furnaces, heat pumps, and air conditioners, so the demand for these items remains rather uniform throughout all seasons. Single exponential smoothing is considered an adequate forecasting method for these items. The inventory manager has data for the past 27 months and wants to select a value of α, through a procedure that is sometimes called "retrospective testing," which will make the single smoothed model fit the past data as well as possible. The MAD is used to measure how well the forecast model performs. The company's management has no reason to believe that any new forces are influencing demand, so it is assumed that the model that minimizes forecast error for the past data will be the best model to use to forecast future demand.

Table 4.5 illustrates the comparison of the MAD for a model with $\alpha = 0.1$ and one with $\alpha = 0.2$. Some initial value is needed to begin the series of forecasts. Demands for the first 3 of the 27 months are averaged to get a mean of 196.2 as the initial forecast of the series. The next 24 months are forecast by a single smoothed model with an α of 0.1. Since the initial mean was not calculated with this model, and it affects the first several forecasts made with a single smoothed model, the inventory manager decides to disregard the first five forecasts made with the model. Therefore, the accuracy of this and the other models was measured by computing the MAD with only the last nineteen forecast values. The same procedure

Table 4.5

CALCULATIONS OF EXPONENTIAL SMOOTHED FORECASTS AND MAD

PERIOD	ACTUAL	$\alpha = 0.1$ FORECAST	ABSOLUTE DEVIATION	$\alpha = 0.2$ FORECAST	ABSOLUTE DEVIATION
1	210	196.2[a]	[b]	196.2[a]	[b]
2	206	197.6	[b]	199.0	[b]
3	181	198.4	[b]	200.4	[b]
4	201	196.7	[b]	196.5	[b]
5	192	197.1	[b]	197.4	[b]
6	186	196.6	10.6	196.3	10.3
7	190	195.5	5.5	194.2	4.2
8	208	195.0	13.0	193.4	14.6
9	190	196.3	6.3	196.3	6.3
10	220	195.7	24.3	195.0	25.0
11	223	198.1	24.9	200.0	23.0
12	175	200.6	25.6	204.6	29.6
13	205	198.0	7.0	198.7	6.3
14	178	198.7	20.7	200.0	22.0
15	214	196.6	17.4	195.6	18.4
16	181	198.3	17.3	199.3	18.3
17	187	196.6	9.6	195.6	8.6
18	217	195.6	21.4	193.9	23.1
19	184	197.7	13.7	198.5	14.5
20	196	196.3	0.3	195.6	0.4
21	202	196.3	5.7	195.7	6.3
22	169	196.9	27.9	197.0	28.0
23	223	194.1	28.9	191.4	31.6
24	190	197.0	7.0	197.7	7.7
			287.1		298.2

$$\text{MAD(with } \alpha = 0.1) = \frac{287.1}{19} = 15.11$$

$$\text{MAD(with } \alpha = 0.2) = \frac{298.2}{19} = 15.69$$

$$\text{SF}_{t+1} = \text{SF}_t + \alpha(A_t - \text{SF}_t)$$
For example, for $\alpha = 0.2$:

$$\text{SF}_2 = 196.2 + 0.2(210 - 196.2) = 196.2 + 2.8 = 199.0$$
$$\text{SF}_3 = 199.0 + 0.2(206 - 199) = 199.0 + 1.4 = 200.4$$
$$\text{SF}_4 = 200.4 + 0.2(181 - 200.4) = 200.4 - 3.9 = 196.5$$
$$\text{SF}_5 = 196.5 + 0.2(201 - 196.5) = 196.5 + 0.9 = 197.4$$
$$\text{SF}_6 = 197.4 + 0.2(192 - 197.4) = 197.4 - 1.1 = 196.3$$

[a]Initial mean estimated prior to these calculations = 196.2.
[b]Omitted to reduce the effect of the initial mean.

is repeated with α values of 0.2, 0.3, and so forth, and the MADs are compared. The model with $\alpha = 0.1$ has the smaller MAD in the comparison shown in Table 4.5. Other values of α were evaluated for forecasting demand for this blower motor, but none produced a lower MAD than the model with $\alpha = 0.1$, so 0.1 will be used in the model to forecast the demand for blower motors. Smoothing constants to use in forecasting other products were selected in the same manner. Since other products had different demand patterns, other values of α were best for some of them.

Double Exponential Smoothing

We saw earlier that both a simple moving average and single exponential smoothing will continually lag behind actual data that have a steady upward or downward trend. *Double exponential smoothing* is a technique sometimes used to obtain short-range forecasts of future values of a time series that contains a trend. Several double smoothing models are available. One model uses only one smoothing constant. The model discussed here uses two smoothing constants. The first constant, α, is used to smooth out randomness in the overall level of the series. A second smoothing constant, β, is used to smooth out variations in the estimates of the slope of the line as more data points are added to the series over time.

The smoothed average or "base" at any period t is found by equation 4.7.

$$SA_t = \alpha A_t + (1 - \alpha)(SA_{t-1} + T_{t-1}) \qquad [4.7]$$

where T_{t-1} is the latest estimate of the smoothed average trend.

The difference between two successive smoothed averages is an estimate of the trend in the data. These estimates can be somewhat erratic if there is randomness in the series. The most recent estimate of the trend is incorporated into the smoothed average trend by equation 4.8 to obtain the latest estimate of the smoothed trend.

$$T_t = \beta(SA_t - SA_{t-1}) + (1 - \beta)T_{t-1} \qquad [4.8]$$

A forecast for the pth period beyond the most recent period can be obtained with equation 4.9.

$$F_{t+p} = SA_t + (p)T_t \qquad [4.9]$$

With this equation, forecasts for periods 1, 2, 3, or more periods beyond the series are obtained by multiplying the smoothed trend by the number 1, 2, 3, or the corresponding number for how far the trend is to be projected and adding this amount to the latest smoothed average.

This two-parameter model permits the forecaster to select a combination of α and β that seems to have a sufficient degree of responsiveness yet maintain stability over changes in the data. To begin forecasting with this model, we need initial estimates for the smoothed average and the trend. As with single smoothing, the first several forecasts are influenced by the initial estimates and do not give a true indication of how well the model works. With these estimates we calculate the first forecast. Then, with the actual value, we can adjust the smoothed average. The difference between the new smoothed average and the initial estimate can be used to calculate a new estimate of the trend. The smoothed average and the trend are used to calculate the next forecast. When another actual demand value becomes available, the procedure is repeated.

Table 4.6
DOUBLE EXPONENTIAL SMOOTHING FORECAST ($\alpha = 0.3$, $\beta = 0.5$)

| PERIOD | Demand | | BASE 90 | TREND 10 | Deviation | |
	ACTUAL	FORECAST			SIMPLE	ABSOLUTE
1	97	100.0	99.1	9.5	−3.0	3.0
2	107	108.6	108.1	9.3	−1.6	1.6
3	125	117.4	119.7	10.5	7.6	7.6
4	140	130.2	133.1	11.9	9.8	9.8
5	132	145.0	141.1	10.0	−13.0	13.0
6	161	151.1	154.1	11.5	9.9	9.9
7	154	165.6	162.1	9.8	−11.6	11.6
8	157	171.9	167.4	7.6	−14.9	14.9
9	175	175.0	175.0	7.6	0.0	0.0
10	166	182.6	177.6	5.1	−16.6	16.6
11	169	182.7	178.6	3.1	−13.7	13.7
12	188	181.7	183.6	4.1	6.3	6.3
13	180	187.7	185.4	3.0	−7.7	7.7
14	180	188.4	185.9	1.8	−8.4	8.4
15	188	187.7	187.8	1.9	0.3	0.3
16	194	189.7	191.0	2.5	4.3	4.3
17	194	193.5	193.7	2.6	0.5	0.5
18	194	196.3	195.6	2.3	−2.3	2.3
19	194	197.9	196.7	1.7	−3.9	3.9
20	194	198.4	197.1	1.1	−4.4	4.4
21	194	198.2	196.9	0.5	−4.2	4.2
22	194	197.4	196.4	−0.0	−3.4	3.4
23	194	196.4	195.7	−0.4	−2.4	2.4
24	194	195.3	194.9	−0.6	−1.3	1.3
25		194.3				
26		193.7				
27		193.1				
28		192.5				
29		191.9				
30		191.3				

Table 4.6 is an example of a spreadsheet used to calculate a series of forecasts with double exponential smoothing. Spreadsheet programs work very well for repetitive calculations of this type.

The values of actual demand in Table 4.6 were obtained from a series with a trend of 10 per period for the first eight periods and a trend of 5 for the second eight periods with random variation about these values. The last eight values were set equal to the value just prior to them and have a horizontal trend with no randomness in the data. Figure 4.12 (pages 150 and 151) shows the forecasts when various values of α and β are used. Notice that both α and β must be large enough to adjust to both the overall level of the data and the rate at which the values are changing. In Figure 4.12*a*, α is so small that the forecast does not adjust to the average level of the data very rapidly and overshoots the actual values, even though the slope of the forecast line becomes horizontal soon after the actual values level off. In Figure 4.12*b*, the value of α is higher, and the forecast values follow more closely the overall values of

Figure 4.12
Double Exponential
Smoothing with Various
Smoothing Constants

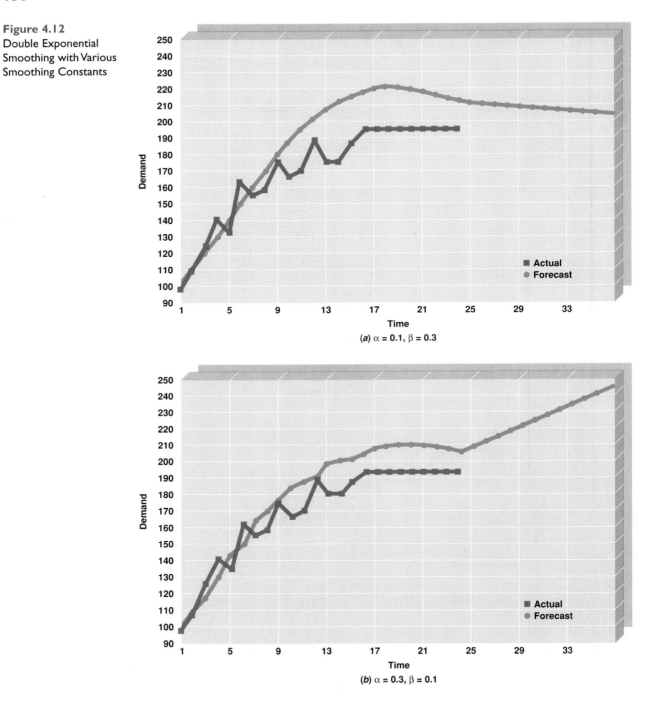

(*a*) $\alpha = 0.1$, $\beta = 0.3$

(*b*) $\alpha = 0.3$, $\beta = 0.1$

the actual data. With a β of only 0.1, however, the trend still had not been completely corrected at the end of the actual values, and the projection beyond the actual values is still trending upward. With both α and β equal to 0.3, the forecast values follow the actual values much better, as shown in Figure 4.12*c*. The forecast values are slightly better with an α of 0.3 and a β of 0.5, as shown in Figure 4.12*d*.

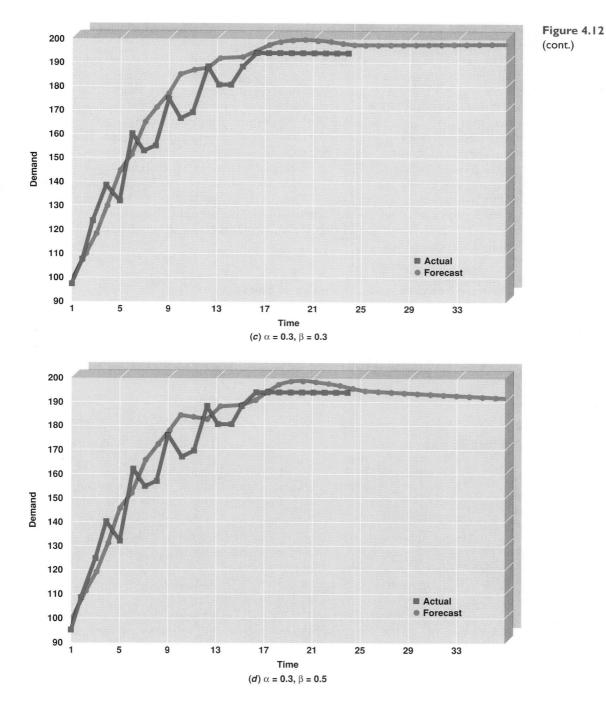

Figure 4.12
(cont.)

(c) $\alpha = 0.3$, $\beta = 0.3$

(d) $\alpha = 0.3$, $\beta = 0.5$

TIME SERIES DECOMPOSITION

Time series decomposition is separation of the overall series into some of its basic components that are more likely to have recognizable and more predictable patterns. These basic components can then be projected into the future and recombined to form a forecast. The four basic components—trend, cyclical, seasonal, and random—were defined earlier and were illustrated in Figure 4.4.

The decomposition approach is based on the assumption that these components act independently of one another. If they are projected into the future, it is assumed that the forces that have caused them to occur in the past will continue. In view of the many factors that influence demand, there is some danger in projecting the past too far into the future. Judgment and experience are needed to recognize when a change has occurred in the forces that have acted on demand in the past. These situations are called *turning points.* For example, consider the rate of increase in U.S. automobile sales before the 1973 oil embargo and the rate of decrease in sales immediately afterward and the increase in demand for larger cars 10 years later, when gasoline prices were stable and the mileage of these cars had improved. When a forecast model has been used for an extended time, one should consider this question: Have the conditions and forces that act on demand changed significantly since the model was developed?

Multiplicative and Additive Models

There are two general forms of time series models. The most common is the *multiplicative model,* in which the components are ratios that are multiplied together to estimate demand. The second type is an *additive model,* in which the components are added together to obtain the estimate. Equations 4.10 and 4.11 are multiplicative and additive models, respectively.

$$\text{TF} = T \cdot S \cdot C \cdot R \tag{4.10}$$

$$\text{TF} = T + S + C + R \tag{4.11}$$

where TF = time series forecast
T = trend component
S = measure of seasonality, either a ratio or an amount to add
C = measure of cyclical adjustment, either a ratio or an amount to add
R = random component, which is any variation in demand not explained by previous factors

Visual inspection of a plotted time series is often helpful to determine the type of model that most appropriately represents the data. The data may appear to fit one of the general patterns presented in Figure 4.13.

If seasonal variation repeats on a 1-year cycle the seasonal and irregular components can often be removed by calculating 1-year moving averages, starting with the first year and moving forward through the data. If many years' data are available, the forecaster may use only the most recent several years because they are more likely to reflect current conditions. The averages can be plotted at the center of the time periods used to compute each average. This plot shows how the combined trend and cycle components are moving. If there is no trend or cycle, the moving averages will appear approximately as a straight horizontal line.

It may take 15 to 20 years of data to define and separate the trend and cycle components. However, very few products remain in stable condition this long—either competitive conditions or the product's life-cycle stage will change well before the end of this period. Decisions cannot be postponed 15 years while managers wait to see what the trend really is. The trend is sometimes estimated from data from 2 or more years. Consequently, in practice many planners identify only the seasonal com-

Figure 4.13
Some Possible Time
Series Patterns

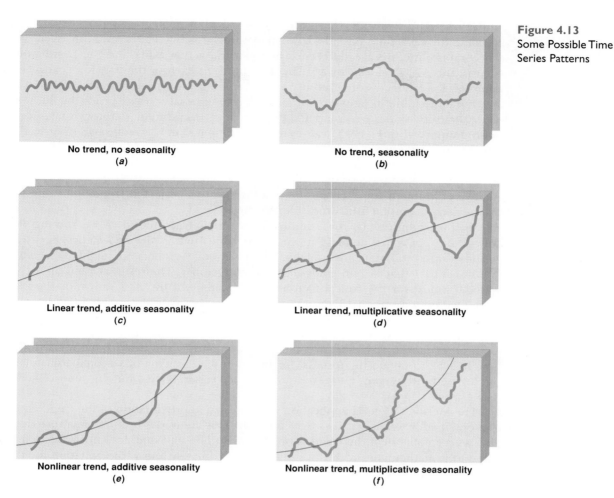

No trend, no seasonality
(*a*)

No trend, seasonality
(*b*)

Linear trend, additive seasonality
(*c*)

Linear trend, multiplicative seasonality
(*d*)

Nonlinear trend, additive seasonality
(*e*)

Nonlinear trend, multiplicative seasonality
(*f*)

ponent and a combination trend-cycle component. The random component is assumed to be averaged out over multiple observations.

The plotted combination trend-cycle component may appear as a straight line or as some form of curve, after the seasonal and irregular components are averaged out. A least-squares curve-fitting program can be run on a computer to determine the equation for a curve. Linear regression (which is presented later with equations 4.12 and 4.13) can be used to find the slope and intercept for a straight line, if the data appear to form a linear function.

The trend-cycle function (which we call the trend) can be extended into the future by visually extrapolating the plotted values or by calculating future values, if an equation has been determined. The trend line should be extended with caution, particularly for long-range projections, because the trend estimate may be distorted by changes in the cycle component which is mixed with the trend.

Extension of the trend line does not provide a complete forecast for each future period if there is seasonal variation about the trend. The pattern of seasonal variation about the trend line must also be projected into the future to form a forecast for the expected sales in each future period. If the data appear to be following an additive model, one must determine the proper seasonal adjustment (positive or negative) to be made for each time period for which a forecast is made. For monthly data, one can compute the average difference between the actual value and the trend value (that is, the $A - T$ values) for a particular month in each of the past few years. This value, say for January, would tell us by what amount the typical January differs from the trend-line value in January. For example, January sales may typically be 86 units above the trend value. We would add 86 units to the trend value to forecast sales for a future January. If the $(A - T)$ values for some other month average −38 (that is, the actual values are usually 38 units below the trend), we would add −38, which is equivalent to subtracting 38 units from the trend value in that month. This procedure can be repeated to find the seasonal adjustment for February and the other months. The additive adjustment for each period is added to the projected trend-line value for that period to compute the forecast for the period.

Seasonal adjustments for a multiplicative model are found by computing the average ratio of actual demand to the trend value (that is, the A/T values) for each period of interest. If data are available for, say, several Octobers, we might average the ratios of A to T that we can compute for each October. The result is a multiplier, or seasonal index, for the typical October. For example, if the A/T ratios for the past three Octobers average 1.18, then the sales in October typically are about 18 percent above the trend value for that month. We multiply the projected trend value for a future October by 1.18 to compute the sales forecast for that month. If the ratios for some other month, say June, average 0.82, we multiply the trend value for a future June by 0.82 to obtain the forecast for that month. This type of seasonal adjustment can be used with weekly, quarterly, or other data series. Such a ratio is often referred to as a *seasonal index*.

The McDoe Cafeteria application illustrates an approximation of the trend equation obtained by reading values from a graph. This method is useful if an approximation is acceptable or if the trend is not a straight line and one does not want to fit a curve to it mathematically. If the trend is approximately linear, the equation for the trend line can be developed by simple linear regression.

Simple linear regression determines the equation for a straight line that passes through a set of points so that the sum of the squared distances from the points to the line will be the minimum amount for any straight line that could be drawn through the points. That is, it determines the "least-squares line," or the line with the minimum squared error. The trend equation has the form $Y_T = a + bx$, where Y_T is the height of the trend line at any particular point x on the horizontal axis. The slope of the line b is found with equation 4.12. The intercept a, or the point where the trend line crosses the vertical axis, can be found by equation 4.13.

$$b = \frac{n\Sigma XY - \Sigma X \Sigma Y}{n\Sigma X^2 - (\Sigma X)^2}$$

[4.12]

$$a = \overline{Y} - b\overline{X} = \frac{\Sigma Y}{n} - b\frac{\Sigma X}{n} = \frac{\Sigma Y - b\Sigma X}{n}$$

[4.13]

where $\overline{Y}$ = arithmetic mean of dependent variable
$\overline{X}$ = arithmetic mean of independent variable
n = number of data points or X, Y pairs
Y = actual values of dependent variable
X = values of independent variable

EXAMPLE OF TIME SERIES DECOMPOSITION

Don McDoe has operated a cafeteria in a small resort town for almost 3 years. He is seriously reexamining his desire to remain in this business because it is time to renew his annual lease and he is not pleased with his attempts to staff the business properly. In the past Don has hired with the intent of having permanent employees as the level of business increased week after week. He later had the agony of laying off employees as the business declined, and he found he was losing money and had idle people on his payroll. Because he is located in a popular resort, Don believes he can employ college students to work during the busy summer season, providing them with employment in a pleasant location and at the same time solving his staffing problems.

Before renewing his lease, Don decided to plot a time series to examine the variations in the volume of business during the first 3 years. He used the number of meals served rather than dollars as a measure of sales or demand, to remove the effect of price changes he had made to adjust for inflation. Sales data are shown in the first three columns of Table 4.7. The sales data from column 3 were plotted against time on a graph, as shown in Figure 4.14. When you look at this graph, you can see why each spring Don thought his business was growing so rapidly that he needed more personnel. Week after week demand continued to climb. You also see why each winter Don thought he was headed for bankruptcy.

A longer-term trend gives a better picture of future prospects for a business. Don computed the 1-year (i.e., four-quarter) moving averages for the demand and plotted them carefully on his graph, with each moving average at the appropriate height and located horizontally at the center of the time periods represented in the average, as shown in column 6 of Table 4.7 (that is, "centered moving averages"). The 1-year moving averages (represented by the blue triangles in Figure 4.14) smoothed out the seasonal variation, making the actual trend more apparent. He drew a dashed line through the approximate center of these points and enjoyed a feeling of confidence that his business was prospering on the average, although it was very seasonal.

Don wanted to compute indices to measure the extent of seasonal variation, which would provide him with general guidelines for planning staffing levels and budgets. He decided to use a ratio of the actual sales to the trend because this ratio for a given season was relatively consistent from year to year. This index is part of a multiplicative time series model $TF = T \cdot S$. No cyclical component was used because Don did not have enough data to measure it and he is interested in projections that look ahead only a year or less. Examination of Don's graph showed that the actual demand was very close to the trend-line value for each spring and each fall, so Don concluded that the seasonal index for spring was approximately 1.0 and for fall it was approximately 1.0.

Table 4.7
TOTAL AND FOUR-QUARTER MOVING AVERAGE OF MEALS SERVED AT McDOE'S CAFETERIA

(1) QUARTER	(2) QUARTER NUMBER	(3) MEALS SERVED	(4) TOTAL MEALS PAST 4 QUARTERS	(5) FOUR-QUARTER MOVING AVERAGE	(6) CENTERED AT PERIOD
Summer	1	11,800			
Fall	2	10,404	41,729 ÷ 4 →	10,432.3	2.5
Winter	3	8,925	42,214	10,553.5	3.5
Spring	4	10,600	42,819	10,704.8	4.5
Summer	5	12,285	43,107	10,776.8	5.5
Fall	6	11,009	43,793	10,948.3	6.5
Winter	7	9,213	44,858	11,214.5	7.5
Spring	8	11,286	45,119	11,279.8	8.5
Summer	9	13,350	46,172	11,543.0	9.5
Fall	10	11,270	47,024	11,756.0	10.5
Winter	11	10,266			
Spring	12	12,138			

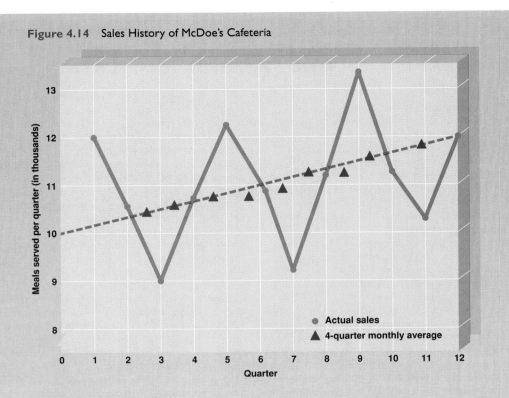

Figure 4.14   Sales History of McDoe's Cafeteria

Don next developed an estimate of the average seasonal index for the level of business in the summer. To estimate the index for the first summer, Don divided the 11,800 actual sales by 10,200, which he read from the graph as the approximate height of the trend line during the first summer (quarter 1), and got a ratio of 1.16. For the second summer (quarter 5) he divided the 12,285 actual sales by 10,850, which he estimated as the height of the trend line for that quarter, and got a ratio of 1.13. Similarly, the seasonal index for the third summer (quarter 9) was estimated as 13,350/11,400 = 1.17. Don averaged the three estimates of the summer index and got 1.15, and he concluded that the level of business in a summer averages about 15 percent above the trend-line value at the middle of that summer.

Similarly, indices of seasonality for the winter quarters were calculated and averaged. The height of the trend line for the first winter (quarter 3) was estimated from the graph to be 10,500. The ratio of actual sales to this value was 8,925/10,500 = 0.85. The ratio for the second winter (quarter 7) was 9,213/11,100 = 0.83, and for the third winter it was 10,266/11,800 = 0.87. By averaging these three estimates of the seasonal index for the winter, Don got 0.85 and concluded that the level of business in a winter averages 85 percent of the trend-line value for that quarter.

Don saw that the swings in the level of demand had been fairly consistent. He can think of no new conditions that will cause the past pattern to change and decides to use this predictable pattern as a forecasting tool. To estimate future demand in a summer, Don can extend the trend line to that quarter and multiply the trend-line height by 1.15. Don can forecast the level of demand in a winter by projecting the trend line to that quarter and multiplying the height of the line by 0.85. He can make a forecast for a fall or spring by reading the height of the trend line in the appropriate quarter, since the seasonal indices for these quarters are 1.0 for his particular business.

He estimated the parameters of an equation for the trend line by the following reasoning. The intercept (height of the line at quarter zero) of the trend line was read directly from the plotted data of Figure 4.14 to be approximately 10,000 meals. The trend line was observed to be at 12,000 meals at quarter 12, so the slope was estimated to be (12,000 − 10,000)/12, or approximately 167 meals per quarter. The equation for the trend line therefore is

Trend value = 10,000 + 167q

where q = the quarter number, as shown on the horizontal scale of Figure 4.14

The trend equation and the seasonal indices were combined by the calculations shown in Table 4.8 to provide a forecast for each quarter of the next year (quarters 13, 14, 15, and 16 on the scale used in Figure 4.14).

Don then decided to try the same procedure, using monthly instead of quarterly data to get more details.

After looking over his figures and admiring the trend, he feels encouraged about the future prospects for his business and has decided to (1) renew his lease, (2) use students as temporary employees in the peak season, and (3) take a vacation (next winter!).

Table 4.8
CALCULATION OF QUARTERLY FORECASTS FOR McDOE'S CAFETERIA

(1) QUARTER	(2) QUARTER NUMBER	(3) TREND VALUE	(4) SEASONAL INDEX	(5) FORECAST (3) × (4)
Summer	13	$10{,}000 + 167(13) = 12{,}171$	1.15	13,997
Fall	14	$10{,}000 + 167(14) = 12{,}338$	1.00	12,338
Winter	15	$10{,}000 + 167(15) = 12{,}505$	0.85	10,629
Spring	16	$10{,}000 + 167(16) = 12{,}672$	1.00	12,672

Equation 4.13 makes use of the fact that the point $(\overline{X}, \overline{Y})$ lies on the line fitted by least squares. Moving a point $(\overline{X}, \overline{Y})$ toward the Y axis a distance of $\overline{X}$ positions it on the Y axis. If we wanted this point to be on the trend line, it would have to be moved vertically a distance equal to the X movement times the slope (that is, b times $-\overline{X}$). For the McDoe Cafeteria data, the regression equation would be developed through the use of a table such as Table 4.9.

The equation for the linear trend line through the moving averages for the McDoe Cafeteria demand data, therefore, is $Y_T = 9{,}956 + 164.18X$, where X is the number of the quarter since the start of the data. This equation is close to the one

Table 4.9
REGRESSION COMPUTATION FOR McDOE'S CAFETERIA

X	Y	X²	XY
2.5	10,432.3	6.25	26,080.75
3.5	10,553.5	12.25	36,937.25
4.5	10,704.8	20.25	48,171.60
5.5	10,776.8	30.25	59,272.40
6.5	10,948.3	42.25	71,163.95
7.5	11,214.5	56.25	84,108.75
8.5	11,279.8	72.25	95,878.30
9.5	11,543.0	90.25	109,658.50
10.5	11,756.0	110.25	123,438.00
$\Sigma X = 58.5$	$\Sigma Y = 99{,}209.0$	$\Sigma X^2 = 440.25$	$\Sigma XY = 654{,}709.50$

$$b = \frac{n\Sigma XY - \Sigma X \Sigma Y}{n\Sigma X^2 - (\Sigma X)^2} = \frac{9(654{,}709.5) - 58.5(99{,}209)}{9(440.25) - 58.5^2} = 164.183$$

$$a = \frac{\Sigma Y - b\Sigma X}{n} = \frac{99{,}209 - 164.183(58.5)}{9} = 9{,}956.03$$

Don McDoe estimated from his graph. The equation could be used to determine values of the trend line by substituting the appropriate number for *X*.

CAUSAL MODELS

The time series analysis method of forecasting and the averaging methods presented previously used time as the only independent variable. However, the use of time alone does not provide a means to identify turning points that are not inherent in past patterns. The time series analysis forecasting method used time as the independent variable (*X* axis) and demand as the dependent variable (*Y* axis). Some forecasting methods use other independent variables to assist the forecaster in estimating future demand. Such methods allow forecasters to use some of the factors they probably would consider if they were making subjective forecasts.

Regression Methods

We may want some measure of external conditions, such as an economic indicator, as the variable to explain demand. The Federal Reserve Board, the Department of Commerce, and many other government agencies publish values of economic indicators. Trade associations, local planning commissions, licensing agencies, and banks also have information related to a company's sales.

The objective is to find an available indicator that moves before the company's sales change (a *leading indicator*) and that has a sufficiently stable relationship with sales to be useful as a prediction tool. Linear regression is a means of finding and expressing such a relationship. Simple linear regression fits a line to a series of points that indicate past values of one *dependent variable* (sales) and one *independent variable* (the indicator). Often the method of least squares is used to fit the line to the data points so that the sum of all the squared deviations from the points to the line will be minimized.

APPLICATION

EXAMPLE OF SIMPLE LINEAR REGRESSION

The Mover City Transit Authority has been examining the demand for its service. Its managers need to know how many vehicles and employees will be needed in the next year so that they can request an adequate subsidy in the budget for the coming fiscal year. They have found that business has declined during the past several years, but the pattern is not obvious. They know that patterns vary within a year and within each week, but the question at hand is one of capacity for the coming year, so seasonal variations are not examined. One department manager has expressed a belief that the year's business should be related to the percentage of the population without automobiles. He has formed a variable, NOCAR, equal to the city population the previous year minus the number of automobile registrations. Some families own two cars, some people who live outside the city use the transit system, others walk or ride bicycles, and the number of trips per user may vary from year to year, so the variable NOCAR may not be exactly related to use of the system. The data for the past 5 years are presented in Table 4.10 and are plotted in Figure 4.15 Equations 4.12 and 4.13 were used along with the computations presented in Table 4.11 to determine the

Table 4.10
DEMAND HISTORY FOR MOVER CITY TRANSIT AUTHORITY

YEAR	PASSENGER FARES COLLECTED (MILLIONS)	NOCAR (THOUSANDS)
1	5.5	77
2	5.1	75
3	4.7	72
4	4.8	73
5	4.6	71

coefficients for a linear equation that expresses the expected number of fares as a function of the variable NOCAR. The equation for the line is

$$Y_T = -6.10 + 0.15X \qquad [4.14]$$

where X is the value of the variable NOCAR for the year before the one in which we wish to forecast the number of fares. The negative intercept has no significant meaning, since the model is to be used for values of NOCAR near the range of the original data.

Since the variable NOCAR (the X in equation 4.14) was 71.0 again this year, the transit authority estimates that the number of passenger rides it can expect to provide next year is 4,550,000, as shown below:

$$Y_T = -6.10 + \times 0.15(71.0)|$$
$$= -6.10 + 10.65$$
$$= 4.55$$

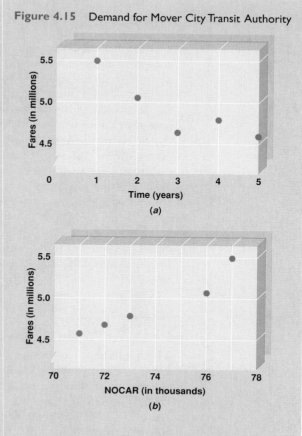

Figure 4.15   Demand for Mover City Transit Authority

(a)

(b)

Table 4.11
COMPUTATIONS FOR REGRESSION ANALYSIS OF MOVER CITY TRANSIT DATA

X (NOCAR)	Y (Fares)	X^2	XY
77	5.5	5,929	423.5
75	5.1	5,625	382.5
72	4.7	5,184	338.4
73	4.8	5,329	350.4
71	4.6	5,041	326.6
$\Sigma X = 368$	$\Sigma Y = 24.7$	$\Sigma X^2 = 27,108$	$\Sigma XY = 1,821.4$

$$\overline{X} = \frac{368}{5} = 73.6 \quad \overline{Y} = \frac{24.7}{5} = 4.94$$

$$b = \frac{n\Sigma XY - \Sigma X\Sigma Y}{n\Sigma X^2 - (\Sigma X)^2} = \frac{5(1,821.4) - 368(24.7)}{5(27,108) - 368^2} = \frac{17.4}{116} = 0.15$$

$$a = \overline{Y} - b\overline{X} = 4.94 - 0.15(73.6) = -6.10$$

Probably the use of other variables in addition to an economic indicator (for example, advertising expenditures or the price of the good or service) will better explain sales. Multiple regression involves the establishment of a mathematical relationship between a dependent variable and two or more independent variables. The complexities of multiple regression are beyond the scope of this book, but an example of simple linear regression provides a general introduction to the concept. The method of least squares is used to fit the line to the data in this example. Remember, the least-squares method was also mentioned as a way to estimate the trend line in time series analysis.

Some measure of the closeness of fit between the line and the actual data is necessary if one wishes to compare the indicator in the example (NOCAR) with other variables we may evaluate. The variable that has the best score for fit will be considered a good candidate for a forecasting model. Two common measures are the coefficient of linear correlation and the standard error of the estimate. These measures will be calculated for the Mover City model.

The *coefficient of linear correlation,* often called the *correlation coefficient,* tells how closely a group of points coincides with a straight line. Using the symbols as defined for equations 4.12 and 4.13, we can calculate the correlation coefficient r from equation 4.15:

$$r = \frac{n\Sigma XY - \Sigma X \Sigma Y}{\sqrt{[n\Sigma X^2 - (\Sigma X)^2][n\Sigma Y^2 - (\Sigma Y)^2]}} \qquad \text{[4.15]}$$

The coefficient can be positive or negative. A positive r means that large values of X generally are associated with large values of $Y;$ that is, as X increases, Y increases. A negative r generally means that Y declines as X increases. The closer the absolute value of r is to 1.0, the better the line fits the points. For the Mover City data the correlation coefficient is +0.9906, which indicates that the points lie very near a straight line and that the line has a positive slope.

Another way of expressing how near the data points are to the regression line is r^2, called the *coefficient of determination.* This number quantifies for the sample data the percentage of variation in the dependent variable (FARES in our example) that is explained by (can be estimated by) the regression line. Another way of viewing the coefficient of determination is to say that it tells, on the average, what percentage of the deviations of the Y's from their mean is explained by the X value for each $Y.$ A computational formula to make calculations by hand or computer more efficient is equation 4.16:

$$r^2 = \frac{a\Sigma Y + b\Sigma XY - n\overline{Y}^2}{\Sigma Y^2 - n\overline{Y}^2} \qquad \text{[4.16]}$$

For the data in our Mover City Transit example, the coefficient of determination is

$$r^2 = \frac{-6.10(24.7) + 0.15(1821.4) - 5(4.94^2)}{122.55 - 5(4.94^2)} = \frac{0.522}{0.532} = 0.981$$

This number shows that a little more than 98 percent of the variation in FARES is explained by the regression line.

The *standard error of the estimate,* s_{yx}, is similar to the standard deviation except that it is based on the mean square vertical deviation of the points from the trend line rather than from their mean. The expression for standard error of the estimate is

$$s_{yx} = \sqrt{\frac{\Sigma(Y - Y_T)^2}{n - 2}} \qquad \text{or} \qquad s_{yx} = \sqrt{\frac{\Sigma Y^2 - a\Sigma Y - b\Sigma XY}{n - 2}} \qquad \text{[4.17]}$$

The standard error of the estimate for the Mover City Transit Authority data when NOCAR is used as the independent variable[2] is 0.0577. If the Mover City Transit Authority tries other models, it can compare the standard errors to see which model fits the data best, that is, which has the smallest standard error. Also there should be some logical relationship or explanation for the variables used in regression models. The model that uses NOCAR as an explanatory variable has a logical relationship and fits the data very well.

USING COMPUTERS TO FORECAST

Forecasting often involves manipulation of great amounts of data, particularly when forecasting models are being developed by trying many variables in many different combinations and when those models involve complex calculations. Computers can greatly reduce the work and time involved in developing and evaluating forecast models and in making routine forecasts. A great deal of work may be involved in evaluating possible forecast models and selecting the one that seems to best fit a demand pattern. Many combinations of independent variables may be examined in the search. The ability to perform repetitive calculations rapidly also makes it feasible to try values of the independent variables one period prior to demand, then two periods prior to demand, and so forth. Thus one can investigate several amounts of "lag" to find the one that best predicts demand.

Manual calculations of regression model coefficients s_{yx} and r^2 can be tedious and time-consuming, particularly for data sets of a realistic size. The values can be obtained much more easily through use of a spreadsheet of the numerous available software packages such as SAS, SPSS, or Microstat. Figure 4.16 shows a printout for the Mover City data obtained with Minitab, one of the popular packages. The top data rows are used to enter the X, Y pairs, then there is a command to regress column 2 on column 1. There also is a command to predict Y for $X = 71$. The program then provides the regression equation. The hypotheses that the slope and intercept are equal to zero are tested. The standard error of the estimate of 0.05773 and r^2 of

---

[2]The left-hand expression of equation 4.17 was used to calculate s_{yx}, as shown in the table below. To use this formula, we must calculate Y_T for all the X values used to develop the trend line. In larger problems, however, the right-hand formulation often is used because it reduces rounding errors.

X	Y	Y_T	$Y - Y_T$	$(Y - Y_T)^2$
77	5.50	5.45	0.05	0.0025
75	5.10	5.15	−0.05	0.0025
72	4.70	4.70	0	0.0000
73	4.80	4.85	−0.05	0.0025
71	4.60	4.55	0.05	0.0025
				$\Sigma(Y - Y_T)^2 = 0.0100$

$$s_{yx} = \sqrt{\frac{\Sigma(Y - Y_T)^2}{n - 2}} = \sqrt{\frac{0.0100}{5 - 2}} = \sqrt{0.0033} = 0.0577$$

Figure 4.16
Minitab Output for the
Mover City Transit Data

```
MTB > read c1 c2
DATA> 77 5.5
DATA> 75 5.1
DATA> 72 4.7
DATA> 73 4.8
DATA> 71 4.6
DATA> end
     5 ROWS READ
MTB > regress c2 1 c1;
SUBC> predict 71.

The regression equation is
C2 = - 6.10 + 0.150 C1

Predictor      Coef       Stdev      t-ratio
Constant     -6.1000     0.8826      -6.91
C1            0.15000    0.01199      12.51

s = 0.05773    R-sq = 98.1%    R-sq(adj) = 97.5%

Analysis of Variance

SOURCE       DF        SS           MS
Regression    1      0.52200     0.52200
Error         3      0.01000     0.00333
Total         4      0.53200


    Fit    Stdev.fit      95% C.I.           95% P.I.
  4.5500     0.0405    ( 4.4212, 4.6788)  ( 4.3256, 4.7744)
```

98.1 percent are shown. The program also provides an analysis of variance table and gives the prediction that was requested. It predicted a Y of 4.55 and provided a confidence interval for the mean of the Y's at $X = 71$. Then it gives a prediction interval for the individual Y values. A great amount of data can be analyzed, and a model can be found in a shorter time, if this type of software is available.

Computers allow immediate access to useful information that would be too cumbersome without the technology. For example, at Mrs. Field's Cookies stores, technology enables immediate feedback from cash register receipts. If sales are down, the computer is programmed to make suggestions. This technology also helps Debbi Fields keep a careful watch on individual stores.

Nubar Alexanian/Stock, Boston

FORECASTING PRODUCT DEMAND

Intelligent systems have become an important tool for improving the quality of operations. These systems, often called expert systems or knowledge-based systems, embed the experience and skills of various personnel: engineers, purchasing agents, shop floor managers, salespeople, and others.

There is an increasing trend toward implementing expert systems. Expert systems allow decisions to be made based not only on shared common data, but also on shared common knowledge.

As an example of using an expert system consider the following. Hewlett-Packard's Networked Computer Manufacturing Operation (Roseville, Calif.) has developed Merlin, an expert system designed to forecast the factory's product demand. The system analyzes and predicts a year-out forecast for more than 500 products and product options in less than 1 hour.

Merlin contains embedded knowledge bases which enable it to make predictions using the latest reasoning process of the forecasting experts. It obtains data from, and passes data to, data base systems residing on HP minicomputers. In producing a product forecast, Merlin uses past order history data as well as product information supplied by the forecasters to drive the expert system. A standard knowledge base is used for the process and is cycled through twelve times as a computer analysis is done for every month to create a full-year's forecast.

Merlin has saved a significant amount of the forecaster's time, according to HP, as well as produced acceptable product forecasts.

Source: David Blanchard, "Making the Smart Choice," *APICS—The Performance Advantage,* January 1995, pp. 32–33.

Computers can be applied to use a forecast model after the model has been selected. Companies sometimes have thousands of items for which they routinely develop forecasts. Automation of much of the forecasting calculations improves the speed and reduces the cost of developing these forecasts. A forecasting program can access a company's data base to process data in a demand history file and routinely make forecasts for products or product families. Some of the references in the Bibliography at the end of the chapter provide information on packages that will perform the types of forecasts we discussed. Some means of monitoring the performance of forecast models is needed, particularly when forecasts are generated routinely without human review. One way to evaluate the performance of a forecast model continually is to use a tracking signal, which is discussed next.

MONITORING AND CONTROLLING FORECASTS

Sales patterns are seldom static, and sales forecasts should strive to move with them or even anticipate their movements. New accounts are gained and old ones lost. The level of activity of existing accounts may rise or fall. Sales forecasts should be reviewed and revised periodically. Sometimes the forecasting method may be changed.

Recall from our previous discussion that many companies revise or update their forecasts for every month or every quarter. As new data become available, they are incorporated into the forecast because usually these recent data are most relevant, at least in short-range planning. New data can also be compared with the forecast values to evaluate the forecasting method's performance. One way of determining whether a forecasting method is performing adequately is, of course, by visually comparing new data and forecast values. Another method is to use a tracking signal.

A *tracking signal* is the ratio of the running sum of forecast errors (RSFE) to the mean absolute deviation (MAD):

$$\text{Tracking signal} = \frac{\text{RSFE}}{\text{MAD}} = \frac{\sum_{t=1}^{n}(A_t - F_t)}{\text{MAD}} \qquad [4.18]$$

where A_t = the actual value of demand for period t
F_t = the forecast value of demand for period t

The tracking signal is recalculated each time the actual demand data for a sales period become available and the forecast is updated. The tracking signal should remain fairly small (near zero) if the forecasting method is performing adequately. Deviations will occur but should balance each other—some deviations will be positive and others negative. If demand departs significantly from the forecast during several periods, the numerator of equation 4.18 will grow, causing the tracking signal to deviate significantly from zero. A graph of a tracking signal indicating poor performance is illustrated in Figure 4.17. When the tracking signal moves outside of some preestablished range, it trips a signal, indicating that it is time to reevaluate the demand pattern and the forecasting method. A company might examine its past data to see what tracking signal limits are appropriate for its needs for forecast accuracy and demand patterns. Limits that permit the tracking signal ratio to be as large as 4 to 8 are often used. The larger limits are used when the penalties for a forecast error are relatively small. The tracking signal is an application of the management-by-exception principle: If things are working all right, don't waste your time trying to fix them; spend your time where it's needed.

A method of checking forecasts is particularly useful if forecasting is done by a computer, as it often is when forecasts must be maintained for a great variety of products. The computer may be programmed to print out only the expected demand unless the tracking signal "trips" a limit (see Figure 4.17). If the tracking signal passes a limit, the computer may print a report showing the past history so that one can decide what to do. When a type of exponential smoothing is used, the computer may be programmed to change the value of α (so the forecast will be more responsive) and to continue forecasting. This technique is called *adaptive smoothing* because the exponential smoothing model is being adapted when the situation warrants.

Figure 4.17
A Tracking Signal

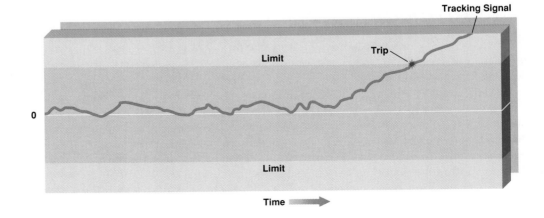

SUMMARY

Forecasting is important in operations management and in other functions within an organization. Long-range, intermediate-range, and short-range decisions must be made, and all require some inferences or assumptions about the future. Forecasting is basic to operations decisions because projections (1) indicate when decisions are needed, (2) determine which alternatives are reasonable, and (3) help to indicate which alternative solution to a problem should be selected.

Demand forecasts are particularly important to operations managers because managers seldom control demand, yet have the responsibility of providing the goods and services in response to it. Demand forecasts also are basic inputs to financial plans, personnel plans, facilities plans, and marketing plans. Companies often have short- to intermediate-range forecasts of demand for specific products or product families. These specific forecasts are used to plan production, to procure inputs, and to schedule transformation of those inputs into products or services. Specific forecasts may be updated with a frequency of a week to a month. Longer-range forecasts may be made quarterly or annually to aid in making long-range plans for facilities, research and development programs, and marketing strategies.

Forecasting methods of several types may be used to estimate future demand. Subjective or qualitative methods may be used to develop forecasts. Subjective forecasting methods include use of the field sales force, jury of executives, users' expectations, and the Delphi method. Time series data can be used to forecast by simple moving averages, weighted moving averages, exponential smoothing, and decomposition. Causal models use regression to express the relationship between demand and some economic index or other variable that changes ahead of demand and is correlated to demand.

Moving average and exponential smoothing methods are useful for short-range forecasts and do not require extensive historical data.

Time series analysis and higher-order exponential smoothing are useful when a knowledge of seasonal variations is important to planning. A considerable amount of historical data should be available (3 or more years) to provide estimates of the consistency of seasonal indices.

Regression analysis is useful to determine trends in time series analysis, which can be extended for estimates of long-range changes. Regression can be used also to estimate the relationship between sales and some index of economic activity. To be useful as a forecast base, the index should change an adequate lead time before a change in sales occurs.

The quantitative model that is appropriate depends on the demand pattern to be projected and the forecaster's objectives. Table 4.12 shows the four combinations of trend and seasonal components and the models that often are found to be appropriate for projecting them.

Extrapolation of any pattern always is subject to the danger of a turning point in the pattern. Some of the forces that have been in effect in the past may change. It is advisable to compare the forecast made by one method with other forecasts and to compare a forecast with what common sense suggests before basing plans on the forecast.

Table 4.12
APPLICATION OF FORECASTING METHODS

COMBINATION OF COMPONENTS IN THE SERIES	OBJECTIVES	MODELS OFTEN APPROPRIATE
Time Series Models[a]		
No trend (horizontal trend), no seasonal variation; that is, a stable average with random fluctuation	To average out randomness and find average	Simple moving average Weighted moving average Simple exponential smoothing
No trend, but seasonal variation	To determine seasonal pattern and project it or to average out seasonality	Time series decomposition Simple moving average
Trend, but no seasonal variation	To make short-term projection of latest trend estimate To make longer-term projection of average trend	Double exponential smoothing Time series decomposition
Trend and seasonal variation	To project trend and seasonal variation around it	Time series decomposition or Winters' triple exponential smoothing[c]
Causal Models[b]		
Pattern of changes not related to time	To identify variables that "explain" level of demand	Simple linear regression Curvilinear regression[c] Multiple regression[c]

[a]If the series of demand data shows a generally consistent pattern over time and the influencing conditions are expected to continue, a time series model often is adequate.
[b]If demand shows very erratic changes over time so that factors other than time must cause them, then causal models should be investigated to see if they are appropriate.
[c]Not discussed in detail in this chapter.

KEY TERMS

Forecast
Technological forecast
Economic forecast
Demand forecast
Business cycle
Product life cycle
Delphi method
Time series models
Causal models

Leading indicators
Time series
Trend component
Seasonal component
Cyclical component
Random component
Mean absolute deviation (MAD)
Mean square error (MSE)

Running sum of forecast errors (RSFE)
Mean forecast error (MFE)
Mean absolute percentage error (MAPE)
Simple moving average (SMA)
Stability
Responsiveness

Weighted moving average
Exponential smoothing
Double exponential
  smoothing
Time series decomposition
Turning points
Multiplicative model

Additive model
Seasonal index
Dependent variable
Independent variable
Coefficient of linear
  correlation

Coefficient of
  determination
Standard error of the
  estimate
Tracking signal
Adaptive smoothing

DEMONSTRATION PROBLEMS

Problem

The following are 3 months of demand data for emergency room service at a hospital. Using $\alpha = 0.2$ and a forecast of 706 for the first month, calculate exponentially smoothed forecasts for the demand in months 2 through 4.

MONTH	ACTUAL
1	721
2	816
3	671

Solution

For the first month, the forecast was 706 and the actual demand was 721, so the error was $A - SF = 721 - 706 = 15$. This information is used to adjust the forecast of 706 upward by $0.2(15)$, or 3, so the forecast for month 2 is $706 + 0.2(721 - 706) = 709$.

The forecast for month 3 is

$$SF_3 = SF_2 + 0.2(A_2 - SF_2)$$

$$= 709 + 0.2(816 - 709)$$

$$= 709 + 21.4 = 730.4$$

Since this is an average level of demand, we can keep the decimal. We will carry one decimal place to know whether to round up or down if we want to estimate an integer value for demand.

$$SF_4 = SF_3 + 0.2(A_3 - SF_3)$$

$$= 730.4 + 0.2(671 - 730.4)$$

$$= 730.4 + 0.2(-59.4)$$

$$= 730.4 - 11.9 = 718.5$$

Notice that in month 3 the forecast was higher than the actual, resulting in a negative forecast error. This negative error causes the forecast or smoothed average to be reduced, and the new average of 718.5 is the forecast for month 4.

Problem

The following numbers are 5 weeks' data in a time series: 38, 41, 39, 43, 44. Starting with a smoothed average base of 35 and an initial trend estimate of 2.0, use $\alpha = 0.3$ and $\beta = 0.5$ to forecast demand for these 5 weeks, and make a forecast for each of the 3 weeks beyond these five.

Solution

To get a forecast for week 1, the initial trend is added to the initial smoothed average to obtain a value of $35 + 2 = 37$. The actual demand in week 1 was 38, so this value is incorporated into the smoothed average with a weight of 0.3, and the prior smoothed average is given a weight of 0.7. The new smoothed average is $0.3(38) + 0.7(37) = 37.3$. In week 1, the latest estimate of the trend is the difference between the smoothed average and the prior one, or $37.3 - 35 = 2.3$. This newest estimate of the trend is given a weight of 0.5 and averaged with the prior smoothed trend to obtain a value of $0.5(2.3) + 0.5(2.0) = 2.15$. The forecast for week 2 is obtained by adding the new smoothed trend to the new smoothed average to get a value of $37.30 + 2.15 = 39.45$. This procedure is continued to forecast each week's demand through week 6. The forecast for week 7 is calculated by extending the trend for 2 weeks beyond the smoothed base of week 5. The forecast for week 8 is calculated by extending the trend for 3 weeks beyond the base in week 5. These calculations are shown in the following table.

WEEK	FORECAST	ACTUAL	BASE = 35.00	TREND = 2.00
1	37.00	38	$0.3(38) + 0.7(37.00) = 37.30$	$0.5(2.30) + 0.5(2.00) = 2.15$
2	39.45	41	$0.3(41) + 0.7(39.45) = 39.92$	$0.5(2.62) + 0.5(2.15) = 2.39$
3	42.31	39	$0.3(39) + 0.7(42.31) = 41.32$	$0.5(1.40) + 0.5(2.39) = 1.89$
4	43.21	43	$0.3(43) + 0.7(43.21) = 43.15$	$0.5(1.83) + 0.5(1.89) = 1.86$
5	45.01	44	$0.3(44) + 0.7(45.01) = 44.71$	$0.5(1.56) + 0.5(1.86) = 1.71$
6	46.42			
7	48.13			
8	49.84			

Problem

The following are a company's quarterly demand figures for the past 2 years.

Year 1		Year 2	
QUARTER	DEMAND	QUARTER	DEMAND
1	26,209	1	25,390
2	21,402	2	19,064
3	18,677	3	18,173
4	24,681	4	23,866

(a) Compute 1-year moving averages centered at the end of quarters 2.5 through 6.5, respectively, to remove the seasonality (i.e., assume the demand figures are at the center of the time periods they include).

(b) Compute a linear regression equation for the trend through the five moving averages.

(c) Compute an average seasonal index (multiplicative) for each quarter of the year.

(d) Forecast the demand for each quarter of year 3.

Solution

(a) The first year's moving average would be centered between the second quarter and the third quarter, that is, at the X coordinate of 2.5. The X coordinate for the next moving average will be 3.5, etc.

The four-quarter moving averages and the corresponding X coordinates are shown in the following table:

ACTUAL DEMAND	SUM OF 4 QUARTERS	SUM ÷ 4	X COORDINATE
26,209			
21,402			
18,677			
24,681	90,969	22,742.25	2.5
25,390	90,150	22,537.50	3.5
19,064	87,812	21,953.00	4.5
18,173	87,308	21,827.00	5.5
23,866	86,493	21,623.25	6.5

(b) We can compute a linear regression equation to show the relationship between the quarter and the trend value of demand.

X	Y	X^2	XY
2.5	22,742.25	6.25	56,855.625
3.5	22,537.50	12.25	78,881.250
4.5	21,953.00	20.25	98,788.500
5.5	21,827.00	30.25	120,048.500
6.5	21,623.25	42.25	140,551.125
22.5	110,683.00	111.25	495,125.000

$$b = \frac{n\Sigma XY - \Sigma X \Sigma Y}{n\Sigma X^2 - (\Sigma X)^2}$$

$$= \frac{5(495,125) - 22.5(110,683)}{5(111.25) - 22.5^2}$$

$$= \frac{2,475,625 - 2,490,367.5}{556.25 - 506.25}$$

$$= -\frac{14,742.5}{50} = -294.8$$

$$a = \frac{\Sigma Y - b\Sigma X}{n}$$

$$= \frac{110,683 - (-294.85)(22.5)}{5}$$

$$= \frac{117,317.125}{5} = 23,463.425$$

(c) The time period at which actual demand occurs corresponds to periods 1, 2, 3, 4, etc., on the time scale . Using these values for X, we can determine the trend value at each of these times so that we can compute seasonal relatives or seasonal indices for a multiplicative model.

YEAR	QUARTER	X COORDINATE	TREND VALUE	ACTUAL DEMAND	ACTUAL ÷ TREND
1	1	1	23,168.6	26,209	1.131
1	2	2	22,873.7	21,402	0.936
1	3	3	22,578.9	18,677	0.827
1	4	4	22,284.0	24,681	1.108
2	1	5	21,989.2	25,390	1.155
2	2	6	21,694.3	19,064	0.879
2	3	7	21,399.5	18,173	0.849
2	4	8	21,104.6	23,866	1.131

$$\text{Average index for 1st quarter of year} = \frac{1.131 + 1.155}{2} = 1.143$$

$$\text{2d quarter} = \frac{0.936 + 0.879}{2} = 0.908$$

$$\text{3d quarter} = \frac{0.827 + 0.849}{2} = 0.838$$

$$\text{4th quarter} = \frac{1.108 + 1.131}{2} = 1.120$$

(d) The forecast for year 3 is found by projecting the trend to quarters 9 through 12 and multiplying each of these figures by the appropriate seasonal index.

YEAR	QUARTER	X COORDINATE	TREND VALUE	SEASONAL INDEX	FORECAST (TREND × SEASONAL INDEX)
3	1	9	20,809.8	1.143	23,786
3	2	10	20,514.9	0.908	18,628
3	3	11	20,220.1	0.838	16,944
3	4	12	19,925.2	1.120	22,316

DISCUSSION QUESTIONS

1. Why is sales forecasting the key to many other types of forecasts?
2. What is meant by a qualitative or subjective as compared to a quantitative or statistical forecast?
3. Is forecasting a skill or a science? Explain.

4. Why do some investments in forecasting yield a negative net return?
5. Why does the marketing function usually make sales forecasts?
6. When should a quantitative forecast be substituted for judgment?
7. Name three subjective methods of forecasting, and give the origin of the data for each.
8. Name three quantitative or statistical forecasting methods that use time as the basis for changes in demand.
9. What cautions should be observed in checking on statistical forecasts? Why?
10. Why are computers often used in evaluating forecast models to select one that appears to be best suited to a pattern of previous demand and for making routine, repetitive forecasts after a company has selected a model?
11. Discuss a possible reason for using *(a)* the MAD, *(b)* the MSE, and *(c)* the MAPE as a measure with which to compare the accuracy of two forecast models.
12. Why do forecasting methods need to be monitored or controlled?

PROBLEMS

1. Given below is a series of weekly demand data that the Zoop Company collected on one of its products and forecasts for the corresponding weeks, made by forecast model 1, which the company is testing.
   a. Compute the mean absolute deviation based on all 6 weeks of data.
   b. Compute the mean squared error based on these 6 weeks' data.

WEEK	DEMAND	FORECAST
1	142	155
2	181	157
3	144	159
4	174	161
5	192	163
6	176	165

2. Forecast model 2, similar to the one used for the data in problem 1, was used by the Zoop Company to forecast demand for a different product. Six weeks of actual data and forecast data are shown below.
   a. Calculate the MAD based on these 6 weeks' data.
   b. Calculate the MSE based on these 6 weeks' data.

WEEK	DEMAND	FORECAST
1	206	240
2	241	250
3	280	255
4	225	240
5	214	240
6	268	250

3. On the basis of the mean absolute percentage error, does it appear that the forecast model in problem 1 or the model in problem 2 does the better job of forecasting? If you worked the two previous problems, discuss the MADs for the two forecast models.

4. Given below is a series of weekly demand for outpatient care at an ambulatory center. Also shown are forecasts of demand calculated by two forecasting methods that are under consideration.

DEMAND	FORECAST MODEL A	FORECAST MODEL B
536	575	550
590	600	580
554	580	545
622	595	600
718	610	670
673	625	645
640	630	650
595	640	645
542	600	565
588	605	570

  a. Compute the MAD for each forecast model.
  b. Compute the RSFE for each forecast model.
  c. Indicate which model you think is better and why.

5. Given below are the actual demand and the forecasts made by two forecast models.

ACTUAL DEMAND	FORECAST MODEL A	FORECAST MODEL B
3,189	3,700	3,480
4,038	3,496	3,594
3,874	3,713	3,708
3,322	3,777	3,822
4,116	3,595	3,935

  a. Compute the MAD for both forecast models.
  b. Compute the RSFE for both forecast models.
  c. Indicate which model you think is better and why.

6. Given below are 2 years of monthly demand data for an item.

	YEAR 1	YEAR 2
January	75	81
February	78	97
March	81	89
April	92	105
May	108	116
June	116	130
July	110	112
August	108	116
September	92	102
October	87	86
November	78	85
December	72	77

  a. Calculate the 3-month moving averages for the data.
  b. Calculate the 6-month moving averages for the data.
  c. Which appears to be more stable? Why?

7. Given below are data on the monthly demand for a product.

MONTH	DEMAND	MONTH	DEMAND	MONTH	DEMAND
1	487	13	528	25	517
2	602	14	622	26	595
3	551	15	608	27	619
4	587	16	592	28	602
5	509	17	536	29	545
6	457	18	504	30	486
7	349	19	461	31	431
8	386	20	391	32	416
9	490	21	437	33	444
10	507	22	503	34	492
11	516	23	562	35	538
12	573	24	570	36	575

a. Compute the 3-month moving average of this demand. Does this series still show seasonal variation?

b. Compute the 12-month moving average of this demand. Does this series of averages still show seasonal variation?

c. Plot the original data and the two moving averages, centered between the periods they represent.

8. The Olde Favorite Ice Cream Shoppe has recorded the demand for a particular flavor during the past 6 weeks, as shown below.

WEEK	GALLONS	WEEK	GALLONS
1st week, May	19	4th week, May	27
2d week, May	17	1st week, June	29
3d week, May	22	2d week, June	33

a. Calculate a 3-week moving average for the data to forecast demand for the next week. *(Three weeks of data are used for each forecast, so you can make only three forecasts for periods where actual data are available.)*

b. Calculate a weighted average forecast for the data, using a weight of 0.6 for the most recent data and weights of 0.3 and 0.1 for successively older data.

c. Compare the forecasts from parts *a* and *b*. Which forecast do you think is more appropriate? Why?

d. Do you think that a regression trend forecast for this product would be appropriate? Why or why not?

9. Demand for a special model of jet ski during the past 5 months is shown below:

April	226
May	301
June	392
July	387
Aug	236

a. Compute the forecast demand for each month from May through September, using single exponential smoothing with $\alpha = 0.2$. Assume that the forecast for April was 325.

b. Compute the MAD for this forecasting model based on the data for May, June, July, and August.

10. **a.** Repeat problem 9 with $\alpha = 0.4$.
    b. Compute the MAD for this forecast model based on the data for May, June, July, and August.
    c. Which appears to be the better value of α, 0.2 or 0.4?

11. The following table represents monthly sales data for a particular model of racing tires for motorcycles.

MONTH	SALES	MONTH	SALES
1	104	7	95
2	104	8	104
3	100	9	104
4	92	10	107
5	105	11	110
6	95	12	109

    a. Calculate the single exponentially smoothed forecast, using an α of 0.20 and an initial forecast of 100.0.
    b. Calculate the single exponentially smoothed forecast, using an α of 0.40 and an initial forecast of 100.0.
    c. Calculate the MAD for both forecasts. (Use all 12 months of data.)

12. The following table represents sales data for gallons of milk (in hundreds) sold by a grocery.

MONTH	SALES	MONTH	SALES
1	96	7	99
2	106	8	115
3	92	9	106
4	114	10	91
5	108	11	102
6	98	12	99

    a. Use single exponential smoothing to forecast demand, with an α of 0.20 and an initial forecast of 100.0.
    b. Use single exponential smoothing to forecast demand with an α of 0.30 and an initial forecast of 100.0.
    c. Calculate the MAD for both forecasts. (Use all 12 months of data.)

13. **a.** Use double exponential smoothing to forecast sales through period 11 for the following data. Use an α of 0.30, a β of 0.50, an initial base of 29.0, and a trend of 1.0.
    b. Also calculate the tracking signal.

PERIOD	SALES
1	33
2	35
3	39
4	32
5	32
6	29
7	38
8	42
9	38
10	30

14. **a.** Use double exponential smoothing to forecast sales using an α of 0.20, a β of 0.50, an initial base of 38.0, and a trend of 2.0.
    b. Extend the forecasts through period 15.

PERIOD	SALES	PERIOD	SALES
1	39	6	48
2	47	7	45
3	39	8	56
4	44	9	53
5	49	10	61

15. **a.** Use double exponential smoothing to forecast sales with an α of 0.20, a β of 0.40, an initial base of 59.0, and a trend of 1.0.
    b. At each period calculate the MAD based on the data available up to and including that period.
    c. At each period, calculate the tracking signal based on data up to and including that period.

PERIOD	SALES	PERIOD	SALES
1	55	7	67
2	62	8	67
3	57	9	75
4	64	10	67
5	66	11	71
6	69	12	71

16. The Deadweight Anchor Company has experienced the following demand for a particular model of boat anchor during the past 2 years:

MONTH	YEAR 1	YEAR 2
January	1,361	1,415
February	1,286	1,325
March	1,230	1,286
April	1,225	1,295
May	1,220	1,275
June	1,250	1,255
July	1,210	1,290
August	1,190	1,240
September	1,240	1,300
October	1,288	1,375
November	1,362	1,422
December	1,438	1,490

a. Compute and plot the 4-month moving average for these data.
b. Compute a 12-month average for the first 12 months and the last 12 months. Plot these points, and draw a trend line that represents the trend of these data. What are the intercept and slope of the line?

17. A Midwest distributor has handled a particular brand of two-cycle motor oil for the past 5 years. The demand data for the product during those years are given below.

YEAR	DEMAND	YEAR	DEMAND
1	428	4	778
2	631	5	841
3	740		

   a. Plot the data. Should the first year's data be included in computing a linear regression model to estimate the trend in annual demand? Give a reason to support your answer.
   b. Calculate a linear regression equation for annual demand based on the data you concluded in part *a* to be most appropriate.
   c. Use your equation to estimate demand for years 6 and 7.

18. Given below are 2 years of quarterly demand data for a particular model of personal computer from a local computer store.

QUARTER	YEAR 1	YEAR 2
1	40	44
2	46	57
3	39	43
4	42	45

   a. Deseasonalize the data with a moving average, and compute a linear regression equation for the trend in demand.
   b. Compute an average multiplicative index for each of the four quarters of a year.
   c. Using the trend and seasonal indices you have developed, compute a forecast for the demand in each of the quarters of the following year.

19. Given below are 2 years of quarterly data on demand for a particular model of luggage at a mail-order warehouse.

QUARTER	YEAR 1	YEAR 2
1	206	226
2	137	128
3	153	173
4	188	191

   a. Deseasonalize the data with a moving average and compute a regression equation for the trend in demand.
   b. Compute the average multiplicative index for each of the four quarters of a year.
   c. Using the trend and seasonal indices you have developed, compute a forecast for the demand in each of the quarters of the following year.

20. Given below are 2 years of quarterly data on demand for a particular model of electric blender at a mail-order warehouse.

QUARTER	YEAR 1	YEAR 2
1	916	902
2	822	794
3	840	818
4	928	902

a. Deseasonalize the data with a moving average and compute a regression equation for the trend in demand.

b. Compute the average multiplicative index for each of the four quarters of a year.

c. Using the trend and seasonal indices you developed, compute a forecast for the demand in each of the quarters of the following year.

21. Assume that the trend line equation for the data of problem 16 is $Y_T = 1,244 + 4.53X$, where X is each month in the series of data beginning with 1, 2, 3, etc.

a. Compute the average multiplicative seasonal index for each month of the year.

b. Compute the trend value for each of the next 6 months, and adjust each month's trend value by the seasonal index.

22. A linear equation for the trend in demand data was found to be $Y_T = 1,524 + 5.2X$, where X is the number of the month as designated in the table that follows.

	Year I		Year 2	
MONTH	MONTH NUMBER	ACTUAL DEMAND	MONTH NUMBER	ACTUAL DEMAND
January	1	1,419	13	1,495
February	2	1,341	14	1,390
March	3	1,275	15	1,319
April	4	1,353	16	1,420
May	5	1,438	17	1,506
June	6	1,547	18	1,627
July	7	1,688	19	1,719
August	8	1,755	20	1,802
September	9	1,862	21	1,921
October	10	1,782	22	1,851
November	11	1,670	23	1,736
December	12	1,576	24	1,659

a. Project the trend values for each month and determine the multiplicative index for each of the 24 months.

b. Determine the additive index for each of the 24 months.

c. Is it obvious whether an additive or multiplicative model is more appropriate?

23. The owners of a beer distributorship want to forecast the level of sales for the next 2 years, so they can determine the requirements for resources such as storage space, refrigerated storage, trucks, workers, and capital. The quarterly sales for the past 2 years and the first half of this year are given below.

QUARTER	YEAR BEFORE LAST	LAST YEAR	CURRENT YEAR
1	24,500	26,200	29,200
2	33,200	36,600	38,100
3	36,900	39,700	
4	26,400	28,500	

a. Average the first year's sales to establish one point on a trend line. Average the second year's sales to determine the second point. Develop an equation for this trend line which expresses sales as a function of the quarter.

b. Determine the average seasonal index as the ratio of the actual demand to the trend value for each quarter, using the data for the first 2 years.

c. Do the sales for the first two quarters of the current year appear to be consistent with the model?

d. Use the model to estimate the quarterly sales for the last two quarters of the current year and for next year.

24. An established photo processing laboratory has experienced a consistent decline in business, owing primarily to the spread of 1-hour photo processing minilaboratories. The following data represent quarterly sales (in thousands of dollars) for the past 2 years.

QUARTER	SALES
1	400
2	406
3	446
4	352
5	328
6	320
7	340
8	264

a. Average the first year's sales to determine the height of one point on a trend line. (The x value will be 2.5.) Average the second year's sales to determine a second point. Develop an equation for this trend line.
b. Determine the average seasonal index for each of the four quarters of a year, as the ratio of the actual sales value to the trend value.
c. Using the trend formula and the indices developed above, forecast quarterly sales for the following year.

25. a. Calculate the five four-quarter moving averages that can be found from the data in problem 24. Determine the linear regression equation for these points, and compare it with the line determined by using just the two endpoints.
b. What is the danger in using only two endpoints to estimate the location of a line?

26. The sales manager of a local building material supply chain suspects that the sales of roofing materials are correlated with the amount of framing lumber sold 1 or 2 months earlier. Use the data given below (in units sold) to see if the correlation is highest between lumber sales and roofing sales in the same month, with roofing lagging lumber by 1 month or with roofing lagging lumber by 2 months.

MONTH	LUMBER SALES	ROOFING SALES
1	96	52
2	116	53
3	119	63
4	127	65
5	146	71
6	145	76
7	153	77
8	143	84
9	137	82
10	122	75
11	111	72
12	103	66

27. **a.** Using the sales data in problem 26, develop a regression equation to express the number of units of roofing that you would expect to sell as a function of the number of units of lumber sold the month before.

b. Forecast the expected roofing sales for the month following a month in which 125 units of framing lumber were sold.

28. Soft Touch Carpet Installers is trying to select a forecasting model to determine the number of carpet installers the company will require each month. A relationship is thought to exist between the demand for carpet installation and the number of building permits issued some months prior to the demand. Given below are the number of building permits issued and the demand for carpet installation in a series of months.

MONTH	BUILDING PERMITS ISSUED	DEMAND FOR CARPET INSTALLATION
1	506	87
2	491	84
3	517	76
4	563	82
5	619	81
6	632	86
7	686	95
8	692	107
9	703	117
10	714	125
11	652	118
12	619	121

a. Using the first 8 months of building permit data, compute the coefficient of linear correlation between demand for carpet installation in a 1-month period and the number of building permits issued 2 months prior to that period (a 2-month lag model).

b. Using the first 8 months of building permit data, compute the correlation coefficient for a 3-month lag model.

c. Using the first 8 months of building permit data, compute the correlation coefficient for a 4-month lag model.

d. The company is considering the development of a linear regression model to estimate demand on the basis of building permits issued in some prior month. Against which month's building permits should the demand data be regressed to develop the best model?

29. **a.** Using the data in problem 28, develop a regression model to express demand for carpet installation as a function of the building permits issued 3 months prior to the demand. (Use the first 8 months of building permit data.)

b. Forecast the demand for carpet installation 3 months following a month in which 693 building permits were issued.

30. A bank in a rapidly growing city is outgrowing its facility. The bank officers feel that the operations (proof, transit, computer, bookkeeping) part of the bank should be moved. They are looking for an existing building to lease or buy or for a site on which to build an operations center. They feel that the current facility will handle a quarterly volume that averages 330,000 checks per day. The lead time to obtain a site and design and construct a new facility is at least 2 years.

Given below are the quarterly averages of the daily check volume, in thousands:

QUARTER	YEAR 1	YEAR 2	YEAR 3	YEAR 4
1	141	157	181	206
2	132	147	166	193
3	152	168	192	222
4	171	192	221	254

a. Determine the four-quarter moving averages, and plot them along with the past quarterly values.

b. Using the graph, determine the average seasonal adjustment (multiplicative) for the peak quarter of the year.

c. When should the bank have its new facility available?

d. What additional information would be helpful in developing this forecast?

COMPUTER-BASED PROBLEMS

FORECASTING DEMAND

1. Use the 36 successive values of demand data given in problem 2 to determine the number of periods to include in a moving average so that the MAD is minimized. You can construct a spreadsheet with columns for month number, demand, sum of n months, forecast, deviation, and absolute deviation. Sum the absolute deviation column for months 13 through 36 to get the numerator for the MAD. Use 450 for the initial forecast, and use a 2-month moving average. Record the MAD, then repeat with a 3-month moving average, etc., until you find the number of months in a moving average that minimizes the MAD. Use the prior month (a 1-month average) as a forecast. Which forecast model seems to fit the data best? Why?

2. Given below are 36 months of sales data from Redwood Rummage Company.

MONTH	DEMAND	MONTH	DEMAND
1	447	19	411
2	652	20	351
3	501	21	477
4	627	22	553
5	549	23	522
6	407	24	610
7	309	25	567
8	436	26	555
9	450	27	669
10	557	28	552
11	466	29	505
12	613	30	436
13	478	31	471
14	662	32	376
15	558	33	394
16	552	34	452
17	586	35	538
18	544	36	575

Construct a spreadsheet to calculate an exponential smoothing forecast for each month, using a forecast of 450 for the first month. Use a column for each of the following: month number, demand, forecast, error, $\alpha \times$ error, absolute error, error squared, percentage error, and absolute percentage error. Sum the appropriate columns from month 13 through month 36 to compute the mean absolute deviation, mean square error, and mean absolute percentage error. Perform the first computations with $\alpha = 0.1$, and record the measures of error for this α. Change α to 0.2 and repeat; then use α of 0.3. When the MAD starts to increase, you have passed the best α (as measured by the MAD). By changing α in steps of 0.02 (use a two-decimal-place value of α), search near the best value of α found so far. Which of these values of α makes the MAD the smallest?

3. Repeat problem 2, but select the forecast model that minimizes the mean square error. Why might the model (value of α) that minimizes the MSE be different from the one that minimized the MAD?

4. Use a spreadsheet template to see how long it takes for the effects of an initial forecast to "wash out." You can develop another template, or you can use the one developed for problem 2, but you will not need all the columns. Use an α of 0.3 and an initial forecast of 350 (your instructor may give you different values of the initial forecast). How many months does it take until the forecast with an initial value of 350 rounds to the same integer as the forecast made when an initial forecast of 447 was used?

5. Repeat problem 4 using an α of 0.5.

BIBLIOGRAPHY

Bowerman, Bruce L., and Richard T. O'Connell. *Forecasting and Time Series: An Applied Approach.* 3d ed. Boston: Wadsworth, 1993.

Chambers, John C., Satinder K. Mullick, and Donald D. Smith. "How to Choose the Right Forecasting Technique." *Harvard Business Review,* July–Aug. 1971, pp. 45–74.

De Lurgio, Stephen A., and Carl D. Bhame. *Forecasting Systems for Operations Management.* New York: Wiley, 1991.

Gardner, Everette S., Jr. "The Strange Case of the Lagging Forecasts." *Interfaces,* May–June 1984, pp. 47–50.

———. "Exponential Smoothing: The State of the Art." *Journal of Forecasting 4,* no. 1 (March 1985): 1–38.

Hanke, John E., and Arthur G. Reitsch. *Business Forecasting.* 4th ed. Boston: Allyn and Bacon, 1992.

Makridakis, Spyros G., and Steven C. Wheelwright, eds. *The Handbook of Forecasting: A Manager's Guide.* 2d ed. New York: Wiley Interscience, 1987.

———, ———, **and Victor E. McGee.** *Forecasting Methods and Applications.* 2d ed. New York: Wiley, 1983.

Ryan, Barbara F., Bryan L. Joiner, and Thomas A. Ryan, Jr. *Minitab Handbook.* 3d ed. Boston: Wadsworth, 1994.

Seitz, Neil. *Business Forecasting Concepts and Microcomputer Applications.* Reston, Va.: Reston, 1984.

Willis, Raymond E. *A Guide to Forecasting for Planners and Managers.* Englewood Cliffs, N.J.: Prentice-Hall, 1987.

Wilson, J. Holton, and Barry Keating. *Business Forecasting.* Burr Ridge, Ill.: Irwin, 1994.

DESIGN OF OPERATIONS SYSTEMS

Companies may evaluate many possible strategic moves and forecast the demand, cost, and profit of each. Based on the projected results, the company may move ahead to implement the most promising alternatives. People in all functions must make numerous decisions and work to make the company successful. The operations decisions discussed in this book can be divided into two major categories. The first type involves decisions that relate primarily to the design of the system (facilities, equipment, work methods, etc.) which will produce the goods or provide the services most advantageously. The second major category involves decisions about how the system will be run, primarily planning and controlling operations. These two categories are related. The design of the system often affects how it can best be run, and the way a system is to be run certainly influences the way it should be designed. We discuss design-related issues in Part II. In Part III, we deal with planning and controlling operations.

Part II contains five chapters and one supplement that discuss issues related to the design of operations systems. The appropriate design for a system is related to several strategic issues we discussed and to the expected level of demand. The type of business, obviously, determines whether to design a restaurant or a movie. But the design must consider determining the size of the facility, number of employees, types of jobs, number and types of equipment, and other matters that are more detailed than our general discussion.

Chapter 5 briefly discusses estimating the size facility that will be required and selecting a location for it. Supplement F discusses methods used to estimate the number of workers required to provide a given amount of work. Chapter 6 discusses the overall flow of work within a facility. It also addresses the impact on design of the general mode by which the processing is to be done—whether the system is to provide a very narrow variety of outputs or is to be very versatile and flexible. Chapter 7 presents some of the issues managers must consider about selecting technology and staying up to date on the relevant technology. Chapter 8 considers some issues related to the design of people's jobs and to compensation of employees. Part II is concluded with Chapter 9 which presents some ideas about redesign of systems so that continuous improvement is more likely.

CHAPTER 5

Facility Location

SUPPLEMENT F:
Work Measurement and Time Standards

CHAPTER 6

General Configuration and Mode of Processing

CHAPTER 7

Application of Technology for Competitive Advantage

CHAPTER 8

Design of Jobs and Compensation

CHAPTER 9

Review and Redesign for Continuous Improvement

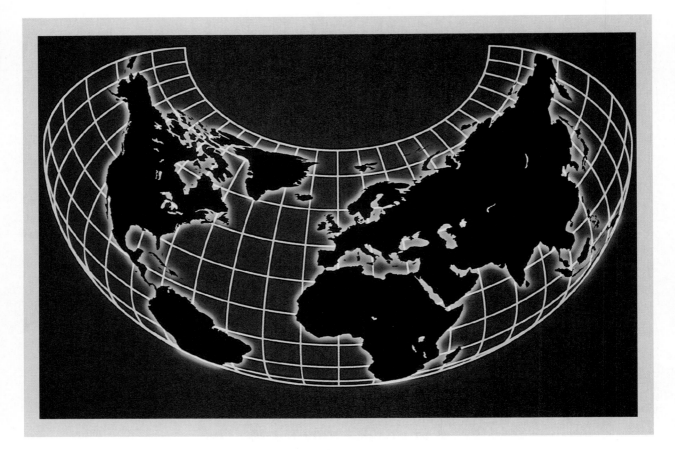

FACILITY
LOCATION

In its strategy formulation, a company determines what type of goods or services it will offer and in what markets it will compete. It makes demand forecasts to estimate the demand in various market areas. Part of the company's strategy consists of selecting the location or locations from which potential markets will be served. The location of a nonmanufacturing operation helps determine how conveniently customers can conduct business with the company. Location of manufacturing and nonmanufacturing operations can have a great impact on operating costs, thereby affecting profit and perhaps the price at which goods or services can be offered.

Long-range forecasts and capacity plans may reveal the need for additional capacity in some areas. If a company has excess capacity in one location or excess shipping costs to some areas, relocation of some facility or facilities may be desirable. At least four aspects of the facility question must be addressed: the types of facilities needed, the location of those facilities, the necessary capacity, and the design or layout of the facilities. The layout of components within a facility is discussed in Chapter 6.

Companies that can select the location at which their operations are performed may face decisions about location and arrangement at various times. A new company may begin operating in a leased facility, later decide to build or buy its own, then expand to multiple locations, and so on. Shifts in the location of demand and the addition of new products or services to those already offered may necessitate the relocation of some facilities or the complete design and construction of new ones. In a dynamic market for its goods and services, an organization may expand, relocate, or add new facilities, which means that location decisions are made occasionally throughout the life of a company.

This chapter discusses general ideas about estimating the size of a facility to be established and some factors and methods involved in selecting locations for operations activities. As will be seen, these decisions often depend on inexact approaches. Naturally, such considerations are appropriate only when the company is free to select the location where service is to be provided. Some service operations (emergency medical or fire fighting, carpet cleaning, and on-site repair services, for example) do not select the location where their services are provided. In such operations, decisions are influenced more by the equipment to be used and by the locations of the bases from which they operate than by where the services are delivered.

DETERMINING THE SIZE AND CAPACITY OF THE FACILITY

When a company considers a new facility, two basic questions that must be considered are what size the facility should be and where it should be located. A facility includes the building and the equipment in it, so an estimate of the size facility that will be needed is an important input into estimating the cost of the facility to determine its economic feasibility. Even if a company is sure of the economic feasibility it is important to determine the proper capacity the facility should have. Too large a facility results in excessive expenses to pay for the investment, maintenance, and so forth. On the other hand, too small a facility may result in poor customer service and the company's missing significant amounts of business.

The facility imposes an upper limit on the company's internal capacity within some intermediate time horizon or longer, until additional internal capacity can be obtained. Sometimes a company can serve a level of demand above its internal capacity by revising its make-or-buy decisions and calling upon its suppliers to perform a larger percentage of the total work. Some service companies can use this option. For example, a restaurant may elect to purchase its breads and desserts already prepared by other establishments or an automobile repair operation may call upon other businesses for wheel alignments or waxing and detailing. However, if the service is one in which the service receiver must be present, the service operation finds fewer opportunities to subcontract part of its work.

Options to subcontract manufacturing work or to use suppliers to perform more of the total process are fairly common. Manufacturing companies may perform only one step in a series of production steps provided by a supply chain. For example, a company may buy thread, which it weaves into cloth, then may sell the cloth to another manufacturer that sews it into clothing. The general trend in many industries, such as auto manufacturing, is to use supplier-partners to provide more of the components that go into the product.

When we discuss running the operations system in Part III, we will consider such matters as changing the size of the work force and the number of hours they work to adjust the internal capacity within the constraint imposed by the facility. In this part we consider the design of the system, which includes estimating the capacity that should be included when a company plans a new facility and factors that may be important in locating it.

A procedure, sometimes called *resource requirements planning,* can be used to make general estimates of the need for key resources in the extended future of an existing facility or in a new facility. Resource requirements planning is used to plan such resources as the work force, equipment capacity, space, working capital, and supplier support. Here we are considering the number of employees, equipment that is to be used, and the space required to house the operation.

The size building a company would buy, build, or lease depends on the forecast level of demand for the goods and services that are to be provided from the facility. A well-founded forecast should be developed for a "reasonable" time horizon into the life of the facility. The length of a reasonable horizon depends upon such matters as the time required to add capacity through additional space, equipment, and trained employees. It may be 2, 5, or more years. For an electric utility the time range may be over 10 years—which means the forecast may involve significant uncertainty. Often companies include allowances for flexibility in their facilities where feasible to allow for forecast inaccuracies. For example, a site that is large enough to allow for expansion would be selected. The building might be designed so that it could be converted to other uses if the market changes significantly. Flexible equipment may be preferred if the company anticipates changes in demand or if the company wants to stress flexibility in its strategy.

Companies normally plan some extra or reserve capacity so they are not stretched to the limit from the beginning. This reserve allows for some forecast error, and the normal random and seasonal variation in demand as well as a growth trend that most businesses desire. If a growth trend occurs, its rate of change (slope) determines how soon additional capacity should be added.

The forecast for finished goods or services must be converted into estimates of the number of employees needed and the amount of equipment and work space they will need to perform the work. We will now look at some approaches to making these estimates.

First, let's assume some overall ratio of worker-hours, or workers, to the level of output can be obtained through experience at another facility. Capacity planning by overall factors (CPOF) can be performed with ratios determined from accounting records at the reference facility to calculate the number of direct labor-hours required per unit produced. The ratio is more reliable if only one product or service is provided at the reference facility and no economies of scale are expected in the new facility. If a variety of goods and services are provided at the reference facility, labor-hours must be allocated to each product—and this could make the ratio less accurate. Suppose that one product is involved and the reference facility can provide 200 units of output per day with 40 direct workers. It could use this information as the basis for an overall ratio of 5 units per day from each direct worker. If the forecast for a new location indicates a demand of 125 units per day, the company might then estimate that it would need 25 direct workers. The number of administrative workers that will be needed might then be determined from considerations about how the business will be organized and how much of the administrative work will be handled by the staff at other locations. This idea of capacity planning by overall factor is straightforward as long as the company has experience at another location in providing the same good or service that is to be offered at the new location. A similar procedure could be used to develop ratios to estimate how many of the employees would be needed in specific departments.

When the new location is to provide a good or service that is different from any available reference facility, the factor for output per worker must be estimated by more complicated means. Perhaps it can be estimated that the new item or service will require, say, about 85 percent of the work required by some other product or service with which the company is familiar.

Estimates of the amount of equipment and employee time required to perform the necessary work are used to calculate the cost to provide the good or service as well as to determine the capacity needed in a facility. As such, the estimates are the basis for evaluating the feasibility of the entire project and are very important, even though they may not be exact. When a large capital investment is to be made and data from a similar facility are not available, some more-detailed basis for estimating capacity requirements may be justified. Sometimes a small pilot operation can be set up and studied to improve the estimates of the work required to produce the intended output.

The following provides an overview of some steps that may be involved in a more-detailed study. The forecast for the final output would be broken down into all the components that must be made or all the service work that must be performed in order to serve the forecast level of demand. The company might then perform make-or-buy comparisons on some components to decide which parts of this work would be performed in-house and which would be provided by suppliers. The company must then develop estimates for how many workers will be required to perform in 1 week the amount of work that must be performed each week to provide its internal work for the planned level of output. The fundamental basis for this estimate is how many worker-hours are required to produce one unit of the product or provide one unit of service work. This ratio of time per unit of work is referred to as a *time standard* or sometimes a *standard time*.

Time standards are used for several important applications in addition to determining the size work force required to provide a given amount of capacity in a facility. They also are useful for estimating the labor cost for products or services, scheduling the completion times for work, determining the degree to which different departments or work centers are loaded with work, and as a basis for evaluating productivity improvements. A variety of methods can be used to estimate the relationship between output and worker time, ranging from very detailed work-measurement studies to development of a general empirical ratio. Supplement F at the end of this chapter contains a detailed discussion of work measurement. The time to provide one unit of output can be multiplied by the expected level of output per week to determine the number of hours that will be needed in a week for each type of skill or process equipment. The total hours can be divided by 40 to determine the number of persons with a particular skill that will be required. In considering the amount of equipment needed, the total hours would be divided by the number of hours the equipment is to be run each week. The number of employees and the amount of processing equipment needed provide a basis for estimating the support staff that will be needed and the amount of space that will be required.

In some instances, particularly with service businesses, the required size of the facility and the location of the facility are interrelated. The level of demand may depend on the convenience of the location so that a different size facility might be considered for each location. Thus, the cost of the facility, the cost of the site, and the anticipated sales revenue must be evaluated for each location under consideration. This matter will be mentioned again later when we focus on the location analysis rather than the size determination.

THE IMPORTANCE OF LOCATION

Location decisions are important and warrant management's careful attention for several reasons. Three important reasons for care in the selection of facility locations are as follows:

Competition

A company's location affects its ability to compete and many other aspects of its operations. In manufacturing companies, location affects direct costs by influencing transportation costs to and from the facility as well as the cost of labor and many supplies used in the production process. In service operations, location can affect the convenience for customers and the amount of drive-by traffic, which have an impact on the demand for the services and the effectiveness of the entire operation. Location can also influence morale, employee relations, and public relations.

Cost

Failures to make good location decisions are expensive and have long-lasting consequences. Decisions to purchase land and construct a building involve significant amounts of money; mistakes may be literally set in concrete. Time and effort spent in doing something wrong and then correcting it will never be recovered. Perhaps even more expensive—if less obvious—is the cost of making a poor location decision and not correcting it.

Hidden Effects

The effects of location are insidious. Since they are not directly observable, management must always be alert to the need to evaluate location. The cost of a poor location is an opportunity cost and therefore is hidden. No checks are written for the opportunity costs; they do not show up in accounting reports. Consequently, they come to the attention of only those who periodically examine and critically evaluate operations.

What's the most important asset for a ski resort? Good accommodations? Good food? A friendly staff? All those things count, but a ski resort isn't a ski resort without the slope and the snow! Geography can provide opportunities for business people. Another example is earthquake fault lines (right). Customers who live near fault lines form a unique market for earthquake preparedness stores.

David Brownwell/The Image Bank

Earthquake Outlet, Albany, California. Photo by Bonnie Sokall Swope.

HOW FACILITY LOCATION CAN HELP ADD VALUE FOR CUSTOMERS

Selection of good facility locations enables a company to provide convenient, dependable service to its customers. Location affects the costs of resources and, for operations that deal in tangible items, it affects transportation costs. Locating in areas where there are sufficient skilled or trainable workers with good work ethics can lead to higher-quality performance and better customer satisfaction. A facility that is located where employees are more dependable will, in turn, be more dependable in its response to demand.

LOCATION DECISIONS

Some basic operations such as mining or timber cutting must be located where the basic raw material is found. For most other types of operations, a wide variety of locations can be considered. The scope and magnitude of a location study can be enormous, even for companies that restrict potential locations to their home country. Many companies, however, are developing global operations and entering multinational markets, so they must consider many more locations and address a broader array of issues in their location studies.

Location selection methods may be very simple decisions or lengthy, complicated studies. The choice of location for small companies may be based on very little in the way of formal location studies. A location may have been selected because the business founder already owned it or could acquire it easily.

In a multinational company, the catalyst for a location study may arise through a proposal from an international subsidiary, a potential joint-venture partner, or some other entity recommending a business opportunity in a particular nation or region of the globe. If a feasibility study shows that the opportunity should be pursued, a site selection team will probably be established. This team identifies all the essential factors needed in a site as well as other desirable characteristics. The foreign associate might then identify sites possessing those essential factors. The team or some other entity, such as the corporate real estate department, evaluates the more appealing sites. Final selection may involve determining which site has more of the desirable factors as well as meeting other social and political criteria. In this chapter we discuss some factors that often are considered in more formal methods of selecting locations.

The Systems View

When the location of facilities is considered, a broad systems view is necessary. The problem may encompass many interrelated factors, and one should be careful to see that all major ones are included in the analysis.

The operations function is part of a larger system—the company. The company in turn is part of a larger system—a logistic chain. Manufacturing companies depend on suppliers for inputs and need to supply their outputs to customers. Thus, several companies or several divisions of a large company may be linked in a *logistic chain* (Figure 5.1). A metallic product may be produced from ore mined at one location, transported to a smelter to be refined, converted to mill products at another factory, fabricated into components at yet another factory, assembled into a finished product

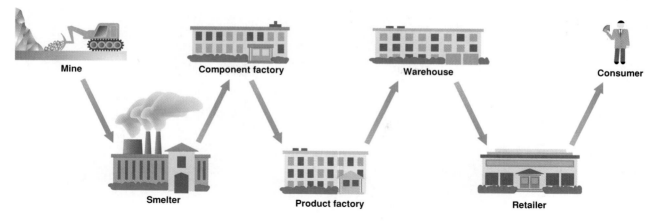

Mine   Component factory   Warehouse   Consumer

Smelter   Product factory   Retailer

Figure 5.1
The Logistic Chain

at an assembly plant, and then shipped to a warehouse. A company is said to be *vertically integrated* if it owns several of the links in the logistic chain.

The best location of one component in the logistic chain depends on the location of suppliers, consumers, and other facilities involved in the production distribution process. Ideally, a company should make location decisions to accomplish the entire production distribution process at maximum profit or minimum cost, at least for that portion of the logistic chain under its control. A *systems view* examines all the components and their interrelationships to try to arrive at an optimal location for all components of the chain. Most companies, however, own only a small portion of the total logistic chain and have little or no control over the location of other components. Even when companies own several links in the logistic chain, many facilities may already exist when a new location is to be picked. Consequently, location decisions are usually, by necessity, made piecemeal, in light of many existing components of the logistic chain.

Service organizations are also part of logistic chains in that they must obtain input services and supply consumers with their services. Service companies must consider the availability of inputs and the location of demand. Many services require direct contact with customers, making location critical to the success of the enterprise. Often operations of this type concentrate on market-related factors, which are discussed next.

LOCATION FACTORS

Location decisions often involve a broad array of factors that can influence revenue, cost, or both, and consequently may affect profits. Other factors may have a less-measurable effect on profits but still are important in location considerations. Several operations location factors are discussed below and for convenience are grouped into three general categories:

1. *Market-related factors:* locations of demand and of competition

2. *Tangible cost factors:* transportation, labor, utilities, site costs, construction costs, taxes

3. *Intangible factors:* international considerations, zoning and legal regulations, environmental factors, local attitude toward industry, room for growth, climate, schools, churches, hospitals, recreational opportunities, and so on

7-Eleven stores are located according to market-related factors. They might be located far away from competitors in areas where the population is too small to support a supermarket. Or, they might be located to meet competitors head on. In highly populated areas the supermarket is more likely to have long lines at the check-out; 7-Eleven stores attract customers with a guarantee of quick service, usually 24 hours a day.

Robert Rathe/Stock, Boston

Market-Related Factors

Market strategies often must be considered in locating facilities. Demand forecasts help determine where goods or services are most likely to be sold. A centroid, or weighted center of demand, exists for each product or product family. A decision on the location of the facility that supplies this demand must take into account the level and location of demand for each product, both now and in the future. The location of competitors will also affect the desirability of a location. Some companies consider it necessary to be located near competition. Other companies wish to avoid competitors. The convenience or inconvenience of a location may affect the number of potential customers and thus revenue. Marketing strategy is an important factor to be considered along with operations factors when a location is to be selected.

Some companies, particularly those that make high-volume purchases over a long term, are changing their purchasing practices to favor suppliers located closer to the purchaser's plant. These companies, seeking the advantages of just-in-time (JIT) manufacturing and intending to operate with much less inventory, may require that suppliers be located within, say, 2 hours' driving distance. Or they may stipulate that the supplier must make multiple deliveries of small quantities of products each day. The purchasing company may offer longer-term contracts in exchange for these extra deliveries and a commitment to high quality. The result is that suppliers who want this business may have to locate within an acceptable range of a particular customer.

Tangible Cost Factors

The cost of some factors that relate to location decisions can be established more directly than others. We will first consider those for which costs can be more easily identified. Remember, however, that the relevant costs are those that the company will incur during the life of the facility, which may be many years.

TRANSPORTATION AND DISTRIBUTION   Transportation and distribution costs can be a major expense for some wholesale, retail, and manufacturing companies that deal in tangible products. It is estimated that American companies spent $670 billion in 1993, or over 10 percent of the GDP, to pack, load, transport, sort, reload, and unload goods. This cost does not include the cost of capital invested in goods in transit, which is also sizable. Some manufacturing companies select *materials-oriented locations,* that is, they locate near their major sources of raw materials, because their major raw materials are concentrated in one area. Mining and forest products companies are examples of these types of companies. When raw materials come from scattered locations and their major customers are primarily concentrated in one area, they may select a *market-oriented location.* A custom manufacturing company like a cabinet shop would probably be market-oriented.

Products may pass through a complicated network from the original factory warehouse, to a distribution center, to a wholesaler, then to a retailer, and on to the final consumer. Numerous links in an inefficient logistic chain, or "supply chain," either within a single highly integrated company or through a series of supplier-customer transactions, can add excessive costs to products. The cost to the ultimate consumer may be higher than the cost of a competing product purchased through some other supply chain. Companies, therefore, will try to select locations for the different parts of their business that are favorable with regard to one another, making an efficient distribution network. Also, supplier location may be an important factor in selecting suppliers, so that a company can keep its costs low and respond more quickly to its customers. Some companies, such as Laura Ashley and National Semiconductor, have found that they can reduce costs and improve their delivery speed and reliability by consolidating their distribution network into one distribution center and outsourcing their distribution to a third-party logistics firm.

Many service companies require customer contact and select market-oriented locations. Some, however, such as the Red Cross when it solicits donations during a blood drive, may locate at least temporarily near their source of supply. Other than for wholesale and retail businesses, the costs of transporting its inputs or outputs is usually not a major factor in selecting the locations for services.

Weyerhaeuser Company

While products come to 7-Eleven stores from scattered locations and are sold to customers in concentrated locations, the reverse is true for Weyerhaeuser. Weyerhaeuser is an example of a company with materials oriented locations. Weyerhaeuser has its mills close to its raw materials in timber areas to reduce transportation costs. Weyerhaeuser's decision saves money not only because timber is found in concentrated areas, but logs are also more difficult to transport than are finished lumber products.

INTERNATIONAL TRANSPORTATION Companies involved in international trade should investigate numerous transportation-related factors. The company should begin by identifying the commodities to be shipped, the countries from which freight will come, and the countries to which freight will probably go. Several modes of transportation may be involved, including truck, rail, air, and ocean. If international air links are anticipated, the nearness to major air gateways may be important to the success of a plant or distribution center. If ocean transportation is contemplated, the company must consider nearness to a suitable port. If the site is not near an ocean container pool, then the cost of obtaining containers and returning empties must be considered. Use of consolidation services might result in significant savings for a company that will not be shipping full containers.

Customs duty or tariffs are transportation-related costs that must be taken into account. It is advisable for companies that import large amounts of components or subassemblies for further assembly in the United States to consider locations in a free-trade zone. Such a location allows the company to delay payment of the duty on the imported components until the finished goods are removed for final sale. Obviously, location can have an impact on many transportation-related costs.

WAGE RATES AND AVAILABLE SKILLS With the trend toward a high percentage of service and information-intensive businesses the important criteria in seeking employees have changed. In many manufacturing operations the cost of direct labor may be less than 10 or 15 percent of costs. Employee skills, flexibility, and work ethic are becoming important. There are fewer companies that require large pools of unskilled or semiskilled workers. A location must be capable of providing sufficient qualified workers who show promise of being capable and dedicated employees. The prevailing wage rates among the qualified locations can be a factor.

The United States has a relatively low unemployment rate despite having a large percentage of the work force that is said to be functionally illiterate. Citicorp has located a data entry operation in Ireland where there is a well-educated work force and the unemployment rate approaches 20 percent and wage rates are lower. American Airlines has an accounting data entry operation in Barbados. Since data can be transmitted anywhere on the globe the number of possible locations for some information-related operations is very broad.

ENERGY AVAILABILITY AND COSTS Many manufacturing plants use large amounts of energy sources, such as electricity or natural gas, to operate production processes. Nonmanufacturing facilities use these resources for heating or air-conditioning the workers' environment. Fuels have become scarce and expensive in many locations and will play an increasingly large part in companies' location selections. To ensure the possibility of future expansion, it is wise to examine the power company's expansion plans and future allocations of fuel to the gas company from its sources.

WATER AVAILABILITY AND COSTS Processes that require large amounts of water are restricted to locations where abundant water resources are available. Water shortages occur in some locations and will probably become more common. If the process overheats or chemically contaminates the water, then the availability of locations will be further restricted; some sites may even be forbidden. Availability of water and the cost of water treatment and pollution control must be considered by operations that make extensive use of water.

OPERATIONS MANAGEMENT IN ACTION

BMW SELECTS SPARTANBURG, S.C.

In June of 1992, automaker BMW announced that it would build its first major production plant outside Germany. The new Beemer plant is in Spartanburg, South Carolina. The corporate director for planning said the arithmetic favored U.S. production and several reasons for its new location were noted.

Market Conditions

The United States is the world's biggest market for luxury cars and the market was expected to grow by another 20 percent when the plant began production in 1995, as the baby boomers enter middle age and are candidates for upscale autos. A strong German mark and a new luxury tax in the United States had made the cost of buying a BMW in the United States high, while new competition such as the Lexus and Infinity had been introduced into the market and had eaten into sales. BMW has reoriented its line with more lower-priced models, which give it a wider selection for customers and a higher volume of business.

Tangible Cost Factors

Initial labor costs will be about one-third less than the $28 per hour the company pays at home. Other production efficiencies could save $2,000 to $3,000 per car. This is a significant reduction on the cars with prices starting in the $20,000's. Shipping costs should drop by about $2,500 also. The company will receive about $135 million in state and local tax breaks and subsidies for locating its plant at Spartanburg.

Intangible Factors

South Carolina will extend a free-trade zone from the Spartanburg airport to the plant so the company will not have to pay duty on imported components. Initially, most of the components will come from Germany. As the local supplier base is developed and internal skills are improved more of the components will be local. The plans are to continue obtaining major components such as the engines and axles from German plants. Being in a free-trade zone can be important because BMW plans to export about half the plant's production, primarily back to Europe and Japan.

Source: "The Beemer Spotlight Falls on Spartanburg, USA," *Business Week,* July 6, 1992.

SITE AND CONSTRUCTION COSTS One cost directly related to facility location is the cost of purchasing the site and building the facility. The cost per acre of land varies widely from site to site within a region and from region to region. The cost per acre is sometimes deceptive, because less costly land may require greater expenditures to prepare the site and construct a building.

TAXES Some localities use tax concessions as incentives to attract business and industry. Tax reductions or exemptions may be allowed to new businesses. Property taxes may be sizable for a company with a multimillion-dollar investment in facilities and inventory. The extent of a company's investment will influence the relative importance of taxes in selection of a location.

Intangible Factors

Not all measures of a location's desirability can be expressed in dollars and cents. People must be induced to come to work there, so the appeal of a locality as a place to live and rear a family is important. The local political environment may also have important effects on a company.

INTERNATIONAL CONSIDERATIONS Companies that are considering foreign locations must assess numerous factors relative to each country under consideration.

Such factors might include trade quotas, language, culture, government stability and cooperation, monetary system, and others.

TELECOMMUNICATIONS AND OTHER SERVICES Sophisticated telecommunications infrastructure is important in some companies' location selections. As traffic problems and commuting costs increase, more employees may opt for alternative work spaces and telecommute. Many information-intensive businesses already require extensive data transmission support. Business parks are providing considerable support to help lure companies to their locations. For example, Paducah Information Age Park in Paducah, Kentucky, features underground utilities, fiber optics, integrated services digital network (ISDN) service, and a digital switching system. A multipurpose resource center provides full videoconferencing and access to the University of Kentucky supercomputer.

ZONING AND LEGAL REGULATIONS Local, state, and federal pollution control regulations may limit the locations available to some companies. Zoning regulations control the types of businesses that may operate in certain areas. Since zoning and legal regulations may restrict the types of future diversification a company can undertake, long-range plans should be considered from both the company's and the community's standpoint.

ENVIRONMENTAL FACTORS Obtaining permits to build and operate some facilities can be a lengthy and expensive process. Detailed technical studies and public hearings may be necessary. These requirements must be anticipated, and the process begun early to achieve timely completion of a project. The availability of suitable waste disposal sites and the cost of waste disposal are important considerations for businesses and the public. Public reaction to hauling or storing hazardous waste will make some sites unfeasible and may even cause some contemplated business projects to be unfeasible.

COMMUNITY ATTITUDES Community relations should be an integral part of location decisions. Public opinion in some areas may be unfavorable to a particular type of business, even though there is no formal legislation against it. A company locating in such an area runs the risk of future restrictions, excessive taxes, or other undesirable public reactions. Problems may arise if the public becomes aroused by unexpected smoke, noise, odor, or some other undesirable impact. It is wise to meet with community leaders and sample opinion before making costly commitments.

SPEED AND RESPONSIVENESS OF SUPPORT Speedy selection and support are becoming more important for some companies in fast-paced businesses like semiconductors. Such companies must move quickly to select a site and construct a facility. Sites that cannot respond quickly with the necessary approvals and upgrades of roads, sewers, electric power, and so on, may be dropped from consideration. For example, several sites were dropped from consideration because they could not respond quickly enough when Intel selected Chandler, Arizona, for a $1.3 billion semiconductor plant.

EXPANSION POTENTIAL A site for a manufacturing or nonmanufacturing facility should offer some flexibility and room for expansion. The size and contour of the plot of land should allow for expansion of the facility without a sacrifice of efficiency. Room for expansion of utility service capacity should be available. Access roads and transportation facilities should also be capable of accommodating increased volume.

SITE SELECTION IN INDIA: A CASE STUDY

The logistics of site selection across national borders are much more complex than locating facilities domestically, and for this reason the task is often handled by a team of experts.

Background

The site selection process for Du Pont Co. differs for international and domestic sites. Domestically, the company controls the total process, with the real estate section performing or coordinating the job. The procedures are quite formalized and structured. Only the real estate section has the authority to execute agreements pertaining to real estate.

Internationally the company does business through myriad separate, independent subsidiaries. In most countries Du Pont has an office primarily for marketing and has a country manager. The impetus for an international site originates with a business need to have a particular product at a particular place to serve a local market, regional market, for worldwide export, or for a combination of reasons.

The international site selection process deals with widely varying circumstances, so the procedures are less structured. In many cases, particularly in the Far East but also in Europe and Latin America, certain products can be produced only in designated areas of countries. In some countries, it is nearly impossible for a nondomestic company to acquire property in its own name. Many times the only way to enter a foreign market is through a joint-venture partnership.

International Site Selection Team

When the list of potential sites has been narrowed to a few, a select group from Du Pont, the site selection team, visits the sites to evaluate them and make recommendations. The team usually consists of the following persons with their particular interests: The real estate representative is interested in making sure that all the bases are covered by the team in evaluating the costs and methods for site procurement. The representative will also investigate possibilities for expatriate housing and any off-site support requirements, such as warehousing and office space. The civil engineer is interested in soil stability, methods of construction, utilities, wind direction, environmental concerns, and so on. The logistics expert evaluates the feasibility of getting raw materials to the site and finished products out. The manufacturing or operations representative concentrates on the work force, work

rules, quality of labor, and overall suitability of the location for the product. The team or subgroups visit plants operating in the area to gather information on the work force, local government, reliability of the electrical service, and so forth. They also visit the utility companies and local schools, which are of great interest to expatriates and their families.

Back home, the site selection team presents its findings to a steering committee made up of management, legal, public affairs, and finance representatives. This committee gives the site selection team guidance on corporate concerns and regarding who will have input into the final recommendation and start-up of the facility.

Site Selection in India

With over 700 million people, India can no longer be ignored as a market for Du Pont's products. In this country, at least for the products Du Pont is interested in manufacturing, it is mandatory to have an Indian joint-venture partner. Also, to manufacture a product in the country, the company must obtain a license from the government for a particular area, which limits the number of alternative sites.

Du Pont gave its joint-venture partner the task of evaluating general areas according to the following criteria:

- Proximity to market
- Proximity to port
- Raw-material transport
- State government stability
- Cooperation expected of state government
- Ease of obtaining license clearance
- Industrial relations
- Labor costs
- Site costs
- The power situation
- Pollution clearance
- Financial incentives
- Proximity to infrastructure
- Proximity to Delhi, the capital of India and the location of headquarters offices of both Du Pont and its Indian partner

Locations with insurmountable obstacles, such as a general lack of acceptance of the chemical plant and state government instability, were excluded. The Indian state of Uttar Pradesh in the foothills of the Himalayas was chosen as a potential location. Even so, this site is located 1,700 kilometers (900 miles) from the nearest ocean port, with road access and driving conditions that are treacherous at many points along the way.

Du Pont's joint-venture partner obtained the license for a manufacturing facility and located the 570-hectare (230-acre) site in Bhang Wan, population 200. This is near Pontseib, which happens to be the sixth most important Seikh shrine in India. Obtaining the license was a very long and arduous process. The site selection team was to determine if there were any fatal flaws that would preclude its use for the intended purpose.

The critical issues were:

- We were dealing with a potentially hazardous raw material, isocyanate (also referred to as NDI in this article).
- It would have to be transported 900 miles inland.
- Possible poor quality or lack of expatriate facilities.
- Unknown quality of the local work force.
- We needed to address local environmental concerns.

An adequate electrical supply is absolutely necessary. Usually we like to have two separate sources of electricity, such as backup from on-site generators.

The permitting process took about 2 years just to get the required okays on the site we are discussing. To go after another site might have delayed plant start-up by another 2 years. The timing was also a factor because three other companies had already gotten licenses to produce the same product.

The Raw Materials: But the main issue for the site selection team had to do with our concern that the isocyanate would be a problem to the Indian government and the people of India after the chemical plant disaster in Bhopal. The isocyanate that would be used at this plant is not at all like the isocyanate involved in the Bhopal tragedy. Du Pont's isocyanate is a solid and has a very high melting point. To make sure that it stayed solid during shipment, the chemical would be transported in 40-foot refrigerated containers all the way from the manufacturer to the plant site.

Du Pont's principal supplier of NDI is Dow in the United States. Alternatively, we could also get it from Bayer in Germany, which is already supplying a polymeric NDI, used by foam-product producers in India. When confronted with the Bhopal problem, the Indian government immediately banned all movement of NDI within the country, regardless of whether the chemical was the same one involved with Bhopal. And it took a month for the foam producers to convince the Indian government that the NDI that they used was entirely different from that which caused the Bhopal tragedy. Then they were able to resume their imports of it.

The other raw material used at this plant presents no real environmental problem. It would be put into

tanks at Du Pont's Niagara Falls plant and moved to the Indian site.

Part of the logistics problem of determining whether Du Pont could make this enterprise work in India has to do with who the NDI carriers would be, what Indian affiliates they have, and what connection they would have with this prospective site. The site selection team found that there were several transportation candidates with good Indian contacts or subsidiaries. Failing shipment from the United States, Du Pont had two alternatives from Europe.

Transportation: One of the factors in considering this site is the long lead time required to get the raw materials to the site from the production point. Shipment would require a certain number of days in the country of origin, plus time for an in-route port clearance. But in the case of India, the shipment process would also have a problem with monsoons.

The site selection team assumed that the raw-material supply trucks would run only during daylight, making the journey to the site from the port a 6-day trip.

The trucks carrying the NDI would come up through Bombay. In this region, the width of the road rapidly narrows from a maximum of 20 feet (6 meters) down to 10 feet (3 meters), and the course contains numerous sharp curves. That means that the trucks with 40-foot containers in tow would probably have trouble getting around some of those curves.

Although there has not been a specific commitment to Du Pont to improve the roads, we noticed that the Indian government was widening some of the roads up to the site.

Our conclusion was that with the right logistical controls, such as driving only during the day and having people on board the trucks who were capable of making any repairs, the site could work.

Other Site Selection Considerations: We considered the possibility of building a residential colony at the site. But it is remote and isolated and currently has no local amenities. Du Pont would have had to put in everything that the plant's staff would have there. An hour's drive from the plant over an adequate but heavily traveled road there is good family housing. This is the place where the British came to seek out cool weather in the hot season during the colonial days.

Two hours' travel from the site within the city of Pontseib there is good family housing. There is apparently a lot of thievery, and so all Westerners living there hire guards. Grocery shopping in the city can be difficult for Westerners. There are specialty stores, you might call them, but they are in a crowded part of town, and they are extremely unsanitary to our way of looking at them.

There is an excellent boys' school in the city, which goes to the secondary level. The city is the site of India's version of West Point or Sandhurst for training of army personnel. On the down side, the big problem with this area is that it contains no major medical facility.

Next, we will discuss the quality of the work force. The plant site is located in Seikh country. One of the important Seikh temples is located very close to the site. And there are many Seikhs living in the local area. Seikhs are, of course, among the best of the work force in India. So the site selection team concluded that the labor pool was adequate and certainly trainable. There are people expert in mechanics from a large cement plant nearby. And there is a lot of light industry in the region.

Plant safety is a real problem because Seikhs will not give up their turbans, particularly in this area which is characterized by a high level of religious enthusiasm. A safety hat will not fit over a turban. And the site selection team observed employees in local plants who needed hearing protection and hard-toe shoes according to our standards, but these safety precautions were not the custom. We would have to impose these safety programs on plant staff.

Regarding environmental factors, the plant would need to dispose of some liquid waste. A river flows right by this site. But the plant would generate a liquid waste that could not be discharged into that river, which is the local source for drinking water. Solid waste disposal did not appear to be a problem.

But from a manufacturer's point of view, the dust generated by a nearby cement plant poses a problem. However, the engineers said that the dust was not an issue in light of the normal wind directions. We would need to drill wells on the site, and there was a question of groundwater allocation rights. But the site selection team concluded that the well would be okay if we got some local support.

The final issue for the site selection team was the monsoon. In July and August, between 25 and 35 inches of rain fall in a single month. The site selection team visited the site in the non-monsoon season. The team visited the site again during the monsoon season.

The Site Acquisition Process

The site had already been designated for industrial use by the state government, so the site selection team did not have that hurdle to cross. Industrial sites in India can be acquired in two ways. First, the government can acquire it, akin to our laws of condemnation. This is, however, a very long process that must go through the courts and frequently results in bad feelings by the people since they may feel unfairly compensated and treated.

The second way of acquiring an industrial site involves direct negotiation with the property owners.

The 570-hectare (230-acre) property consisted of 100 individual parcels owned by members of twenty-seven different families. We estimated that it would cost a million dollars, or $4,300 per acre, to purchase the land and another $100,000 to relocate the people living there. Their homes were grass huts. We were required to give the displaced families a small piece of land for their sacred cow on a section of the site away from the plant. We also agreed that the plant's clinic would provide medical service to the community and that the plant would hire members of the displaced families. Du Pont did not have to hire all the people who had lived on the site. Generally, one person from each family would be hired. These people would be placed in jobs such as landscaping, grounds maintenance, and cleaning the plant—work appropriate for people who are not literate.

Du Pont's joint-venture partner felt that the land purchase negotiations would take anywhere from 1 to 6 months but could take longer. Negotiations would generally be held with the head of the village and his counselors, who would make the decision for others.

When the site selection team got back to the United States and we put our heads together and talked to management, we had many concerns. But we thought that we could manage all those concerns. The general conclusion was that the site selection team found no fatal flaws in the site, and we recommended that Du Pont acquire it.

Source: Adapted from Harry Thomes and Robert Fulton, "Site Selection in India: A Case Study," *Site Selection 34,* no. 5 (August 1989): 16–19. Reprinted by permission of Conway Data, Inc.

QUALITY OF LIFE   Often a company's top-echelon personnel are obtained from other branches or other companies. Today some people decline promotions with their own company or offers from other companies because they do not want to move to the job location. The costs of living—housing, food, clothing, power, and other essentials—are important to all employees. And areas noted for high crime rates, to mention another example, are not conducive to easy recruiting.

Table 5.1 *Quality of life* (handwritten)

MOST CRITICAL QOL FACTORS IN NEXT 5 YEARS

1. Education K–12	48%
2. Availability of affordable housing	43%
3. Reasonable cost of living	38%
4. Nearby colleges and universities	31%
5. Availability of career opportunities for two-career families	24%
6. Attractiveness of an area's physical environment	19%
7. Day-care facilities for working parents	19%
8. Low crime rate	12%
9. Absence of drug-related problems	10%
10. Climate of service area	7%

Source: Jack Lyne, "Firsthand Observation, Education Ranked as Key Element in Quality-of-Life Equation," *Site Selection 34,* no. 4 (August 1989): 946. Reprinted by permission of Conway Data, Inc.

A location's appeal to potential employees may be an important consideration. People are interested in the environment in which they and their families will live. Most want above-average schools for their children and opportunities for further study for themselves. The climate and recreational opportunities may also influence the appeal of a location. Table 5.1 lists ten of the most important quality-of-life (QOL) factors as reported in one study.

LOCATION EVALUATION METHODS

Location decisions are strategic and are interrelated with other strategic decisions. They involve large amounts of funds and they affect a company's ability to compete. For example, a manufacturing company may operate from one central factory and have the risk of a fire, flood, or strike closing down the entire operation. Alternatively, it could operate several smaller plants, which might cause it to lose some economies of scale and to have higher distribution and coordination problems. Most location decisions involve trade-offs or compromises of various good points and less desirable points. Much of the relevant data for reaching these decisions are estimates of future costs and intangible factors. The number and diversity of factors involved, such as those mentioned earlier, make location selection an inexact science. Consequently, location decisions are "satisficing" decisions rather than provable optimal decisions. Fortunately, some types of business can be successful in a variety of settings. For example, there are electronics manufacturers and insurance companies in many parts of the world.

How does a person or a group of people arrive at a location selection? No doubt, there are many methods. We will discuss some of the features of the location problem and some approaches to a solution. We first discuss factors that often are considered by retail establishments and then evaluations that may apply to service businesses or to manufacturing businesses.

Retail Considerations

Retail location decisions typically are more market-oriented than supply-oriented. A retail business will have determined the product line it handles or will handle and the type of clientele to whom it wishes to sell. The criterion for selecting a site frequently is its market potential. If the retailer's strategy is to sell at nationally advertised retail prices and to compete through service and convenience, this decision will favor some locations over others. Convenience is more important for retailers than for wholesalers, particularly for items that are purchased frequently, such as groceries. Customers may be willing to go to more trouble to purchase durable goods that do not have to be purchased often.

A retailer would be interested in determining the trading area—that is, the geographical section from which a store draws customers—around potential sites. The age distribution, occupations, incomes, and life-styles of the people in this area are also important. Some of the factors about a site in relation to its potential as a store location are listed below.[1]

1. Competition: the types and nearness of competing stores. Stores that are part of a chain have more name recognition, broader advertising, and the financial strength to be tough competition.

2. Other establishments that can help or hurt. A children's shop is better located near a women's clothing shop than near a bar or an auto parts shop. Parks, museums, and other attractions may draw customers for some types of businesses.

3. Availability of a site or existing building near the desired location.

4. Traffic counts and convenience of the entrance and exit. Nearness to public transportation may also be important.

5. Visibility of the site or store.

6. Convenient secure parking nearby.

7. Regulations about construction, appearance, signs, and other matters.

8. Miscellaneous factors, such as police and fire protection and banking support in the area.

Data of this sort may be obtained and evaluated. Census track data can be used to determine much of the information about occupants in the trading area. Traffic counts on the streets and surveys of automobiles in the parking lots of nearby stores or a shopping center will provide a measure of how busy the area is. Personal interviews of shoppers in the area will provide some indication of their shopping patterns and preferences. Again, a major objective is to assess the profit potential of each potential location. The business owners may have to invest more or sign a more expensive lease for a site that will earn more. Some methods of evaluating retail sites are presented in the Mason and Mayer reference listed in the Bibliography. We now discuss some of the considerations that are more related to the location of manufacturing facilities.

Usefulness of Geographic Information Systems (GIS)

Geographic information systems are software designed to store, analyze, integrate, and display data in regard to particular geographic areas. By use of color-coded maps these systems can display location-related data in a form that is easily understandable and powerful. These systems are useful for screening locations to see which

---

[1]Melvin Morgenstein and Harriet Strongin, *Modern Retailing*, 3d ed. (New York: Wiley, 1992), Chap. 8.

Geographic information systems use color coding to indicate characteristics such as population density, family income, or age distribution of various locations.

Charles Feil/Stock, Boston

meet some initial screening criteria or for further analysis. For example, one might analyze the impact of reduced transportation costs by locating near a large population center versus the higher wage rates and taxes these locations may have. Data requirements are extensive if many possible sites are in the analysis.

Banks, retail outlets, and restaurants are among the leading users of GIS software. Location decisions for these establishments are based on such factors as traffic volume, population growth, income levels, shopping habits, and other variables that often can be obtained in data bases. Often only one community or part of it is considered so data can be sorted by block number or zip code. Industrial site analysis may consider an entire nation or continent and may require data on wages, utility rates, taxes, transportation costs, construction costs, and other factors. The data base cost for this type analysis may be large. But these systems can perform powerful analyses quickly and provide useful displays to location selection teams that can give insight into the patterns with which relevant factors vary.

General Procedure for Location Selection

Location decisions often are made by a management team. Such teams may include representatives from logistics, real estate, operations, human resources, and marketing. The process of selecting a location may follow many steps of evaluation. The sequencing of these steps may vary with the situation, but a frequently used sequence is listed below. A global company would first select the nation(s) of interest.

1. Select the general region.
2. Select generally acceptable communities.
3. Select appropriate sites within the communities.
4. Determine a method of evaluating community-site combinations.
5. Compare sites and select one.

Step 2 may sometimes be omitted; an organization may search for sites within the desired region and proceed to steps 3 and 4. General approaches other than the one outlined above may be followed. Marketing considerations, *distribution costs,* wage rates, and the availability of raw materials may lead to selection of a general region. An evaluation of available labor skills, highways, railways, waterways, docks, or air-

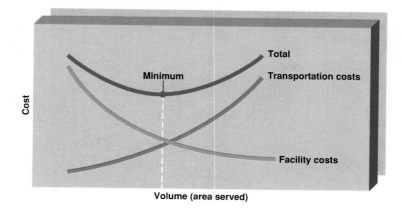

ports will lead to a list of communities within the region. Intangible factors may eliminate some or move them to the bottom of the list. The company can then survey the acceptable communities to determine if suitable sites are available.

Grouping of Service Areas

When the company produces more than one product or provides several services, the problem of location becomes rather complicated. Managers must decide whether to have small plants and warehouses located in areas ideal for each product or to group products into larger facilities in locations that represent a compromise for some items but are best for the group as a whole. Trade-offs must be evaluated to decide which products to group and where to locate facilities. Economies of scale must be compared with the cost of nonoptimal locations.

As the volume of products handled by a regional warehouse is increased, the warehouse cost will be spread over a greater volume. Hence the warehouse cost per unit will decrease. Introducing additional products into the facility, however, means that a broader geographic area must be covered by it, and delivery costs will therefore be increased. A graphical model of these costs has a generally familiar appearance, as shown in Figure 5.2. The same structure may be applied to service operations by comparing travel costs for a location to the facility savings that result from combining smaller regions.

Sound judgment is a vital part of any decision. A broad array of models or techniques are available to assist those responsible for reaching a decision. Four of the models or techniques that may be beneficial in reaching a location decision are discussed below.

Cost-Profit-Volume or Break-Even Analysis

Since the volume of business available is one of the variables that affect a location's desirability, *cost-profit-volume analysis,* sometimes called *break-even analysis,* may be a useful tool in selecting a location. Some of the costs of having a facility in a location will be fixed, and others will vary with the volume of business. The cost structures will probably be different for each location being considered. So will the volume of sales. A graphical model such as Figure 5.3, showing the relationship of cost and volume in two locations, may therefore give a significant insight into the situa-

Figure 5.3
Relationship of Cost and
Volume at Two
Locations

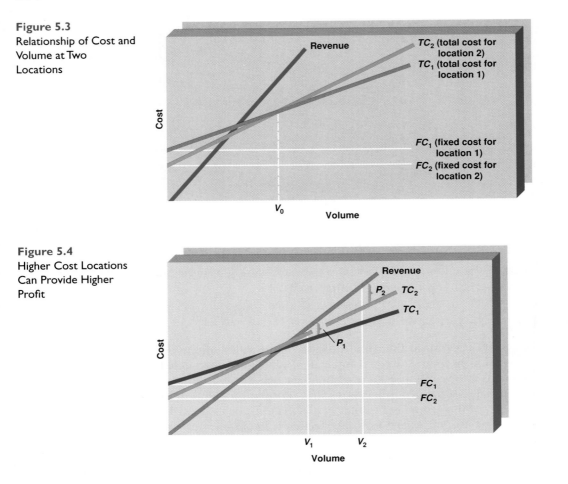

Figure 5.4
Higher Cost Locations
Can Provide Higher
Profit

tion. Only one revenue line is shown, since it is assumed that the product will sell for the same price no matter which location is selected. As long as the location does not affect the volume sold and the volume is above V_0, location 1 is preferable to location 2, because TC_1 is lower than TC_2 for all volumes greater than V_0.

One should not conclude that the lowest-cost location will always be the maximum-profit location, unless the price and volume are to be the same for all locations. Some location other than the one with minimum costs might result in sufficient additional volume to increase revenue more than costs. Figure 5.4 shows the same costs as Figure 5.3. Assume, however, that the company will experience a sales volume of V_2 in location 2 and a sales volume of V_1 in location 1. For this particular set of conditions, the higher-cost location will result in a greater profit.

Many manufactured products are purchased by people who don't know where the goods were manufactured or stored before they were shipped to the point of purchase. Location of a factory or warehouse has no effect on the volume of demand. Location may have a great effect, however, on the volume of sales for a retail establishment or a service operation. Consider, for example, a laundry and dry cleaning establishment. A customer has to make two trips, one to leave dirty clothes and another to pick them up after they have been cleaned. A convenient location can often increase volume significantly, and the effect on profit must be considered.

The discussion in this section has been somewhat simplified in order to illustrate the basic idea of cost-profit-volume analysis in relation to location selection. The method can be used to compare many more than two possible locations, and the curves representing costs and revenue can often be more complicated than straight lines.

Point Rating

In selecting a site, companies have several objectives, but not all are of equal importance. The relative weight a company assigns to each type of objective or to each location factor may be represented by the number of points a perfect site would receive in each category. Each potential site then is evaluated with respect to every factor a company is looking for, and points are assigned to each factor. The site with the highest total points is considered superior.

Of course, implementing an organized system such as this for evaluating multiple goals requires careful judgment. As the *point rating* has been described thus far, a high score in any factor can overcome a low ranking in any other. However, because some factors may be essential, any site that does not have at least a specified number of points for that factor will be excluded from further consideration. For example, the existing labor force may be sufficient, but the projected growth of other businesses in the area may be so large that the company foresees a lack of growth potential or an expensive wage payment contest. Another matter that must be worked out to implement a point rating system is the relative importance of tangible cost factors compared to intangible factors. Points are usually assigned only to the intangible factors, and an evaluation is made to determine whether the difference between the intangible scores is worth the difference, if any, between the tangible costs of the competing locations.

Consider this example: After evaluating two potential sites by comparing costs and finding them approximately equal, a pipe manufacturer decided to evaluate the intangible factors for sites A and B by point rating. Comparative ratings were assigned to major location factors to determine the relative importance of each. Each site was assigned a percentage of the maximum possible points, and these points were totaled. The results of the point rating, presented in Table 5.2, indicate a slight preference for site B.

Table 5.2
POINTS ASSIGNED TO ALTERNATIVE LOCATIONS

FACTORS RATED	MAXIMUM POSSIBLE POINTS	Location A	Location B
Future availability of fuel	300	200	250
Transportation flexibility and growth	200	150	150
Adequacy of water supply	100	100	100
Labor climate	250	220	200
Pollution regulations and tax stability	30	20	20
Site characteristics	50	40	30
Living conditions	150	100	125
Total		830	875

APPLICATION

USE OF THE TRANSPORTATION METHOD IN LOCATION ANALYSIS

Table 5.3

PLANT CAPACITY AND SHIPPING COSTS TO ACTUAL AND HYPOTHETICAL DESTINATIONS, ATLANTIS POOL SUPPLY COMPANY

PLANT	CAPACITY	Shipping Cost To:			
		GLENDALE	DALLAS	ATLANTA	CHARLOTTE
Phoenix	800	$ 5	$9	$16	$17
Little Rock	800	9	4	8	9
Columbus	600	15	8	3	5

The Atlantis Pool Supply Company began with a factory in Phoenix in 1981. It produces and distributes a line of swimming pool accessories that are sold to pool supply stores in many major cities, primarily in the South and Southwest. Soon after starting the company, Splash Gordon, the owner, expanded by opening a distribution warehouse near Glendale, California. Next he opened a second factory in Little Rock, Arkansas, and a distribution warehouse just outside Dallas, Texas.

Splash has just returned to the company's Phoenix headquarters from getting operations under way at a new factory in Columbus, Georgia. He has decided to open a distribution warehouse in the Southeast. Splash and several of his upper-level managers have gone through a point rating evaluation of several cities and have concluded that either Atlanta or Charlotte will be suitable. We shall look over his shoulder as he compares the cost of operations in the two cities.

In order to use the transportation method, Splash first obtained the costs for shipping from all the sources to all the possible destinations. He also estimated the amount of capacity available at the sources. The estimated demand was 700 in Glendale and Dallas and 700 at Atlanta or Charlotte. The other data are presented in Table 5.3.

In certain instances, this type of problem could be solved by including both Atlanta and Charlotte in the same transportation method tableau and adding a dummy source. If either of the proposed locations is excluded from the solution (that is, receives only dummy products), it is obviously the wrong location. When the optimal solution indicates that both proposed locations should receive some actual product and some dummy product, it is not clear which location is preferred. Splash decided to solve this problem by considering each proposed location separately.

Figure 5.5 Optimal Solution to Atlantis's Transportation Problem if Atlanta Is Used as a Warehouse Location

Plant	Warehouse				Capacity
	Glendale	Dallas	Atlanta	Dummy	
Phoenix	5 / 700	9	16	0 / 100	800
Little Rock	9	4 / 700	8 / 100	0	800
Columbus	15	8	3 / 600	0	600
Demand	700	700	700	100	

First, the problem was worked under the assumption that Atlanta was chosen. The final solution is shown in Figure 5.5. Notice that the plants have 100 units of excess capacity, so a dummy location requiring 100 units is included in the tableau. The cost of supplying the dummy location from any plant is zero. The total cost of this allocation can be found by multiplying the amount in each occupied cell by the unit shipping cost for that cell and summing these amounts for all the occupied cells. The monthly shipping cost if Atlanta is used as a location will be 700($5) + 700($4) + 100($8) + 600($3) + $0 = $8,900.

The procedure was then repeated, using the appropriate numbers for Charlotte. The optimal solution is presented in Figure 5.6. This tableau indicates the same shipping pattern, but the total monthly shipping cost if Charlotte is selected as the warehouse location will be 700($5) + 700($4) + 100($9) + 600($5) + 100($0) = $10,200.

After going through these calculations, Splash asked his assistant to find the name of a good industrial real estate firm in Atlanta and to place a call to it. He then left to go to the product testing laboratory for a quick swim.

Figure 5.6   Optimal Solution if Charlotte Is Used as a Warehouse Location

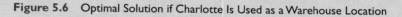

Plant	Warehouse				Capacity
	Glendale	Dallas	Charlotte	Dummy	
Phoenix	5 / 700	9	17	0 / 100	800
Little Rock	9	4 / 700	9 / 100	0	800
Columbus	15	8	5 / 600	0	600
Demand	700	700	700	100	

The Transportation Method of Linear Programming

When only one source will be used to supply the location under consideration, the cost of supplying it can be found by adding the production cost at the supply point and the shipping cost from there to the potential location. When a network of several supply points can supply a potential location, however, the cost is more difficult to compute. Interaction between existing facilities and the proposed facility must be considered. The total cost for one location must be compared with the total cost for another location. To make this type of comparison, we must first find the best match of capacity and demand for one potential location, then the best match for another, and so on for every location under consideration, so that the costs and profits for all of them can be compared.

The transportation method of linear programming can be used to match capacity and demand. This method derives its name from its ability to minimize the cost of transporting products from source locations to distribution centers. The transportation method can be used to allocate productive capacity at various factories to a group of field warehouses, to allocate materials at field warehouses to customer accounts in various cities, and to assign service accounts to service centers, each of which has some specified capacity.

The location of a facility may affect its operating cost. For example, the location of a repair center will affect the cost of transporting all the necessary repair parts. If several sources of supply are available and several other existing repair centers also are to be supplied, the best allocation or distribution of the repair parts probably will not be obvious. If revenue is not affected by location, its contribution to profit and overhead can be maximized by finding the minimum-cost location. Here the transportation method may be put to good use, although a computer might be employed to solve large-scale problems.

Simulation

The previous application of linear programming considered only the inbound transportation cost for the swimming pool equipment. The Atlantis Company may feel that the rise in outbound freight cost caused by moving a location in one direction will be offset by an equivalent reduction in the cost of freight going in the opposite direction. Besides, Atlantis charges the outbound delivery cost to the customer.

A company must take a more holistic, systems view when both the inbound and outbound freight costs are relevant to a location decision. In multiple-location operations, materials may be moved around from one warehouse to another because demand is greater than expected in some areas and less than expected in others. Inventory levels within each facility fluctuate with a probabilistic demand. Different levels of safety stock may be required at different locations. When, in addition, a company stocks and sells hundreds or thousands of products, analysis of the system requires considerable time and effort. Several variables and their interactions must be considered.

Computers have made possible the storage of vast amounts of data and the rapid computation necessary to keep track of the many variables involved in such complex problems. Simulation is sometimes used as a tool in selecting the location for such complex systems. Further, simulation can provide useful information about the system in addition to indicating the results of alternative locations. Simulation can also be used in analysis of operations that do not distribute or manufacture tangible products.

SUMMARY

Location decisions are important because they may affect cost, profit, and even the success or failure of operations. They are likely to be complex, often involving myriad factors and interrelationships among numerous components of a total system. The impact of location on operations is not always obvious because some cost components represent opportunity costs rather than out-of-pocket costs. Since facilities generally are long-term investments, decisions regarding their locations usually have long-term effects.

Three major categories of factors have important influences on location decisions: market-related factors, tangible cost factors, and intangible factors. These factors may have varying degrees of influence, depending on the type of operation. Since a service operation is likely to involve direct contact with the consumer, its location, even the aesthetics or appearance of the facility, can have a significant impact on demand. Manufacturing operations usually have less direct contact with customers, so their location is usually based on operating costs.

Several models and techniques may be used in evaluating potential locations. Four of these techniques are cost-profit-volume analysis, point rating, linear programming, and computer simulation.

KEY TERMS

Time standard   Market-related factors   Market-oriented location
Logistic chain   Tangible cost factors   Distribution costs
Vertical integration   Intangible factors   Cost-profit-volume analysis
Systems view   Materials-oriented location   Point rating

DISCUSSION QUESTIONS

1. Why should location decisions be considered from a broad systems view?
2. Why can location seldom be selected on the basis of tangible cost alone?
3. What three major categories of factors influence operations location?
4. How may tangible costs and intangible factors be compared to arrive at a location decision?
5. Why do various organizations emphasize different location factors?
6. What trade-off is made as the area serviced by a distribution center is expanded?
7. When should profit be considered in location analysis? Discuss the usefulness of cost-profit-volume analysis in locating a service operation.
8. What are the steps in solving the location problem?
9. Is monetary cost or profit always the appropriate criterion for location decisions? Why?
10. Which of the factors discussed in the chapter are most important in determining the location of the following? Briefly explain the reason for your answer.
    a. A garment plant
    b. A paper mill
    c. An automobile repair shop
    d. A distribution warehouse
11. a. What factors would lead a company to be market-oriented rather than materials-oriented in selecting its location?
    b. What factors favor a materials orientation?

PROBLEMS

1. Each factor used in evaluating potential sites was assigned a weight to represent its relative importance for a particular facility to be constructed. Four potential sites were then assigned points on a scale between 0 and a best possible score of 100, to express how well the site scored in regard to a particular factor. Rank the four sites shown in the table below on the basis of the total weighted points for each site.

		Site			
FACTOR	WEIGHT	A	B	C	D
Site and construction cost	0.10	90	60	80	85
Operating cost	0.10	90	80	90	80
Traffic count	0.30	60	90	85	70
Convenient access	0.20	80	75	90	90
Parking area	0.20	90	80	90	80
Surrounding population	0.10	60	90	85	70

2. Donald Donavan is comparing two sites for his sales and repair shop, which he has decided to relocate from its present location in a declining downtown business district. Both the sites he is considering have high traffic counts, which Donald feels is an important factor. From reading trade magazines and talking with people in similar

businesses, he estimates that the average number of customers each day will be about 0.5 percent of the daily traffic count. Donald estimates that the value of the average sale per customer will continue to be $25 worth of goods and services—the average value of goods and services sold at his present location. The average cost of the goods and services he sells is equal to 60 percent of the retail price.

Donald wants to recover the building and site costs over 10 years with a 14 percent return on the unrecovered investment. The capital recovery in 10 years with a 14 percent return will be treated as a fixed annual cost equal to 19.17 percent of the initial investment. The cost estimates and traffic count for the two sites are shown in the following table. The business will be operated 260 days per year. Compare the annual before-tax profit for the two sites.

FACTOR	SITE I	SITE 2
Average weekday traffic count	20,260	24,870
Cost of site	$125,000	$150,000
Site preparation	$ 10,000	$ 14,000
Building cost	$125,000	$125,000
Operating costs (clerical, maintenance, insurance, taxes, utilities, etc.)	$50,000	$50,000

3. Your company is considering expanding into the Sun Belt. Your industry is heavily dependent on water transportation, so the preliminary research has narrowed the location to three sites near port facilities in Memphis, New Orleans, and St. Louis. On the basis of the following data, which site is preferable? Show your computations.

RELEVANT FACTORS	MEMPHIS	NEW ORLEANS	ST. LOUIS
Variable costs per unit	$1.80	$2.00	$1.95
Fixed costs/year	$150,000.00	$300,000.00	$400,000.00
Price per unit	$3.00	$3.00	$3.00
Volume (units/year)	300,000	250,000	325,000

4. The Michael Corporation has plants in three cities. It distributes products from these plants to some customers and to two distribution centers. The company is planning to open a third distribution center in either Oklahoma City or Amarillo. The costs of shipping products from the company's plants to its present and prospective distribution center locations are given in the following table along with the plant capacities and requirements for each distribution center.

SHIPPING COSTS FROM PLANTS TO CURRENT AND POTENTIAL DISTRIBUTION CENTERS

DISTRIBUTION CENTER	SAN JOSE	SALT LAKE CITY	LITTLE ROCK	DEMAND AT DISTRIBUTION CENTER
St. Louis	$17	$13	$ 5	900
Phoenix	6	9	11	700
Amarillo	9	8	7	600
Oklahoma City	10	7	7	600
Capacity at plant	800	900	800	

a. Determine the best distribution pattern if Amarillo is selected as the location for the new distribution center.

b. Determine the best distribution pattern if Oklahoma City is selected.

c. Compute the total distribution cost for parts *a* and *b*, and determine which location yields the lowest total distribution cost.

d. What other factors might be important in the selection of a location for the new distribution center?

5. Nancy Andrews is president of the Andrews Electronic Company, which assembles pocket calculators and minicomputers. The company currently has plants in Los Angeles, California, and Richmond, Virginia. Ms. Andrews is evaluating the merits of opening a third plant in a more central part of the United States. She wishes to compare Denver and Omaha as potential locations.

Up to 1,000 units of raw material each month can be obtained from any of three locations: Oakland, Dallas, and Minneapolis. The monthly requirements for each of the present and potential locations are given in the following table along with the combined cost to purchase a unit of raw material at a specified source and ship it to the indicated plant location.

SOURCE OF MATERIALS	Cost per Unit at Destination				TOTAL UNITS AVAILABLE AT SOURCE
	LOS ANGELES	DENVER	OMAHA	RICHMOND	
Oakland	$ 6	$9	$10	$12	1,000
Dallas	9	8	7	8	1,000
Minneapolis	11	9	7	9	1,000
Requirements	600	550	550	500	

a. Decide whether the selection of Denver or Omaha would minimize the company's total cost of obtaining raw materials.

b. How much will these costs be if Denver is selected? If Omaha is selected?

c. What other factors do you think should be considered in reaching the decision?

6. The Hi Sun Chemical Division of a Taiwanese trading company is evaluating potential sites for an additional factory so it can better access the low labor costs and high potential demand of mainland China. The company currently operates factories in the Philippines and Malaysia. Hi Sun has narrowed the selection of a site for the new factory to two potential locations, Shenzhen and Xiamen. The costs of supplying these locations from the company's existing Asian facilities and the amounts of the available supplies and requirements are given in the following table.

SOURCE OF MATERIALS	Cost ($/Ton) from Source				AVAILABLE TONS/YEAR AT SOURCE
	MALAYSIA	PHILIPPINES	XIAMEN	SHENZHEN	
Thailand	$19	$22	$20	$19	8,000
Korea	28	23	18	20	5,000
Taiwan	16	18	15	17	4,000
Requirements	4,000	6,000	2,000	2,000	

a. By use of the transportation method, compute the lowest cost arrangement for supplying the factories if Shenzhen is selected for the site.

b. Repeat the analysis for Xiamen.

c. Which site will provide the lowest cost, and how much is the cost?

7. The Theodore Corporation supplies its entire market from its location in Kansas City. Orders of sufficient size are shipped by rail where rail service is available at the destination. Mr. Theodore is considering a revision in the way smaller orders are transported. All smaller orders (about 30,000 tons) are now delivered by truck from the Kansas City warehouse. Mr. Theodore is considering opening distribution centers in Salt Lake City and Pittsburgh to serve the western and eastern regions, respectively. These distribution centers would be supplied by rail from Kansas City and would then serve small-order customers in their regions by truck. The company would continue to serve small-order customers in the central region by truck from Kansas City. Under the new plan each of the three locations would have a volume of about 10,000 tons of small orders.

If the distribution system is changed, some equipment will be moved to the new distribution centers. Under the current system, the Kansas City operation has fixed costs of $1,000,000 per year. These costs would be reduced to $800,000 if the distribution centers were opened. Each of the two new distribution centers would have fixed costs of $300,000. Under the present system, the Kansas City operation carries an average inventory of 800 tons of product at a cost of $240 per ton per year. This inventory can be reduced to 500 tons if the distribution centers are operated. Each distribution center will carry an average inventory of 200 tons, and the carrying cost is estimated to be $240 per ton per year at these locations also. If the distribution centers are used, there will be additional costs of $4 per ton to load the railcar loads and $4 per ton to unload and handle the product at the distribution centers. A cost of $5 per ton to load the truck shipments will be paid under either distribution alternative.

A major cost difference will result from shipping by rail rather than by truck from the plant to the distribution centers. The cost to ship from Kansas City to Salt Lake City is $3.31 per cwt (hundredweight) by rail and $7.90 per cwt by truck. The cost to ship from Kansas City to Pittsburgh by rail is $2.03 per cwt; by truck it is $2.48 per cwt. It is assumed that the truck costs for delivery from the distribution center will be approximately the same as the distribution costs in each region if the items were shipped directly instead of going through the distribution centers.

   a. Compare the costs of the two alternatives.

   b. What factors other than costs might be important in this comparison?

8. A company is performing a simplified analysis to determine approximately how far apart it should locate its warehouses. The company estimates that the fixed costs of operating a warehouse are $400,000 per year. It wants to determine how large an area to serve with the warehouse. The company estimates that 10 orders per year will be received per square mile served by the warehouse and that the shipping cost is $0.02 per mile for each order.

   a. Begin with a 50-mile radius around the warehouse, and compute the number of orders to be served. Assume that each order in this circle will be shipped an average of 25 miles. Compute the total cost and cost per order in this 50-mile-radius area to be served by the warehouse.

   b. Add a ring to the service area by extending the radius an additional 50 miles. Assume the order within this ring must be shipped an average of 75 miles. Compute the cost per order if the warehouse services a 100-mile radius.

   c. Continue adding rings until you determine the radius at which the cost per order is minimized. What is the best radius?

   d. In what ways would an actual analysis differ from the simplification used in this analysis?

CASES

I. THE DOWNTOWN NATIONAL BANK

The Downtown National Bank (DNB) is located in a city of about 500,000. Mr. James, the chairman of the board, was the major force behind the chartering of the bank 5 years ago. He had been president and chief executive officer of one of the other top five banks in the state—the Empire Trust Company.

Empire had become so large, with mergers throughout the state through its holding company, that Mr. James felt its business and personal customers were becoming dissatisfied with the resulting "impersonal" relationship between them and the bank. With these and other circumstances in mind, Mr. James was convinced he could start a new bank that within a short time could compete with the top banks in the state.

The result was awe-inspiring; DNB's growth was nationally heralded. Within the first 2 years the bank's assets had grown to fifteen times the original capitalization. Mr. James's bank had exceeded even his own optimistic expectations. At the most recent board meeting he complimented everyone in the bank for believing in his convictions and making them work so effectively. Every person associated with the bank felt a personal pride and hoped to be able to take a breather after this accomplishment.

Mr. James, however, announced a plan to seek new personal accounts as aggressively as the bank had sought—and would continue to seek—accounts with correspondent banks and businesses. Mr. Chase, who had spearheaded the marketing department in its initial record-breaking program, was selected to devise a plan of attack on the new expansion policy. Currently the DNB operates from a single downtown location, and everyone knew that the new policy meant suburban branches. Mr. Chase was directed to find the three best suburban locations.

In narrowing his general criteria, Mr. Chase defined his goal as finding those locations that could provide the greatest potential for personal deposits. Going a step further, he evaluated his product—money; there was no doubt that money was the basic product. But money from one bank was the same as money from another. Service—what a bank did with money, how and when it received and disbursed it, and the related services it provided—made the important difference. He made a mental note to check the services offered by competing branch banks, but he rationalized that site selection should be unrelated to services. Regardless of location, the bank would determine the services it would offer as an independent issue. Going back to his basic product, Mr. Chase tried to evaluate its nature. People use money daily, so it is a convenience good rather than a durable good. He needed the three most convenient locations—convenient to the best deposit potential!

Mr. Chase decided to take a personal survey of some of his friends and neighbors to find out what they felt were the requirements of a convenient location for a branch bank. His responses revealed three criteria for convenience:

1. It must be near where I live.
2. It must be near where I shop.
3. It must be near where I work.

Mr. Chase realized that his survey responses described any area in the county. Slightly frustrated, he decided to see what other banks were doing in terms of branch locations. He obtained a map and located every branch bank in the county. Recognizing

Table 5.4
BRANCH BANKING MARKET SEGMENT ANALYSIS

MARKET SEGMENT	NO. OF BANKING FACILITIES	TOTAL ANNUAL FAMILY INCOME (MILLIONS OF DOLLARS)	AVERAGE TOTAL FAMILY INCOME PER BANKING FACILITY (MILLIONS OF DOLLARS)	FAMILY INCOME PER BRANCH WITH ONE ADDITIONAL BRANCH BANK (MILLIONS OF DOLLARS)	GROWTH RATE (PERCENT)
Valley Hills	2	$ 98.6	$49.3	$32.9	+48.8%
Woodland	2	86.8	43.4	28.9	−2.2
Crestville	2	80.2	40.1	26.7	+3.2
Gardenside	1	34.0	34.0	17.0	+24.5
East Thomas	1	32.2	32.2	16.1	−12.5
Pleasant Grove	1	31.1	31.1	15.5	+16.2
Five Points West	4	122.4	30.6	24.5	−11.4
Cahaba	1	28.9	28.9	14.5	+10.5
Trusstown	1	28.3	28.3	14.2	+12.2
Avondale	1	27.6	27.6	13.8	+5.7
Ironwood	4	103.2	20.6	20.6	+8.9
Hueyville	2	49.0	24.5	16.3	+11.7
Herbert	3	67.5	22.5	16.9	+52.8
Tarrance	2	40.4	20.2	13.5	−11.7
Montdale	4	76.4	19.1	15.3	+42.9
Forestdale	2	34.8	17.4	11.6	+19.2
Wyman	3	49.8	16.6	12.5	−1.1
Homeville	6	90.6	15.1	12.9	+5.3
Graysville	1	15.1	15.1	7.6	+14.3
Centerville	3	38.7	12.9	9.7	+27.8
North Morgan	2	24.2	12.1	8.1	−16.5
Downtown	22	182.4	8.3	7.9	−52.3

that competing branches tended to cluster in certain areas, primarily shopping areas, he decided to segregate the clusters into market segments. He then went through the tedious process of determining, through census data, the number of families living in each segment and the amount of average family income earned per segment. Mr. Chase then developed the information shown in Table 5.4, which identified the total number of branches in a segment and the total annual income of those families per bank branch. He also noted on the table the population growth rate for the previous 10 years for each segment and the family income per branch if a new branch were added in the segment.

He reasoned that for two given segments with the same total annual family income, the deposit potential of a new branch would be greater where more potential deposit funds were available.

1. Is a bank materials-oriented or market-oriented?
2. Discuss the "systems approach" as it relates to this case.
3. What other data would you suggest that Mr. Chase evaluate before making his recommendations?
4. Which three market segments would you recommend as the best locations on the basis of the information presented in this case? Why?
5. Within each of Mr. Chase's three recommended market segments, what criteria would you use in selecting the actual sites for the branches?

2. A LOCATION DECISION USING A POINT RATING SYSTEM

A growing chemical processing company, Excellent, with its home office in Tulsa, Oklahoma, is considering opening an oil refinery on either the Atlantic Coast or the Gulf Coast. Company executives have selected two potential sites for location of the new facility, one near Norfolk, Virginia, and the other near Mobile, Alabama.

Shipment from the rich oil fields of the Middle East would be less costly with a Norfolk location, and currently most of the company's oil comes from the Middle East. But the prospects of future availability of this supply at competitive prices are not encouraging. The possibility of further restrictions on tanker shipments, import duties, and another oil embargo make investment with the Middle East supply in mind less desirable. The potential on the Gulf Coast is much better. In fact, recent testing indicates that the Alabama site may be within a few hundred miles of one of the most productive oil fields of the 1990s.

It is obvious that proper evaluation of this situation is crucial to the success of the company as a whole. Much time and money must be spent to resolve the issue. But this is not the only location consideration; other costs must also be considered. What would be the comparative costs of such things as construction, utilities, transportation, and labor?

Property and labor have been found to be less costly in Mobile. Indeed, almost every cost is lower in Mobile. Mobile is located farther from the manufacturing centers of the North, however, and therefore most materials and supplies are more expensive there as a result of the additional shipping and transportation costs.

After construction is completed, operating costs will become crucial. They may make the difference between success and failure for the new plant. For Excellent the most important of these costs are labor, materials, utilities, transportation, pollution control, and taxes. Data have been collected and statistical forecasts made to determine the possible future impact of each factor on operating costs. Mobile has been found to have lower total operating costs.

Norfolk, however, is located nearer much of the planned market, and therefore shipping costs would be less from an Atlantic Coast plant. In addition, less competition exists along the Atlantic seaboard. Several refinery plants have been opened recently along the Gulf Coast, and regional competition for everything from product demand to professional employees will be more difficult there.

If Excellent goes through with its proposed expansion, many key personnel from the Tulsa office will be asked to transfer to the new location. A poll of those employees indicated that most would prefer to move to Norfolk. Data from the Norfolk Chamber of Commerce shows that there are more hospitals, schools, and recreational opportunities there.

In sum, more than 200 factors and considerations have been studied. Those of prime importance are outlined above. Other considerations of some relevance are labor union strength, climate (Mobile is located in a potential hurricane path, and Norfolk could have winter storms that would completely halt operations and cost Excellent many thousands of dollars), public opinion, and water supply.

After this exhaustive study, the company executives are still undecided as to which location to select. But one of the top executives at Excellent has worked out a point rating evaluation of relevant factors for Excellent, using statistical methods plus his own personal judgment. The results of his ratings are listed in Table 5.5 and indicate that Mobile is a slightly more desirable location for Excellent's new plant. The executive realizes that this conclusion is, of course, based on the proper assignment

Table 5.5
POINTS ASSIGNED TO TWO LOCATIONS, BY FACTOR

FACTOR	MAXIMUM POSSIBLE POINTS	Location	
		NORFOLK	MOBILE
Availability of raw materials	1,000	700	800
Construction and site costs	500	300	400
Operating costs	1,000	700	900
Relevant market factors	900	800	600
Living conditions and desirability	400	300	200
Labor union strength	50	40	30
Climate	100	70	80
Public opinion	50	40	40
Water supply	70	60	50
Total		3,010	3,100

of points. So he has explained the system and his point assignments to several other executives in the Tulsa office, and most agree with his findings. This conclusion is based primarily on the lower operating and construction costs in the Mobile area. The potential availability of an adequate supply of domestic crude oil also contributes significantly to the decision.

1. Should Excellent locate in Mobile on the basis of this study?
2. Is the total point difference between Norfolk and Mobile significant?
3. Do you agree with the point assignments?

BIBLIOGRAPHY

Ballou, Ronald H. *Business Logistics Management: Planning and Control.* 2d ed. Englewood Cliffs, N.J.: Prentice-Hall, 1985.

Best, William J., and Mamoru Watanabe. "Logistics Planning for Japanese Firms Seeking U.S. Sites." *Site Selection,* August 1989, pp. 1317–1321.

Bowersox, Donald J., David J. Closs, and Omar K. Helferich. *Logistical Management: A Systems Integration of Physical Distribution, Manufacturing Support, and Materials Procurement.* 3d ed. New York: Macmillan, 1986.

Canary, Patrick H. "International Transportation Factors in Site Selection." *Site Selection,* October 1988, pp. 1217–1219.

Carlson, Richard A. "What You Should Know before Choosing New Office Spaces." *Administrative Management,* June 1981, pp. 28–30.

Cooney, James L. "Expand or Move: Some Intangible Factors in Making the Choice." *Industrial Development,* May–June 1980, pp. 2–4.

Doyle, P., I. Fenwick, and G. P. Savage. "A Model for Evaluating Branch Locations and Performance." *Journal of Bank Research,* Summer 1981, pp. 90–95.

Francis, Richard L., Leon F. McGinnis, Jr., and John A. White. *Facility Layout and Location: An Analytical Approach.* 2d ed. Englewood Cliffs, N.J.: Prentice-Hall, 1992.

Johnson, Eric. "New Rules to Use in Site Location Today." *Dun's Business Month,* November 1986, pp. 73–87.

Johnson, James C., and Donald F. Wood. *Contemporary Physical Distribution and Logistics.* 3d ed. New York: Macmillan, 1986.

Lambert, Douglas M., and James R. Stock. *Strategic Physical Distribution Management.* 2d ed. Homewood, Ill.: Irwin, 1987.

Lyne, Jack. "Quality-of-Life Factors Dominate Many Facility Location Decisions." *Site Selection Handbook,* August 1988, pp. 868–870.

Mason, J. Barry, and Morris L. Mayer. *Modern Retailing: Theory and Practice.* 5th ed. Plano, Tex.: Business Publications, 1989.

Morgenstein, Melvin, and Harriet Strongin. *Modern Retailing.* 2d ed. New York: Wiley, 1987. Chap. 8.

Rees, Terry L. "Site Selection in Europe—A Case Study." *Site Selection,* October 1988, pp. 1223–1225.

Schmenner, Roger W. *Making Business Location Decisions.* Englewood Cliffs, N.J.: Prentice-Hall, 1982.

Sharman, Graham. "The Rediscovery of Logistics." *Harvard Business Review,* September–October 1984, pp. 71–79.

Tompkins, James A., and John A. White. *Facilities Planning.* New York: Wiley, 1984.

WORK MEASUREMENT AND TIME STANDARDS

W hen a company designs jobs and other elements of the operations system, it establishes the employees' work activities. The time required to perform different work activities is important for several reasons, which we discuss. This supplement presents an overview of many of the more common methods that companies use to estimate the time required to perform jobs.

WORK MEASUREMENT

Work measurement is the application of techniques to determine the time necessary for a qualified worker to perform a particular task. The time that a job is expected to take is expressed as a "time standard," "work standard," "production standard," or simply "standard." A time standard states the time a qualified worker, working at a normal rate of speed, will require to perform the specified task. It may be expressed as minutes per unit of output, units of output per hour, or some other ratio of time to work.

Uses for Time Standards

Time standards are useful for several purposes such as the following:

- *Capacity planning:* to know how much capacity is required for a given level of output
- *Scheduling:* to know when a customer's work will be ready and when employees will be available to work on other assignments
- *Loading:* to see that sufficient but not excessive work has been planned to effectively utilize available processes, and to equitably distribute work among employees
- *Cost estimating:* to know how much the wage portion of cost is for providing goods and services
- *Evaluation:* to compare improvement suggestions such as alternative methods or process steps to see if they facilitate better performance or to provide a baseline for determining if employees have attained some basic skill level

Where Work Measurement Can Be Applied

Many jobs in offices and factories can be studied and measured. There are three general criteria for measurable jobs:

1. The work should be identifiable in terms of the number of units a person performed.
2. The work should be performed in a reasonably consistent manner.
3. There should be a sufficient volume of the work to justify performing a study and keeping counts and records.

Work measurement is widely used in manufacturing operations where the work or at least some parts of the work are repetitive. Fewer service operations use work measurement. Slowness in making use of work measurement in service settings has been attributed to several characteristics, generally related to the fact that the work is typically more variable and much of it is mental. It is difficult to count mental work or to performance-rate it.

METHODS USED IN SETTING STANDARDS

Work measurement can be performed by several methods, some of which are briefly discussed in the following sections.

Time Study

Fundamentally, stopwatch time study or *time study* is performed by timing a worker as the job is performed, summing the times for the necessary elements of the job, adjusting this time if an abnormal work pace was observed, and then adding time for personal and rest breaks.

Analysts who perform time study should select an operator who is properly trained and uses the proper work method. They should tell the worker that they want to observe and time the job through a considerable number of cycles and should try to allay any fears or suspicions the worker may have. After an analyst has observed the job sufficiently to identify the necessary work involved, he or she lists the necessary *work elements* and begins to record the amount of time each element requires. Dividing the work into elements can be helpful for several reasons:

1. The list of elements and their times helps describe the work method and shows how the time for performing the job is distributed among the elements. Longer work elements often are the targets for methods improvement efforts because they account for the greatest portion of the total.

2. A worker's rate of performance may not be the same for all elements of a job. The time-study analyst must adjust the operator's time to represent the time that the average worker would take. If the operator is much faster than the average worker for some work elements, these elements should be given a different performance rating than those performed more slowly.

3. Machine-paced elements should be separated from those that are under the control of the operator.

4. Some elements may not be repeated every cycle but may recur every tenth cycle, every sixteenth cycle, or at some other interval.

5. Times for similar work elements from several jobs may be compared to help keep standards uniform.

6. Element times can be collected and cataloged into "standard data" that can possibly be combined to arrive at standards for other jobs without the need for time study.

Figure F.1 shows a time-study observation form for the task of posting inventory records. Notice that the task has been divided into elements and that one of the elements was not repeated during every cycle that was observed. It was observed in this study that element 3 occurred during only about 8 percent of the inventory transactions that were processed. Therefore, 0.08 times the time to perform element 3 was added to the standard. The study period must be long enough to obtain a good estimate of the delays and interruptions that confront workers.

DETERMINING THE NUMBER OF CYCLES TO TIME The number of cycles that should be timed increases with the degree of accuracy desired for the standard and with the variability of the observed times. After 10 or 15 cycles have been timed and some preliminary calculations have been made, the total number of cycles that should be timed can be determined by use of a formula or graph. Extreme time values, both high and low, for any element should be discarded and not used in estimating the variability of data because they might represent erroneous readings.

FORMULA FOR SAMPLE SIZE Assuming that a normal probability distribution applies, a confidence interval may be constructed that has a given probability (that is, "confidence") that the interval will contain the actual mean time to perform the task. A 95 percent confidence interval means that intervals developed by this procedure will contain the actual mean in about 95 percent of the cases, so the probability is 0.95 that the actual mean is estimated within the desired accuracy A, expressed as a decimal fraction

Figure F.1 Example of a Time-Study Observation Sheet

Operation Posting Inventory Records	Date 3/9/81	Operator B. Ratliff	
Department Inventory Control	Shift 1	Observer R. Baker	
Part	Study		
Size	Sheet 1 of 1		

REMARKS Telephone interruptions and delays during study = 9.6%

ELEMENT DESCRIPTION	1	2	3	4	5	6	7	8	9	10	11	12	13	14	15	Rating	Normal Time	Minutes per Cycle
1. Read part number from record, find and pull card	0.14	0.15	0.21	0.17	0.19	0.14	0.17	0.18	0.18	0.21	0.18	0.17	0.18	0.20	0.18	1.10	(2.65/15)(1.10) = 0.1943	0.1943
2. Transfer usage or receipt from requisition or receiving report to card and compute new inventory balance	0.45	0.42	0.50	0.51	0.43	0.48	0.54	0.44 missed	0.49	0.43	0.49	0.50	0.43	0.48		1.00	(6.59/14)(1.00) = 0.4707	0.4707
3. Write purchase requisition if on hand and on order below reorder level (8% of transactions)	0.88	0.92	1.06	0.90	0.82											1.00	(4.58/5)(1.00) = 0.916	0.0733
4. Replace inventory record card in file	0.07	0.08	0.11	0.09	0.05	0.07	0.06	0.08	0.06	0.05	0.07	0.11	0.05	0.05	0.06	1.10	(1.06/15)(1.10) = 0.0777	0.0777
																	NORMAL	0.8160
																	x 1.206	
																	STANDARD	0.9841

ALLOWANCES:
Personal & fatigue 11.0%
Delays 9.6%

20.6% TOTAL ALLOWANCE

of the actual mean. The equation for the required number of observations is

$$n = \left(\frac{Zs}{A\bar{x}} \right)^2 \qquad \text{[F.1]}$$

where n = total number of observations that should be taken to provide desired accuracy

$\bar{x}$ = mean of the times already collected

A = accuracy desired expressed as decimal fraction of the true value

Z = standardized normal deviate that has (1 − confidence) /2 as the area remaining in the tail of the distribution beyond the value of Z

s = estimated standard deviation of distribution of element times, based on observations already made

A time-study analyst would observe several cycles, say 10 or 15, and compute n on the basis of the data obtained at that stage of the study. Sampling would then be continued until n observations were obtained. If the element times are to be used to develop a catalog of times required to perform given parts of the cycle, the calculation of n should be based on data for the most constraining element—the one that yields the largest value of n (that is, the one with the largest coefficient of variation).

Suppose we are interested in estimating the actual mean time to perform element 4 of the task represented in Figure F.1. Assume that we wish to provide 95 percent confidence that the true mean time to perform element 4 is estimated within 10 percent accuracy. To simplify the calculations, only the first six observations are used, even though at least two or three times this number of observations probably would be used in an actual study. The observed times for the six observations are shown in Table F.1. The calculations used to estimate the sample size required to yield 10 percent accuracy with 95 percent confidence are also shown. This sample size is 26 observations.

DETERMINING SAMPLE SIZE BY GRAPH Alternatively, the number of observations for a given accuracy can be determined from a graph such as Figure F.2. Suppose that we had taken 10 observations of some task and the trial mean was 4.21 minutes with a standard deviation of 0.73 minute. The coefficient of variation for these data is 0.73/4.21 = 0.173, or about 17 percent. Referring to Figure F.2, we see that approximately 40 observations should be taken to establish 95 percent confidence that we have esti-

Table F.1
OBSERVED ELEMENT TIMES FOR SIX OBSERVATIONS

OBSERVATION	OBSERVED ELEMENT TIME X_i	X^2_i
1	0.07	0.0049
2	0.08	0.0064
3	0.11	0.0121
4	0.09	0.0081
5	0.05	0.0025
6	0.07	0.0049
	0.47	0.0389

$$\bar{x} = \frac{\Sigma x_i}{n'} = \frac{0.47}{6} = 0.07833$$

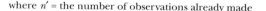

$$s = \sqrt{\frac{\Sigma x^2 - (\Sigma x)^2/n'}{n' - 1}} = \sqrt{\frac{0.0389 - 0.47^2/6}{5}} = 0.0205$$

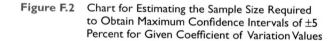

$$n = \left(\frac{Zs}{A\bar{x}} \right)^2 = \left[\frac{1.96(0.0205)}{0.10(0.07833)} \right]^2 = 26.31$$

where n' = the number of observations already made

Figure F.2   Chart for Estimating the Sample Size Required to Obtain Maximum Confidence Intervals of ±5 Percent for Given Coefficient of Variation Values

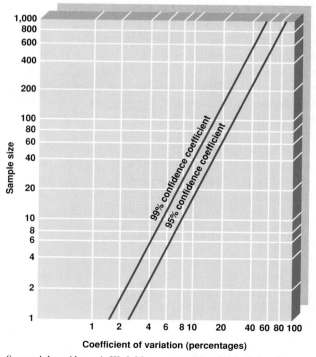

Source: Adam Abruzzi, *Work Measurement* (New York: Columbia University Press, 1952), p. 161. Reprinted by permission of the publisher.

mated the true mean cycle time within 5 percent of its value.

ADJUSTMENT FOR WORKER'S PACE The objective of a time study is to arrive at a standard that is suitable for the normal employee; yet the employee who was timed may not have been working at a normal rate of speed. An adjustment called *performance rating,* pace rating, leveling, or normalizing is made to adjust the observed times to the time required by someone working at a "normal" pace. Rating is the process of comparing the worker's rate of performance with the observer's concept of a normal work rate. Notice that each element of the task in Figure F.1 was assigned a rating before the normal time was computed. The normal pace is not some optimal rate that only the best workers can achieve. Generally a standard is established so that most employees can achieve it without overexertion. A *normal work pace* should be one at which qualified workers can work all day without undue fatigue.

Even though it is a company's prerogative to determine what it considers a normal pace, it is important that the company be consistent in its rating so as to provide equitable expectations for all its employees.

NORMAL TIME The *normal time* for a job is the time it should take a qualified worker to perform the essential elements of a job while working at a normal pace. The *actual time* is the amount of time taken by the particular worker who was studied, at the pace he or she worked during the study. The normal time (NT) can be found by multiplying the observed actual time (AT) for the essential elements of the job by the overall performance rating for the job as a ratio to the normal efficiency rating (usually 100 percent).

$$\text{NT} = \text{AT} \times \frac{\text{performance rating}}{\text{normal efficiency rating}} \qquad \text{[F.2]}$$

A worker who was working 15 percent faster than what is considered a normal pace would be given a performance rating of 115 percent. Equation F.2 would add 15 percent to this worker's time to determine the time that would be expected for the job when a worker was working at the normal pace. If we assume that an analyst had measured an actual time of 4.23 minutes for this job, the normal time would be

$$\text{NT} = 4.23 \times 1.15 = 4.86 \text{ minutes}$$

Working at the normal pace, a worker would be expected to take 4.86 minutes to perform the job.

ALLOWANCES Even though it would take only 4.86 minutes to perform the above job at a normal pace, a company would be unrealistic to allow only this amount of time for each job cycle. Workers need rest breaks during the day, and some delays are bound to occur. *Standard times* that are used for scheduling and pricing products should include time for unavoidable delays, personal time, and rest time to relieve fatigue. *Personal, fatigue,* and *delay allowances* are added as a percentage of the normal time so that the standard time (ST) is found by equation F.3:

$$\text{ST} = \text{NT} \ (1 + \text{allowances}) \qquad \text{[F.3]}$$

where the allowances are expressed as a decimal fraction of the normal time. Some guidelines for personal and fatigue allowances are shown in Table F.2.

DELAYS Delays may occur on a job through no fault of the operator. He or she may have to wait for a crane to come and remove a work item from the machine and place another on it, for a computer to respond, or experience some other unavoidable delay. A company should incorporate time for unavoidable delays in standards. Conversely, time for avoidable delays should not be included in a standard. The percentages that should be allowed for unavoidable delays can be determined by a method called *work sampling* or *ratio delay studies.*

DETERMINING DELAY ALLOWANCES BY WORK SAMPLING Work sampling has been used extensively to determine allowances used to convert normal times to standard times. An *allowance* is a percentage of the normal working time that is allowed for unavoidable delays. Work sampling involves observing a worker at random times during the day and noting the type of activity in which he or she is engaged. The basis for work sampling is sampling theory, according to which an adequate-sized random sample should contain observations of various subcategories of work effort in the same proportion as the proportion of time consumed by these subcategories. A

Table F.2

PERCENTAGES TO BE ADDED TO THE NORMAL TIME FOR AN ELEMENT TO MAKE ALLOWANCES FOR ITS WORK CONDITIONS

1. Constant allowances		
(a) Personal allowance	5	
(b) Basic fatigue allowance	4	
2. Variable allowances		
A. Standing allowance	2	
B. Abnormal position allowance		
(a) Slightly awkward	0	
(b) Awkward (bending)	2	
(c) Very awkward (lying, stretching)	7	
C. Use of force or muscular energy (lifting, pulling, pushing)		
Weight lifted, pounds		
5	0	
10	1	
15	2	
20	3	
25	4	
30	5	
35	7	
40	9	
45	11	
50	13	
60	17	
70	22	
D. Bad light		
(a) Slightly below recommended	0	
(b) Well below	2	
(c) Quite inadequate	5	
E. Atmospheric conditions (heat and humidity)—variable	0–10	
F. Close attention		
(a) Fairly fine work	0	
(b) Fine or exacting	2	
(c) Very fine or exacting	5	
G. Noise level		
(a) Continuous	0	
(b) Intermittent—loud	2	
(c) Intermittent—very loud	5	
(d) High-pitched—loud	5	
H. Mental strain		
(a) Fairly complex process	1	
(b) Complex or wide span of attention	4	
(c) Very complex	8	
I. Monotony		
(a) Low	0	
(b) Medium	1	
(c) High	4	
J. Tediousness		
(a) Rather tedious	0	
(b) Tedious	2	
(c) Very tedious	5	

Source: Benjamin W. Niebel, *Motion and Time Study,* 8th ed. (Homewood, Ill.: Irwin, 1988), p. 416.

work-sampling study to determine the proper allowance should include observations of workers at random times to note whether they are engaged in normal work activities, unavoidably delayed, or involved in some other activity such as breaks or other avoidable delays. The subject of interest is the ratio of unavoidable delay time to normal work time, so we will know how much time should be added to the normal time to allow for delays over which the operator has no control.

Suppose that an analyst observes a lathe operator at 150 randomly selected times. During some of those times the operator may be waiting for a supervisor or inspector to give directions or check the work, waiting at a toolroom to get some tool or attachment needed to perform the job, waiting for someone to help lift an object on or off the machine. These times are recorded as unavoidable delays. At each observation the analyst makes a tally mark in one of three categories, indicating the activity of the operator at that moment. Suppose that the total tally marks in each category are as shown in Table F.3. Obviously an allowance must be provided for delays that cannot be prevented. This allowance as a percentage of the normal work time for the observed job is $16/112 = 14.3$ percent.

Table F.3

OBSERVED FREQUENCIES OF ACTIVITIES

ACTIVITY	OBSERVED FREQUENCY
Normal work activities	112
Avoidable delays	22
Unavoidable delays	16
Total observations	150

Standard Data

Several jobs in a company may contain the same work element. It is not necessary to time these work elements in every job if a reasonable standard already has been determined from one or more previously studied jobs. A company can maintain a data base of work element durations obtained through previous time studies conducted at its facilities, that is, *standard data*. If the times required for all the elements of a new job are available in standard data, they can be totaled to arrive at the normal time for the job. Personal, fatigue, and delay allowances have to be added to the normal time to arrive at a standard for the new job.

Sometimes an element time is determined by interpolation of standard data among existing element times. A company might plot the time required to sand the surface on each of several different sizes of wooden shelves. The graph, as shown in Figure F.3, could then be used to determine the time for sanding various other sizes of shelves.

Standard data have some advantages over stopwatch time study. Since the standards from which the data base of element times is taken have been used previously, a company can have some assurance that the times are acceptable to both management and workers. Standard times can save the cost and interruption involved in having a time-study analyst go to the workplace, talk with the operator, and study the job. Besides, some workers resent being timed as they work. Another advantage of standard data is that standards can be determined for jobs that are not yet in operation. Production of new products or potential changes in work methods can be evaluated without the time, disruptions, and expense that would occur if they all had to be tried.

Predetermined Motion Times

Any manual task is composed of basic motions such as reach, grasp, move, turn, or other short motions arranged in a particular sequence. Just as any word in the English language can be composed from only twenty-six letters of the alphabet, most manual tasks can be described by a list of the sequence in which relatively few basic motions occur and recur. Through thousands of measurements under controlled conditions, researchers have recorded the time required to perform each basic motion. By summing the appropriate entries from tables that list these *predetermined motion times,* an analyst can determine the time required to perform various manual tasks. It does not matter whether a person is reaching for a pencil, a scalpel, or a wrench; the time required to reach a certain distance is approximately the same. Some adjustments may be required to allow for the particular conditions under which the reach occurs. Appropriate allowances should be added to arrive at a standard time for the job.

Predetermined motion times differ from standard data in that the predetermined motion-time technique breaks a job into much finer detail than the job elements that are used for standard data, and the times for these minute parts of a person's motions are determined through observing a large number of persons outside the using company. The advantages for predetermined motion times are similar to those for standard data.

METHODS-TIME MEASUREMENT One of the better-known predetermined motion-time systems is *methods-time measurement (MTM)*. Figure F.4 shows MTM tables for some basic motions and the conditions under which these motions can occur. A trained analyst would break a manual task into the basic motions required to perform it and judge the conditions under which each motion will occur, then sum the appropriate predetermined times for all the basic motions involved.

Figure F.3   Standard Data for a Work Element Graphed to Facilitate Interpolation

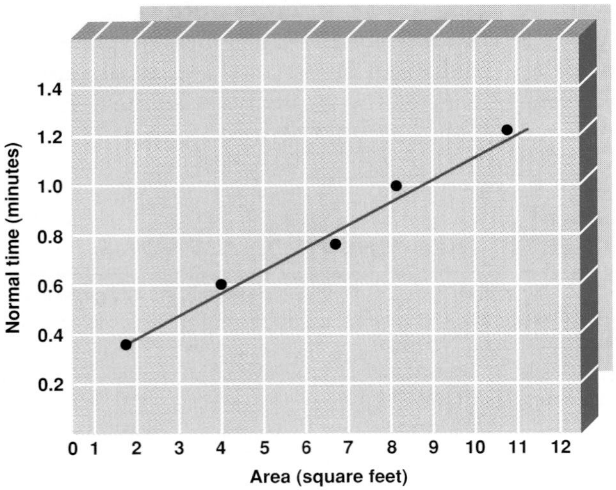

Figure F.4 Methods-Time Measurement Application Data
(times in TMUs)

> Do not attempt to use this chart or apply Methods-Time Measurement in any way unless you understand the proper application of the data. This statement is included as a word of caution to prevent difficulties resulting from misapplication of the data.

1 TMU	= .00001	hour		1 hour	= 100,000.0 TMU
	= .0006	minute		1 minute	= 1,666.7 TMU
	= .036	seconds		1 second	= 27.8 TMU

TABLE I — REACH — R

Distance Moved Inches	Time TMU				Hand in Motion		CASE AND DESCRIPTION
	A	B	C or D	E	A	B	
3/4 or less	2.0	2.0	2.0	2.0	1.6	1.6	**A** Reach to object in fixed location, or to object in other hand or on which other hand rests.
1	2.5	2.5	3.6	2.4	2.3	2.3	
2	4.0	4.0	5.9	3.8	3.5	2.7	
3	5.3	5.3	7.3	5.3	4.5	3.6	**B** Reach to single object in location which may vary slightly from cycle to cycle.
4	6.1	6.4	8.4	6.8	4.9	4.3	
5	6.5	7.8	9.4	7.4	5.3	5.0	
6	7.0	8.6	10.1	8.0	5.7	5.7	
7	7.4	9.3	10.8	8.7	6.1	6.5	**C** Reach to object jumbled with other objects in a group so that search and select occur.
8	7.9	10.1	11.5	9.3	6.5	7.2	
9	8.3	10.8	12.2	9.9	6.9	7.9	
10	8.7	11.5	12.9	10.5	7.3	8.6	
12	9.6	12.9	14.2	11.8	8.1	10.1	
14	10.5	14.4	15.6	13.0	8.9	11.5	**D** Reach to a very small object of where accurate grasp is required.
16	11.4	15.8	17.0	14.2	9.7	12.9	
18	12.3	17.2	18.4	15.5	10.5	14.4	
20	13.1	18.6	19.8	16.7	11.3	15.8	
22	14.0	20.1	21.2	18.0	12.1	17.3	**E** Reach to indefinite location to get hand in position for body balance or next motion or out of way.
24	14.9	21.5	22.5	19.2	12.9	18.8	
26	15.8	22.9	23.9	20.4	13.7	20.2	
28	16.7	24.4	25.3	21.7	14.5	21.7	
30	17.5	25.8	26.7	22.9	15.3	23.2	
Additional	0.4	0.7	0.7	0.6			TMU per inch over 30 inches

TABLE III A — TURN — T

Weight	Time TMU for Degrees Turned										
	30°	45°	60°	75°	90°	106°	120°	136°	150°	165°	180°
Small - 0 to 2 Pounds	2.8	3.5	4.1	4.8	5.4	6.1	6.8	7.4	8.1	8.7	9.4
Medium - 2.1 to 10 Pounds	4.4	5.5	6.5	7.5	8.5	9.6	10.6	11.6	12.7	13.7	14.8
Large - 10.1 to 36 Pounds	8.4	10.5	12.3	14.4	16.2	18.3	20.4	22.2	24.3	26.1	28.2

TABLE V — POSITION* — P

CLASS OF FIT		Symmetry	Easy to Handle	Difficult to Handle
1-Loose	No pressure required	S	5.6	11.2
		SS	9.1	14.7
		NS	10.4	16.0
2-Close	Light pressure required	S	16.2	21.8
		SS	19.7	26.3
		NS	21.0	26.6
3-Exset	Heavy pressure required	S	43.0	48.6
		SS	46.5	52.1
		NS	47.8	53.4
SUPPLEMENTARY RULE FOR SURFACE ALIGNMENT				
P1SE per alignment: >1/16<1/4"			P2SE per alignment: <1/16"	

TABLE II — MOVE — M

Distance Moved Inches	Time TMU			Hand in Motion B	Wt. Allowance			CASE AND DESCRIPTION
	A	B	C		Wt. (lb.) Up to	Dynamic Factor	Static Constant TMU	
3/4 or less	2.0	2.0	2.0	1.7				
1	2.5	2.9	3.4	2.3	2.5	1.00	0	**A** Move object to other hand or against stop.
2	3.6	4.6	5.2	2.9				
3	4.9	5.7	6.7	3.6	7.5	1.06	2.2	
4	6.1	6.9	8.0	4.3				
5	7.3	8.0	9.2	5.0	12.5	1.11	3.9	
6	8.1	8.9	10.3	5.7				
7	8.9	9.7	11.1	6.5	17.5	1.17	5.6	**B** Move object to approximate or indefinite location.
8	9.7	10.6	11.8	7.2				
9	10.5	11.5	12.7	7.9	22.5	1.22	7.4	
10	11.3	12.2	13.5	8.6				
12	12.9	13.4	15.2	10.0	27.5	1.28	9.1	
14	14.4	14.6	16.9	11.4				
16	16.0	15.8	18.7	12.8	32.5	1.33	10.8	**C** Move object to exact location.
18	17.6	17.0	20.4	14.2				
20	19.2	18.2	22.1	15.6	37.5	1.39	12.5	
22	20.8	19.4	23.8	17.0				
24	22.4	20.6	25.5	18.4	42.5	1.44	14.3	
26	24.0	21.8	27.3	19.8				
28	25.5	23.1	29.0	21.2	47.5	1.50	16.0	
30	27.1	24.3	30.7	22.7				
Additional	0.8	0.6	0.86					TMU per inch over 30 inches

Source: Copyrighted by the MTM Association for Standards and Research. No reprint permission without written consent from the MTM Association, 1411 Peterson Avenue, Park Ridge, Illinois 60068.

Historical Records

Standards are sometimes developed by counting the output of a department, person, or work center over some time during which a consistent type of work is being performed, then dividing the output by the number of worker-hours expended. The method is simple, but it tends to be less accurate than most other methods because it disregards adjustments for the worker's pace and for delays. That is, it is assumed that the level of diligence while the records were collected was satisfactory.

The accuracy of standards set by this method can be improved by conducting work sampling while historical data are being collected so that the work pace and percentage of time lost to delays can be estimated. The data can then be adjusted for delays or an abnormal work pace.

Work Sampling

Recall that work sampling is a method of analyzing work by taking a large number of observations, usually at random times, to see the relative frequency with which various activities occur. The percentage of the total observations a person or facility is engaged in a given activity approximates the percentage of the total work time spent in that activity. Assume, for example, that during a 2-hour study period an analyst made a total of 50 observations, and 10 of those observations showed the worker making entries in a customer contact log. It would be assumed that $10 \div 50$, or 20 percent, of the time was spent making entries in the log. Twenty percent of 2 hours is 24 minutes. If the log showed that 38 entries were made by the worker during the study, then it would be assumed that each entry took an average of $24 \div 38 = 0.632$ minute. The analyst might adjust this time by a performance rating established while the observations were made.

Some of the advantages and disadvantages of work sampling are presented in Table F.4.

NUMBER OF OBSERVATIONS REQUIRED   The number of observations required to estimate the proportion of time spent in delays or in any element of a job depends on the accuracy desired and the variability of the data. We may wish to know the proportion of work time spent in an activity within some given percentage of its true value. To keep the relative accuracy the same, the absolute accuracy must be increased if an activity represents only a small portion of the total time. Very large samples must be taken to estimate small proportions accurately.

Frequently a normal distribution is used as an approximation to the binomial distribution of a proportion. If we assume a normal approximation, the sample size needed to provide a specified accuracy and confidence is given by equation F.4.

$$n = \frac{Z^2}{A^2}\left(\frac{1-p}{p}\right) \qquad \text{[F.4]}$$

where A = accuracy desired as a decimal fraction of true proportion
p = proportion
Z = value from a standardized normal distribution required to give desired confidence interval
n = sample size

A small random sample of 50 or so observations can be used to make an initial estimate of p. Then equation F.4 can be used to see how large the total sample should be. Sampling is then resumed until the total sample is large enough to give the desired accuracy.

Table F.4
SOME ADVANTAGES AND DISADVANTAGES OF WORK SAMPLING IN COMPARISON WITH CONTINUOUS TIME STUDY

Advantages
Does not require extensive training to perform
Can simultaneously study several operators
Takes less of the observer's time and is less costly, particularly if the work cycle is lengthy
Observations are made over a more extended time, so they are more likely to take variations into account

Disadvantages
Does not permit as detailed a breakdown of types of activities
Study of a group provides an average but no measure of individual differences
Workers might intentionally change activity upon seeing the analyst, whereas this distortion is more difficult to produce under the continuous observation of time study

Suppose that work sampling in a hospital has been conducted, and 16 of 100 observations have shown a nurse to be working with charts and other papers. Suppose we want 95 percent confidence that we have estimated the true proportion within 10 percent. The preliminary estimate of the proportion is 0.16, so

$$n = \frac{1.96^2}{0.10^2} \times \frac{1-0.16}{0.16} = \frac{3.84}{0.01} \times 5.25$$

$$= 2{,}016 \text{ observations}$$

A random-number table could be used to select, say, 100 or so times during a day that observations should be made. Several nurses should be observed at each of these times so that the study will not be continued for an extremely long time. If the nurses' activities vary from day to day during the week or during the month, however, the observations should be spread over a representative time span.

Employee Self-Timing

Sometimes standards can be established by asking the workers to record the time required to perform their jobs. A simple form showing two columns, one for time of day and another for activities, is sufficient for recording data. Some companies make lists of possible activities and assign a code to each activity so that data recording is simplified. Each time a different activity is started or completed, the employee indicates the time and a code or brief description indicating the type of activity. A record of the number of work units provided during each activity is also made. Later the time data are summarized to construct a distribution or ordered array of the time required for each activity. Management then must decide which value of the distribution of times for a task to use as a standard—the mean, the mode, the 66th percentile, or whatever.

This method of developing standards is simple and requires little training. It provides a general index of work performed during a period of time and is useful for some service jobs and knowledge work where an analyst cannot observe the start and stop of work tasks. However, the method does not make allowances for inefficiencies or interruptions that might have occurred during the data-collection period. Data collection may also upset the normal work routine because the employees do much of the data collection.

SUMMARY

Productivity is vital to competitors in the marketplace. Companies must keep their prices reasonable and competitive, and they must be able to respond quickly to changes in demand. The productivity of both labor and capital is important in keeping companies competitive. In recent years the rate of productivity improvement in several industrialized nations has exceeded that of the United States, and many U.S. companies have lost part of their market. Both manufacturing and service companies in the United States are working to increase their rates of productivity, which in turn has improved the current and projected rate of improvement in the country's overall productivity.

At the individual worker level, the productivity of labor is measured in terms of a time standard, sometimes simply called a *standard,* that expresses output per unit of time. Work standards are determined through some means of work measurement, such as stopwatch time study, standard data, predetermined basic motion times, historical records, work sampling, or employee self-timing. Stopwatch time study, called simply *time study,* is the most common method of establishing standards. After informing the worker of the study, a time-study analyst observes the worker long enough to understand the elements of the job and to see that proper work methods are being used. The analyst times the necessary elements of the job for a sufficient number of cycles. The normal time for the job is the actual time adjusted for any difference between the observed worker's pace and a normal pace. Allowances for personal time, fatigue, and unavoidable delays are then added to the normal time to determine the standard time.

KEY TERMS

Work measurement
Time study
Work elements
Performance rating
Normal work pace
Normal time
Actual time

Standard time
Personal allowance
Fatigue allowance
Delay allowance
Ratio delay studies (work sampling)
Allowance

Standard data
Predetermined motion times
Methods-time measurement (MTM)

DEMONSTRATION PROBLEMS

Problem

A job has been time-studied for 20 observations. The mean actual time was 5.83 minutes, and the standard deviation of the times is estimated to be 2.04 minutes. How many total observations should be taken for 95 percent confidence that the mean actual time has been determined within 10 percent?

Solution

$$n = \left(\frac{Zs}{A\bar{x}} \right)^2 = \left(\frac{1.96(2.04)}{0.10(5.83)} \right)^2$$

$$\left(\frac{3.998}{0.583} \right)^2 = 6.858^2 = 47.03$$

Therefore a total of 47 observations should be made. Since 20 observations have already been made, only 27 more are necessary.

Problem

An analyst has observed a job long enough to become familiar with it and has divided it into five elements. The element times for the first four cycles and a performance rating for each element are given in the following table.

ELEMENT	CYCLE 1	CYCLE 2	CYCLE 3	CYCLE 4	PERFORMANCE RATING (PERCENT)
1	1.246	1.328	1.298	1.306	90
2	0.972	0.895	0.798	0.919	100
3	0.914	1.875	1.964	1.972	100
4	2.121	2.198	2.146	2.421	110
5	1.253	1.175	1.413	2.218	100

(a) Do any of the times look like "outliers," that is, probable errors in reading or recording data that should not be included in the analysis?

(b) Compute an estimated normal time for the job based on the data available at this stage of the study.

(c) On the basis of the data available, what size sample should be taken to estimate the time for element 2 within 5 percent of the true mean time with 95 percent confidence?

Solution

(a) The times for element 3 in cycle 1 and for element 5 in cycle 4 are suspect and should be disregarded.

(b) The following estimates are made on the basis of the remaining times:

ELEMENT	MEAN ACTUAL TIME	PERFORMANCE RATING (PERCENT)	NORMAL TIME
1	1.295	90	1.166
2	0.896	100	0.896
3	1.937	100	1.937
4	2.222	110	2.444
5	1.280	100	1.280

Normal time for total job = 7.723.

(c) For element 2:

$$\bar{x} = 0.896$$

$$s = \sqrt{\frac{\Sigma x^2 - (\Sigma x)^2/n'}{n' - 1}}$$

$$= \sqrt{\frac{3.227174 - 3.584^2/4}{3}} = \sqrt{0.005303}$$

$$= 0.0728$$

$$n = \left(\frac{Zs}{A\bar{x}}\right)^2 = \left[\frac{(1.96)(0.0728)}{(0.05)(0.896)}\right]^2$$

$$= (3.185)^2 = 10.14$$

The analyst probably would want to use more than 10 observations so that workers would have more confidence in the standard. A company might make it a general practice to use at least, say, 15 or more observations.

DISCUSSION QUESTIONS

1. What is a work standard? State two ways that standards may be expressed.
2. What are four basic criteria for determining jobs most suitable for measurement?
3. What are the steps in performing a stopwatch time study?
4. What factors should be considered in the determination of a standard?
5. Why do time-study analysts break jobs into elements?
6. Distinguish between actual time, normal time, and standard time.
7. What are predetermined motion times?
8. Distinguish between work sampling and time study.
9. How can historical records be used in the development of standards?
10. **a.** What are standard data?
    b. What are some advantages of using standard data?
11. What are some of the characteristics that differentiate office work from factory work?

PROBLEMS

1. A job has been time-studied for 30 observations. The mean actual time was 3.66 minutes, and the coefficient of variation (CV) was found to be 20 percent (CV = 0.20). How many total observations should be taken for 95 percent confidence that the mean actual time has been determined within 5 percent?
2. A job has been time-studied for several cycles, and the mean actual time was found to be 1.84 minutes. The standard deviation of the actual times was estimated to be 0.38 minute. How many observations should be taken to estimate the true actual time within 10 percent with 95 percent confidence?
3. Time-study observations of a job have been completed, and the mean actual time was found to be 6.28 minutes. The analyst estimated that the observed worker had a performance rating of 110 percent during the study. Personal and fatigue allowances of 13 percent are appropriate for the job, and unavoidable delays are estimated to be 10 percent.
   a. Compute the normal time for the job.
   b. Compute the standard time for the job.

4. An analyst has become familiar with a job and has divided it into four elements. The element times for the first four cycles are given in the table below with a performance rating for each element.

ELEMENT	CYCLE 1	CYCLE 2	CYCLE 3	CYCLE 4	PERFORMANCE RATING (PERCENT)
1	1.38	1.58	1.71	1.49	100
2	0.29	0.35	0.30	0.38	120
3	0.61	0.58	0.53	0.57	105
4	0.77	0.82	0.74	0.88	90

a. On the basis of the times observed through four cycles, determine the normal time for the job.
b. How many observations would be required to estimate the true time for element 1 within 10 percent with 90 percent confidence?

5. An analyst has observed a job long enough to become familiar with it and has divided it into four elements. The element times for the first five cycles are shown in the following table with a performance rating for each element.

ELEMENT	CYCLE 1	CYCLE 2	CYCLE 3	CYCLE 4	CYCLE 5	PERFORMANCE RATING (PERCENT)
1	1.51	1.63	1.48	1.55	1.72	110
2	2.46	2.34	2.33	2.36	2.30	95
3	1.79	3.02	1.84	1.78	1.77	90
4	1.25	1.11	1.40	1.15	1.29	115

a. Compute an estimated normal time for the job based on the data available at this stage of the study.
b. On the basis of the data available, what size sample should be taken to estimate the time for element 1 within 5 percent of the true mean time with 95 percent confidence?

6. The analyst in problem 4 performed a work-sampling study for the same task and recorded the counts shown in the following table for three categories of activities. What allowance should be made for unavoidable delays?

ACTIVITY CATEGORY	OBSERVED FREQUENCY
Normal work activity	126
Avoidable delays	15
Unavoidable delays	16

7. The analyst in problem 5 performed a work-sampling study for the same task and recorded the counts shown in the following table for three categories of activities. What allowance should be made for unavoidable delays?

ACTIVITY CATEGORY	OBSERVED FREQUENCY
Normal work activity	132
Avoidable delays	25
Unavoidable delays	13

8. Ajax Car Rental Service has attempted to streamline the process of completing a rental contract so that customers may obtain cars with minimum delay. The manager has timed 20 transactions from the time the agent begins talking with the customer until the customer is handed the keys and a completed agreement. The mean time is 8.2 minutes, and the estimated standard deviation is 2.63 minutes. How many observations are required to estimate the mean time with 95 percent confidence within an accuracy of 1 minute?

9. Arrow Airlines has attempted to streamline the process of booking flight reservations in order to service the maximum number of on-site customers. The manager has timed 40 transactions from the time the agent begins talking with the customer until tickets are prepared and paid for and luggage is checked in. The mean time is 4.7 minutes, and the estimated standard deviation is 1.8 minutes. How many observations are required to estimate the mean time with 95 percent confidence within an accuracy of 0.50 minute?

10. The Donnelly Company owns 100 machines for lease by the day to customers. Randomly selected records of 30 days show that on average 44 machines are rented each day. How many records should be observed to estimate the utilization of these machines within 10 percent accuracy and with 95 percent confidence?

BIBLIOGRAPHY

Barnes, Ralph M. *Motion and Time Study.* 7th ed. New York: Wiley, 1980.

Hamlin, Jerry D., ed. *Success Stories in Productivity Improvement.* Atlanta: Industrial Engineering and Management Press, 1985.

Harris, Melvin F., and G. William Vining. "The IE's Future Role in Improving Knowledge Worker Productivity." *Industrial Engineering 19,* no. 7 (July 1987): 28–32.

Issues in White-Collar Productivity. Atlanta: Industrial Engineering and Management Press, 1984.

Karger, Delmar W., and Walton M. Hancock. *Advanced Work Measurement.* New York: Industrial Press, 1982.

Kearney, A. T., Inc. *Measuring and Improving Productivity in Physical Distribution.* Oak Brook, Ill.: National Council of Physical Distribution Management, 1984.

Kendrick, John W. *Improving Company Productivity.* Baltimore, Md.: Johns Hopkins University Press, 1984.

Landel, Robert D. *Managing Productivity through People: An Operations Perspective.* Englewood Cliffs, N.J.: Reston, Prentice-Hall, 1986.

Niebel, Benjamin W. *Motion and Time Study.* 8th ed. Homewood, Ill.: Irwin, 1988.

Sitnek, Larry N. "Performance Rating." *Industrial Management,* January–February 1977, pp. 11–16.

GENERAL CONFIGURATION AND MODE OF PROCESSING

CHAPTER 6

The building(s) and equipment within the operations system play a major role in the accomplishment of the work that is to be done by operations. The building and equipment are often referred to as facilities and, as the word facility implies, they should facilitate or make the work easier. The facility plus the people, their jobs, work methods, and procedures really make up the operations system. In designing the operations system, managers and designers must give consideration to the interplay of many factors. Strategic planning and quality management considerations of the customers' needs, desires, and expectations establish what goods and services would be offered to external customers. Good design practice and team design efforts during the initial design of the product or service package give general consideration to feasible processing methods that will be needed to produce the desired output. Demand forecasts provide estimates of the level of output that the operations system should be capable of providing. Based on this information, more-detailed decisions can be made in regard to the design of the operations system to provide the desired output in the desired volume.

The business must determine the configuration of the departments, work groups, and individual work stations within the facility so that work will flow smoothly and efficiently and so communication and coordination can easily be accomplished. This relative location of units within the facility is often referred to as the "layout" of the facility. Selection of a particular type of configuration or layout usually involves much more than just determining where things are placed with respect to the other entities. Generally, selection of a layout carries with it the selection of the types of processing equipment that will be most appropriate. In manufacturing it is also related to the type of materials-handling equipment that will generally be appropriate. For example, a type of layout that is more appropriate for a high-volume output of a standard good or service is more likely to be associated with special-purpose processing equipment. If the system is to produce a tangible product that must be transported to various work locations, fixed-path handling equipment is likely to be used. Conversely, a layout for a system that is to provide a wide variety of products or services is more likely to be associated with more flexible general-purpose processing equipment and, if handling equipment is involved, it will be more flexible with variable paths of movement.

In designing the operations system, many other matters must also be considered—such as defining all the work steps that must be performed, the sequence in which they will be performed, how technology and human effort will be employed to perform these steps, and how the work tasks will be grouped and assigned to individuals as reasonably satisfying jobs are also related. We will discuss some factors related to technology in Chapter 7 and some considerations about job design will be discussed in Chapter 8. In this chapter we will discuss some options for layouts with the recognition that they are also related to decisions about the selection of equipment for value-adding operations and perhaps materials movement.

DIFFERENT LAYOUTS FOR DIFFERENT OPERATIONS

We see numerous ways in which a facility is designed to support the work to be done. Health care facilities provide examples of some general ways in which facilities are designed to support their differing needs. A general hospital has operating rooms, postsurgery recovery rooms, laboratories, an emergency room, private and semiprivate patient rooms, and so forth. A 1-day surgery hospital does not include much space for overnight patients and would not have an emergency room. A nursing home is designed with some recreation areas and little provision of treatment areas. Many more specific differences also exist to make each health care facility better serve its function.

Restaurants provide other examples of variations in layouts. A restaurant may be designed to serve customers at the counter, as in a fast food restaurant; to have customers serve themselves at a service line, as in a cafeteria; or to provide service at the tables. Within each facility numerous factors must be considered, often beginning

Offices are designed to facilitate the work process. Because form and function go hand in hand, the offices that "work" best are often aesthetically pleasing.

Tom Tracy/The Stock Market

with the amount of space available and its shape. Within the available space, many trade-offs are made. A general increase in construction and lease costs creates pressure to reduce the amount of space used, and restaurants are not likely to reduce the amount of seating space and thus lose revenue. Therefore, the kitchen receives careful attention. Along with the desire to make it compact, there must be sufficient space to allow people to work efficiently and to move freely and rapidly without mishap, such as knocking dishes off a tray. Many restaurants are willing to pay for more frequent deliveries and use waste compactors or waste disposal systems to reduce space requirements. A concise objective is provided in this advice:

> "Use your head, not your feet" is a common bit of advice for foodservice employees. Waiters, cooks, and, indeed, their managers know that efficiency rides upon the purposeful movement of people and the materials they handle. Kitchen designers call this movement "flow," and they strive to coordinate equipment, people and products along sensible flow lines to minimize the time, effort and expense of production.[1]

This design objective is very important in a restaurant chain because the design may be duplicated in hundreds of locations. An example of some considerations in such a situation is given in the following application.

[1] "Variations on a Theme," *Restaurants & Institutions,* June 24, 1988, p. 38.

KENTUCKY FRIED CHICKEN'S NEW PROTOTYPE

To remain competitive in today's quick-service industry, chains must look to the future. A good design must anticipate future change. Designers of Kentucky Fried Chicken's latest Series 38 prototype restaurant have attempted to do just that. The company wanted its restaurants to be more contemporary. The decor scheme lends itself to current tastes, and the kitchen will be able to accommodate menu changes over the next few years.

The design began by looking at the exterior in terms of drive-by traffic. Larger windows and lighter, brighter colors were selected to make the restaurants easily visible and readily accessible to motorists. The dining areas in older restaurants had too much emphasis on dark woods, so better lighting and pastel colors were introduced. A mixture of booths, two-top tables, and four-top tables is used to offer diners a choice. The design will accommodate 52 diners in a 2,400-square-foot model and up to 77 persons in a 2,700-square-foot model. A floor plan (layout) of the prototype is shown in Figure 6.1.

The angled counter is immediately accessible to the customer entering the store. The angle allows 21 feet rather than 15 feet of counter, so there is more space for service persons and cash registers to reduce waiting time. Wording on the menu behind the counter has been minimized to shorten selection time also. The angled counter provides more room for the drive-through service area, which accounts for about one-third of the average unit's sales. It also provides room for the manager to be near what's happening up front, in the kitchen, and in the drive-through area.

A computer system with screens in each location links the front counter, manager's office, drive-through window, and kitchen. Electronic headsets are used so workers in the drive-through area can move around and still talk with their customers.

One goal was to make the entire operation more user-friendly, and the employees are certainly some of the users. The lighting in the kitchen was increased, and the aisles were widened from 3½ to 5 feet. Wider aisles make better working conditions and allow room for the

Figure 6.1 Kentucky Fried Chicken's Series 38 Prototype

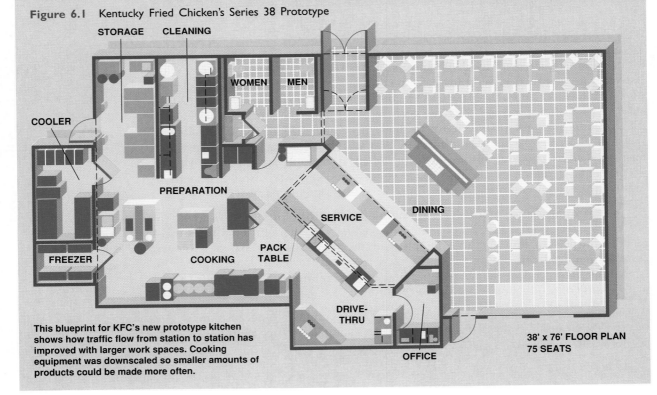

STORAGE CLEANING

WOMEN MEN

COOLER

PREPARATION

DINING

SERVICE

FREEZER

COOKING PACK TABLE

DRIVE-THRU

OFFICE

38' x 76' FLOOR PLAN
75 SEATS

This blueprint for KFC's new prototype kitchen shows how traffic flow from station to station has improved with larger work spaces. Cooking equipment was downscaled so smaller amounts of products could be made more often.

equipment needed to prepare new menu items that the company may add. Other changes were made to accommodate current demand. Previously most of the demand came at dinner, so large amounts had to be cooked at one time. Now the business is spread more evenly, since lunch business has increased. The cooking equipment has been down-scaled so that smaller quantities are often cooked in smaller, more efficient fryers. Use of this cooking method also creates a fresher product. The new focus on sandwich business required a separate sandwich station near the main counter. Chicken is cooked and carried to the sandwich station for further preparation. In looking for efficiency,

the designers replaced the old type of fixed-shelf storage with dense-packed rolling shelves. Now there are six shelves in the space that previously accommodated four.

The previous design had been used for about 7 years, so clearly these businesses have to reexamine their designs and look for improvements. Sales at the prototype stores are running about one-third higher than the average unit.

Source: "KFC's New Prototype," *Restaurant Business,* August 10, 1989, pp. 139–141. Reprinted with permission of Restaurant Business.

Retail Layout

In the examples above we see that the facility helps support an important objective of the organization—serving the customers' needs. In businesses and not-for-profit organizations, this should be done in an efficient, cost-effective manner. The impact of layout on cost or profit is often difficult to measure precisely. Nevertheless, businesses that survive must perform their work to receive a profit. An example in which the arrangement of items in the facility clearly has an impact on the "bottom line" is a retail establishment, such as a supermarket. A customary objective is to maximize profit per square foot of space or per linear foot of aisle. Shelf space is allocated to items depending on how fast they sell. Space can be reallocated based on current sales data collected through bar code scanners at the point of sale.

Necessary purchases that bring customers to the store (called "power items") are dispersed throughout the store, to draw shoppers past other items not on their shopping lists. The end of the aisle space is often used to give best exposure to high-margin nonessentials, or impulse items. Items that are easily stolen are placed in highly visible areas. The aisles are made wide enough to restock merchandise easily and allow shoppers to move freely and feel comfortable. There are numerous subtle principles of effective merchandising related to layout in supermarkets or other retail businesses that we will not go into. You can see how layout is important in such a business.

HOW FACILITY LAYOUT CAN HELP ADD VALUE FOR CUSTOMERS

A good layout can keep costs low by reducing materials-handling costs and time lost while people move from one location to another. Layout also can affect quality and dependability by improving the ease of coordination and by making people's work easier. Flexible layouts such as U-line cells can make a company more flexible and responsive to changes in demand. The appearance and layout of service facilities can improve customer convenience and satisfaction, thus enhancing customers' perception of service quality.

Distribution and Warehouse Areas

Some portions of facilities in businesses and nonprofit organizations may also hold items in shelves or racks, not for display and selection by customers, but to store for future use. In some cases the intent is long-term storage or warehousing, such as storing repair and replacement parts, so they will be available if needed. In other cases, such as a Wal-Mart distribution center (discussed in Supplement D), the intent is to achieve flow of the items. Items are to move in and out rapidly (high turnover). An objective is to minimize the travel involved in placing the items in storage racks and retrieving them later. The items that turn over fastest will be located nearest to the loading and unloading dock, the next fastest-moving items will be located in areas slightly farther from the loading and unloading area, and so on. If items are moved to the loading dock by conveyor or other automated means after they are selected to be shipped, as in the Wal-Mart example, then it is primarily important to consider locating the items with respect to the area where they are unloaded manually. This minimizes the time workers spend moving items. If some items are much heavier than others, a company may calculate the sales volume of each item times its weight and try to minimize the number of ton-miles of movement.

Office Layout

Usually the weight of items to be moved is not the major consideration in the office areas of many service businesses and in the administration areas of manufacturing companies. Much office work is knowledge work that involves interchanging and processing information. Some departments or subgroups have to be located in the vicinity of others because they have to converse, use the same hard-copy files, or exchange original documents. Information technology such as the use of distributed computers with access to central data bases, electronic mail, facsimile transmission (fax) machines, and electronic data interchange (EDI) has greatly reduced the need to locate some types of work near others. Some workers such as programmers and analysts "telecommute" or work in their homes at least part time and interface with the remainder of the organization through electronics. But, for the most part, office workers have a work location "at the office," and such a space must be provided.

The general approach to office layout involves several steps. The volume of work is forecast, and this is translated to capacity required (the number of workers and the amount of equipment) for each department or work group. The amount of work space each department will require to house this number of workers is then determined. Space is added for conference rooms or other meeting areas and for support functions such as rest rooms, break rooms, cafeteria, mail room, maintenance, and storage. The necessary space is found or the available space is allocated to the work groups based on the calculated needs. The location of each group with respect to the others depends on some criteria such as the need for face-to-face communication or to deliver documents between groups.

The need for one group to be near another is sometimes called a *nearness priority*. Figure 6.2 presents a convenient grid, developed by Richard Muther, to show nearness priorities. The diamond-shaped boxes at the right of the grid are formed by the intersection of bars representing two departments. The letters *(a, e, i, o, u,* or *x)* are used to indicate the degree to which it is important for the two departments to be near each other. Sometimes a number is also used in the diamond, to indicate the reason for the nearness priority.

Figure 6.2
Nearness Priorities in
a Muther Grid

Department A					
Department B	o 3	i			
Department C	i	o 3	i a		
Department D	e	o 3	e x 5		
Department E	i	u	u		
Department F	e	x 5			

Nearness Priority Code	Degree of Importance	Reason Code	Possible Reasons
a	Absolutely necessary	1	Use same equipment
e	Very important	2	Use same records or personnel
i	Important	3	Work flow facilitated
o	OK, ordinary importance	4	Ease of communication or supervision
u	Unimportant	5	Unsafe conditions
x	Undesirable		

Offices have become more flexible. Many companies are using an "open-plan" concept with modular office partitions erected to separate work stations. This concept offers more economy and flexibility than fixed-partition construction. Care must be taken to use sound-absorbent materials to keep noise below annoying levels. Some modular office partitions are shown in Figure 6.3.

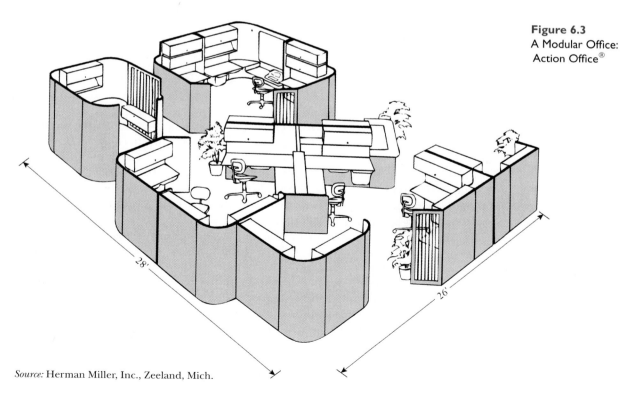

Figure 6.3
A Modular Office:
Action Office®

28'

26'

Source: Herman Miller, Inc., Zeeland, Mich.

APPLICATION

EXAMPLE OF AN OFFICE LAYOUT

Noah Sark owned and managed a small brokerage firm. His company had outgrown its offices, so Noah planned to move into new facilities. He had found an ideal location but was not sure that the available space would provide everything that he desired. Besides, the area was square—a shape different from that presently occupied by his company.

Noah discussed the situation with his son, Alec, when he was home from school for a weekend. Noah said that he had thought about the layout for some time but just did not see how it could be achieved in the square office space. He had to sign a lease on the space early the next week if he wanted it. Noah explained his many objectives, some of which appeared to conflict with others. His senior brokers all wanted privacy and quiet, yet wanted to be able to see the ticker display from their offices. Both the senior and junior brokers wanted to be able to see the customer reception area, so they could greet customers who came in. Noah wanted the receptionist area near the entrance and near his office so the receptionist could also serve as his secretary. Noah believed there should be a customer seating area where customers could watch the ticker display and that this area should be near the brokers' offices. The operations and bookkeeping department should be near Noah's office and easily accessible to all the brokers. A large storage room for

records and office supplies should be near bookkeeping. Noah also told Alec that the employees needed a lounge for coffee breaks, snacks, or lunch. He would also like a conference room, but he might not be able to have that and all his other objectives, too. If a conference room were added, it should be near the lounge so that coffee could be served easily. Alec developed a matrix to express the priorities that should

Figure 6.4   Matrix for Sark Layout Analysis

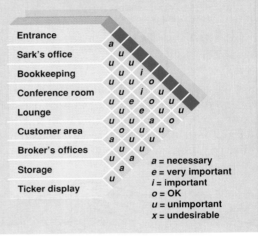

a = necessary
e = very important
i = important
o = OK
u = unimportant
x = undesirable

COMPUTER USE IN OFFICE LAYOUT   An integrated approach that makes use of several computer programs has been applied to office layout. This approach involves considerable interaction between the analyst and a series of three computer programs to develop candidate layouts. The initial phase involves the collection of data by questionnaire to determine communication patterns and the use of common data, equipment, or meeting areas. These data are obtained both for individuals and for subunits of the organization.

The next phase of analysis involves grouping entities into clusters that have a high degree of interaction. A great deal of flexibility is afforded by the system. The analyst can select from five different heuristic procedures to partition up to 100 entities into groups. Entities can be selected to be individuals, sections, departments, or other organizational subunits. The system supplies data to compare the number of intergroup and intragroup interactions. The analyst must use judgment to determine when desirable groupings have been found.

The last phase of the approach supplies alternative office layouts for location of the groups. The analyst must supply the input used to determine the floor space required by the groups and specify any locations that must remain fixed. Another be observed in the designing of the office (Figure 6.4). He then went to work designing the office.

The available office space was an open square area with the entrance near one corner and rest rooms at the opposite corner. Alec knew his father's office should be near the receptionist, so he put it at the corner near the door. The bookkeeping office should also be adjacent to his father's office. The storage area was located in the corner adjoining the bookkeeping office, so, at this stage, that wall of the office area was completely utilized. The ticker display, which displays stock quotations on a wall, is the center of attention in a brokerage office. Any wall where the ticker is located is not suitable for brokers' offices, because the ticker would not be visible from them. Therefore Alec placed the ticker along the outer wall of the bookkeeping office. He then located the lounge and conference room on the opposite wall, leaving a large open space, from any point in which the ticker display was clearly visible. Alec then drew nine offices along the sides of this space. Each office could be open, or it could be separated from the open space by a glass partition without loss of view of the ticker display. The remaining space was left open so that customers could sit and observe the ticker display, yet have easy access to brokers or to the bookkeeping department.

The next morning Alec told his father how silly he was for not being able to develop a layout that met all his objectives. Alec handed his father the layout

Figure 6.5   Alec Sark's Layout

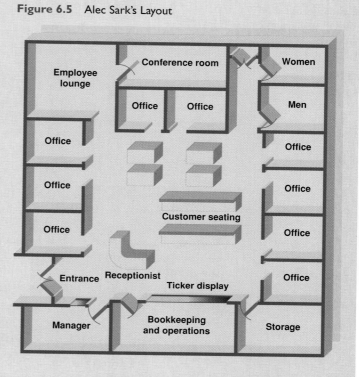

presented in Figure 6.5 and said that any student in his class could do almost as well, but none, naturally, quite so well. Noah looked at the layout and marveled at how smart Alec was.

program generates block diagram layouts, using the product obtained when interactions are multiplied by the distances between the interacting entities to measure effectiveness.[2]

CONSIDERATION OF MAJOR LAYOUT TYPES

There are different kinds of service businesses and different designs of facilities to support their work. Likewise, there are different designs for factories to support the strategic needs of different manufacturing businesses. We discuss primarily two classical types of layout from manufacturing and a hybrid layout that combines some of the advantages of these two. Also some applications of similar layout concepts in service businesses are mentioned. We only mention the third classical layout type,

[2]F. Robert Jacobs, John W. Bradford, and Larry P. Ritzman, "Computerized Layout: An Integrated Approach to Special Planning and Communication Requirements," *Industrial Engineering*, July 1980, pp. 56–61.

Figure 6.6
Characteristics of
Three Manufacturing
Types

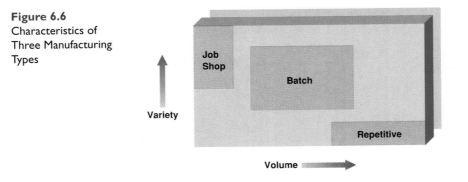

called *fixed-position layout.* It means that the work object is not moved and all materials, tools, and people come to it.

In Chapter 1 we discussed three general types of manufacturing businesses: job shop, batch, and repetitive. It is useful to classify these according to two dimensions to show the differing needs in their facilities. One important dimension is variety, or the number of unique parts or products they make. The other dimension is volume, or the average quantity they produce of each unique part or product. A graph of the relationship is shown in Figure 6.6.

Job Shop Layout or Layout by Function

Job shops contract to make items that are nonstandard, so they usually are not produced in high volumes. Job shops therefore must contract to make a wide variety of such items in order to have a sufficient level of sales. The factory for such a business should offer a great deal of flexibility but need not be designed for efficiency at high volumes. These companies purchase general-purpose equipment that can be set up to perform a variety of operations and employ persons who can do a variety of tasks. People and equipment that perform the same general function are grouped in the same area. That is, all the grinding would be in one area, all the welding in another, all the milling in another, and so on, as shown in Figure 6.7. The job shop arrangement is also called *layout by function, functional layout,* or *layout by process.*

Any particular item made in a job shop may require a unique sequence of operations to convert the raw material to the desired end item. Consequently the flow

Figure 6.7
Layout by Function

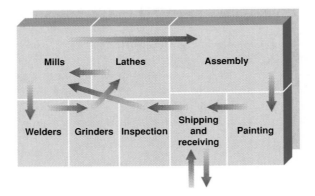

paths through the facility, from one functional area to another, may vary from item to item. Some paths may be lengthy and involve considerable backtracking, as shown in Figure 6.7. Flexibility is required in the materials-handling equipment used to move items from one work station or machine to another. Since the volume is low, manually operated equipment that can transport items to various locations will probably be used. Forklifts are common materials-handling equipment for this type of operation, as shown in Figure 6.8.

Figure 6.8
Forklift Truck
(Counterbalance Type)

Some of the advantages and disadvantages of layout by process are given below.

ADVANTAGES

1. Flexibility of equipment and personnel.
2. Smaller investment in equipment because duplication is not necessary unless volume is large.
3. Expertise. Supervisors for each department become highly knowledgeable about the functions under their direction.
4. Diversity of tasks. Work assignments make work more satisfying for people who prefer variety.

DISADVANTAGES

1. Lack of materials-handling efficiency. Backtracking and long movements may occur in the handling of materials.
2. Lack of efficiency in timing. Work must wait between tasks.
3. Complication of production planning and control.
4. Cost. Workers must have broader skills and must be paid higher wages than assembly-line workers.
5. Lowered productivity. Because each job is different, it requires different setups and operator learning.

APPLICABILITY TO SERVICES   Services also may be arranged according to process. Since materials handling is not an important factor in many such operations, the distances between successive operations and the need for backtracking are not severe penalties. Offices that handle large volumes of paperwork, such as insurance claims, may be arranged to facilitate the high-volume flow of lightweight materials (paperwork). In many offices, however, ease of face-to-face communications and supervision are often more important than the flow of papers. When several people must use the same equipment or have access to the same records, they are usually located in the same area.

Since the customer is often a participant in service operations, customer convenience is important. Facilities should be arranged for easy access and should enable customers to find easily the persons they wish to see.

Many services arrange facilities by function. Retail stores group all similar products such as hardware, sporting goods, and photographic equipment in separate departments for ease of supervision and to enable shoppers to locate merchandise easily. Jobs in offices are grouped into departments or sections, such as accounts receivable and accounts payable. Universities often locate together the separate schools and departments that have frequent communications with one another. Hospitals have obstetrical wards, cardiac units, surgical wards, X-ray departments, and pathology laboratories, with similar functions performed within each department. Some automotive repair facilities have a designated area for paint and body work, and another for engine work. Since different equipment and skills are needed for these types of work, the functions are separated. Banks frequently have separate components, such as loan and mortgage departments, and sometimes have separate teller windows for savings and checking accounts.

Layout by Product or Flow-Line Layout

If a company produces a high volume of one or a few items, the facility can be arranged to achieve efficient flow of materials and lower cost per item. Special-purpose equipment that quickly and reliably performs a specific task is purchased for each production step needed to convert the input material to the desired end item. The equipment is closely placed along a line in the sequence that each piece of equipment is used in the processing. The work item is moved along the line from work station to work station where each operation is performed. An objective is to make the path of movement no longer than necessary. Internally produced components or subassemblies should be made near the locations where they are used in the process. Purchased items should be delivered to the locations where they are to be used. If items must be stored, they should be stored close to their point of use. Since the sequence of work tasks required by the product dictates the layout, this arrangement is sometimes called *layout by product*. It is also called a flow line, production line, or assembly line. The flow path does not have to be a straight line; it might be curved to fit the shape of an available space or to make it more compact. In some cases multiple lines are combined, as shown in the lower part of Figure 6.9, where an assembly line is fed by lines that make subassemblies.

Lightweight items such as small radios or tape players may be passed along the line manually. Since there is a fixed path of travel and a large volume of items to move, an investment in automated materials-handling equipment is often justified. Overhead conveyors or floor-mounted conveyors (as shown in Figure 6.10) may be

Figure 6.9
Schematics of
Production Lines

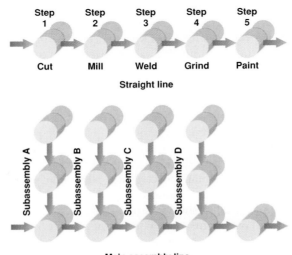

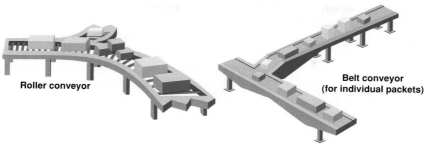

Figure 6.10
Use of a Conveyor

Roller conveyor

Belt conveyor
(for individual packets)

used. Robots also may be used to move materials or to perform value-adding work tasks, such as painting or welding. The Nissan factory discussed in Supplement B is an example of a facility that is laid out by product.

Some of the advantages and disadvantages of layout by product are given below.

ADVANTAGES

1. Reduced materials handling

2. Small amounts of work in process

3. Reduced total processing time

4. Simplified production planning and control systems

5. Simplification of tasks, enabling unskilled workers to learn tasks quickly

DISADVANTAGES

1. Lack of process flexibility. A change in product may require facility modification.

2. Lack of flexibility in timing. The product cannot flow through the line faster than the slowest task can be accomplished, unless that task is performed at multiple stations.

3. Large investment. Special-purpose equipment is used, and duplication is required wherever that type of processing is performed along the line.

4. Dependence of the whole on each part. A breakdown of one machine or the absence of enough operators to staff all work stations may stop the entire line.

5. Worker monotony. Workers may become bored by the endless repetition of simple tasks.

APPLICABILITY TO SERVICES Some services are arranged in a flow-line layout. When you go through a cafeteria line, you pass from one type of operation to another (silverware to salad to entrée, and so on). When large numbers of people are to give blood, the facilities are arranged so that donors move from one station to another: medical history to blood pressure to temperature check, and so on. When a large number of people are to be served through successive steps, some advantages may be gained by use of such a flow-line arrangement.

Flow lines reduce both the time people spend in going through all the steps and backtracking. Fewer people must wait, and each waits a shorter time. It is simple to direct people through the facility because the flow and sequencing are built into the arrangement of the facilities.

AUTOMATION IN PRODUCTION LINES Traditionally there has been a great deal of mechanization and fixed automation in production lines. A high volume of standard items will often provide sufficient utilization of dedicated equipment. Special-purpose equipment might be designed and built if the volume to be produced is very high. For lower volumes or where standard production equipment will serve the purpose, special tooling is installed on a machine to enable it to perform a specific operation. It would be a lengthy task to change such a line to make a slightly different item. Each machine would have to be stopped, the tooling would be unbolted, then new tooling would be installed and adjusted to perform a new operation. Traditional production lines had little flexibility to change products.

Programmable automation has improved the flexibility of machine tools and has made possible flexible production lines that can be changed over ("set up") much more quickly. These lines might have tooling for a set of similar items. Software commands to the controlling computer can cause the machines to switch from one combination of tooling and machine setting to another. The flexibility may be more costly than a line that can make only one item but less costly than a separate line for each item, where the volume is not sufficient to utilize each of the separate lines. Another way some companies achieve some flexibility is through the use of hybrid layouts.

Hybrid Layouts

Some manufacturing operations use a combination of classical layouts. For example, some of their products may have low demand volumes but may contain common components that are needed in high volume. The volume of a common component may be high enough to justify dedicating a flow line to its production. Thus, within a facility one might find some areas with layout by process and others with layout by product.

Assembly operations in many batch manufacturing factories are performed on manual assembly lines that can be shifted from one product to another relatively easily. Parts used in the assembly line may, however, be fabricated in shops that are arranged by function to provide the flexibility of making several kinds of components.

Batch manufacturers sell intermediate volumes so they typically produce in larger lots than a job shop to reduce the number of setups and trips between departments. Production and movement in large lots, however, cause some disadvantages, such as requiring higher work-in-process inventory and excess space, and imposing erratic or lumpy work loads on work centers as the lots move through the facility. Consequently, many batch manufacturers have reduced their lot sizes and revised their layouts from being totally laid out by function to using manufacturing cells where they apply. High-volume factories are also using dedicated cells in some places.

Manufacturing Cells or Cellular Manufacturing

Parts that look similar but may vary in some of their dimensions or other features often are produced with the same sequence of steps through the same types of equipment. Parts that have the same general characteristics are called "part families." Companies have found that they can lay out a *manufacturing cell* or close grouping of the equipment required to produce a part family and gain many of the advantages of a flow-line layout for that group of parts. Where at least some of the items are produced in cells a company is said to use *cellular manufacturing*. Consider, for example, a company that might require a variety of parts made from flat pieces of steel. Many of these items might be made by cutting off a piece of steel plate, milling flat surfaces so the part has a specified thickness, and drilling holes in the plate. The specified widths, thicknesses, and the hole diameters and locations might be different from one part to another. All of them, however, could be made by using a cutoff saw, milling machine, and drill press, in that sequence. These three equipment items could be grouped into a small cell. Instead of sending members of this part family on what might be a long journey from a saw to a milling department, and then to a drilling department, they could all be produced in the cell.

Parts that are produced in a cell can be handed or moved easily from one step to another because the equipment is nearby, so materials-handling time and cost is much lower. Since the parts move one at a time instead of waiting for a large enough load to be worth moving to another department, the work-in-process inventory and storage space requirements will be lower. Without these delays the time to complete a part will be less. Consequently the use of cells or cellular manufacturing can provide many of the advantages of layout by flow lines, yet it has much of the flexibility that is found in functional layouts. Cellular manufacturing is considered a hybrid or combination of layout by product or flow lines and layout by process or functional layout because it has some of the characteristics of each.

Such companies as Caterpillar, Briggs and Stratton, Cummins Engine, Hewlett-Packard, Deere and Company, and Martin Marietta use cellular manufacturing to advantage. Deere, for example, produces several models of farm equipment, with some of the parts in one model being similar in shape but a different size from the same type of part in another model. Such a company is likely to have many parts families. Accompanying photographs (page 248) show a collection of parts from John Deere and the same parts grouped into part families. Once part families are identified, the appropriate machines can be grouped into cells for their production. Deere uses cells in its factories in Wisconsin, Illinois, and Iowa. One cell at its engine plant in East Moline, Illinois, uses a cell to produce various sizes of hydraulic cylinders. After shifting to the cell, the time for cylinders to flow through production dropped from 28 days to 10 minutes and work in process, rework, materials handling, and scheduling were reduced.

GROUP TECHNOLOGY   The process of identifying similar parts and grouping parts into families is sometimes referred to a *group technology*, presumably because it develops groups of items that require similar production technology. Some companies have tens of thousands of parts so it is difficult to identify all that are similar. Numeric codes can be used to describe the basic features such as the size and shape of each part. A computer search of these codes will reveal the collection of parts that are similar. Design engineers can sometimes describe a part that is needed in some assembly and find that the company already has a part that will work satisfactorily. If a part already exists it reduces the design time and allows the use of common parts. An alternative method that is sometimes used to identify part families for cellular manufacturing is to examine the route sheets that list the sequence of production steps the part goes through and find those with common routings.

Random Parts

John Deere and Company

A Family of Parts

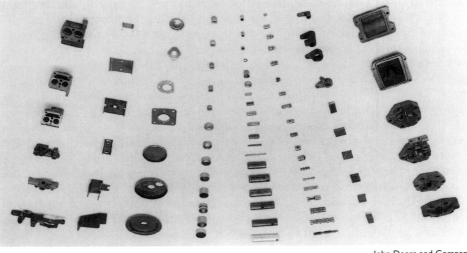

John Deere and Company

Some Common Cell Arrangements

One form of cell that often can be used to advantage, particularly if a robot does parts handling, has the machines arranged in the shape of a C, with the robot in the opening of the C. The robot can swing through an arc and reach any machine. The robot loads parts on the first machine, transfers parts between machines, and unloads parts from the last machine. The parts must, of course, be arranged at locations where the robot has been programmed to find them. An example of a robot used in a C-shaped cell is presented in the following box.

Two other forms of cells are used by manufacturing companies that employ multiskilled workers who are capable of operating multiple types of equipment in a cell. These types of cells often are found in companies that apply just-in-time production methods. These layouts are the rabbit-chase cell and the U-line cell.

OPERATIONS MANAGEMENT IN ACTION

A CUSTOMIZED, ROBOTIZED MACHINING CELL

At Kurt Manufacturing Company in Minneapolis, a robot handles a 90-pound part between a trio of machine tools to produce a deck that will become part of a hard-disk drive assembled by a subsidiary of Control Data Corp. Kurt, a precision-machining job shop with some 300 employees, bids each year for the contract to make this part and has made the part since 1975. Over the years, Kurt has developed a close relationship with the customer and has recommended design enhancements to improve manufacturability. As the production quantities increased, Kurt Manufacturing moved to a cell to achieve production efficiencies.

The part starts out as a 90-pound aluminum casting, and Kurt performs operations to mill a smooth surface

Kurt Manufacturing's Robotized Cell

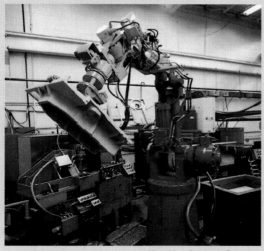

Kurt Manufacturing Company

to within 0.0005 inch, mill other parts of the item, and drill 97 precisely located holes, about 70 of them being tapped with threads for screws. The heavy workpiece would be slow and strenuous for a human operator to maneuver on and off the machines and would require an overhead hoist. Instead, a robot moves the parts between the equipment, arranged as shown in the accompanying photograph. Two workers operate the cell, where eight were required to operate the cluster of machines previously required to produce the part. One loads the carts and moves them to and from the cell. The other serves as a parts inspector and checks for broken taps or other machine problems.

The robot takes the part from the input cart to the first milling operation, where seventeen work spindles operate on five sides of the part. The part is moved next to the ready rack and then to the machining center. The part is removed from the machining center and washed in a custom tank, to remove any metal chips from locating surfaces so the part can be precisely located for the final operations. The part is then moved to the drilling and tapping machine. When this operation is complete, the part is washed again and placed in the output cart for shipment to the customer.

The first milling machine and the drilling and tapping machine were custom-designed by Kurt engineers. Kurt also developed the overall system arrangement and programmed the control of the equipment. This robot-tended cell reduces direct labor requirements. You can see how this creative use of a cell also minimizes the move distances and lost time between operations, reduces WIP, and makes very compact use of floor space.

Source: Information courtesy of Kurt Manufacturing Company and from Ingo Wolfe and Richard K. Wallin, "Customizing a Machining Cell," *American Machinist,* October 1984, pp. 86–89.

RABBIT-CHASE CELL   In a *rabbit-chase cell* (shown in Figure 6.11) the machines are arranged in a circle, with the operator side of the machines facing the center. By moving around in a small circle, a worker can operate all the machines. If the worker must perform all the operations manually, the cycle time for the cell is the sum of all the operations' times and the handling time. The cycle time can be shortened if some of the machines perform their operations automatically. The worker moves around the circle, loading and unloading the automatic machines, and can perform other work while automatic machines are working. Different parts can be produced in this type of cell by changing the setups on the machines. If an extensive setup is

Figure 6.11
Rabbit-Chase Cell

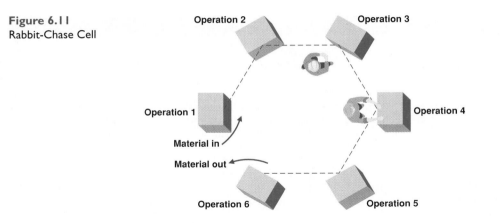

required on some machine for a part that is run fairly often, the machine may be duplicated in the cell. One of the duplicate machines remains set up with the difficult setup and is used only when the appropriate part is being run.

Another way to increase the rate of output from this type of cell is by having two workers move around the circle, one behind the other, sharing the equipment. The rate can be increased even further if three or more workers are in the chase. But the workers have to be capable of performing all the operations in the cell. And the work can proceed only as fast as the slowest worker moves around the circle.

U-LINE CELL   Sometimes a cell is formed by placing the machines in the shape of a narrow U. A worker with sufficient skills can perform all the operations on a part by stepping along one side of the U, around the closed end, and back up the other side of the U. The rate of output can be increased by having two (or more) workers in the U with each simultaneously performing part of the work cycle. The first worker would process a part through the operations down one side of the U, maybe halfway, then leave the part and turn to the other side of the aisle to pick up a part that had been left by the second worker, and finish processing it back up the other side of the U. The second worker would take the part that had been left by the first worker and process it through the machines down one side, around the closed end of the U, and up the other side, to the place where it is to be picked up and finished by the first worker. A *U-line cell* with the paths that might be followed by two workers is shown in Figure 6.12. Use of multiple workers in this manner can reduce the number of skills required of each worker.

Materials Handling with Cellular Manufacturing

A variety of methods can be used to move materials when cellular manufacturing is employed. As we saw, a robot can be used in a cell to move the work item from one operation to another. Manual handling is common for items that are not heavy. A conveyor, a table over which small carts can be rolled, or a table with rollers mounted into its top surface enables heavy objects to be rolled from one operation to another.

Movement between cells can be accomplished with manual trucks or, if the volume justifies, with conveyors. Since cells are used to gain flexibility in many cases, flexible materials handling is often used. One materials-handling method that is sometimes used is the *automatic guided vehicle (AGV)*. These vehicles are usually battery-powered and are guided by computer signals pulsed through wires on or in the

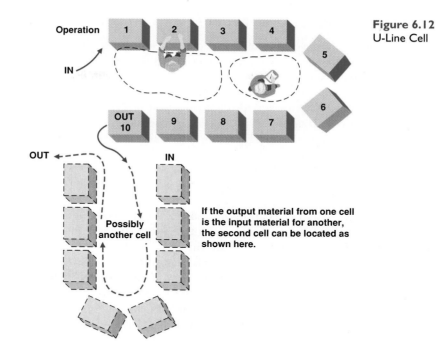

Figure 6.12
U-Line Cell

floor, so they do not require an operator. They can respond to commands of where to turn, speed up, stop, load, or unload. AGVs are another form of programmable automation.

Application of Cellular Configurations in Services

Many service businesses apply the concept of cells by grouping in one work area all of the equipment to work on a variety of similar jobs. Often performing the work in this way is so natural in these settings that we don't recognize that any other approach might be considered. When you watch a short-order chef turn out a broad assortment of meals at one counter area you are watching a service equivalent to cellular manufacturing. The barber shop, beauty shop, and dentist's operatory often are much like cells. A secretary's work area may contain a telephone, typewriter, computer, printer, and perhaps a fax machine and a photocopy machine providing the capability to produce a wide variety of letters, reports, and so forth. A quick oil change shop has bays that are essentially cells. An automobile dealer or auto service shop may contain a cell for oil, grease, and filter changes; another cell for wash, wax, vacuum, or other clean-up work; and another cell for wheel and tire work. Probably you can think of other settings where several kinds of similar work can be performed with equipment that is grouped in one area.

FACTORS THAT INFLUENCE LAYOUT SELECTION

Not every situation will fit exactly the conditions that make one type of layout fully suited to the operation and other types undesirable. Myriad factors should be considered in designing a work facility.

Volume of Production

The volume of items to be produced usually is very important in selection of an appropriate layout. A job shop has the flexibility to produce many types of items, so its design is not optimized for any one particular item. Consequently, as the volume of a specific item increases, the job shop layout suffers disadvantages in comparison to a layout designed for production of items similar to the one under consideration. A cell designed to produce this type of item will contain equipment that is purchased or adapted to perform the necessary operations efficiently. The pieces of equipment will be located close to one another in order to reduce materials-handling costs. Production workers will be more knowledgeable about the work because it is repeated more often, and the advantages of the learning-curve effect are more likely to be realized.

When cells are used to make components of an assembly, there will be some WIP and extra materials handling between the various cells and the assembly area. Thus, when the volume is high, the cost per unit can be higher when cells are used than it would have been if a dedicated production line or assembly line were used. Production lines use special-purpose equipment designed to perform a particular operation very efficiently. Material moves are very short, and there is very little work in process along the line. The general relationships between volume and cost for the three layouts discussed are shown in Figure 6.13.

Other Factors

Volume is certainly not the only factor to consider in selecting a layout. Each business has many other factors, and their relative importance will vary from one organization to another. Some commonly considered factors are:

The weight of the item to be produced

The nature of the service to be provided

The cost of the building to house the operation

The product mix that must share a facility

The fragility of a product or component

Figure 6.13
Effect of
Volume on Cost with
Classical Layouts

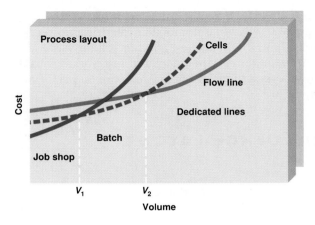

SUPPORT SERVICES

No discussion of layout would be complete without consideration of the space necessary for support services. The plant or service facility per se is important, and its layout influences profit. Support activities must be carried on in such a way that the direct operations can function smoothly. It is estimated that about one-third of a plant or department may be devoted to support facilities.

Floor space in any facility costs money. The space required for direct production is always considered justified, but all other space is sometimes considered an unnecessary expense, even though support services are essential to the primary operation. The space occupied by support services should be arranged with care to ensure their efficiency, so that indirect expenses are minimized. Crowding a department into such small quarters that its operations are hampered is false economy.

Some support services need ready access to the direct work areas whereas others do not. With the move to greater employee participation, it is important to include team meeting areas and training rooms. Some of the ancillary departments to be considered in a layout are:

Inventories of components, materials, and supplies

Toolrooms or tool cribs

Inspection and quality control

First aid

Shipping and receiving

Maintenance

Supervisory offices

Washrooms and locker facilities

Refreshment areas and cafeteria

Security and safety

Clerical and bookkeeping

Design and development

The inventory storage area is one service area whose layout has received considerable attention. When a manufacturing operation has 100,000 or more different inventory items, the movement of such items into and out of inventory involves much materials handling. The primary activities of some operations, such as distribution centers, are materials handling and storage. Warehouse design has changed in recent decades, with increased use of high-rise storage, stacker cranes, and computer-directed storage and picking of stock. Storage racks may be 80 feet or more high, with several layers of storage lines above the floor level. The objective is to achieve the maximum amount of storage per square foot of floor space.

Layout considerations involve three dimensions in high-rise storage. Items may be stored in any location as long as the bins are large enough to accommodate them. High-rise stacker cranes may be operator-controlled or automatically controlled through a punched card, magnetic tape, or computer input. Storage may be random, so that a locator file must be maintained to identify the location of each item. With automated storage and retrieval systems, the computer stores in memory the address at which each item is placed. When the item is to be retrieved, the computer will search its memory, find the item's location, and dispatch the crane to pick it from the rack. Generally, more frequently used items should be stored at the lower levels near the front, in order to reduce storage and retrieval time. Energy can be saved by storing heavier items at the lower levels.

ANALYSIS FOR LAYOUT BY PRODUCT

Some of the design for a production line facility (that is, layout by product) is established when each part of the product is designed and a process engineer determines the steps required to make it. The volume to be produced may determine the process that is most economical, and the process technology may then dictate the sequence in which the steps must be performed. The equipment and work stations to perform the work are then arranged in the sequence in which they are needed. For example, a printed-circuit board for an electronic assembly, such as a television set, must be produced before the electronic components can be mounted on it. Components that can withstand the heat of an automatic soldering process are mounted on the board (perhaps by a robot or automatic "board stuffer"). The electrical connectors for all these components can be soldered automatically at the same time. Components that should not be exposed to the heat of automatic soldering might then be added manually. Another example might be a metal part that requires a hole to be drilled and threaded and a bolt installed. These steps must be performed in that sequence. The pieces of equipment required to perform the operations are placed along a line in the sequence in which they are required. The line might be curved so that it fits within the available space or within an economical structure, if one is to be built.

In some cases the task sequence is not dictated by the technology, and a line may be arranged with work stations and equipment in many possible sequences. This situation is common in manual assembly operations where items may be installed in many sequences. When many options exist, mathematical models such as line-balancing models are useful in determining the appropriate ways to group the tasks to be performed at each work station.

Line Balancing

The total amount of work to be performed on a line must be broken into tasks and the tasks assigned to work stations, so the work is performed in a feasible sequence within an acceptable cycle time. The *cycle time* for a line (time between completion of successive items on the line) is determined by the maximum time required at any work station. Work cannot flow through the line any faster than it can pass through the slowest stage (the bottleneck of the line). If one work station has a great deal more work than others, assign some of this work to stations with less work so that there are no bottlenecks in the line.

Ideally, there will be equal amounts of work at work stations, that is, a balanced line. All stations of a balanced line are fully utilized if it is run at its fastest cycle time. If it is run at a slower rate, the idle time on the line will be equitably distributed among all the workers along the line. This idle time might be used as a rest pause and to allow for variability of work requirements from one cycle to another. Consider an automobile assembly line. Installing an automatic transmission may require more time than installing a standard transmission, and the products flowing down the line may have some different transmission requirements. It is desirable to have the average work loads balanced at each station, even though some variation around the expected times will occur.

Line balancing involves selecting the appropriate combination of work tasks to be performed at each work station so that the work is performed in a feasible sequence and approximately equal amounts of time are required at each of the work stations. The objective is to minimize the required labor input and facility investment for a given amount of output. This objective is sought by either:

1. Minimizing the number of work stations (workers) required to achieve a given cycle time (that is, a given production capacity)

2. Minimizing the cycle time (maximizing the output rate) for a given number of work stations

The first objective is more appropriate when one is considering the initial scheduling or rescheduling of a line. The second objective is more appropriate if demand equals or exceeds the rate that can be achieved with the available resources (space, equipment, people, etc.).

The total idle time (IT) for the line is given by

$$IT = nc - \sum_{i=1}^{k} t_i \qquad\qquad \text{[6.1]}$$

where IT = total idle time for line
 n = number of work stations, assuming one worker per work station
 c = cycle time for line
 t_i = time for ith work task
 k = total number of work tasks to be performed on ith production line

A line is perfectly balanced if IT = 0 at the minimum cycle time. Sometimes the degree to which a line approaches this perfect balance is expressed as a percentage or a decimal, called the line efficiency. As a percentage, the line efficiency, e, is found by

$$e = \frac{100\left(\sum_{i=1}^{k} t_i\right)}{nc} \qquad\qquad \text{[6.2]}$$

A well-balanced line has a very high efficiency.

The number of task combinations that could be assigned to a work station rapidly becomes large and unwieldy as the number of work tasks increases. Consequently, algorithms have been programmed to develop approximate or satisficing solutions by use of computers. Line-balancing problems have been solved by various approaches such as trial and error, heuristic methods, computer sampling until a good solution is found, linear programming, and dynamic programming. The last two of these are optimizing methods that will require considerable computation for any reasonable-sized problem.

Before assigning work tasks to work stations, the analyst must take several preliminary steps.

1. Identify all the work tasks that must be done to produce the product.

2. Identify the time required to perform each task.

3. Identify the precedence requirements for each task. In other words, which task(s) must be performed before a particular task can be performed?

4. Define the target cycle time (which must be greater than or equal to the largest task) or define the target number of work stations. If we know Σt_i and n, then we can find the target cycle time: $c_t = \Sigma t_i / n$.

After these four requirements are completed, the analyst can begin to assign work tasks to work stations. We shall discuss heuristic methods of line balancing. A *heuristic method* uses rules of thumb that lead to a feasible, though not necessarily optimal, solution.

Some tasks must be performed before others can begin. For example, a hole must be drilled or punched in a piece of metal before a bolt can be put through it. The task that must be performed immediately prior to another is called its predecessor. Often a precedence diagram is drawn to show the order of performance of work elements to assist in their selection.

Usually tasks are assigned to the first work station, then the second, and so on until the final assembly tasks are assigned to the last work station. A complete set of work tasks is selected and assigned to one work station before assignments are made to the next station. At any stage of assigning work tasks, some tasks have already had their predecessors assigned and therefore can be assigned themselves. This subset of the total task list is called the *available list*.

A rule or set of rules is needed to guide the selection of tasks from the available list for assignment to the work station being loaded with work tasks. A simple rule is to select tasks in the order in which they occur on the list as long as the time required by the tasks is less than or equal to the remaining available work time at the work station. Tasks that are too lengthy are skipped, and assignments continue to be made by working down the list until it is exhausted or until the available time at the work station is filled. Each time a task is assigned, its successor tasks are added to the available list. Once the available cycle time for a work station is filled, assignments to the next are begun.

This or some other heuristic method is usually used to select work elements for assignment, although several computerized line-balancing packages are available, some of which use a combination of rules. Some heuristic methods are:

1. Select from the available list the task with the largest time that will fit within the work station's available time.

2. Select the task with the most successors (as long as it will fit within the work station's available time).

3. Select the task with the greatest sum of the task times of its successor tasks (as long as it will fit within the work station's available time).

Example of Line Balancing

Let's go through an example of a line-balancing problem, using heuristic method 1 mentioned above. The company wants to achieve a production rate of 160 units per 8-hour day utilizing a production line. Table 6.1 lists the nine work tasks that must be performed to produce the item and indicates the sequence in which these tasks must be performed. The specified production rate of 160 per 8-hour day is 20 per hour. This rate converts to a cycle time of 3 minutes, which is 180 seconds per unit. No station can work on the item (or delay it) for more than 180 seconds if the target production rate is to be achieved. If the line is balanced and a minimum

Table 6.1

**TASK TIMES AND SEQUENCING
REQUIREMENTS FOR LINE-BALANCING
PROBLEM IN EXAMPLE**

WORK TASK	PREDECESSOR(S)	TIME (SECONDS)
A	None	60
B	A	80
C	None	30
D	C	40
E	B, D	40
F	None	50
G	F	100
H	D, G	70
I	E, H	30

number of stations are to be used, each work station should have about this amount of work. The nine work tasks must be assigned to work stations in such a way that they will be performed in the proper sequence. All work stations will have about the same amount of work to perform, and the desired cycle time will be achieved.

For manual solution, it is often helpful to display the sequencing requirements in the form of a network, such as that shown in Figure 6.14. Each work task is shown as a node (circle), and the sequence requirements are indicated by arrows. With the time required to perform each task indicated above its node, the entire problem is contained in the network.

STATION I ASSIGNMENTS   The available list before any assignments are made is *A, C,* and *F* because they require no prior work task. *A* is selected because the 60-second time is the greatest task. *A* is removed from the available list, and *B* is added because its predecessor has been assigned.

Next *B* is selected because its time is the longest and it will fit in the unassigned portion of the cycle time at station I. The available list now contains *C* and *F.* Notice that *E* was not added to the available list because only one of its two predecessors has been assigned.

Next task *F* is tried because its time is the longest. Task *F* is too large, however (its time is longer than the unassigned cycle time at station I). It is found that the next larger time will fit, and task *C* is assigned to work station I.

Assigned tasks: *A, B, C*

Total work time: 170 seconds (and 10 seconds idle time)

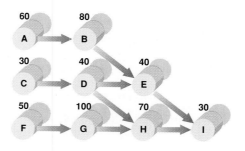

Figure 6.14
Precedence Diagram
for Line Balancing

STATION II ASSIGNMENTS The available list is *F* and *D* because their precedence requirements have been fulfilled. The longest task, *F*, is assigned to the second station. The available list is now *D* and *G*. Task *G* is assigned because its time is longer and it will fit within the remaining time. The available list is *D*, and it will *not* fit into the remaining time.

Assigned tasks: *F, G*

Total work time: 150 seconds (and 30-second idle time)

STATION III ASSIGNMENTS The available list consists of only task *D*, so it is assigned to the third station. The available list becomes *E* and *H*, so *H* is assigned. The available list becomes *E*, and *E* will fit within the available time at the work station, so *E* is assigned. The available list now consists of task *I*. Sufficient time for *I* remains, so it is also assigned to this station.

Assigned tasks: *D, H, E, I*

Total work time: 180 seconds (and no idle time)

EVALUATION OF THE LINE BALANCE The line will be paced by the 180-second time of work station III. The idle time for the line will be

$$IT = nc - \sum_{i=1}^{k} t_i$$

$$= 3(180) - (60 + 80 + 30 + 40 + 40 + 50 + 100 + 70 + 30)$$

$$= 40 \text{ seconds}$$

The efficiency of the line is

$$e = \frac{100(\Sigma t_i)}{nc} = \frac{100(500)}{3(180)} = 92.6 \text{ percent}$$

Other Considerations

We have assigned work tasks to work stations solely on the basis of the time the tasks are expected to take. Sometimes other factors must be taken into consideration. The skills required for one task may be much different from those required for another. Hence, tasks requiring different skills should be assigned to the same person only if the staffing and training difficulty can be met. Regardless of the operator's skills, some processes are incompatible and should be performed in different areas. Grinding and painting probably should be separated. Processes involving flames or sparks, such as welding, should be located away from flammable operations, such as cleaning with solvents. Lines are sometimes zoned into areas, and certain classes of work elements are assigned only within certain zones.

In addition to the technical and physiological considerations, psychological factors should be considered. The worker's need for a sense of accomplishment suggests that the elements assigned to him or her should be somewhat related and should make a recognizable contribution to the total job. Factors of this sort are discussed in Chapter 8.

Potential Increases in Production Rate

Various actions are possible if demand increases beyond the capacity of a production or assembly line. If a line is unbalanced, there is potential for increased capacity without modification of the entire line. Many of the work stations in an unbalanced line may have capacity to service demand slightly beyond the capacity of the line as a whole. Remember, the slowest work station, or "bottleneck," determines the minimum cycle time of the line. Careful study of the work methods and equipment at the limiting work station may reveal opportunities to reduce the cycle time of the entire line. If the line is balanced but demand greatly exceeds capacity, it may be replaced by a higher-capacity line or complemented by an additional facility. Sometimes the cycle time of a line can be changed by the addition or elimination of work stations and reallocation of tasks.

A balanced line with some manual work stations and some machine-paced stations may become unbalanced over time. Operators may become more skilled and may develop shortcuts in performing their work. The machine times will remain relatively constant, leading to differences of capacity, or throughput rate. The phenomenon of reduced production time as more and more units are produced—the learning curve—is discussed in Chapter 15.

ANALYSIS FOR LAYOUT BY PROCESS

Determining Department Size

Layout by process is generally associated with versatile operations that must provide nonstandard products or services. The typical product mix must be forecast in order to determine what sort of facility will be appropriate for the operation. Facility decisions may be based on those types of products that are most frequently produced or most greatly affected by the layout.

After a forecast is made, it must be converted to the space required in each department. For a manufacturing operation, the routing of each product or component must be determined. The number of production hours required for each product (that is, "time standards," discussed in Supplement F) or component should be multiplied by the expected number of items to be produced each month, to arrive at an estimate of the number of production hours needed in each department. The production hours per month indicate generally the number of people and machines that should be available. Of course, some provisions should be made for seasonal and random fluctuations in work load. This additional capacity also allows for catch-up work needed because of scrap, absenteeism, equipment breakdowns, and other causes.

Determining Department Location

After the necessary department sizes have been determined, the departments can be arranged within an existing structure (if space permits) or in a desired pattern in some new facility. The relative location of departments depends on such factors as the space required, the shape of any existing structure, and the sequence of steps through which each product must be processed. Some structural shapes are more economical or better suited to the site than others. This stage of layout by process presents an extremely large number of options and makes the layout process very challenging.

To illustrate the wide variety of arrangements that can be made, consider the example shown in Figure 6.15. Assume that we are to arrange six equal-size departments (1 through 6) in a building, and to simplify the matter, consider only square departments. Assume that the building is rectangular. There are six spaces in which

Figure 6.15
Six Square Department
Spaces in a Rectangular
Building

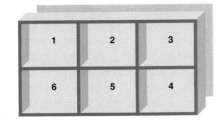

we could place department 1. Once 1 is placed, there are five spaces in which to place the next department. The next department will have four available spaces, and so on. In all there are 6!, or 720, ways in which we could arrange this facility. If we added one more department, we would have $7 \times 720 = 5,040$ ways. The number of ways we can arrange n square departments is $n!$ Of course, some of these arrangements are mirror images (left-to-right or top-to-bottom reversals) of other arrangements. If we begin to change both the shapes and the locations of departments, however, the number of options becomes limitless. You can see that identifying and arranging a realistic number of departments would take a long time unless we used some heuristic (rule of thumb) to limit the options we try. Of course, we would need some criterion or objective before we could know which alternative to select, and this criterion would reduce the number of options that must be evaluated.

Transportation Cost as a Criterion for Layout

A large number of factors usually influence the final selection of a layout. A frequently used factor, although it is seldom the sole factor considered, is transportation. To begin, let us concern ourselves only with transportation cost. The cost of transportation between two departments may arise because of the need to move material or correspondence between departments or the need of personnel to walk from one department to another to confer, inspect, supervise, or perform direct work activities.

It is frequently assumed that transportation costs for a given type of object are proportional to the distances between two departments—at least, the incremental costs that can be influenced by layout. In a factory, for example, the load-and-unload cost is fixed if the size of the lot to be moved is fixed. Manufacturing layouts often are selected by finding the layout that minimizes the total movement M, which is the product of the volume V, the weight W, and the distance D, as shown in equation 6.3.

$$M = \sum_{i=1}^{N} \sum_{t=1}^{T_i} (V_{it} \times W_{it} \times D_{it}) \qquad \text{[6.3]}$$

where M = measure of materials handling
$\quad i$ = product or component
$\quad N$ = number of products or components that must be considered
$\quad t$ = individual transfers that must be accomplished between departments
$\quad T_i$ = total number of transports that must be accomplished for the ith product or component

Sometimes only those items produced or used in large volumes or those of great weight are considered. Computer programs are available to perform this step. Flow matrices may also be used. Some of these methods are discussed in more detail later.

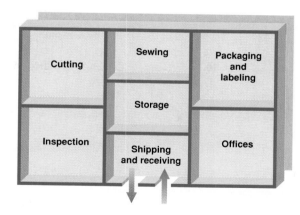

Figure 6.16
Layout for a Dominated Flow Pattern

The only way to change the transportation cost once the layout is established is to change the volume of products moved in each trip, thus also changing the number of trips necessary between two departments. The cost per unit of distance moved will sometimes be different at different stages of production. In a plant that makes chairs, for example, it is more expensive to move a load of wood for chair frames than to move the frame padding. When costs per unit of distance vary, we work with dollars rather than distance.

DOMINATED FLOW PATTERN   We consider first a fully *dominated flow pattern,* then a flow that is not fully dominated by any pattern. Assume that we wish to lay out a contract sewing facility. There is no standardized product; the company bids to manufacture a specified number of garments. Each contract can be for a different garment in a different quantity, in different colors and sizes. The material for every contract is received, stored, released to the cutting room, cut, sewn into garments, packaged, stored until a truckload is accumulated, and then shipped. The inspectors move through the plants and inspect each operation where it occurs. Since every movement from any department always goes to only one other department, we can minimize the transportation cost by making those departments adjacent. The resulting arrangement could be a straight line of departments. Since shipping and receiving activities are carried out by the same department, however, an O or U shape would be better (see Figure 6.16). The sizes of the departments may vary with the capacity required and the shape of the building. For this type of operation, we are arranging entire departments along some path in the same way that we would arrange machines or work stations along a flow line.

NONDOMINATED FLOW   When flow is equal among all departments, no particular arrangement is superior to any other as long as they all fit into the available space—unless, of course, some moves are more costly than others. We consider a company that has some reason for desiring a particular layout but for which the most desirable layout is not as obvious as in a fully dominated situation. Job shops have such a broad variety of jobs that the flow of work leaving any department may go in any of a number of directions—a *nondominated flow.*

Assume that we have a forecast of demand throughout some reasonable portion of the lifetime of a facility. Knowing the anticipated product mix and quantity enables us to know the necessary size of each department and the anticipated average number of trips, say, per month, between the departments. Figure 6.17 shows a hypotheti-

Figure 6.17
Average Number of
Trips per Month
Between Departments

To	Departments					
From	A	B	C	D	E	F
A	0	217	418	61	42	180
B	216	0	52	190	61	10
C	400	114	0	95	16	20
D	16	421	62	0	41	68
E	126	71	100	315	0	50
F	42	95	83	114	390	0

Figure 6.18
Cost per 100 Feet to
Move an Average Load
(in Dollars)

To	Departments					
From	A	B	C	D	E	F
A	0	0.15	0.15	0.16	0.15	0.16
B	0.18	0	0.16	0.15	0.15	0.15
C	0.15	0.15	0	0.15	0.15	0.16
D	0.18	0.15	0.15	0	0.15	0.16
E	0.15	0.17	0.16	0.20	0	0.15
F	0.15	0.15	0.16	0.15	0.15	0

cal number of trips among six departments to be housed in a new facility. Next we need the cost per unit of distance (per 100 feet, per 1,000 feet, per 100 meters, whatever) to move the average-size load between each pair of departments. This information is shown in Figure 6.18. Notice that Figure 6.18 uses all the matrix except the diagonal. If cost were considered proportional to distance from each department to every other, we could use only the portion of the matrix above or below the diagonal. But a variety of objects are to be handled (because a different transformation is made in each department), and each department's output may be handled by a different method and in a different load size. Therefore we do not assume that the cost to move a load from department *A* to department *D* is equal to the cost to move a load from department *D* to department *A*, and so on.

Multiply the number of trips in the trips matrix (Figure 6.17) by the number in the same cell of the cost-per-unit-of-distance matrix (Figure 6.18). The resulting product represents the cost of each 100 feet of travel from one department to another. When we add the numbers below the diagonal, for cost of movement in one direction, to the numbers above the diagonal, for cost of movement in the opposite direction, we determine the cost per month for each foot of distance between pairs of departments.

The numbers in Figure 6.19 were developed by multiplying the hypothetical numbers in Figures 6.17 and 6.18. The numbers below the diagonal in Figure 6.19 were added to those above the diagonal to find the monthly moving cost per unit of distance, as presented in Figure 6.20. If the cost to move a unit of distance were the same between each pair of departments, we would not have needed the matrices in Figures 6.18 and 6.19; we could have looked at the number of trips to determine which departments should be near each other. Since the cost to move a unit of distance varies between pairs of departments, Figure 6.20 provides a basis for locating departments so as to minimize transportation cost.

To	Departments					
From	*A*	*B*	*C*	*D*	*E*	*F*
A	0	32.6	62.7	9.8	6.3	28.8
B	38.9	0	8.3	28.5	9.2	1.5
C	60.0	17.1	0	14.3	2.4	3.2
D	2.9	63.2	9.3	0	6.2	10.9
E	18.9	12.1	16.0	63.0	0	7.5
F	6.3	14.3	13.3	17.1	58.5	0

Figure 6.19
Monthly Cost per
100 Feet Between
Departments
(Direction of Movement
Considered)

Between	Departments					
And	*A*	*B*	*C*	*D*	*E*	*F*
A	0	71.5 ③	122.7 ①	12.7	25.2	35.1
B		0	25.4	91.7 ②	21.3	15.8
C			0	23.6	18.4	16.5
D				0	69.2 ④	28.0
E					0	66.0 ⑤
F						0

Figure 6.20
Total Monthly Moving
Cost per 100 Feet
Between Departments

The nearness priorities (transportation costs) are indicated by circled numbers in cells of Figure 6.20, in descending order. If transportation cost were our only criterion, we would want (1) department *A* near *C*, (2) *B* near *D*, (3) *A* near *B*, (4) *D* near *E*, and (5) *E* near *F*. Using these heuristics (rules of thumb) as guides, we could develop a resulting layout that looks like Figure 6.21. The double arrows indicate the nearness priorities. Several arrangements would place departments with high nearness priorities adjacent to each other.

Nontransportation Factors

One department may be placed near another or away from another for many reasons other than transportation cost. In a hospital we want contagious diseases away from the nursery and the surgery wing. Obviously we want the recovery room near the operating room. In a factory, we want a painting department (with flammable solvents) located away from the welding department (with its sparks and flames). Common sense will provide a few guidelines to prevent the need to try all possible arrangements.

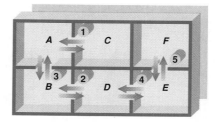

Figure 6.21
Layout to Satisfy
Transportation Cost
Nearness Priorities

ARRANGEMENT OF FACILITIES WITHIN DEPARTMENTS

As mentioned above, one of the first major steps in layout analysis is to determine the space needed in each department. This is accomplished by the conversion of a sales forecast into capacity requirements. A second major step is determining the relative location of the departments by seeing how well each arrangement meets some established criteria. This second step can be assisted by computer analysis. The remaining step is arranging equipment and people within the departments.

Arranging facilities within a department may be looked on as a miniature layout problem. One must consider intradepartmental as well as interdepartmental flows. Actually much of the intradepartmental layout may be determined before the relative departmental locations are considered. Earlier analysis of the layout within departments will help identify their desired size and shape and perhaps reduce the number of alternative arrangements to be considered in arranging their location.

The placement of individual pieces of furniture within a clerical department or of individual machines within a factory may be determined by use of graphical models. Scale drawings of the space and equipment or movable scaled templates may be used to evaluate alternative arrangements. Sometimes templates are used during deliberations, and drawings are made after the layout is decided upon. An example of a factory layout drawing is shown in Figure 6.22.

Computers may be used to assist in the layout within departments, although most applications probably do not justify the effort. The layout analyst would need to treat each major piece of equipment within a department as though it were a department. Flow between these subcomponents of departments or nearness priorities for the

Figure 6.22
Section of Sketch of Equipment Layout within a Department

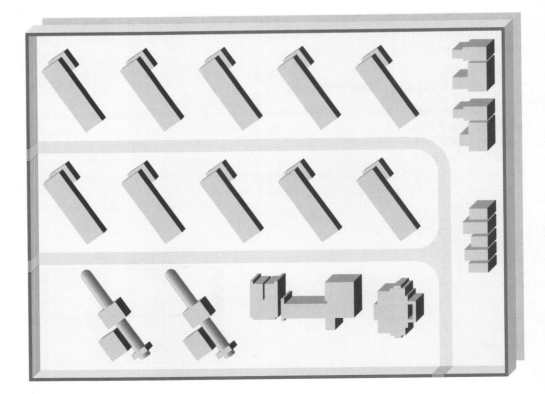

subcomponents must be identified, just as for other applications of computerized layout packages.

The Need for Versatility

Mass communications, mass marketing, broad travel, and other factors have led to rapid shifts in consumption patterns and operation methods. Change is part of the life of any organization in a dynamic economy. Factories are designed with broad open areas that can be adapted to a wide variety of uses. Because of their flexibility and economy of construction, metal buildings have become popular as factories, showrooms, warehouses, and even offices.

SUMMARY

If a company is to achieve its full potential for success, its facilities should facilitate the work to be done. Usually the work involves movement, flow, and interaction with equipment or between people. Retail establishments for food or other items try to provide attractive and functional surroundings; however, each business may work to achieve specific differences. Restaurants try to make the distances short because their employees have to make the trips many times. Stores may try to make customers move longer distances, passing attractive, high-margin items to get to the item desired. In each type of operation there is a trade-off among various objectives.

Manufacturers also work to make layouts as efficient as possible—ensuring that there is adequate but not excessive work space and that no bottlenecks impede movement. Layout by process and layout by product (two of the three classical layout types) were discussed in some detail. Layouts involve trade-offs of some advantages and disadvantages. The primary advantage of layout by process is its flexibility to make a variety of items in small volumes, so it is usually used in job shops. Layout by product is most suitable for high-volume production of one item or a very few similar items. Consequently, it is used by repetitive manufacturers. Many operations, such as batch manufacturers, try to gain both efficiency and flexibility through cellular layouts.

The location of equipment in a flow line is dictated by the necessary sequence of production steps. Line-balancing algorithms can be used to determine how many work stations will be needed. The location of departments in a process layout may depend on the compatibility of processes, requirements for utilities or ventilation, ease of supervision, employee safety, or transportation (materials-handling) costs. Overall transportation costs are frequently calculated in the evaluation of potential layouts. The moving cost to be minimized is proportional to the product of the number of moves, the weight to be moved each trip, and the distance for each trip.

KEY TERMS

Nearness priority	Cellular manufacturing	Heuristic method
Fixed-position layout	Group technology	Available list
Layout by function	Rabbit-chase cell	Dominated flow pattern
Functional layout	U-line cell	Nondominated flow
Layout by process	Automatic guided vehicle	
Layout by product	(AGV)	
Manufacturing cell	Cycle time	

DEMONSTRATION PROBLEM

Problem

A production line is to be established to produce 300 modems per day (460 minutes). The production tasks, their times, and their precedence requirements are shown in the table below.

TASK	TIME (MIN.)	PREDECESSOR(S)
a	0.6	—
b	0.3	a
c	0.8	—
d	0.7	—
e	0.4	c, d
f	0.8	b, e
g	0.5	f
h	0.9	f
i	0.2	g
j	0.1	h, i

(a) Using a heuristic that assigns the longest available task that will fit within the remaining work station time, assign the tasks to the minimum number of work stations required to meet the cycle time.

(b) Determine the efficiency of the line.

(c) How might the balance be improved?

Solution

(a) The target cycle time is 460 minutes/300 units = 1.533 minutes. A precedence diagram is useful to show how the tasks can be divided.

For Station I

The initial available list is a (0.6), c (0.8), d (0.7); so c is selected. No tasks are added to the available list. Next d is selected, and no other task will fit within the remaining work station time if the cycle time is to be 1.533 minutes. The first station has a cycle time of 1.5 minutes.

Tasks assigned: c, d. Work station time: 1.5 minutes.

For Station II

The available list is a (0.6), e (0.4); so a is selected, and b (0.3) is added to the available list. Next e is selected. Task b is the only task on the available list, so task b is selected. Task f is added to the available list, but it will not fit in the remaining time at station II.

Tasks assigned: a, e, b. Work station time: 1.3 minutes.

For Station III

The available list is f (0.8); so f is selected, and g (0.5) and h (0.9) are added to the available list. Task g is selected because it is the only one that fits the remaining time. Task i is added to the available list, and it is selected because it will fit in the remaining time.

Tasks assigned: f, g, i. Work station time: 1.5 minutes.

For Station IV

The available list is h (0.9), j (0.1); so h is assigned, then j is assigned.

Tasks assigned: h, j. Work station time: 1.0 minute.

It is helpful to mark a boundary around and label the assigned tasks as each station is loaded. These enclosed areas are shown on the diagram.

(b) The idle time for the line is $nc - \Sigma t_i = 4(1.5) - 5.3 = 0.7$ minute, if the line is run at its minimum cycle time. The line efficiency would be $\dfrac{100(5.3)}{4(1.5)} = 88.3$ percent.

(c) The work loads at the four stations would be closer to equal if task a were moved to station I, task d moved to station II, and task i moved to station IV. The cycle time could be reduced to 1.4 minutes if these changes were made.

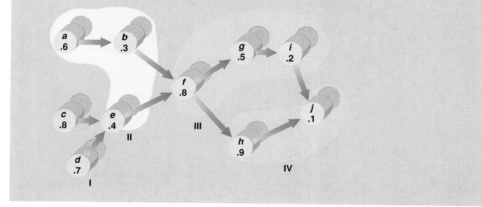

DISCUSSION QUESTIONS

1. Define layout.
2. Under what circumstances might a layout study or evaluation be warranted?
3. Discuss some of the objectives of a good layout.
4. Describe five major types of materials-handling methods, and name some advantages of each.
5. What are three classical types of layout? Give an example of each.
6. What are five advantages and five disadvantages of layout by product (flow line)?
7. What is a manufacturing cell or "cellular manufacturing"?
8. Briefly describe how a U-line cell operates.
9. Briefly describe how a rabbit-chase cell operates.
10. Differentiate between manufacturing and service layouts.
11. Several factors usually should be taken into account in the attempt to develop an optimal layout. What are some of these factors?
12. Why are some offices utilizing the open plan with broad expanses of space that have no permanent partitions?
13. Why are many factories utilizing large, preengineered metal buildings with broad expanses of unobstructed floor space?
14. Why are many offices being built as multistory buildings whereas single-story factories are more common?

PROBLEMS

1. The Baud Electronics Company produces electronic calculators and is planning to begin production of a new model. An assembly line is to be developed that will produce 500 units per 7.5-hour workday. The tasks, task times, and precedence requirements are given in the following table.

   a. Group the tasks into work stations by selecting the shortest remaining time from the available list at each selection, so long as that time will fit within the remaining available time at the work station.

   b. How well balanced is the line? How many work stations are used?

   c. Balance the line by selecting the longest task time that will fit within the available time for the work station. Is this assignment much different from part a? Why, or why not?

TASK	TIME (SECONDS)	PREDECESSOR
A	32	None
B	35	A
C	15	A
D	22	A
E	35	B
F	38	B
G	12	D
H	16	G
I	31	G
J	20	I

2. Shown below are the tasks, times, and precedence requirements for the work required to assemble a portable video game. The company wants to produce 340 units in a 460-minute shift.

TASK	TIME (MIN.)	PREDECESSOR(S)
A	0.3	—
B	0.6	—
C	0.4	—
D	0.8	A
E	0.7	B
F	0.3	C
G	0.9	D
H	0.1	F
I	0.3	H, E
J	0.4	G, I

   a. Draw a diagram showing the precedence requirements, and list on it the times with the tasks.

   b. Divide the tasks to achieve a balanced line. Use the heuristic of selecting the longest time that will fit in a work station.

3. The Apollo Toy Company is a small new toy manufacturer. The company is to produce a toy rocket and can assign three people to its assembly.

a. Develop a three-station assembly line for the following tasks.

TASK	TIME (SECONDS)	PREDECESSOR(S)
A	30	None
B	20	None
C	8	A
D	14	A
E	16	B
F	20	B, D
G	25	E
H	6	G
I	16	E
J	20	H
K	12	H
L	6	J

b. What is the cycle time?

c. What is the efficiency of the line?

d. What would be the expected output of this line per 8-hour production shift (assume the line is run at its minimum cycle time)?

4. The Montana Appliance Company is installing an assembly line to produce one of its small appliances, and you have been asked to balance the line. The tasks that are to be performed are listed below, along with the time required to perform each task and its immediate predecessor(s). The line is to produce 300 units in a full 8 hours of work.

a. Assign tasks to work stations by selecting the longest task that can be assigned at each opportunity.

b. Compute the efficiency of the line you developed in part *a*.

TASK	TIME (SECONDS)	PREDECESSOR(S)
A	51	None
B	22	A
C	28	A
D	32	A
E	39	A
F	20	B
G	20	C
H	16	D
I	12	E
J	42	F, G
K	44	H, I
L	20	J
M	20	K
N	12	L, M

5. Use the same target cycle time, task times, and precedence requirements given in the previous problem.

a. Assign tasks to work stations by selecting the shortest task that can be assigned at each opportunity.

b. Compute the efficiency of the line as assigned in part *a* of this problem.

6. Arrange six square departments in a grid like the one shown, so as to meet the objectives listed:

Department A near E
A near D
A near C
B near C
B near D
F near D
E near F

7. The grid shown here is an initial layout of four square departments within a square office building. The number of moves each week between departments is as follows: A–B = 200, A–C = 300, A–D = 400, B–C = 200, B–D = 500, C–D = 100. All movements are assumed to occur from the center of the sending departments to the center of the receiving departments. These moves are made along aisles that run parallel to the exterior walls. Therefore the average move distance between diagonally located departments is assumed to be 200 feet, and between adjacent departments it is assumed to be 100 feet. Enumerate the layouts that can be made through pairwise interchanges, and determine the total movement distance that results from each layout. Which layout minimizes movement?

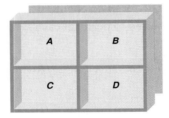

8. Arrange six square departments 1 through 6 in a 2 × 3 grid like the figure in problem 6 so that the nearness priorities shown in the matrix below are satisfied.

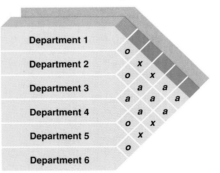

a = absolutely necessary
e = very important
i = important
o = OK, ordinary importance
u = unimportant
x = undesirable

9. Draw the resulting layout for each possible pairwise interchange of departments that can be made in the departmental arrangement shown.

10. A factory with four major departments is to be arranged so that the cost of moving materials between the departments will be at or near the minimum. The product mix for the next 2 years has been forecasted and the number of trips that will result between departments has been estimated. Based on the anticipated load sizes and the materials-handling methods that are to be used, the cost per unit of distance between the departments has been estimated. This data is shown in the table that follows. Develop the nearness priorities for the pairs of departments.

Movement		EXPECTED NUMBER OF TRIPS	COST PER UNIT OF DISTANCE
FROM	TO		
A	B	300	$0.16
A	C	100	0.16
A	D	150	0.12
B	A	100	0.15
B	C	350	0.18
B	D	200	0.18
C	A	425	0.16
C	B	300	0.15
C	D	100	0.12
D	A	30	0.25
D	B	50	0.22
D	C	100	0.26

11. You are called in as a consultant for a firm that produces sporting goods. The manager wants you to arrange the plant to minimize transportation. The number of trips between departments and the cost per unit of distance for the typical load are given in the table below. Develop the nearness priorities for the departments.

Movement		EXPECTED NUMBER OF TRIPS	COST PER UNIT OF DISTANCE
FROM	TO		
A	B	200	$0.10
A	C	300	0.10
A	D	200	0.10
A	E	150	0.10
B	A	100	0.18
B	C	80	0.18
B	D	60	0.18
B	E	90	0.18
C	A	100	0.11
C	B	25	0.11
C	D	80	0.11
C	E	150	0.11
D	A	50	0.12
D	B	75	0.12
D	C	300	0.12
D	E	100	0.12
E	A	200	0.16
E	B	50	0.16
E	C	90	0.16
E	D	100	0.16

12. Departments *A, C, D,* and *E* should be 40×40 feet. Department *B* should be 40×80 feet. Arrange these five departments in a space 80×120 feet so that the layout meets the conditions specified in the matrix.

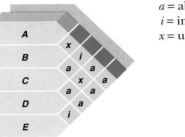

> *a* = absolutely necessary
> *i* = important
> *x* = undesirable

13. Locate nine square departments 1 through 9 in a 3×3 grid so that the priorities in the matrix are satisfied.

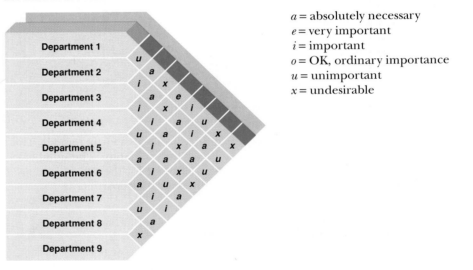

> *a* = absolutely necessary
> *e* = very important
> *i* = important
> *o* = OK, ordinary importance
> *u* = unimportant
> *x* = undesirable

14. The X-Calibre Company wishes to rearrange its six departments within a recently enlarged 160×240 foot building. The departments are to be equal in size, 80×80 feet, and arranged in a 2×3 grid. Assume that the average move distance between two departments is equal to the straight-line distance between the centers of the departments. For two departments beside each other the distance is 80 feet. Use the squared distance of the two sides to find the square of the distance between the centers of departments that are located diagonally. Assume that the cost per unit of distance is the same for all moves, so cost is not needed. The following table shows the number of trips per week that are expected to occur between departments.

	Number of Trips per Week				
DEPARTMENT	**2**	**3**	**4**	**5**	**6**
1	60	200	170	30	50
2	—	50	90	40	0
3	—	—	40	20	25
4	—	—	—	100	20
5	—	—	—	—	10

a. Identify the top five priorities for locating departments near each other.

b. Make at least one attempt to locate the departments in accordance with these priorities.

c. Calculate the total distance moved in a week with this arrangement.

d. In class, compare your solution with the solutions found by others.

15. The Spruce It Up furniture plant wishes to rearrange its six departments within a recently enlarged 200 × 300 foot building. The departments are to be equal in size, 100 × 100 feet, and arranged in a 2 × 3 grid. Assume that the average move distance between two departments is equal to the straight-line distance between the centers of the departments. For two departments beside each other the distance is 100 feet. Use the squared distance of the two sides to find the square of the distance between the centers of departments that are located diagonally. Assume that the cost per unit of distance is the same for all moves, so cost is not needed. Given below is a table showing the estimated number of trips per week between departments.

a. Identify the top five priorities for locating departments near each other.

b. Make at least one attempt to locate the departments in accordance with these priorities.

c. Calculate the total distance moved in a week with this arrangement.

d. In class, compare your solution with the solutions found by others.

	Number of Trips per Week				
DEPARTMENT	**2**	**3**	**4**	**5**	**6**
1	80	20	10	75	30
2	—	50	30	40	35
3	—	—	20	10	90
4	—	—	—	45	80
5	—	—	—	—	60

16. Six equal-size rectangular departments are to be placed in locations I through VI in the building sketched below. Aisles and corridors will be parallel to the exterior walls so that no diagonal travel will occur, and it is assumed that all travel will be from the center of one department to the center of another. For example, the following distances (in feet) between locations are assumed: I to II = 80; I to III = 60; I to IV = 80 + 60 = 140; I to V = 60 + 60 = 120; and I to VI = 80 + 60 + 60 = 200. The cost per unit of distance moved is the same for any move. Estimates of the average number of trips per week between departments are provided in the table.

a. Make an initial assignment of departments A through F to the six locations so that it appears that the travel distance will be minimized.

b. Exchange the locations of departments E and D, and compute the net effect on the total move distance.

		Weekly Number of Trips between Departments					
FROM	**TO**	**A**	**B**	**C**	**D**	**E**	**F**
A		—	90	50	90	80	20
B		30	—	20	60	30	60
C		50	20	—	90	90	30
D		70	30	80	—	20	60
E		80	30	60	60	—	10
F		50	80	10	60	30	—

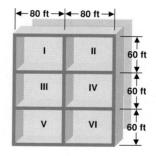

17. Determine which of the following two layouts will result in a lower product of trips times distance traveled per year if the numbers of trips between pairs of departments are as given in the table preceding the layouts. Assume that all movements are between the centers of the specified departments and are made parallel to the walls of the building and all turns must be at right angles, since there are no diagonal aisles.

EXCHANGING DEPARTMENTS	LOADS PER YEAR
A–C	1,100
A–B	1,300
D–E	1,600
C–D	2,100
A–D	2,500
B–C	3,200
B–D	3,800
A–E	4,200
C–E	4,300
B–E	4,600

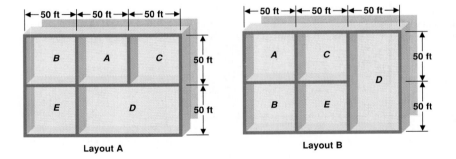

Layout A   Layout B

18. The MTL Company wishes to arrange stock within its warehouse (see layout at top of next page) so that the items with the highest use times weight (about 20 percent of the items in this company) are in zone A, nearest the loading dock. Items with the next highest use times weight (about 30 percent of the items) will be stored in zone B, and the remainder in zone C. Select from the items listed in the table below the items that should be in zones A, B, and C.

ITEM NUMBER	ORDERS PER MONTH	WEIGHT	ITEM NUMBER	ORDERS PER MONTH	WEIGHT
1	610	410	11	25	17
2	320	107	12	71	52
3	500	12	13	490	51
4	840	29	14	55	3,000
5	900	650	15	900	1,160
6	250	400	16	250	18
7	560	19	17	120	73
8	1,000	84	18	50	91
9	350	63	19	370	271
10	770	59	20	1,700	318

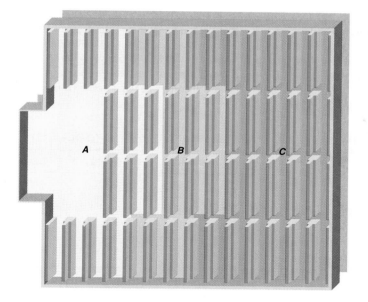

19. The Gingersnap Company is interested in designing a new plant. Forecasts of the future product mix and demand levels indicate the floor-space requirements for the six production departments shown in the following table. The company does not want the space occupied by any department to be more than twice as long as it is wide. The company plans to use a metal building that has a width of 120 feet and can be constructed in any length. The building site will accommodate a building up to 300 feet long.

The expected numbers of trips among the departments each week are indicated in the second table that follows. Assume that the transportation costs per foot traveled are equal between all pairs of departments. Suggest a layout of these departments that will fit the building, provide the desired floor space, and minimize transportation costs.

Floor-Space Requirements
for Six Departments

DEPARTMENT	SPACE REQUIRED
A	4,000
B	5,000
C	3,600
D	7,500
E	2,500
F	4,000

To	Departments					
From	A	B	C	D	E	F
A	—	80	10	5	2	20
B	20	—	5	90	6	10
C	6	0	—	6	0	120
D	10	18	100	—	0	30
E	20	16	20	2	—	18
F	4	20	25	18	95	—

20. The Marengo Machine Company is a job shop that produces a great variety of items. Flow within its plant is varied. Some departments deal with heavy items that are expensive to transport. The materials usually transported between some departments require only hand trucks, while a large industrial truck is usually required for the items moved in other parts of the plant. The costs for moving between various pairs of departments are shown in Table A. The expected number of trips between the departments is shown in Table B.

Table A
COST PER UNIT OF DISTANCE BETWEEN DEPARTMENTS (DOLLARS)

FROM TO	LATHE	MILLS	DRILLS	CASTING	FINISHING	ASSEMBLY
Lathe	—	0.02	0.02	0.02	0.02	0.02
Mills	0.05	—	0.05	0.05	0.05	0.05
Drills	0.03	0.03	—	0.03	0.03	0.03
Casting	0.08	0.08	0.08	—	0.08	0.08
Finishing	0.05	0.05	0.05	0.05	—	0.05
Assembly	0.10	0.10	0.10	0.10	0.10	

Table B
EXPECTED NUMBER OF TRIPS BETWEEN DEPARTMENTS PER WEEK

FROM TO	LATHE	MILLS	DRILLS	CASTING	FINISHING	ASSEMBLY
Lathe	—	300	100	10	100	100
Mills	200	—	300	10	150	150
Drills	50	150	—	10	200	300
Casting	50	350	300	—	50	100
Finishing	20	20	20	10	—	500
Assembly	10	10	10	0	0	

a. Develop a matrix of nearness priorities by computing the cost the company will incur for each unit of distance between the various departments.
b. Assume the departments are equal-size squares, and arrange them in a 2 × 3 grid so that the transportation costs will be minimized.

21. A small college is designing a new campus and has studied the average flow of students between buildings as classes change. The number of students moving between buildings is shown in the matrix to the right. Arrange the eight buildings around the perimeter of a square block so that the amount of walking between buildings will be near minimal.

	Mathematics	Chemistry	Physics	Behavioral Sciences	Language	History	Art	Gymnasium
Mathematics		220	220	160	100	150	220	200
Chemistry			240	180	170	150	180	140
Physics				200	190	200	160	100
Behavioral Sciences					100	180	260	180
Language						100	220	100
History							260	100
Art								100

BIBLIOGRAPHY

"Bakers Concept Keeps Shoppers on Their Feet." *Chain Store Age Executive,* February 1988, pp. 76–77.

Buffa, Elwood S., and Jeffrey G. Miller. *Production-Inventory Systems: Planning and Control.* 3d ed. Homewood, Ill.: Irwin, 1979.

"A Dozen Motor Factories under One Roof." *Business Week,* November 20, 1989, pp. 90–94.

Flynn, Barbara B., and F. Robert Jacobs. "An Experimental Comparison of Cellular (Group Technology) Layout with Process Layout." *Decision Sciences,* Fall 1987, pp. 562–581.

Francis, Richard L., Leon F. McGinnis, Jr., and John A. White. *Facility Layout and Location: An Analytical Approach.* 2d ed. Englewood Cliffs, N.J.: Prentice-Hall, 1992.

Gallagher, C. C., and W. A. Knight. *Group Technology Production Methods in Manufacture.* Chichester, England: Ellis Howard, 1986.

Hall, Robert W. *Attaining Manufacturing Excellence.* Homewood, Ill.: Dow Jones-Irwin, 1987.

Hyer, Nancy Lea. "The Potential of Group Technology for U.S. Manufacturing." *Journal of Operations Management 4,* no. 3 (May 1984).

———, **and Urban Wemmerlöv.** "Group Technology and Productivity." *Harvard Business Review,* July–August 1984, pp. 140–149.

Jacobs, F. Robert, John W. Bradford, and Larry P. Ritzman. "Computerized Layout: An Integrated Approach to Special Planning and Communications." *Industrial Engineering,* July 1980, pp. 56–61.

Milas, Gene H. "Assembly Line Balancing . . . Let's Remove the Mystery." *Industrial Engineering,* May 1990, pp. 31–36.

Pesch, Michael J., Larry L. Jarvis, and Loren Troyer. "Turning Around the Rust-Belt Factory: The $1.98 Solution." *Production and Inventory Management Journal,* 2d quarter 1993, pp. 57–62.

Rosenblatt, M. J. "The Dynamics of Plant Layout." *Management Science,* January 1986, pp. 76–86.

Schonberger, Richard J. *Japanese Manufacturing Techniques: Nine Hidden Lessons in Simplicity.* New York: Free Press, 1982.

Shafer, Scott M., and John M. Charnes. "Cellular Versus Functional Layouts under a Variety of Shop Operating Conditions." *Decision Sciences 24,* no. 3 (May–June 1993): 665–681.

Usher, John S., C. A. Ciesielski, and Ralph A. Johanson. "Redesigning an Existing Layout Presents a Major Challenge—and Produces Dramatic Results." *Industrial Engineering,* June 1990, pp. 45–49.

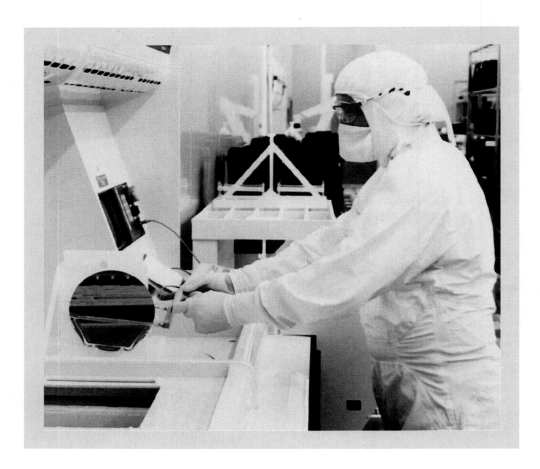

APPLICATION OF
TECHNOLOGY FOR
COMPETITIVE ADVANTAGE

CHAPTER 7

CHAPTER OUTLINE

TECHNOLOGY IS IMPORTANT FOR SEVERAL REASONS
New Goods and Services • Improved Ways to Provide Goods and Services • Improve the Structure and Functioning of the Organization • *How Technology Can Help Add Value for Customers*

MANAGEMENT SUPPORT FOR TECHNICAL PROGRESS
Encouraging Technical Awareness • Foster Idea Acceptance

INFORMATION TECHNOLOGY HAS BROAD IMPACT ON BUSINESSES AND LIVES
Overview of Some Changes from Information Technology

SOME APPLICATIONS OF TECHNOLOGY IN BUSINESS
Operations Management in Action: Information Technology in Travel Services • Office Automation • Electronic Data Interchange (EDI)

ARTIFICIAL INTELLIGENCE (AI)
Expert Systems

AUTOMATED DESIGN SUPPORT
Computer-Aided Design (CAD) • Finite-Element Modeling—Computer Testing of Prototypes • Automated Drafting (and Reducing the Need for It)

COMPUTER-AIDED MANUFACTURING (CAM)
Indirect CAM • Integrated CAD/CAM • Direct CAM

FLEXIBLE MANUFACTURING SYSTEMS (FMS)
Advantages of FMS • Limitations of FMS

COMPUTER-INTEGRATED MANUFACTURING (CIM)
Operations Management in Action: A Breakthrough in Automating the Assembly Line • Integration Challenges

TRENDS

Summary • Key Terms • Discussion Questions • Bibliography

I n broad terms, technology is the application of knowledge. In a business, technology includes the skills, techniques, procedures, equipment, and systems used to perform the work. As companies strive to improve, they seek the most appropriate technology to accomplish their work. Firms can also apply knowledge to develop improved products. High-technology firms try to incorporate the more advanced technology into their products in order to find new market niches and reap available profits before other firms introduce competing products. Lower-technology firms also must remain competitive, so they must use the most appropriate technology, even though these firms may not use the latest state-of-the-art in scientific knowledge. Thus, technology can be used to advantage through improved processing methods and improved goods and services that are offered in the market.

When a business designs or redesigns its production or operations system, it makes choices about the methods and equipment, hence the technology, that will be used in producing goods and providing services. Selecting or failing to select the most appropriate technology or failing to manage technology properly can have serious implications for a business. Michael Porter, a noted author on competitive strategy, remarked that technological innovation is perhaps the single most important source of major changes in market share among competitors and probably the most frequent cause for the demise of entrenched dominant firms.[1] Technology can provide a way to build competitive advantage for a company that can manage technology well.

Managers must see that their companies remain current and competitive. Clearly operations managers must consider technology in the initial design of an operations system, and they must continually evaluate technological threats and opportunities and be open to changing and adopting new ways. Technology can be improved through major strategic changes in processes and equipment which necessitate upper-management decisions. But the success of these major efforts and many smaller-scale changes, which are often powerful forces for improvement, depends on the efforts of the direct work force and front-line supervisors to change how the technology is applied. Remarkable improvements have been achieved through the efforts of improvement teams, suggestion programs, and other forms of employee participation. Small, continual refinements to apply knowledge to improve performance and customer satisfaction are important to remain competitive. Managers have to develop and nurture within the organization the ability to understand how major technical advances can be applied, and they must keep the organization open and motivated to change. It is difficult for a company to improve if its employees are resistant to change.

TECHNOLOGY IS IMPORTANT FOR SEVERAL REASONS

Businesses must remain aware of the potentials offered by technology and work to apply it if they do not want to fall behind their competitors. Technology can be applied by businesses in at least the three ways outlined below.

New Goods and Services

Technology can lead to new products or services that offer the customer something new and desirable. We often think of companies operating large research and development laboratories that work to develop new products to gain sales as older products enter the declining portion of their life cycles. High-tech firms try to com-

---

[1]Michael E. Porter, "The Technological Dimension of Competitive Strategy," in *Research on Technological Innovation, Management and Policy*, R. S. Rosenbloom, ed. (Greenwich, Conn.: JAI Press, 1983), p. 3.

mercialize technology in products by rapidly bringing out new products before the same company or one of its competitors introduces some other improved version. At Hewlett-Packard, for example, 70 percent of sales come from products that have been introduced or revamped within the past 2 years. A decade ago only 30 percent of sales came from recently developed or redesigned products.

There are many examples of new products that companies are introducing or are working to introduce. Consider a bubble jet printer that also serves as a fax machine. Or it could be movies on demand through a television set so that customers do not have to go to the video store twice, once to rent the movie and then to return it. Operations plays a major role in developing, introducing, and providing new goods and services.

Improved Ways to Provide Goods and Services

Technology can provide new processes or new ways of providing goods or services. For example, an artificial joint could be implanted by a robot—a "surgeon" whose hands do not shake—thereby giving a closer fit to the implant. Certainly operations will be different if "Robodoc" is to perform part of the procedure. Another possibility in the biotechnology field is to have kidney stones removed by introducing special bacteria that devour them. Banks provide service through automatic teller machines and manufacturing companies use computer-controlled machine tools to make parts.

Improve the Structure and Functioning of the Organization

Technology can be used to change the way the organization communicates, interacts, and coordinates the activities of its members. Employees may connect through telephone lines to telecommute to a virtual office where they access shared data bases and communicate with fellow employees through E-mail and videoconferencing. A department or section of a company may "work together" but may literally be scattered all over the world. Technology can be used in the logistics of linking a company to its suppliers and customers (such as the use of satellite communications at Wal-Mart, discussed in Supplement D).

We will not elaborate in detail about all the uses of technology. Certainly, one chapter cannot catalog all the dazzling goods and services that incorporate some recently developed wonder of science and invention. If such a catalog could be prepared, it would be obsolete tomorrow. Of course, not all technology is high technology or recently invented. Sometimes the technology has been available for years and businesses discover new applications for it. Sometimes companies negotiate mergers, acquisitions, and license agreements so they can apply technology that other companies have developed.

The intent of this chapter is to stress the point that technology is changing the world in which businesses operate and it will change almost any business. One's competitors may be seeking ways to employ technology to gain competitive advantage. A company and its competitors can supply new goods or services, provide them in better ways, and make the organization function better through the proper application of technology. Managers must lead their organization in such a way that it remains alert to new opportunities for technology application and is capable of employing it to the fullest potential.

HOW TECHNOLOGY CAN HELP ADD VALUE FOR CUSTOMERS

Technology includes all the work methods a company uses, whether high technology or otherwise. Improvements in technology offer opportunities for new products or services that will give customers more value. Automation, such as expert systems, can give quicker responses in manufacturing and services. It can improve quality by providing the knowledge base of several experts for much lower cost when the system is to be used for sufficient volume to justify developing these types of systems. Automated manufacturing is often more consistent than humans and can improve quality in some applications. Programmable automation, such as robotics and flexible manufacturing systems, can provide more flexibility than conventional automation and can reduce costs in some settings.

MANAGEMENT SUPPORT FOR TECHNICAL PROGRESS

Neither the success of new technology nor the failure of older technology is ensured. Companies are finding varying degrees of success. Competitiveness can be impaired by overinvestment of money and time in sophisticated technology that the company lacks the capability to use effectively. A company must evaluate its needs and must first ensure that it develops the ability to implement such changes as automation effectively enough to enhance its competitiveness. Much training and preparation for change are required along with modifications in technology. Behavior often alters along with technology, and the behavioral implications of a contemplated change must be analyzed and dealt with. Managers' technical knowledge and behavioral skills can be used to support an environment of advancement throughout the organization.

Companies that apply technology will naturally need some appropriate number of technically trained people. A company must devote the necessary resources to hiring and training so that it develops and nurtures the necessary knowledge within certain parts of its formal organization. To exploit technical advances in its products, for example, a company must effectively integrate marketing research efforts to assess customer desires with efforts in applied research and product development. Employees in product development must have broad understanding of scientific principles and technology in order to apply technology in ways that will better serve customer needs. Those who design production and service-delivery processes must also understand the available technology and look for innovations in the ways goods or services are produced. Aside from the technical staff and other parts of the formal organization charged with seeking technological improvements, a company must have a culture that respects and embraces technology and the progress it can provide. For greatest success in exploiting technology to the company's advantage, managers must maintain an environment that not only accepts technical change but also seeks and encourages it.

Encouraging Technical Awareness

How do managers develop an organization that discourages inertia and does not allow people to become complacent in the same old rut of routine procedures? Here are a few ideas about how to create an environment that values, accepts, and encourages new ideas.

1. Seek ways to bring value-adding ideas into the organization. Provide meaningful learning experiences through such methods as sponsorship of speakers and attendance at conferences that pertain to the business.

2. Circulate information on new ideas that are relevant.

3. Hold sessions to discuss what has been learned, the merits of applying it within the company, or how it might be applied by competitors. A company might hold meetings of small groups of managers and technical specialists so they can share ideas and opportunities. Such meetings are more productive if they focus on the mission and are not permitted to wander in all directions.

4. Sometimes great value is achieved through casual conversations in the hallways or at lunch. But good working relationships such as these must be facilitated and nurtured. Managers can help foster these relationships through such factors as organizational design, physical facilities, planning sessions, management style, and the culture or environment.

Foster Idea Acceptance

A few ideas on how managers can help build a positive attitude toward improvement projects might also be helpful.

1. The environment should encourage change where there is a good chance for improvement. Yet a company should steer away from fads that are not solid improvements—don't change just to be different.

2. Don't change everything all at once; the result can be confusion. Have a few improvement projects going, and make sure they are well thought out.

3. Managers should show genuine support and commitment to projects and should help minimize any barriers or difficulties. Once part of a company is organized to do things one way, it may require considerable persuasion to try something new.

4. Praise and publicize the successes, and do not allow anyone to be stigmatized for an honest attempt that did not work out well. People will be reluctant to try new ways if there is personal risk in failing.

There is considerable advice to be found in change theory. Much depends on management skills and insights into the specific situation and the people involved. It is apparent that there are many things that managers in all parts of the organization must do to make improvements work.

In the next section of the chapter we review information technology and its impact on businesses and lives. Then we discuss some applications of technology in business and artificial intelligence.

We will now discuss some applications of technology in providing services and in manufacturing goods. As we mentioned earlier, the focus is not on managing research and developing technology for new products as the outputs of businesses. Our focus is on technology used by businesses in performing their work. Of course, much of the technology that one company uses in its processes is likely to be the product of another company. Many of the topics discussed below are directly part of information technology or made possible by developments that are related to information technology.

INFORMATION TECHNOLOGY HAS BROAD IMPACT ON BUSINESSES AND LIVES

Information technology is very pervasive and is used in many parts of companies in a wide variety of types of business. Table 7.1 gives some indication of how widespread computers are in the workplace in regard to persons who directly use them. Many people benefit from applications of computers without being aware that computers are there working for them. A computer can be whatever it is programmed to be. For example, a computer can be a calculator, equipment controller, traffic controller, telephone switch, automatic engine tuner, a provider of animated displays on a television screen, or fantasy games, simulated virtual experiences, or many other things. Information technology is having a great impact on how companies provide goods and services and how they operate and are managed. Much of the progress in automating manufacturing and services is related to progress in the ability to transmit, store, and execute digital data and commands. Let us take a greatly simplified overview of some of the impact information technology has had over the past 40 years and then we will look at more specific applications of this and other technology in services and manufacturing.

Overview of Some Changes from Information Technology

Early applications of information technology provided little improvement in a business's overall or total factor productivity. Centralized data processing units used mainframe computers to perform analyses and provide reports for many persons. The organizations depended on distributing all of the relevant information to the proper employees and, of course, these persons must interpret the information, reach decisions, and direct communications so that the appropriate actions would be taken. The organizational structure was not modified as this level of computerization was implemented, only the clerical labor required to produce the reports was changed. Expensive capital equipment (that became obsolete rather quickly) had been substituted for clerical labor and total-factor productivity had been helped very little.

Computers steadily became much less expensive and much more powerful. Computer hobbyists, computer companies, publications, and company training programs helped more people learn to use the computer's capabilities. Employees in many

Table 7.1
WORKERS USING COMPUTERS ON THE JOB, BY INDUSTRY

Finance, insurance, and real estate	71%
Public administration	62%
Transportation, communication, and other public utilities	40%
Services	39%
Manufacturing	36%
Mining	31%
Wholesale and retail trade	28%
Construction	13%

Source: Ira Sager, "The Great Equalizer," *Business Week: The Information Revolution 1994*, p. 106. Reprinted from May 18, 1994 issue of *Business Week* by special permission, copyright © 1994 by The McGraw-Hill Companies.

Table 7.2
HOW THE INFORMATION AGE IS CHANGING BUSINESS

The advance of digital technology is having a dramatic impact on businesses, their workers, and the suppliers and customers who trade with them. Here's how:

Organization	New electronic systems are breaking down old corporate barriers, allowing critical information to be shared instantly across functional departments or product groups—and even with workers on the factory floor.
Operations	Manufacturers are using information technology to shrink cycle times, reduce defects, and cut waste. Likewise, service firms are using electronic data interchange to streamline ordering and communication with suppliers and customers.
Staffing	New systems and processes have eliminated management layers and cut employment levels. Meanwhile, companies are using less costly computers and communication devices to create "virtual offices" from workers in far-flung locations.
New Products	The information "feedback loop" is collapsing development cycles. Companies are electronically feeding customer and marketing comments to product-development teams so that they can rejuvenate product lines and target specific consumers.
Customer Relations	No longer simply an "order entry" job, customer-service representatives are tapping into companywide data bases to solve callers' demands instantly, from simple changes of address to billing adjustments.

Source: Ira Sanger, "The Great Equalizer," *Business Week: The Information Revolution 1994*, p. 101. Reprinted from May 18, 1994 issue of *Business Week* by special permission, copyright © 1994 by The McGraw-Hill Companies.

parts of businesses recognized applications for small computers and businesses began using PCs and small computers for decentralized applications.

A very major part of the progress in business benefits from information technology is in data communication and the ability to network computers. Computers gained the ability to exchange data, sometimes even at great distances, and many employees could work with a common data base. Employees can now generate, test, and exchange ideas that help a business perform better and quicker. Improved performance and productivity are not simply a matter of reducing the clerical cost of handling data. The payoff comes from being able to do things the organization could not do previously, or doing them faster, better, and cheaper.

Companies that are most successful at reaping the benefits of information technology are achieving this success by implementing organizational changes as they accomplish technology changes. Companies are "reengineering" the ways they work to take advantage of the powerful tools that are becoming available. Many have found that they can reduce the number of layers of managers used to collect and interpret information and communicate results and instructions up and down a hierarchy. The information can be interpreted and steered to the proper places faster through information technology, so organizations have become flatter and faster. Much of the impact of this technology on business is summarized in Table 7.2. Advances in technology are occurring with increasing speed and companies are applying technology in a multitude of innovative ways. No doubt, companies will continue to employ these advances in their pursuit of continuous improvement. Let us now look at a few more-specific tools and applications toward the goal of improving business efficiency and effectiveness.

SOME APPLICATIONS OF TECHNOLOGY IN BUSINESS

A good example of the way technology can change service delivery is found in the respiratory therapy department at the University of California San Diego Medical Center. The therapists carry miniature computers in the pockets of their lab coats. Patient records and instructions can be transmitted to these computers by radio frequency signals from a central computer. The therapists can spend more time with patients instead of traveling to and from their offices and nursing stations to obtain this information.

Coopers and Lybrand, an international accounting and consulting firm, is an example of how information technology is being used to improve and speed the reactions of a business. The company has purchased some 28,000 copies of a software package to enable employees to network their computers and exchange ideas and data. Consider one way in which this capability benefits the company. A data base contains previous work assignments of the company's consultants. A consultant working on a particular type of assignment and desiring some advice can query the data base and find other employees who have experience with similar types of problems. With E-mail, faxes, and the network, the firm can pull together team input from other employees in any part of the world.

We are directly familiar with some applications of automation and computer applications. Food and beverage vending machines, automated teller machines, machines for vending insurance, and automatic car washes fall into this category. Another familiar example is the operation in which the clerical function is supported by automation. A clerk in a grocery or other retail store can scan a bar code label to quickly and accurately enter information about the item being sold. Bar codes are most appropriate when the task is highly repetitive identification of numerous items, perhaps in multiple locations. The Red Cross, for example, uses bar coding to identify and track its blood inventory.

Other methods for automating data collection include optical character readers, magnetic-strip readers (for high density of data or for data that can be updated), and voice recognition (which is being developed but currently recognizes only a very limited number of voices and can understand a limited vocabulary). Computer vision systems are being developed to determine what an object is by direct observation rather than by reading a coded label.

The types of data collection methods mentioned above can be used in customer service areas and in office operations and manufacturing. Bar codes are often used in automated materials-handling systems in distribution centers and other warehouses. Avon reported doubling the order-filling rate of its distribution center at Pasadena, California, through the use of bar code scanning to direct the flow of shipping cartons. The U.S. Postal Service uses automatic zip code scanning on some letters to speed the sorting of mail for various locations.

Technological advances are applied to improve the processes used to provide services. For example, satellite-borne lasers can provide profiles of atmospheric wind, temperature, and humidity at different altitudes. Doppler radar can measure wind

OPERATIONS MANAGEMENT IN ACTION

INFORMATION TECHNOLOGY IN TRAVEL SERVICES

Over 85,000 computer terminals at travel agencies in 47 countries are linked in one of the world's largest privately owned computer networks, called Sabre (Semi-Automated Business Research Environment). Sabre, developed by American Airlines, is powered by seven massive IBM mainframe computers in an underground concrete bunker outside Tulsa, Oklahoma. American began marketing the system to outsiders in 1975 after talks between travel agents and major carriers failed to develop an industrywide reservation system. Analysts estimate that American earns a higher return on investment by booking tickets than it does by flying airplanes.

In addition to booking tickets, the system calculates flight plans, and since it knows how many passengers are on each flight, it figures the aircraft's weight and balance, fuel requirements, and takeoff power settings for about 2,300 American flights each day. Sabre maintains prices for up to eight fare classes for each possible trip. When price wars rage, nearly 1.5 million new fares may be loaded into the system each day.* A travel agent can access the system through a computer terminal and specify the travel dates, origin, and destination of a potential traveler. The system will search and within a short time provide the flights that can be used to link the two cities with feasible travel schedules. The availability and prices of the tickets are given along with dates by which flights must be booked to obtain the various fares. If the client wishes to purchase the ticket, the system can be used to make seat assignments and print tickets and boarding passes on most U.S. carriers and many international flights. Since the reservation system works in real time, it enables agents at many locations to know the current availability and to reserve seats on particular flights. Several agents could book the same seat if the response time were not rapid.

The features and capabilities of such a system are impressive and enable travel agents to provide many services beyond ticketing. One can find what movies will be shown on the flights and can order special meals. The system can arrange for assistance for children or handicapped persons to change planes or can have a limousine meet a particular passenger. It gives current attractions in many cities (for example, what's playing on Broadway) and can even order tickets to many such events. The system can reserve rental cars and book cruises, tours, and hotel accommodations. It may also give the weather in many cities, news of political unrest, or other travel advisories. For international travelers, the system can provide currency exchange rates, obtain foreign currencies, and provide information on visa requirements. The system will also provide the agency with periodic accounting reports on the business it has done.

*"The Computer Network that Keeps American Flying," *Fortune*, September 24, 1990, p. 46. © 1990 The Time Inc. Magazine Company. All rights reserved.

---

speeds in distant storms. Infrared images from satellites can be used to track hurricanes. The results are better weather forecasts from the National Weather Service.[2]

Since a large part of many services is knowledge work, computers are used to perform or to support at least part of the work. The rapid communication and data search capabilities of computers have been applied to provide remarkable capabilities in the field of airline reservation systems (see box). Micros, minis, and mainframes are at work in many places that provide services, from accounting and architecture to zoning consultants and zoos. Automobile dealerships have computer diagnostics of engine functions, computerized wheel balancing, and computers that control the parts inventory. Utility companies use computers to switch telephone circuits when calls are dialed, help control power plants, and compute customer's bills. Computers are everywhere, even in satellites overhead! We discuss only a few applications.

[2]Gordon Graff, "Tomorrow's Weather: New Accuracy in Forecasting," *High Technology 6*, no. 4 (April 1986): 27–31.

Itron's Mobile Automatic Meter Reading (AMR) system uses low-power radio to remotely read utility, electric, gas, and water meters from a vehicle equipped with a data collection transceiver called the DataCommand © Unit. Mobile AMR can read up to 24,000 meters in 8 hours.

Itron, Inc., photo by Robert Barros

Office Automation

One aspect of automation that affects both manufacturers and services is office automation. Paperwork is a major part of the processing in many service industries, and often it is the end product. Office automation technology in manufacturing companies usually has the greatest effect on workers in the support functions. In either case, however, classical office automation procedures are designed to assist personnel with repetitive physical tasks, even though the work the automation supports may be highly cognitive.

Office automation can have applications at all levels of the organization. A word processor, for example, can be used at many levels in the organization and for a variety of purposes. A secretary can produce a letter, a quality control engineer can create a file of fault experience for a given part, and a CEO can create a 10-year plan for the firm. Many of these applications can be especially useful if the word processor is linked to a data base program that can provide specialized searches of the data.

Just as manufacturing operations link machines into a system to pass physical work, machines that assist in knowledge work can be linked to interchange data to enhance their effectiveness. This capability allows data to be transmitted at the speed of light rather than at the much slower rate of reducing information to hard copy and sending it through the mail. Hard-copy data might then have to be reentered into a machine for further analysis. Networking is an especially important area of office automation, because it can help a company become better coordinated and more quickly responsive. Some standardization of signals and equipment is necessary to enable machines to "talk" to each other. *Technical and office protocol (TOP)* is a standard designed to meet the needs of office communication. If vendors make their equipment to the same standard, the machines can exchange data.

Electronic Data Interchange (EDI)

Companies are finding that *electronic data interchange (EDI)* has certain advantages. EDI involves the use of standard formats and compatible equipment so that computers in two companies can exchange messages. A computer at a large retailer, for example, can scan inventory records to determine which items are below their reorder levels. A buyer can indicate which items are to be purchased. The computer can prepare purchase orders, sort them, and store them electronically in designated "mailboxes" in its memory or in a data base at a timeshare data service. Through a data link, a computer at a vendor company will periodically check the mail in its box. The vendor's computer then enters the purchase order into its order entry system, prepares a pick list to withdraw the proper items from its inventory, and prepares the packing slip to ship it. This processing eliminates the handling and keying of data and is much faster. Later the vendor's computer can transmit back to the retailer's computer data regarding the items that have been shipped. The retailer knows what goods are in transit, so the price tickets can be prepared and ready when the goods arrive. Naturally, such applications of EDI require standardized formats and communication protocols, just as communication within a company does.

ARTIFICIAL INTELLIGENCE (AI)

Artificial intelligence (AI) is a branch of computer science that attempts to give computers the ability to understand language, to solve problems that call for reasoning, and to learn—in sum, to emulate human methods of learning and of solving problems. To approximate the way humans reason, AI systems manipulate symbols, in contrast to conventional systems, which manipulate numbers and rely on algorithms to solve problems. Rules, networks, graphs, and other data structures are used to show the relationships among the symbols that represent objects, persons, events, and their characteristics.[3]

These systems can "make assumptions" and simulate inductive reasoning by comparing incomplete data to ideal models. Systems that use a combination of these simulated inductive processes and conventional routines with set algorithms resemble the intuitive and logical thought that humans use to solve problems. AI systems are able to perform some tasks that otherwise would be done by humans and are able to produce adequate solutions.[4]

For tasks that involve creativity or for which new rules or insights must be developed, however, computers may not be as successful as humans. The ability to use incomplete data makes AI systems more flexible than conventional computer systems. As a result, AI-based control systems will perform better than conventional control systems in situations that demand flexibility. This ability allows the systems to perform some knowledge work, so they are being applied in both services and manufacturing.

The general field of artificial intelligence has been divided into six areas: expert systems, software development, natural language processing, robotics control, speech recognition, and computer vision. Expert systems are the most widely used, followed

[3]Ronald J. Meyer, "AI and Expert Systems: In Pursuit of CIM," *CIM Technology*, February 1987, pp. 15–16.
[4]Eliezer Geisler, "Artificial Management and the Artificial Manager," *Business Horizons*, July–August 1986, p. 19.

by software development. Considerable work is also being done to develop natural language processing so that AI-based software and conventional computer applications will be readily accessible to end users. We will primarily discuss expert systems.

Expert Systems

Expert systems are computer programs designed to make the knowledge of experts in a particular field available to users. They can be used to aid experts or less-knowledgeable persons in making decisions. The basic core of an expert system contains an inference engine and a knowledge base, or data base. Usually there is a natural language interface that permits the user to communicate with the system. The core components of an expert system are shown in Figure 7.1.

The system's knowledge base consists of traditional knowledge—facts and other information—as well as "if-then" rules that determine how the data are related both to other data and to potential solutions. These inference rules are rules of good judgment and reasoning that characterize expert-level decision making and problem solving. The rules are established by interviewing experts in the field to determine how they make decisions. The other major component of an expert system is the *inference engine,* or control mechanism, which does the actual problem solving. It contains programming that allows the system to evaluate the rules in the knowledge base. The inference engine determines which rules to invoke, depending on what has been determined so far about the problem. Since this control code is separate from the knowledge base, a single inference engine or "shell" can be used to drive different knowledge bases, creating expert systems for a wide range of disciplines.

Some of the earliest practical expert systems were developed in the medical field. One such system helps physicians diagnose bacterial infections. When supplied by the physician with the patient's symptoms and test results, the system offers a number of possible diagnoses, assigns confidence levels to each, and can even suggest additional tests. In addition, it can explain the reasoning behind a particular diagnosis. The same shell, or inference engine, with different knowledge bases has also been

Figure 7.1
Core Components of an Expert System

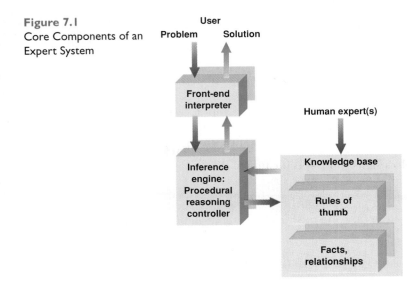

Table 7.3
SOME APPLICATIONS OF EXPERT SYSTEMS

Medical diagnoses	Integration of heterogeneous software for spacecraft design
Evaluation of loan applications	Design of image-forming optical systems
Insurance underwriting	Generation of programs to control a computer-controlled machine tool
Securities analysis	
Financial planning	Generation of process plans for fabricated parts
Tax consulting	Assistance of analysts in scheduling orders
Configuration of computer systems	Monitor and control of an automated materials-handling system
Automated design of forged parts	Visual recognition of parts
Design of digital logic circuits	

used to drive an expert system to aid in aircraft wing design, assist in mineral exploration, and serve as an expert tutor.[5]

Both direct and indirect activities in manufacturing also benefit from developments and improvements in artificial intelligence. Expert systems can act as interpreters to aid communication between various automated systems. This capability helps remove the barriers between what has been referred to as "islands of automation." Table 7.3 shows some of the types of applications where expert systems have been used.

Closely related to expert systems is the AI field of systems development tools. A common development tool is the interpreter, which allows a programmer to write a program in one language, then translate it to another. Most software of this kind is designed to translate general-purpose languages to newer, more specialized programming languages that allow the program developer to write in a language that is more natural to him or her.

Many applications of AI, such as those in training and in software development, can be used in manufacturing firms and in service firms as well. The developing field of AI will have a broad impact on many firms, and many people's jobs.

As this type of technology becomes more commonplace, it should become more user-friendly and less expensive, so that it will be feasible to automate tasks that previously were impractical to automate. We will now look at some of the applications of computers in the design and manufacturing of parts and products.

AUTOMATED DESIGN SUPPORT

Computer-Aided Design (CAD)

Computer-aided design (CAD) provides interactive graphics that assist in the development of product and part designs, tool designs, and specifications. A designer, working at a work station with a high-resolution graphics screen, can generate various views of an assembly or components. Wire-frame models can be used to represent three-dimensional figures and contours. Figure 7.2 provides an example of such a figure. More recently developed techniques for shading also are used to represent

[5]Wally Rhines, "Artificial Intelligence: Out of the Lab and into Business," *Journal of Business Strategy 6,* no. 1 (Summer 1985): 53.

Figure 7.2
Wire-Frame CAD

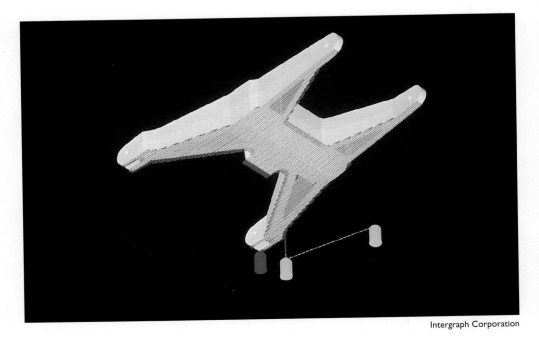

three-dimensional views of the object. The designer can zoom in on portions of an assembly, rotate it, or enlarge it to check for interference and examine other geometric features. These graphical models provide opportunities for manufacturing engineers, marketing specialists, and even customers to view the item and offer suggestions before further work is done. This type of design activity enables the product to be introduced rapidly, but it also helps overcome flaws that could give the product a poor reception that may never be surmounted.

Finite-Element Modeling—Computer Testing of Prototypes

Finite-element modeling is another technology that can speed the product development cycle. It is a type of simulation that enables engineers to test certain physical characteristics of an object in the computer, without the costs and delays required to construct and test prototypes. The object is described as a collection of small finite elements that are joined together. The stress and deflection characteristics of each element are then described by equations. The behavior of the total structure is determined by simultaneous solution of the equations for all the elements. A design can be revised, and performance of the improved design can then be tested.

Automated Drafting (and Reducing the Need for It)

Once the design is finalized by use of CAD, it can be stored in a computer data base that may be used to drive plotters to make drawings of the parts. That is, the physical acts of detail drafting can be automated. In a conventional manufacturing setting, information is transmitted by paper blueprints and specifications. When a design is changed, a goal (and one that is not always achieved) is to replace all old copies with the new design, so that all parts of the organization are working on the same object. The CAD data base enables other functions to access the same data and with much less paperwork. Such functions as tooling design, quality, and purchasing can access the same data base to ensure coordinated use of the latest product definition. An additional benefit of integrated data and communication is the ability to use this same data base to plan production and generate the detailed instructions needed to drive numerically controlled equipment that will produce the parts. That is, the common data base can also support computer-aided manufacturing, which we discuss next.

COMPUTER-AIDED MANUFACTURING (CAM)

Computer-aided manufacturing (CAM) means the use of computers directly to control the processing equipment or materials-handling equipment or indirectly to support manufacturing operations.

Indirect CAM

Indirect CAM involves the application of computers for capacity planning, scheduling, purchasing, inventory control, material requirements planning, shop-floor control, quality reporting, shipping and distribution, and other activities—most of which are discussed in other parts of the book. Indirect support systems may capture data about the flow of items in the shop (perhaps through bar codes or other automatic means) and use this information to support planning and scheduling. This kind of monitoring may also be used to update inventory use, scrap rates, or other quality information. Another indirect application of the computer to support manufacturing is process planning.

COMPUTER-AIDED PROCESS PLANNING   *Computer-aided process planning (CAPP)* helps determine the processing steps required to make a part after CAD has been used to define what is to be made. CAPP programs develop a process plan or route sheet by following either a variant or a generative approach. The variant approach uses a file of standard process plans so it can retrieve the best plan in the file after reviewing the design. The plan can then be revised manually if it is not totally appropriate. The generative approach to CAPP starts with the product design specifications and can generate a detailed process plan complete with machine settings. CAPP systems use design algorithms, a file of machine characteristics, and decision logic to build the plans. Expert systems are based on decision rules and have been used in some generative CAPP systems.[6]

Integrated CAD/CAM

Manufacturing performance is enhanced by the ability to consider such manufacturing matters as processing steps, machine capabilities, tool changes, holding fixture requirements, and assembly requirements, when a part or assembly is designed. Successful products must have designs that serve the function and that can be manufactured satisfactorily and economically. Both design engineering and manu-

---

[6]Philip M. Wolfe, "Computer-Aided Process Planning Is Link between CAD and CAM," *Industrial Engineering*, August 1985, pp. 72–73.

facturing engineering are based on a definition of the part as recorded in its design. There are, however, some fundamental differences in the approaches these two types of engineering activities take. For example, consider a part that is to be made by a machining process such as milling, drilling, or turning on a lathe. The design engineer looks at the design with an interest in the material that is in the part—its strength, its shape, and the function it will perform. The manufacturing engineer, however, looks at the part with an interest in the material that is *not* there and that has to be cut away to form the part. He or she also has to determine the proper places to hold the part while the material is being cut away. Successful automation of design activities must also consider the manufacturability of the parts being designed. For this reason, the ability to analyze and interchange information rapidly between a CAD system and a CAM system is a distinct advantage.

When CAD and CAM are combined in a totally integrated package for *computer-aided design and manufacturing*, it is written as one acronym—*CAD/CAM.* Computer-to-computer communication linkage is an important part of both an effective CAD/CAM system and a more broadly integrated system such as computer-integrated manufacturing, which is discussed later. All functions of a CAD/CAM system revolve around a data base that contains information, drawings, bills of materials, routings, and any other necessary data. The interrelationships of functions with the CAD/CAM data base are depicted in Figure 7.3.

Direct CAM

Direct CAM applications link a computer directly to one or more pieces of production equipment so that signals to and from the computer enable it to monitor and control the actual production processes. This technology can be applied in several kinds of manufacturing, but we illustrate it with applications in metal machining. Computer numeric-controlled (CNC) machines can store in their own computers

Figure 7.3
Data Base for CAD/CAM
Function Wheel

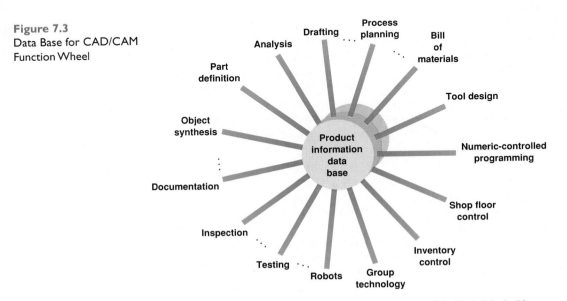

Source: James H. Greene, ed., *Production and Inventory Control Handbook,* 2d ed. (New York: McGraw-Hill, 1987), p. 20.11. Reprinted by permission of McGraw-Hill, Inc.

Six legs and a computer-controlled motor are a powerful combination in the Giddings & Lewis Variax machining center. The legs provide the stability and the computer the brains to allow the cutting head to remove material from all sides of the part being machined. Weighing in at 15,000 pounds, the hexapod is one-third the weight of its more conventional ancestors.

Bob Sacha

instructions for making parts and can use this information to control their actions. These instructions are read into the machine from magnetic tape or disks. More recently, direct numeric-controlled (DNC) machines have been developed so that one or more machines can be linked to a remote computer that supplies instructions to control the machine's movements.

With this technology, software commands can cause rapid changes in the machines' activities. Automatic tool changers can position any of more than 100 tools into the cutting spindle and change the cutting speed and pattern in which the tool will cut. The changeover from one operation to the next can be rapid. This type of *flexible automation* has great competitive advantages over earlier forms of *hard automation* in many applications. Hard automation relies on such devices as mechanical stops and limit switches to sense and control the machine's position. Changeovers with hard automation are often a time-consuming series of trial-and-error adjustments.

Machine tools and robots can operate under direct control of their own dedicated computers but can take supervisory commands from a host mainframe or mini-computer that coordinates activities in the shop. The machine must be informed of what kind of item it is to work on next, so the machine can retrieve the appropriate instructions from its data base or these instructions can be downloaded from a host computer. Machines can be informed of the next kind of part that they are to work on by such means as information manually keyed in, a bar code label that they can scan, signals from a video sensor, or signals from a robot loader that can sense the difference in the item's weight or shape. The ability to interchange physical workpieces between machines and to interchange coordinating signals makes it possible to have such integrated systems of machines and handling devices as flexible manufacturing systems.

FLEXIBLE MANUFACTURING SYSTEMS (FMS)

The concept of grouping equipment that can produce a variety of related parts can be extended and automated to form what is often called a *flexible manufacturing system (FMS)*. A flexible manufacturing system is a group of machines with reprogrammable controllers linked by an automated materials-handling system and integrated through a central computer so that the system can produce a variety of parts that have similar processing requirements. An FMS can be constructed with various amounts and combinations of equipment. An example of a small system might be two lathes that share a robot as the materials-handling system. A large system might contain a dozen or more machines connected by an elaborate conveyor network or an automatic guided vehicle system (AGVS) that can move parts from one machine to another in any order. Generally, an FMS will contain at least four machines—to provide enough volume and variety to make the concept really effective and to justify the great amount of work required to develop an integrated system. A diagram of an FMS is shown in Figure 7.4.

Since the Industrial Revolution, the general trend has been toward more specialization of processes to achieve the advantages of automation. A typical and effective way to employ automation has been to use "hard automation" such as a *transfer line*—a fixed-path conveyor with single-purpose equipment mounted along the sides. The conveyor of the transfer line moves the parts forward one work station, where they are indexed accurately into position for the machines to perform work; the machines operate; then the parts are all moved forward one more work station. A transfer line is a very economical way to produce large volumes of identical or nearly identical

Figure 7.4
Example of a Flexible
Manufacturing System
(FMS)

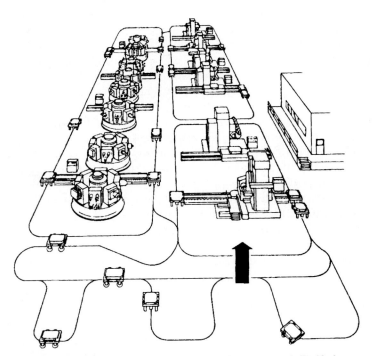

Source: Kearny and Trecker Corp., West Allis, Wisconsin, *KT's World of Advanced Manufacturing Technologies*, 2d ed., 1983, p. 19. Courtesy of KT-Swasey.

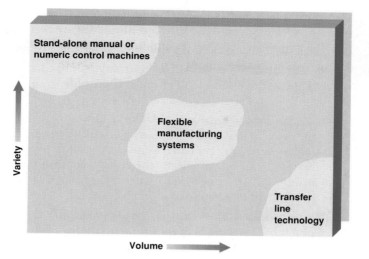

Figure 7.5
Combinations of Volume and Variety Best Served by Alternative Production Methods

items. An FMS offers more flexibility than a transfer line, but it, in turn, is not as flexible as individual machinists working with conventional or numeric-controlled (NC) machines. Appropriate applications for FMSs are in companies that produce intermediate volumes of a variety of parts that require the same type of processing. FMSs and nonautomated cells thus help fill the gap between individual machines and transfer lines, as shown in Figure 7.5. Therefore, they are most suitable for batch manufacturing.

Presently most FMSs are utilized in machining—cutting metal chips away from a block of raw material to leave an item of the desired size and shape. A general overview of the operation of an FMS involves the following steps. The central computer contains the routings for all the parts to be run on the FMS. A person or robot loads a part on a pallet, and the computer is told what has been loaded. The computer retrieves the appropriate routing for the part and directs the conveyor to transport the part to the machine that is to perform the first operation. The conveyor signals the computer when the part is at the machine, and the computer tells the machine which part is there. The machine then retrieves the appropriate program of instructions to work on that part and steps through the specified tool changes and operations to complete its work. The central computer is informed when this work is completed. The central computer checks the status of the machines that can perform the next operation on the routing and directs the conveyor to deliver the part to an available machine, and processing is continued. When all operations on the part are completed, the part is sent to an unload station, where it is removed from the pallet and another part can be loaded on the pallet for processing.

Advantages of FMS

Some companies have experienced great success with FMS installations. Many of the early successes were applications with large workpieces, such as axle housings for large earthmovers. Moving these parts between machines and fixturing the parts at each machine would be expensive without an FMS. Parts such as these are expensive and would result in a large work-in-process inventory investment if they were produced in batches. An FMS could be used to make the left housing, the right housing,

FLEXIBLE MANUFACTURING SYSTEM

then the center part. The parts could then be assembled and used, resulting in little accumulation of inventory. More recently, FMSs are being applied to smaller parts.

The advantages of FMS are summarized briefly below.

Reduced direct labor. Reduced fixturing, reduced materials handling, and automatic control of machines make it possible to operate an FMS with less direct labor in many instances.

Reduced capital investment. Machine utilization with FMS can be about three times as high as with conventional machining, so fewer machines are required. Since there are fewer machines, less tooling is required to equip them. Since materials move directly to the next machine, there is a lower investment in inventory. Since there are fewer machines and less inventory, a smaller amount of floor space is required.

Shorter response time. Setup or changeover time is relatively low with FMS, since much of this work is accomplished automatically in response to software commands. With low WIP there are almost no queues to delay jobs. The result is a very short flow-through time. One application reported 1.5 to 3 days instead of the 35 to 90 days required with conventional production.

Consistent quality. Much of the human variability and error is removed, so quality is more consistent. One FMS installation visited by the author reported that the scrap rate had been reduced from 10 percent to 3 percent.

Better control of work. With few jobs waiting to be worked and a smaller area to survey for problems, it is easier to keep track of the work. Priorities do not change much when jobs flow through in a few days instead of taking months. The flow of much of the work in an FMS is controlled by computer, so it is more consistent.

Limitations of FMS

Not all situations in which an intermediate variety of items are produced at intermediate volumes are suitable for FMS. There needs to be a family of parts that require about the same size machines and the same accuracy, which must be within the tolerances achievable with NC machines. The variety of types and sizes of cutting tools must be kept within the capacity of the automatic tool changers. The limitation may require some standardization of part designs to reduce the number of tools required.

An FMS takes the place of several machines that do not all wear out at the same time. Companies often prefer to make a series of smaller investments over time to replace their machines piecemeal, rather than make a larger investment in a technology with which they are not familiar. FMS requires a long planning cycle and a long development cycle to ensure that the system will be a success. Many managers, however, are oriented to shorter-term decisions and payoffs. The elevated complexity of developing an integrated system may cause some companies to shy away from flexible manufacturing systems. Often the best approach is to evolve into a system. A company can begin using CNC machines, then install a linking materials-handling system, and later develop the central computer and software to coordinate the system.

FMS concepts are a step toward linking some of the activities in manufacturing—primarily materials handling with processing—but sometimes inspection is included. Further integration is achieved if CAD/CAM is used to develop the data base that contains the design data and process plans. An even further degree of integration, computer-integrated manufacturing, is discussed next.

COMPUTER-INTEGRATED MANUFACTURING (CIM)

Computer-integrated manufacturing (CIM) is a concept of linking and coordinating a broad array of activities in a manufacturing business through an integrated computer system. Its purpose is to enable the company to transform product ideas to high-quality products in minimum time and at minimum cost. CIM goes beyond the scope of an FMS or an integrated CAD/CAM system. The concept is to integrate information from the core manufacturing activities and possibly to include information from marketing, order entry, maintenance, accounting, and shipping as well.[7] Figure 7.6 provides a view of many of the functions that are included in CIM.

The core manufacturing activities fall into two major groups: (1) engineering support, which may include computer-aided engineering, computer-aided design, group technology coding, computer-aided process planning, and manufacturing engineering; and (2) operations management, which may include subsystems for master scheduling, capacity planning, material requirements planning, inventory control, purchasing, direct numerical control, shop-floor control, quality reporting, shipping, and distribution.

A full CIM system connects all the activities the company uses, providing a common data base and bidirectional communication to enable the entire operation to work together as an integrated whole.[8] The chief goal of CIM is not to reduce direct labor cost, as one might first assume. Many products made in the United States have a direct labor content of only 10 to 15 percent. CIM helps reduce indirect costs such as materials handling, inspection, and middle management, which may account for 40 to 50 percent of total costs. Rapid production allows a company to operate with very little WIP and finished-goods inventory, yet respond quickly to customer orders. Allen-Bradley, Inc., was able to slash its costs 35 percent by incorporating CIM and JIT production for one of its products (see box).

---

[7]Mikell P. Groover, *Automation, Production Systems, and Computer-Aided Manufacturing* (Englewood Cliffs, N.J.: Prentice-Hall, 1980), p. 75.
[8]James H. Greene, ed., *Production and Inventory Control Handbook,* 2d ed. (New York: McGraw-Hill, 1987), Chap. 19.

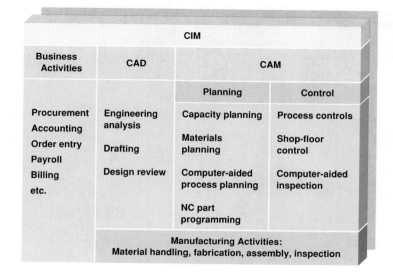

Figure 7.6
Relationship Between Some Functions in CIM

OPERATIONS MANAGEMENT IN ACTION

A BREAKTHROUGH IN AUTOMATING THE ASSEMBLY LINE

With its futuristic assembly line, which began in April 1985, Allen-Bradley has achieved a milestone in the development of computer-integrated manufacturing (CIM) or the ability to make different versions of a product at mass production speeds in lots as small as 1. The line produces contactors and relays that serve as starters and controllers for industrial electric motors. Allen-Bradley's specialty is industrial controls. Recent competition from Europe and Japan had changed the relay and contactor business, which accounted for about 10 percent of Allen-Bradley's $1.2 billion annual sales, and these items are a crucial part of the other electrical equipment the company sells. European or Japanese contactors and relays, built to International Electrotechnical Commission (IEC) standards, were about one-third the size and one-third the price of the Allen-Bradley products manufactured to the U.S. standard. The market elsewhere represented about $700 million a year.

Allen-Bradley looked into offshore production and joint ventures and scoured the world to learn how other companies made their contactors and relays. Executives finally decided to invest $15 million in the new CIM line. A team of nearly thirty specialists tackled the project. The contactors and relays were redesigned for easy automated manufacture. Meanwhile part of the team developed the entire manufacturing process, including the assembly machinery. Allen-Bradley built about 60 percent of the machinery.

Most orders that are received during one day will be produced the next. During the night, orders are transferred into the scheduling computer. At 7:30 A.M. the assembly line comes to life with pneumatic sighs and birdlike whistles. Lights flash. Without human intervention, plastic casings the size of pocket transistor radios start marching through twenty-six complex automated assembly stations.

Bar code labels, computer-printed on the spot and pasted on each plastic casing by a mechanical arm, tell each station which of nearly 200 different parts to install in what combination. As the casings move along a conveyor belt, tiny mechanical fingers insert springs,

A contact insertion machine automatically places lower contact and pressure plates in the correct configuration on relays and contactors.

Allen-Bradley, a Rockwell International Business

another mechanical arm places covers over the casings, and automatic screwdrivers tighten the screws. At the end of the line, a laser printer zaps detailed product information onto the side of each finished plastic box. The boxes are then packaged, sorted into customer orders, and shunted into chutes ready for shipment—all automatically. The four technicians who stand by to unclog jams are rarely needed. Elapsed time per box from start to finish: 45 minutes.

Contactors and relays of different sizes and types freely intermingle on Allen-Bradley's assembly line. Flexible assembly machines responding to specific bar codes make nearly instantaneous changes without slowing production. For example, when a bar code tells a screwdriver assembly that a larger contactor frame is approaching, the screwdriver moves upward and puts a larger screw higher on the frame.

Scrutiny by scores of computer-controlled sensors helps ensure quality control. As a grinding machine processes the faces of tiny magnets for the controllers, for instance, a laser gauge measures the surfaces to keep them within tolerances as small as one-sixth the diameter of a human hair. In conventional manufacturing, magnets would have been first ground and then put into an inspection machine that culls the bad ones. Here there are no defective magnets. At Allen-Bradley, 3,500 automatic inspection steps have boosted product quality far beyond what less-automated production can achieve.

Turning out variegated products at 600 per hour in any mix allows Allen-Bradley to do away with most of its parts inventory. The company manufactures everything it needs for the contactors and relays except springs, electrical coils, and screws. A local supplier delivers springs on a just-in-time basis. Screws and coils, ordered in economically large quantities, are stored until needed. The four technicians load assembly machines overnight with just enough raw materials and parts to take care of the next day's run.

Other companies can suit a customer's specialized needs on their assembly lines. But they cannot do it automatically without slowing down or stopping. Thanks to its automated line, Allen-Bradley has been able to come late to a highly competitive world market and establish itself as a leader. To be sure, contactors and relays are not as complex as cars and farm machinery, but Allen-Bradley's remarkable assembly line points the way toward making more complicated products rapidly in lots of 1.

Source: Gene Bylinski, "A Breakthrough in Automating the Assembly Line," *Fortune,* May 26, 1986, pp. 64–66. © 1986 The Time Inc. Magazine Company.

A nine-alley reservoir of different-sized molded housings dispenses the type of housing that is specified by the bar code on the base.

Allen-Bradley, a Rockwell International Business

The Allen-Bradley application shows how the company applied technology to achieve a significant strategic advantage. The company broadened the market for its product; at the same time it reduced cost, improved quality, and gained great flexibility to shift product mix and volume, and the company has been able to achieve reliable delivery performance. This is an example of a situation where a business covers a greater volume in all directions within the pyramid of performance measures that we discussed in Chapter 2.

Integration Challenges

The integration of all the hardware and software involved in running a manufacturing operation poses numerous challenges. A company may have difficulty integrating equipment made by several vendors into a network that can communicate. The meaning of a particular set of electronic impulses for one vendor's equipment may not be recognized by another vendor's equipment, or they may be recognized as meaning something other than the intended message. Postprocessors or special translators may be required to convert data to the proper form. Data communication requires some standardization of signals and equipment. *Manufacturing automation protocol (MAP)* is evolving as one of the standards that will enable better communication between manufacturing equipment such as conveyors and robot welders. Planning and coordinating the work of several machines that perform varying mixes of jobs also is a challenge. Many decisions will be so complex that they require decision support at the human interfaces so the system operates at machine speed instead of waiting for slow human analysis. We have looked at only a few highlights of technology's impact on the business world. Before moving to the next chapter let us reflect on the trends that appear to be occurring.

TRENDS

Manufacturing will continue to become more high tech and less labor-intensive.[9] Many of the manufacturing job opportunities will therefore be in management, purchasing, distribution, and technical support.

Services, many of which remain labor-intensive, will account for most of the employment. If the overall productivity of the country is to increase, then services will have to become more productive. Developments in information technology offer opportunities to improve productivity in some services that deal with knowledge work. Many service jobs, such as retail sales, require direct personal contact and will continue to be performed primarily by humans. Part of the challenge of competitiveness in services is to enable workers to be more productive, perhaps through supporting technology.

Much of the discussion in this chapter has referred to the improvement of competitiveness. It is important to recognize that competitiveness does not mean just productivity and cost advantage. The trends in competition based on quality, flexibility, and customer service will no doubt continue. In evaluating new ways to apply technology, managers must seek ways to improve quality and responsiveness. One very desirable feature of software-driven automation is its flexibility. Improvements in this

---

[9]William Van Dusen Wishard, "The 21st Century Economy," *Futurist*, May–June 1987, pp. 24–25.

technology, in artificial intelligence, and other fields of information technology should add further to organizations' flexibility.

One can see that jobs will continue to be challenging and changing. Those who design operations systems and jobs that people perform must consider the types of technology that are available and how technology can help employees perform their jobs. In the next chapter the focus turns to the design of jobs.

SUMMARY

Companies must improve both their products and their productivity to remain competitive. Managers must guide these improvements and must ensure the long-term success of their companies through continued investments in technology and personnel training. They must nurture an environment or culture that accepts change as a way of life and that seeks and encourages improvement.

New technologies are available, and others are constantly being developed which, if properly applied, can improve performance. For almost any company and product there are small innovations that can be applied to advantage. Managers must remain alert for occasional technological breakthroughs that provide major opportunities and challenges. Many potential advantages are understood only by persons who have studied a particular business and the science and technology that support it, so the intent of the chapter has been not to discuss all new technology but to review some of the changes that can affect the way operations are managed.

Services also face the challenge of finding new ways to serve customers better and be more competitive. Technology is being applied in this quest. Information processing and office automation have done much to improve paperwork handling. Automatic data entry by bar code and optical character recognition provide some automated assistance for many operations. Voice input to computers will provide further improvement for some work. It is hoped that developments in artificial intelligence will provide opportunities to increase the performance of knowledge workers in many kinds of businesses.

Some developments in manufacturing that are discussed in this chapter include computer-aided design (CAD), computer-aided process planning (CAPP), and direct and indirect computer-aided manufacturing (CAM). Flexible manufacturing systems (FMS) combine direct CAM applications to control processing equipment and materials-handling devices under the same host computer. Computer-integrated manufacturing (CIM) seeks to integrate indirect computer support of manufacturing with direct CAM so that many of the systems can pass data and work as a coordinated system.

Data communication and networking multiply knowledge and improve coordination for better teamwork in both small and large organizations.

In today's world, numerous competitors will be trying to do a better job than your company for the same customers. Opportunities to use technology to competitive advantage should be considered in the original design and throughout the life of a business. Remember that the design or revision of a production system is more than just a way to use technology. It involves development of a sociotechnical system that reflects the nature of people and the way they work together. In the next chapter we discuss some considerations in regard to job design.

KEY TERMS

Technical and office
protocol (TOP)
Electronic data
interchange (EDI)
Artificial intelligence (AI)
Expert systems
Inference engine
Computed-aided design
(CAD)
Finite-element modeling

Computer-aided
manufacturing (CAM)
Indirect CAM
Computer-aided process
planning (CAPP)
Computer-aided design
and manufacturing
(CAD/CAM)
Direct CAM
Flexible automation

Hard automation
Flexible manufacturing
system (FMS)
Transfer line
Computer-integrated
manufacturing (CIM)
Manufacturing automation
protocol (MAP)

DISCUSSION QUESTIONS

1. Is it reasonable to think that people's creative drives and capabilities can be influenced by management efforts? Why, or why not?
2. What are some ways managers can try to keep organizations current on technology?
3. How can managers help encourage positive attitudes toward improvement projects?
4. Why should persons in manufacturing care about the way design engineers perform the design activities?
5. What are CAD and CAM? How do they differ from integrated CAD/CAM?
6. What are some advantages of using a common data base for multiple activities in a manufacturing company?
7. What are some advantages of using a common data base for multiple activities in a service company?
8. What is finite-element modeling, and why is it useful?
9. What is the difference between the variant approach and the generative approach to computer-aided process planning (CAPP)?
10. For very large production volumes, flexible automation often is less efficient than hard automation. Why might a company opt for flexible automation?
11. What are some advantages of flexible manufacturing systems?
12. What are some ways in which artificial intelligence differs from conventional computer applications?
13. How can an expert system assist a person who is already considered to be an expert in the field?
14. Why might artificial intelligence be valuable in automating services?
15. What impact do expert systems have on operations management decision making?

BIBLIOGRAPHY

Ayres, Robert U. "Future Trends in Factory Automation." *Manufacturing Review,* June 1988, pp. 93–103.

Burrus, Daniel, with Roger Gittineo. *Technotrends: How to Use Technology to Go Beyond Your Competition.* New York: HarperCollins, 1993.

Bylinski, Gene. "Turning R&D into Real Products." *Fortune,* July 2, 1990, pp. 72–77.

Choobineh, Fred, and Rajan Suri, eds. *Flexible Manufacturing Systems: Current Issues and Models.* Atlanta: Industrial Engineering and Management Press, 1986.

Cross, Kelvin F. "The Factory of the Future Depends on Successful Integration of Automation and Job Design." *Industrial Engineering 18,* no. 1 (January 1986): 14–18.

Crowe, Edward R., and Costas A. Vassiliadis. "Artificial Intelligence: Starting to Realize Its Practical Promise." *Chemical Engineering Progress,* January 1995, pp. 22–31.

Gunn, Thomas G. *Manufacturing for Competitive Advantage: Becoming a World Class Manufacturer.* Cambridge, Mass.: Ballinger, 1987.

Horwitch, Mel, ed. *Technology in the Modern Corporation: A Strategic Perspective.* New York: Pergamon, 1986.

The Information Revolution: How Digital Technology Is Changing the Way We Work and Live [Special bonus issue]. *Business Week,* 1994.

Jelinek, Mariann, and Joel D. Goldhar. "The Strategic Implications of the Factory of the Future." *Sloan Management Review 25,* no. 4 (Fall 1984): 25–43.

Leonard-Barton, Dorothy, and John J. Sviokla. "Putting Expert Systems to Work." *Harvard Business Review,* March–April 1988, pp. 91–98.

Liebowitz, Jay. *Introduction to Expert Systems.* Santa Cruz, Calif.: Mitchell Publishing, 1988.

Madu, Christian N. *Management of New Technology for Global Competitiveness.* Westport, Conn.: Quorum, 1993.

Meyer, Ronald J. "AI and Expert Systems: In Pursuit of CIM." *CIM Technology,* February 1987, pp. 15–26.

Monroe, Joseph. "Strategic Use of Technology." *California Management Review,* Summer 1989, pp. 91–110.

Naisbitt, John, and Patricia Aburdene. *Re-inventing the Corporation: Transforming Your Job and Your Company for the New Information Society.* New York: Warner, 1985.

Nevens, T. Michael, Gregory L. Summe, and Bro Uttal. "Commercializing Technology: What the Best Companies Do." *Harvard Business Review,* May–June 1990, pp. 154–163.

Oliff, Michael D., ed. *Intelligent Manufacturing: Proceedings of the First International Conference on Expert Systems and the Leading Edge in Production Planning and Control.* Menlo Park, Calif.: Benjamin Cummings, 1988.

Quinn, John J. "How Companies Keep Abreast of Technological Change." *Long Range Planning 18,* no. 2 (April 1985): 69–76.

Rhines, Wally. "Artificial Intelligence: Out of the Lab and into Business." *Journal of Business Strategy 6,* no. 1 (Summer 1985): 50–57.

Teresko, John. "Remaking the Way We Make Things." *Industry Week,* April 8, 1988, pp. 59–60.

Tushman, Michael, and David Nadler. "Organizing for Innovation." *California Management Review 28,* no. 3 (Spring 1986): 74–92.

Vajpayee, S. Kant. *Principles of Computer-Integrated Manufacturing.* Englewood Cliffs, N.J.: Prentice-Hall, 1995.

Weston, Frederick C., Jr. "Computer Integrated Manufacturing Systems: Fact or Fantasy?" *Business Horizons,* July–August 1988, pp. 64–68.

Wiig, Karl M., George B. Rockwell, and Thomas J. Martin. "Artificial Intelligence in Banking." *Bankers Magazine,* March–April 1986, pp. 47–51.

Wolfe, Philip M. "Computer-Aided Process Planning Is Link between CAD and CAM." *Industrial Engineering 17,* no. 8 (August 1985): 72–77.

DESIGN OF JOBS AND COMPENSATION

D esigning the operations system includes several aspects that are interrelated. Selecting the overall work-flow pattern and the technology that will be utilized in performing the work certainly has an impact on the work roles of employees. These matters must not be considered separately although we focus primarily on one at a time in our discussions. In this chapter we focus especially on the work roles or jobs that are assigned to employees and on the compensation methods used to reward employees for their efforts. Successful companies must have employees who are capable and motivated to efficiently perform the work that must be done to provide the value the customers seek, and excellent companies must do this better than the rest. The degree to which employees are motivated to perform their jobs is greatly influenced by the activities and responsibilities that are part of the jobs and by the intrinsic and extrinsic rewards associated with their jobs. Therefore, companies should give careful consideration to job design and compensation methods.

INTRINSIC AND EXTRINSIC REWARDS

It is generally recognized that people may receive two major categories of rewards from work. One is *intrinsic rewards,* which are rewards that are internal to workers and which they give themselves. Intrinsic rewards include self-esteem, a sense of accomplishment, and a feeling of growth or development of special skills and talents. Many of these rewards are derived from the work itself. Intrinsic rewards are related to the worker's perception of the job and, hence, are affected by job design, which we will discuss in the first part of the chapter.

A second category is *extrinsic rewards,* which are external to workers and are given by the organization or someone else. Extrinsic rewards include direct pay and such fringe benefits as insurance, vacations, company cars, payments to retirement plans, and so on. Being an extrinsic reward, compensation is more easily controlled by managers than are intrinsic rewards. The later part of the chapter reviews several aspects of employee compensation methods, with particular attention to wage incentive plans.

JOB DESIGN

Job design encompasses the formal specifications and informal expectations of an employee's work-related activities, including both the structural and interpersonal aspects of the job. A job should be more than just a list of tasks that the organization needs performed on a regular basis. The job should be carefully planned, and the needs of both the jobholder and the organization should be taken into consideration in designing the job. Many aspects of an organizational system relate to workers' jobs and should be taken into account when jobs are designed. They may be grouped into two broad categories.

1. Technical-physical factors
   a. Task content—the operations that must be performed to convert inputs to the desired output
   b. Physical context—the heat, light, noise, fumes or pollution, appearance, and safety precautions that surround the jobholder

2. Sociopsychological factors
   a. Social factors—the personal interactions that occur because of the organizational structure and job assignments
   b. Intrinsic factors—the internal psychological feelings that are engendered as a result of performing the job

A full-time job traditionally specifies a set of tasks that the organization expects a person to perform each workday. Naturally, the company would like the employees to perform their jobs with commitment and enthusiasm. Employees are more willing and more motivated to perform their jobs if the jobs themselves have satisfying ele-

Both intrisic and extrinsic rewards are the results of self-directed work teams at Saturn. Teams at Saturn enjoy the autonomy to make hiring, budgeting, and purchasing decisions. Team members are expected to take charge of product quality; a percentage of their salaries depends on it.

Ted Thai, *Time* Magazine

ments. The basic premise is reasonable: If employees like their work, they will be more willing to do the work or to do more work than if they do not like it. A basic challenge of job design is to develop jobs that get the necessary work done, yet, to the extent that it is feasible, contain more elements that people like about work and fewer elements that they dislike.

The rapidly changing conditions of the current economy affect the extent to which a company can specify all the tasks an employee must do to provide what the customer expects. The economy exposes many companies and their employees to constantly and rapidly changing conditions. In some companies employees have gone through stressful upheavals of downsizing, delayering, job sharing, turning routine work over to computers, using a shifting group of temporary workers as work changes, and other revisions to their employment pictures. One article said that the United States is becoming "de-jobbed"; that is, traditional jobs as workers have known them are disappearing.

Job security has declined and probably will decline further. The unwritten social contract whereby companies give job security in exchange for employee loyalty is being revised. There are no lifetime jobs as a structured set of tasks to be performed because companies' work is often changing. In a world that is changing rapidly, the company cannot rewrite the job descriptions and redraw the organization chart every week or two. It looks as though employees will be expected to earn employment security (but not necessarily job security) by continuously finding new ways to add value for the company.

This emerging work situation means that workers must be given more freedom and training so they can find ways to grow and adapt to shifting demands on the company. Capable, motivated people must react at the level where there is the greatest familiarity with the requirements and nuances of the work. In many instances this

HOW JOB DESIGN CAN HELP ADD VALUE FOR CUSTOMERS

Job design affects the motivational components of jobs, which means that it affects the amount of physical and intellectual capabilities of the person drawn into performing the job. Workers who are motivated by their jobs usually perform their jobs better and are more likely to contribute improvement ideas. Job design can, therefore, help to improve quality and cost. Workers who are pleased with their jobs deal with customers better than disgruntled employees and help provide better service and service quality. Motion efficiency and ergonomics in job design help reduce worker fatigue and costs and can lead to improved employee alertness so that quality is better. Compensation and other extrinsic rewards align employees' interests with the welfare of the company and its customers. Group incentives can help support teamwork. Well-designed compensation plans encourage employees to provide better customer service and control costs.

entrepreneurial role is facilitated through the use of self-directed work teams, which provide many of the desirable job characteristics we will discuss later. In *The Wisdom of Teams,* Katzenbach and Smith define a *team* as a small number of people with complementary skills who are committed to a common purpose, performance goals, and approach for which they hold themselves mutually accountable. Workers within such teams confer and plan their work so that, to some degree, they design at least parts of their own jobs to improve team results. In many self-directed teams the members interview and approve new employees who are assigned to the team and provide informal and often formal peer review input for performance appraisals.

Work teams remain together unless their part of the company is reorganized and they have significant responsibility for their work area. For example, at Kodak the employees who work with X-ray cassettes and spools, canisters, and cartons for film arrange their own hours, keep track of their production, and fix their own machines. They also coach fellow team members in statistical quality control, interview prospective employees, meet with suppliers, and manage just-in-time inventory.

Some companies in dynamic, high-tech fields use other approaches to deal with the dynamic demands of their markets. Intel, EDS, and Microsoft, for example, use projects as the basic unit to organize work. They define sets of projects and assign workers to project teams. As the work that needs to be done changes, the project missions are changed and workers are shifted to new projects. Workers may simultaneously be members of more than one project team.

This is considerably different from traditional, narrowly defined jobs. In the past, however, job descriptions often ended with a familiar catchall, "and other duties as assigned." In the new approach to work a new phrase may be substituted or added—"and other activities you determine will add value and lead to improved customer satisfaction and competitiveness."

MULTIPLE OBJECTIVES IN JOB DESIGN

It usually is not feasible to design a job so that going to work is more fun than any other activity a person might pursue. A job must be a reasonable compromise of at least three types of factors. The job must be technically, behaviorally, and economically feasible. These types of feasibility are discussed briefly below.

TECHNICAL FEASIBILITY   A job is a set of tasks or duties assigned to be performed. The person who holds the job must be capable of performing the assignment with the equipment and systems available, and the job must make the necessary transformations of inputs into outputs. A job must not be beyond the reasonable limits of a person's skills or physical and mental endurance. Proper selection of processes and equipment as well as proper selection and training of employees help ensure technical feasibility.

ECONOMIC FEASIBILITY   Businesses and other organizations are subject to pressures to keep costs and prices at reasonable levels. As a whole, the collection of jobs within an organization must remain solvent. The costs of compensating the jobholder, providing the equipment to perform the job, and maintaining the environment where the job is performed must not be too high.

BEHAVIORAL FEASIBILITY   Some characteristics of a job may affect the jobholders' perception of themselves, their perception of others, and their relationships with others. A task role may give people a feeling of great worth—of being an important part of the organization. The feelings that people derive from a job affect their motivation to perform it. Since a job is often more than just a set of mechanical motions to be performed, it requires motivation and mental stimulation to be performed successfully. Unstructured jobs often require so much of a person's creativity and mental attention that a good attitude is vital to its satisfactory performance. Even routine, structured jobs require that a person be motivated enough to be present at the job and contribute the necessary effort.

Beyond the individual, jobs carry with them social interactions that may lead to group reactions. Informal organizations or work groups have a large impact on the effectiveness of an organization, for good or bad. Attitudes are contagious, and peer relations or peer pressure may be responsible for many of the motivational reactions of workers.

The Balancing of Objectives

An organization must achieve economic feasibility to survive. This pressure may cause a company to stress technical efficiency at the expense of employee satisfaction and motivation. Jobs may become so unrewarding that they go unfilled or are filled by employees who are not motivated or cooperative. Halfhearted effort on the job, absenteeism, high labor turnover, and/or strikes may lead to excessive costs and even to lack of economic feasibility. On the other hand, a company cannot afford to make jobs too inefficient just to make them satisfying. One objective in making jobs satisfying is to increase the worker's motivation so that there is no reduction in efficiency and perhaps even an improvement in quality and cost performance. The relationship between the three types of feasibility is shown schematically in Figure 8.1. The most darkly shaded portion represents the objective sought in job design.

Managers and social scientists are still seeking keys to achieving optimal job design. Capabilities, backgrounds, expectations, and aspirations vary widely among people. Technical needs and organizational cultures differ from company to com-

Figure 8.1
Objectives of Job Design

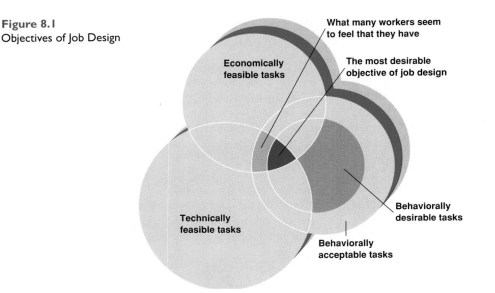

pany, so one theory probably will not be successful in all settings. Many of the theories that have been proposed seek to prevent or to overcome overspecialization. The appropriate degree of specialization in a company is one factor to consider.

Specialization

Specialization has both its good and bad points. Becoming a specialist in some particular area can provide a person with a great deal of pride. Some fields, such as medicine, are so broad that one has to specialize in order to keep up with the latest findings, treatments, and techniques. A medical specialty is broad enough, and so many changes occur over time that one would not be likely to find it boring. But some jobs, such as a short, repetitive task on an assembly line, can be so specialized that some people find them boring, or at least not very motivating. Yet other people seem to like or tolerate specialized jobs fairly well. Table 8.1 summarizes some of the possible beneficial and adverse aspects of extreme job specialization.

SOME APPROACHES TO JOB DESIGN

Several approaches have been taken to reduce the amount of specialization in jobs. Some approaches which have been successful in many, but certainly not all, settings are discussed below.

Herzberg's Two-Factor Theory

Frederick Herzberg offered some general insights into the types of features that increase jobholder motivation and satisfaction. He postulated two major sets of factors: *motivators* and *hygiene factors.* The hygiene factors or satisfiers should be present, or else the jobholder will become dissatisfied. The hygiene factors are extrinsic to the

Table 8.1
POSSIBLE ADVANTAGES AND DISADVANTAGES OF JOB SPECIALIZATION

Advantages

Qualified workers are easier to find because fewer skills are required.
Worker training time is shorter.
Production time is shortened by the "learning-curve effect" due to repetition.
Wage rates are generally lower because skill level is lower.
Work instructions and production control are simpler because worker assignments are consistent.
Scheduling of completion times and staffing requirements is more predictable because the worker has performed the work before.
A higher degree of mechanization or automation is often possible.

Disadvantages

Flexibility is reduced; it is difficult to shift work load to available workers if they do not have a variety of skills.
Workers may be overqualified for jobs and may not feel self-esteem for accomplishing them.
Workers may feel less sense of accomplishment because the job makes a small contribution to the product or service.
Workers may be bored because they perform the same operation repeatedly.
Workers may manifest feelings of dissatisfaction through high absenteeism, high turnover rates, grievances, demands for higher wages, strikes, sabotage, etc.

work and primarily relate to the environment in which the work is done. Company policy, working conditions, supervision, salary, and relationships with peers are some of the more important hygiene factors. If these factors are not handled properly, employees will become dissatisfied. Hygiene factors can keep employees on the payroll and coming to work, but they do not motivate employees to give outstanding performance.

A different set of factors, the motivators, provides the real motive to excel or to perform the job at exceptional levels. The motivators are more intrinsic to the work itself. Recognition, responsibility, advancement, and a feeling of personal growth are some factors believed to be most effective in motivating people to superior effort.

Job Characteristics Model

The motivators express something about the feelings that people get from jobs they find motivating, but the list of motivators does not give specific recommendations about how to structure jobs. The job characteristics model provides some suggestions on how to structure jobs to include more motivators. This model proposes that five characteristics are important in the motivational makeup of a job:

- *Skill variety:* the degree to which a job requires a range of abilities
- *Task identity:* the degree to which a job requires completion of an identifiable unit of work from beginning to end, with visible outcome
- *Task significance:* the degree to which the employee perceives the job to have a substantial impact on the lives of others inside or outside the organization

- *Autonomy:* the degree to which the job provides the employee freedom and discretion in scheduling and determining procedures
- *Feedback:* the degree to which the job provides direct and clear information about the effectiveness of the employee's performance

Several approaches to job design and job redesign have been used to bring these desirable job characteristics into people's work.

JOB ROTATION   *Job rotation* involves having a worker periodically exchange jobs with another worker to break the monotony of performing the same job every day. This can introduce some skill variety into workers' activities, but it actually does not improve the design of the jobs. A worker may feel that performing two overspecialized, boring jobs is little or no better than performing only one. Sometimes, however, a job rotation program can add job challenge and improve worker esteem by helping workers develop new skills.

QUALITY CIRCLES AND IMPROVEMENT TEAMS   *Quality circles* are groups of about five to twelve workers from the same work area who meet voluntarily on a regular basis to identify and solve problems related to their work. Participation in these groups provides some of the desirable characteristics to their experience. Participants often can use a variety of skills not used on their regular jobs. Also by solving problems they can gain a feeling of significance and personal growth from this activity. To identify problems and solve them, the groups need feedback on how well the work progresses and on the effectiveness of their efforts to solve problems. Workers gain some autonomy by having a say about what they perceive as a problem and having input into the solutions.

Improvement teams are not standing committees, but are formed on an ad hoc basis and assigned special problems. Participation on a team has the same advantages as participation in a quality circle. In addition, being named to a team is a form of recognition, which is also a motivator.

JOB ENLARGEMENT   *Job enlargement* involves horizontal expansion of a job to add related tasks but without the addition of prework planning or postwork inspection. Enlargement can permit the worker to perform a whole unit of work so that the job has task identity and task significance in addition to the skill variety that is added.

JOB ENRICHMENT   *Job enrichment,* like job enlargement, increases the number and diversity of tasks that the worker performs, but it also adds vertical loading; that is, it adds responsibility for prework planning and/or postwork inspection. Workers must be given feedback about the work if they are to plan the work and verify its performance. Jobs that are enriched can provide all five of the desirable job characteristics.

Sociotechnical Systems Theory

The term *sociotechnical systems* recognizes the interrelationships between the technical system required to perform tasks and the social organization in which the tasks are performed. Any production system is both a social system and a technical system. The system must provide some technology to convert its inputs into the desired outputs. But the system also is a group of humans who interact in some way to carry out

Job enrichment at European Collision Center, an auto body shop in Cambridge, Massachusetts, means that each car is under the watch of one person who bears responsibility for its service. Regular skills training is part of the package. Workers love the empowerment, customers love the results.

Brian Smith

its function. Operations managers must be interested in both aspects of the sociotechnical system, since they are responsible for coordinating the efforts of groups of people to perform technical tasks.

Sociotechnical systems theory is very general and does not define one specific approach to organizational change. Usually it includes formation of *autonomous work groups,* each responsible for a significant part of the work. A group's members share much of the decision making in regard to planning and executing the group's work. An objective is for group members to develop close ties with one another and build a joint commitment to the work.[1] Thus, many of the interpersonal roles and relationships of the social system are worked out by the group, rather than being specified by the formal organization. The members may vary the roles they play in performing the work. These efforts can result in a close social group that is effective at the technical task.

Some recommendations are that the work have reasonably demanding content, variety, learning opportunities, discretion in decision making, a relationship to one's social life, and a feeling that the job leads to some desirable future. Additional recommendations are that the job design carry only minimum specifications about how the job will be done, that variances be controlled as close as possible to their origin, and that feedback information be provided to the place where the action occurs. The groups may have input into support activities such as selection, training, performance assessment, and promotion, so these activities will reinforce the behavior that the organization desires.

Many leading companies, including Procter & Gamble, Cummins Engine, GM, GE, Westinghouse, IBM, Xerox, and Polaroid, have developed work teams that oper-

[1]Frederick Herzberg, "One More Time: How Do You Motivate Employees?" *Harvard Business Review,* September–October 1987, p. 120

Table 8.2
THE CHANGING APPROACH TO ORGANIZING WORK

	OLD WAY	NEW WAY
What management assumes about workers	Worker wants nothing from the job except pay, avoids responsibility, and must be controlled and coerced.	Worker desires challenging job and will seek responsibility and autonomy if management permits.
How the job is designed	Work is fragmented and deskilled Worker is confined to narrow job. Doing and thinking are separated.	Work is multiskilled and performed by teamwork where possible. Worker can upgrade whole system. Doing and thinking are combined.
Management's organization and style	Top-down military command with worker at bottom of many supervisory layers; worker is expected to obey orders and has no power.	Relatively flat structure with few layers; worker makes suggestions and has power to implement changes.
Job training and security	Worker is regarded as a replaceable part and is given little initial training or retraining for new jobs. Layoffs are routine when business declines.	Worker is considered a valuable resource and is constantly retrained in new skills. Layoffs are avoided if possible in a downturn.
How wages are determined	Pay is geared to the job, not the person, and is determined by evaluation and job classification systems.	Pay is linked to skills acquired. Group incentive and profit-sharing plans are used to enhance commitment.
Labor relations	Labor and management interests are considered incompatible. Conflict arises on the shop floor and in bargaining.	Mutual interests are emphasized. Management shares information about the business. Labor shares responsibility for making it succeed.

Source: "Management Discovers the Human Side of Automation." Reprinted from September 29, 1986, issue of *Business Week* by special permission, copyright © 1986 by The McGraw-Hill Companies.

ate under sociotechnical principles. The use of teams and other work reforms in conjunction with technology is credited with the fact that, in some of these plants, productivity is 30 to 50 percent higher than in conventional plants. These productivity gains are being achieved mainly in new plants designed specifically for sociotechnical methods and equipped with new technology.[2] An interesting summary comparison of the old and new look in jobs is seen in Table 8.2.

Job Enrichment Opportunities Differ

Jobs in some service companies and manufacturing companies already provide front-line and direct-labor employees with considerable variety and discretion in their jobs. Job shop manufacturers, for example, often have work of many types, and skilled workers have to determine some of the methods that will be used to perform

---

[2]John Hoerr, "Getting Man and Machine to Live Happily Ever After," *Business Week*, April 20, 1987, p. 61.

the work. Customer service and sales personnel in some service businesses also have variety in their contacts and job activities.

Batch manufacturing companies have some variety in the items they make. A worker may run only one machine if the company is organized by function. Producing in large batches causes the worker to perform the same job over and over for an extended time. The trend toward production in small batches permits the operator to change the type of work more often. Arrangement of this type of company into cells, such as rabbit-chase cells, can enable workers to learn several steps in making an item. With cellular manufacturing a worker can produce an entire part or subassembly; thus the worker's job provides more task identity and significance.

Jobs in mass production and very specialized services such as making sandwiches or separating recyclable trash items are more difficult to enlarge, especially without special plant equipment. If the volume of demand in an automobile plant is one per minute, then it might require two production lines to allow each worker to perform 2 minutes' work on each automobile. New United Motors Manufacturing, Inc. (a joint venture between General Motors and Toyota), in Fremont, California, uses an assembly line but provides workers with many of the job characteristics mentioned earlier. Workers are assigned to teams. Each team is responsible for the work done in one section of the line. They have some say as to how work in their section is divided among them, and the team develops ways to improve the work in its section of the line. A worker can exchange jobs with another on the team every 2 hours. The team is given feedback about how well it is performing and how the overall plant is doing. Thus, the workers have variety and feedback, with some autonomy and participation in decisions.

APPLICATION

JOB ENRICHMENT AT SHENANDOAH LIFE INSURANCE CO.

Service jobs can be enriched in some instances. Consider the following example of a successful job redesign. Shenandoah Life Insurance Co. experienced a change in the mix of policies it sold, so that more universal life policies were being processed. An analysis revealed that the universal life policies were being processed through thirty-two sets of hands that included nine sections in three departments. Work, such as marketing services, receiving, premium accounting, policy issue, policy records underwriting, reinsurance, and so on, was performed by a series of specialists in an assembly-line fashion. In 1983, the company revised this procedure and formed its first experimental self-managed team.

The team was assigned responsibility for all tasks related to health insurance and universal life business generated in the state of Virginia. Management expected the team to be self-managed to the extent possible, so no supervisor was appointed. The team had advisers in such areas as human resources, methods and procedures, and personnel. The team's responsibilities included all tasks involved in policy issue, premium accounting, and policyholder relations for its business area. All team members were encouraged to develop the skills necessary to handle independently any part of the team's business. In addition the team made final selection of its members, made job assignments, scheduled vacation times, designed its office layout, determined the basics of its pay system, and corrected members who did not do their share. Members trained each other or arranged for training. After about a year other teams were formed, and the experimental team continued to handle its assigned business responsibilities. The company saw a 13 percent increase in business with no increase in employees. The company also has experienced a marked decline in complaints about errors or service. The team approach has allowed the company to be more flexible and responsive to rapidly changing business requirements.

Managers should realize that job enrichment is not some magical elixir that will cure all motivational and employee problems in their companies. A company should review several conditions in determining the likelihood of success of a job enrichment program. The technology of the work must have enough flexibility that the work can be changed into more-enriched assignments. Employees must be favorably disposed to enriched jobs and perceive them as an improvement. Some employees have higher growth needs than others. There should be no general problems such as an authoritarian management culture that will not accept the idea of yielding some authority to workers. The perceived level of hygiene factors must be adequate to support the success of the program.

Not all jobs can be restructured to be enriched, and not all workers want enriched jobs. Probably all workers, however, want to be treated as human beings with brains and emotions as well as a pair of hands. This is a general theme of many of the ideas that are presented. Good companies recognize that, whether jobs are specialized or not, workers respond more positively when they are kept informed and treated with respect. With these ideas on how to make jobs more satisfying and motivating in mind, we now consider some ideas on how to make jobs more efficient. One aspect of job design is the consideration of automation or mechanization.

WHEN SHOULD MACHINES BE UTILIZED?

In designing and redesigning jobs, companies often must decide whether a job or part of a job should be performed by machine. Companies are seeking ways to gain competitive advantage through the use of automation. As low-wage countries increase their participation in global markets, companies in higher-wage countries are seeking ways to reduce labor costs through automation. Machines can be employed in numerous applications. Table 8.3 provides a general comparison of some capabilities of machines and humans. Companies may apply automation for a variety of reasons, such as the following.

IMPROVED SPEED AND RESPONSIVENESS   Grocery stores can use bar code scanners to reduce clerical work and customer waiting time at the checkout counter. Retailers, wholesalers, and manufacturers use electronic data interchange (EDI) to link their computers to their suppliers' computers. Orders and confirmations are exchanged rapidly, and clerical errors are reduced.

IMPROVED JOBS   Machines may be used to perform jobs that are highly repetitive and boring; where fumes, sparks, or radiation make a job hazardous; or to lift loads that are too heavy for humans. For example, some automobile plants use robots in areas where there is a high concentration of spot welding and it would be too crowded and unsafe for humans among all the flying sparks.

IMPROVED COST   The long-term cost is sometimes reduced for automated operations, particularly for simple repetitive operations performed during two or three shifts per day. Machines can work almost 24 hours a day, and they do not require payments for health insurance, vacation, retirement, and so forth. Automation has been used in light assembly and in fabricating components for items such as typewriters and printers. Computers perform much of the switching of telecommunications.

Table 8.3
RELATIVE CAPABILITIES OF HUMANS AND MACHINES

Humans Generally Are Better in Their Abilities to:

- Sense very low levels of certain kinds of stimuli: visual, auditory, tactual, olfactory, and taste
- Detect stimuli against high- "noise"-level background, such as blips on cathode-ray tube (CRT) displays with poor reception
- Recognize patterns of complex stimuli that may vary from situation to situation, such as objects in aerial photographs and speech sounds
- Sense unusual and unexpected events in the environment
- Store (remember) large amounts of information over long periods (better for remembering principles and strategies than masses of detailed information)
- Retrieve pertinent information from storage (recall), frequently retrieving many related items of information; but reliability of recall is low
- Draw upon varied experience in making decisions; adapt decisions to situational requirements; act in emergencies (Humans do not require previous "programming" for all situations.)
- Select alternative modes of operation, if certain modes fail
- Reason inductively, generalizing from observations
- Apply principles to solutions of varied problems
- Make subjective estimates and evaluations
- Develop entirely new solutions
- Concentrate on the most important activities when overload conditions require it
- Adapt physical response (within reason) to variations in operational requirements

Machines Generally Are Better in Their Abilities to:

- Sense stimuli that are outside the normal range of human sensitivity, such as X rays, radar wavelengths, and ultrasonic vibrations
- Apply deductive reasoning, such as recognizing stimuli as belonging to a general class (but the characteristics of the class need to be specified)
- Monitor for specified events, especially infrequent ones (but machines cannot improvise in case of unanticipated types of events)
- Store coded information quickly and in substantial quantity (for example, large sets of numerical values can be stored very quickly)
- Retrieve coded information quickly and accurately when specifically requested (although specific instructions need to be provided on the type of information to be recalled)
- Process quantitative information following specified programs
- Make rapid and consistent responses to input signals
- Perform repetitive activities reliably
- Exert considerable physical force in a highly controlled manner
- Maintain performance over extended periods (Machines typically do not "fatigue" as rapidly as humans.)
- Count or measure physical quantities
- Perform several programmed activities simultaneously
- Maintain efficient operations under conditions of heavy load (Humans have relatively limited channel capacity.)
- Maintain efficient operations under distractions

Source: Mark A. Sanders and Ernest J. McCormick, *Human Factors in Engineering and Design,* 6th ed. (New York: McGraw-Hill, 1987), pp. 526–527. Reprinted by permission of McGraw-Hill, Inc.

At the Twentymile Mine in Colorado, workers position the mining equipment that will shear a 30-inch slab of coal from the longwall. Push-button controls allow them to get out of the way when the machine goes to work and the coal dust flies. After a conveyor pulls out the newly cut slab, the workers go back in to reposition the machine for a deeper cut. Massive jacks support not only the equipment, but also the roof of the mine, helping to protect workers from mine cave-ins.

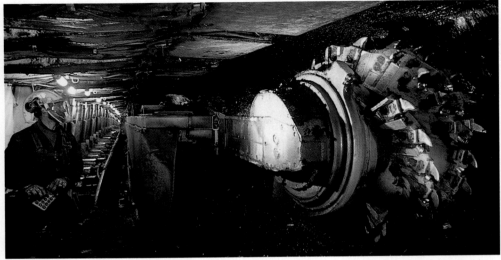

Jeffrey Aaronson/Network Aspen

IMPROVED QUALITY   Machines can provide high repeatability, so they can produce items with less variability in high-volume production. This leads to better fit of parts in an assembly, so the assembly, such as an electric motor, will perform better. Some semiconductor production requires automation because it must be done in such a clean environment that the pollution from human breathing, hair, and microscopic skin particles cannot be permitted.

Applications and Potential Applications Should Be Reconsidered

Companies should continue to evaluate possible applications of automation as competition, job requirements, and the available technology change. Many current applications of automation in services and in manufacturing are impressive, and many new applications will continue. Robert Ayres estimates that we probably have achieved 1 percent or less of the potential applications of robots, FMS, CAD/CAM, and machine vision in manufacturing.[3] Even if the current accomplishments are as high as 10 percent of the potential, what will be done in the future will be far greater than what is available today. Job requirements in companies will change as more technology becomes available. In manufacturing, the percentage of direct labor will decline further. New jobs will be in developing applications and tooling for automated equipment and in maintaining this type of equipment. The percentage of jobs involved with developing, modifying, and maintaining software to operate automated equipment for clerical and production applications will probably increase. As artificial intelligence is developed further, more office and service activities will be performed or assisted by automation. Training and retraining, which even now should be designed into jobs in a rapidly changing business world, will become more vital portions of many jobs.

[3]Robert U. Ayres, "Future Trends in Automation," *Manufacturing Review 1*, no. 2 (June 1988): 101.

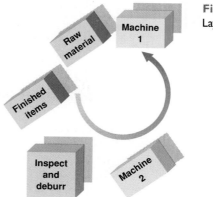

Figure 8.3
Layout of Coverplate Cell

which is the most desirable. Charts like the multiple-activity chart are useful in evaluating the initial design of a job and in evaluating jobs periodically to consider possible redesign or improvement.

MOTION ECONOMY AND WORK EFFICIENCY

Most workers do not enjoy making wasted motions, particularly if they result in unnecessary fatigue. In addition to providing some social and psychological rewards, a job should be reasonably efficient. Although motion study was developed in the early days of scientific management, it still has relevance today in helping to reduce fatigue and waste. In some instances, workers are trained in the principles of work efficiency and are responsible for developing their own efficient work methods.

Motion study and micromotion study usually are applied to analyze work performed at a fixed location, as opposed to analysis of work flow or movement, which is discussed in the next chapter. The movements of each worker's hands are noted and recorded on a chart, called an operations chart, or left-and-right-hand chart. The hand motions may be listed with a different degree of detail, but frequently the elements of reach, grasp, transport, position, and assemble are used to describe them. The chart may include a sketch describing the workplace, and distances the hands move may be indicated on the chart to assist in describing and analyzing the work.

The objectives of *motion study* are to examine the motions performed by a worker and to find improvements that will lead to a more productive (that is, less time-consuming) and/or less fatiguing pattern. A systematic attempt is made to eliminate all unnecessary elements and to arrange the remaining elements in the best sequence. Each step should be examined to see if it can be eliminated, simplified, combined with some other step, replaced by a simpler motion, or rearranged so that an improved motion pattern is achieved.

Figure 8.4 shows an example of a left-and-right-hand chart, or operations chart, for an improved method of assembling a lock washer, a flat steel washer, and a flat rubber washer on a bolt. In the method used previously, the left hand held the bolt while the right hand slipped each washer on it. Use of a hand as a holding device is poor motion economy when a mechanical device can be used. (See principle 12 in Table 8.4.) The hole in the rubber washer is slightly smaller than the diameter of the

Figure 8.4
Left-and-Right-Hand
Chart of Bolt and
Washer Assembly—
Improved

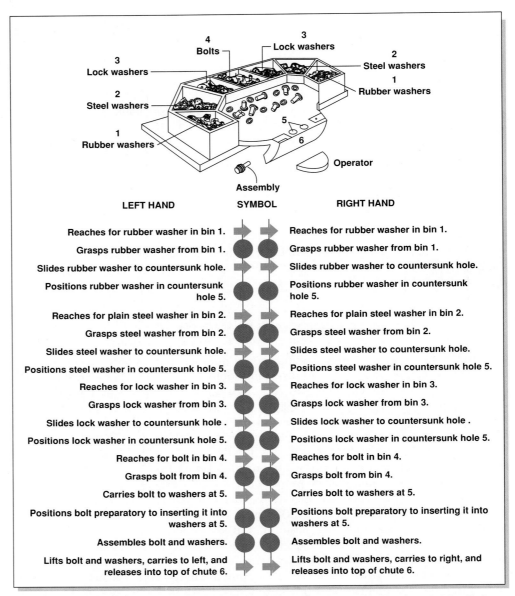

LEFT HAND	SYMBOL	RIGHT HAND
Reaches for rubber washer in bin 1.		Reaches for rubber washer in bin 1.
Grasps rubber washer from bin 1.		Grasps rubber washer from bin 1.
Slides rubber washer to countersunk hole.		Slides rubber washer to countersunk hole.
Positions rubber washer in countersunk hole 5.		Positions rubber washer in countersunk hole 5.
Reaches for plain steel washer in bin 2.		Reaches for plain steel washer in bin 2.
Grasps steel washer from bin 2.		Grasps steel washer from bin 2.
Slides steel washer to countersunk hole.		Slides steel washer to countersunk hole.
Positions steel washer in countersunk hole 5.		Positions steel washer in countersunk hole 5.
Reaches for lock washer in bin 3.		Reaches for lock washer in bin 3.
Grasps lock washer from bin 3.		Grasps lock washer from bin 3.
Slides lock washer to countersunk hole .		Slides lock washer to countersunk hole .
Positions lock washer in countersunk hole 5.		Positions lock washer in countersunk hole 5.
Reaches for bolt in bin 4.		Reaches for bolt in bin 4.
Grasps bolt from bin 4.		Grasps bolt from bin 4.
Carries bolt to washers at 5.		Carries bolt to washers at 5.
Positions bolt preparatory to inserting it into washers at 5.		Positions bolt preparatory to inserting it into washers at 5.
Assembles bolt and washers.		Assembles bolt and washers.
Lifts bolt and washers, carries to left, and releases into top of chute 6.		Lifts bolt and washers, carries to right, and releases into top of chute 6.

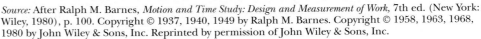

Source: After Ralph M. Barnes, *Motion and Time Study: Design and Measurement of Work,* 7th ed. (New York: Wiley, 1980), p. 100. Copyright © 1937, 1940, 1949 by Ralph M. Barnes. Copyright © 1958, 1963, 1968, 1980 by John Wiley & Sons, Inc. Reprinted by permission of John Wiley & Sons, Inc.

bolt, so the bolt will not slip off unless intentional force is exerted. In the improved method, the worker produces two assemblies simultaneously by making a stack of washers with each hand, then forcing a bolt through each. This new method utilizes principles of work efficiency 2, 3, and 4 noted in Table 8.4 by having both hands work simultaneously and by using fixed locations.

The fifteen principles of work efficiency listed in Table 8.4 are useful criteria to guide the development of efficient motion patterns. These rules or principles may be profitably applied to shops, services, and office work alike. Although not all are

Table 8.4
PRINCIPLES OF WORK EFFICIENCY

Use the Human Body the Way It Works Best

1. Work should be performed by machines if machines are more suitable or if the work is unsafe for humans.
2. Tools and materials should be placed in fixed locations in a sequence that permits a natural rhythm of motions and close together so movements are short and eye fixations are minimized.
3. Hands should begin and complete motions together when possible, and both should not be idle except during rest times.
4. Simultaneous arm motions should be in opposite directions with symmetric patterns.
5. Smooth continuous arcs of motion are preferable to straight-line movements involving abrupt changes in direction.
6. Motions should be confined to the lowest classification to involve as few muscle groups as are required to perform the job satisfactorily. The ascending order of motion classifications is:
   (a) Fingers only
   (b) Fingers and wrists
   (c) Fingers, wrists, and lower arms
   (d) Fingers, wrists, lower and upper arms
   (e) Hands, arms, and body

Arrange the Workplace to Improve Performance

7. Worker safety is a primary consideration in workplace design.
8. Chairs, tables, ventilation, illumination, and all features of the workplace should be suitable for the task and the worker.
9. Gravity feed chutes or other automatic conveyance devices should be used where appropriate to deliver objects close to the point of use.
10. Tools, materials, and controls on equipment should have set locations, close to the point of use and arranged to permit the best sequence and paths of motion.

Use Equipment to Improve Human Productivity

11. Computers, automation, and mechanical assistance should be employed where they can improve productivity.
12. Vises or clamps can be used to hold work precisely and relieve the hands for performing more valuable work than simply holding.
13. Mechanical guides might be used to reduce the time, effort, and attention required to position work.
14. Automatic controls and foot-actuated devices should relieve the hands for higher-value work or to reduce fatigue, where practicable.
15. Mechanical systems should be designed to require minimal operator motion and only reasonable amounts of force to use them.

Source: Based on ideas from Frank C. Barnes, "Principles of Motion Economy: Revisited, Reviewed, and Restored," *Proceedings of the Southern Management Association,* 1984; and Ralph M. Barnes, *Motion and Time Study,* 7th ed. (New York: Wiley, 1980).

applicable to every operation, they do form a basis for improving efficiency and reducing fatigue in manual work. Companies may train employees on efficiency principles and methods improvement techniques. Employees are then better prepared to design their own jobs and to suggest methods improvements.

Micromotion Study

Micromotion study is a much more detailed form of motion analysis that sometimes is used to examine high-volume jobs. Micromotion analysis uses a "simo chart," which is like a left-and-right-hand chart except that the activities are described in terms of seventeen basic elements of motion called *therbligs*. Therbligs are very small parts of motions that can be sequenced to form any task, just as various combinations and sequences of only twenty-six letters can be used to form any word in the English language. *Therblig* is derived from *Gilbreth* spelled backward; the name recognizes the contributions of Frank and Lillian Gilbreth to the early development of time and motion study.

Seventeen therbligs, or minute basic elements of motion, are listed below.

1. Search—locate an object visually or by groping for it.
2. Select—choose one part from among several.
3. Grasp—close the fingers around a part.
4. Transport empty—motion of the empty hand.
5. Transport loaded—motion of the hand while carrying an object.
6. Hold—manual support or control of an object.
7. Release—relinquish manual control.
8. Position—locate an object in specific position.
9. Preposition—orient object correctly.
10. Inspect—compare object with standard.
11. Assemble—unite mating parts.
12. Disassemble—disunite mating parts.
13. Use—manually implement production procedure.
14. Unavoidable delay—idleness beyond operator's control.
15. Avoidable delay—idleness for which operator is responsible.
16. Plan—mentally determine next action.
17. Rest to overcome fatigue—a periodic delay due to operator fatigue.

The first fifteen micromotions are so short that they might go undetected in normal observation. For this reason, micromotion study is performed by use of slow-motion photography.

Micromotion study is not widely used because the extra expense is not often justified and because filming is likely to distort the observed work and distract other workers. Most workers do not want to have such detailed descriptions of their work.

Inefficient uses of the hands can be detected by motion study and micromotion study. Analysts look for such things as idle time, long or unnecessary transports, and the use of hands for activities that could be performed by such mechanical devices as jigs and fixtures. Revision of the motions may result in more productive and/or less fatiguing work.

HUMAN FACTORS AND ERGONOMICS

In addition to the psychological effects of work, discussed under "Specialization," physical effects of work on the worker should be considered in job design. Some of these effects are taken into account in the design of the equipment that workers use. Additional allowances for the physical effects of work are taken into account in work measurement and in the setting of work standards. *Human factors engineering,* or *ergonomics,* endeavors to apply relevant information about human characteristics and behavior to the design of things people use, the methods by which they are used, and the environment in which people work and live.

Human factors engineering is applied in two major areas: the physical devices that people use in performing work and the environment in which work is performed.

Design of Physical Devices

We stated earlier that a worker is part of a system containing many elements, including the tools and equipment he or she uses. These combinations sometimes are called machine-worker systems because they are interrelated components that form a subsystem in the total collection of factors that affect operations. Since the human part of the machine-worker system cannot be redesigned and reconstructed in an effort to increase its effectiveness, the machine must be adapted to the worker. To be able to operate a piece of equipment, a person must be able to sense the operating conditions, reach the controls, and apply the necessary force to them. The average person is capable of reaching many locations, but the speed of reach and accuracy of adjustment are affected by the location of the object for which one is reaching; therefore, a determination of the best location requires considerable investigation and understanding of human capability and limitations.

ANTHROPOMETRIC DATA People vary in size, weight, strength, and skill. Considerable *anthropometric data* on the dimensions of various parts of the human body have been collected and serve as a basis for the design of tools and systems. Investigators have tabulated data on the reach, range of motion, speed of response, strength, sitting height, working height, and other variables in the machine-worker relationship. The reach required to operate a piece of equipment should be no greater than the shortest reach of all persons who are expected to operate it.

Just as the driver's seat in an automobile can be adjusted through a range of positions to accommodate a variety of drivers, seating arrangements and work heights may need to be adjustable. The work may be repositioned with respect to the worker or vice versa. Some companies use participative ergonomics so workers can improve working conditions that are particularly awkward or difficult. At its Livonia, Michigan, transmission plant, for example, Ford Motor Co. lowered the height of a conveyor by 11.5 inches so the workers would have only to reach out instead of reaching out and up with a 33-pound transmission housing in hand.

All controls and information displays should be located for clear access and visibility. Switches should be located so that all the off positions are in the same direction. Gauges should be arranged so that the indicators point in approximately the same direction when the device is operating normally. Thus the operator can quickly spot deviations from normal. Levers and hand wheels should be of the proper size and located so that sufficient operating force may be applied in the appropriate direction.

One aspect of physical devices with which employees work that is receiving increased attention is the matter of *repetitive stress injuries (RSI)*. The number of reported cases increased tenfold between 1982 and 1992. Autoworkers and meat packers are among the workers with the highest rates of reported cases. It is also high among workers who extensively use keyboards, cash registers, and electronic checkout scanners. Some of these persons develop pain in their fingers, hands, wrists, elbows, or shoulders. The incidence rate for this disorder is often higher where there is repeated use of force and/or extreme range of motion in joints. Often vibration is also involved. Some manufacturing companies provide motorized screwdrivers, wrenches, and so on, and braces to limit the range of motion in the joints involved in repetitive tasks that might give problems. Since it is thought to be associated with repetition, this ailment may be another reason for breaks, job rotation, and readjusting work positions periodically.

The Work Environment

The environment in which people work can affect their comfort, health, and productivity. Some environmental variables to be considered are temperature, noise, and lighting.

TEMPERATURE Humans can perform under various combinations of temperature, humidity, and air movements. The effects of these variables depend on the strenuousness of the work task and individual adaptation to the conditions. A comfortable temperature may range from 65 to 80°F (18.3 to 26.7°C), depending on other conditions (humidity and air movement, for example).

NOISE Unwanted sound in the workplace not only may be distracting but also may cause damage to the worker's hearing. The intensity of sound is measured in decibels (db); an increase of 10 decibels represents a tenfold increase in sound intensity. Workers may become so accustomed to a low level of noise that it does not impair their ability to perform mental or physical tasks. The Occupational Safety and Health Act of 1970 states that workers should not be exposed to noise above 90 db for more than 9 hours at a time. A lathe or a motorcycle emits a noise intensity of about 90 db. Higher sound intensities are permitted for shorter exposures, but no sound as high as 130 db (a painful intensity) should be experienced. Ear protection devices should be worn, and/or the duration of exposure should be limited when sounds are above 85 to 90 db.

LIGHTING Good illumination on work items or on the work surface is necessary for proper work performance without eyestrain. The color content of light and amount of glare are also important. The recommended illumination for various tasks is shown in Table 8.5.

DESIGN OF COMPENSATION METHODS

Employees of a company can exhibit a wide range of commitment and performance, ranging from the bare minimum necessary to remain employed to their full maximum effort. Operations depend on the efforts of employees to produce the products or services they offer for sale. Managers are responsible for gaining employees' cooperation in seeing that the company's objectives are achieved and hence are interested in directing their behavior. Human behavior is energized, directed, and sustained by *motivation*. An employee's motivation is to some degree related to the rewards the employee receives through participation in the organization.

Table 8.5

SOME RECOMMENDED ILLUMINATION LEVELS

VISUAL TASK	SAMPLE ACTIVITIES	RECOMMENDED ILLUMINATION (FOOTCANDLES)
High contrast or large size	Reading printed material, typed originals, handwriting in ink; rough bench or machine work; ordinary inspection; rough assembly	20–50
Medium contrast or small size	Reading medium-pencil handwriting, poorly reproduced material; medium benchwork or assembly; difficult inspection	50–100
Low contrast or very small size	Reading handwriting in hard pencil, very poor reproduction; highly difficult inspection; fine assembly;	100–200
	very difficult inspection; fine bench and machine work	200–500
Very prolonged and exacting tasks	Most difficult inspection; extra-fine bench and machine work; extra-fine assembly	500–1,000

Source: Mark S. Sanders and Ernest J. McCormick, *Human Factors in Engineering and Design,* 6th ed. (New York: McGraw-Hill, 1987), p. 408. Reprinted by permission of McGraw-Hill, Inc.

Time-Based Pay or Incentive Pay

Organizations may elect to pay employees on the basis of the amount of time spent on the job or on the basis of the production they achieve. Obviously, to be paid according to their production, employees must be involved in some activity for which there is an objective means of measuring the employees' output. For this and other reasons, which are discussed later, most employees are paid on the basis of time. Employees are said to work on a *daywork* plan if they are paid by the hour, day, or other unit of time without any production standards or measurement of their output. The pay plan is called *measured daywork* when production standards are used and output is measured but pay remains at a fixed hourly rate for some period of time.

Companies may, on the other hand, elect to pay employees by some type of incentive program, which ties employees' pay to some measure of individual or group output. *Wage incentive plans* are methods of remuneration by which employees, individually or as a group, are paid automatically and promptly an amount related to their output, according to some preestablished formula.

It is estimated that slightly more than 25 percent of the manufacturing work force is paid under some type of individual incentive plan. Few office workers are paid on incentive plans, so that less than 20 percent of the total work force receive individual wage incentives. Survey results indicate that the use of individual wage incentives has declined over the past two decades in most industries except iron and steel and footwear.[4] Yet the use of indirect bonuses through profit sharing appears to be increasing. Certainly, direct incentives are not suitable for every situation. In the remainder of the chapter we review several types of incentive plans used by some companies.

[4]Eric Seiler, "Piece Rate vs. Time Rate: The Effect of Incentives on Earnings," *Review of Economics and Statistics,* August 1984, p. 364.

SOME TYPES OF INDIVIDUAL WAGE INCENTIVE PLANS

An individual's pay may be tied to his or her productivity in innumerable ways. We briefly discuss some payment plans that relate individual pay to individual output. Individual wage incentives are intended to encourage each worker to produce as much as he or she can. At times this aim may run counter to other objectives of a company. The just-in-time (JIT) production concept calls for making only what is needed to keep inventory low and maintain flexibility. Paying a labor bonus to create further costs for inventory is not consistent with waste reduction. The emphasis in many JIT plants is on teamwork, mutual support, and quality. Group incentives (discussed later) seem more appropriate in these settings, particularly where tasks are interdependent. When employees' pay is tied to their output, care should be taken to ensure that pay is based only on work that is of acceptable quality.

Piece-Rate Plan

A *piece-rate plan* or *piecework* pays the employee a stated amount per unit produced, regardless of the number of units produced. This is probably the oldest type of payment plan; it was used in ancient days before clocks were widely available, and it became widely used in the early days of the scientific management era. The primary advantage of piecework is simplicity: Neither the company nor the employee has any difficulty computing the worker's pay. The piece-rate method is not common today because of government minimum wage requirements. The *standard-hour wage plan* is more common.

Standard-Hour Wage Plan

The standard-hour incentive plan is like a piece-rate plan except that each employee is guaranteed some base wage even if his or her average hourly output during a pay period is less than the standard for that particular job. Output can be expressed as the number of standard hours of output produced. Pay for the period is equal to the base rate times the number of standard hours of output produced during the period.

If the standard production is 8 units per hour and an employee produces 10 units, he or she will have 1.25 standard hours of production. If the base wage for the job is $10.00 per hour, the employee will receive $10.00(1.25) = $12.50 for the hour. It is more likely that the production will be counted for a day or a week, as long as the employee is working on the same product during the pay period. The standard-hour plan is a one-for-one plan, since the employee is paid 100 percent of the pay per unit that would be received at the standard rate for each unit above standard. The relationship between production and wages that begin at 100 percent of standard (standard-hour plan) is shown in Figure 8.5.

Workers who are employed under a one-for-one plan and produce above the level at which the bonus is paid receive pay just as though they were being paid at a piece rate. The pay per unit is equivalent to the unit pay for the production level where bonus earnings begin. Suppose that a worker is employed under an agreement that provides a one-for-one bonus for all hourly production above 80 percent of the standard rate. The worker would receive 1.5 times the base rate for production that

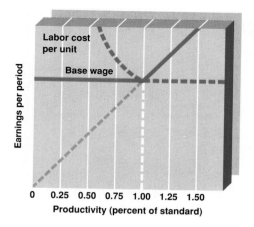

Figure 8.5
One-for-One Standard-Hour Plan with Bonus Beginning at Standard

was 120 percent of the standard. The pay at any level of performance above the point at which incentive pay begins is found by the following equation:

$$\text{Pay} = \frac{\text{base hourly wage} \times \text{hours worked} \times \text{actual production rate}}{\text{production at which bonus begins}}$$

Or, for production below the rate at which bonus pay beings, the worker's pay is

$$\text{Pay} = \text{base hourly wage} \times \text{hours worked}$$

Gain-Sharing Plans

A *gain-sharing plan* guarantees a base rate, but the wage is increased less than 1 percent for each percentage point that the employee produces above standard. Thus the employee and the company *share* the gain or bonus for work above standard. The employee may receive 70 percent, 50 percent, or some other percentage of the bonus earnings; the remainder may be retained by the company to help defray the cost of setting standards, counting production, and other administrative expenses associated with the incentive plan. Sometimes the part of the bonus that the direct worker does not receive is divided among the supervisors and indirect employees who support the production worker.

Like one-for-one plans, gain-sharing plans may begin paying a bonus at some level of production other than 100 percent of standard. Pay may be determined by multiplying the percentage of sharing by the amount of bonus production, then adding this amount to the base pay for the period. For example, if an individual produced 130 percent of the rate at which bonus pay begins, then he or she would have a 30 percent bonus production. Under a 60 percent sharing plan the worker would be credited with 0.6×30 percent, or 18 percent, bonus pay for the period. If the employee worked 8 hours at the job while achieving this average level of output, then he or she would be paid for $8 \times 1.18 = 9.44$ hours at the base rate. The relationships between production level and wages for some gain-sharing plans with sharing beginning at 75 percent of standard are shown in Figure 8.6.

Some wage incentive plans are based on nonlinear relationships between production and wages. It is apparent that an infinite variety of plans can be devised by having different slopes and changing the relationship between pay and productivity at

Figure 8.6
Gain-Sharing Plans with
Bonus Beginning at Less
than Standard

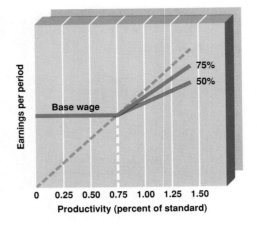

different levels of productivity. Usually this type of plan provides for a decreasing rate of bonus as output increases, so that bonus earnings will level off at, say, twice the standard wage.

Many factors other than pay have significant effects on motivation and performance. Social interactions with other workers influence workers' attitudes and behavior. Influential coworkers become opinion leaders, head informal organizations, and have more direct contact with workers than the official managers of the formal organizations. Contacts with peers influence the worker's attitude and the degree to which he or she accepts the company's expectations about performance. Peer pressure can overcome many of the positive or negative effects of a wage program. Social pressure is sometimes applied to any worker who exceeds an informally established quota that sets what is considered a "reasonable" level of work above the company standard. Workers may fear that managers will raise the standard if the workers exceed the standard by very much. Obviously, mutual trust between workers and managers is necessary if an incentive plan is to succeed.

GROUP INCENTIVE PLANS

Financial incentives may be paid to individuals or to groups. Group plans simplify the measurement and compensation decisions, particularly when a group of employees work as an interdependent team to produce a product or service. Group plans can provide financial recognition for support persons who move material, sharpen tools, maintain facilities, or contribute in other ways.

Direct-Wage Group Incentive Plans

Any of the individual plans discussed previously could also be applied to groups of employees. Group incentive plans that determine the direct wages on the basis of the output of the group simplify the production counting and administration process and reduce overhead expenses. A group incentive plan divides the bonus among the group members in proportion to each member's base wage. Such plans may lead to peer pressure from members of the group to see that each group member does his or her share of the work. Group plans still depend on the efforts of management, however, to motivate employees. No wage incentive plan should be viewed as a substitute for management efforts. Some proponents of wage incentive plans favor individual plans in settings where a worker performs independent work because they feel that it strengthens the incentive appeal.

Profit-Sharing and Cost-Reduction Plans

Companies are interested in earning enough profits to ensure that they can survive and grow. These objectives should be shared by owners, managers, and workers alike. Many companies have instituted profit-sharing plans to help secure the interest of workers in the soundness of the company and its profit picture. Profit sharing simplifies the job of administering an incentive plan because it does not require that each employee's contribution be measured. Since it is less likely to cause employees to feel a direct relation between their effort and their financial reward, profit sharing is as much an employee relations program as an incentive program.

Profit sharing is defined by the Council of Profit Sharing Industries as "any procedure under which an employer pays or makes available to regular employees, subject to reasonable eligibility rules, in addition to prevailing rates of pay, special current or deferred sums based on the profits of business." Profit-sharing plans have become increasingly popular in recent years. They may pay a bonus quarterly, semiannually, annually, or at some other interval. Some plans pay the bonus as direct income; others pay the employee's share into a retirement fund or provide a combination of payments.

Profit-sharing plans can be influenced by variables other than employee efficiency—variables beyond the control of workers. Changes in demand level, in product mix, in technology, in the cost of materials, and in executive salaries and bonuses affect the amount of revenue left to be divided among owners and workers. In some years employees may do well with no extra effort while in other years they may work extra hard and have no bonus. The business cycle and competitive maneuvers are facts of life for entrepreneurs and can also become unpleasant facts for employees who are on profit-sharing plans. Cooperation with management and other workers, however, can lead to improved production methods that give the company a sounder position in the marketplace, enabling everyone to enjoy better security in the long run and perhaps more pay in the short run.

The Scanlon Plan

The *Scanlon Plan* was developed by the late Joseph Scanlon in 1936, but World War II postponed its implementation at Lapointe Machine Tool Company until 1947. Scanlon, who had been a union official, proposed the plan as a means of keeping a financially troubled company afloat. The initial use was successful, and numerous other companies have adopted some form of this plan. The Scanlon Plan is as much an employee relations plan as an incentive plan. It is based on a philosophy of building a single team of management and labor, striving for increased productivity by reducing cost and improving efficiency. Labor is to share in the savings effected by reduced labor cost per unit of output. The employee's bonus is based on a ratio of total labor cost to the sales value of production. As labor cost declines in relation to sales value, the bonus increases. Since increases in material costs, taxes, fuels, and other expenses can reduce the proportional value of labor costs even when labor efficiency has not increased, the base ratio must be revised from time to time. By collective bargaining and negotiation, management and labor agree on a normal proportion of total cost to represent labor cost. Management may be included in the bonus or may be considered to benefit from increased sales and output relative to plant overhead.

Employee participation is an important aspect of the plan. One major component is the use of production committees to review suggestions for improved operations. Each production committee can implement improvements that involve no other departments and that require no capital expenditures. A second major component is the use of a screening committee composed of employee representatives and members of the top plant management group. The screening committee reviews and approves suggestions that involve more than one department or capital investments.

The Lincoln Electric Plan

The Lincoln Electric Company of Cleveland, Ohio, has a broad incentive plan that includes elements of profit sharing, participative management, and job enlargement. The basic concepts of the plan evolved between 1914 and 1934 under the direction of James F. Lincoln, the company's president, and no doubt the plan still undergoes occasional refinement. The objective of the plan is for management and labor to work together to produce the best product at the lowest price. Employees serve on job evaluation committees that seek suggestions for improvement in productivity. Lincoln's philosophy is that making money for someone else has never been a great motivational tool, so several methods of distributing financial rewards to the employees are used.

The *Lincoln Electric Plan* has three major components: (1) a piecework system, (2) a yearly bonus, and (3) a stock-purchase plan. In addition to these components of the pay scheme, the company provides enriched jobs and participation in decisions. Employees serve on evaluation committees involved in the plan. Independent work groups plan their own production processes and perform their own quality control evaluations.

The employees at Lincoln Electric are among the highest paid factory workers in the world in their lines of work. They also are among the most productive. Some of Lincoln's products sell today for little more than their prices in the 1930s, despite the dramatic inflation in material prices since that time. The Lincoln system has achieved some results that many companies should find worthy of serious study.

SUMMARY

Engineers and managers must realize that when they select and combine components of a technical system to be used by humans, they are designing a social system. This chapter has presented material on several physical and behavioral aspects of job design and redesign. A job may be examined before it is assigned to a worker or reexamined at any time during the life of a company. Important questions should be raised regarding both the technical-physical and sociopsychological aspects of a job.

Several theories of motivation and job satisfaction were discussed. The job characteristics of skill variety, task identity, task significance, autonomy, and feedback can help improve motivation. Job enrichment is a program of adding variety and decision making to a job.

Motion economy and human engineering are more traditional approaches to designing efficiency into jobs and concentrate primarily on the technical-physical aspects of the job.

Efforts to improve methods should never cease. Managers should strive constantly to encourage members of their organizations to look for improvements. Changes in technology, volume, product mix, and human inventiveness lead to opportunities for improvement. Competitive pressures and/or potential growth of profits encourage methods studies.

Individual or group wage incentives are used in some companies as a means of motivating employees and as a way to share with employees the benefits of their productivity. Individual incentives may pay the full labor rate for units that the employee produces above the standard. An alternative is gain sharing, which pays less than 100 percent for units above the standard. Profit sharing or other group incentives are used in some instances, such as where administration of individual incentives would be cumbersome or where work depends on interrelated activities of worker groups. Two group incentive plans that have been acclaimed as highly successful in some installations are the Scanlon Plan and the Lincoln Electric Plan.

KEY TERMS

Intrinsic rewards
Extrinsic rewards
Job design
Team
Motivators
Hygiene factors
Skill variety
Task identity
Task significance
Autonomy
Feedback
Job rotation
Quality circles

Improvement teams
Job enlargement
Job enrichment
Sociotechnical systems
Autonomous work groups
Multiple-activity chart
Motion study
Micromotion study
Therbligs
Human factors
    engineering
    (ergonomics)
Anthropometric data

Repetitive stress injuries
    (RSI)
Motivation
Daywork
Measured daywork
Wage incentive plans
Piece-rate plan or
    piecework
Standard-hour wage plan
Gain-sharing plans
Profit sharing
Scanlon Plan
Lincoln Electric Plan

DISCUSSION QUESTIONS

1. What is job design?
2. What three criteria should be considered in job design?
3. Discuss the relevance of feedback in job design.
4. How do you think most jobs are designed today?
5. What are some of the hygiene factors mentioned in Herzberg's two-factor theory?
6. What are some of the motivators?
7. How do motivators and hygiene factors compare to extrinsic rewards and intrinsic rewards?
8. Name and discuss three methods that are used to provide variety in jobs.
9. Discuss the use of quality circles.
10. Discuss some of the differences between horizontal and vertical job expansion.
11. Under what conditions is job enrichment likely to be successful?
12. Can all jobs be enriched successfully? Briefly discuss the reasons for your answer.
13. Discuss briefly some physical factors that should be taken into account in job design.

14. How are anthropometric data and human engineering useful in the design of some jobs?
15. What are the objectives of motion study?
16. How is it possible to perform micromotion study at the extremely detailed therblig level?
17. Why is motivation important to organizations?
18. Briefly describe two categories of rewards that people may derive from their jobs.
19. Define a wage incentive plan.
20. For what reasons might a company elect to use a wage incentive plan?
21. Distinguish between a piece-rate plan and a standard-hour plan.
22. What is gain sharing?
23. Under what conditions is a group incentive plan generally more appropriate than an individual incentive plan?

PROBLEMS

1. Go through the following list of tasks and indicate alongside each whether it would be better performed by a human or a machine.

   Make rapid and consistent responses to input signals.
   Recognize patterns of complex stimuli that may vary from situation to situation.
   Adapt decisions to situational conditions.
   Retrieve coded information quickly and accurately.
   Develop entirely new solutions.
   Detect small amounts of light or sound.
   Store coded information quickly and in substantial quantity.
   Perform repetitive activities reliably.
   Select alternative modes of operation if certain modes fail.
   Reason inductively, exercise judgment.
   Apply great force smoothly and precisely.
   Store information briefly and erase it completely.
   Develop concepts and create methods.
   Perform many different functions simultaneously.

2. Prepare a multiple-activity chart to show the activities involved in preparing two pieces of bacon, two scrambled eggs, two pieces of buttered toast, and four cups of coffee with a coffeemaker, an oven, a stove, and one skillet. Estimate the time required for each activity. Compare your time estimates with those of other members of your class.

3. An office of the state employment service in a city is responsible for interviewing persons seeking employment, placing the applicants' qualifications in a file, and searching a file of job openings to determine if a suitable match between job and applicant can be found. The three persons presently employed in this activity enjoy interviewing clients more than they enjoy searching files. Employees are displeased because they are overloaded with work, have shortened their breaks, and work some unwanted overtime.

   During the typical 8-hour day, clients arrive with an average interarrival time of 8 minutes. The times required to perform the interviews are normally distributed with a mean of 30 minutes and a standard deviation of 5 minutes. Searching the list of job openings requires approximately 7 minutes for each applicant to review files that are in a room next to the interview rooms. No more than three persons can use the files at the same time.

The office manager is planning to add the necessary personnel. She also is considering how to assign work to individuals. All the employees could continue to interview applicants and perform the associated file searches. Or one or more employees could be permanently assigned to interview applicants, and one or more could be assigned permanently to search files. As a third alternative, the jobs could be rotated each hour, half day, day, week, or month.

a. How many employees should be assigned to the office to perform the average work load without overtime? Employees are paid for 8 hours but are permitted a 15-minute break in the morning and in the afternoon.

b. Discuss the advantages and disadvantages of the alternative ways that work can be assigned to structure jobs in this office.

4. The Blitz Corporation employs six workers in painting stripes on parking lots. The employees are paid by a daywork plan at $6.80 per hour. On the basis of past contracts, the manager, Ruby Smith, has established a standard of 50 yards of striping per hour for each painter. The company has just accepted a contract for a new shopping center parking lot with 6,600 yards of stripes.

a. Determine the labor cost for the contract if the painters work at efficiencies of 85, 95, 105, and 115 percent.

b. The manager is concerned about completing the contract before the new shopping center opens. She can use only three painters, so she has offered to pay $0.12 per yard for each yard of striping above standard. What will be the labor cost if the three workers finish the lot in a 40-hour week?

c. What will each painter earn per week, before deductions? How does this figure compare with the pay for an ordinary 40-hour week?

5. The Eagle Mountain Hospital pays employees in its laundry according to a standard-hour plan. The standard rate of ironing is 31 bedsheets an hour. Currently employees in this department are paid $5.40 per hour as a base wage and work 40 hours a week. Ellie Davis, one of the more skilled workers in the department, regularly irons 36 sheets per hour. Determine her weekly (40 hours) pay if she works at 90 percent of standard, a pace that is easy for her; at 100 percent; if she works a little harder, at 110 percent; if she really applies her skill and achieves 120 percent of the standard.

6. Darnell Corporation pays employees in its billing office according to a one-for-one standard-hour plan with a bonus beginning at 100 percent of standard. The standard rate of billing is 22 bills an hour. Currently employees in this department are paid $6.50 per hour as a base wage and work 40 hours a week. Jeff Baker, one of the more skilled workers in the department, regularly types 27 bills an hour. Determine his weekly (40 hours) pay if he works at 90 percent of standard, a pace that is easy for him; at 100 percent; if he works a little harder, at 110 percent; if he really applies his skill and achieves 120 percent of the standard.

7. Employees in the manufacturing department of Michael Metals Company are paid on a one-for-one incentive plan beginning at 85 percent of standard. Bob Darver works in this department and earns a base wage of $8.50 per hour for a 40-hour week. The standard for Bob's job is 20 units per hour. Last week Bob produced 890 units.

a. How many standard hours did Bob earn last week?

b. How much gross pay did Bob earn for this work?

8. Employees in the assembly department of McDaniel Microwave Corporation are paid on a one-for-one incentive plan beginning at 90 percent of standard. Tom Minor works in this department and earns a base wage of $9.20 per hour for a 40-hour week. The standard for Tom's job is 7 units per hour. Last week Tom produced 310 units.

a. How many standard hours did Tom produce last week?

b. How much gross pay did he earn for this work?

9. Samantha Smith works 40 hours a week at the Cato Custard Company. Samantha is paid on a 70 percent gain-sharing plan, with bonus earnings beginning at standard. The base wage for her job is $7.35 per hour, and the standard is 36 units per hour.
   a. What is Samantha's weekly (40 hours) pay if she works at standard, and what is the company's labor cost per unit?
   b. What is her weekly pay if she produces 1,800 units in the 40 hours? What is the labor cost per unit at this production rate?

10. Charles Curtis works 40 hours a week at Sunnydale Dairy. Charles is paid on an 80 percent gain-sharing plan, with bonus earnings beginning at standard. The base wage for Charles' job is $6.75 per hour, and the standard is 43 units per hour.
    a. What is Charles's weekly (40 hours) pay if he works at standard, and what is the company's labor cost per unit?
    b. What is his weekly pay if he produces 1,950 units in the 40 hours?

11. The Bio Company pays its workers on a 70 percent gain-sharing plan, with bonus pay beginning at 90 percent of standard. The standard is 400 units per 40-hour week. Caroline Demarco, whose pay is $7.10 per hour, produced 440 units last week.
    a. What is Caroline's gross pay for the week?
    b. What is the unit labor cost at 60 percent of standard?
    c. At standard?
    d. At Caroline's rate of work last week?

12. The Omega Corporation pays its workers on a 75 percent gain-sharing plan, with bonus pay beginning at 80 percent of standard. The standard is 1,250 units per 40-hour week. Leslie Blount, whose pay is $6.90 per hour, produced 1,385 units last week.
    a. What is Leslie's gross pay for the week?
    b. What is the unit labor cost at 70, 85, and 100 percent of standard?
    c. What is the unit labor cost at Leslie's rate of work last week?

13. Alton's Auto Repair pays mechanics one-half the labor bill charges for the repair work they perform, or $8 per hour, whichever is higher. Repair work is billed at $24 per hour for each standard hour as stated in a reference catalog. A skilled mechanic can perform 48 standard hours of work in a 40-hour week. Mechanics at this shop are not paid a percentage of the price for parts they install. Barton's Auto Repair charges $22 per standard hour and pays mechanics $10 per hour plus 10 percent of the price for parts used on the repair work they perform. Each of Barton's mechanics installs an average of $2,400 worth of parts in a week.
    a. What are the average earnings at each shop?
    b. Where would you prefer to have your automobile repaired and why?

CASES

I. RON AND CROCKETT EQUIPMENT COMPANY

Crockett Equipment Company is a 4-year-old company involved in the development and sale of equipment for drilling oil and gas wells. The company is small but has pioneered a new type of equipment and is growing rapidly, with thirty-four employees involved in marketing, sales, engineering, and purchasing. Because of its rapid growth, capital is limited, so the company has not established its own production shop. Crockett has signed an agreement with RON Company, a small machine shop that is to perform the machining (lathe and milling) operations. Crockett performs the design and final assembly operations.

Sales have skyrocketed, and RON has had difficulty in keeping enough capacity to serve the needs of Crockett. The Crockett work now accounts for almost half of RON's total business. Crockett has purchased machines and placed them in the RON plant to help RON deal with the booming production requirements. RON provides the skilled operators and has set up a special production line using some of the Crockett equipment and some of its own, and RON has added a second shift to help meet the production demands.

Competition between Crockett and its competitors is fierce. Several newly designed products are being introduced. These new products and design changes for units already partially produced are being rushed through the production line along with the other Crockett products. Often these new items require that Crockett engineers and RON production supervisors work alongside the machine operators to direct them during the machining process. Machine operators feel pressured and intimidated by the close supervision. The RON supervisors feel as if they are losing control of their shop. Production rates and time schedules are being impaired, so the pressures are increasing to make production quotas because of the competition. Most workers on the production line feel frustrated because they want to complete the models for which there are no design changes, but they are continually interrupted to make changes in several of the developmental models. Yet, the parts will be unsalable if the design changes are not made immediately.

The RON employees feel they have a right to control what is made in their shop because their company owns most of the machines. Heated arguments erupt from time to time between the RON supervisors and the Crockett engineers, sometimes in the presence of subordinates. The situation is affecting morale and undermining authority. Both sides feel they are performing their duties and responsibilities, yet tensions are building.

What should be done to revise the jobs so that the problems are reduced and order is restored to the two companies?

2. EAGLE MOUNTAIN RADIOGRAPHY DEPARTMENT

The Eagle Mountain Hospital has recently added a new wing to its older, over-crowded building. The Radiology Department was one of the most crowded in the old facility. The department occupied three diagnostic examination rooms and one darkroom, all of which adjoined a large office with a desk for each radiographer. The six radiographers kept a coffeepot in this office and enjoyed a congenial relationship extending to social activities outside the hospital.

The new radiology department is located at the end of the hall on the first floor of the new wing. Each radiographer has a small office opening to the hall, and there is a lounge halfway down the hall. There are four examination rooms, two on each side of the hall, with a darkroom between each pair of examination rooms.

The supervisor in this department has assigned three radiographers to each pair of examination rooms and suggested that they could rotate the assignment of working in the darkroom. The supervisor is not pleased with the performance of the radiographers. They spend too much time down the hall in the lounge and are seldom in their offices when she wants to talk with them or when patients arrive. Despite the attractive surroundings, the employees seem less happy and less motivated than they were before the move. One radiographer has submitted his resignation, and the others have complained about having to do so much more walking in the new location.

The supervisor is wondering what can be done to improve the situation in her department. What do you think may be hurting the efficiency and morale of the department? Can you suggest some improvements?

3. ELMOR PRODUCTS, INC.

Elmor Products, Inc., employs 500 people in producing a variety of products, one of which is a small electric saw. The company has been experiencing unusually high absenteeism and employee turnover in several departments, and productivity is low. The problem is most serious in one of the older departments. The pay scale in this department is equal to the pay scale in the others. David Emhoff, the new assistant manager, has studied one work center within this department and has identified several relevant facts.

The layout for the saw assembly work center is shown in Figure 8.7. Although the work areas are well lighted, there is little control of the temperature in the room. The workers use considerable movement during the assembly process. All the work tasks except the drill press operations are performed by hand. Each worker has a work table that is 30 inches high (about the height of a desk).

The assembly process consists of the following six steps:

1. Worker A walks from his assembly table to the stamped parts department and returns carrying a box of 20 frames. He then hand-files all the rough edges left from the stamping process.
2. Worker A then drills six holes of two different sizes, using the two drill presses.
3. Worker B obtains a set of retaining pins from the stock bin. While worker C holds the frame in position, worker B presses the retaining pins into the frame.
4. Worker C then carries the frame to her worktable and attaches a handle, which she obtains from the stock bin.
5. Worker B then takes the frame and attaches a saw blade, which he obtains from the blade production department.

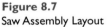

Figure 8.7
Saw Assembly Layout

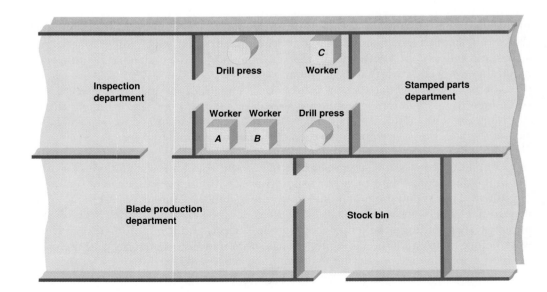

   6. Worker *C* then carries the completed assembly to the inspection department.
      a. What improvements in the physical arrangements can you recommend?
      b. What improvements in the work assignments can you recommend?
      c. Why do you think employee turnover is high in this work center?

4. ALK MANUFACTURING, INC.

ALK Manufacturing, Inc., is a medium-size manufacturing firm making arc welding equipment, electric motors, and generators. The plant design is a typical assembly-line layout: Various components are added to the item as it moves down a conveyor line until the completed product is assembled. Each worker is assigned to a work station along the assembly line and performs a specific task on the item at his or her station. The tasks are extremely repetitive with little flexibility for the employee.

   The manufacturing facility itself is large, noisy, and poorly ventilated (hot in the summer and cold in the winter). There is little interaction among the employees or the supervisors during the day. Management style has always been authoritarian, and since the plant is a nonunion shop, there is no employee representation to management. Product quality has always been a problem at ALK but has gotten out of hand over the last few years. Returns from distributors have greatly increased, along with customer complaints. Productivity of the workers is well below industry standards for this type of facility. Absenteeism and employee turnover are extremely high, which has begun to hamper the plant's ability to meet production deadlines.

   The plant was recently purchased by an outside investor group, the former owner having decided to sell the business because of the problems outlined above. You have been hired as the new plant operations manager, with a firm directive from the investors to improve all phases of operations. Suggest some specific methods you would employ to accomplish the objectives given to you by top management.

BIBLIOGRAPHY

Bridges, William. "The End of the Job." *Fortune,* September 19, 1994, pp. 62–64, 66, 72, 74.

Champagne, Paul J., and R. Bruce McAfee. *Motivating Strategies for Performance and Productivity: A Guide to Human Resource Development.* New York: Quorum Books, 1989.

Cunningham, J. Barton, and Ted Eberle. "A Guide to Job Enrichment and Redesign." *Personnel,* February 1990, pp. 56–61.

Dumaine, Brian. "Who Needs a Boss?" *Fortune,* May 7, 1990, pp. 52–60.

Griffin, Ricky W., and Gregory Moorehead. *Organizational Behavior.* Boston: Houghton Mifflin, 1986. Chap. 8.

Hackman, J. Richard, ed. *Groups That Work (and Those That Don't).* San Francisco: Jossey-Bass, 1991.

Hellriegel, Don, John W. Slocum, and Richard W. Woodman. *Organizational Behavior.* 4th ed. St. Paul, Minn.: West, 1986. Chap. 13.

Herzberg, Frederick. "One More Time: How Do You Motivate Employees?" Reprinted with "Retrospective Commentary" in *Harvard Business Review,* September–October 1987, pp. 109–120.

Horwitz, Tony. "9 to Nowhere: These Six Growth Jobs Are Dull, Dead-End, Sometimes Dangerous." *Wall Street Journal,* December 1, 1994, pp. A1, A8.

Katzenback, Jon R., and Douglas K. Smith. *The Wisdom of Teams.* New York: HarperCollins, 1993.

Kovach, Kenneth A. "What Motivates Employees? Workers and Supervisors Give Different Answers." *Business Horizons 30,* no. 5 (September–October 1987): 58–65.

Larson, Carl E., and Frank M. LaFasto. *Teamwork: What Must Go Right/What Can Go Wrong.* Newbury Park, Calif.: Sage, 1989.

Lawler, Edward E., III. *Strategic Pay: Aligning Organizational Strategies and Pay Systems.* San Francisco: Jossey-Bass, 1990.

———. *High-Involvement Management: Participative Strategies for Improving Organizational Performance.* San Francisco: Jossey-Bass, 1986.

Miller, Christopher S., and Michael H. Schuster. "Gain-sharing Plans: A Comparative Analysis." *Organizational Dynamics,* Summer 1987, pp. 44–67.

Nichel, James E., and Sandra O'Neal. "Small-Group Incentives: Gain Sharing in the Microcosm." *Compensation and Benefits Review,* March–April 1990, pp. 22–29.

Niles, John L. "Group Compensation for Continuous Flow Manufacturing Systems." *1990 International Industrial Engineering Conference Proceedings.* Atlanta: Institute of Industrial Engineers, 1990, pp. 619–625.

O'Reilly, Brian. "The New Deal, What Companies and Employees Owe One Another." *Fortune,* June 13, 1994, pp. 44–52.

Ost, Edward J. "Team-Based Pay: New Wave Strategic Incentives." *Sloan Management Review,* Spring 1990, pp. 19–27.

"The Payoff from Teamwork." *Business Week,* July 10, 1989, pp. 56–62.

Perlman, Stephen L. "Employees Redesign Their Own Jobs." *Personnel Journal,* November, 1990, pp. 37, 38, 40.

Rollins, Thomas. "Productivity-Based Group Incentive Plans: Powerful but Use with Caution." *Compensation and Benefits Review,* May–June 1989, pp. 39–50.

Sanders, Mark A., and Ernest J. McCormack. *Human Factors in Engineering and Design.* 6th ed. New York: McGraw-Hill, 1987.

Schmid, Richard O. "Structuring Gainsharing for Success." *Industrial Engineering 26,* no. 7 (July, 1994): 62–65.

Schultz, Duane P., and Sydney Ellen Schultz. *Psychology and Industry Today.* 4th ed. New York: Macmillan, 1986. Chap 11.

Verespej, Michael A. "Ergonomics: Taming the Repetitive Motion Monster." *Industry Week,* October 7, 1991, pp. 26–32.

———. "Yea Teams? Not Always." *Industry Week,* June 18, 1990, pp. 104–105.

REVIEW AND REDESIGN FOR CONTINUOUS IMPROVEMENT

Japanese businessmen who have returned to the United States and revisited factories they had visited 25 years earlier as some of the world's foremost manufacturing facilities, have expressed surprise and disappointment that these factories have changed very little. They were surprised that, rather than building upon their strong base in order to continue in their position among the world's foremost factories, management had simply attempted to preserve the status quo. They had fallen behind many more-advanced factories in other parts of the world. In a competitive world, those who do not move forward will fall behind.

Several reasons can be offered to explain why many American companies did not have continuous efforts underway to modify and improve their facilities and work methods. Companies often use long-term analyses to justify their investment in plant and equipment and do not include continuing additional investments for improvement in the study. In order to meet their numbers they make no additional investments. Another possible financial reason is that they may be overly attracted to the return on book value that occurs as the facility is depreciated and the income is maintained at about the same level. During the 25-year era referred to in the preceding paragraph the level of competition was not as fierce as it is today and, in many industries, the competition was primarily domestic. Many of a company's competitors had the same management training, accounting methods, capital markets, and operating methods. The pace of improvement among competitors did not force rapid and continuous improvement. Frequently, major improvements involve some investment and a temporary loss of productivity to revise old equipment, install new equipment, retrain employees and allow them to become proficient at the new methods. It may take several months or more before the change proves itself a true improvement in performance. Some managers (particularly those who are on a fast-track promotion program and have good chances to make it to high levels in the company) have been reluctant to take a chance at showing a decline in performance, even though it is intended to be temporary. By the time such a manager had been in a job long enough to understand what improvements should be made it was time to be concerned about the next promotion. Perhaps another reason is the mindset discussed in the next paragraph.

In his book *Serious Creativity,* Edward de Bono points out that a very common and dangerous saying is, "If it ain't broke, don't fix it." That is, if it is running right do not bother it. He seems to think this guiding principle is responsible for much of the decline of U.S. industry because, under this guidance, a company would hold its creative energies in reserve until something breaks. In the event of a breakdown the company's energy and creativity would be expended to get back to where it was before the breakdown. Consequently the company would never get better.

It seems that a better guiding principle, or motto, for companies these days is, "If it ain't perfect, find ways to improve it." As global markets have emerged and global competition has grown, companies have recognized that the pace of competition has increased and the status quo has to be continuous efforts to improve. Change within a company is necessary. Market demographics change, people's tastes change, technology changes, new competitors appear, old ones try new tactics, and other forms of change and challenge occur. Companies must also seek change in the form of improvements if they are going to remain competitive. With or without a motto as suggested above, many companies today are seeking continuous improvement, and even then some are struggling to stay even with or ahead of competition. Even companies that are changing and improving may fall behind their competition, if they do not improve fast enough.

Home, hearth, and . . . computers? Redesigning for "home appeal" is something computer companies, including Apple, are willing to try. Thinking about improving a product's aesthetics is part of the continuous improvement process.

Andy Freeberg

HOW CONTINUOUS IMPROVEMENT CAN HELP ADD VALUE FOR CUSTOMERS

The driving force for most improvements is to improve competitiveness. That means the change has to result in something the customer likes better, that is, that the customer values more. A company's improvement activities can enhance value in several ways. Improvement efforts can enhance any of the multiple dimensions of quality, lead to quicker response, provide more service and dependability, and reduce cost. Basically a company can improve any of the performance capabilities mentioned in Chapter 2.

BREAKTHROUGHS AND INCREMENTAL IMPROVEMENTS

The literature on improvement often compares two major approaches. One approach to improvement looks for *breakthroughs*—major innovations or significant changes that make such a large improvement that it is obviously worthwhile to disrupt the established routine or status quo in a company. An employee suggestion that shows a major cost-saving or quality improvement, new technology that becomes available from some vendor, or a new process that a company develops in its R&D laboratory are examples of the types of improvements that are considered major breakthroughs. Breakthrough improvements may require significant investment on the front end. The proposed changes are carefully studied through a series of formal reviews which include an analysis of the return on investment to ensure that it is sufficient before such a change can be implemented. These types of improvements are very important to companies. Many companies, therefore, have R&D departments and maybe a small group of staff specialists such as industrial engineers or internal consultants who are permanently assigned the job of looking for and developing improvements. Major improvements occur relatively infrequently because only a small percentage of the employees are charged with looking for them. In addition, some of the proposed improvements are turned down for causes such as a company's lack of experience with the technology, an insufficient rate of return, and so forth. Breakthrough improvements would lead to a set of upward jumps in a company's performance over time or to discontinuous jumps in its improvement spiral, as discussed in Chapter 1. This pattern shown in Figure 9.1*a*, with a series of jumps in performance as companies implemented major improvements and with horizontal lines between, is considered to be typical of what U.S. companies tried to achieve up until a decade or two ago. Some authors suggest that companies that just wait between breakthroughs probably experience some regression, so the actual progress is more like Figure 9.1*b*.

Many leading Japanese companies, in comparison, have operated with a culture of *kaizen,* which means continuous improvement involving everyone. Now leading U.S. companies are also developing a culture that encourages all employees in the company to seek numerous small improvements. Staff specialists can work on only a few projects at a time. But when all employees are working on improvements the aggregate result can be immensely impressive even though each improvement may be relatively small. When each department or work unit improves only 1 or 2 percent a year, the company can become an awesome competitor in a few years. For a contin-

Figure 9.1
Improvement through
Breakthroughs and with
Regression

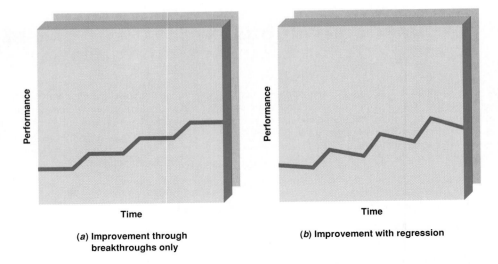

(*a*) Improvement through
breakthroughs only

(*b*) Improvement with regression

uous improvement situation, the graph of a company's improvement over time is more like a continuing upward ramp as shown in Figure 9.2*a*. Of course, *kaizen* does not preclude occasional breakthroughs, so the ideal objective is to achieve the type of progress graph shown in Figure 9.2*b*.

The motivational climate can be high in a company that stresses continuous small improvements and accepts a large percentage of suggestions. In an environment where only a few major suggestions are accepted, employees might feel that it is unlikely they can develop a suggestion that is outstanding enough to be accepted, so fewer of them try. Breakthroughs and incremental improvements are not mutually exclusive. A company can have the best of both worlds by forming groups to find breakthroughs and having all employees participate in other improvement efforts. Both breakthroughs and incremental improvements become more likely when most of the work force is highly motivated and mentally active in seeking improvements.

Figure 9.2
Improvement through
Small Incremental Steps
and Breakthroughs

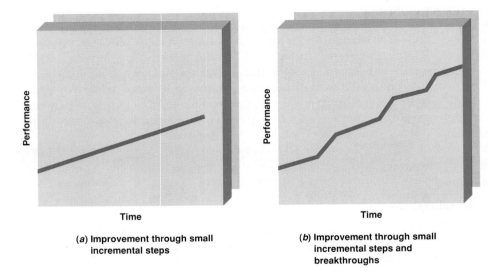

(*a*) Improvement through small
incremental steps

(*b*) Improvement through small
incremental steps and
breakthroughs

The result could be an improvement spiral or ramp with some discontinuous jumps in company performance, which certainly is a very desirable pattern.

Incremental steps often result from the efforts of individuals, quality circles, or temporary teams established to focus on small group improvement activities. These types of groups often study the work of one department or work area. Occasionally these groups develop large-impact improvements, but typically develop more-numerous small improvements. Companies may also establish improvement teams with a broader scope to study major processes that involve a series of work steps that flow through multiple departments or work areas. Either of these types of improvement teams can use the same general procedures and many of the same types of tools and techniques. We will discuss a general procedure for work improvement and present some of the tools that frequently are used in improving processes and work methods.

A GENERAL PROCEDURE FOR IMPROVEMENT

A formal improvement study often begins with a broad view that may uncover areas for more detailed study. For example, an initial review might examine a manufactured product's design to see if the number of parts can be reduced or if the processing can be reduced or simplified. The general flow or layout may be examined to determine if it can be revised to advantage. This overview may reveal locations where a more concentrated study may be needed. For example, a bottleneck might become the focus of a detailed improvement study, or availability of new technology to perform some of the work might require redesign of several jobs in a processing sequence.

The overall procedure for performing a methods improvement study may be summarized in the five basic steps listed below:

1. Observe and understand the current method.
2. Document the current method. It is usually helpful to have a detailed description of a method to be studied. Charting methods, such as the multiple-activity chart discussed earlier, may be useful. The flow process chart, discussed below, is also helpful.
3. Critically evaluate the current method and any proposed changes in it. This is the most important step in a methods study because it is here that any ideas for improvement will occur. Creativity, ingenuity, and persistence can pay off at this stage. A broad, total-system view is helpful and should include consideration of the layout, training or retraining, required investment, and any other factors that may affect performance and costs.
4. Implement the improvement. Naturally, ideas alone will accomplish little; an improvement must be put into effect before any benefit will be achieved. Someone must specify a plan of action, assign responsibilities, and follow up to see that the new method is used. Any new method that is implemented should show promise of a potential cost savings or an improvement in quality that is at least large enough to pay for its cost.
5. Reevaluate the new method after sufficient time has passed to see that it is working as intended.

This general procedure is similar to several described in the literature. One source describes a six-step methodology that has an initial step of commitment to performance improvement before the five steps described above. We will now discuss some common tools that can be used in conducting a performance improvement study.

SOME TOOLS AND TECHNIQUES FOR PERFORMANCE IMPROVEMENT

A variety of tools and techniques can be used in conducting improvement studies. Some of these have been presented earlier. When the focus of the study is an individual job, tools such as motion study and micromotion study, discussed in Chapter 8, can be used for improvement studies or for evaluation in the original design of jobs. Likewise, the left-and-right-hand chart can be used in developing an initial job design or analyzing for improvements in an existing job. The multiple-activity chart, also presented in Chapter 8, is a means of documenting more than one job when the jobs are to be synchronized or coordinated in some way. The multiple-activity chart can be used in the initial design of jobs or for jobs that are being analyzed for improvement. It is not uncommon for different persons to have different perceptions of how jobs are performed. By observing and asking questions, a team or individual can develop an accurate description of how a specified part of the company's work is performed. Once it is documented it can be reviewed with various workers and supervisors to clear up any misunderstandings and ensure that the description is accurate. Once there is a common understanding of what the current method is, the group can examine and question the steps and look for improvements.

Often, improvement studies involve a broader scope than just the work performed at one location. Flowcharts or flow process charts are useful devices to describe these types of work activities and the people conducting the improvement study can understand what is involved and focus on various parts of the work that might be improved. We will first discuss the flow process chart.

Flow Process Chart

Flow process charts are useful in documenting the flow of people or materials in some operations. A material flow process chart displays actual or potential movements of material. Each activity that is performed is classified as one of the five types shown below with their symbols.

Operation: ◯ An operation is an intentional change in the physical or chemical characteristics of an object; the receipt or dissemination of information; the making of calculations or plans.

Inspection: ☐ An inspection is the examination of an object or group of objects to verify that they have certain characteristics or to ascertain their quantity.

Transportation: ⇒ Transportation is the movement of an object from one location to another; it does not include movements that are part of an operation or inspection.

Delay: ◗ A delay is any occurrence that prevents the immediate performance of the next planned activity.

Storage: ▽ Storage is an intentional delay in which an object is kept and protected against unauthorized removal.

Documentation of work methods in some form, such as a flowchart, provides an opportunity for people to study some part of the operation and look for ways to improve it. The real payoff is not in the documents but in the critical evaluations of methods and creative exploration of possible improvements. Extensive checklists may be used to trigger ideas that might improve some part of the process under study. Sample questions in several categories that might be reviewed in an operations analysis are provided in Table 9.1.

Many questions beyond the sample in Table 9.1 can be asked to uncover possible weaknesses in the proposed method of performing a new or an existing operation. Such a review can reveal opportunities to improve the process at the macro level. It may also suggest places where the process should be studied at a more micro level. Motion study can be used to make a detailed study of a job.

Improvement activities are most likely to be effective if they are based on careful analysis of factual data, rather than on someone's opinion about what will improve performance. Once an improvement team has defined the work they will study, they can use several tools to record and analyze data in order to determine problem areas that might be corrected or improved. Several tools that often are used in evaluating quality problems are presented in the following sections.

Table 9.1
SAMPLE ITEMS FROM AN OPERATION ANALYSIS CHECKLIST

1. Material
   - (a) Can a cheaper material be substituted?
   - (b) Is material used to the fullest extent?
2. Materials handling
   - (a) Can the number of times the material is handled be reduced?
   - (b) Is the material received, moved, and stored in suitable containers?
   - (c) Can the operator be relieved of handling by use of a conveyor or other device?
3. Tools, jigs, and fixtures
   - (a) Are tools the best kind for this work?
   - (b) Are both hands occupied by productive work in using the tools or fixtures?
4. Machine setup
   - (a) Should the operator set up his or her own machine?
   - (b) Are all the necessary items obtained before the setup is begun?
5. Operation
   - (a) Can the operation be eliminated?
   - (b) Can two or more operations be combined into one?
   - (c) Can the sequence of operations be improved?
   - (d) Can the parts be prepositioned at the prior operation or for the next operation?
   - (e) Can interruptions be reduced or eliminated?
   - (f) Can an inspection be combined with an operation?
6. Operator
   - (a) can the operator's performance be improved by further training?
   - (b) Can unnecessary fatigue be eliminated by changing the layout, tooling, working conditions, etc.?
7. Working conditions
   - (a) Are any unnecessary hazards involved in the operation?
   - (b) Is good housekeeping maintained throughout the facility?

Source: Adapted from Ralph M. Barnes, *Motion and Time Study: Design and Measurement of Work,* 7th ed. (New York: Wiley, 1980), pp. 102–104. Reprinted by permission of John Wiley & Sons, Inc.

APPLICATION

USE OF A FLOW PROCESS CHART

The Ace Construction Company had a procedure for paying invoices that sometimes led to excessive delays. Some invoices offered a discount on the amount due if paid within 10 days. The old procedure involved making copies of the invoice and coding it so that it could be entered into the company's information system before the entire package was sent to the project manager for approval. Since the project manager was usually at a construction site or sites, it sometimes took 3 or 4 days to obtain approval of an invoice. The company did not want to pay invoices unless the project manager agreed that the material had been received at the job site and was of acceptable quality.

Ace has adopted an improved method that shortens the time between receipt and payment of invoices. A copy is sent to the project manager before all the coding and checking are done. The invoice can wait or be checked by the project manager while the additional accounting work is being performed. If the project manager disapproves an invoice—this rarely happens—the payment may be stopped. Otherwise the trade discounts are obtained.

The old method for reviewing and paying invoices is shown on the flow process chart in Figure 9.3, and the new procedure is shown in Figure 9.4. The revised procedure has reduced the time for processing invoices from 9 or 10 days to 4 or 5 days. A time reduction of a few days results in a significant reduction in the cost of materials and supplies for the company and the new method is no more costly to perform than the old one.

Figure 9.3 Old Procedure for Reviewing and Paying Invoices

DETAILS OF ☑OLD ☐NEW METHOD	CHART SYMBOLS	DIST. IN FEET	TIME IN MINS	NOTES
1 Invoice received, date stamped				By mail clerk
2 To mail clerk		20		
3 On first payable clerk's desk			1/2	
4 Purchase order attached				
5 To cost accountant		25		
6 On cost accountant's desk			1/2	
7 Coded to appropriate job				
8 To first payable clerk's desk		25		
9 On first payable clerk's desk			1/2	
10 Copies made				
11 Original to project manager		110		
12 On project manager's desk			3	
13 Examined and approved by project manager				
14 To second payable clerk's desk		90		
15 On payable clerk's desk			1/2	
16 Vendor number & due date added, extensions checked			1	
17 Data keyed to magnetic tape			1	
18 INVOICE PAID				
19 To file clerk's desk		30		
20 On file clerk's desk			2	
21 Invoice filed				
22				
23				
24				

Figure 9.4   Current Procedure for Reviewing and Paying Invoices

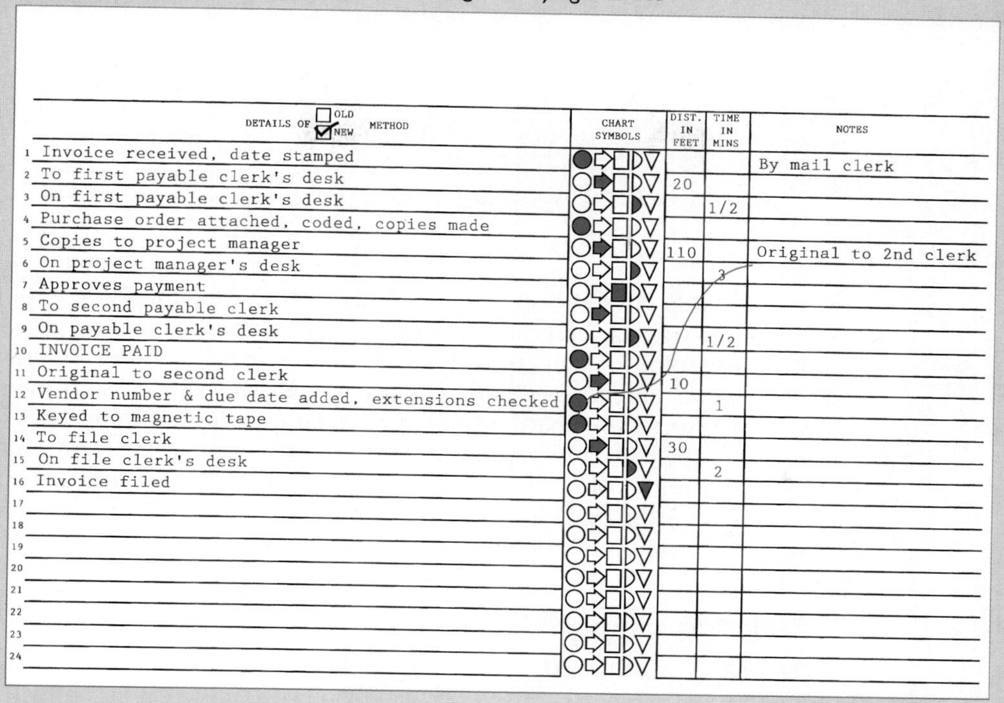

DETAILS OF ☐ OLD ☑ NEW METHOD	CHART SYMBOLS	DIST. IN FEET	TIME IN MINS	NOTES
1 Invoice received, date stamped	●⟹☐∇			By mail clerk
2 To first payable clerk's desk	○⟹☐∇	20		
3 On first payable clerk's desk	○⟹☐∇		1/2	
4 Purchase order attached, coded, copies made	●⟹☐∇			
5 Copies to project manager	○⟹☐∇	110		Original to 2nd clerk
6 On project manager's desk	○⟹☐∇		3	
7 Approves payment	○⟹■∇			
8 To second payable clerk	○⟹☐∇			
9 On payable clerk's desk	○⟹☐∇		1/2	
10 INVOICE PAID	●⟹☐∇			
11 Original to second clerk	○⟹☐∇	10		
12 Vendor number & due date added, extensions checked	●⟹☐∇		1	
13 Keyed to magnetic tape	●⟹☐∇			
14 To file clerk	○⟹☐∇	30		
15 On file clerk's desk	○⟹☐∇		2	
16 Invoice filed	○⟹☐▼			
17	○⟹☐∇			
18	○⟹☐∇			
19	○⟹☐∇			
20	○⟹☐∇			
21	○⟹☐∇			
22	○⟹☐∇			
23	○⟹☐∇			
24	○⟹☐∇			

Checksheets, Histograms, and Location Plots

Data collection techniques can be used to simplify the recording of the types of problems that have occurred and where. Figure 9.5 shows an example of a *checksheet* for the types of problems that occurred in a day's production of a particular printed-

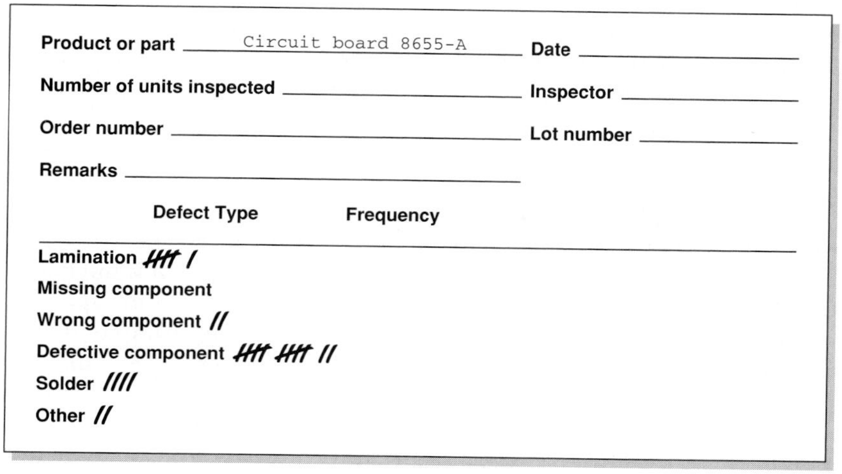

Figure 9.5
A Checksheet for
Recording Data

Product or part _____ Circuit board 8655-A _____ Date _____

Number of units inspected _____ Inspector _____

Order number _____ Lot number _____

Remarks _____

Defect Type	Frequency
Lamination	卅 /
Missing component	
Wrong component	//
Defective component	卅 卅 //
Solder	////
Other	//

Figure 9.6
A Location Plot for
Circuit Board 8655-A

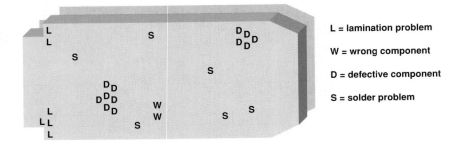

L = lamination problem

W = wrong component

D = defective component

S = solder problem

circuit board that goes into a television. A checksheet with equal-size frequency marks can be used to construct a crude histogram rather simply.

A location plot for defects in the same circuit board is shown in Figure 9.6. The most frequent problem was defective components. This particular problem occurred at the two places on the board where a particular capacitor is mounted. The problem was traced to the capacitor supplier who had an equipment problem on the day this batch of capacitors was produced. The supplier instituted a more frequent check on the capacitor-bonding pressure and a procedure to screen all items produced after a problem is detected until the process is known to be in control again.

Pareto Analysis

Pareto analysis utilizes the Pareto principle, or 80-20 rule, as it is sometimes called. It is based on a theory expressed by an Italian economist that 20 percent of the people control 80 percent of the wealth. This same idea is often used to identify the more critical inventory items, since a small percentage of the items usually deserve special attention because they account for a large percentage of the annual expenditure for all items. Pareto analysis determines the relative frequency of various problems or causes for problems so that primary attention can be focused on the most important ones. If the problems do not result in about the same cost, the frequencies can be multiplied by the average cost of that kind of problem. Such a procedure can help establish priorities in terms of the costs of the problems. Suppose that a quality circle decided to investigate an excessive scrap rate for part 1088-2. The circle members want to identify the major reason the part is being scrapped. A Pareto diagram of their data, which is useful for displaying this type of information, is presented in Figure 9.7. You can see from this figure that the most frequent problem with part 1088-2 is dents.

Cause-and-Effect Diagrams

Cause-and-effect diagrams are useful in identifying and isolating the cause, or the major causes, of a problem. This diagram, sometimes called a "fishbone diagram," lists the problem at one end of a horizontal line. Diagonal branches are drawn from this line for each major category of possible causes. More specific, contributory causes are added to the branch for each category. An example of a cause-and-effect diagram for part 1088-2 is shown in Figure 9.8. Cause-and-effect diagrams, such as the one in Figure 9.8, are useful in focusing the attention of an individual or improvement team on each specific possible cause of a problem and on possible solutions. Teams often find the technique of brainstorming useful as they deliberate and seek

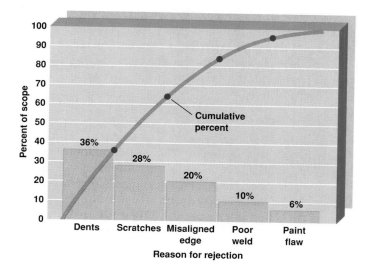

Figure 9.7
A Pareto Diagram
for Part 1088-2

to uncover the basic underlying cause of a problem and as they try to discover the most effective solution to identified problems.

Brainstorming

Brainstorming is a useful technique for generating ideas about problems on which a group might focus its activities, about possible causes of problems, and about potential solutions to problems once they have been identified. The objective of a brainstorming meeting is to generate lots of ideas on a particular subject. No criticism of ideas is permitted during brainstorming because it might stifle creativity, thought flow, and expression. The good ideas are selected later, so that judgments are not passed while creativity is the objective. One seemingly useless idea may stimulate another one that is valuable.

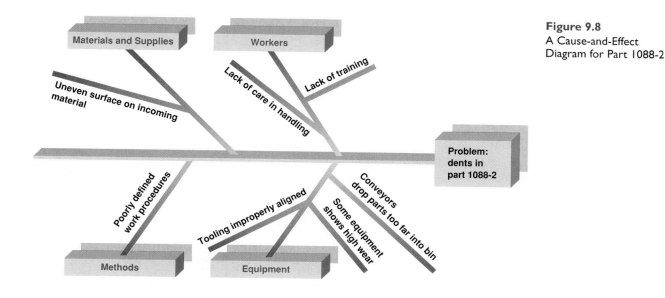

Figure 9.8
A Cause-and-Effect
Diagram for Part 1088-2

Many tools other than the ones we have discussed are also used in analyzing situations to better understand them and evaluate factors that might improve them. In some cases designed experiments are conducted to gain understanding and to evaluate the effect of some of the variables involved in a process. One relatively simple tool that can help show relationships is the scatterplot.

Scatterplots

A *scatterplot,* or *scatter diagram,* is useful in evaluating whether there is a relationship between two variables and what that relationship is. Often a person is interested in finding some quality variable and another factor that affects it. One would collect several observations of paired data (that is, a value of the *x* variable and the value of the *y* variable that occurred with it) and plot them. A linear correlation coefficient can be calculated if a numerical value is desired. (Sometimes, however, the relationship may be a curve.)

Figure 9.9 is an example of a scatterplot where a linear relationship exists. This plot suggests that the longer the solution is in the mixing vessel, the more impurities are absorbed. It indicates that the cause of a contamination problem is probably somewhere in the mixing operation. Further investigation may be done to find a vessel material that is not dissolved by the solution, clean the vessel better, cover the vessel when it is empty and during mixing, or keep the air surrounding the mixing operation cleaner. This plot also suggests that the company probably should establish a standard procedure for as short a mixing operation as will do a satisfactory job. This would help reduce contamination and possibly lead to higher productivity.

Ideas and innovations are valuable and many tools or techniques can help develop data and present them so that new insights can be gained about problems and opportunities. Much of the work in improvement, however, requires human creativity. Team members must gain new insights about the needs and methods of the business. They also must conceive of new ways to apply the available resources, reduce the resources required, improve quality, or make the company's responses faster. The environment should be one that will accept occasional "wierd" suggestions and one that accepts occasional failures of what seems like a "logical" improvement. Otherwise people may be reluctant to share their ideas.

Figure 9.9
Scatterplot of Mixing
Time Versus Impurities

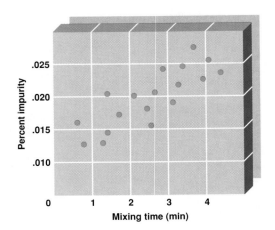

The tools and techniques we have discussed can be applied in a narrow-focused study of a small segment of the company's overall work, often leading to small incremental performance improvements. Many of these techniques can also be applied in improvement studies that have a much broader view. Some companies have achieved outstanding improvements through business process reengineering which we will discuss in the following section.

BUSINESS PROCESS REENGINEERING

Business process reengineering (BPR) is a fundamental rethinking and a radical redesign of a business process to achieve dramatic improvements. The basic idea is to start from ground zero with no assumptions accepted as essential. The first step is to question what things a company *must* do, before even beginning to seek ways to do it. Then, with a clean slate, seek the best way to accomplish that work and only that work. In other words, it attempts to ignore what *is* and concentrates on what *should be*.[1] Reengineering is intended to overcome the shortcomings of seeking incremental improvements or solving problems at one part of an existing process. Instead, it says "Let's not patch up the old one—let's replace it with the best we can develop." This shifts the focus from a particular type of activity to the result that is to be accomplished and opens the minds of the people involved (often a reengineering team) to more-creative possibilities. Reengineering is a useful tool in seeking larger, breakthrough improvements since it can be applied to include a large portion of a company's work in a study.

A *process* is defined as a collection of one or more types of work activities that add value to some input(s) to provide an output for some external or internal customer. We can see from this definition that the operations function itself is a process. It also contains many subprocesses that could be examined at a detailed level. An overall business is also a web of many interrelated processes. One noted reference points out, however, that hardly any company contains more than ten principal processes and provides a high-level process map for Texas Instruments. The map indicates the six principal processes for Texas Instruments, as listed in Table 9.2. The operations function can play a role (along with other parts of a business) in making the processes of a company effective and efficient. The fact that processes operate across functional lines and may involve many departments makes it important to consider work from a process perspective.

[1] Michael Hammer and James Champy, *Reengineering the Corporation: A Manifesto for Business Revolution* (New York: Harper Business, 1993), p. 32.

Table 9.2
PRINCIPAL PROCESSES AT TEXAS INSTRUMENTS

Customer communications	Manufacturing capability development
Strategy development	Design adaptation for custom needs
Product development	Order fulfillment

Source: Michael Hammer and James Champy, *Reengineering the Corporation: A Manifesto for Business Revolution* (New York: Harper Business, 1993), pp. 118–119.

Table 9.3
SOME SYMPTOMS AND UNDERLYING PROBLEMS IN PROCESSES

SYMPTOM	PROBLEM
Extensive information exchange, data redundancy, and rekeying	Arbitrary fragmentation of a natural process
Inventory, buffers, and other assets	Using system slack to cope with uncertainty
High ratio of checking and control to value adding	Fragmentation
Rework and iteration	Inadequate feedback along the chain
Complexity, exceptions, and special cases	Adding too many options to one basic process

Source: Michael Hammer and James Champy, *Reengineering the Corporation: A Manifesto for Business Revolution* (New York: Harper Business, 1993), pp. 122–126.

Viewing work as a process helps identify all the interrelated steps that must be planned in the system. It also helps keep only the necessary steps in the system. Sometimes no one person has ownership for an entire process when it includes work in several departments. It is possible that the work will not be performed in the most efficient manner if each part of it is planned as a relatively independent work step within the domain of a single part of the business. Over time, better methods might become available to perform the process or parts of it and these potential improvements might go unnoticed or unimplemented because no one is supervising and analyzing the process as a whole. Many companies today are engaging in business process improvement or business process reengineering and studying their work from a process perspective to try to improve their work methods. Viewing work as a series of interrelated steps either in the initial design or in improvement efforts is more likely to improve the coordination of all the parts and result in a smoother working system.

Each company has its own core processes and supporting processes and may find its own unique ways to improve them. Selection of a process as a candidate for improvement might consider at lease three criteria. A company might look for the process that seems to be working poorest, the one that has the most impact on its customers, or the one that seems most feasible to improve. Hammer and Champy point out several symptoms of dysfunctional processes and the basic problems those symptoms may indicate. Some of these are listed in Table 9.3.

Characteristics that often appear in reengineered work are listed below to give some indication of the types of changes that are sometimes made.

Several jobs are combined into one.

The workers make more decisions.

The steps in the process are performed in a natural manner.

Processes have multiple versions for flexibility.

The work is performed where it makes the most sense.

Checks and controls are reduced.

Reconciliation is minimized.

A case manager provides a single point of contact.

Hybrid centralized/decentralized operations are prevalent.

Generally the objective is to overcome a fractionalized organization where people focus only on a part of the work and to achieve a more-integrated, better-coordinated organization. Hammer and Champy reported an interesting example of a total rethinking and redesign of the way work is performed. The accounts payable department at Ford Motor Company employed over 500 persons in the early 1980s. Managers thought that by automating some of the existing manual procedures (not a reengineering) they could reduce the number of required workers by about 20 percent. After finding that Mazda accomplished its vendor payment with only five employees Ford focused on reengineering the total procurement process.

The old process at Ford, which was fairly typical, involved three documents. When the buyer in the purchasing department issued a purchase order to a supplier, a copy of the document was also sent to accounts payable. When a shipment arrived, a clerk in receiving sent a description of what was received to accounts payable. When the supplier sent an invoice to accounts payable, an employee would check to be sure the three documents agreed. Most of the time the documents agreed. But when they did not agree, it took a great deal of employee time, sometimes weeks, to trace the problem and solve it.

In the new process, the buyer enters an order into an on-line data base when it is sent to a supplier. When goods arrive at receiving, an employee there keys in what was received. If the receipt matches an outstanding order the clerk pushes a button and the goods are accepted, added to the inventory data base, and a check is issued to the supplier. Otherwise the goods are returned to the sender. Basically, payment is now authorized in receiving instead of accounts payable. Instead of 500 people involved in vendor payment, Ford now accomplishes the job with about 125 people. The head count in accounts payable at the Ford Engine Division is down to about 5 percent of its former level. Some Ford divisions and some other companies simply pay when they use the supplier's item. When they assemble or ship a finished item their system will pay the suppliers for the parts required to make the item. This is a radical redesign or reengineering of the way the work is performed with the focus on accomplishing the intended result rather than attempting to merely improve the work in some way.

SOME COMPETITIVE IMPROVEMENTS COMPANIES ARE MAKING

Much of our discussion in this chapter has concerned tools, techniques, and methods companies can use to improve in some way. The approach that was implied was one of looking at a work step or a work process. Companies are also working to improve competitiveness by changing various features of the way they do business. We will close the chapter with a look at some of the facets that companies are changing in order to become more competitive. Numerous companies in the United States have already made impressive improvements in their performance and are continuing their efforts to improve even further. Each company is faced with its own competitive challenges as well as its own set of employee skills, technology, financial resources, and other resources, so not all companies necessarily attempt the same set of improvements. There is, however, a fairly consistent set of characteristics that will include many of, if not all, the changes that the leading companies have made. These characteristics are outlined in the following paragraphs. Fortunately, these methods provide a review of many important topics discussed in this book.

Strategy

It is important for a company to evaluate its competitiveness in its strategy. Leading companies take a long-range view of developing markets, customers, and capabilities, rather than just working to keep a string of quarterly earnings. A company should try to select good long-term markets and be in businesses in which it can compete successfully. To do this, a company should evaluate the competitors in a field and seek open niches and ways in which it can differentiate itself to serve the targeted market segments.

After identifying the appropriate long- and short-term goals, the company should identify all the capabilities the company will need to achieve them. Then the company moves to develop or acquire any that are missing. The capabilities of the operations function are used to competitive advantage just as marketing efforts seek to gain advantage. Common long-range goals are used throughout the company to help build continuity and teamwork.

Nucor's "slabcaster" opened up new markets for minimill steel plants. The slabcaster allows minimills, which were previously restricted to making small structural shapes, to make the thin sheets of steel used by appliance and auto makers.

Nucor Steel, a division of Nucor Corp., photo by Gerin Choiniere

Product Design

Leading companies try to take the customer's view in product development and improvement. The goal is to understand customer needs and to have products that are appealing and that effectively and reliably serve those needs. Faster product development times are sought. Since design determines 30 to 70 percent of a product's controllable cost, considerable attention is paid to the design phase. *Concurrent engineering* is used to design production processes and products that are compatible and cost effective. Representatives from marketing, purchasing, quality, field service, production, and other appropriate areas often serve on teams that review and offer various design suggestions. These teams seek designs that have customer appeal, cost-effective materials, ease of component production, ease of assembly, good performance, durability, and reliability. Good design simplifies products so that they use as few parts as necessary and seeks ways to use parts that are common with other models where practical.

Logistic Network

Leading companies recognize that they are part of a supply chain for their customers and maybe their customers' customers. They establish an effective and efficient network to serve the customer. The distribution channel must respond quickly to the customer, so the company should establish effective sharing of information with the customer to assist the planning and coordination of both companies. The trend is toward having long-term partnership relationships with both customers and suppliers. Early involvement of capable suppliers as advisers in the design process has benefited many companies.

Processes and Equipment

Process selection is an important part of the design phase for new products. New processes and process improvements become available over time for existing products. Leading companies seek and evaluate improvement suggestions from employees, equipment suppliers, and process engineers. They create a culture or environment that strives for continuous improvement.

Many companies have found that a very effective way to begin process improvement is to simplify the processes where this is possible. Simpler processing equipment often is easier to maintain and more reliable. Simpler processes are easier to learn, and they reduce opportunities for confusion and the need for coordination effort. Simple processing steps can also improve the throughput velocity. After processes have been simplified, companies may seek ways to automate them for further improvement in cost and quality. The goal, however, is not to wait for or seek only major breakthroughs such as automation or other equipment that may require large investments. Leading companies constantly work to improve little by little. They also are willing to spend money on maintenance and to invest in refurbishment or replacement to upgrade equipment and keep their processes in top working condition. In the past, too many companies have had a tendency to run equipment until it almost fell apart before it was reworked. The requirements for quality and for reliable deliveries necessitate new views on maintenance and capital investment.

Arrangement and Layout

The way people and equipment are arranged within a facility is an important factor in producing goods or services efficiently. If a company has been in operation for some time, often the best place to begin improvement is in housekeeping. Leading companies remove what is not needed, organize the rest, and arrange it neatly. Support items, such as tools and tooling, that are used together are located together and often are color-coded so they can easily be identified and kept together near the point of use. Inventories of components also are maintained near their points of use to reduce materials handling and to facilitate coordination by sight.

Many leading companies that make a variety of items have benefited greatly by grouping equipment into manufacturing cells that run families of items requiring similar processing steps. Production items flow through these cells in small lots or as single items, so work in process (WIP) is kept low. Machines and people can be located near each other to facilitate coordination and to reduce space requirements and capital investment needs. Leading companies arrange cells and other equipment to eliminate long moves and movement bottlenecks. Cells or other logical groupings of processes can be used as a basis for forming self-directed work teams.

Systems, Scheduling, and Control

Leading companies work to reduce WIP by employing just-in-time production in small lot sizes, which usually requires the capability for rapid setups. Setup reduction programs are important in many companies in which a variety of items are run on shared equipment. The throughput time or velocity quickens as small lots are run and queues of WIP are reduced. As the throughput time is reduced, forecast horizons are shorter and the company becomes more responsive to market changes. Many companies try to level the production schedule and use mixed-model assembly to match the product mix to the rate at which products appear to be demanded, so that less finished-goods inventory is required.

Less inventory on the shop floor allows people and equipment to be located closer together so that some coordination by sight is possible. Simple visual signals, such as the return of kanban cards or empty containers, can be used by one work center to signal its supplying work center that more of a particular component is needed. Other simplification or data automation can be used to reduce paperwork in reporting work activities and in other applications. Information systems may be revised to support coordination among manufacturing cells and among self-directed teams instead of trying to direct every operation. Also information is shared with suppliers to support visibility and coordination. Electronic data interchange (EDI) can be used to speed communication so that supply lead times are shorter and data accuracy is improved.

Employees

Human resources are considered the major asset that makes a company work. Training and development to improve human resources are an important basis for improving the company. Leading companies are organized to support overall teamwork and portions of the company may operate as self-directed teams. Employees are made part of improvement teams, and their ideas are sought. Companies recognize that experienced employees often have detailed insights into the operation of processes and can provide valuable input into improvement efforts.

The number of layers of management between the top and the frontline worker is reduced. Employees have broadened job responsibilities and participate in decisions and improvement activities. Coordination efforts and information systems can be geared to fewer details because much of the planning and coordination occurs within the cells and work teams.

Quality

Quality-related activities are the vehicle through which many of the improvements in leading companies are made. When a company sets out to reduce waste, often much of it is found to be scrap and rework. Often it is less expensive to make items correctly the first time than to make them over. In the past, particularly where there is pressure to make shipment dates and budgets, companies have not dug deeply enough to correct the root causes of their problems. They have made amends for the symptoms of the problem or perhaps corrected the symptoms without really solving the root cause of the problem. Leading companies are devoting more attention to understanding the causes of problems and correcting their weaknesses.

The quest for continuous improvement can lead to design improvements, process upgrades, employee training, supplier programs, or other beneficial activities. Many leading companies have included taking a careful look at customer requirements and desires as an early step in their efforts to improve.

A goal is to develop a culture of quality consciousness so that every part of the company is involved in quality improvement activities. Utilizing statistical quality control at the operator level gives employees some job enrichment, can instill a greater sense of responsibility and pride, and can increase the motivation for improvement. Teamwork and quality consciousness are enhanced by instilling in employees the idea that every employee has a customer or customers to serve. The next person to handle what one employee works on is his or her immediate customer. Each employee should strive to understand the needs of that customer and to serve those needs well.

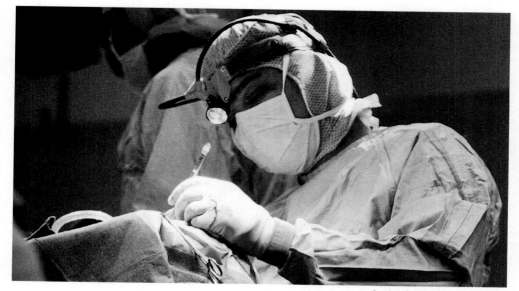

The quest for quality works for many types of design improvements. A technology called magnetic source imaging (MSI) has improved surgical techniques for brain surgery. Using MSI, a surgeon can pinpoint precise regions of the brain, reducing the risk of damage to healthy tissue. Clearly, customers benefit when companies strive for continuous improvement.

Stephen Simpson/FPG, International

OPERATIONS IMPROVEMENTS AT VICTORY MEMORIAL HOSPITAL

Victory Memorial Hospital in Waukegan, Illinois, is committed to continuous improvement as a way to provide quality health care and to better manage costs. During 1992 and 1993 the hospital reduced the length of stay for Medicare patients from 9.1 to 6.7 days, receivables from 73.6 days to 59.3 days, average inventory from $270,000 to $200,000, and patient satisfaction scores have improved by up to 30 percent. One improvement project is to reduce the time patients spend waiting in the emergency department. The emergency department has several challenging aspects because patients do not arrive for scheduled appointments but at randomly erratic rates and their medical problems range from minor to life threatening.

The first step in the emergency department study was to form a cross-functional team with representatives from the emergency department, quality assurance, telemetry, admitting, diagnostic imaging, environmental services, laboratory, and patient registration. The team developed a flowchart (Figure 9.10) to show all the key steps, waits, and decision points in the process that contribute to the total time a patient spends in the emergency department. Previous studies had shown that level two acuity (degree of illness) had longer waits than level one or level three, and complained more about delays. Level one patients, because of the severity of their illnesses, frequently are admitted to the critical care units of the hospital without waiting for all their test results and do not stay in the emergency department long. Level three patients often can be treated and released in a shorter time than the level two patients. Level two patients, however, typically require a variety of examinations and laboratory tests and must wait for test results and image analysis reports before being treated.

The team initially focused on level two patients and found that the average times in the emergency department ranged from a low of 1.2 hours for removal of a foreign body to a high of 2.6 hours for a patient with a suspected urinary tract infection (UTI). A Pareto diagram of the average time required for categories of level two patients is shown in Figure 9.11. UTI is not the most frequently occurring level two illness but it is the one that averages the longest time per patient. The most frequent (fractures and strains) and the second most frequent (lacerations) usually do not require as much diagnostic work before treatment.

The Improvement Working Team constructed a detailed cause-and-effect diagram (Figure 9.12) that identified possible causes of delays. Three items were selected as the most probable causes of delays:

- Waiting for laboratory results
- Waiting to get a sample from patients with suspected UTI
- Waiting for a physical examination

The team then used force field analysis to identify possible solutions to the three likely causes of delays. *Force field analysis* is a tool to display the forces acting to restrain improvement in a situation and forces that can help drive the situation toward improvement. This type of analysis helps break the cause of a problem into smaller, more-manageable pieces so that possible improvement actions can be identified. An example of a force field diagram used by the improvement team is shown in Figure 9.13. When doctors need an additional blood sample for further testing, there can be delays until a nurse is available and then until a sample is drawn. Now nurses draw an extra tube of blood when the initial sample is collected. Some delays in getting urinary samples from suspected UTI patients can be reduced by giving them liquids as soon as the admitting nurse recognizes the symptoms. One cause of the delay in waiting for a physical examination was the wait for an examination room to become available. An emergency treatment room with an examination table was added to the emergency department.

The next steps are to continue to analyze other causes identified as contributing to excessive wait times for emergency services and to identify appropriate solutions. The objectives are to reduce patient delays and to contribute to the efficient operation of the emergency department. The hospital has developed a new medical record form to collect data on patient wait times and total length of stay in the emergency department. These data will be used to monitor the effect of these and other improvements on an ongoing basis.

Source: Deborah Davis, "Victory Memorial Solves Operations Problems with TQM," *Target,* vol. 9, no. 6 (November–December 1993):14–19. Reprinted from *Target* with the permission of The Association for Manufactoring Excellence.

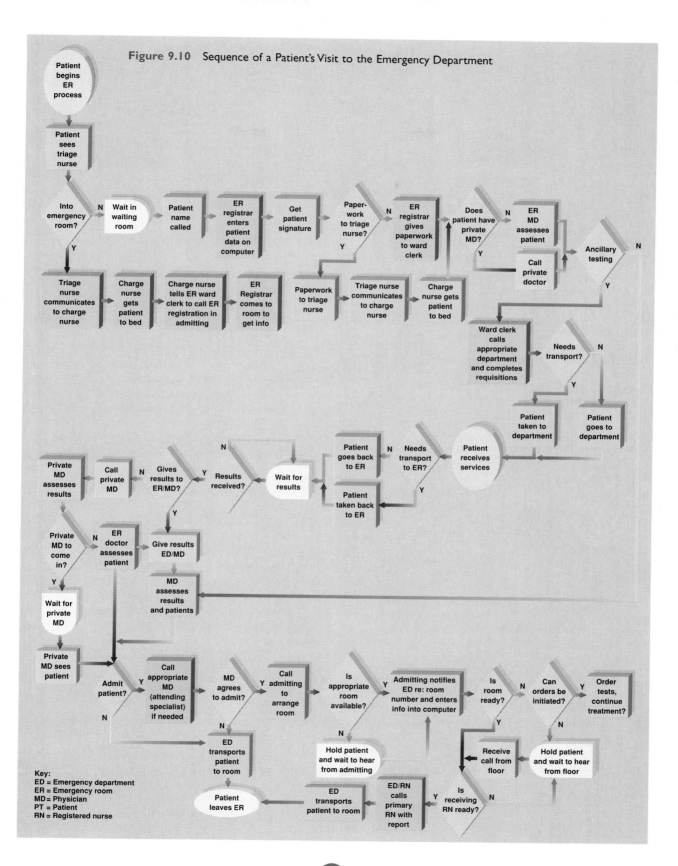

Figure 9.10   Sequence of a Patient's Visit to the Emergency Department

Key:
ED = Emergency department
ER = Emergency room
MD = Physician
PT = Patient
RN = Registered nurse

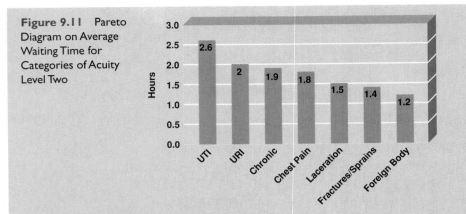

Figure 9.11 Pareto Diagram on Average Waiting Time for Categories of Acuity Level Two

Figure 9.12 Fishbone Diagram of Possible Causes of Delay

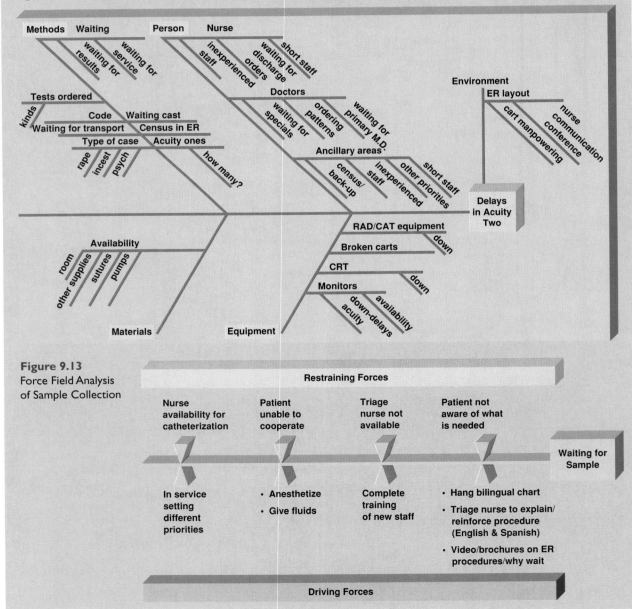

Figure 9.13 Force Field Analysis of Sample Collection

SUMMARY

Companies are always under the gun to improve their goods and services and the ways they are produced. Competitors try to surpass their performance and customer expectations continue to rise. Today, companies that do not improve can quickly fall into a competitive tailspin. A useful motto today is, "If it ain't perfect, look for ways to improve it." Companies should seek both large jumps in improvement, called breakthroughs, and smaller incremental improvements that can occur more frequently. A culture of *kaizen* in a company can be very stimulating and can lead to awesome results over time.

A useful procedure for improvement is to first observe and understand the current method, document it, critically evaluate it and any methods that can be developed that seem better, implement the best ideas that are developed, and then collect data to verify the performance of the new method.

Tools that can be used in improvement studies include flowcharting, the principles of motion economy, left-and-right-hand charts, multiple-activity charts, flow process charts, checksheets, histograms, location plots, Pareto analysis, cause-and-effect diagrams, brainstorming, and scatter diagrams.

Business process reengineering (BPR) is a methodology for seeking major breakthroughs in broad processes. A process is a collection of one or more types of work activities that add value to some input(s) for a customer. The major or core processes in a company often cut across organizational boundaries. Sometimes parts of a process are neglected since no one person is responsible for the entire process. BPR focuses on the desired result and seeks new ways to accomplish that result, instead of examining the steps of an existing process. A process focus can lead to a smoother working organization.

Companies try to improve many parts of their approach to doing business. In addition to working to improve detailed work steps and processes, companies are striving to improve their strategy, quality, products (goods and services), logistic networks, equipment, layouts, scheduling and control systems, and employees. Numerous improvement opportunities continue to occur as markets, technology, and competitors change.

KEY TERMS

Breakthroughs	Storage	Business process
Kaizen	Checksheet	reengineering (BPR)
Flow process charts	Pareto analysis	Process
Operation	Cause-and-effect diagrams	Concurrent engineering
Inspection	Brainstorming	Force field analysis
Transportation	Scatterplot, or scatter	
Delay	diagram	

DISCUSSION QUESTIONS

1. A company's facilities (buildings and equipment) last for many years. Is it reasonable to expect that they may be revised after only a few years of use?
2. Why is change inevitable for most companies?
3. What is *kaizen*?

4. Why might a graph of improvement over time show a decline between improvement steps if the company concentrates only on finding major improvements?

5. In an improvement study, what are some reasons for or advantages of documenting the current methods of performing the job or process that is being studied?

6. In developing a flow process chart, what are the five types of activities used to describe the steps involved in the job or process?

7. **a.** How is a Pareto analysis useful in guiding the selection of areas where improvement efforts will be directed?

   b. Give two selection criteria other than frequency of occurrence that could be plotted in a Pareto diagram and used to select the problem that should be improved.

8. Do cause-and-effect diagrams have any advantages over a simple list of possible causes of a problem? Why?

9. In brainstorming, why is it recommended that a group not evaluate ideas as they are generated in order to keep ideas more realistic and practical?

10. What, if anything, is the difference between process reengineering and process improvement?

11. Why is it beneficial to view work from a process perspective?

12. Why would a company restudy its processes after they have been carefully designed and debugged initially?

13. Other than improving work steps and processes, how are companies improving their competitiveness today?

BIBLIOGRAPHY

Barnes, Ralph M. *Motion and Time Study: Design and Measurement of Work.* 7th ed. New York: Wiley, 1980.

Christopher, William F., and Carl G. Thor, eds. Handbook for Productivity Measurement and Improvement. Portland, Oreg.: Productivity Press, 1993.

de Bono, Edward. *Serious Creativity: Using the Power of Lateral Thinking to Create New Ideas.* New York: Harper Business, 1992.

Dumaine, Brian. "Payoff from the New Management." *Fortune,* December 13, 1993, pp. 103–110.

Haas, Elizabeth. "Breakthrough Manufacturing." *Harvard Business Review,* March–April 1987, pp. 75–81.

Hammer, Michael, and James Champy. *Reengineering the Corporation.* New York: Harper Business, 1993.

Harrington, H. James. *Business Process Improvement: The Breakthrough Strategy for Total Quality, Productivity, and Competitiveness.* New York: McGraw-Hill, 1991.

Hayes, Robert H., and Kim B. Clark. "Why Some Factories Are More Productive than Others." *Harvard Business Review,* September–October 1986, pp. 66–73.

Imai, Masaaki. *Kaizen: The Key to Japan's Competitive Success.* New York: Random House, 1986.

Powell, Cash. "Process Reengineering at Westinghouse." *Target 10,* no. 3 (May–June, 1994): 28–31.

Robinson, Alan, ed. *Continuous Improvement in Operations: A Systematic Approach to Waste Reduction.* Cambridge, Mass.: Productivity Press, 1991.

————, **editor-in-chief.** *Modern Approaches to Manufacturing Improvement: The Shingo System.* Cambridge, Mass.: Productivity Press, 1990.

Robson, George D. *Continuous Process Improvement: Simplifying Work Flow Systems.* New York: Free Press, 1991.

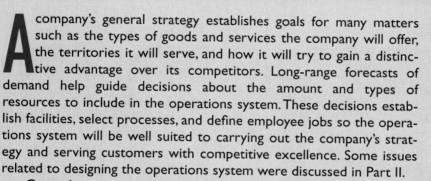

PLANNING AND CONTROLLING OPERATIONS

A company's general strategy establishes goals for many matters such as the types of goods and services the company will offer, the territories it will serve, and how it will try to gain a distinctive advantage over its competitors. Long-range forecasts of demand help guide decisions about the amount and types of resources to include in the operations system. These decisions establish facilities, select processes, and define employee jobs so the operations system will be well suited to carrying out the company's strategy and serving customers with competitive excellence. Some issues related to designing the operations system were discussed in Part II.

Once the operations system is established, a great deal of management activity is concerned with planning and controlling the work that takes place within it. These decisions focus on a shorter time horizon than designing and establishing the operations system, and often are more detailed and specific. Part III consists of nine chapters and two supplements that primarily discuss planning and controlling the work performed by the operations system.

A primary responsibility in planning and executing work in any part of a company is to ensure that high-quality work will be performed. Part III begins with Chapter 10, which deals with statistical quality control. Having established methods to ensure high quality, a company can plan and control work that will be timely and efficient while providing customer satisfaction. A company must have the appropriate capacity to perform the work required in a timely and cost-effective manner. Chapter 11 discusses several aspects of planning operations and capacity. Many companies (e.g, wholesalers, retailers, and manufacturers) must have materials in order to serve their customers. Chapter 12 overviews many of the activities involved in managing the availability of the appropriate amounts of the appropriate materials. Chapters 13 and 14 present more-detailed methods of controlling inventories of materials.

Companies must have effective methods to control the detailed work steps they perform. Chapter 15 reviews traditional methods of scheduling and controlling work activities in manufacturing, while Chapter 16 discusses more-recent approaches. Chapter 17 examines some challenges of planning and controlling work in services, and Chapter 18 focuses on projects and special assignments.

CHAPTER 10

Statistical Quality Control

CHAPTER 11

Planning for Operations and Capacity

CHAPTER 12

Overview of Materials Management

CHAPTER 13

Managing Independent-Demand Inventory

CHAPTER 14

Managing Dependent-Demand Items and Capacity

CHAPTER 15

Scheduling and Controlling Manufacturing

CHAPTER 16

The Just-in-Time Philosophy of Seeking Excellence

   SUPPLEMENT G:
   Total Productive Maintenance

CHAPTER 17

The Nature and Scheduling of Services

   SUPPLEMENT H:
   Simulation

CHAPTER 18

Scheduling and Controlling Projects

STATISTICAL QUALITY CONTROL

H eightened global competition and increasing customer expectations have made it more important for companies to improve and emphasize their quality capabilities if they are to increase customer satisfaction and gain competitiveness. The achievement of outstanding quality requires that a company excel in three major types of activities: quality of design, quality of conformance, and quality of performance and service to support customers' needs. In Chapter 3 we discussed the importance of understanding customer needs and using procedures such as quality function deployment (QFD) to ensure that the design of goods and services will meet the customer's needs, desires, and expectations. In this chapter we primarily discuss methods used to control quality so that it conforms to the levels of quality that have been designed.

Management applications of the control concept involve three major elements. First, there is the establishment of a target or a planned level of performance. Then there is a measurement of the actual performance and comparison of these measurements to the target value. The third element is some type of corrective action if the actual measurements are not within some established range near the target value. This concept is applied in several areas of business such as budgetary control, inventory control, and quality control. Some applications in quality use sampling or other statistical techniques to assess the actual performance and are referred to as statistical quality control (SQC).

This chapter primarily focuses on statistical methods for controlling quality. Before we explore the techniques for controlling quality to ensure that it conforms to the plan, we first discuss some considerations about planning for quality.

PLANNING FOR QUALITY

A great deal of planning is necessary to make an organization's quality efforts consistent and successful. Planning for quality occurs at all levels of the organization. Top management establishes the conditions and fosters the culture that encourages quality. Strategic planning at this level also establishes goals regarding the degree to which quality will be emphasized in developing the competitive strengths of the organization. Middle managers plan the more-detailed matters about the methods and procedures by which quality will be achieved. Planning is also required to establish how control will be achieved—what will be tested or measured and how often. At a lower level, planning is required in developing training programs for the necessary skills, planning work methods, and devising work assignments that will result in quality work.

The basis for quality planning is a clear understanding of customers' needs and expectations. It is unlikely that a company can develop services and a delivery process or design a product and a production process that will provide customer satisfaction unless it first has an understanding of this important input. A company must plan methods that will provide customer input on a continuing basis. The initial development and design phase defines what the company plans to provide to the customer in terms of services or goods. Planning for product quality in the design phase considers establishing the reliability, durability, serviceability, appearance, and other dimensions of product quality as mentioned in Chapter 3. Planning for service quality in the concept phase would include considerations about the types of personnel, facilities, and equipment that would be needed to consistently provide prompt service to meet customer expectations.

Definition of the service concept or product design establishes the goals for developing production processes and service delivery methods. Managers and possibly process engineers and others must plan the details of how the work necessary to provide the intended output will be accomplished. Consistency and error prevention are important considerations in this planning. Planning for training programs to prepare workers to be high-quality performers is also a part of the planning process that affects quality.

The total quality management philosophy makes planning for quality a consideration in all parts and activities of a company. The company also must establish an organization and assign responsibilities so that all the necessary efforts are accomplished to ensure quality, rather than just saying it is everybody's job. Some activities that are not part of the work performed in the value-adding processes are necessary in order to achieve quality. Often a department of the company with a title like Qual-

HOW STATISTICAL QUALITY CONTROL CAN HELP ADD VALUE FOR CUSTOMERS

Statistical quality control (SQC) can be a very effective means of preventing quality problems or detecting them as soon as they occur. In most cases, it is less expensive to prevent problems than it is to correct them after the fact. As with total quality management, SQC can improve quality and reduce costs so that a company can provide greater value to its customers. Companies that quickly spot problems and correct them use less of their capacity making things wrong and reworking them, so they can provide more-dependable goods and service. For example, Harley-Davidson instituted statistical quality control as part of its Material as Needed program. The company had a 46 percent reduction in scrap and rework and a 35 percent reduction in warranty cost.

ity Assurance Department helps coordinate and facilitate the quality efforts of the company. The types of activities that such a department might perform are mentioned below. The list is not exhaustive, but it shows some important quality matters for which planning must occur. Usually a company will prepare a quality manual that spells out for employees and customers how the company will deal with such matters so that quality is ensured.

A company must plan methods and assign responsibilities to see that the following is done:

- Maintain the latest versions of all pertinent drawings, specifications, procedures, and instructions for performing work and provide them to all appropriate persons.

- Review all recruiting and training materials and purchase agreements to see that quality issues are appropriately addressed.

- Provide suppliers with and see that they understand and comply with all appropriate drawings, specifications, and standards.

- Review and approve the capabilities of suppliers to provide work that will meet the expectations of customers.

- See that all incoming materials and subcontracted work conform to the appropriate specifications.

- Identify and control all raw materials and supplies so that only the proper materials are issued for each job.

- Identify potential trouble spots in processes, devise procedures or devices to prevent problems, perform inspections at appropriate spots to detect problems as early as possible, and follow up to prevent recurrence of problems.

- Maintain and calibrate all necessary gauges, testing, and measuring devices required to verify that equipment is working properly and that products meet specifications.

- Maintain information from customer satisfaction ratings, warranty claims, returned items, inspection records, control charts, material certifications, supplier performance reports, inspection reports, and other information that pertains to quality.

For McDonald's, quality means the same thing all over the world. Before opening its first restaurant in Moscow, McDonald's spent $50 million to make sure its suppliers would meet its quality standards. A food processing factory was built to assure that food was handled according to the high standards of sanitation McDonald's maintains in the United States. Russian farmers were even introduced to a new strain of potato to guarantee the perfect McDonald's fries.

Frank Siteman/Stock, Boston

- Use available information to help identify any problems and notify the appropriate parties.
- Control all rejected materials and items to see that they do not get into the product and are properly disposed of or reworked.
- Follow up with suppliers to see that causes of any problems are identified and corrected.
- Plan and perform final inspections, assembly inspections, and functional testing of completed products.
- Establish standards and instructions for packaging and shipping.

After planning how these and any other requirements will be met the organization then has to instruct and motivate persons who are charged with the responsibility. When activities of this type are performed satisfactorily quality can be controlled. We will now consider the matter of controlling quality, primarily when statistical methods are employed.

USES OF STATISTICS IN QUALITY CONTROL

Statistical techniques are applied to three major types of applications in the field of quality control, as summarized in Figure 10.1. Statistics can be used in statistical process control to monitor critical parameters of processes, with the goal of keeping them operating within desired levels that are known to provide quality results. Statistics may be applied in acceptance sampling with the goal of screening and separating batches of items that contain an unacceptable number of defective items from acceptable batches. The defective items in the rejected batches are then discarded or

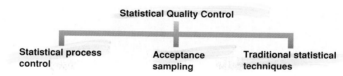

Figure 10.1
Groups of Techniques in Statistical Quality Control

reworked so they will not be processed further or sold to customers. In addition to these two applications of sampling, traditional statistical techniques (such as histograms, correlation, regression, and analysis of experiments) can be used to analyze and improve quality levels.

Acceptance sampling is a corrective approach to quality, which means that the company may have already wasted the resources required to make some items incorrectly and then must use more resources to sort products and rework what can be salvaged. Generally, it is better to concentrate on preventive approaches that keep processes working properly so that defective items will not be made. Consequently, many companies are working to make broader use of process control. With the increasingly competitive global market, companies are also interested in the design of experiments and other investigative techniques that might help them improve quality. In this chapter we primarily review applications of sampling for process control and acceptance sampling.

SOME CONSIDERATIONS ABOUT CONTROLLING PROCESSES

A process is a series of steps that *(if working properly)* add value to input(s) to provide output(s) for internal or external customers. Through such efforts as careful process design, worker training, and equipment improvement, companies work to maintain processes that reliably perform the work necessary to add value and provide customer satisfaction. Some processes are very complex and involve a large number of steps to perform their intended work. Companies seek to make their process "robust" so they can tolerate some variation from the ideal level of performance at each work step and still produce high-quality results. Designed experiments are sometimes used to evaluate various settings of process parameters to determine how sensitive the quality of the output is to the level at which the process parameters are set and to small variations in performance of the various process steps. Such experiments help show the best level to run a process so it is more robust and indicate which steps in the process are more temperamental in terms of their potential to cause quality problems. Those process steps that can be most damaging to the process' performance must be controlled carefully. Once a company has identified the key process steps and the parameters that are important to control at those steps, it may develop process control procedures to help ensure that the output of the process will have high quality.

Some steps in a process may be monitored carefully even though they may not be the steps that usually have a major impact on quality. Items may be inspected just prior to a process step that is very expensive to perform, to ensure that no defective items are sent through these expensive steps. Also, care may be taken to see that only good items are fed into a bottleneck operation where capacity is limited, to ensure that none of this scarce capacity is wasted in running already defective items.

At Du Pont, sophisticated computers control the movement of products between work centers and help maintain process control.

The Du Pont Company

Mistake Proofing

Companies that seek to excel also work to mistake proof their products and processes so that good quality is achieved the first time and there is no wasteful scrap and rework. Efforts can be made in the design of products and their components so that the parts can only be installed into the assembly the right way. Similarly, processing equipment can sometimes be designed so that it is very difficult to use the equipment improperly. For example, a device that holds a part while a machine performs some operation on it may be constructed so that the part will fit into the holding device only the right way. In some cases machines are equipped with automatic sensors that will sound an alarm or turn off the machine if they sense that a defective part has been fed into the machine. The Japanese call this technique poka-yoke.

Simple logic can be used to errorproof some operations. Workers who assemble the same type of item many times a day sometimes don't remember after they have built up an assembly if they installed the right number of each component inside. A simple error prevention method is to have a tray that has a compartment for each part that goes into the assembly. The tray is loaded with the right number of the right parts before beginning the assembly operation. If there are no parts in the tray when the assembly is completed, they must have been installed in the assembly, so none has been left out.

When machines or operators perform quality checks as an integral part of each process step, they provide 100 percent checking of quality. This prevents further processing of items that are not repairable and it prevents having to rework more than just the most recently performed step. When automatic self-checking can be economically applied it can lead to very high levels of quality with low cost. Wise application of these techniques can achieve a prevention cost that is lower than the cost of internal and external failure. An example of automatic checking was presented in Chapter 7 when we discussed computer-integrated manufacturing at Allen-Bradley's plant that manufactures starters and controllers for electric motors. In some other applications of quality control not all steps are checked every time and the company relies on sampling to control quality.

WHY USE SAMPLING?

Often organizations use statistical sampling to infer the quality of a batch of products or to infer whether a process is working properly. There are several reasons companies may prefer to take samples instead of checking every item or constantly measuring the process parameters as every item is made:

1. Sampling often is faster. A company may not need to know an exact measure of some characteristic. It may just need to know whether the characteristic is within some acceptable limits and to know this quickly enough to take corrective action if needed. A sufficient sample may provide sufficient accuracy more quickly.

2. Some tests require that the product be damaged or destroyed. Destructive testing might involve a procedure such as placing the item in a special holding device and increasing a force applied to it until the item breaks. The amount of force required to break the item is recorded and compared to standards. In other instances, such as services, the relevant data may be customer satisfaction surveys. Collection of these data may annoy the customers, so it may be preferable to use only a sample.

3. The test may be very expensive to conduct. Obtaining data from some sample of the product may be much more economical than testing all the products.

4. Data from 100 percent inspection may give a false sense of accuracy. When people test items in high-volume production, they often miss some errors. In some studies inspectors found as few as 80 percent of the defectives present. When these people test many fewer items, such as samples from the larger production runs, their accuracy rate increases.

Since sampling can be very helpful in quality control, let us look at some of the ways it is employed. The first method we review is statistical process control.

STATISTICAL PROCESS CONTROL

Information from samples can be used in *statistical process control (SPC)* to infer something about the proper functioning of the processes through which items have been, or are to be, run. SPC is very important in quality control because it helps keep the processes running correctly so that defective items are seldom produced. That is, SPC helps maintain high-quality operations where quality is built into the product

Figure 10.2
Feedback Loop Used to
Control a Process Step

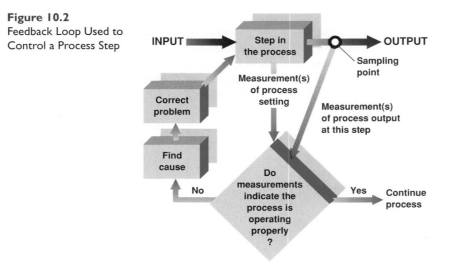

the first time. After all, quality must be built into the product when it is made to be achieved. Inspection and testing do not directly add quality to an item. They just check after an item is made to see if the quality is there or not. Statistical data from product tests can also be used to infer whether the processes appear to have been working properly when the items were made.

Figure 10.2 depicts some of the feedback that can be obtained from a process step or the output of a step, and used to monitor the processes' performance. If the feedback indicates that a problem is likely in the process, the process is checked. Corrective action such as changing the process settings or changing a procedure is taken if the need is indicated.

To practice SPC, a company should identify all the key quality characteristics that must be controlled in order for its goods and services to have the intended level of quality. Some means of measuring each of these characteristics must be devised. The company then runs the process under carefully controlled conditions to ensure that no identifiable causes of variation are introduced into the process. Repeated measures of some process parameter or of some measurement on items that have been through the same step in the process will show variation even when the process is run under these conditions.

Chance Causes and Assignable Causes of Variation

Not all the work performed by a process will be identical even when the process is working properly and no changes are made in the work methods, machine settings, or other factors that would be expected to change the result. The differences may be very small, but if they are measured closely enough, there will be some variation in the results. These variations are due to a stable system of *chance-cause variation* that leads to some inherent variability in the process. Chance-cause variation is due to small changes in many variables that are difficult or impossible to remove and therefore are considered inherent in the process. Consider, for example, a grinding operation that is intended to grind metal objects to a target dimension. Even when the work procedure and the machine settings are kept the same, many small variations may occur in this process because of such factors as changes in temperature, vibrations in the machine, wear on the grinding wheel, and small variations in the chemical composition and hardness of the metal. If the metal objects were measured closely enough some variation in size would be found. However, if the process is "capable" (as we discussed in Chapter 3) and if the process is correctly aimed for the target measurement, all the objects will be within the acceptable tolerances for that dimension on the item.

The process can be run so that just its stable system of chance-cause variation is present and the dispersion of this inherent variability can measured. Based on the dispersion in the inherent variation, limits (called control limits) can then be calculated so they will be near the extremes of the chance-cause variation in the measurement that is to be controlled. Usually in process control, these limits are plotted on a *control chart* for the measurements that are to be controlled. A control chart is a simple graphical method to display a series of data points in chronological order on a scale that shows the control limits for that measurement. The general form of a control chart is shown in Figure 10.3.

Subsequently, the control chart is used to record and compare data that is collected as the process is run. Sample data are collected at selected times. Values from the samples are plotted on the control chart and compared to the control limits to see if the process is operating within what has been shown to be its normal dispersion. If the sample data are within the control limits and show only the usual random pattern of variation there is no evidence that the process is not operating normally. Under these conditions the process is said to be *in control.*

If the sample data are outside the control limits or some other suspicious pattern is seen in the data, the process is said to be *out of control.* This means that some *assignable cause of variation* is suspected. An assignable cause of variation is some change in the process beyond its chance-cause variation. The process usually is stopped when such a signal is observed and the process is checked to determine the problem. If problems are found, they are corrected and the process is restarted.

Notice in Figure 10.3 that sample number 7 is above the *upper control limit (UCL).* Such an event would cause the production personnel to conclude that the process was probably "out of control," that is, not working as it should. A similar interpretation would be made if a sample value fell below the *lower control limit (LCL).* An out-of-control signal would cause the responsible persons to begin looking for an assignable cause of the variation and to correct it. Occasionally the process could be working properly, a sampling error might cause the suspicious data, and no assignable cause is found in the process.

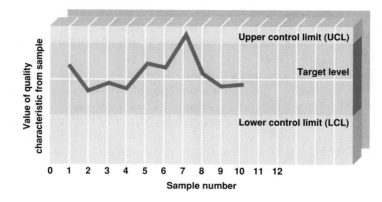

Figure 10.3
Example of a
Control Chart

One of the functions of Motorola University is teaching employees the math necessary for using statistical process control. At Motorola, all levels of employees are expected to be able to control for quality.

Motorola

Type I and Type II Errors

Relying on sample data as the basis for decisions about the process involves some risk that sampling errors will lead to the wrong conclusion. The sample may differ from the actual population to the extent that it may lead to either of two types of errors, a type I or a type II error. The quality control program should be designed and sampling done so as to keep the probability of errors reasonably low. Let us look at more details about type I and type II errors.

TYPE I ERRORS   A sample from the output of a process may lead to the conclusion that the process is out of control when, in fact, it is operating as intended. Such an error might involve only the cost of rechecking some adjustments to the process when there really is no need for the inspection. It might also, however, lead to a very expensive and embarrassing result, such as recalling everything produced since the last sample was taken. The probability of making a type I error, α, should be established with due consideration of the cost that would result from such an error.

TYPE II ERRORS   A type II error occurs when the process is not working as it should, but sampling error causes one to infer that the process is satisfactory. In a manufacturing plant the risk of a type II error, β, may lead to investing lots of money in further work on items that are defective. It may also result in product liability suits if the defects go undetected and the product harms a user. The cost of a type II error must be considered in establishing control limits.

Table 10.1 is a contingency table showing the conditions that exist with type I and type II errors. Examples of type I errors are the conviction of an innocent defendant, being led by a blood test to believe that one has a disease when one does not, and paying for automotive repairs one does not need. Some examples of type II errors are the failure to convict a guilty defendant and getting a false-negative result from a blood test.

Table 10.1
TYPE I AND TYPE II ERRORS

CONDITIONS	Decision to:	
	SEARCH FOR DEFECT IN PROCESS AND TRY TO CORRECT IT	LEAVE THE PROCESS AS IT IS
Process is working properly	Type I error	Correct decision
Process is defective	Correct decision	Type II error

Attribute Data and Variable Data

The general concepts of the control chart that were presented are major keys to process control. Use of the proper chart, calculation of the proper control limits, and accurately monitoring sample data from the process are important. These factors provide the information to keep the process in control. When possible problems are indicated, the process should be stopped immediately and any assignable causes of variation should be corrected. By use of different control charts these concepts can be applied to control either of two major types of data: attribute data and variable data.

An attribute describes whether an item has a particular characteristic or falls into a particular classification. *Attribute data* simply tell whether an item being evaluated has a particular attribute or list the number of times that a particular attribute occurred. A binary comparison is made: An event occurred, or it did not. An electric switch works, or it does not. A part conforms to specifications, or it does not. A customer complains or does not. In some instances attribute data are a count of how many times a particular event occurred. These evaluations often are easier to make than evaluations of variable data. Either a p chart or a c chart can be used to control processes that are recorded as attribute data. We discuss these types of charts later.

Variable data record the particular reading that was obtained for some measurement which can take on any value within some range of possible values. This tells (as closely as the measurement device shows) which of many possible numbers occurred. With variable data, one knows how far the actual measurement is from some ideal target value, in addition to seeing whether or not it falls into the acceptable category. Examples of variable data are the temperature of a baking oven, the time it takes a bank teller to process a transaction, or the thickness of a part that must fit into some assembly, such as the diameter of a shaft that must fit into a bearing in an electric fan.

If a quality characteristic is measured as variable data, it is important to maintain control over both the mean and the variability of the quality characteristic. A *control chart for the mean,* or $\bar{X}$ *chart,* can be used to determine whether the mean of the distribution of measurements being produced by the process is located at (or at least very near) the target value. A *control chart for the range,* or R *chart,* often is used to monitor the variability of the process. We will discuss constructing the $\bar{X}$ chart and the R chart after a brief discussion of the statistical basis for them.

Table 10.2 summarizes the types of charts that were mentioned above and the type of data for which they are used. We will discuss the development and use of each of these types of charts in statistical process control beginning with the control charts for variable data. Before we go into the details of making the charts we will first review some of the relevant concepts from statistics.

Table 10.2
FOUR COMMON CONTROL CHARTS

CHART	TYPE OF DATA	MEASUREMENT IT IS USED TO CONTROL
$\bar{X}$ chart	Variable	The central location of a distribution of variable data
R chart	Variable	The range as a measure of the dispersion of variable data
p chart	Attribute	Proportion of items that are defective (nonconforming)*
c chart	Attribute	Number of defects (nonconformities) found in some specified amount of the output

*In some standards, *nonconforming* means that the associated product or service does not meet the specifications, and *defective* means that the associated product or service differs so severely that it will not satisfy its intended, normal usage requirements. Since our purpose is to simplify and illustrate the general concepts and methods, we do not make a distinction in this chapter and sometimes use the terms interchangeably.

Brief Statistical Background

Assume that a process produces a quality characteristic, which we call X, that is normally distributed with a mean of μ and a standard deviation of σ. Repeated random samples of n units (the sample size is n) are taken from the population, and $\bar{X}$, the mean, is computed for each sample. The $\bar{X}$'s will also be normally distributed. The mean of the distribution of all the possible $\bar{X}$'s, given the symbol $\mu_{\bar{x}}$, is equal to the mean of the population, and the standard deviation of the distribution of $\bar{X}$'s is $\sigma_{\bar{x}} = \sigma/\sqrt{n}$. Therefore, if we take a random sample from the population and calculate its $\bar{X}$ we have some member of this distribution of possible $\bar{X}$'s. The probability is $1 - \alpha$ that this $\bar{X}$ falls within $Z_{1-\alpha/2}$ of the $\mu_{\bar{x}}$ and hence the mean of the population μ. This property is the basis for using a random sample to test a hypothesis that μ has a particular value. We do not reject the hypothesis if the difference between the hypothesized mean and the $\bar{X}$ of the random sample is less than $Z_{1-\alpha/2}$ times the standard deviation of the distributions of the $\bar{X}$'s. That is, the evidence we got from the sample is not different enough from what we hypothesized to make us believe that the hypothesis probably is false. We reject the hypothesis if the $\bar{X}$ of the random sample is farther than this from the hypothesized value of the mean. The value of α establishes the risk that we will reject the hypothesis when the mean μ actually is at the hypothesized value.

The relationship between the hypothesized location of the population and the distribution of $\bar{X}$'s that can occur if the hypothesis is true is shown in Figure 10.4. If an $\bar{X}$ from the random sample is outside the limits indicated on the distribution of $\bar{X}$'s, the hypothesis that the population is in this location is rejected. There is a risk equal to α that the hypothesis will be rejected when it is true.

Control Charts for Variable Data: The $\bar{X}$ and R Charts

A control chart for $\bar{X}$ is similar to a series of tests of a hypothesis that the mean of the process is in the right place. The hypothesis is tested repeatedly as the process is run by collecting a series of $\bar{X}$'s and comparing them to the control limits. It is assumed that the $\bar{X}$'s will be approximately normally distributed. The control limits are usually drawn as horizontal lines, so visualize that Figure 10.4 has been rotated 90 degrees. The upper control limit for $\bar{X}$, $UCL_{\bar{x}}$, would correspond to the upper rejection limit in Figure 10.4, and the lower control limit for $\bar{X}$, $LCL_{\bar{x}}$, would correspond to the lower rejection limit. The control limits for $\bar{X}$ will then be similar to the limits on the right-hand side of Figure 10.5.

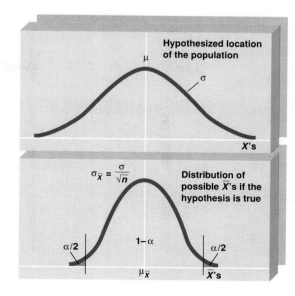

Figure 10.4
Relationship Between Hypothesized Population and the Values of $\bar{X}$ That Can Occur If the Hypothesis Is True

If the target value of the mean (equivalent to the hypothesized value) is μ and the standard deviation of the population of measurements is σ, then the values for the control limits are calculated by equations 10.1 and 10.2.

$$\text{UCL}_{\bar{x}} = \mu + Z_{1-\alpha/2}\sigma_{\bar{x}} \qquad\qquad [10.1]$$

$$\text{LCL}_{\bar{x}} = \mu - Z_{1-\alpha/2}\sigma_{\bar{x}} \qquad\qquad [10.2]$$

where $\sigma_{\bar{x}} = \dfrac{\sigma}{\sqrt{n}}$

Often the value 3 is used for Z in calculating control limits, and these limits are referred to as the 3σ ("three sigma") limits. Assuming a normal distribution, these limits include 99.7 percent of the area under the probability distribution for the $\bar{X}$'s. The probability then is only 0.003 that a random $\bar{X}$ will fall outside the limits if the population mean is at the target value. If an $\bar{X}$ occurs that is outside these limits, either the population mean is not at the target value or a sample has been drawn that has only a probability of 0.003 of occurring.

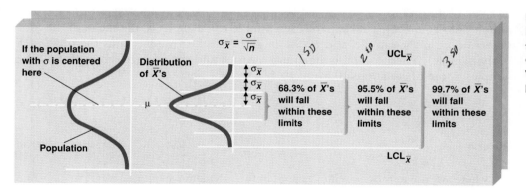

Figure 10.5
Relationship Between the Population and Control Limits When the Process Is in Control

Figure 10.6
Sampling Distribution of $\overline{X}$ Approaches Normal, and Standard Deviation Decreases, as n Increases

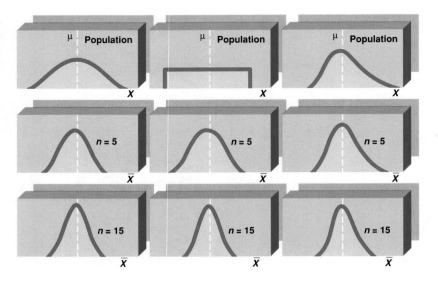

POPULATION PARAMETERS OFTEN MUST BE ESTIMATED   Usually, μ and σ are not known precisely and must be estimated from samples taken from the population. Even if the population is not exactly normal, the distribution of $\overline{X}$'s will be closer to normal than the population because of the central-limit theorem. Thus, probability statements about the values of $\overline{X}$ that may occur are based on the assumption that the distribution of the $\overline{X}$'s is normal. As long as the population is close to normal, this assumption is satisfactory even for small sample sizes. Figure 10.6 shows that as long as the population is not badly skewed, the distribution of $\overline{X}$'s will be close to normal for samples as small as $n = 5$. Use larger samples if a population is highly skewed.

Samples as small as $n = 4$ or 5 observations are often used in quality control. Small samples reduce the time and cost for each sample, so samples can be taken more often for the same cost. Also, with small samples, there is less chance for the process to change during sampling and cause the within-sample variability to be high.

DEVELOPING TRIAL LIMITS   Suppose that we wish to establish control limits for a process for which we do not know μ and σ. The process should be operated with careful attention not to introduce any assignable causes of variation, and preliminary samples should be taken. In manufacturing, for example, an experienced operator should use the proper procedure, the equipment should be in proper working order, and raw materials of the proper quality should consistently be used. At least 20 to 25 samples of the size to be used in subsequent sampling should be taken. Assume that samples of size $n = 4$ are taken. For each sample calculate its $\overline{X}$, the mean of the four observations in the sample, and R (the largest X in the sample minus the smallest $\overline{X}$ in the sample). Then compute the grand mean $\overline{\overline{X}}$ and the average range $\overline{R}$ of all the samples by use of equations 10.3 and 10.4:

$$\overline{\overline{X}} = \frac{\Sigma \overline{X}}{K} \qquad\qquad\qquad\qquad\qquad\qquad\qquad\qquad \textbf{[10.3]}$$

$$\overline{R} = \frac{\Sigma R}{K} \qquad\qquad\qquad\qquad\qquad\qquad\qquad\qquad \textbf{[10.4]}$$

where K = the number of samples used in the calculations

Relationships between R and σ have been developed for a normal distribution, so that control limits can be established under the assumption of normality. Trial limits for the R chart should be established first by use of equations 10.5 and 10.6. The constants D_3 and D_4 required to establish 3σ control limits for R using various sample sizes are given in Appendix V at the back of the book. (Other constants for the $\bar{X}$ charts are also provided.)

$$\text{UCL}_R = D_4\bar{R} \qquad\qquad [10.5]$$

$$\text{LCL}_R = D_3\bar{R} \qquad\qquad [10.6]$$

The ranges of the preliminary samples (the R's) should be tested to see that they fall within these trial limits. If more than 3 of the R's are outside the limits, then an investigation should be made to remedy assignable causes of variation in the process and new samples should be taken after the process is corrected. (If the process is not in control, we should not use the data from the process to establish control limits.) If only 2 or 3 of the R's are outside the limits, a search should be made for assignable causes that those samples were out of control. If reasons can be found why these samples were not in control, these R's can be discarded and the rest of the R's used to construct new trial limits. The $\bar{X}$'s that were calculated from the samples with the discarded R's should also be discarded. If the R's are in control, then the data can be used to construct limits for $\bar{X}$. Development and application of control limits for $\bar{X}$ and R are illustrated in the application box on pages 387–388.

The 3σ control limits for $\bar{X}$ can be found by use of equations 10.7 and 10.8 if the grand mean $\bar{\bar{X}}$ is located at or near enough to the desired target value. (Values of A_2 for various sample sizes are provided in Appendix V.) If it is desired to control the central value of the process at some other target value, that value is substituted for the grand mean. This should be done only if it is reasonable to assume that the variability of the process will not be different if the process is readjusted to this new target value.

$$\text{UCL}_X = \bar{\bar{X}} + A_2\bar{R} \qquad\qquad [10.7]$$

$$\text{LCL}_{\bar{X}} = \bar{\bar{X}} - A_2\bar{R} \qquad\qquad [10.8]$$

USE OF THE $\bar{X}$ AND R CHARTS   The limits for R usually are drawn on one chart, and the limits for $\bar{X}$ are drawn on another. Samples are taken at selected times as the process is run, and the values of R from these samples are plotted on the R chart to see if they fall within the control limits. If any R is outside the limits, the process is suspected of being out of control. If you examine the values of D_3 in Appendix V, you will notice that for sample sizes smaller than 7, the value of D_3 is zero, which means that the lower limit for R will be zero for samples of fewer than 7 observations. You might wonder why there would ever be any other lower limit. That is, why would anyone want a signal that the variability might have gotten significantly smaller, since consistency in the process is a goal? A company would probably want to find the assignable cause for the improvement and standardize the improved method. A new value of R should also be calculated and new limits established for $\bar{X}$ so the probability of a type I error will remain at the established level.

The $\bar{X}$'s from samples are plotted on the $\bar{X}$ chart to see if they are within the control limits and to observe any nonrandom pattern that might appear in the data. Various guidelines have been developed regarding what evidence on the $\bar{X}$ control chart leads to a suspicion that the process is out of control. When a process is suspected of being out of control, the process is investigated to see if any assignable cause of varia-

Figure 10.7
Patterns on an $\bar{X}$ Chart
That Trigger a Suspicion
That the Process Is Out
of Control

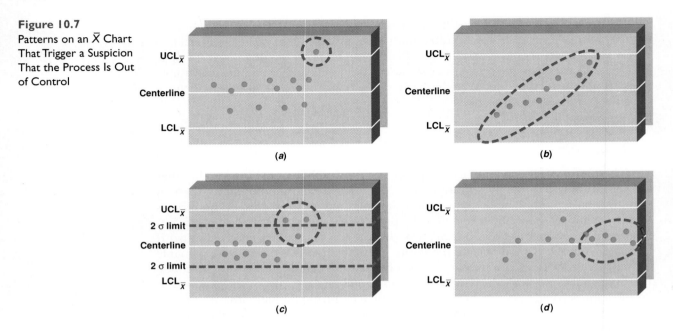

tion can be found. Some of the commonly used guidelines for indications on an $\bar{X}$ chart that a process may be out of control are shown in Figure 10.7. The suspicion indicators shown are, respectively, *(a)* any point outside the 3σ limits, *(b)* a trend of 7 or 8 points that do not decrease or increase, *(c)* 2 out of 3 points beyond the 2σ limits if these limits are included on the chart, and *(d)* a run of 5 or more points that all fall on the same side of the centerline.

Over time a significant amount of data from the process may be accumulated. If the data are kept as individual measurements, they can be used to calculate σ′ as an estimate σ, the process standard deviation. Equation 10.9 can be used to compute this estimate.

$$\sigma' = \sqrt{\frac{\Sigma(X - \bar{\bar{X}})^2}{N - 1}} \qquad \text{[10.9]}$$

where N = total number of observations of X that are used in this calculation

The population standard deviation can also be estimated from data that may be available if numerous values of the sample range have been accumulated. Equation 10.10 can be used to compute this type of estimate:

$$\sigma' = \frac{\bar{R}}{d_2} \qquad \text{[10.10]}$$

Here d_2 is a constant that is appropriate for the particular sample size used to collect the R's. These constants are tabulated in Appendix V.

The standard deviation of the process is useful, you may recall from Chapter 3, to estimate the capability of the process to meet the specifications for a particular operation. If the company has a good estimate of the process standard deviation, the estimate can be used in equations 10.1 and 10.2 to establish control limits for $\bar{X}$. The calculation and use of control limits for $\bar{X}$ and R are illustrated in the following box.

APPLICATION

ESTABLISHING CONTROL LIMITS FOR $\bar{X}$ AND R

Pearl Choppers owns a small toothpaste factory in which she uses automatic equipment to fill the toothpaste tubes. The automatic machine can be set to dispense a desired amount, and the company is starting to produce a new 6-ounce tube (previously it produced only 12-ounce tubes). Ms. Choppers feels that the variability of the amount dispensed by the machine might be different at a 6-ounce setting from what it had been at the 12-ounce setting so the process variability will be estimated near the 6-ounce setting. She wants to set up $\bar{X}$ and R charts to help monitor and control the amount of paste in the 6-ounce tubes. If the tubes are too full, toothpaste is wasted and the consumer will get upset if a 5- to 8-inch ribbon of paste flows out the first time the container is opened. If the container is not sufficiently full, the consumer will be unhappy and the company will be guilty of false advertising. Ms. Choppers wants the probability of a tube's containing less than 6 ounces to be very small.

The machine was set so that approximately 6.35 ounces would be dispensed (to be sure the tubes contained at least 6 ounces) and an initial trial was run. Samples of $n = 4$ tubes were taken at random intervals during the initial processing. When the data from 25 samples were available, trial control limits were established. The data are given in Table 10.3.

Before control limits were set for future production, the test data were compared with trial control limits to ensure that the process was in control when σ was estimated.

Trial control limits for R were set at

$$LCL_R = D_3(\bar{R}) = 0(0.1496) = 0$$

$$UCL_R = D_4(\bar{R}) = 2.282(0.1496) = 0.341$$

Trial control limits for $\bar{X}$ were set at

$$LCL_{\bar{x}} = 6.35 - 3\,\frac{\sigma'}{\sqrt{n}} = 6.35 - 3\left(\frac{0.0727}{\sqrt{4}}\right)$$

$$= 6.35 - 0.109 = 6.241$$

$$UCL_{\bar{x}} = 6.35 + 3\,\frac{\sigma'}{\sqrt{n}} = 6.35 + 0.109 = 6.459$$

All the past data points were within these limits, so the estimates of σ and R were considered valid for controlling future production. If any points had been outside the trial limits (such points are called "outliers"), they would have been removed and new limits would have been computed.

Once an estimate of σ was available, control limits for future production could be established. Nearly all the population—99.7 percent—should fall between the mean $+3(0.0727)$ and the mean $-3(0.0727)$. The process mean should be set at least $3(0.0727)$, or 0.2181, ounce above 6 ounces so that very few tubes would be produced containing less than 6 ounces. The process mean could, therefore, be set closer to 6.218 ounces than at 6.35 ounces without the inherent variability of the process causing many tubes to contain less than 6 ounces. Therefore, Ms. Choppers ordered the machine

Table 10.3
DATA FROM 25 RANDOM SAMPLES OF TOOTHPASTE

SAMPLE NO.	$\bar{X}$	R	SAMPLE NO.	$\bar{X}$	R	SAMPLE NO.	$\bar{X}$	R
1	6.36	0.10	9	6.37	0.16	18	6.35	0.13
2	6.38	0.18	10	6.33	0.13	19	6.34	0.18
3	6.35	0.17	11	6.32	0.18	20	6.34	0.16
4	6.39	0.20	12	6.30	0.10	21	6.33	0.12
5	6.32	0.15	13	6.34	0.11	22	6.36	0.09
6	6.34	0.16	14	6.39	0.14	23	6.32	0.17
7	6.40	0.13	15	6.37	0.17	24	6.33	0.10
8	6.33	0.18	16	6.36	0.15	25	6.35	0.20
			17	6.35	0.18			

$\sum \bar{X} = 158.72 \qquad \bar{\bar{X}} = 6.35 \qquad\qquad \sum R = 3.74 \qquad \bar{R} = 0.1496$

$$\sigma' = \frac{\bar{R}}{d_2} = \frac{0.1496}{2.059} = 0.0727$$

set at 6.25 ounces. The control limits were moved to center on 6.25 ounces with $3\sigma_{\bar{x}}$ control limits established about this value. The new control limits for $\bar{X}$ and R are shown in Figure 10.8. Data for the next 15 samples are shown, and you will notice that the $\bar{X}$ for sample number 12 was outside the control limits. A search for assignable causes revealed that the orifice was partially clogged, so that the paste could not flow out of the machine at the ordinary rate. After this condition was corrected, new samples indicated that the process was back in control.

Figure 10.8   New $\bar{X}$ and R Charts for Pearl Choppers' Toothpaste

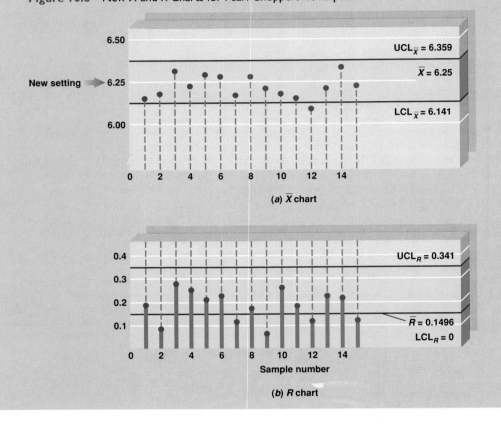

(a) $\bar{X}$ chart

(b) R chart

Control Charts for Attribute Data

CONTROL CHARTS FOR THE FRACTION DEFECTIVE   Control charts for $\bar{X}$ and R are usually not appropriate for attribute data. Attribute data record only a determination of whether or not an item falls into a particular category or a count of the number of occurrences of some defect. For example, the characteristic that is recorded may be whether an ambulance arrived within 6 minutes of a call or not, whether a customer complained or not, whether a light bulb burns or not, and so forth. Consequently, there is no set of values from the sample for which a mean and range can be calculated. The data available may tell how many items in the sample conform to some specification and how many do not conform. These data can be

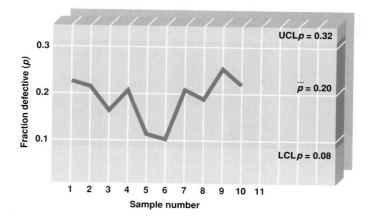

Figure 10.9
Example of a *p* Chart

used to calculate *p*, the fraction of the sample that is defective—sometimes called the proportion defective or the proportion nonconforming. The *p* chart is a control chart to monitor some process to see whether the fraction defective appears to have changed beyond the natural or inherent variation of this statistic.

An example of a *control chart for the fraction defective,* or *p chart,* is shown in Figure 10.9. The *p* chart can be used to see if a process is remaining stable, that is, producing consistent results within normal variation. And $\bar{p}$, the target level of *p*, may be based on historical data from a time when the process was known to be in control, or it may be a target established by management. Care should be taken to establish $\bar{p}$ at attainable levels, or people may not take it seriously. In fact, unrealistic goals may create some animosity. Often *p* charts are based on full 100 percent inspection. The sample size must be large enough to expect inclusion of at least one defective item; so if $\bar{p}$ is 0.05, the sample size should be at least 20, preferably larger.

APPLICATION

DETERMINING CONTROL LIMITS FOR THE FRACTION DEFECTIVE

Suppose that an airline has found that its passengers whose flights culminate at a particular airport report an average of 0.48 percent of their luggage as lost or damaged. On a typical day the airline's passengers claim about 1,000 pieces of luggage at that airport. Yesterday was no busier than usual but ten pieces of luggage were reported as lost or damaged. An attendant stated that something must have gone wrong with the system because this is about twice the normal level of claims.

The control limits for the fraction defective for a process with $p = 0.0048$ and samples of 1,000 follow.

$$UCL_p = 0.0048 + 3\sqrt{\frac{0.0048(0.9952)}{1,000}}$$

$$= 0.0048 + 0.00656 = 0.0114 \quad \text{or } 1.14 \text{ percent}$$

which is about eleven bags per thousand. The lower limit would be zero.

This 1-day result does not fall outside the control limits, which means it is not beyond the inherent variability that would be expected to occur in this process.

The 3σ control limits[1] for p should be set as indicated in equations 10.11 and 10.12.

$$UCL_p = \bar{p} + 3 \sqrt{\frac{\bar{p}(1 - \bar{p})}{n}}$$ [10.11]

$$LCL_p = \bar{p} - 3 \sqrt{\frac{\bar{p}(1 - \bar{p})}{n}} \quad \text{or 0, whichever is larger}$$ [10.12]

where $\bar{p}$ = the mean proportion defective for the process
n = the size of samples used in monitoring the process

CONTROL CHARTS FOR DEFECTS PER UNIT   Another example of an attribute that is counted, rather than a variable that is measured on a continuous scale, is the number of defects found in some specified amount of a product. This discrete variable is often referred to as the defects per unit (or nonconformities per unit). A distinction should be made between the terms *defective* and *defect*. A defective item is one that does not conform to specifications. It may contain one or more defects. In many instances, the opportunities for defects in a unit are indeterminable, so the idea of a fraction defective is meaningless. A company may decide to use a *control chart for defects per unit,* or *c chart,* in a situation such as this.

Consider the number of pinholes or small bubbles in the paint on a sheet of paneling that is 4 feet by 8 feet. The number of places where a small defect could appear is countless, yet we can count the number that are detected. One can monitor the number of crimes that occur in a given neighborhood within, say, a 1-week period. No one knows the number of opportunities that crimes could have been committed. The number of reported crimes per week may be monitored to see if there is a need for additional police patrol, for example. One might monitor the number of errors

---

[1] The probability of a type I error, α, may not be the same as that provided by the 3σ limits for $\bar{X}$ because the p and c charts are not based on a normal distribution.

APPLICATION

A CONTROL CHART FOR DEFECTS PER UNIT

The Mover City Transit Authority receives complaints from customers about the way drivers drive, their lack of courtesy, and so on. On several occasions, the drivers who have received the most complaints have told the manager that they carry many more passengers than other drivers, so they can be expected to receive more complaints. The manager has constructed a control chart for defects per unit c. In this case a complaint is a defect, and a unit of work is 500 fares collected on the bus. The c chart has been posted on the office wall, and the complaints reported are posted each week for each group of 500 fares that the driver collected. An average of 28.2 defects per unit occurred before the chart was posted. Control limits on the chart are

$$LCL_c = 28.2 - 3 \sqrt{28.2} = 12.3$$
$$UCL_c = 28.2 + 3 \sqrt{28.2} = 44.13$$

Two weeks have passed since the chart was posted, and the average number of complaints per unit is 17.1. Do you believe that the chart has made a significant difference in the care and courtesy of the drivers?

per page of typing, the number of accidents per month on a given stretch of highway, the number of scratches per yard of picture-frame molding, or the number of leaks per mile of pipe. The c chart is used to display sample data on defects per unit.

Control limits for the defects per unit are based on the Poisson probability distribution, which has a variance equal to its mean. Therefore the standard deviation σ is equal to $\sqrt{\bar{c}}$, where $\bar{c}$ is the mean number of defects per unit. The 3σ control limits for $\bar{c}$ are given by expressions 10.13 and 10.14.

$$\text{UCL}_c = \bar{c} + 3\sqrt{\bar{c}} \qquad\qquad \textbf{[10.13]}$$

$$\text{LCL}_c = \bar{c} - 3\sqrt{\bar{c}} \qquad \text{or 0, whichever is larger} \qquad \textbf{[10.14]}$$

where $\bar{c}$ = the mean number of defects per unit of output.

ACCEPTANCE SAMPLING

Acceptance sampling by attributes involves extracting a random sample from some larger lot of material to determine whether to accept or reject the entire lot or whether to subject it to 100 percent screening and separate the good products from the bad. The process may be used in receiving, in-process, or final inspection, but the terminology used is most appropriate for receiving inspection. A rejected lot may be returned to the supplier, or the supplier may be charged for 100 percent screening of rejected lots, after which only the defective items are returned for a refund. A high rate of rejections may be expensive for the supplier even if it does not lead the buyer to find another source of the goods or service. It may be less expensive for the supplier to increase its expenditures for prevention of quality problems and appraisal and have these costs more than offset by reductions in the costs of quality failures.

Many companies deal only with suppliers that consistently have high quality. The purchasing companies expect the suppliers to have effective SPC and to achieve quality at the source as the items are produced. A supplier who demonstrates consistent high quality may become a certified supplier. Items from certified suppliers are given little or possibly no receiving inspection. Sometimes items from certified suppliers are delivered directly to the point where they are installed into the purchasing company's product, and there is no receiving inspection. Relationships such as this develop over a long term between companies that have a high regard for quality and mutual trust.

When materials are to be inspected by sampling, the company can choose from many possible approaches to sampling. A lot may be evaluated on the basis of one sample through what is called *single sampling* or on the basis of more than one sample through *double sampling* or *sequential sampling*.

Single Sampling

A sampling plan for a single sample is specified by two numbers, n and c. The number of items that should be included in a single random sample from the lot being inspected is the *sample size, n*. The *acceptance number, c,* specifies the maximum number of defectives that may be found in the sample if the lot is to be accepted. If more than c defective items are found in the sample, the entire lot will be rejected or fully screened.

Double Sampling

Sometimes the quality of a lot of material is so good or so bad that it can be detected by a smaller sample than that normally used in a single sampling plan. Time and expense are spared when such lots are accepted or rejected on the basis of a small sample and only the questionable materials are subjected to larger sampling.

Double sampling uses the following procedure. First a random sample of size n_1 is taken. If the number of defectives in n_1 is less than c_1, the lot is accepted. If the number of defectives in n_1 is greater than c_2, the lot is rejected. If the number of defectives in n_1 is between c_1 and c_2, a second random sample of n_2 items is taken. The lot is accepted if the cumulative defectives in the two samples still does not exceed c_2. Otherwise the lot is rejected.

Sequential Sampling

The concept of double sampling can be extended to triple sampling and to other forms of multiple sampling. The limit of reducing the sample size and sampling until a clear decision is reached is sampling one unit at a time. In sequential sampling, units are randomly selected from a lot and tested one by one, and the cumulative sample size and cumulative number of defectives are recorded. If the cumulative number of defectives is above a certain limit for a given cumulative sample size, the lot is rejected. The lot is accepted if the cumulative number of defectives is below some other limit for the cumulative sample size. Figure 10.10 illustrates a sequential sampling plan. Sampling will continue as long as the cumulative number of defectives is between the acceptance limit and the rejection limit for the cumulative sample size taken thus far. Some lots that are close to the borderline of acceptable quality might eventually be sampled 100 percent without being rejected. Some multiple and sequential sampling plans provide for rejection (which may lead to 100 percent inspection) if the cumulative sample size reaches some number without the lot's being accepted. Of course, the lot could automatically be accepted if it still had not been rejected at some cumulative n if the cost of accepting defectives were fairly low.

Figure 10.10
A Sequential Sampling Plan

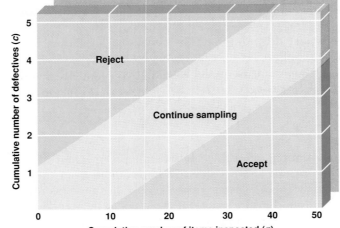

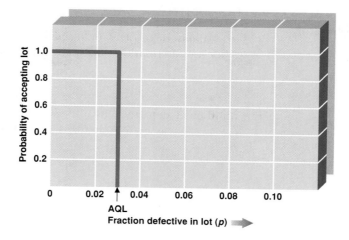

Figure 10.11
Perfect Discrimination
of an Inspection Process

Selecting a Single Sampling Plan for Sampling by Attributes

Acceptance sampling is frequently applied to screening of incoming purchased items. Sampling is particularly appropriate when the cost of inspection is high in relation to the cost of allowing defectives to enter the operation or when inspection requires destructive testing. It is generally expected that lots will not always consist of 100 percent good items and that lots with some fraction of defectives will be accepted. Suppose the acceptable fraction or percentage of defectives in a lot is 3 percent. If the inspection process were perfect, 100 percent inspection would provide a probability of 0.0 for accepting lots with more than the acceptable fraction of defective items. The probability would be 1.0 that a lot with less than the acceptable fraction of defectives would be accepted. The discrimination ability of 100 percent sampling with a perfect inspection process when the acceptable fraction of defectives is 0.03 is illustrated in Figure 10.11.

Inspection by sampling yields something less than perfect discrimination because of possible sampling error, even if we assume that the test is 100 percent accurate. There is a chance that the random sample will contain much less than the average percentage of defectives in the lot and cause us to conclude that the lot is good when it is not. On the other hand, a random sample may occasionally contain much more than the average percentage of defectives in the lot and cause a good lot to be rejected. The desirability of a sampling plan may be judged by how closely it approaches ideal discrimination. A plot of the probability of acceptance versus the fraction of defectives in a lot provides what is called the *operating characteristic curve*, or *OC curve*, for a sampling plan.

THE OPERATING CHARACTERISTIC CURVE As Figure 10.12 illustrates, the operating characteristic curve for a sampling plan will not be a sharp stairstep like the OC curve for 100 percent sampling and no inspection error. Larger sample sizes make the curve steeper when the acceptance number is kept at the same proportion of the sample size. Increasing n for the same c will steepen the curve and move it closer to the origin. To approach the ideal curve, a sampling plan would have a large n so that it would have a high likelihood of representing the composition of the lot

Figure 10.12
Effect on the OC Curve of Increasing the Sample Size and the Acceptance Number

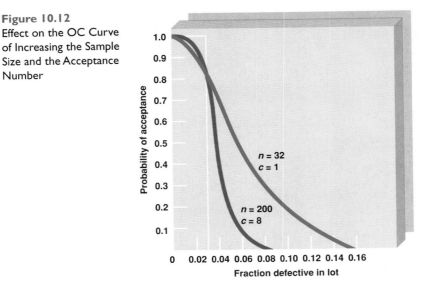

and a *c* large enough so that lots of acceptable quality or better would have a high probability of being accepted. The effect of changing both the sample size and the acceptance number is shown in Figure 10.12. The best sampling plan to use at a given inspection station depends on a trade-off of the cost of inspecting a larger sample versus the risk that results from smaller samples.

PRODUCER'S RISK AND CONSUMER'S RISK   Because a random sample does not always reproduce the exact composition of a lot from which it is taken, there is some risk in using sampling data as the basis for acceptance of an entire lot. One might mistakenly reject a good lot (a type I error) or mistakenly accept a bad lot (a type II error). These two kinds of risk are taken into account when a sampling plan is selected. The *acceptable quality level (AQL)* is the maximum percentage (or fraction) defective that is considered satisfactory as the overall average for the process for acceptance sampling purposes. The AQL must be greater than zero (but some companies expect very low numbers, such as a few defective parts per million). The producer wants a high probability that lots of this quality will be accepted. There is, however, some probability—called the *producer's risk* and symbolized by α—that a lot as good as the AQL will be rejected by use of a particular sampling plan. Not all lots will have the same degree of defectiveness as the process average—some will be better, and others will be worse. For acceptance sampling, however, there is some upper limit to the percentage of defective products in an individual lot that the consumer is willing to tolerate, even if the process average is acceptable. This limit is called the *lot tolerance percent defective (LTPD)*, or *lot tolerance proportion nonconforming*. (We use the term LTPD even though we may at times be referring to a fraction defective.) The *consumer's risk*, symbolized by β, is the probability that a lot with the percentage (or fraction) of defective products equal to the LTPD will be accepted by a sampling plan.

How do we find a sampling plan that will meet the desires of the consumer and the producer? A combination of α and AQL specifies a point that should fall on the

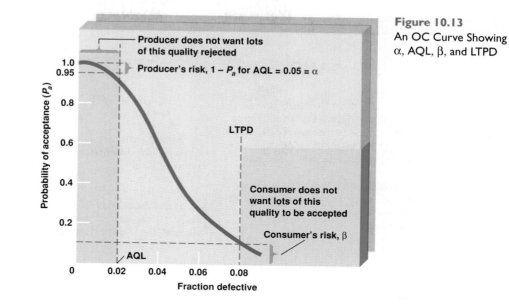

Figure 10.13
An OC Curve Showing
α, AQL, β, and LTPD

operating characteristic curve. Specifying a value of β at a particular LTPD defines another point that should be on the OC curve for the plan we seek. The objective, then, is to find a plan with an OC curve that passes through or almost through these two points. Bear in mind that if the AQL and LTPD are close to the same percent defective, the OC curve will have to be steep, which means the sample size n may be too large to be practical for sampling, so 100 percent inspection may be used. Figure 10.13 shows an OC curve with the values of α, β, AQL, and LTPD on it.

Searching for a sampling plan with an OC curve through the desired points could lead to many trials and errors. One might have to solve the appropriate probability equation many times to find the sampling plan that had the desired characteristics.[2] Fortunately, tables are available that permit one to find a suggested sampling plan in most instances without detailed calculations.[3] Since a sampling plan uses integers for n and c, the OC curve for a particular plan may not go exactly through the specified points; but a plan should be available with characteristics fairly close to those desired. (When the allowable number of defectives is only a few hundred per million, it may require 100 percent inspection for most reasonable lot sizes.[4]) Automatic testing of items while they are in process is often the best way to achieve quality control in this type of situation.

The calculations performed in the application can be greatly reduced when a table of Poisson probabilities is available. Such a table is presented in Appendix III. To find the probability of accepting a lot, look in the row for the expected number of defectives in the sample and read the probability of finding c or fewer defectives.

[2]The hypergeometric distribution is appropriate, but it can be approximated by the Poisson distribution if the sample is not a significant portion of the lot size. Joseph Juran suggests that the sample size should be at least 16, less than one-tenth the lot size, and p should be less than 0.1 [Joseph M. Juran and Frank M. Gryna, Jr., *Quality Planning and Analysis,* 2d ed. (New York: McGraw-Hill, 1980), p. 412].
[3]H. F. Dodge and H. G. Romig, *Sampling Inspection Tables,* 2d ed. (New York: Wiley, 1959).
[4]Gerald Hurayt, "Sample Size of PPM," *Quality,* March 1985, p. 75.

FINDING α AND β FOR A STATED SAMPLING PLAN

The Granite Isle Insurance Company is interested in buying 10,000 simulated granite paperweights to give to new customers. Rocky Davis, a new Granite Isle buyer, got two quotations that he felt were too high. Hoping to get a better price, Rocky said that he did not expect to get perfect quality and would consider 3 percent defectives as reasonable. He requested that the two potential vendors give new quotations with the understanding that a random sample of 60 items would be taken from each lot of 1,000 units, and if no more than 2 defectives were found, the lot would be accepted. The potential suppliers asked him to specify a LTPD that was higher than the 3 percent defectives he considered reasonable. Rocky replied that 5 percent would be acceptable. The suppliers said they would use 0.02 for the AQL. When the new quotations arrived, Rocky was surprised to find that the price was the same as before.

Assume that Rocky knows you are familiar with quality control and has asked for your help. He wants you to find the producer's risk and consumer's risk for the proposed plan and explain why the price was not reduced.

The Poisson probability distribution can be used because the sample is small in comparison with the lot size, and the probabilities are less than 0.10. The approximate probability of finding x defectives in a random sample is given by the Poisson expression

$$P(x) = \frac{(np)^x}{x!}\, e^{-np}$$

where x = number of defectives for which we wish to find the probability
n = sample size

p = actual proportion of defectives in lot
e = base of natural logarithms = 2.71828

Rather than solving this equation for each value of x for which we need a probability, we look in Appendix III which is a tabulation of values for the Poisson distribution. The probability that a lot as good as the AQL (that is, with 2 percent defectives) will be accepted is the probability that 0, 1, or 2 defectives will be found in a sample of 60 units. The expected value for a sample of 60 from a lot that has 2 percent defectives is $np = 60 \times 0.02 = 1.2$. Looking in the row of Appendix III that has 1.2 for the np value, we find that the probability that 2 or fewer will occur is 0.879. This is the probability that a lot would be accepted, so the producer's risk α (the risk it will be rejected) is $1 - 0.879 = 0.121$.

The consumer's risk β is the probability that a lot with 5 percent defectives will be accepted. This is the probability of getting 2 or fewer defectives when the expected number is $0.05 \times 60 = 3.0$. Looking in the appropriate row of Appendix III, we find the probability of 2 or fewer to be 0.423. Therefore the value of β for the sampling plan that Rocky arbitrarily proposed is 0.423. This is the probability that the Granite Isle Insurance Company would accept a lot of paperweights that contained 5 percent defectives.

Rocky considered the risk to both parties. He could understand that a supplier would not reduce its price if there were a 12 percent chance that very good products would be rejected. Rocky decided that in the future, instead of arbitrarily selecting a sampling plan, he would examine the operating characteristic curves for several plans and propose one that had a reasonable risk to both parties.

Average Outgoing Quality (AOQ) and Its Limit

Suppose the output of some process is passed in lots to an inspection station where the lots are subjected to acceptance sampling according to some sampling plan. If the sample from a lot does not meet the acceptance criterion, the lot is screened by checking 100 percent of the items and the defective units are either replaced with good ones or they are simply removed, depending on the established policy. Over the long run, the average quality leaving the inspection station (called the *average outgoing quality* or *AOQ*) would be better than the average quality being sent to this station, unless the incoming quality were perfect, making the two quality levels equal.

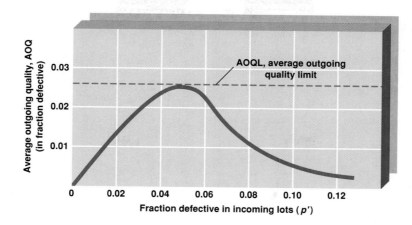

Figure 10.14
An AOQ Curve

For a specified sampling plan the probability that an incoming lot would be rejected and upgraded depends on the number of defectives in the incoming lot. We will use p' to represent the average proportion or fraction defective in the incoming lots. If the average incoming quality is very good, that is, p' is small, the sampling plan in unlikely to reject many lots and cause them to be upgraded. The outgoing quality will still be good and somewhat better than the incoming quality if any lots are upgraded. If the incoming quality is very bad, most lots will be rejected by the sampling plan and will be upgraded by removing or replacing the bad items, resulting in a very good AOQ. Somewhere between very good incoming quality and very poor incoming quality the sampling plan does its worst job of upgrading quality, resulting in what is called the average outgoing quality limit (AOQL). At this level of incoming quality some of the lots are not very good but some of the poor ones are undetected by the sampling plan. Figure 10.14 shows what is called an AOQ curve, which is a plot of the average incoming quality versus the average outgoing quality. Notice that very good quality is at the origin of the graph. As the average incoming quality gets worse the outgoing fraction defective goes up, then reaches a peak, and then improves as it moves to the right. The AOQL is the height of the peak of this curve. Each possible sampling plan will have a different AOQ curve. One method of evaluating and selecting sampling plans is to compare the AOQL's for various plans and select the one that gives the best protection over the long run.

Dodge-Romig Tables

The Dodge-Romig sampling tables, cited in footnote 3, are organized so that the user can select a sampling plan based on either of two criteria. Some plans are arranged so that the user can select a plan based on choice of AOQL; others are arranged so that the user can select a plan based on choice of a particular LTPD that will give a consumer's risk of 0.10.

If only occasional lots of an item are purchased, the purchasing company might prefer to select a plan based on the LTPD to provide the specified degree of protection from accepting a bad lot. For higher-volume items that are purchased in a continuing series of lots, the company might be primarily interested in controlling the average level of quality and might select a plan on the basis of the AOQL.

Military Standard 105D

Other sampling plans can be found in Military Standard 105D, a quality standard prepared for U.S. government procurement and sometimes used for commercial contracts. This standard provides plans based on the AQL and is oriented to specifying the producer's risk. Single-, double-, and multiple-sampling plans are given. The plans provide for normal sampling under normal circumstances, with a shift to tightened sampling if quality appears to have deteriorated. The plans permit reduced inspection if quality is very good for a series of prior samples and the process is running at a steady rate.

SUMMARY

Quality involves all the activities necessary to ensure that the customer receives satisfactory performance, including assurance that the product or service is adequately designed and conforms to the design. It may also include efforts to train consumers in proper use, to design safeguards to prevent misuse, and to ensure that reasonable service and repair capabilities are available to the user.

Statistical techniques often are used to help control and improve quality. Three general types of statistical techniques used are process control, acceptance sampling, and traditional techniques. Process control applications are employed to infer whether the processing operations are performing within the usual amount of chance-cause variation. Acceptance sampling is used to infer the acceptability of the particular lot or batch from which the sample was extracted. Traditional techniques are employed to measure the extent of variation, understand the relationship between variables, and seek the causes of problems or potential problems. The objective of process control is prevention of off-quality results, while the objective of traditional analysis is often to improve quality still further. Consequently, both of these applications are increasing in importance and popularity.

Both process control and acceptance sampling may be based on either attribute data or variable data. Attribute data simply classify the inspected goods or services as either acceptable or unacceptable. Variable data involve a measurement of the extent to which an actual characteristic varies from some target measurement for that characteristic.

Process control can be performed by direct workers and is a very effective means of preventing defective work. Hence it often improves both quality and productivity. Process control relies on control charts and limits to indicate the adequate (or otherwise) performance of the processes that produced the measured characteristic. Control charts for the mean $\bar{X}$ and the range R are used for control when sampling is done by variables. Process control for sampling by attributes may employ a control chart for p, the fraction of the items that are defective, or a control chart for c, the number of defects within some amount of output.

Acceptance sampling requires some sampling plan, such as single, double, or sequential sampling. Since sampling cannot guarantee 100 percent accuracy in the assessment of quality, there is some risk to the producer that good products will be rejected and some risk to the consumer that defective products will be accepted.

Efforts to control, understand, and improve quality require methods that can provide insights into numerical data which usually contain some unexplained dispersion. Providing employees with an understanding of basic statistical methods gives them tools for collecting and interpreting this type of data. Then actions are more likely to be based on facts instead of guesses or assumptions.

KEY TERMS

Statistical process control (SPC)

Chance-cause variation

Control chart

In control

Out of control

Assignable cause of variation

Upper control limit (UCL)

Lower control limit (LCL)

Attribute data

Variable data

Control chart for the mean, or $\bar{X}$ chart

Control chart for the range, or R chart

Control chart for the fraction defective, or p chart

Control chart for defects per unit, or c chart

Single sampling

Double sampling

Sequential sampling

Sample size, n

Acceptance number, c

Operating characteristic curve, or OC curve

Acceptable quality level (AQL)

Producer's risk

Lot tolerance percent defective (LTPD)

Consumer's risk

Average outgoing quality (AOQ)

DEMONSTRATION PROBLEMS

Problem

Incoming steel to be used in processing is tested to see that it is of the right chemical composition before it is machined. Dimensions of the machined parts are inspected prior to the heat-treating operation. An automatic heat-treating furnace is set at a temperature which hardens the parts. The temperature is set so that the average force required to break the part is 32,000 pounds. The inherent variability of the heat-treating process produces a standard deviation of the breaking force of 3,000 pounds. Establish the control limits for $\bar{X}$ so that $\alpha = 0.10$ when samples of size $n = 4$ are taken.

Solution

$$\sigma_{\bar{X}} = \frac{\sigma}{\sqrt{n}} = \frac{3,000}{\sqrt{4}}$$

$$= 1,500 \text{ pounds}$$

$$Z_{1-\alpha/2} = Z_{0.95} = 1.645$$

$$\text{UCL}_{\bar{X}} = \mu + Z\sigma_{\bar{X}}$$

$$= 32,000 + 1.645(1,500)$$

$$= 32,000 + 2,467.5$$

$$= 34,467.5 \text{ pounds}$$

$$\text{LCL}_{\bar{X}} = \mu - Z\sigma_{\bar{X}} = 32,000 - 2,467.5$$

$$= 29,532.5 \text{ pounds}$$

Question for Further Consideration

What is the probability that an $\bar{X}$ from a random sample of 4 observations ($n = 4$) will fall within these limits if the mean of the population actually is at 31,000 pounds? That is, what is β (that is, the probability of a type II error) if $\mu = 31,000$? What is β if $\mu = 30,000$?

Problem

Establish the 3σ control limits for R for the process described above.

Solution

From Table 1 of Appendix V, we find that d_2 for samples of size $n = 4$ is 2.059. Since $d_2 = \bar{R}/\sigma'$, we can find an estimate of $\bar{R}$ for samples of 4 taken from this process.

$$2.059 = \bar{R}/3,000 \quad \text{so} \quad \bar{R} = 2.059(3,000) = 6,177$$

From Table 2 of Appendix V we can obtain the constants D_3 and D_4 for samples of size 4. Using these values, we can compute the control limits for R.

$$\text{UCL}_R = D_4\bar{R} = 2.28(6,177) = 14,083.6$$

$$\text{LCL}_R = D_3\bar{R} = 0(6,177) = 0$$

Problem

The radiology department at a large hospital has an average retake rate of 8.8 percent; that is, 8.8 percent of its X-rays must be repeated because the picture is not sufficiently clear. Errors can occur because of incorrect patient measurement, improper calibration or setting of the machine, poor film quality, incorrect film processing, or other reasons. During the past month 9,000 X-rays were taken, and 11.2 percent had to be repeated. Does the process appear to be within its 3σ limits, or does it appear that there may be some assignable cause for variation?

Solution

$$\bar{p} = 0.088$$

Control limits for p when a sample of 9,000 is taken are

$$\bar{p} \pm 3 \sqrt{\frac{\bar{p}(1 - \bar{p})}{9,000}}$$

$$= 0.088 \pm 3 \sqrt{\frac{0.088(1 - 0.088)}{9,000}}$$

$$= 0.088 \pm 0.00896 = 0.0970 \text{ and } 0.0790$$

The value of 11.2 percent defective is very much outside the 3σ limits for the process.

Problem

Twenty samples were taken from a cable-weaving machine while it was being operated under closely controlled conditions. The number of defects per 100 meters for the samples is recorded in the chart below. Determine the control chart limits for the machine.

4	4	5	3
6	2	2	4
5	3	4	2
3	2	4	5
5	7	5	3

Solution

$$\bar{c} = \frac{\Sigma c}{n} = \frac{78}{20} = 3.9$$

Control limits for the number of defects per 100 meters are $\bar{c} \pm 3\sqrt{\bar{c}}$. So

$$\text{UCL} = 3.9 + 3\sqrt{3.9} = 9.8$$

$$\text{LCL} = 3.9 - 3\sqrt{3.9} \qquad \text{or} \qquad 0,$$

whichever is greater. Therefore, LCL = 0.

DISCUSSION QUESTIONS

1. What are three general areas in which statistics can be applied to control and improve quality?

2. Give four reasons why companies may use samples instead of checking every item. When might a company prefer to check every item?

3. Which is generally considered better, preventive or corrective approaches to quality control? Why?

4. What is the purpose of SPC?

5. What are the meanings of the terms *in control* and *out of control?*

6. In establishing trial control limits, why are the limits for *R* established first?

7. **a.** What is meant by the consumer's risk?
   b. What is meant by the producer's risk?

8. Supplier selection and supplier relations are considered important to the purchasing department. Should the quality assurance department ever become involved in these issues? Why, or why not?

9. Under what conditions would a *p* or *c* chart be used instead of $\bar{X}$ and *R* charts?

10. How does the precision or exactness of the testing or measuring method that is used affect the applicability of control charts? What does variability in the testing method do to α? To β?

11. Would it ever be advisable for control limits to be placed much beyond the $3\sigma_{\bar{X}}$ control limits? When?

12. **a.** Can you inspect quality into a product? Explain.
    b. Can extreme care in production offset a poor design? Explain.

13. Can proper application of quality control methods actually reduce costs while improving quality? Give a reason for your response.

PROBLEMS

1. An experienced operator has operated a machine over several days, being careful to keep assignable causes of variation absent from the process. Twenty-five random samples of $n = 6$ were taken during this time, and $\Sigma \bar{X} = 75.186$ cm and $\Sigma R = 4.270$ cm. Compute control limits for $\bar{X}$ and R that are 3 standard deviations from their expected value. Assume the process mean was correctly set.

2. Samples of size 6 were taken from a process while it was operated under carefully controlled conditions, and the following measurements were found: $\bar{\bar{X}} = 5.240$ cm, and $\bar{R} = 0.0026$ cm. Establish 3σ control limits for the mean and the range.

3. Thirty samples of size $n = 8$ were taken from a process, and the following measures were calculated: $\Sigma \bar{X} = 44.682$ and $\Sigma R = 0.114$.
   a. Determine the 3σ control limits for $\bar{X}$, using Appendix V.
   b. Determine the 3σ control limits for R, using Appendix V.

4. A machine for bagging hard candy will drop at least one more piece into a bag if the contents weigh 8 ounces or less. Twenty-five samples of size $n = 4$ were taken, and the following sums were calculated: $\Sigma \bar{X} = 205.513$ and $\Sigma R = 2.325$ ounces.
   a. Establish 3σ control limits for $\bar{X}$.
   b. Establish 3σ control limits for R.

5. A process is set so that it coats roofing with a layer of material that weighs an average of 6 pounds per square yard. The standard deviation of the process, under controlled conditions measured on a square yard of roofing, is 0.124 pound. Determine the upper and lower control limits for $\bar{X}$ so that $\alpha = 0.05$ when samples of size $n = 6$ are taken.

6. A process is to produce a product that will stand an average force of 20,000 pounds. The variance of the product's strength is 727,618 pounds-squared.
   a. Specify the control limits for $\bar{X}$ so that $\alpha = 0.05$ when samples of size 4 are used.
   b. Establish control limits for $\bar{X}$ when samples of size 5 are to be taken and the desired probability of a type I error is 0.03.

7. The specifications for a shaft diameter call for it to be 2.000 inches with a tolerance of ±0.005 inch. The processing equipment has an inherent variation that is normally distributed with $\sigma = 0.002$ inch.
   a. When the process is correctly set at 2.000 inches and maintained in control, what percentage of the products will fall outside the product tolerance?
   b. What percentage will fall outside the product tolerance when the process is centered at 1.995 inches?

8. Specifications call for a dimension to be 1.285 ± 0.005 inches. The variation in the equipment and processing results in a standard deviation of 0.003 inch for this dimension.
   a. What percentage of the parts will be outside the specification if the process is centered properly?
   b. What percentage of the parts will be out of spec if the process is actually centered at 1.282 inches?

9. Suppose the company in problem 8 works to reduce the process standard deviation to 0.002 inch.
   a. What percentage of the parts will be out of spec if the process is properly centered?
   b. What percentage of the parts will be out of spec if the process is actually centered at 1.282 inches?

10. Specifications for a plastic material call for one of its ingredients to be between 6.20 and 6.40 percent with a target composition of 6.30 percent. The current measuring and mixing procedures result in a normally distributed variation of this ingredient with a standard deviation of 0.040 percent. The properties of this material are very

inconsistent, and the company is to begin reducing the variability of this troublesome ingredient. The company will buy its supplies from fewer suppliers so there will be less variation in their compositions, maintain its equipment so it operates more consistently, and have all employees follow a standardized mixing procedure.

a. Before the above-mentioned improvements are implemented, what percent of the material will be out of specification if the process is centered correctly on target?

b. If the improvements are made and reduce the variation in the amount of the troublesome ingredient so the standard deviation is 0.030 percent, how much reduction will this make in the percent of out-of-spec material when the process is correctly centered?

11. Specifications for an item call for it to have a strength of at least 900 kilograms per square centimeter. The ingredients and processing that raise the item's strength are expensive, so the intent is to center the process so that the mean strength will be 1,100. The process has a σ of 100 and is normally distributed.

a. Construct 95 percent control limits for $\bar{X}$ when samples of size 6 are taken.

b. What portion of production will be below the specifications limit if the process is properly centered?

12. Find the probability that the $\bar{X}$ of a random sample of 6 observations will fall inside the control limits for $\bar{X}$ that were found in problem 11 if σ remains equal to 100 kilograms but the mean of the process shifts to (a) 1,050, (b) 1,000, (c) 950.

13. Refer to the data in problem 11. Suppose that the process is correctly centered at 1,100 kilograms but σ increases to 150. What portion of production will be below the specifications limit?

14. A process is known to have a σ of 1.27 kilograms. Control limits have been established at 3 standard deviations on either side of a target weight of 20 kilograms for samples of size $n = 4$. What is β if the process is actually centered at 19.82 kilograms?

15. A process has been operating for several weeks and found to produce an average of 1.22 percent defectives. Establish the 3σ limits for the proportion defective when samples of 1,000 units are to be taken.

16. The supervisor of a stenographic pool is developing control charts for typing reports and memorandums. Random samples of 30 pages of the daily output have been selected and proofread. The fractions defective for 15 samples were recorded as follows: 0.067, 0.10, 0.133, 0.133, 0.067, 0.0, 0.10, 0.033, 0.10, 0.033, 0.067, 0.167, 0.200, 0.067, 0.033. Does the process appear to be in control? (Use 3σ control limits.) Under what circumstances would a chart of these control limits be useful?

17. Silverware at the Riverview Restaurant is washed by an automatic washer. It is inspected as employees select 24 pieces of tableware to set a table and return any that are not satisfactorily cleaned to a container for dirty silver. Normally this procedure averages 1 unsatisfactorily cleaned item out of 24. Today an average of 4 out of 24 were unsatisfactory. Does this suggest that something is amiss in the washing process—that is, does 4 fall outside the control limits for samples of 24?

18. A sharpening machine at the Carolina Electric Razor Company sharpens the blades on rotary cutter heads for electric razors. If there is a burr on any of the cutter blades, the razor will not operate properly, so random samples of 50 parts are inspected regularly to see if the machine is operating properly. The results of 10 samples are 0.08, 0.08, 0.04, 0.12, 0.20, 0.24, 0.04, 0.12, 0.08, 0.04. Establish the 3σ control limits for the proportion defective for this process.

19. A production process makes large sheets of plate glass with an average of 2.42 defects per sheet. Establish 3σ control limits for the defects per unit for this process.

20. A process produces microminiature circuit chips with a reject rate of 11.2 percent when it is operating satisfactorily. During a day when the process was operated with materials from a new supplier, 12 defective chips were found in 50 randomly selected chips. Is there cause to suspect that the process is not functioning properly?

21. A police department wants to establish control limits for the number of crimes per week within certain neighborhoods so that they will recognize when and if patrol protection should be increased. If an average of 4.38 crimes per week occurs within a neighborhood, establish 95 percent control limits for the crime process.

22. Spools of wire have been tested and found to contain an average of 3.71 defects per spool. Establish the 3σ control limits for the defects per unit when the wire-making process is in control.

23. Twelve bolts of printed fabric have been carefully examined to determine the number of defects in each bolt. The number of defects found in each was 4, 3, 5, 3, 7, 4, 6, 5, 3, 1, 8, and 6, respectively. Careful attention was paid to see that the process was in control when these samples were taken. Establish limits that can be used to determine if the process remains in control.

24. Cases of a particular type of computer disks have been found to contain an average of 1.62 defects per case. Construct the 3σ limits for the number of defects in a case of these disks.

25. Rocky Davis has stated that a sampling plan of $n = 100$, $c = 4$ will be used for purchasing simulated granite paperweights. Find the probability that a lot with the AQL of 0.02 defective will be rejected. Find the probability that a lot of 0.03 defective will be accepted. Find the probability that a lot with the LTPD of 0.05 defective will be accepted. Use the Poisson table in Appendix III. How do these probabilities compare to those shown in the Granite Isle application presented in this chapter? Why?

26. Develop the OC curve for the sampling plan $n = 40$, $c = 2$, and for the plan $n = 80$, $c = 4$. Assume that the Poisson distribution can be applied. What are the α's for the two plans if AQL = 0.02? What are the β's for the plans if LTPD = 0.08?

27. A single-sampling plan uses $n = 30$, $c = 1$. What is α at AQL = 0.01? What is β at LTPD = 0.06? Assume the Poisson approximation can be used.

28. A single sampling plan uses $n = 60$ and $c = 2$. The lot size of 600 is large enough that the Poisson table in Appendix III can be used. Construct the OC curve for this sampling plan.

COMPUTER-BASED PROBLEMS

1. Construct a spreadsheet template to compute the 3σ control limits for $\bar{X}$ and R from 15 samples of size $n = 3$. You will need 15 rows and 3 columns to record the data given in the table below. Determine $\bar{X}$, the maximum, the minimum, and $\bar{R}$ for each sample; then compute $\bar{\bar{X}}$ and $\bar{R}$. Store the appropriate constants in the program so that the limits are calculated and displayed.

2. If graphics are available, plot the control limits and the $\bar{X}$ and R values from the samples.

SAMPLE	OBSERVED DIMENSIONS (CM)			SAMPLE	OBSERVED DIMENSIONS (CM)		
1	4.843	4.863	4.859	9	4.904	4.863	4.866
2	4.925	4.882	4.891	10	4.921	4.920	4.894
3	4.866	4.914	4.873	11	4.914	4.884	4.899
4	4.852	4.883	4.880	12	4.892	4.896	4.887
5	4.920	4.884	4.821	13	4.866	4.829	4.880
6	4.915	4.902	4.898	14	4.850	4.875	4.872
7	4.887	4.892	4.858	15	4.867	4.900	4.885
8	4.868	4.888	4.842				

BIBLIOGRAPHY

Banks, Jerry. *Principles of Quality Control.* New York: Wiley, 1989.

Berry, Leonard L., Valarie A. Zeithmal, and A. Parasuraman. "Quality Counts in Services, Too." *Business Horizons 28,* no. 3 (May–June 1985): 44–52.

"Buying Quality" (a series of articles). *Purchasing 104,* no. 2 (January 28, 1988).

Deming, W. Edwards. *Out of the Crisis.* Cambridge, Mass.: MIT CAES, 1986.

DiPrimio, Anthony. *Quality Assurance in Service Organizations.* Radnor, Pa.: Chilton, 1987.

Dodge, H. F., and H. G. Romig. *Sampling Inspection Tables.* 2d ed. New York: Wiley, 1959.

Enrick, Norbert L. *Quality, Reliability, and Process Improvement.* 8th ed. New York: Industrial Press, 1985.

Evans, James R. *Statistical Process Control for Quality Improvement: A Training Guide to Learning SPC.* Englewood Cliffs, N.J.: Prentice-Hall, 1991.

"Facing Up to the Quality Issue" (a series of articles). *Purchasing 103,* no. 8 (November 5, 1987): 37–63.

Feigenbaum, Armand V. *Total Quality Control.* 3d ed. New York: McGraw-Hill, 1983.

Gitlow, Howard, et al. *Tools and Methods for the Improvement of Quality.* Homewood, Ill.: Irwin, 1989.

Glossary and Tables for Statistical Quality Control. Milwaukee: American Society for Quality Control, 1983.

Ishikawa, Kaoru. *Guide to Quality Control.* Tokyo: Asian Productivity Organization, 1982.

———. *What Is Total Quality Control? The Japanese Way.* Trans. David J. Lu. Englewood Cliffs, N.J.: Prentice-Hall, 1985.

Juran, Joseph M. *Quality Planning and Analysis.* 3d ed. New York: McGraw-Hill, 1993.

Just-in-Time/Quality Conference Proceedings. Falls Church, Va.: American Production and Inventory Society, 1987.

Mitra, Amitava. *Fundamentals of Quality Control and Improvement.* New York: Macmillan, 1993.

Montgomery, Douglas C. *Introduction to Statistical Quality Control.* 2d ed. New York: Wiley, 1991.

"The Push for Quality" (a special report series). *Business Week,* June 8, 1987, pp. 131–143.

Smith, Gerald. *Statistical Process Control and Quality Improvement.* Englewood Cliffs, N.J.: Prentice-Hall, 1995.

PLANNING
FOR OPERATIONS
AND CAPACITY

CHAPTER 11

A large portion of management activities involves working with others to develop plans that appear to be best for their organization's success and to see that the plans are executed. Other members of the organization may participate in the planning process, but it is management's responsibility to see that plans are developed that will lead to the organization's success. Once good plans are developed, managers work to see that the plans are well executed.

If the organization is to carry out its plans it must have all the resources that are needed to ensure successful performance. A part of good planning, therefore, includes developing plans to provide sufficient, but not excessive, amounts of all the right resources when they are needed. A business will need sufficient people with the proper skills, building space, power, telephones, and perhaps computers and other equipment necessary to serve its customers well. The matter of planning for facilities was discussed in Chapter 5 since it is closely related to the subject of location selection. It was pointed out there that establishment of the facility often requires a long lead time and usually is considered in the long-range planning of a company. A company's buildings are usually considered to represent a relatively fixed upper limit to a company's internal capacity within the near- or intermediate-range time horizon (with some exceptions where an existing building can be leased, purchased, or expanded).

United Airlines has a work scheduling system called the Station Manpower Planning System (SMPS). The SMPS combines management science and computers to arrive at the optimal utilization of its labor force. The system not only ensures that the right number of people are on the job at the right time, it also allows employees more flexibility in their schedules.

United Airlines

In this chapter we discuss planning the adjustable work capacity within the short- or intermediate-range time horizon. The resources to provide adjustable capacity that are considered and discussed are:

1. The work force size (whether temporary, "permanent," part time, or full time)
2. The number of hours they work in a day or week
3. The amount of work that will be performed with outside capacity through purchasing items made elsewhere or through subcontracting
4. Possible inventory

Inventory is considered when a company's work products can be stored, because this inventory provides a way to use capacity in one time period to serve demand in some later time period. It is, in essence, storing capacity.

The basic approach to capacity planning can be summarized as follows. Upper management determines in general terms the level of business that the company is to be prepared to conduct. Each function then plans the resources it will require to perform at the planned level. Usually there is a great deal of interaction among the parts of the company and with top management to develop plans and coordinate them and to get approval for adding resources, but the general approach outlined above is often followed. The general planning with top management is often referred to as business planning and it will be discussed first in the chapter. Then we will discuss production planning, which is the highest, or most general, level of planning that takes place in the operations function. After that we discuss aggregate planning, which is the planning efforts to provide sufficient capacity to carry out the production plan in a cost-effective way. Considerable discussion will elaborate on some methods and examples of aggregate planning. The later part of the chapter discusses the more-specific planning that must be done for the near portion of the company's plans. For a service company the detailed near-term plan may be called the work schedule or simply the schedule. It designates the specific jobs that are to be performed in the near future and when. In a manufacturing company this nearer-range plan is often called the master production schedule. It specifies which products are to be made, how many, and when they are to be completed. The chapter ends with a discussion of rough-cut capacity planning, which is a more-detailed method of ensuring that the schedule is within the capacity of the company and makes reasonable use of the company's capacity.

We use manufacturing examples primarily because they usually require more detail and span a longer time horizon than plans in many services. Manufacturers must plan for obtaining every component and raw material required, in addition to planning all the work activities that are necessary to convert these inputs into products. Some services do not require materials, so their planning focuses on just the work activities. But planning capacity for the work activities in these services is similar to the capacity planning discussed in this chapter.

Manufacturing operations must plan to make both the capacity and the materials available so a product can be produced. Since capacity is usually less flexible than materials deliveries, the usual approach is to first develop plans that make sufficient capacity available and that use the capacity wisely. The company can then plan supplier deliveries of materials to facilitate execution of the plan. Although the primary focus in this chapter is on planning capacity, remember that the capacity plans must be coordinated with materials plans for manufacturing operations and for some services. This need to coordinate capacity and materials plans is mentioned only occasionally in this chapter. Chapters 12, 13, and 14 discuss materials management in greater detail.

BUSINESS PLANNING

Strategic planning which was discussed in Chapter 2 involves the creation of a long-term plan for the overall business. The strategic plan defines such issues as the types of goods and services that will be offered, the territories in which the company will serve customers, and the performance characteristics to be developed and emphasized. This plan and the company's mission give overall guidance regarding how the company will operate and try to attract demand. Forecasts provide estimates of the level of demand that the company expects to result from its efforts. Based on these forecasts of demand, the company can formulate plans for investments and other aspects of running the business.

Many manufacturing companies use a formal *business planning* process. Business planning addresses both the long- and intermediate-range decisions for running the overall business. Usually, the conditions and decisions are evaluated in terms of their financial impact on the business, and the plans are expressed in financial terms. Plans are considered for such matters as new product introductions, levels of sales in dollars, new process requirements, capital investments, and new distribution strategies. The long-range aspects of business planning may be evaluated quarterly, semiannually, or annually with an assessment of conditions and formulation of a general plan for a horizon out as far as 5 years or more.

Long-range business planning has an impact on operation's activities and capacity. Capital budgets for new or expanded facilities and major equipment purchases must be developed in the general, long-term business planning. Forecasts of the amount and type of facilities needed in distant time periods are relatively vague and uncertain, because economic and competitive conditions can change significantly during the intervening time. Nevertheless, long-lead-time activities such as facility construction must be begun early so they can be available at future dates. Frequently it takes years to design a facility, acquire the site, construct the building, and purchase the necessary furnishings and equipment. Since facilities usually cannot be changed in the intermediate horizon, they represent an approximate upper limit of the company's internal capacity and are sometimes referred to as *fixed capacity*. This limit can sometimes be "stretched" by leasing facilities that may be available outside the company and by changing make-or-buy decisions to purchase a larger amount of its inputs from suppliers and subcontractors.

More-frequent (usually monthly) meetings are held to develop greater detail for the intermediate-range portion (maybe 18 months or more) of the business plan. These meetings, sometimes referred to as "sales and operations planning," seek to coordinate the operating decisions and intermediate-range plans of the various functions within the business. This type of business planning typically involves the general manager, such as the chief executive officer (CEO), and the managers of functions such as manufacturing, marketing, finance, and engineering—particularly if the company is a make-to-order manufacturing company. Materials management is often represented because much of the planning relates to activities involving materials. This committee meets to review conditions, reach coordinated execution decisions for the near periods, and formulate coordinated intermediate-range plans for the various functions, so that all plans are aimed at the goals established in the long-range business plan. These plans have to be achievable within the constraints of the facilities made available as a result of long-range decisions made earlier.

The group reviews marketing's assessment of what can be sold, operation's assessment of what can be produced, and finance's assessment of monetary needs and the financial impact of alternative plans. Engineering may present plans for product modifications and possible new products. The result of this planning is a more-

It took long-range planning to design and construct the Weyerhaeuser Norpac plant in Longview, Washington, but the goal was speed. At 45 mph, it takes 10 seconds to convert pulp into finished newsprint.

Kevin Horan/Stock, Boston

HOW CAPACITY PLANNING CAN HELP ADD VALUE FOR CUSTOMERS

Planning ahead to make the necessary amount of the right types of skills and equipment available can help achieve high quality. Sufficient capacity to allow adequate time for production and maintenance operations improves operation's dependability. Sufficient capacity also provides for flexibility to change product mix and production volume in response to customers' desires, thus allowing operations to respond quickly with what customers value.

detailed business plan for the intermediate horizon, or the "sales and operations plan," which is based on anticipated sales in dollars for the time periods in the intermediate planning horizon. Accounting data can be used to project the cost of sales, payroll costs, inventory levels, and pro forma profits. This information is used as a basis for planning budgets for the various departments and activities.

Business planning is sometimes referred to as the manager's handle on running the business. One CEO remarked after the business planning sessions had been held for several months that he felt more like a coach guiding the parts of the business in a coordinated game plan. Before initiating the process, he had felt as if he were a referee trying to settle problems and disputes, after the fact, when some mismatch occurred among certain functions in the company.

THE PRODUCTION PLAN

The business planning process guides each function in coordination with the others. The portion of the intermediate-range business plan which the operations function is responsible for implementing is usually called the *production plan* in a manufacturing company. Sometimes it is called an operations plan, particularly in a service company. The production plan states, in general terms, the total amount of output that is the responsibility of manufacturing to produce for each period in the planning horizon. The output may be expressed as worth in dollars, tons, gallons, or units of a *pseudoproduct,* which is a fictitious product that represents the weighted average of all the products in the product line. The production plan is manufacturing's commitment to support the overall business plan which has been agreed to by the general manager and coordinated with the other functions.

The production plan is useful for top-level coordination of plans for various parts of a company. Toward the intermediate- or near-term horizon this plan is manufacturing's authorization to produce products at a rate consistent with marketing plans, financial resources, and other parts of the overall business. Since the production plan is expressed in dollars or some other general measure of output, it is not specific enough to be the basis for purchasing the specific materials and scheduling production of all the individual product models. While time periods are still far enough into the future, the production plan for those periods must be developed into a detailed master production schedule (MPS) which states specific products to be produced and when. Figure 11.1 shows the planning steps involved in developing the general business plan and refining it into the specific master production schedule.

Figure 11.1
Development of More-
Detailed Levels of Plans

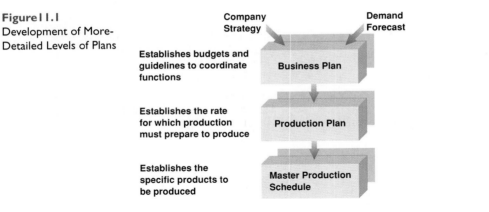

Establishes budgets and
guidelines to coordinate
functions

Establishes the rate
for which production
must prepare to produce

Establishes the
specific products to
be produced

Consider, for example, a company that manufactures televisions. The production plan might be expressed as "units," or the number of televisions that the company plans to produce each month for the next 12 months, without regard to the type of televisions they are. The product line can be described in various levels of detail as shown in Figure 11.2. The overall aggregation of the product line is shown at the top of the figure as the average television, a pseudoproduct. This product line could be broken into various levels of detail by dividing it into groups such as portable and console models, or by other classifications. At some point in the planning, the specific models that are going to be produced must be identified so purchasing can buy the right components and raw materials for their production. That is, the production plan must be "disaggregated," or divided, into how many of each specific model of televisions are going to be made in each time period.

Until time periods move close enough to forecast them reasonably accurately there is no need to develop a master production schedule stating in detail a specific mix of product operations plans for production, because the forecast and the schedule will probably change before the company begins work to carry out the schedule. As time periods get closer to the current date, the quantity in the production plan for a period will be disaggregated, or subdivided, into the specific items and quantities that will be produced in that period. Thus for the near portion of the planning horizon there is a detailed MPS. For periods beyond the MPS the production plan is the best estimate of the amount of capacity the operations function will need to make available. So capacity plans for the more distant periods in the intermediate time horizon are based on the production plan. Typically make-to-stock companies, particularly if they have seasonal demand, plan capacity for periods beyond the MPS to allow sufficient lead time for such changes as building up and training the work force

Figure 11.2
Aggregation of the
Product Line for a
Television Manufacturer

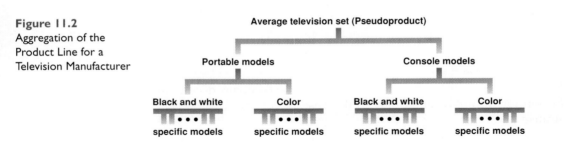

or building seasonal inventory, and so forth. Such companies must develop general or aggregate-level capacity plans based on the production plan. This plan can be adjusted or "fine-tuned" for the near portion of the planning horizon after the MPS for those periods has been developed. We will now discuss planning capacity based on the production plan. Later we will discuss the master production schedule in detail and present some specifics about disaggregating the production plan into the MPS and a more-detailed method of determining capacity requirements for periods in the near portion of the planning horizon for which the MPS is developed.

AGGREGATE PLANNING: PROVIDING CAPACITY FOR THE PRODUCTION PLAN

It is important that operations have sufficient capacity to carry out the commitment stated in the production plan. Operations must evaluate the plan and determine the best general strategy for providing in a cost-effective way the proper amount of capacity to produce at the level in the production plan. It is advisable to check the amount of capacity required by the production plan in certain periods while those periods are far enough in the future to change the capacity in some departments, if necessary. This is particularly true for businesses that have significant seasonal variations in demand. A procedure called capacity planning or aggregate planning is used to evaluate the capacity requirements and to plan the best way to make the capacity available. We use primarily the latter term. *Aggregate planning* is the process of aggregating (that is, consolidating or grouping) all the requirements for capacity for each period in the intermediate horizon and determining the best way to provide the needed capacity. The objectives are:

1. *Feasibility.* The internal capacity needs must be within the capability of the operations system.

2. *Optimality.* It is desirable to determine the least costly way to meet the capacity needs.

Aggregate planning considers the variables that can be used to adjust the capacity within the intermediate horizon. The most common variables in *adjustable capacity* are the work force size, the production rate in terms of the number of hours worked per day or week (this amounts to the use of overtime work or idle time), and inventory if it can be used to "store capacity" in one period so it can serve demand in some later period. (Services usually cannot store inventory of their output.) Sometimes back-ordering and subcontracting are used. If only one variable is adjusted to deal with a nonuniform demand within the planning horizon, it is called a "pure strategy"; the adjustment of more than one variable is called a "mixed strategy." Table 11.1 presents some cost factors and other considerations related to some variables that may be used to adjust operations capacity.

Aggregate planning can be a significant challenge when there is a varying demand pattern such as seasonality that results in a varying production plan. Engaging in this type of planning can lead to significant savings in some situations, however. Consider the demand pattern shown in Figure 11.3a. If the company decides to match the production rate to the demand rate, so that inventory is not used (this is called a "chase strategy"), it will require capital investment in sufficient fixed capacity to serve the peak demand. (Many service companies cannot use inventory and face

Table 11.1
SOME STRATEGIES THAT MAY BE USED FOR MEETING NONUNIFORM DEMAND

1. Strategy: Absorb Demand Fluctuations by Varying Inventory Level, Back-Ordering, or Shifting Demand

METHODS	COSTS	REMARKS
Produce in earlier period and hold until product is demanded.	Cost of holding inventory	Service operations cannot hold service inventory. They must staff for peak levels and/or shift deman
Offer to deliver the product or service later, when capacity is available.	Delay in receipt of revenue, at minimum; may result in lost customers	Manufacturing companies with perishable products often are restrained in the use of this method.
Exert special marketing efforts to shift the demand to slack periods.	Costs of advertising, discounts, or promotional programs	This is another example of the interrelationship among functions within a business.

2. Strategy: Change Only the Production Rate in Accordance with the Nonuniform Demand Pattern

METHODS	COSTS	REMARKS
Work additional hours without changing the work force size.	Overtime premium pay	The time available for maintenance work without interrupting production is reduced.
Staff for high production levels so that overtime is not required.	Excess personnel wages during periods of slack demand	Sometimes work force can be utilized for deferred maintenance during periods of low demand.
Subcontract work to other firms.	Continuing company overhead plus subcontractors' overhead and profit	The capacity of other firms can be used, but there is less control of schedules and quality levels.
Revise make-or-buy decisions to purchase items when capacity is fully loaded.	Waste of company skills, tooling, and equipment unutilized in slack periods	All these methods require capital investments sufficient for the peak production rate, which will be underutilized in slack periods.

3. Strategy: Change the Size of the Work Force to Vary the Production Level in Accordance with Demand

METHODS	COSTS	REMARKS
Hire additional personnel as demand increases.	Employment costs for advertising, travel, interviewing, training, etc.; shift premium costs if additional shift is added	Skilled workers may not be available when needed, as they are likely to seek employment elsewhere.
Lay off personnel as demand subsides.	Cost of severance pay and increases in unemployment insurance costs; loss of efficiency due to decline in morale as high-seniority workers are moved into jobs for which they are inexperienced, "bumping" workers with less seniority	The company must have adequate capital investment in equipment for the peak work force level.

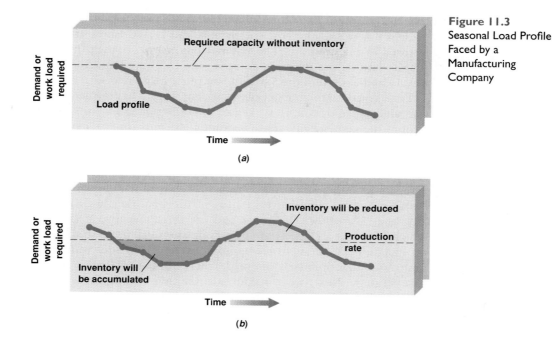

Figure 11.3
Seasonal Load Profile
Faced by a
Manufacturing
Company

this situation.) The full capital investment is utilized only during the peak-demand period, and the company will have a high payroll cost or employees will be uncertain about stable employment.

If inventory can be used, the company can operate with a lower level of capital investment, as shown in Figure 11.3*b*, and have a higher level of utilization of its capacity. Also, employees have more stable jobs. Inventory could be accumulated during the periods of low demand and sold to make up the difference between demand and capacity during the periods when demand is higher than capacity. It is called a "level strategy" when a uniform production rate is used and inventory is accumulated and reduced to absorb the difference between demand and production.

Aggregate planning can be performed by a variety of methods. The most common method is the trial-and-error or intuitive approach. We will illustrate this method and provide further insight into the nature of aggregate planning in the next section.

The Trial-and-Error Method

Trial and error is probably the most widely used method of aggregate planning. This method simply evaluates the cost of alternative ways of using resources to provide the necessary production capacity. Managers evaluate options until they arrive at the one that seems most desirable. The method does not involve elaborate mathematics to develop the best plan, so it is relatively easy to understand and use. The method does, however, involve tedious repetition of simple calculations to evaluate the costs of alternative plans. It is helpful to develop a table to display these calculations. In an actual application, such a table would be developed and the calculations repeated for several trials during each planning session. The planning process would be repeated at each planning session, say, every month. This repetition of calculations makes it desirable to develop a computer program or electronic spreadsheet to perform this work. The cost coefficients and relationships among the variables can be stored in the program. The planner has only to change the values of the desired variables and let the program compute the resulting cost. Alternative plans can thus be evaluated easily and quickly with computer assistance.

Let's go through an example of trial-and-error aggregate planning by evaluating some alternative operating strategies for Imperial Sail Company, which experiences seasonal demand for its original equipment and replacement boat sails. The estimated demand per period has been moved earlier to the period in which the production would have to occur and these production requirements are shown in Table 11.2. Often a graph helps one visualize the demand pattern and suggests possible aggregate planning strategies. Figure 11.4 shows the cumulative production requirements versus the cumulative months in the planning horizon, represented by the black line. Also shown in Figure 11.4 are the alternative strategies we will evaluate. We consider first a chase strategy, varying the work force so that cumulative production matches the cumulative requirements and coincides with the black line in the graph. Note that the black line represents both the production requirements and the chase strategy. Next, we consider maintaining a uniform production rate, represented by the orange line in the graph, so that all the variation in demand is accommodated by inventory that will be accumulated during part of the year. Finally, we consider a mixed strategy. This mixed strategy, represented by the blue line in the graph, changes the production rate and accumulates some inventory during the year.

Imperial's management estimates that the typical sail, the "pseudoproduct," requires 20 hours to produce. Each employee is estimated to contribute 168 hours per month, so each employee can produce about $168 \div 20 = 8.4$ average sails per month. No scrap or rework is assumed for their aggregate planning. Estimates indicate that it costs \$300 to hire an employee and \$400 to lay off an employee. It has been found that about 1,000 units should be available as work in process and safety stock, at least during peak production months, and this amount will be on hand at the start of the planning horizon. It costs \$6 per month to hold a unit in inventory.

Table 11.2
PRODUCTION REQUIREMENTS FOR IMPERIAL SAIL COMPANY, BY MONTH

(1) MONTH	(2) MONTHLY FORECAST PRODUCTION REQUIREMENTS (UNITS)	(3) CUMULATIVE PRODUCTION REQUIREMENTS
April	1,600	1,600
May	1,400	3,000
June	1,200	4,200
July	1,000	5,200
August	1,500	6,700
September	2,000	8,700
October	2,500	11,200
November	2,500	13,700
December	3,000	16,700
January	3,000	19,700
February	2,500	22,200
March	2,000	24,200

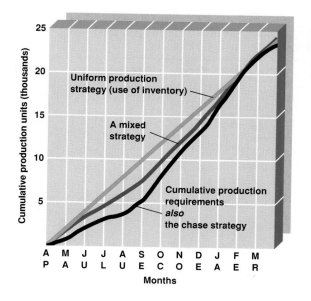

Figure 11.4
Cumulative Production Requirements and Cumulative Production vs. Time

Imperial's management expects the demand pattern in the years preceding and following the planning year to be about the same as the demand pattern for the year we are planning. Therefore, the number of employees at the beginning of the planning year is set equal to the number of employees at the end of the planning year. This condition is also assumed for all the alternative strategies evaluated in this example.

In actual situations, the company might need to evaluate the cost of changing the work force and inventory levels from current levels to the levels considered for the beginning of the planning year. The expectation of a different demand level for the year after the planning year might cause the company to plan to end the year with work force and inventory levels that differ from their levels at the beginning of the year. The conditions assumed in this example are only that the year start and end with the same work force level and with approximately the same inventory level. These conditions are sufficient to show how the trial-and-error method could be employed to evaluate alternative aggregate plans.

COST OF VARYING ONLY THE WORK FORCE One pure strategy that Imperial might consider is that of changing only the size of the work force. This strategy assumes that persons with the necessary skills can be employed when they are needed and that they will be hired or laid off to keep the direct labor hours that are available equal to the demanded production hours. The graph of cumulative production during the year will coincide with the black line representing cumulative production requirements in Figure 11.4. The cost to implement this strategy is developed in Table 11.3 and is estimated to be $238,600.

COST OF VARYING ONLY THE INVENTORY LEVEL Another strategy to meet the varying demand is to set a uniform production rate that will produce in 1 year the amount forecasted as needed during that year. This strategy is feasible if back-ordering (delivering the product in some period after the one in which it is ordered) is permitted or if inventory is held. The aggregate plan in this example begins with a

Table 11.3
COST TO VARY WORK FORCE IN ACCORDANCE WITH MONTHLY PRODUCTION REQUIREMENTS

(1) MONTH	(2) MONTHLY PRODUCTION REQUIREMENTS	(3) DIRECT EMPLOYEES NEEDED DURING MONTH (ROUNDED)	(4) EMPLOYEES ADDED AT START OF MONTH	(5) EMPLOYEES LAID OFF AT START OF MONTH	(6) COST OF CHANGING EMPLOYMENT LEVEL ($300 × COL. 4 OR $400 × COL. 5)
April	1,600	190	0	48	$ 19,200
May	1,400	167	0	23	9,200
June	1,200	143	0	24	9,600
July	1,000	119	0	24	9,600
August	1,500	179	60	0	18,000
September	2,000	238	59	0	17,700
October	2,500	298	60	0	18,000
November	2,500	298	0	0	0
December	3,000	357	59	0	17,700
January	3,000	357	0	0	0
February	2,500	298	0	59	23,600
March	2,000	238	0	60	24,000
			238	238	$166,600

Cost of changing employment level	$166,600
Cost of maintaining 1,000 units of inventory	72,000
Total cost	$238,600

Note: It is assumed that the company has 238 direct employees just prior to this year and at the end of this year since no trend is assumed in the data. This analysis considers just seasonal variation. If there were an up trend, we would end the year with more than 238 direct employees.

period after the peak demand. This beginning point makes it more obvious that surplus inventory can be accumulated in some early period, when demand is less than the production rate, to be sold in some later period, when demand is higher than the production rate.

Since the company needs to produce 24,200 units in 12 months, it must produce at an average rate of at least 2,016.67 units per month. A work force of 240 persons will be required. The cost to hold an item in inventory is $6 per month for the average amount in inventory, including work in process. The monthly inventory levels and the resulting cost of $192,912 are developed in Table 11.4.

CONSIDERATION OF OTHER STRATEGIES   Other strategies can be used to meet a nonuniform demand for the outputs of the operations function. For the example being considered, a wide variety of pure and mixed strategies could be used. The company could consider staffing at some intermediate level and using overtime and undertime (idle time). Or perhaps the company could subcontract some work during the season of peak demand. Mixed strategies might include a combination of subcontracting and overtime, or overtime and inventory, and so on. When you consider the possibility of mixing three or more strategies and the infinite variety of ratios for blending strategies, you see how challenging the problem is.

CONSIDERATION OF A MIXED STRATEGY   Let us consider a mixed strategy for the Imperial Sail Company. The company might want to set a relatively low uniform

Table 11.4

COST TO USE INVENTORY WITH A UNIFORM WORK FORCE AND PRODUCTION RATE

(1) MONTH	(2) CUMULATIVE MONTHS OF PRODUCTION	(3) CUMULATIVE UNITS PRODUCED (2) × 2,016	(4) CUMULATIVE FORECAST DEMAND	(5) ENDING INVENTORY (3) − (4) + 1,000	(6) INVENTORY HOLDING COST @ $6 × (BEGINNING + ENDING)/2
April	1	2,016	1,600	1,416	$ 7,248
May	2	4,032	3,000	2,032	10,344
June	3	6,048	4,200	2,848	14,640
July	4	8,064	5,200	3,864	20,136
August	5	10,080	6,700	4,380	24,732
September	6	12,096	8,700	4,396	26,328
October	7	14,112	11,200	3,912	24,924
November	8	16,128	13,700	3,428	22,020
December	9	18,144	16,700	2,444	17,616
January	10	20,160	19,700	1,460	11,712
February	11	22,176	22,200	976	7,308
March	12	24,192	24,200	992	5,904
					$192,912

production rate for the first 5 months of the year and a higher uniform rate for the latter part of the year. This would reduce the amount of inventory accumulated early in the year, resulting in lower inventory costs than a pure strategy involving only inventory. Since some inventory would be used, the production rate changes would not be as extreme as under a pure strategy of changing only the work force, and the cost of changing the work force would not be so great. Following is a calculation of the cost of one possible mixed strategy of this type.

The first month of the planning horizon Imperial will need to produce at least 1,600 units, if no inventory was accumulated. This requires more than 190 employees. The planner arbitrarily selects 200 employees for the first part of the year. The production rate will be 200 × 8.4 or 1,680 units per month. At the end of 5 months, the company will have produced 5 × 1,680 = 8,400 units. (Again, we are not considering absenteeism, scrap, or other matters that might occur in actual situations.) At the end of 12 months Imperial needs to have a total production of 24,200 units, so, the company will need to produce 15,800 units during the last 7 months of the year, or an average of about 2,257 units per month. The work force required for this production rate is approximately 269 direct employees, which will provide a production rate of 2,259.6 units per month. So, 69 people should be hired at the beginning of September and laid off at the end of the year to achieve these employment levels and to end the year with the same number of employees as were on the payroll at the start of the year.

By using the mixed strategy just analyzed, Imperial Sail Company will accumulate some inventory for part of the year. It is assumed that the average inventory for a month is halfway between the starting and ending inventory for the month, and it costs $6 per average unit on hand during the month. The cost of this mixed strategy, which is developed and presented in Table 11.5, is estimated to be $181,261. Notice that the cost of this mixed strategy is lower than the cost of using only inventory or work force changes, discussed above.

Table 11.5
COST OF MIXED STRATEGY—VARYING WORK FORCE AND USING INVENTORY

(1) MONTH	(2) EMPLOYEES	(3) MONTHLY PRODUCTION RATE (UNITS)	(4) CUMULATIVE PRODUCTION	(5) CUMULATIVE DEMAND	(6) ENDING INVENTORY (4) − (5) + 1,000	(7) INVENTORY COST @ $6 × (BEGINNING + ENDING)/2	(8) COST OF CHANGING WORK FORCE
April	200	1,680	1,680	1,600	1,080	$ 6,240.0	
May	200	1,680	3,360	3,000	1,360	7,320.0	
June	200	1,680	5,040	4,200	1,840	9,600.0	
July	200	1,680	6,720	5,200	2,520	13,080.0	
August	200	1,680	8,400	6,700	2,700	15,660.0	
September	269	2,259.6	10,659.6	8,700	2,959.6	16,978.8	$20,700
October	269	2,259.6	12,919.2	11,200	2,719.2	17,036.4	
November	269	2,259.6	15,178.8	13,700	2,478.8	15,594.0	
December	269	2,259.6	17,438.4	16,700	1,738.4	12,651.6	
January	269	2,259.6	19,698	19,700	998	8,209.2	
February	269	2,259.6	21,957.6	22,200	757.6	5,266.8	
March	269	2,259.6	24,217.2	24,200	1,017.2	5,324.4	27,600
						$132,961.2	$48,300

Total cost = $132,961.20 + $48,300 = $181,261.20

LESSONS FROM THE IMPERIAL SAIL COMPANY EXAMPLE The Imperial Sail Company example illustrates several points worth elaborating. For one thing, it shows the lengthy calculations necessary to evaluate possible aggregate production plans by the trial-and-error method. (You can see why an electronic spreadsheet or other computer program would be useful in an actual situation.) It also illustrates some of the many strategies that may be employed. It makes clear that a combination strategy can be even more economical than a pure strategy. But a pure strategy might be better if the cost of one variable, such as carrying inventory, was much less than the cost of other variables. We probably did not find an optimal solution. We would have to try many strategies that seem reasonable and see which is most economical.

APPLICATION TO SERVICES If the operation in question is service, the same type of analysis can be done. The major difference is that inventory accumulation is not a permissible variable to use in smoothing capacity requirements. Other variables, such as changes in the employment level and use of overtime and idle time, still apply. A cost penalty for delayed delivery of the service to the customer is analogous to a back-order penalty. Back-ordering is delivering the demanded item at a later time. This is what service companies do when they tell you that they can get to your job late next week. There may be no significant cost penalty to such a delay unless the customer decides to go elsewhere.

After finding the number of workers that seem best in each period of the planning horizon a company might then decide whether to use part-time, temporary, or "permanent" employees. Consideration may be given to whether the demand forecast indicates temporary needs for employees or a long-term growth trend. The relative costs, union agreements, and company policy also are factors to be considered. The effect on employees and their families is an important matter to consider in addition to the cost of overtime versus adding to the number of employees (see box).

OPERATIONS   MANAGEMENT   IN   ACTION

SOME DISGRUNTLED WORKERS SAY BOSSES ORDER TOO MUCH OVERTIME

News accounts during the past several years have reported closings of many U.S. factories and others have reduced their employment levels and shortened their work hours. Workers in some industries still complain of idle factories and short shifts. During 1994, however, the average work week for those who are employed hit its highest level since the years of World War II. Manufacturing workers averaged 4.4 hours of overtime a week that year. This average comes from some workers who work more than 20 hours overtime a week and many who work none. Some workers like the extra income and volunteer for extra shifts while others prefer more free time. During 1994 workers struck at companies including Caterpillar, General Motors, and Allegheny Ludlum to protest issues that included mandatory overtime and excessive overtime. Workers want the right to refuse overtime if it interferes with their personal plans. However, on a production line all the work stations have to be staffed for the line to run. All the workers are needed or none of them are.

The problem is not confined to manufacturing. Variations on the burnout theme are increasingly widespread in service organizations and throughout our society. A woman who works for a Fortune 500 company recently wrote Ann Landers to tell of her problem. She works a 60-hour week, brings work home, and checks messages from home on her personal computer. She stated that this puts a burden on her family and, since she and the workers in her office are exhausted, it is not best for the company. A July 1994 article in *Fortune* referred to "burned-out bosses" who had the psychological pain of firing waves of coworkers in addition to the stress of heavier workloads as additional victims of downsizing.

When workers are committed to serving their customers they may have to work overtime when rush orders occur or during temporary peaks in demand. In some cases companies would rather use a smaller group of skilled workers who work overtime on a regular basis instead of hiring and training new employees. This suggests that they believe they cannot find new workers as good as the ones they have. In other cases it is a matter of cost. The average cost of fringe benefits is over $5 per hour, so if the existing workers earn $10 an hour or less, it costs less to pay a 50 percent premium for overtime and spread the work among them instead of having another worker on the payroll.

The trend is toward using a smaller percent of permanent employees. A 1994 Cahners Economic survey of manufacturers showed that less than one-third of the respondents who planned to increase their work level were planning to use permanent hires. Forty-one percent planned to use overtime and 28 percent planned to use temporary or contract workers.

Sources: "60-hour Workweeks Are Taking Toll on 'Burnt-Out,'" "Dear Ann Landers," *Birmingham Post-Herald*, September 15, 1994; and Lee Smith, "Burned-Out Bosses," *Fortune*, July 25, 1994, pp. 44–46, 50, 51.

Mathematical Analysis or Optimization Methods

The trial-and-error or intuitive method of aggregate planning provides some insight into the nature of the problem and some tradeoffs that may be considered. It is one method by which companies evaluate alternative plans. In evaluating alternatives, it was necessary to identify the costs for changing the variables that were considered. Management scientists have developed various forms of equations, or mathematical models, for the total cost of a capacity plan as a function of the variables that are considered, multiplied by the appropriate cost for that variable. The analysts then can perform mathematical operations to find the values of the variables that will minimize the total cost of making the necessary capacity available. One approach to mathematical analysis assumes that the total cost is a linear function of the number of units of a variable, such as overtime hours worked or units held in inventory. Mathematical techniques such as linear programming and goal programming have been

Work force size is one of the variables of adjustable capacity. Temporary employees, many in the guise of students on vacation, help retailers get through the holiday season. Forecasting employment needs requires estimating seasonal indices, discussed in Chapter 4.

John Eastcott/Yva Momatiuk/Stock, Boston

used to achieve the desired level of output for the planning horizon at the lowest cost, according to the assumed model.

Another method, called the *linear decision rule,* assumes that the total cost might not be a linear function of the variables involved. This approach uses quadratic equations for the cost as a function of the variables such as the number of employees added or the number of overtime hours worked. Matrix manipulations are used to develop two equations, or linear decision rules. One gives the best work force size for next month as a linear function of the forecast for the next several months. Another equation gives the best production rate, or number of work hours, for the upcoming month as a linear function of the forecast for the next several months.

Another approach considers that realistic equations for the cost of making capacity available often are so complicated that they defy mathematical optimization, so a computer technique, called a *search decision rule,* is employed. The computer is programmed to try various alternatives, much like a trial-and-error method, except that it successively improves the solution in a patterned search. It finds the direction to change variables that will reduce costs at the greatest rate. Then it will change in the best direction and check again. It continues to move the solution in the direction of greatest cost reduction until it can find no direction that will make the solution better. This search technique does not guarantee an optimal solution because it may have found a local minimum rather than the "global minimum," or absolute minimum-cost combination of the variables that are considered.

It is worthwhile to keep in mind that the formulated problem is based on a forecast which in all likelihood is different from the actual demand that will occur. Also, the problem is based on a pseudoproduct, and the average mix of actual products that is demanded may differ from it. Consequently, extensive efforts to find an exact solution to the assumed problem may not be necessary.

Now that we have considered the matter of planning capacity for the production plan, we will discuss why the detailed master production schedule must be developed a considerable time into the future for many companies, followed by the development of the master production schedule (MPS). After we consider development of the MPS, we will discuss rough-cut capacity planning (RCCP), which is a more-detailed method of estimating and planning for the capacity that will be required to produce the items in the MPS.

PLANNING MUST FOCUS BEYOND SOME MINIMUM HORIZON

Most planning for products that are to be completed in a particular time period has to be done while that period is far enough into the future to allow sufficient time for execution of the plan. Considerable time may be required for a product's execution cycle, that is, the time required for all the procurement activities and production tasks that must occur to complete a product. The requirements for materials and purchased components must be determined, and these must be ordered. Suppliers may require weeks or months to complete their work and to deliver the materials. After the materials are received, they must be processed through all the steps to make them into components, to assemble these components into the finished product, and perhaps to perform testing and packaging. Figure 11.5 shows the cumulative procurement and production time, or execution cycle, for an assembled product.

Assume that time is being measured in weeks in Figure 11.5, and visualize time as passing from left to right during a 1-week period every week. The best time to plan which items are to be completed during a particular week is while that week is to the right far enough to be beyond the duration of execution cycles for most of, preferably all, the company's products. Once activities have begun for the product with the longest execution time, the amount of capacity and possibly the materials available for making other products are affected. Companies often consider that there is a *time fence* just beyond the longest execution cycle and that most of the planning has to be focused on periods while they are beyond this minimum planning horizon. Execution of the plan must begin once a time period "slides under the time fence" on its way to becoming the current period, so the planning should be completed to the level of detail that tells which specific products are to be made. Also, the plan should

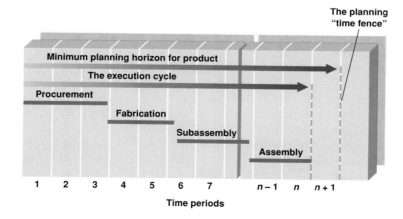

Figure 11.5
The Minimum Planning Horizon for a Product Must Be Longer Than Cumulative Procurement-Production Time

be rather firm. Some changes can be made within this horizon, but they may be expensive (overtime work, cancelled orders, expedited shipments, etc.). Other changes cannot be made, such as increasing the production quantity when it is just too late to obtain the necessary raw materials or components.

Make-to-order companies will take orders for items to be delivered in periods beyond the execution lead time. Make-to-stock companies must forecast the demand expected in periods within the planning horizon, but to the right of the time fence, and must plan in response to this anticipated demand. If companies can shorten their procurement cycles and production times, then the time fence will be closer, they can respond faster to changes, and the forecasts for the periods just beyond it should be more accurate.

THE MASTER PRODUCTION SCHEDULE

Each individual product, model, or unique item a company produces may require a unique set of materials and components and a unique series of work tasks. Procurement of materials requires that the plan specify precisely what is to be made; so, while the planned period is beyond the time fence, a company must plan the particular product mix it will produce. The *master production schedule (MPS)* is the plan that states what is to be produced, how many are to be completed, and when they are to be completed. It should include all planned production that will place significant demands on manufacturing resources. The MPS for a make-to-stock firm is stated in end items (the item at the stage where the plant is through with its work) rather than in lists of every component to be produced. Examples of items that usually are master scheduled are finished products, service and replacement parts to be produced to support products already in the field, and components or subassemblies that are sold to customers or shipped to other plants. A typical master production schedule looks like a matrix with a list of end items down the side and sequential weeks across the top. Numbers in any block of the matrix under a week represent how many of the items heading that row are to be completed in that week.

An assemble-to-order firm would master schedule the major subassemblies or modules that can be assembled to make the particular product options a customer may order. For example, an automobile manufacturer would plan to produce an adequate supply of each engine option and transmission option and would purchase enough of the sound systems it offers, various paint colors, and so forth. Then the automobile manufacturer could assemble any particular combination of options a customer might order. A final assembly schedule is developed later when customer orders are received. The master schedule for the modules is based on a forecast of the overall demand level and the relative ratios in which the modules are used. This planning can be facilitated by a "planning bill," similar to a bill of materials, which states the fractional part of each module in the average assembly. If the total number of units to be made is multiplied by the planning bill, it will tell how many of each module should be made or purchased.

While a period is still beyond the time fence, the total quantity of products represented in the production plan for a period must be subdivided into the specific items to be produced. A good master schedule should make enough product to serve customer demand but should not overproduce and create excessive inventory. This is why the production plan is coordinated with marketing's sales plans during the business planning process. The sum of the specific items in the MPS should be consistent with the rate of production promised by manufacturing in the overall business plan. Execution of the master production schedule must also be possible within the capacity that is available for production. Yet the capacity should not be much in excess of the amount required, or it will result in unnecessary expense. We now discuss dividing or "disaggregating" the production plan into the MPS; then we address the matter of planning the capacity that must be made available to produce the items in the MPS.

Disaggregating the Production Plan into the MPS

As mentioned before, the production plan is expressed in general terms, such as dollars' worth of product to be made in each of a series of fairly gross time periods, such as quarters or months. This general plan must be broken down to the level of detail required for initiating specific purchasing and shop activities. A procedure like the following can be used. The quarterly time blocks are divided into months and then into weeks. The quantity of each product family to be produced in a quarter is divided by the weeks in the quarter. The total quantity of a product family to be made in a week is divided among individual product models in that family, based on the mix of those products in the current demand pattern and adjusted for the current inventory level of each product. The MPS can be reviewed each week to check that the proper mix of products is to be produced, particularly for the week that is about to enter the time fence. For this reason, it is often advisable for the MPS to be developed with input from marketing. Thus, the MPS can be developed as a specific plan of items to produce that sums to be consistent with the general production plan. Development of a detailed MPS that adds to the general production plan is depicted in Figure 11.6.

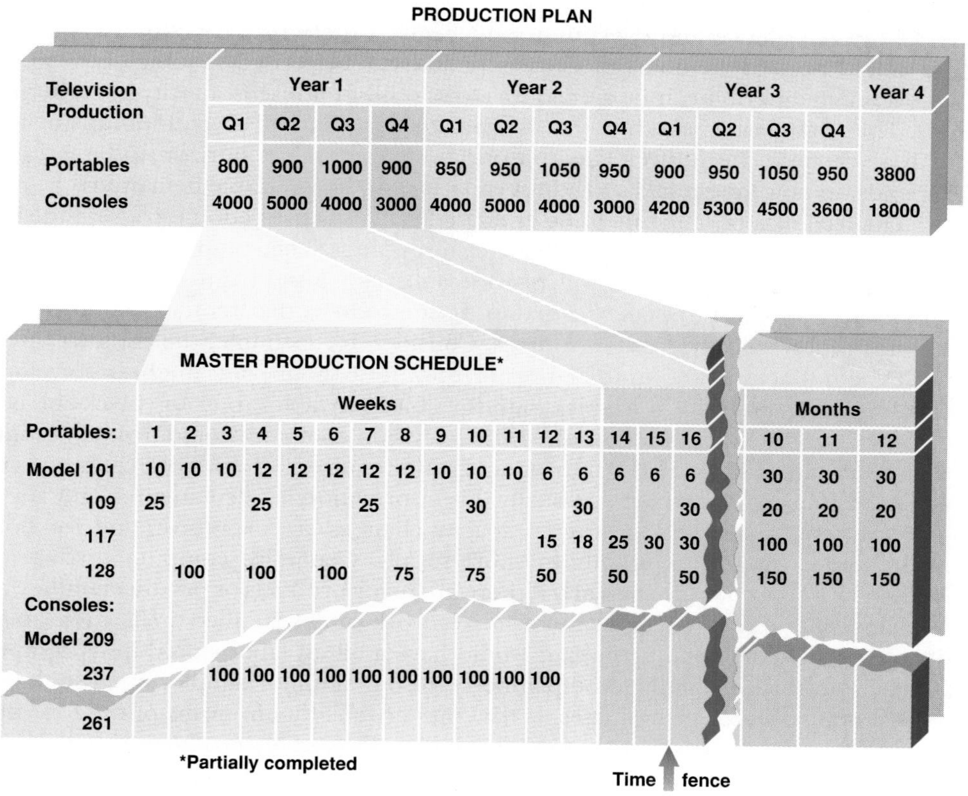

Figure 11.6
MPS Develops Details of Production Plan

PRODUCTION PLAN

Television Production	Year 1				Year 2				Year 3				Year 4
	Q1	Q2	Q3	Q4	Q1	Q2	Q3	Q4	Q1	Q2	Q3	Q4	
Portables	800	900	1000	900	850	950	1050	950	900	950	1050	950	3800
Consoles	4000	5000	4000	3000	4000	5000	4000	3000	4200	5300	4500	3600	18000

MASTER PRODUCTION SCHEDULE*

Portables:	Weeks																Months		
	1	2	3	4	5	6	7	8	9	10	11	12	13	14	15	16	10	11	12
Model 101	10	10	10	12	12	12	12	12	10	10	10	6	6	6	6	6	30	30	30
109	25			25			25			30			30			30	20	20	20
117												15	18	25	30	30	100	100	100
128		100		100		100		75		75		50		50		50	150	150	150
Consoles:																			
Model 209																			
237		100	100	100	100	100	100	100	100	100	100								
261																			

*Partially completed

Time fence

The example in Figure 11.6 is for the television company whose product line was depicted in Figure 11.2. The production plan is broken into specific product models so the company will have a detailed and coordinated plan of what it intends to produce. With such a plan, purchasing can then obtain the right amounts of the right components from suppliers and production control will know what items to release for work and when. Each work center can be informed which components and sub-assemblies to make and when. Basically all parts of the company that need to be coordinated will be working from the same plan. The plan must be feasible, that is within the capacity of each work center to perform its part of the work. Aggregate planning performed a general analysis of the capacity that should be made available to perform the intended work. After the MPS is developed a technique called rough-cut capacity planning is often used to analyze the capacity requirements with a more-detailed analysis. This technique can be used to plan capacity at the product-family level or even at a more-detailed level of individual product models. We will now discuss rough-cut capacity planning.

ROUGH-CUT CAPACITY PLANNING

Rough-cut capacity planning (RCCP) involves planning production quantities at some lower level in the breakdown of a company's product mix and then aggregating the capacity requirements of these more-detailed plans. Plans may be developed for individual products or logical groups of products, and then the capacity required for these subgroups can be summed to reveal the aggregate requirements and how the capacity needs can best be met. RCCP can be used to evaluate the feasibility of a trial MPS and plan how to make the needed capacity available before the time periods enter the time fence and execution must begin. If periods are evaluated while they are well in front of the time fence, the schedule can be revised so some of the work in an overloaded period can be spread forward to fill in unused capacity in earlier periods. The trial master schedule that is evaluated may extend several months or more than a year into the future. The appropriate length of the horizon to be evaluated depends on how long it takes to adjust capacity and how variable demand is.

The trial master schedule to be evaluated can be expressed in terms of individual products, product families, or other logical groupings. The company must determine which groupings of products will provide sufficient insight into its capacity needs. Certainly it is logical to plan as a group those products that require about the same amount of work on the same resources. Consider, for example, the product line for the TV manufacturer shown in Figures 11.2 and 11.6. Four plans might be developed: one for black-and-white portables, one for color portables, one for black-and-white consoles, and one for color consoles. The television company would need an estimate of the amount of work that each product group requires in each work center where it wishes to consider the capacity. Usually this information is calculated for only the key work centers, such as those where capacity changes are expensive, and for bottle-necks where capacity is usually in short supply. Generally, computations are performed by a computer, particularly if there are many products or product families.

The list of capacity required in each key work center is called a *bill of labor*, or bill of capacity. The television company would have a bill of labor stored in its computer for each product or family to be planned. For our simple example, suppose that the television manufacturer evaluates its trial master schedule in terms of the four product families identified above, before developing the master production schedule for

Table 11.6
SAMPLE BILL OF LABOR

Product Family: Color Console Televisions	
WORK CENTER	**STANDARD HOURS PER UNIT**
Printed-circuit board	0.22
Cabinet	1.04
Power supply	0.41
Assembly	0.28

individual product models. The bill of labor for the color console family might look like Table 11.6. The average color console television requires 0.22 hour of work in the printed-circuit board department, 1.04 hours in the cabinet department, and so on. There would be a different bill of labor for each of the other three product families: black-and-white consoles, black-and-white portables, and color portables.

To determine how much capacity a product family would use in a particular work center during a period under consideration, the quantity of the family to be produced in that period is multiplied by the appropriate number in the bill of labor for that family. For example, if the company plans to produce 400 color consoles during week 19, it will require $400 \times 0.22 = 88$ hours of work in the printed-circuit board department, $400 \times 1.04 = 416$ hours in the cabinet department that week, and so on. For each work center, the capacity required by all families is summed in each period, say each week, to determine the total amount of work that work center would have for each week throughout the planning horizon. This series of capacity requirements is called a *load profile* or load report and may be displayed as a table, like Table 11.7, or as a graph, like Figure 11.7.

The load profile for each work center is examined to see if it is within the available capacity of the center and appears to make wise use of the capacity. The load in any period must be within the maximum capacity of the center. Preferably the load will be within the normal (no overtime) capacity of the work center. A uniform work load is desirable, rather than one that requires overtime in some periods and has idle time in others. If there is a serious problem in the load profile of one or more work centers, the trial master schedule will probably be revised to move some of the planned work to another period. The new MPS is then evaluated. This iterative process might be continued with improvements being made to the trial master schedule each time, until a schedule is developed that is good enough for the company to implement. The refined MPS is then developed in further detail, if necessary, and

Table 11.7
EXAMPLE OF A TABULAR LOAD PROFILE OR LOAD REPORT

Load Report								
Work Center: R 58								
Normal Capacity (Hours per Week): 300								
Week number	8	9	10	11	12	13	14	15	16
Load (hours)	380	275	200	265	225	175	160	140	120

Figure 11.7
Example of a Graphical
Load Profile or Load
Report

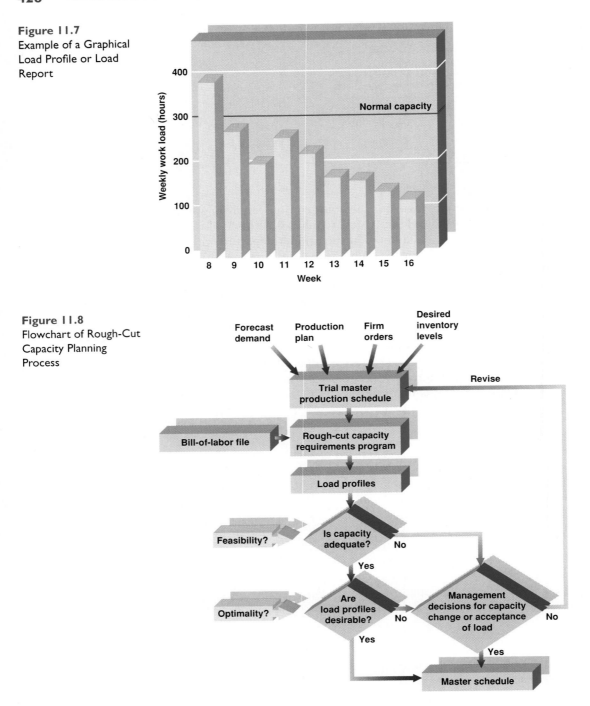

Figure 11.8
Flowchart of Rough-Cut
Capacity Planning
Process

implemented. A flowchart of this process is shown in Figure 11.8. If the load profiles cannot be leveled within the current capacity, the problem will be brought to management's attention in time for some adjustments to be made. A decision may then be made to revise the plan by such means as the following:

1. Miss some potential sales.

2. Work overtime.

3. Subcontract some of the work.

4. Add a shift.

5. Hire more people.

6. Schedule alternative routing of work (that is, transfer some work to another work center).

7. Transfer personnel into the overloaded work center.

SUMMARY

This chapter provides an overview of many of the concepts related to capacity planning for the intermediate-range planning horizon. Capacity planning in operations is driven by the company's overall business plan. The operations portion of the business plan, called the production plan, is expressed in general units of output. The production plan is the best estimate of required output in the more-distant portion of the planning horizon and is the basis for planning the aggregate, or total, capacity operations will need to fulfill its commitments as expressed by the production plan. Variables considered in this type of analysis include the work force size, the number of hours employees are to work per week, the use of inventory for manufacturing companies, and the use of subcontracted work. Aggregate planning often is performed by the trial-and-error method. Some other methods use mathematical analysis to find a minimum cost strategy to make the necessary capacity available. Linear programming or computer search techniques have been applied to the problem.

As time periods get closer to the present time the production plan is refined into a detailed master production schedule (MPS) for the periods in the nearer portion of the planning horizon. The MPS states how many of each specific product model are to be made and when. A more-detailed technique called rough-cut capacity planning (RCCP) is used to make a more-accurate estimate of the capacity required to meet the MPS. RCCP multiplies the number of each product or product family that is to be made in a period by the hours required in each key work center to make one unit of the item. All the work hours in a work center are then summed for each time period to provide a load profile for each key work center. The load profiles are then evaluated subjectively to see if they are within the capacity of the work center and if they can be improved to make the cost of meeting the MPS lower. Usually a good load profile is uniform so that it does not result in idle time in some periods and overtime in others. If there is a ramp up it should allow time for adding and training workers. An ideal down trend would allow for natural attrition.

KEY TERMS

Business planning	Linear decision rule	Rough-cut capacity
Fixed capacity	Search decision rule	planning (RCCP)
Production plan	Time fence	Bill of labor
Pseudoproduct	Master production	Load profile
Aggregate planning	schedule (MPS)	
Adjustable capacity		

DEMONSTRATION PROBLEMS

Problem

The following is a tentative master schedule for 4 weeks at a small company:

	Week			
PRODUCT	**1**	**2**	**3**	**4**
A	2,000	4,000	1,000	2,000
B	3,000	1,000	4,000	3,000

The bill of labor in the key work centers for the company's two major products is as follows:

	Product	
DEPARTMENT	**A**	**B**
4	0.21	0.07
11	0.06	0.10
14	0.11	0.08

Determine the load on department 4 over the next 4 weeks.

Solution

The load profile for department 4 over the next 4 weeks is found by multiplying the labor requirement in department 4 for each product by the quantity of that product to be produced in each week and summing the hours required for all products in each week.

Hours required in each week

Week 1

For product A	$0.21(2{,}000) = 420$
For product B	$0.07(3{,}000) = \underline{210}$
Total load for week	630

Week 2

For product A	$0.21(4{,}000) = 840$
For product B	$0.07(1{,}000) = \underline{\ 70}$
Total load for week	910

Week 3

For product A	$0.21(1{,}000) = 210$
For product B	$0.07(4{,}000) = \underline{280}$
Total load for week	490

Week 4

For product A	$0.21(2{,}000) = 420$
For product B	$0.07(3{,}000) = \underline{210}$
Total load for week	630

Notice this load profile is not very uniform, even though 5,000 units of product are produced each week.

Problem

A manufacturing company has a seasonal demand pattern, with the forecast demand for each month next year equal to 1,300, 1,000, 800, 700, 700, 700, 800, 900, 1,000, 1,200, 1,400, and 1,500 units, respectively. The company plans to end the current year with about 800 units in inventory. The company requires a minimum of 500 units in inventory for safety stock and work in process. It costs $1.10 per month to hold a unit in inventory.

The company will end the current year with 40 employees, and it costs $400 to hire and $600 to lay off an employee. It takes an employee 5 hours to make a product. Employees are paid $9.00 an hour for regular-time work and $13.50 per hour for overtime work. For simplified planning, each month is considered to have 20 days. Employees can begin or end employment on any day of the month, so an employee can work fractions of a month.

(a) Compute the cost of a chase strategy, in which the number of employees is changed so the monthly production rate is made equal to the monthly demand rate.

Use the following method to find the approximate number of employees to be hired or laid off in each month: Find the unrounded employment level (to two decimal places) needed for each month by dividing the number of units to be produced that month by the number of units an employee can produce in a month. Determine the integer number of employees on the payroll at the end of each month, and find the difference between successive values to determine how many employees would be hired or laid off. Estimate the integer employment level at the end of the month as follows: When employment is decreasing, round the approximate employment level down to the next lower integer. Decreasing is when the unrounded employment level before a particular value (or before the series of equal values of which it is part) is higher than it and the value after it (or after the series of equal values of which it is part) is lower.

For increasing employment (the reverse case), round up. When the employment cycle is reversing at a peak or valley, round up if the decimal is greater than 0.50 and down if the decimal is less than 0.50. If one of these values has a decimal equal to 0.50, round down if it is at a peak and up if it is at a valley.

(b) Compute the cost of a pure inventory strategy, with the work force and production rate held constant at the average demand rate and the variation in demand rate accounted for by accumulating and depleting inventory. A part-time employee can be used to provide any fractional employment level to obtain the desired production rate.

Solution

(a) Since the company will begin the year with 800 units in inventory and needs only 500 in inventory for a chase strategy, the production required in the first month was reduced by 300 units. The production required in each month is shown in column 2 in the table at the top of page 432.

CHASE STRATEGY COST FOR PART a

(1) MONTH	(2) REQUIRED PRODUCTION	(3) UNROUNDED EMPLOYMENT LEVEL (COL. 2 ÷ 32)	(4) COL. 3 ROUNDED	(5) LAYOFFS	(6) HIRES
1	1,000	31.25	31	9	
2	1,000	31.25	31	0	
3	800	25.00	25	6	
4	700	21.88	22	3	
5	700	21.88	22	0	
6	700	21.88	22	0	
7	800	25.00	25		3
8	900	28.13	29		4
9	1,000	31.25	32		3
10	1,200	37.50	38		6
11	1,400	43.75	44		6
12	1,500	46.88	47		3
				18	25

Total cost $10,800 $10,000

Hiring and layoff cost $20,800
Inventory cost   6,600
Total $27,400

Each employee contributes 160 hours each month, and it takes 5 hours to make a unit, so each employee can produce $160/5 = 32$ units per month. Column 3 in the table shows the demand divided by 32 to show the unrounded number of employees required to make the number of units needed in any month. These numbers must be rounded to determine the number of employees to be hired or laid off in the month. If the company is reducing employment, we round down to find the number of employees at the end of the month and how many layoffs there would be during the month. If the company is expanding its employment, we round up. At the lowest level of production, we round up so that the company will have at least the required capacity. Column 4 shows the rounded number of employees. The change in employment level is shown in column 5 if the number of employees is being reduced and in column 6 if the number is being increased. The first number in column 5 is found by subtracting 31 from the number of employees at the end of the prior year (40). The sum of column 5 is multiplied by $600 to get the total layoff cost, and the sum of column 6 is multiplied by $400 to get the total hiring cost. (If you are familiar with a spreadsheet program, you can see how the table could easily be developed.)

The company needs a minimum of 500 units in inventory each month. If it is assumed that this inventory will be carried, there is an additional cost of $550 each month to hold this inventory—at $1.10 to hold a unit for a month. The cost to hold this inventory for a year will be $500 \times \$1.10 \times 12 = \$6,600$. The total cost of this strategy will be $\$20,800 + \$6,600 = \$27,400$.

(b) Since the total demand for the year is 12,000 units, the company should produce 1,000 units each month to keep the production rate uniform. It will require $1,000/32 = 31.25$, which is rounded to 31, and a part-time employee will be used to provide this production rate. Column 4 shows the change in the inventory level that will occur each month if the demand and production rate occur as planned. Since the minimum inventory must not get below 500 units, the company will need to start the year with 800 units, as is planned.

The inventory that will be on hand at the end of each month is shown in column 5. The average inventory during the month, shown in column 6, is found by averaging the ending inventory for the month with the ending inventory for the previous month. The sum of column 6 is the total unit-months of holding inventory. This is multiplied by $1.10 to get the total inventory cost. There is an additional one-time cost to adjust the employment level from 40 employees at the end of the prior year to 31 employees being considered for this strategy. These 9 layoffs will cost 9 × $600 = $5,400. The total cost of this strategy will be $16,500 + $5,400 = $21,900.

INVENTORY STRATEGY COST FOR PART b

(1) MONTH	(2) DEMAND	(3) PRODUCTION	(4) INVENTORY CHANGE	(5) ENDING INVENTORY	(6) AVERAGE INVENTORY
1	1,300	1,000	−300	500	650
2	1,000	1,000	0	500	500
3	800	1,000	200	700	600
4	700	1,000	300	1,000	850
5	700	1,000	300	1,300	1,150
6	700	1,000	300	1,600	1,450
7	800	1,000	200	1,800	1,700
8	900	1,000	100	1,900	1,850
9	1,000	1,000	0	1,900	1,900
10	1,200	1,000	−200	1,700	1,800
11	1,400	1,000	−400	1,300	1,500
12	1,500	1,000	−500	800	1,050
				Total-unit months	15,000

Inventory cost	$16,500
Layoff cost	5,400
Total	$21,900

DISCUSSION QUESTIONS

1. List the titles of the managers who are likely to be involved in developing the intermediate-range business plan or sales and operations plan.
2. **a.** Describe the relationship between the business plan and the production plan.
   b. Describe the relationship between the master production schedule and the production plan.
3. Why is there some minimum horizon or time fence beyond which production should be planned?
4. Why should some companies have longer planning horizons than others? What are some of the factors that determine how far ahead a company should plan?
5. What is aggregate planning?
6. What are some methods that nonmanufacturing companies use to smooth the level of demand by removing seasonality and short-term variations in demand?

7. What are some dangers of planning production rates and work force sizes on the basis of an aggregate product?
8. Describe in your own words the steps involved in rough-cut capacity planning.
9. Discuss some advantages and problems associated with planning overall employment by summing all the requirements for individual items in the company's product line.
10. Discuss the advantages and disadvantages of various aggregate planning methods.
11. Why is the trial-and-error method of aggregate planning widely used?
12. Discuss some advantages and disadvantages of relying on overtime work to meet a significant portion of demand.
13. Discuss some of the advantages and disadvantages of hiring and laying off employees as demand increases and subsides. Should a company employ workers with the intention of laying them off within a few months? Should it just hire temporary personnel who are not expecting permanent employment?
14. How does detailed scheduling relate to aggregate planning?

PROBLEMS

1. The Adirondack Supply Company produces two major product families, group A and group B, both of which can be inventoried. The average cost to hold a unit of group A in inventory is $2 per month and for group B it is $4. The company has the following forecast of demand for the next 6 months.

	Month					
GROUP	**1**	**2**	**3**	**4**	**5**	**6**
A	800	650	800	900	800	850
B	425	300	500	500	400	500

The hours required to process a typical unit of each product group in the three major departments of the company are:

	Department		
GROUP	**X**	**Y**	**Z**
A	1.3	0.7	1.1
B	1.6	1.3	0.8

a. Determine the load profile for department X if both groups of products are produced in the quantities forecasted.
b. Since it costs twice as much to hold a unit of B, Mr. Donald, who does the master scheduling, has decided to produce the number of B's that were forecast in each month. He wants to schedule production of group A products so that the total work load in department X will be uniform over the 6-month horizon. Develop a schedule that achieves these goals.

2. For the Adirondack Supply Company data in problem 1:
a. Determine the load profiles in departments Y and Z for the schedule developed in problem 1b.
b. Give three possible reasons why Mr. Donald might have selected department X in preference to either of the other two departments as the place to make the load uniform.

3. A manufacturing company produces two products, *A* and *B*. The bills of labor for these products are shown below along with a trial master schedule for a 6-month horizon. The production cycles for the products are so short that the lag between the loads on the work center and the final production operation shown on the master schedule need not be considered in rough-cut capacity planning.

Bill of Labor, Product A		Bill of Labor, Product B	
WORK CENTER	**HOURS REQUIRED**	**WORK CENTER**	**HOURS REQUIRED**
16	2.1	10	2.8
19	6.8	18	1.3
25	4.1	19	3.6
41	7.2	35	2.1
52	3.9	52	1.7

TRIAL MASTER SCHEDULE (Units to Be Completed)

	Month					
PRODUCT	**1**	**2**	**3**	**4**	**5**	**6**
A	400	200	250	350	200	100
B		300	350	200	300	300

a. Determine the load profiles for work centers 19 and 52 caused by the trial master schedule.

b. Adjust the trial master schedule so that it provides more uniform load profiles yet meets the following conditions: At least 400 *A* units must be available by the end of period 1; and additional 750 *A* units must be available by the end of period 5; and 1,100 *B* units must be made by the end of period 5.

4. Mr. Baker, the scheduler at Idaho Manufacturing Company, has developed the following tentative master schedule for the next 6 months and wants to evaluate it.

	Month					
PRODUCT	**1**	**2**	**3**	**4**	**5**	**6**
A	160	300	350	520	400	280
B	175	197	216	224	206	190
C	420	420	410	380	350	325
D	400	400	460	500	560	600

The following bill of labor gives the hours required in each of the company's five key work centers to make one unit of the company's products.

	Product			
DEPARTMENT	**A**	**B**	**C**	**D**
2	0.56	0.19	0.22	0.71
3	0.41	0.42	0.68	1.74
4	0.80	0.41	0.59	0.00
6	0.22	0.00	0.24	0.61
8	0.36	0.61	0.28	1.06

Develop the capacity requirements for each of the next 6 months—that is, the load profile—for department 2.

5. For the data in problem 4:
   a. Develop the load profile over the 6-month horizon for department 3.
   b. For which product or products would you revise the schedule so the company would produce the product early and hold it in inventory until it is needed, resulting in more uniform load requirements in department 3?

6. For the data in problem 4, compute for each month the total load in all the company's key work centers.

7. Roberta Mawin, a planner at the Riviera Manufacturing Co., is working on a tentative master production schedule. The production plan stated the amounts that were to be produced in each quarter for a product family that is made in one small department, called a work cell. The product family has been broken down into the following quarterly schedule for the three products in the family.

| | Quarterly Schedule | | | | Production Data | |
	1	2	3	4	SETUP TIME	RUN TIME/UNIT
Product *A*	300	350	400	320	4 hr.	6.0 min.
Product *B*	2,100	2,000	1,800	2,000	3	5.1
Product *C*	7,500	8,000	8,000	6,000	2	5.2

The procedure is to divide the quarter directly into weekly time blocks without considering monthly quantities. The first and last quarters of the year she is planning are considered to be 12 weeks, and the middle quarters are considered to be 13 weeks. The company normally works two 8-hour shifts a day for 5 days a week. The goal is to have a level schedule that calls for production of the same amount of a product in each week of the quarter, without working overtime. Ideally, a week's supply of each product would be produced each week. The forecast for the coming year is considerably higher than in the past, and Roberta has doubts that the goal can be achieved. The schedule will be developed for the first quarter and reevaluated each month. The schedule for the second quarter will be developed later. With regard to only the first quarter:
   a. Can the company set up and run all three products each week without overtime work?
   b. If no overtime is permitted, which product(s) do you think should be run less often and how often should they be run?
   c. For which product would it be most advantageous to reduce the setup time?
   d. For which product would it be most advantageous to reduce the run time?

8. The Keep It Trucking (KIT) Company provides routine preventive maintenance and minor repair service at a fixed charge for clients within a 20-mile radius. The company's customers have seasonal businesses and try to postpone some maintenance until their slow seasons. This results in a seasonal demand for KIT services. The number of jobs forecast for the four quarters of next year are 840, 1,060, 940, and 1,180, respectively. The typical service call requires 7.4 hours, including travel and paperwork. Employees are paid $9.20 per hour, and the typical employee provides 490 hours of direct work per quarter but will be paid for 2,080 regular hours per year plus any overtime worked.

Skilled workers who are reliable enough to make these service calls are scarce, and KIT wants to provide permanent employment to its work force. The company is considering the use of overtime, paid at time and a half, to meet some of the peak demand.

a. Compute the payroll cost if the company maintains a constant work force of sufficient size so that overtime during the peak demand will be 15 percent of regular-time capacity.

b. Repeat part *a*, allowing 20 percent overtime.

c. Repeat part *a*, allowing 25 percent overtime.

9. Suppose that KIT Company described in problem 8 can employ temporary employees who are less skilled than its normal work force. These temporary employees work at 85 percent efficiency (that is, they require 7.4 ÷ 0.85 hour to provide the typical unit of service), yet they are paid $9.20 per hour, as are permanent employees. It is estimated to cost $500 to find, hire, and indoctrinate one of these employees and an equal amount when one is terminated.

   Compare the cost for hiring-related expenses, labor, and severance pay for two optional strategies. The company will staff with permanent employees with capacity for the average demand of 1,000 calls per quarter and (*a*) use overtime or (*b*) use temporary employees for demand above this level. Temporary employees will be paid for the entire quarter (490 hours) that they are employed, but will not be retained at the end of a quarter if they are not needed in the next quarter.

10. A service company has the following demand forecast for the next year, expressed in six bimonthly (2-month) periods:

PERIOD	FORECAST DEMAND (STANDARD UNITS OF WORK)
1	400
2	380
3	470
4	530
5	610
6	500

a. Graph the cumulative demand vs. cumulative workdays, assuming that each month has 22 working days.

b. Assume that an employee contributes 176 regular working hours each month and that each unit requires 20 standard hours to produce. How many employees will be needed during the peak bimonthly period if no overtime production is to be scheduled?

c. What will be the average labor cost for each unit if the company pays employees $6 per hour and maintains for the entire year a sufficient staff to meet the peak demand without overtime?

d. What percentage above the standard-hour cost is the company's average labor cost per unit in this year due to the company's decision to maintain stable employment sufficient to serve the peak bimonthly period without overtime?

11. Assume that the company in problem 10 can use overtime up to a maximum of 25 percent of regular-time hours. Each overtime hour costs $9. What is the average cost per unit produced during this year if the work force is maintained at a level so that overtime can be used to the maximum during the peak period?

12. The company discussed in problems 10 and 11 wants to determine the cost of meeting the demand for its services through changes in the number of employees and the use of overtime work. To keep from adding too many temporary employees during the peak demand period, the company will use overtime equal to up to 25 percent of the regular-time hours available. As soon as the company believes that 50 percent of a new employee's regular-time capacity could be utilized during the current period and the following period, it will add an employee and will continue to hire up to the maxi-

mum employment level. Overtime will be discontinued before employees are laid off during the decline in demand after the seasonal peak. The company wants to end this year with 23 employees. It costs $400 to hire and $500 to lay off an employee. Overtime hours are compensated at $9 per hour. Assume that all changes in the employment level occur at the end of a bimonthly period and that the company already has the desired number of employees at the start of the year.

   a. Find the employment level for each bimonthly period.

   b. Find the total payroll-related costs for the year.

   c. What cost per unit results from these payroll-related costs?

13. Assume that the company in problem 10 is a manufacturing operation and that its product can be inventoried. Assume that it costs $3 per month ($6 per bimonthly period) to hold an item in inventory. The company plans to maintain a constant production rate, begin and end the year with the same inventory level, and absorb all demand fluctuation by accumulating and depleting inventory. The number of employees will be set at a level so that no overtime will be required. What will be the average cost per unit due to the cost of labor and the additional inventory held during the year?

14. The Decota Manufacturing Company forecasts demand for its product during 12 months (expressed in units needed per month) as 418, 414, 395, 381, 372, 359, 386, 398, 409, 417, 421, 425. The current production work force level is 40 employees, and each employee can produce 10 units per month. An employee can produce 11 units per month by working 10 percent overtime and 12 units per month by working 20 percent overtime. The cost of hiring an employee is $500, and the cost of laying off an employee is $450. Regular-time pay for the employees is $1,250 per month, and they earn time-and-a-half pay for overtime. The cost to hold a unit in inventory for a month is $4, and the current level of inventory is 800 units, which is the approximate amount of inventory that the company wants to maintain.

   a. Develop a mixed strategy for meeting the forecast demand.

   b. What is the cost of this strategy?

   c. Do not revise the strategy, but recommend types of changes that you think would provide a lower cost strategy.

COMPUTER-BASED PROBLEMS

AGGREGATE PLANNING

1. Construct an electronic spreadsheet to perform aggregate planning by the trial-and-error method. Use the Imperial Sail Company example in the chapter. Enter the beginning inventory, desired ending inventory, regular-time production per employee-month, beginning number of employees, cost to hire, cost to lay off, regular-time wage rate, and overtime wage rate in blocks at the top of the template, and refer to these locations. This will allow you to change the problem easily if you want to analyze other problems with this template.

   You may want additional columns, but you will find these helpful: demand per period, employees needed for chase strategy, employees used (the variable you will change), cumulative demand, cumulative regular-time production, overtime required (if cumulative demand is greater than cumulative production), inventory cost (if cumulative production exceeds cumulative demand), hiring cost (when employees are added), and layoff cost. Accumulate the appropriate columns, and develop the cost of payroll + overtime + hiring and layoff + inventory. Use $8.50 per hour as the regular-time wage rate and $12.75 for overtime.

Use the spreadsheet to compare at least three employment patterns. Compare the total cost of your best plan with the costs and best plans that have been developed by others.

2. The Three River Manufacturing Company forecasts monthly demand for its product for the next year as 418, 414, 395, 381, 372, 359, 386, 398, 409, 417, 421, 425.

On average there are 22 production days in a month. The work content for one unit of the product is 3 worker-days. The current production work force level is 50 employees. The cost of hiring an employee is $500, and the cost of firing an employee is $450. Regular-time pay for the employees is $1,250 per month. The cost to hold a unit in inventory for a month is $4. The current level of inventory is 800 units. As protection against unforeseeable demand fluctuations, the ending inventory for each month is planned at no less than 800 units. However, exception to the ending inventory rule is permitted as long as it does not fall below 800 units for more than three periods in the year and the average annual inventory is at least 800. Set up a worksheet for this aggregate planning problem, and consider the following:

a. Develop a production plan, following each of the three strategies: chase, level, and mixed.

b. What is the cost for each production plan?

c. For each plan develop a graph of cumulative demand and cumulative production, and show the accumulation and depletion of inventory.

BIBLIOGRAPHY

Barnett, F. William. "Elastic Capacity and Skin-Tight Costs. Low-Budget Production Improvements." *Sloan Management Review*, Spring, 1990, pp. 65–71.

Blackstone, John H., Jr. *Capacity Management.* Cincinnati, Ohio: South-Western, 1989.

Burch, E. Earl, Michael D. Oliff, and Robert T. Sumichrast. "Linking Level Requirements in Production Planning and Scheduling." *Production and Inventory Management*, 2d quarter 1987, pp. 123–131.

Campbell, Kenneth L. "Rough-Cut Capacity Planning—What It Is and How to Use It." *Conference Proceedings.* American Production and Inventory Control Society, 1982.

Connell, Bertrum C., Everett E. Adam, Jr., and Aimee N. Moore. "Aggregate Planning in a Health Care Food-service System with Varying Technologies." *Journal of Operations Management 5,* no. 1 (1984): 41–55.

Nelson, Mel. "Capacity Planning and Execution: The Other Half of the Equation." *29th Annual International Conference Proceedings.* American Production and Inventory Control Society, 1986, pp. 173–177.

Proud, John F. *Master Production Scheduling: A Practical Guide to World Class MPS.* Essex Junction, Vt.: Oliver Wight, 1994.

Sill, Brian T. "Capacity Management: Making Your Service Delivery More Productive." *The Cornell H.R.A. Quarterly,* February 1991, pp. 77–87.

Smith, Spencer B. Computer-Based Production and Inventory Control. Englewood Cliffs, N.J.: Prentice-Hall, 1989.

Vollmann, Thomas E., et al. *Manufacturing Planning and Control Systems.* 3d ed. Homewood, Ill.: Dow Jones-Irwin, 1992.

OVERVIEW
OF MATERIALS
MANAGEMENT

I n Chapter 11 we reviewed some important factors that companies consider in wisely managing the inputs that provide their capacity to perform work activities. Another important input for many operations is materials. Many businesses have to obtain and wisely use materials and supplies if they are to serve their customers with competitive distinction. Hospitals and other health care organizations need supplies such as drugs, linens, food, and laboratory chemicals to care for their patients. Materials are the major basis for attracting and retaining customers in service businesses such as wholesale and retail distributors as well as grocery and department stores. Repair shops need adequate supplies of all the necessary materials if they are to serve their customers. In some cases the material inputs are not part of the output product, but still are vital to serving customers. Consider that airlines must have suppliers of fuel at reasonable prices and at all the necessary locations so the airlines can provide transportation services and still be competitive. Manufacturing businesses must schedule the simultaneous availability of appropriate material items and the appropriate work capacity so that the materials can be transformed to goods that will provide customer satisfaction.

No matter what performance characteristics they emphasize in their strategy, companies like those mentioned above will probably need to select and work with capable suppliers to execute their strategy. It requires the support of capable and conscientious suppliers to achieve quality, cost efficiency, dependability, and flexibility. It also requires the efficient, well-coordinated work of numerous units within the business. Outstanding companies must have superior performance in managing their supply chain, from finding outstanding sources and buying materials and components, through processing and distributing to customers the results of their processing.

Various terms, such as *logistics* and *materials management,* are used as overall labels for the full scope of all the activities required to manage materials flow from suppliers through company activities to the final use of the material or to the customer. We use the terms interchangeably, but *materials management* is probably used more often because it is so descriptive of the objective. Materials management is defined as "the groupings of management functions supporting the complete cycle of material flow, from the purchase and internal control of production materials to the planning and control of work in process to the warehousing, shipping, and distribution of the finished product."[1] Some companies place most, or all, of these activities under one executive to facilitate coordination. Regardless of how companies are organized, they must have effective teamwork to be successful, and activities related to materials flow are no exception.

We discuss many activities that are performed in companies to achieve effective materials management. Several activities are briefly described to provide an overview of where they apply. Some companies do not have production control because they do not produce the items they sell. Others are not involved in the shipping and physical distribution of materials because they consume materials in providing a service. Probably all companies that deal in materials will have purchasing and inventory. These two subjects are discussed in more depth.

[1]James F. Cox III, John H. Blackstone, Jr., and Michael S. Spencer, eds., *APICS Dictionary,* 7th ed. (Falls Church, Va.: American Production and Inventory Control Society, 1992).

HOW MATERIALS MANAGEMENT CAN HELP ADD VALUE FOR CUSTOMERS

Dependable suppliers of quality inputs help a company improve its quality and reliability. Rapid response of suppliers and rapid flow of items through operations achieved by keeping work-in-process inventories low helps a company provide good service, keep its costs lower, and be more flexible so it can shift products in response to demand. Responding quickly with improved products and improving the use of resources in providing them allow a company to offer more value to its customers.

MATERIALS FLOW IS A MAJOR OBJECTIVE

An end result of effective materials management is to have the right items where and when they are needed. This end result could be achieved by at least two general approaches: (1) have plenty of all the items you may want, or (2) synchronize the flow of items to make them available when needed. The general goal is to have a flow of items from suppliers to consumers with no unjustified delays or costs. The flow of goods is preferred over the possession of excess goods. Even banks, which are often thought of as "storehouses of wealth," are successful only if they can keep money flowing from depositors or other institutions to borrowers willing to pay for use of the funds.

The discussion of Wal-Mart's distribution system in Supplement D provided an outstanding example of achieving materials flow. Wal-Mart supplies its own stores with a consistent pattern of daily deliveries. Some wholesale distributors receive orders for widely varying assortments of items with no consistent pattern to the needed delivery times. Such demands place a challenge on any logistic system. The drug division of Bergen Brunswig of Orange, California (see box on pages 444–445), is a fine example of the use of a logistic system as a competitive weapon to gain and retain customer loyalty in such a challenging environment. The importance of logistics or materials management for this type company is clear because it is almost the entire operations function. The activities that these materials support are located in other companies. The effectiveness and efficiency of materials management directly impact the company's ability to attract and retain customers and make a profit.

Its customers depend upon Bergen Brunswig to provide a reliable flow of all items ordered, and this is a key to the distributor's winning business. Efficient logistics is also a key to the company's profits. It has no retail markup or manufacturing margins to cover the costs of inefficient logistics. In many companies the logistics activities may be more obscured than in Bergen Brunswig because other types of processing are going on. In manufacturing, more business units are involved in materials management, and other activities are aimed more directly at serving the customer. Materials management in these companies is just as important to the support of the units it supplies, even though the supplying units and the using units are both internal to the same company. Manufacturing presents a broad array of logistics needs.

Materials Flow in Manufacturing

In the past, particularly in North America, companies have tended to manage materials by having an overabundance of materials available. Stockpiles of raw materials and large buffer inventories between internal operations reduced the need for close coordination with suppliers or among various internal operations. But having goods sit idle in inventory does not add value, and it does add cost. The objective to be achieved is a *flow* of items from their sources through the necessary processing and on to the customers with no unjustified delays or costs.

One of the most apparent features of large factories is *movement*. A factory is a dynamic, vibrant center of activity. Trucks, barges, railroad cars, or other vehicles arrive with supplies and leave with completed or partially completed products. Large numbers of people and a wide variety of equipment may be involved in materials handling within the factory. Materials are moved from one operation to another as the inputs are transformed to outputs by the manufacturing process. Of course, the purpose of the factory's existence is to make the utility and value of the outputs greater than those of the inputs.

OPERATIONS MANAGEMENT IN ACTION

BERGEN BRUNSWIG'S LOGISTICS

The drug unit of Bergen Brunswig is a major distributor of pharmaceuticals and health care products. It ships to approximately 10,000 independent, chain, and hospital pharmacies from 32 distribution centers that serve an area covering more than 80% of the U.S. population. As a distributor, the drug unit relies 100% on logistics for profits and value added, because there is no contribution from manufacturing. The unit has a staggering 100,000 stock-keeping units.

"We manufacture a service, and as such we must listen to our customers," says Dr. Bernard J. Hale, Bergen Brunswig's vice president for distribution services. "We let the customer set the standards that we must meet instead of us setting the standards."

This simple quote, perhaps more than anything else about Bergen Brunswig's operations, distinguishes it.

"They [Bergen Brunswig] seem to be able to combine the best features of decentralization and centralization in a single logistics solution," says Michigan State's Prof. Bowersox. "Their people, from the dock to the boardroom, really understand why they are doing the things they are doing. They have developed an extraordinary merger of technology and human resources. The net result is the empowerment of people to take initiatives locally and still stay within the company's broad policy guidelines."

Bergen Brunswig provides service levels that meet or exceed customer needs while keeping the cost of providing the service low enough so that virtually all measures of financial performance are continuously improving.

"Our distribution system is designed to operate at a low cost because our margins are low, like those of the food industry," says Dr. Hale. "In our business you must minimize cost and keep service high. Some people might think we are nuts to want both. We disagree. If we can keep costs going down and productivity going up, we will be successful."

To lower cost, order entries from customers have been 99% automated using electronic data interchange. The orders from pharmacies typically reach a Bergen Brunswig distribution center between 5 P.M. and 10 P.M. Company associates pick the orders, and they are delivered the following morning.

The order-cycle time—from when an order is placed until it arrives at one of 10,000 pharmacies in the U.S.—is a remarkable 12 hours.

"This is difficult to achieve," Dr. Hale says. "Most companies [in the wholesale health care and drug business] don't provide deliveries on a daily basis."

And considering that orders placed with Bergen Brunswig are for three Ben-Gays, four Tylenols, three Bayers at a time—not cases of the product—their system is even that much more remarkable.

Why on earth would a company go to all this trouble? "It's done this way because the customer wants it this way," Dr. Hale says simply. "This second reason we do it this way is because if we supply the customers well, they don't need a safety stock or have to carry inventory in their back room."

The $3.4 billion company has long been an industry leader in applications of new technology to reduce distribution costs and improve customer service.

In December 1989, Bergen Brunswig introduced an automated ordering system, called PrimeLine, designed in partnership with customers. Through the use of this software package, pharmacies can contact a Bergen Brunswig distribution center and determine if an item or items are in stock. If they are, the pharmacy locks in an order.

"With this system in place, our customers can rely on a wholesaler for carrying inventory; so they don't have to worry about carrying the stock themselves," says Dr. Hale. "We call this value-added. Our customers can lower their investment by reducing their safety stocks because they know they can rely on prompt delivery from us."

"We intend to increase market share by providing a high level of service in line with a sound cost structure that must for competitive reasons remain very close to its competition." (Bergen Brunswig has 16% of the wholesale drug market.)

Bergen Brunswig achieves its service levels by working in concert with suppliers of product and with its final customers. The wholesale distributor has 221 of its 600 suppliers on-line with its computer-purchasing system. These suppliers represent 94% of Bergen Brunswig's purchasing dollars. Invoices from suppliers are electronically sent to and electronically paid by Bergen Brunswig.

"Our competition pushes us toward excellence. That's healthy for us," says Dr. Hale. He doesn't foresee Bergen Brunswig's easing off on service. The company will use more bar coding, other technology tools, and larger facilities with more automation.

In addition, the company is looking for ways to shorten the lead time between itself and its suppliers. "We are looking at ways to improve inbound freight deliveries to our distribution centers," notes Dr. Hale.

The wholesale distributor uses its own private truck fleet in order to minimize the inbound freight time and to minimize the company's investment in inventory. "A leaner, lower level of inventory equals lower cost," reasons Dr. Hale.

Bergen Brunswig has already achieved some noteworthy results from its logistics operation:
- Its sales per employee are $1.52 million (results for fiscal 1989 ending in August). The average for firms with more than $120 million in sales in the industry is $1.4 million.
- The average number of items picked per warehouse person-hour is 43 for the industry; Bergen Brunswig picks 52 an hour, and some distribution centers have already topped 70 picks per hour.
- The average firm in the industry turns inventory 7.6 times a year. Bergen Brunswig turns it 8.8 times.
- The average total operating expense as a percent of sales for the industry is 4.83%. For Bergen Brunswig, it's 4.64%.

- Bergen Brunswig matches the industry average of 7.6% gross profit margin.

In the future Bergen Brunswig hopes to achieve even greater results from the unleasing of the brainpower of its 3,000 associates. The company started a formal continuous quality improvement (CQI) program in 1988.

"We didn't ignore the customer before, but now we want to think about the customer 24 hours a day," says Dwight A. Steffensen, executive vice president and a director of Bergen Brunswig and a driving force behind the team problem-solving approach of the firm's CQI.

"CQI should lead us to substantial increases in market share and differentiation from the rest of the industry," adds Mr. Steffensen.

Source: "Logistics Gets Some R-E-S-P-E-C-T." Reprinted with permission from *Industry Week,* June 18, 1990. Copyright, Penton Publishing, Inc., Cleveland, Ohio.

Movements of tangible inputs and outputs into, through, and out of a manufacturing operation are summarized in Figure 12.1. The input portion of materials flow involves such activities as purchasing, traffic control, and receiving. Activities associated with materials and their flow within the factory may include production control, inventory control, and materials handling. Output-related activities may include packaging, shipping, and warehousing. Let us look in more detail at some of the units involved in achieving materials flow in manufacturing.

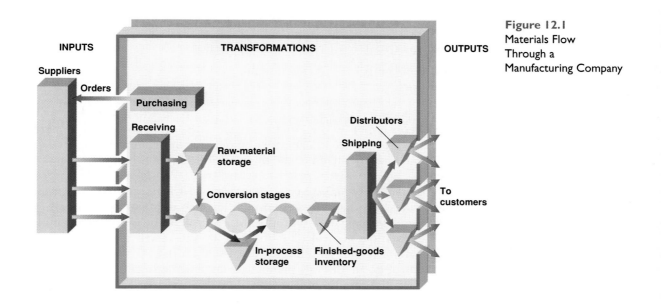

Figure 12.1 Materials Flow Through a Manufacturing Company

The automobile industry has always provided cutting edge thinking in materials handling. Overhead assembly racks make the car's underbelly accessible to workers as it moves along the assembly line.

Gary Cralle/The Image Bank

UNITS THAT SUPPORT MATERIALS FLOW

The organizational structure of a company and the responsibilities assigned to its units depend on the capabilities of employees and the needs of the company as its decision makers perceive them. Regardless of the way a company is organized, several materials-related functions probably are performed in some parts of the company. Some activities that relate to the flow of materials are listed below:

Purchasing	Materials handling
Inbound traffic	Packaging and shipping
Receiving	Outbound traffic
Inventory control	Outside warehousing
Production control	Distribution
In-plant storage	

Whether the people responsible for the functions report to a materials manager, a purchasing manager, or an operations manager, these functions must be performed and coordinated to ensure efficient operations. An operations manager must know how these functions are linked in the organization so that the company can perform effectively.

Since companies organize in a variety of ways, it is impossible to name specific department titles and the exact responsibilities such departments will have. We discuss materials-related activities in production control, traffic, receiving, shipping, purchasing, and inventory control. The first four are most likely to occur only in manufacturing operations and are briefly discussed in that context. Purchasing and inventory control occur in both manufacturing and nonmanufacturing operations. Since these activities are almost universal, they are discussed in greater detail after the first four topics have been outlined.

Production Control

Production control develops short-range operations plans and schedules from longer-term plans. In doing so it performs the following functions:

1. Scheduling production operations in accordance with the scheduled availability of materials, the anticipated backlog of work, the criticality of need for the product, and the lead time for production
2. Dispatching or directing the production departments and materials control to perform the necessary operations to meet the production schedule
3. Issuing materials to operating departments, when this function is not performed by a materials control department
4. Monitoring the progress of work in operating departments, expediting the work of those that are behind schedule, and deexpediting the work of some departments when schedules are changed

Traffic

The cost of transportation and the time it takes to receive their inputs or deliver their outputs are important to both manufacturing and nonmanufacturing firms. Selection of locations for a firm's facilities is inherently related to these costs and lead times. After the location for a facility has been selected, the cost and transportation time for its inbound and outbound shipments can be controlled to some extent by the firm's traffic department.

The traffic department is responsible for selecting and contracting with carriers to transport incoming and outgoing shipments. This responsibility may include:

1. Selecting the transportation mode: parcel post, bus service, air freight, rail freight in full carloads (CL) or less than full carloads (LCL), motor freight in full truckloads (TL) or less than full truckloads (LTL), freight forwarder, water freight, the company's own fleet, or other means of transportation.
2. Arranging shipping terms, such as FOB (free on board) the seller's plant or FOB the buyer's plant. FOB the seller's plant means the seller loads the goods and the buyer pays all other transportation costs. FOB the buyer's plant means the seller pays the cost of shipping the goods there.
3. Maintaining familiarity with regulations of the Interstate Commerce Commission or other agencies and with freight rates between various points for the commodity classifications of interest, so that the best routing and mode may be selected consistent with the cost and criticality of need for the item.
4. Auditing of freight bills to see that billing is proper.
5. Coordinating arrivals and departures of shipments so that demurrage costs—charges for delay of rail cars beyond some normal time allowed for unloading—are reasonable.

Receiving

Some subunit of the organization—usually a *receiving department*—must be responsible for receiving shipments of incoming materials and for maintenance, repair, and operating (MRO) supplies. The receiving department is responsible for:

1. Unloading and identifying incoming shipments

Getting materials in and out of the plant are a major consideration for any manufacturing facility. In this photo of the Saturn plant in Springhill, Tennessee, you can see how trucks and cars are able to easily access all sections of the plant. Even employee parking does not block service roads.

Edward Bower/The Image Bank

2. Preparing a receiving report
3. Dispatching the items to the point where they are to be inspected, stored, or used.

Sometimes materials handling is reduced by performing inspection of purchased goods in the receiving department or at the point where the items are to be used rather than moving the items through some inspection area. Suppliers who have demonstrated consistent high quality may become certified and often make deliveries directly to the point of use without any receiving inspection.

Shipping

The responsibilities of the *shipping department* may include:

1. Selecting from inventory those items to be shipped to the customer ("order picking")
2. Packaging and labeling the shipment
3. Loading shipments onto vehicles
4. Managing the company's fleet of vehicles

A growing trend is to use a third-party logistics service company. These companies contract to provide such services as inbound and outbound traffic, loading, storage, and sometimes even packing.

PURCHASING

Purchasing has the primary responsibility for dealing with other companies or divisions that supply the purchased services, components, materials, and supplies to operate a company. Companies often rely on outside suppliers for many of these inputs since their production has become more complex in many instances and requires special knowledge and equipment. Consequently, purchasing spends a large percentage of the money in many companies. Figure 12.2 shows that in a typical manufacturing company the expenditures for purchased materials and services is more than half the cost of sales. The percentage is even higher in a company such as Bergen Brunswig where the main business is purchasing and reselling items.

Purchasing activities are important in almost any company, but they can quickly make a large impact on profit or lead to disaster in companies where purchases are as large a percentage of costs as those mentioned above. Some of the activities and responsibilities of the *purchasing department* are outlined below:

1. To locate, evaluate, and develop sources of the materials, supplies, and services that the company needs.

2. To ensure good working relations with these sources in such matters as quality, delivery, payments, and exchanges or returns.

3. To seek out new materials and products and new sources of better products and materials so that they can be evaluated for possible use by the company.

4. To purchase wisely the items that the company needs at the best price consistent with quality requirements and to handle the necessary negotiations to carry out this activity. The best value does not always represent the lowest initial cost, so products should also be evaluated for their expected lifetime, serviceability, and maintenance cost.

5. To initiate if necessary and to cooperate in cost-reduction programs, value analyses, make-or-buy studies, market analyses, and long-range planning. Purchasing should keep abreast of trends and projections in prices and availability of the inputs that a company must have.

6. To work to maintain an effective communication linkage between departments within the company and between the company and its suppliers or potential suppliers.

7. To keep top management aware of costs involved in the company's procurements and any market changes that could affect the company's profits or growth potential.

The goal of making items flow from suppliers to consumers with no unjustified costs or delays makes it very important that a company have reliable suppliers. Deliv-

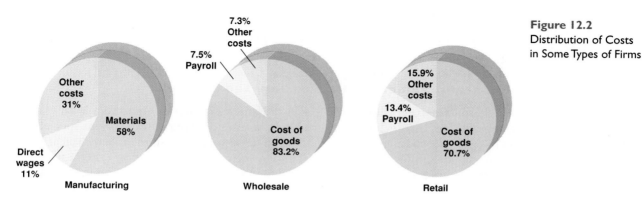

Figure 12.2
Distribution of Costs in Some Types of Firms

Source: U.S. Department of Commerce, Bureau of the Census, *1987 Census of Manufacturers: General Summary, Census of Retail Trade, Census of Wholesale Trade* (Washington, D.C.: Government Printing Office, 1991).

ery schedules have become much more precise to keep companies operating without the added costs of keeping high inventories just in case deliveries are late. To supply their customers with high-quality outputs, companies are vitally dependent on their suppliers to provide high-quality components and materials.

In the past some companies viewed the role of purchasing in a somewhat narrow manner as primarily passing messages from other parts of the company to suppliers and processing the paperwork required for legal contracts. The approach was to find numerous companies as potential suppliers to bid on the order each time an item was to be restocked. This practice increased the probability that one would need the business and bid low on the item being purchased at a particular time. This approach, however, often was not to the long-run benefit of either the buyer or the seller. A supplier who receives only an occasional order for an item, with no assurance that it will receive future order, can hardly afford to invest in the best equipment and devote extensive training and improvement effort to production of the item. Each supplier's bid would have to include some start-up overhead. The purchaser would have several suppliers, none of which could get very far down the learning curve. Progressive companies have achieved remarkable improvements by working in long-term partnerships with fewer highly qualified suppliers. Purchasing has a more strategic involvement in companies which operate with these types of agreements. Purchasing's role is to establish and nurture long-term partnerships with reliable suppliers who will serve the needs of the company.

We will now review some facets that are used in developing partnerships with suppliers.

Reduced Number of Suppliers

Companies are reducing the number of suppliers they have for each item. In some cases they are even going to a single source for all their purchases of the item. A 1990 survey by *Purchasing* magazine[2] showed that the respondents had reduced the number of production suppliers per plant from 402 to 252, with plans to further reduce to 160 by 1992. Another article offers three main reasons for reducing the number of suppliers.

1. Supplier development is expensive, so it is cost-effective only if considerable volume goes to the supplier.

2. A close working relationship requires that there be only a few suppliers to work with.

3. It ensures that the committed suppliers are rewarded with substantial business.[3]

Careful Selection, Monitoring, and Support

Supplier-partners are carefully selected and monitored. Often there is an extensive evaluation that includes on-site visits by a team of experts from various specialties within the purchasing company. A broad review of the company's technical and financial capabilities is made. For example, consider the evaluation criteria used by the Joy Technologies mining machinery division in Franklin, Pennsylvania (see box). At one time Joy had 16 suppliers of machined parts, but it has been reduced to 5.

[2]Ernest Raia, "JIT Delivery: Redefining 'On-Time'," *Purchasing,* September 13, 1990, p. 69.
[3]James Morgan and Susan Zimmerman, "Building World-Class Supplier Relationships," *Purchasing,* August 16, 1990, p. 65.

OPERATIONS MANAGEMENT IN ACTION

JOY TECHNOLOGIES' SUPPLIER EVALUATION

Twenty-five distinct elements of supplier performance are pinpointed in Joy Technologies' rating/certification program. Each element is worth a top of 4 points and is further defined in a glossary-like list used by both multidiscipline rating teams and by suppliers. Note that key quantitative measures under "quality" and "responsiveness and cooperation" require scores in the high 90s to earn certification.

Human Resources

1. Management is trustworthy and committed in every respect.
2. Integrity, information sharing, and open communication are practiced throughout the organization.
3. Personnel are professional and competent.
4. Management depth and succession planning exists.
5. High morale and a stable labor environment prevail.

Capabilities

1. Key management personnel are strong in product knowledge.
2. Increased business levels can be supported with growth potential.
3. Logical long-range strategic plans are developed and maintained.
4. They are knowledgeable about our products, services, and business.
5. They utilize technology in tools, methods, and systems applications as necessary to provide best total value to Joy.

Quality

1. Quality system is maintained to assure consistent product or service.

2. Inspection equipment and controls meet or exceed our Quality Assurance Standards No. 1.
3. Inspection records are documented and retained for a minimum of 6 months.
4. Trailing average acceptance rate of Joy products is 98% or better.
5. Manufacturing equipment and facilities are efficient and properly maintained.

Financial and Pricing

1. Financially strong in profitability and debt service capabilities.
2. Cost-conscious in all areas and provides practical value analysis ideas on a continual basis.
3. Willing to enter into long-term agreements that provide methods for negotiating price increases or decreases.
4. Competes effectively in respect to total value/cost relationship.
5. Partners are important to each other.

Responsiveness and Cooperation

1. Inventory breadth and depth, compressed lead times, and delivery methods provide ability to maintain 95% on-time delivery performance.
2. Schedule changes and emergencies are given top priorities with results achieved.
3. Willing to develop a business partnership with Joy that reaps mutual benefits.
4. Forms partnerships with suppliers to minimize business risks and protect common interests.
5. Suppliers' organization is flexible and facilitates change to accommodate our needs.

Source: "Fine-Tuning the Big Picture," in *Purchasing*, March 8, 1990. Reprinted by permission of Cahners Publishing Co., Inc.

Overall the number of supplier-fault rejects has reduced by 48 percent, delivery performance from suppliers has improved 25 to 30 percent, and their inventory turnover rate has gone from 5 to 13.[4]

Early Supplier Involvement

The partnership between a manufacturing company and its suppliers may involve the supplier in the design of the purchasing company's products. If an outstanding supplier is selected, as should be the case, then the supplier obviously has great

[4]Somerby Dowst, "Define What You Want to Get What You Need," *Purchasing*, March 8, 1990, pp. 84–85.

Table 12.1
THE BIGGEST BENEFITS OF ESI

INDICATED BY:	Percentage Indicating the Benefit			
	BETTER QUALITY	BETTER MANUFACTURING	LOWER COST	LATEST TECHNOLOGY
Purchasing managers	61	60	51	43
Design engineers	41	70	39	37

expertise in the field. The purchasing company often can benefit from this knowledge through early supplier involvement (ESI). The supplier's engineers participate as part of the team during the time that a new product is being designed. Up to 70 percent of the controllable manufacturing cost of a product is established by its design. Thus, there is great potential for cost reduction and quality improvement through ESI. This cooperation can shorten the product development cycle because suppliers do not have to wait until the item is designed before they can plan the best way to produce it. Data in Table 12.1 from surveys of 1,000 design engineers and 1,000 purchasing managers show that there are several other benefits to ESI.[5]

Information Sharing and Rapid Communication

The purchasing companies provide their production schedules to their suppliers so the suppliers can plan their own work. In some instances the contracts or agreements cannot be stated for exact quantities of specific items for distant horizons. The purchasing company may agree to purchase a given number of hours of the supplier's capacity per month, plus or minus some tolerance such as 20 percent. The actual mix of items to be delivered is specified at some agreed-upon lead time prior to delivery.

Information technology can be employed to ensure rapid communication between the two companies. Electronic data interchange (EDI) may be used. EDI enables computers to exchange messages between the two companies. The purchasing company can place orders for all items from a supplier in memory in its computer. The supplier's computer can then call in and have the data transmitted to it. This prevents delays for mailing orders and possible errors that can be made in multiple data entry steps. Some companies simply use FAX machines to transmit the type and amount of items to be delivered on the next release against a long-term blanket purchase order.

Companies track supplier performance in many of the same areas covered in the initial supplier survey. The quality of the product is tracked, but it includes missing paperwork or incorrect labels. Whether the supplier makes delivery within a delivery window is tracked. These windows are getting smaller. In the past most companies expected 10 to 12 days early to 4 or 5 days late. Now their expectations average from 5 days early to 2 days late according to one survey. At Toyota's assembly plant in Georgetown, Kentucky, the window is less than an hour.[6] Technical support service is also evaluated. The suppliers are given report cards, so they know the score. Special training and technical assistance may be provided to suppliers who want help. Suppli-

---

[5]Somerby Dowst and Ernest Raia, "Teaming up for the 90's," *Purchasing*, February 8, 1990, p. 59.
[6]Ernest Raia, "JIT Delivery," p. 65.

ers who consistently perform very well may become *certified suppliers,* and their products bypass receiving inspection unless problems arise.

The preceding discussion shows some of the changes that are taking place in purchasing and in supplier relations to build superior materials management. In addition to working closely with supplies, the purchasing department must work closely with other departments and units in the company to be successful in keeping the cost of materials and supplies low. Two activities in which purchasing works with other parts of the company are value analysis and make-or-buy analysis, which are discussed briefly in the following sections.

OPERATIONS MANAGEMENT IN ACTION

PURCHASING MAGAZINE'S MEDAL OF PROFESSIONAL EXCELLENCE SWEPT AWAY BY TENNANT

We can gain some insight into the trends and priorities in purchasing and supplier relations by looking at companies that are recognized and respected in these types of activities. Tennant Co., Milwaukee, Wisconsin, is the smallest company ($221 million sales) to win the Purchasing excellence award but it is a highly respected company. The company has twice been named by Forbes magazine as one of the best small companies in the United States. Tennant manufactures commercial and industrial floor scrubbers and sweepers.

Tennant is very serious about satisfying customer needs in a very cost-effective way. For example, in 1980 their typical sweeper had an average of one small leak per 100 joints in the hydraulic hose lines. By 1985 the number of leaks was down to one per 1,000 joints and by 1990 it was down to 8 per 100,000 joints. The company stopped counting leaks in 1992. Ten years ago the cost of quality was 17 percent of sales. Since purchased parts represent over 65 percent of the cost of a typical sweeper, Tennant realized early the important connection between quality supplier relations and product quality. By selecting only high-quality suppliers and working closely with them to improve processes, the cost of quality has now been reduced to 5 percent.

Tennant's supplier relations have shown a tendency to work very closely with just a few suppliers to develop close partnerships. Tennant seems to prefer single sourcing many of its items even though many of the company's suppliers are larger than it. One supplier now provides over 90 percent of Tennant's coatings, where it used to have six coatings suppliers. Prior to 1986 Tennant purchased steel from twenty-two suppliers. Today 95 percent of its steel business goes to

two companies. In 1980 the company had sixteen suppliers of hydraulic hose and fittings. By 1982 there were only two. In 1985, Parker Hannifin became the only hose and fittings supplier. Overall the supplier base has been reduced from about 1,100 in 1980 to about 250 active suppliers. Fully qualified suppliers get the first chance at any new business. The practice of developing close working relations with suppliers has led to improvements in quality and having supplier participation in effective product teams that improve product design and speed the development process.

Tennant borrowed a page from Chrysler and established multifunctional product teams to oversee new products from the initial concept until the product is replaced by another. Each team is lead by a senior manager of the company and suppliers are assigned to the new projects before the design is begun. Tennant relies on the suppliers to provide much of the technical expertise. This means sharing a lot of information about future produce plans that in the past would have been considered sensitive information. The result has been much faster development of new products. It used to take Tennant a little over 4 years to develop a new product. Now, it takes about 2 years and the vice president of operations is shooting for 18 months. The goal is to introduce 2 new products per year, which is a considerable increase from the current rate of 1.3 per year. If the company is to grow by entering new markets it must use the best expertise and develop new products that have high quality and competitive cost. At the same time the company must continue to improve its current products and service.

Information sharing and rapid communication are important in services too. Wal-Mart Stores, Inc., discussed in Supplement D, use computers to track exactly what is selling. This enables them to direct their suppliers more accurately, slashing inventory cycles and keeping what's selling in stock. Grocery stores, originally using scanners at checkout counters as a means of customer convenience, are now using the information gathered from scanners to determine what they need to order from suppliers. Ultimately, orders may be communicated between the grocery and the supplier's computers, without manual processing.

Mel Digiacomo/The Image Bank

Value Analysis

Value analysis is an organized effort to reduce the costs of purchased parts and materials. It involves a study of items or services that are to be purchased in sufficient quantities to justify study. Value analysis seeks to answer such questions as: What is the function of the item? Is the function necessary? Are all its features necessary? Can a standard part that will serve the function be found? What does the item cost? What else will perform the equivalent function? What does this substitute cost? The concept sometimes is applied by a team or task force that may involve engineering, production, and purchasing in a review of existing and new products to ensure that expenditures result in the receipt of appropriate value.

Make-or-Buy Analysis

An important issue that must be addressed is the *make-or-buy decision*. A company must decide if it is going to perform the actual manufacturing operations or contract with another company to be a supplier. If the company uses only a few units of a particular item and special equipment is needed to produce it, the company probably will look for a vendor. If several companies purchase the item from the same vendor, the volume of demand may be great enough that the vendor can sell it at a lower cost than the purchasing company would have to pay to produce it. A small volume of demand for a product that no other companies are buying, however, may not be attractive enough to induce a vendor to produce it. Some companies both make and buy to ensure that they will have a source of supply if the vendor has a strike or goes out of business. Several factors are involved in the make-or-buy decision. Some of those that may lead a company to make a product or component internally instead of purchasing it are:

1. Lower cost, because the company does not have to pay the vendor's overhead and profit
2. Assurance of availability
3. Opportunity to control quality
4. Availability of equipment and expertise
5. Desire to preserve confidentiality
6. Savings on transportation costs

The decision to obtain supplies and components from outside, either by subcontracting or by purchasing components from vendors, enables a company to utilize its own capacity for other purposes. It also allows a company to focus on its own core competencies and to gain the advantage of core competencies the suppliers have. In some cases companies contract with other companies to produce their complete product. General Mills' granola bars, for example, are made by Coosa Baking. Dell Computers does not make any computer components. It just assembles components made by various suppliers. (The subcontracting of work to other firms as a means of varying capacity was discussed in Chapter 11, on capacity planning.) On the other hand, it also makes a company dependent on the vendor's effectiveness in such activities as scheduling and quality control.

INVENTORY

Whether a company buys components and products or produces them, it is faced with decisions about inventory. Inventory is any idle resource held for future use. Whenever the inputs and outputs of a company are not used as soon as they become available, inventory is present. Service operations and job shops tend to have small investments in inventory. For many companies, however, inventory accounts for a large percentage of assets. Wholesale distributors and retail companies may own little more than inventory, particularly if they lease their buildings.

Each unique entity—such as a part, subassembly, or type of raw material—that a company identifies for purposes of control may be called a *stockkeeping item,* simply an *item,* or sometimes a *stockkeeping unit (SKU).* The first two terms are preferred. The latter term can cause some confusion, because the word *units* is used to express the quantity of a particular stockkeeping item. We use the term *units* to refer to an amount or quantity of an item. The term *item* will be used to refer to a unique type of material that is inventoried.

Large manufacturing companies may have 100,000 or more different items to maintain in inventory and control. This number alone is large, but when it is multiplied by the number of units of each item that may be on hand, the number of units and the investment in inventory of such a company are tremendous.

For 1993 the value of inventory in the average manufacturing company was equivalent to about 1.47 months' sales or 12.2 percent of annual sales; in a retail company it was equivalent to about 1.50 months' sales or 12.5 percent of annual sales; in a wholesale company it was equivalent to about 1.31 months' sales or 10.9 percent of annual sales.[7] In 1992 the after-tax profits for manufacturing companies averaged

[7]U.S. Department of Commerce, Bureau of Economic Analysis, *Survey of Current Business,* February 1994, Table S.2.

5.95 percent of sales. This figure indicates that they had over 2 years' profits invested in inventory.[8] Why do companies invest so heavily in idle resources? Many companies have found that they did not need the amount of inventory that they were holding. In fact, many have found that they operate better after they have reduced their inventories.

Reasons Companies Hold Inventory

Inventories are neither totally good nor totally bad. Many of the problems of running out of materials and products are obvious. Many of the problems of having too much inventory are less obvious, which is a reason why companies sometimes carry more than they need. Too much inventory causes excessive holding costs, extra space requirements, and product obsolescence, and it hides other problems the company should find and solve. We discuss these matters in more detail later in this chapter and in Chapter 16 when we discuss just-in-time manufacturing.

Companies hold inventory for a variety of reasons, some of which are mentioned here. In Chapter 11, we discussed how companies can accumulate and deplete *finished-goods inventory* to help level the production schedule when demand is not uniform. Inventories of finished goods or finished subassemblies may be held so the company can respond to customer demand in less than the lead time required to obtain the inputs and produce the products. Finished-goods inventories also protect a company from the error of underforecasting demand.

Inventories of inputs protect a company against interruptions of supply due to strikes, weather, or other natural disasters. Companies now try to deal with reliable suppliers who are nearby to reduce this risk, instead of just looking for the supplier with the lowest price.

Accumulation of *in-process inventories* between stages of production allows some processes to run at rates that differ from those of the processes that feed them or that use their output. Many companies gear their processes to the same pace so that these inventories do not accumulate.

Companies often accumulate inventories as a result of buying large quantities to spread order costs over more units, or as a result of producing large quantities on each production run, to spread the cost of setting up the equipment over more units. It is even better, however, to reduce the costs associated with ordering or with setting up the equipment. The firm will save money not only in these costs but also in the costs of holding inventory.

Movement Inventory

Some inventory is not readily apparent because it is not intentionally being held in a warehouse, but still it represents goods that are owned and not being used. If a company moves goods between several stock locations or if transportation times are long, the company may have sizable amounts of goods in transit—or "pipeline inventory." Suppose that before its goods are actually sold, a company moves them from the factory to a central warehouse, then to a regional warehouse, and eventually to the customer. If the average transportation time required for all these moves is 8 days and the company sells an average of 1,000 units per day, there will be an average of 8,000 units in transit. A company might try to ship by a faster mode of transportation or reduce the number of shipment steps to reduce the costs of its *movement inventory*.

---

[8]Ibid., July 1994, Table S.17c.

The Trend toward Operating with Less Inventory

Even though there are reasons why a company might want to have some inventory, it must be on guard to see that it does not accumulate a great investment in inventory that is expensive to maintain. As a company tries to use its resources wisely, it should explore alternatives that reduce some of the reasons for holding inventory, rather than simply holding more inventory "just in case." A trend in the past several years has been for companies to try to hold less inventory than they previously did. Companies have found that they can sometimes reduce the lead times required to obtain materials and to produce products, so that they can operate with less inventory and still serve their customers effectively. Sometimes companies can reduce their setup or procurement costs so that they can economically operate with more numerous but smaller lots, thus keeping inventory low. Many companies have worked with their suppliers to build more reliable sources of quality materials so that it is not necessary to keep so much inventory to protect against supply shortages or scrap losses.

Inventories that are to be held might not all be managed in the same way. Selection of an inventory control method depends on a number of things: the length of time the company intends to maintain the inventory, the type of demand it is to serve, the cost of the item, the degree of control desired, and so on. We now examine some types of inventories and how they can be managed.

SINGLE-PERIOD AND MULTIPLE-PERIOD INVENTORIES

Single-period inventory involves items that will be stocked only once, with no intention of restocking them after they are consumed. *Multiple-period inventory* involves items that will be maintained in inventory long enough that units which have been consumed may be replenished. The amount and timing of future replenishments can be varied to adjust the inventory level in response to demand. Multiple-period inventories are kept for most finished products and their components and are much more common than single-period inventories.

Marginal Analysis for Single-Period Inventories

Consider a business that is to select the quantity of an item to buy when there is only one period in which demand for the item can occur and the level of that demand is not known. Assume, however, that a probability distribution for the various levels of demand that might occur is available or can be estimated. Assume also that the company will not be able to purchase additional quantities of the item if it does not buy enough the first time. If a unit of the product is not sold, there will be a cost to the company of C_o for overstocking. This cost is the amount spent for the unit less any salvage value. The company will suffer an opportunity cost of C_u per unit for understocking, where C_u is the contribution to profit from a unit. The company should add units to the order quantity as long as the expected cost of adding the last unit is less than the expected gain. That is, the order should be increased as long as the expected cost of overstocking for the next unit is less than the expected cost of understocking for it. The objective, then, is to find which unit is the last that the company should add to the order.

Let $P(D)$ be the probability that the level of demand will be greater than or equal to a particular number of units, D. Then $P(D)$ is a value from a cumulative probability distribution with cumulation beginning at the right-hand tail or highest possible level of demand. The company should add the Dth unit if the expected cost of understocking for this unit is greater than the expected cost of overstocking for it. That is,

$$P(D) \times C_u > [1 - P(D)] C_o \qquad \text{[12.1]}$$

And $P(D)$ will decrease as the order size is increased from the minimum possible level of demand until, at some point, the two sides of expression 12.1 become equal. The optimum order size is associated with the $P(D)$ that makes the two expected costs equal. Let us identify the *critical probability* that makes the two costs equal as $P(D)^*$.

$$P(D)^* C_u = [1 - P(D)^*] C_o$$

$$P(D)^* C_u = C_o - C_o P(D)^*$$

$$P(D)^* (C_u + C_o) = C_o$$

$$P(D)^* = \frac{C_o}{C_u + C_o}$$

APPLICATION

EXAMPLE OF MARGINAL ANALYSIS TO DETERMINE THE AMOUNT OF SINGLE-PERIOD INVENTORY TO STOCK

The Lake Nocee Department Store has an opportunity to purchase a special shipment of tableware at $28 a set. These sets of tableware are to be sold for $35 as a special promotion during the store's thirty-fifth anniversary sale. Nocee must purchase the item in units of a dozen sets. Tableware is not part of the store's normal product line, so if the items are not sold during the anniversary sale, they will be sold to The Bargain Basement for $22.50 per set. Caleb McKinney, a buyer for the store, has estimated the probability distribution for demand for the item, as shown in Table 12.2. McKinney solved for

$$C_o = \$28 - \$22.50 = \$5.50$$

$$C_u = \$35 - \$28 = \$7.00$$

Then

$$P(D)^* = \frac{C_o}{C_u + C_o} = \frac{\$5.50}{\$7.00 + \$5.50} = 0.44$$

By referring to the cumulative probability column in Table 12.2, McKinney found the largest quantity with $P(D) \geq 0.44$ was 8, so he ordered 8 dozen sets of tableware.

Table 12.2
PROBABILITY OF DEMAND FOR TABLEWARE, LAKE NOCEE DEPARTMENT STORE

DEMAND (D) (DOZENS)	PROBABILITY OF DEMAND [P(d)] (PROBABILITY DEMAND WILL EQUAL THIS LEVEL)	CUMULATIVE PROBABILITY OF DEMAND [P(D)] (PROBABILITY DEMAND WILL EQUAL OR EXCEED THIS LEVEL)
4 or fewer	0	1.00
5	0.10	1.00
6	0.15	0.90
7	0.25	0.75
8	0.20	0.50 ←
9	0.15	0.30
10	0.10	0.15
11	0.05	0.05
12 or more	0	0

The best quantity to stock is the highest possible quantity that has a cumulative probability of demand greater than or equal to the critical probability.

Multiple-Period Inventory Systems

Wholesale and retail establishments and many batch and repetitive manufacturing operations have standardized products that are sold for many sales periods. Some job shops have repeat orders for the same or similar items, so they have fairly stable utilization of certain raw materials and components. Single-period analysis is not appropriate for such situations, so other models and inventory systems have been developed to assist in the management of these inventories. The type of demand that is to be supplied from inventory determines the type of inventory system that is appropriate. Multiple-period inventories can be classified according to whether they are intended primarily to serve independent demand or dependent demand. This distinction has become increasingly important in the past decade because advances in data processing equipment and software have made it possible for large, complex companies to take dependencies of demand into account.

INDEPENDENT DEMAND   *Independent demand* is demand for an item in its current form (rather than for a kit or an assembly of which the item becomes a part) from some user outside the organization that has the inventory. The item may be a finished good, sold for use as is; a repair or service part; or a subassembly that some other organization will further transform into a final product. Independent demand is the demand for outputs of the operations system, shown in Figure 12.1 as arrows leaving the transformation block. Since the demand rate is determined by some entity outside the producing organization, demand is not known for certain and must be forecast. Independent demand forecasting was the primary topic of Chapter 4.

DEPENDENT DEMAND   *Dependent demand,* as the name implies, is directly related to the demand for another item or other items. It is the requirement for any of the parts or materials necessary to make some other item. Therefore, instead of requiring forecasts, dependent demand for an item can be derived or calculated from the demand for the assembly or assemblies of which it becomes a part. Dependent demands are shown in Figure 12.1 as input arrows and arrows connecting processing stages or in-process inventories within the transformation block. Most use rates other than the rate of final output from the operations system are dependent on other use rates (that is, dependent demands).

DIFFERENCES BETWEEN INDEPENDENT AND DEPENDENT INVENTORY SYSTEMS   Independent-demand systems supply demand outside the organization; dependent-demand systems supply requirements inside the organization. Consequently the need for independent-demand items must be estimated. A large percentage of many independent-demand inventories may therefore consist of items accumulated to provide protection from uncertainty. Independent-demand inventories enable the organization to supply an external user—to make a sale. Lack of sufficient available products may result in significant loss of profit from the direct sale, and future sales that may be lost as a result of customer ill will. Since companies don't know exactly when a customer will want a product, independent-demand systems are designed to keep material available almost all the time. About the only time material is not available is when sales are greater than anticipated and a stockout occurs.

Most dependent-demand items are used to produce independent-demand items. Since dependent-demand inventories supply requirements within the organization, there is less uncertainty about the amount required. The requirements for dependent items occur only when the company produces salable products or subassemblies that go into salable products. The number of dependent items required is directly related to the number of higher-level assemblies the company intends to make (plus allowances for scrap and other losses). The company may forecast inaccurately the number of salable products that should be made. But once a company decides how many finished products it will make, it can determine fairly accurately the number of dependent items it needs.

Some items are demanded both independently and dependently. That is, some items are used within the organization, and also sold externally. Some items may be used in a variety of products, so that the demand for them is fairly uniform over time. Often, these items are managed as independent items even though all or part of their use is dependent. We describe and compare some of the general features of independent-demand inventory systems in Chapter 13 and then briefly discuss material requirements planning (MRP), the system for managing dependent-demand items, in Chapter 14.

Inventory Systems for Independent-Demand Items

An inventory system is a set of procedures that indicate how much material should be added to inventory at what time and the necessary personnel and equipment to carry out the procedures effectively. Sometimes mathematical models are used to determine the most economical amounts to add to inventory and when they should be added. Mathematical models to help manage independent-demand inventory items have been used since approximately 1915. Since then, many complex and sophisticated models have been developed and proposed for use. Complex models, however, often apply to a rather specialized, restrictive set of conditions. We discuss only the more general characteristics of basic models and the types of systems that employ them.

Some companies must have available the exact item that the customer calls for or the exact item that is used at some stage in the company's processing. They cannot select an item that is somewhat similar. For example, if a person needs a picture tube for a 19-inch brand X color television, it is not feasible to substitute a 21-inch replacement tube.

Since companies may stock thousands of different items, they need some fairly simple and reliable way to indicate when each item should be purchased and in what quantity. Remember that the usual objective of systems to control independent-demand items is to make the item available most of the time.

FIXED-QUANTITY SYSTEM A *fixed-quantity inventory system* adds the same preestablished amount to the inventory of an item each time it is replenished. Chapter 13 discusses in detail how the lowest-cost replacement quantity—that is, the economic order quantity (EOQ)—is determined. Orders are placed when the inventory on hand and already on order is reduced to an amount called the *reorder level*. A graph of the inventory level over time in a fixed-quantity system is shown in Figure 12.3. The amount on hand and on order should be considered if the replenishment lead time is long enough that the time to place another order may occur before some previous order has arrived. Notice that the same amount is added to inventory level at each replenishment cycle. The time between replenishments varies in accordance

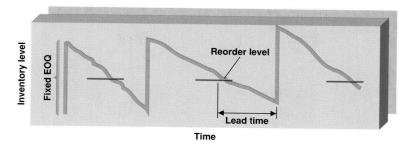

Figure 12.3
Inventory Level in a
Fixed-Quantity System

with the rate of use between orders. The reorder level normally is set high enough that the system does not run out of stock unless the use rate during the reorder lead time (that is, the time between placing an order and the time it arrives) is much greater than expected.

The fixed-quantity system is appropriate for many items that have relatively constant use rates. This type of system requires some means of determining when the reorder level has been reached. When the item is expensive enough to justify the expense of reporting each inventory transaction (that is, additions and withdrawals), a running balance may be maintained. These perpetual inventory records may be kept by manual methods or by computer systems. A bar code or other data entry method can be used to report the part number and the amount withdrawn or added. When the inventory balance reaches the reorder level, the computer may print out a purchase order.

Sometimes other methods are used to signal when the reorder level has been reached. A ring may be painted at a certain height in the storage bin, or a colored paper may be placed at the appropriate level in a stack of material, or some other method may be used to reduce the paperwork required to maintain inventory.

One inventory system with a very simple way to signal that more material should be ordered is the *two-bin system.* This system is useful for inexpensive items that cost more to count and monitor than it costs simply to use some approximate reorder level. A two-bin system has a designated location such as a physically separate bin, a hold area with a painted outline on the floor, or a portion of the larger bin below a painted line, to hold stock for use during the reorder lead time. The reorder level is signaled, and a replenishment order is placed when the normal working stock is exhausted and the company begins using stock from this "second bin." When the order arrives, the second bin is refilled, and the remainder of the order is placed in working stock.

FIXED-INTERVAL SYSTEM Replenishment of inventory can be triggered by the passage of a given amount of time rather than by inventory level. In a *fixed-interval inventory system,* the inventory level is checked on a uniform time frequency, say every 2 weeks. The quantity ordered is the amount necessary to bring the inventory level up to some maximum target level. A graph of the inventory level over time for a fixed-interval system is shown in Figure 12.4. Notice that the order size varies with the number of units used since the last order.

This type of system is best suited for *joint-replenishment items,* that is, items that are purchased at the same time from the same source. The frequency of orders for each item can be established so that the average order for the item or for a group of jointly ordered items is for some economical amount. Ordering groups of items at the same time reduces the ordering cost per item, may reduce the shipping cost per

Figure 12.4
Inventory Level in a
Fixed-Interval System

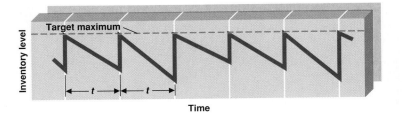

item, and may increase the value of each purchase sufficiently to qualify for price discounts. Perpetual monitoring of inventory is not necessary with the fixed-interval system, since the inventory clerk merely has to count the stock on hand each time the ordering date occurs. Ordering dates for various items can be spaced at particular intervals to smooth the work load for the inventory clerks and buyers.

MINIMUM-MAXIMUM SYSTEM   The fixed-interval system can sometimes result in the placing of very small orders. A *minimum-maximum inventory system* (sometimes called an *S, s system*) eliminates the handling of quantities considered too small to be economical. This system combines some features of the fixed-quantity and fixed-interval systems. A maximum target level *(S)* and a minimum target level *(s)* are established. The inventory is reviewed at fixed intervals *(t)*, and an order is placed only if the inventory is found to be below the minimum level. If it is not below the minimum level, no material is ordered because the quantity on hand is probably sufficient for the next review period and the quantity ordered would be small.

A graph of the inventory level for a minimum-maximum system is shown in Figure 12.5. This type of system is suitable for items that are not expensive, so that holding sizable inventory levels is less costly than keeping track of just how many are on hand and spending more to place frequent orders for small amounts.

BUDGET ALLOCATION   A *budget allocation inventory system* is more of a general guideline than a precise set of operating rules. Systems of this general nature are used to control inventories in retail establishments—gift shops, furniture stores, department stores, and the like. The budget allocation method relies on the discretion of a buyer or department manager to determine how many of which items should be in stock. General allocations of a total budget to various categories of merchandise may be made to keep a balanced selection available to customers. Within these allowable investment amounts, the company's buyers observe what is selling and order replenishments from vendors. Buyers also may decide to purchase items that currently are not stocked if they believe the products will sell. Some companies

Figure 12.5
Inventory Level in a
Minimum-Maximum
Inventory System

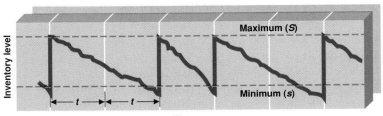

have agreements with suppliers whereby the suppliers' representatives periodically visit the store, check the inventory on hand, and replenish the stock to some target level. Budget allocation methods are useful when customers have some latitude in selecting products.

ABC Classification

We have seen that there are a variety of types of inventory systems that a company may use to manage its inventories of independent-demand items. More than one type of system may be used within the same company—a fixed-quantity system for some items, a fixed-interval system for others. The interval between orders may be relatively short for some items and much longer for others. Selection of the type of independent-demand inventory system to use may be influenced by several factors, such as the variability of demand, the cost of operating the inventory system, the unit cost of the item, or the seriousness of the problem if the item is not available.

Some companies have 100,000 or more inventory items, so it would be very time-consuming to examine thoroughly the characteristics of each item and select an appropriate inventory system for it. Often *ABC classification,* or *distribution by value,* is used to provide an initial sorting of items into groups according to the annual expenditures they cause. Items that represent the highest inventory expenditures are identified through this procedure so they can be given the greatest amount of attention, and so on. Some items may warrant the expense of perpetual inventory records to ensure that they are being carefully controlled because even 1 extra month's supply of these particular items is very costly. For other items, it may be less expensive to keep an extra 3 months' supply than to pay for operating an inventory system that would carefully control the amount on hand. Items with a very low cost and a small use rate would fall into this latter category.

The following procedure is one approach to ABC classification:

1. Multiply the cost of each item by forecasted use of the item for the coming year to get the *annual dollar use* (annual expenditure) for each item.

2. List all the items in descending order of annual dollar use, keeping their identity.

3. Number the items from top to bottom of the list, and determine the cumulative percentage of the items at and above each item on the list. For example, the 280th item in a list of 1,000 would represent 28 cumulative percent of the items.

4. Starting at the top and moving item by item down the list, compute the cumulative total annual dollar use represented by the item and all the items above it.

5. Determine the percentage that each item's cumulative annual dollar use represents out of the entire annual dollar use for all items (that is, the cumulative annual dollar use for the last item on the list).

The distribution by value can be visualized if the cumulative percentage of annual dollar use is plotted against the cumulative percentage of the items. A relationship similar to that shown in Figure 12.6 is usually obtained when these data are plotted. As little as 10 to 20 percent of the items may account for 60 to 80 percent of the annual dollar use. In a wholesale or technical industry (such as a distributor of electronic components) where the product line includes both major products and

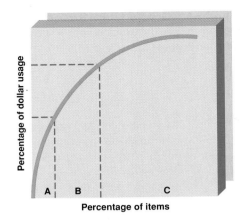

Figure 12.6
Relative Value of Items
vs. Relative Percentage
of Items

minor replacement parts, 10 percent of the products may account for 80 or 90 percent of the annual dollar use.

The items with the highest annual dollar use are called A items. Buying a few months' extra supply of these items means that many unnecessary dollars will be invested in inventory. Even keeping just one or two extra units in inventory may be very expensive. The A items should be controlled closely. They often justify perpetual inventory records in a fixed-quantity system or frequent review in a fixed-interval system.

The B items, those with the second-highest annual dollar use, may represent 20 to 30 percent of the items a company keeps and may account for about the same percentage of annual cost of use. These items would be reviewed less frequently than A items if a fixed-interval system were used. A minimum-maximum system could be used.

APPLICATION

EXAMPLE OF ABC CLASSIFICATION

Since she was a young child, Stephanie Stanton has enjoyed working with boats and being near the water. She is working with her father and will eventually take over operation of the family's wholesale boat and trailer parts business, Stanton Equipment Company. The company's inventory consists of about 12,000 different items that are sold to boat manufacturers, dealers, and hardware stores in the region. Several groups of items are produced by the same manufacturer, so the company controls its inventory with a fixed-interval inventory system. This system permits counting on a particular day the group of items that come from a common supplier and purchasing them all on the same order. This joint replenishment has worked well to help Stanton receive quantity discounts for large purchases and economies on shipping costs.

The business has grown to the extent that the stock clerks who keep track of the inventory are working excessive overtime to count inventory and order items. They do not have time to store items properly and keep accurate records. The usual procedure has been to count all items once a week. Stephanie has found that many of the items that are counted do not need to be ordered because no sales of these items were made during the week, yet very large orders are made for some items. Stephanie has recommended that she and her father determine the "moderate movers," which could be counted, say, every other week, and the "slow movers," which could be counted less often, say every third week. This would reduce the stock clerks' work load so they could work more accurately, and it would reduce overtime costs.

Stephanie obtained an ABC analysis program that would run on the company's computer. The program accessed the company's purchasing files to obtain the latest estimate of the use rate (col. 2, Table 12.3) and the average price paid (col. 3) for each item on the last three buys. The purpose of running the program was to determine which items were A items (those that should be counted each week), which were B items (those that could be counted maybe every other week), and which items were C items (those that could be counted less often). Table 12.3 shows a small sample (one-thousandth of the file), for which the use was multiplied by the cost

of the item. The program then sorted the list in the "Annual Use in Dollars" column to arrange the list in descending order of that variable. The results of the sort are shown in Table 12.4. Stephanie and her father discussed the list and determined that the first two items in Table 12.4 definitely were A items. The next three were considered to be B items, and the remainder were considered C items. They concluded that not all items had to be controlled by the same procedure and that they would try to develop new inventory levels and ordering frequencies for the B and C items so the company could make better use of its resources.

Table 12.3
CALCULATION OF USE IN DOLLARS, STANTON EQUIPMENT

(1) ITEM NUMBER	(2) ANNUAL USE RATE	(3) AVERAGE COST PER UNIT	(4) ANNUAL USE IN DOLLARS
4837	6,850	$ 1.20	$ 8,220.00
9261	371	8.60	3,190.60
4395	1,292	13.18	17,028.56
3521	62	91.80	5,691.60
5223	12,667	3.20	40,566.40
5294	9,625	10.18	97,982.50
6081	7,010	1.27	8,902.70
4321	5,100	0.88	4,488.00
8046	258	62.25	16,060.50
9555	862	18.10	15,602.20
2926	1,940	0.38	737.20
1293	967	2.20	2,127.40
			$220,597.66

Table 12.4
LISTING IN DESCENDING ORDER OF ANNUAL DOLLAR USE, STANTON EQUIPMENT

ITEM NUMBER	ANNUAL USE IN DOLLARS	PERCENTAGE OF SUM	CUMULATIVE PERCENTAGE
5294	$ 97,982.50	44.42	44.42
5223	40,566.40	18.39	62.81
4395	17,028.56	7.72	70.53
8046	16,060.50	7.28	77.81
9555	15,602.20	7.07	84.88
6081	8,902.70	4.04	88.91
4837	8,220.00	3.73	92.64
3521	5,691.60	2.58	95.22
4321	4,488.00	2.03	97.26
9261	3,190.60	1.45	98.70
1293	2,127.40	0.96	99.67
2926	737.20	0.33	100.00
	$220,597.66		

The C items represent a large percentage of the items a company may keep in inventory—perhaps half of them but usually less than one-fourth of the annual dollar volume. Very simple, approximate inventory control methods may be used to control C items. A company may have a crude minimum-maximum system whereby, whenever the inventory gets down to 2 months' supply, an additional 6 months' supply is ordered. Frequently it is less expensive to have extra inventory of C items than to keep track of the inventory balance and purchase frequently.

It is important to recognize that the cost of use is the basis for only a first approximation to classification of items. An item may be an essential part of a company's product, even though it does not cost much. The list of C items should be reviewed to see if any of these items should be moved to a higher classification.

Management of Dependent-Demand Inventories

Consider an independent-demand manufactured product that is controlled by a fixed-quantity, fixed-interval, or minimum-maximum system. Assume that the demand for this product is fairly uniform (perhaps the result of many consumers making fairly small purchases). Components of the final assembly (dependent demand) will be required only when the inventory of the final assembly reaches its reorder level. Consequently, requirements for a component will be zero for each week between reorders, then it will be equal to the number of components required for the number of assemblies that the company plans to produce. For example, an order to produce 1,000 bicycles might trigger orders for 2,000 tires and 72,000 spokes along with orders for other components. This "lumpy" demand for the component is much different from the pattern of demand for the finished product.

MATERIAL REQUIREMENTS PLANNING   Remember that independent-demand inventory systems keep items on hand almost constantly because demand might occur at any time. Dependent demand for components of a product occurs only when the company is in the process of assembling the product. It is less expensive to have these items available only when they are needed, instead of stocking them constantly. The company schedules when assemblies are to be produced and therefore controls when dependent components will be needed. It is possible to schedule backward from the date at which the assembly will be completed to determine when each component will be needed and should be available. A large amount of data must be processed if the company produces a broad line of products with many components. *Material requirements planning (MRP)* is a technique that takes dependent-demand relationships into account. MRP, which is discussed in Chapter 14, can be used to schedule purchases of components or to schedule various levels of fabrication or assembly in the production of products.

JUST-IN-TIME PRODUCTION

Japanese repetitive manufacturers have become very effective at operating with very small inventories through an approach called *just-in-time (JIT) production, zero inventories,* or *stockless production.* This approach to production is now used in many countries. Just-in-time production involves purchasing or producing exactly what is needed at the precise time it is to be used and conveying it directly to the point where it is needed. When a company has no standard product or when its products are demanded spasmodically in large quantities, there is little or no way to prevent lumpy demand for component parts. Lumpy demand and irregular flow of materials are likely to cause accumulations of inventory, unless production is carefully timed by some method such as MRP to occur precisely when materials are needed.

Repetitive manufacturing companies, which have a high demand for a standard product, can prevent lumpy demand for components by producing or ordering the products in numerous small lots instead of in larger, infrequent lots. The result is a smooth, uniform flow of small amounts of the appropriate components to the assembly department and a smooth flow of products from the assembly department, with the accumulation of very little inventory at any stage of production. Coordination of production activities in these companies is often achieved through the use of a card system called a *kanban system*. Just-in-time production and the kanban system are discussed in Chapter 16.

SUMMARY

This chapter provides an overview of materials flow and some of the organizational units involved with materials. A variety of organizational schemes can be used to direct materials-related activities, depending on the type of company, the talents and ambitions of the available personnel, the objectives of managers, and other factors. The various activities involving materials in manufacturing companies may account for a significant portion of the total manufacturing cost. Purchasing activities may involve buying raw materials and components, which, in turn, involves supplier relations. The traffic department controls incoming shipments. The receiving department unloads, and the inspection department checks the quality of materials that are received. In addition, materials handling involves moving the shipment to inventory control or to a stores department. The materials are then moved through various stages of processing, as capacity is available; usually there are some quality inspections among some operations. The transformed materials then go through final assembly, and the finished goods are sent by the shipping department to a distribution center. From there they move to a sales center and on to the customer.

Two of the activities mentioned above, purchasing and inventory, were discussed in greater detail than the others. Purchasing is responsible for most expenditures in many manufacturing companies, and inventory control is responsible for controlling much of the companies' assets. Buying and maintaining supplies are also important activities in many nonmanufacturing operations, such as repair service companies. Wholesale and retail organizations are greatly dependent on their wisdom in procuring and holding the proper items in inventory. For some operations, such as the postal system, materials handling is the primary service.

Inventory items can be classified as either single-period or multiple-period inventory. The latter, those that are replenished from time to time, are further classified as either independent-demand or dependent-demand items. Independent items supply demand that comes from outside the organization. They can be managed by fixed-quantity, fixed-interval, minimum-maximum, or budget allocation inventory control systems. Dependent-demand items supply requirements inside the organization. They subsequently become part of an assembly or kit, so that their rate of use is dependent on the production schedule and the rate of use of other items. Dependent-demand items often are managed by material requirements planning (MRP).

Some companies use the just-in-time approach to keep inventories as low as possible. The following two chapters examine some details of managing independent-demand inventory and dependent-demand inventory. Chapter 16 discusses just-in-time manufacturing in more depth.

KEY TERMS

Logistics
Materials management
Production control
Receiving department
Shipping department
Purchasing department
Certified suppliers
Value analysis
Make-or-buy decision
Finished-goods inventory
In-process inventories
Movement inventory
Single-period inventory

Multiple-period inventory
Critical probability
Independent demand
Dependent demand
Fixed-quantity inventory
    system
Reorder level
Two-bin system
Fixed-interval inventory
    system
Joint-replenishment items
Minimum-maximum
    inventory system

Budget allocation inventory
    system
ABC classification, or
    distribution by value
Annual dollar use
Material requirements
    planning (MRP)
Just-in-time (JIT)
    production
Zero inventories
Stockless production
Kanban system

DEMONSTRATION PROBLEMS

Problem

A style product must be ordered by a store several months before the season and can be purchased at $16.25 per unit. The retail price for the item will be $26.95 during the season. No "fill-in" stock can be ordered during the season if the store runs out of stock. Any excess stock left at the end of the season will be sold for $14.95. The buyer estimates the following probability distribution for selling various numbers of the product. Determine the number of dozens to order that will maximize the store's expected profit.

NUMBER THAT MAY BE DEMANDED (DOZENS)	PROBABILITY OF THIS DEMAND
6	0.03
7	0.05
8	0.07
9	0.15
10	0.20
11	0.20
12	0.15
13	0.07
14	0.05
15	0.03

Solution

If the store overstocks, the loss per unit for every excess unit at the end of the season will be $16.25 − $14.95 = $1.30, that is, $C_o = 1.30. If the store understocks, the opportunity cost for every unit the company could sell but did not stock will be $26.95 − $16.25 = $10.70, that is, $C_u = \$10.70$. The critical probability is

$$P(D)* = \frac{C_o}{C_u + C_o} = \frac{1.30}{10.70 + 1.30} = 0.108$$

The level of stock that will maximize expected profit is the highest level of stock that has a probability greater than or equal to 0.108 that it will be sold. We begin at the upper end of the probability distribution to develop the cumulative probabilities that demand will be greater than or equal to each level, so we can see what level of demand has a probability greater than or equal to 0.108 that it will sell. If the store stocks 15 dozen, the probability of selling that amount is only 0.03, which is less than the critical probability. If 14 dozen are stocked, the probability of selling that amount is 0.03 + 0.05 = 0.08, which still is less than the critical probability. If 13 dozen are stocked, the probability of selling that amount is 0.08 + 0.07 = 0.15, which is greater than the critical probability, so 13 dozen should be stocked. (Often it is useful to construct the greater-than-or-equal-to cumulative probability distribution and examine it to find the highest level that has a cumulative probability equal to or greater than the critical probability.) You can see that 13 is the highest level with a probability greater than 0.108.

Problem
Assume the same cost and sales prices for the item in the previous problem, but assume that the probability distribution is stated a different way. It is estimated that the probability distribution of demands that may occur is expressed by a normal probability distribution with a mean μ of 140 and a standard deviation σ of 25. Determine the stock level that will have a $P(D)*$ of 0.108.

LEVEL THAT MIGHT BE STOCKED	PROBABILITY THAT DEMAND WILL EQUAL OR EXCEED THIS LEVEL	
6	1.00	
7	0.97	
8	0.92	
9	0.85	
10	0.70	
11	0.50	
12	0.30	
13	0.15	←0.108
14	0.08	
15	0.03	

Solution
We are looking for the value in the probability distribution of possible levels of demand that has 0.108 as the area under the curve to the right of the value. Since the normal distribution table at the end of the book (Appendix I) provides the area under a normal curve to the left of Z, we subtract 0.108 from 1.000 to get 0.892 as the area to the left of the Z we seek. Reference to Appendix I shows that this value of Z is between 1.23 and 1.24 and interpolation gives the value as 1.237.

A *Z* value from a standardized normal distribution can be converted to a particular value *X* in a normal distribution with mean μ and standard deviation σ by the equation $X = \mu + Z\sigma$. Therefore,

$$X = 140 + 1.237(25) = 140 + 30.925$$

$$= 170.925$$

Since we must buy an amount that is an integer value, this number should be rounded *down* to 170. As with a discrete distribution, we want to stock the last unit that had a probability greater than or equal to the critical probability. We would place 170 units in stock. Theoretically, the 171st unit would have slightly less than the critical probability of being sold.

DISCUSSION QUESTIONS

1. What is materials management? How does materials management in a manufacturing operation differ from that in a nonmanufacturing operation?
2. Obtain information from a nearby company, or one with which you are familiar, about how materials management activities are organized. Present your findings in class, and compare the organization you surveyed to the organizations surveyed by others in the class.
3. Why is purchasing such an important part of materials management?
4. **a.** List some reasons for having inventory.
   b. Why might companies in some industries have nearly a year's sales in inventory, while companies in other types of business keep only a few weeks' sales or less in inventory?
5. Discuss some examples of single-period inventories.
6. State two general differences between independent and dependent demand.
7. What is an inventory control system?
8. Briefly describe four systems for controlling independent-demand inventory items.
9. Why are dependent-demand items often managed by a different type of inventory system from that used for independent-demand items?
10. **a.** Describe three categories of purchases that a company may make.
    b. Why should some be made by the purchasing department and others not?
11. Why would the purchasing department be involved in value analysis?
12. What are some changes a company may make in the way it operates so that it will require less inventory?

PROBLEMS

1. The Lob Sport Shop has an opportunity to purchase tennis rackets from the bankrupt Foot Fault Manufacturing Co. However, Foot Fault produced the rackets with a very poor quality of strings, so that they will need new strings by the next season. The rackets can be purchased for $19, and Lob plans to sell them for $40 as a special promotion (with the hope of selling the restring jobs in the near future). If the rackets are not sold this season, Lob must restring them before selling them next season. But the price next year should be less than $40 because customers will know that this was the price previously—and because the Foot Fault rackets will be known as having poor-quality strings even though this will not be true of the rackets Lob tries to sell next year. Lob figures it will lose $10 per racket that is not sold this season.

The probability of selling various quantities of rackets this season has been estimated and is shown in the following table. How many rackets should Lob buy?

RACKETS SOLD	PROBABILITY OF SELLING EXACTLY THIS NUMBER	RACKETS SOLD	PROBABILITY OF SELLING EXACTLY THIS NUMBER
50	0.05	100	0.12
60	0.10	110	0.09
70	0.15	120	0.06
80	0.20	130	0.03
90	0.20		

2. Ozark Sportswear can purchase a special shipment of wool caps for $1.85 each. The caps can be sold for $4.95 during the fall season, but any that have not been sold by Christmas will be reduced to $1.50. The following probability distribution has been estimated for demand for these caps prior to Christmas. Caps must be purchased in dozens. Assume that any caps unsold by Christmas can be sold at the lower price.

DEMAND (D) (DOZENS)	PROBABILITY THAT DEMAND WILL EQUAL THIS NUMBER [P(d)]	DEMAND (D) (DOZENS)	PROBABILITY THAT DEMAND WILL EQUAL THIS NUMBER [P(d)]
4	0.05	8	0.15
5	0.15	9	0.10
6	0.25	10	0.05
7	0.25		

How many caps should Ozark purchase?

3. Sour Dough Bakery stocks fresh-baked bread that costs the store 74¢ per loaf. The bread is sold for $1.39 a loaf on the day it is baked and for 59¢ a loaf if it remains at the end of that day. All the old bread can be sold at the discount price. The probabilities of various levels of daily demand for fresh bread are given below. How many loaves of bread should Sour Dough stock?

LEVEL OF DEMAND (DOZENS OF LOAVES)	PROBABILITY OF LEVEL	LEVEL OF DEMAND (DOZENS OF LOAVES)	PROBABILITY OF LEVEL
6	0.03	11	0.12
7	0.09	12	0.09
8	0.16	13	0.06
9	0.24	14	0.03
10	0.18		

4. The Great Newsstand stocks copies of the Sunday newspaper published in a larger city in the region. The papers cost the newsstand 50¢ each and are sold for $1.50. If they are not sold during the week, the papers are sold as scrap paper for approximately 3¢ each. Demand for the paper is distributed according to a normal distribution with a mean of 60 and a standard deviation of 15. How many papers should the newsstand stock?

5. A style item can be purchased for $32.50 a unit before the season, and no additional units can be ordered. The product will sell for $64.95 during the season, and any units left at the end of the season will be sold for $24.95. The probability distribution

of demand during the season is estimated to be normally distributed with a mean of 160 and a standard deviation of 45. Determine the amount of stock to order that will give the maximum expected profit.

6. For the data in problem 5, determine the amount to order if the company decides to use a selling price during the season of $59.95 and all other factors remain the same.

7. A special style of sweater can be purchased by a retail store for $18.25 on a one-time opportunity. The store plans to offer the sweater at a retail price of $34.95 during the season. Any sweaters left at the end of the season will be sold for $14.95. It is estimated that demand for this item at this location will have a normal probability distribution with a mean of 70 and a standard deviation of 20. How many of these sweaters should the store stock?

8. A local band is to order promotional T-shirts with the band's logo to sell during its appearance at a local festival. The shirts will cost $7.00 and will be priced at $17.00 during the festival. Any shirts not sold during the festival will be sold for $6.00. The band's manager estimates that the probability distribution for sales during the festival is normally distributed with a mean of 250 and a standard deviation of 75. How many shirts should the band's manager order if the shirts must be ordered in increments of a dozen?

9. A florist wishes to stock small bouquets of flowers for the last day of Secretary's Week. She estimates that the demand will have a normal probability distribution with a mean of 40 and a standard deviation of 15. Each bouquet will cost approximately $3.00 to prepare and will retail for $7.50. Any that remain at the end of the day will be donated to a local nursing home, and no tax deduction is planned. How many bouquets should be prepared if the florist wants to maximize the expected profit?

10. Bonito's Seafood sells fresh snapper received each morning from the coast for $4.49 per pound. If the fish is kept overnight, it will be priced at $3.95 per pound the second day. All the snapper that remains at the end of the second day is sold for cat food at 25¢ per pound. About 82 percent of the snapper that is not sold the first day will be sold the second day. Snapper costs Bonito's $3.60 per pound delivered to the store. Demand for fresh snapper during its first day in the store is normally distributed with a mean of 32 pounds and a standard deviation of 6 pounds. How much snapper should Mr. Bonito order each day?

11. The owner of the Mother Goose toy factory is planning stock levels and inventory review policies for next year. The entire product line consists of 16 products, each of which costs less than $50 to produce. On the basis of the forecast for next year and the cost of the items, determine the expected dollar volume for next year, arrange the items in descending order of dollar volume, and group them into A, B, and C categories.

PART NUMBER	COST	VOLUME	PART NUMBER	COST	VOLUME
k95	$ 4.65	7,400	m89	$16.30	3,200
i66	6.25	17,200	u43	15.95	2,250
d01	12.45	3,200	c22	32.88	26,000
s56	14.25	8,000	h32	48.50	9,000
h39	5.82	9,100	f43	16.22	17,000
a22	7.00	20,000	u23	14.25	4,200
v67	21.50	4,000	n92	11.88	16,000
e87	47.75	7,400	s44	9.95	19,000

12. A company uses a very small number of items in its business. The items are listed in the following table, as are their cost and annual use in units.

PART NUMBER	ANNUAL USE (UNITS)	COST PER UNIT	PART NUMBER	ANNUAL USE (UNITS)	COST PER UNIT
M602	31,000	$ 0.10	D277	400	$3.35
W101	5,200	10.00	R802	800	2.40
F310	1,500	0.65	D780	600	0.36
H884	100,000	0.14	M029	30,000	1.18
F400	60	255.00	B150	60,000	0.25

a. Determine the annual dollar use, and determine which appear to be the A, B, and C items.

b. Arrange the list in descending order of annual dollar use, then plot the cumulative percentage of annual dollar use versus the cumulative percentage of items.

13. A random sample of 10 items was selected from the 10,000-item inventory in the Sahara Marine Manufacturing Company. The following data were obtained.

PART NUMBER	ANNUAL USE (UNITS)	COST PER UNIT	PART NUMBER	ANNUAL USE (UNITS)	COST PER UNIT
Q10	10,000	$13	V60	5,000	$ 7.50
R20	5,000	5	W70	2,000	2
S30	2,000	6	X80	200	12
T40	1,000	18	Y90	25,000	10
U50	100	55	Z07	500	4

a. Group the data in order of descending annual dollar use.

b. Select A items, B items, and C items.

14. Apollo Distributors handles only 10 items in its inventory. The annual use and cost of these items are listed below.

PART NUMBER	ANNUAL USE (UNITS)	COST PER UNIT
095	5,000	$ 17
186	17,000	62
277	4,000	17
368	4,000	75
459	11,000	125
579	52,000	9
631	12,000	60
722	28,000	50
813	6,000	18
904	3,000	25

a. Calculate the annual dollar use of each item, and arrange the list in the order of descending annual dollar use.

b. Plot the cumulative percentage of annual dollar use against the cumulative percentage of items.

c. Select the A, B, and C items.

COMPUTER-BASED PROBLEMS

I. ABC ANALYSIS

Following is a list of raw materials and parts used in the manufacture of light lawn equipment. The annual requirement and average unit cost are given for each item. Set up the data in a spreadsheet, and categorize the items into A, B, and C classes.

ITEM	ANNUAL USE	UNIT COST	ITEM	ANNUAL USE	UNIT COST	ITEM	ANNUAL USE	UNIT COST
A110	1,000	$ 1.00	C150	2,000	$ 5.50	E111	5,000	$22.00
A135	1,300	2.30	C158	2,000	3.00	E120	15,000	0.10
A155	2,000	20.00	C160	150	14.00	E133	12,500	0.20
A175	200	25.00	C171	220	22.00	E136	12,500	0.20
A180	200	230.00	D111	2,000	2.60	E149	6,000	8.00
B110	150	100.00	D115	2,000	2.00	E151	900	90.00
B120	2,000	25.00	D120	30,000	6.00	E156	900	0.50
B150	1,400	11.00	D125	3,000	0.30	E166	500	25.00
B160	2,500	1.25	D133	1,400	2.20	F120	1,100	23.00
B165	3,000	3.50	D142	1,500	1.50	F163	2,500	1.25
B170	3,300	1.80	D148	1,500	1.50	G110	1,400	11.00
B180	500	120.00	D153	2,500	1.50	G170	3,300	4.00
C120	1,100	3.00	D160	3,000	1.10	H110	4,000	0.50
C135	10,000	0.25	D162	3,000	1.10			
C140	13,000	8.00	E110	2,000	22.00			

2. ABC ANALYSIS

Following is a list of raw materials and parts used in the manufacture of construction equipment. The annual requirement and average unit cost are given for each item. Set up the data in a spreadsheet, and categorize the items into A, B, and C classes.

ITEM	ANNUAL USE	UNIT COST	ITEM	ANNUAL USE	UNIT COST	ITEM	ANNUAL USE	UNIT COST
A120	2,000	$ 10.00	C122	4,000	$ 0.50	D163	3,000	$ 1.10
A130	1,300	2.30	C125	1,100	3.00	E112	5,000	1.20
A140	200	25.00	C130	10,000	7.50	E122	15,000	11.50
A150	1,000	1.00	C132	10,000	0.25	E123	15,000	0.10
A160	1,000	1.00	C145	13,000	0.40	E130	12,500	0.20
A165	2,000	20.00	C147	13,000	8.00	E140	6,000	0.55
A170	1,300	22.30	C153	2,000	5.50	E147	6,000	8.00
B115	150	100.00	C169	150	14.00	E150	900	50.00
B125	150	15.00	C170	220	28.00	E160	500	0.50
B130	3,000	1.50	D110	2,000	45.00	E167	500	25.00
B135	2,000	25.00	D122	3,000	0.30	F150	1,400	11.00
B140	500	2.00	D130	1,400	2.20	F160	150	14.00
B145	2,000	25.00	D136	1,400	2.20	F170	3,300	4.00
B155	3,000	4.00	D140	1,500	1.50	G120	220	26.00
B175	500	2.00	D150	2,500	1.50	G150	2,500	1.50
						G160	2,500	1.25
						H115	4,000	0.50

BIBLIOGRAPHY

Bowersox, Donald J. *Logistical Excellence.* Englewood Cliffs, N.J.: Prentice-Hall, 1991.

Bowersox, Donald J., David J. Closs, and Omar K. Helferich. *Logistical Management: A Systems Integration of Physical Distribution, Manufacturing Support, and Materials Procurement.* 3d ed. New York: Macmillan, 1986.

Dobler, Donald W., David N. Burt, and Lamar Lee, Jr. *Purchasing and Materials Management: Text and Cases.* 5th ed. New York: McGraw-Hill, 1990.

Dowst, Somerby, and Ernest Raia. "Teaming Up for the 90's." *Purchasing,* February 8, 1990, pp. 54–59.

Hall, Robert W. *Attaining Manufacturing Excellence.* Homewood, Ill.: Dow Jones-Irwin, 1987.

Henkoff, Ronald. "Delivering the Goods." *Fortune,* November 28, 1994, pp. 64, 66, 70, 74, 76, 78.

Johnson, James C., and Donald F. Wood. *Contemporary Physical Distribution and Logistics.* 3d ed. New York: Macmillan, 1986.

Measuring and Improving Productivity in Physical Distribution. Oak Brook, Ill.: National Council of Physical Distribution Management, 1984.

Moody, Patricia E. *Breakthrough Partnering: Creating a Collective Enterprise Advantage.* Essex Junction, Vt.: Oliver Wight, 1993.

Morgan, James P., and Susan Zimmerman. "Building World-Class Supplier Relationships." *Purchasing,* August 16, 1990, pp. 62–77.

Moskal, Brian S. "Logistics Gets Some R-E-S-P-E-C-T." *Industry Week,* June 18, 1990, pp. 14–22.

Raia, Ernest. "JIT Delivery: Redefining 'On-Time.'" *Purchasing,* September 13, 1990, pp. 64–76.

Schonberger, Richard J. *Japanese Manufacturing Techniques: Nine Hidden Lessons in Simplicity.* New York: Free Press, 1982.

Tersine, Richard J. *Principles of Inventory and Materials Management.* 4th ed. Englewood Cliffs, N.J.: Prentice-Hall, 1993.

Tully, Shawn. "You'll Never Guess Who Really Makes. . . ." *Fortune,* October 3, 1994, pp. 124–128.

Wight, Oliver W. *The Executive's Guide to Successful MRP II.* Englewood Cliffs, N.J.: Prentice-Hall, 1982.

Witt, Clyde E. "Third-Party Logistics: First Choice for Managers." *Material Handling Engineering,* February 1994, pp. 47–50, 52.

MANAGING
INDEPENDENT-DEMAND
INVENTORY

CHAPTER **13**

A major objective of materials management is to flow items reliably from suppliers to customers with no unjustified delays or costs. Certainly reasonable time delays to perform the value-adding operations required to produce items are justified. In some cases the costs and delays to hold at least some quantity of an item as inventory are justified and inventory can sometimes improve competitiveness. For example, inventory of raw materials can ensure supply when there is uncertainty about the reliability of a supplier or inbound transportation. Some inventory of components as work in progress or an inventory of finished goods can enable a company to fulfill customer orders in less than the lead time that would be required for the full production cycle.

In far too many instances, however, companies have tended to hold excess inventory for protection from problems rather than solving the problems that encourage high inventories. For example, improving operations by such means as developing reliable working relationships with suppliers, shortening production and procurement times, developing more reliable processes, and achieving consistent high quality reduce the need for protective inventory. In addition to excessive cost, large amounts of inventory can reduce the flexibility and responsiveness of a company. The company may have to delay introducing a new or improved item until it sells its existing inventory of similar items. Otherwise the company would make some of its own inventory obsolete. Perhaps one reason U.S. companies have not applied more efforts to operate with lower inventories is that for many accounting purposes inventory is considered an asset.

We have seen that inventory has its good and bad points. A company wants to have sufficient inventory to provide a high likelihood of covering its independent demand, yet it does not want to have excessive amounts of inventory. In this chapter we review a very basic inventory system to see how these conflicting forces have been traded off to reach decisions about inventory. An inventory system is a collection of people, equipment, and procedures that function to keep account of the quantity of each item in inventory and to determine which items to purchase or produce in what quantities and at what times. The goal of an inventory system is to see that a company has items on hand when they are needed without ever having too much inventory. An inventory system should indicate when the level of inventory is low enough that it is time to reorder an item. This level of inventory is often called the *reorder level* or *reorder point.* Some systems use perpetual inventory monitoring to determine if the reorder level has been reached. Perpetual monitoring, which may not be justified for all items, requires reporting every inventory transaction when some of an item is used or when more units are received into inventory. Good inventory management also should order only the right quantity of each item when it is ordered. Much of the discussion in this chapter deals with the development and application of the economic order quantity (EOQ), which provides a conceptual model of the types of conflicting forces that inventory managers often must deal with. The material provides an example of developing a mathematical model that represents certain assumptions and the use of such a model to reach decisions. The assumptions upon which the order quantity models are based are not correct in all cases, and many companies are finding it economic to order smaller amounts than recommended by the traditional model. In this chapter and several following chapters we point out some of the shortcomings and adaptations of this basic conceptual model and the effects of inventory decisions on costs.

HOW INDEPENDENT-DEMAND INVENTORIES CAN HELP ADD VALUE FOR CUSTOMERS

Independent-demand items serve customers directly. Sufficient, but not excessive, inventories of these items provide customers with a dependable source of rapid supply. Managing these inventories wisely helps prevent excess stocks and keeps costs low, so a high level of customer service can be maintained at reasonable costs.

RELEVANT INVENTORY COSTS

Having inventory costs money. But not having at least a certain amount of inventory can also cost money. As a company increases its inventory, some costs increase, other costs decrease, and still other costs are unaffected. Those costs not affected by the decision at hand can be ignored in the analysis. The costs affected by the decision are called *relevant costs* and definitely should be considered in reaching a decision if the amounts are not trivial. We consider first some costs that are increased when the average inventory level is increased.

Inventory Increases Some Costs

COST OF INVESTED FUNDS A company pays either out-of-pocket costs or opportunity costs for the funds it keeps invested in inventory.

COST OF STORAGE SPACE Another cost of holding inventory is the cost of a warehouse or other facility used for storage. Just as there is a cost for the warehouse space for finished goods or for raw materials, there is a cost for any extra plant space required for excess work-in-process inventory.

TAXES AND INSURANCE Many state and local governments collect ad valorem taxes, or taxes on assets, which include inventory. Also, when a company increases its insurance to cover an increase in the value of its inventory, the premiums rise.

QUALITY COSTS If a quality problem arises at one operation when a company produces in large lots, it takes a long time for the total lot to be processed and moved to some subsequent operation where defective units often are discovered. Defective units are discovered more quickly and fewer of them are made if the company produces in smaller lots. Therefore there are some added costs for poor quality if a company operates with large production lots that create more inventory.

COORDINATION COSTS Larger lots take longer to process, so they move more slowly through a factory. More product will be stacked up behind those lots, and they must be tracked, scheduled, and coordinated. Smaller work-in-process (WIP) inventories mean there are fewer jobs to coordinate. The WIP inventories flow through the factory and are out of the way, so the company does not have to coordinate as many jobs.

COST OF POOR RESPONSIVENESS Since jobs flow through a factory more quickly if a company keeps its work-in-process inventories low, there are some competitive advantages in the resulting responsiveness. High WIP inventories prevent a company from quickly introducing innovations or from responding quickly to shifts in customer demand.

OBSOLESCENCE COSTS High finished-goods inventories can become obsolete, resulting in additional costs if demand shifts. Some food items have rather short storage lives. Drugs are assigned dates after which their potency or purity is considered inadequate to allow their sale. Other products also may deteriorate or be damaged in handling and storage. Pilferage may also decrease the value of the stock of some products.

Inventory Decreases Some Costs

ORDER COST Some costs are incurred each time a company places an order to a supplier and receives the resulting shipment of goods. It costs money to solicit and evaluate bids, negotiate prices, prepare purchase orders, and expedite or follow up to ensure that the shipment will arrive on time. Delivery costs may be paid by the purchaser and very likely will have economies of scale. Often it is necessary to unpack, inspect, and move items into storage, then later move them to the point at which they are to be used. Companies that use just-in-time concepts have been successful at developing long-term supply contracts with reliable suppliers that have very high quality ratings. In some cases, after they have attained high-quality ratings, these suppliers deliver directly to the point of use, so the purchasing company does not have to uncrate and inspect them. Development of supplier-partner relationships where an order may be placed with just a fax, telephone call, or electronic data interchange (EDI) can reduce order cost to very little. When orders are placed for the company's own shop to produce and supply an item, the order costs are called setup costs.

SETUP COSTS Manufacturing companies incur certain *setup costs* each time they begin a production run on an item the equipment was not producing the last time the equipment was used. The equipment on which the parts of the product are to be produced must be prepared. The machines are idle during this period, and additional costs are incurred for the setup workers who install and adjust the necessary attachments. Sometimes trial products are produced, adding the cost of additional labor, additional nonproductive machine time, and the materials turned into defective parts until the equipment is properly adjusted.

If a company produces a greater quantity of the product each time it initiates production (that is, if it increases the lot size), fewer setups will be needed per year to provide the year's required production. The cost of each setup will be spread over more units, thus reducing this portion of unit cost.

Many companies in the past have tended to treat setup cost as a fixed quantity and have adjusted the lot size to be the best to go with that setup cost. More recently, particularly with just-in-time manufacturers, the approach has been to try to make lot sizes small and to work on reducing the setup cost so that it is appropriate for small lots. Remarkable reductions in setup costs have been achieved and have been used with just-in-time manufacturing (discussed in Chapter 16) to keep lot sizes and inventories very low. It is important that all inventory-related costs be kept as low as practicable, instead of more inventory being kept just to make the setup cost per unit low.

Flexible automation can reduce setup costs. Setup costs can, in essence, be eliminated in appropriate situations by dedicating one lower-capacity machine to production of one product and another lower-capacity machine to production of another product, rather than shifting a higher-capacity machine back and forth.

ITEM COST Prices for some purchased items may be reduced as the order size is increased. Item cost becomes a relevant cost factor if quantity discounts are available. However, if the cost of each unit remains constant regardless of the size of an order, the item cost can be disregarded in determining lot sizes.

COST OF MISSED SALES Availability of inventory can eliminate delays in supplying customers. Forecasts are seldom fully accurate, so extra inventory helps a company meet unanticipated demand. Customers do not like to wait for a product to be back-ordered, and often they will not tolerate a delay. They may revise their requirements or acquire the item from a competitor if it is not available in stock (that is, if a stockout occurs). As a result, the company misses a sale and loses the profit it would have made. Sometimes customers become so dissatisfied as a result of missed shipments that they take all future business elsewhere. The cost of missed future business (the cost of ill will) may be considerable. These *stockout costs* are difficult to estimate because of the difficulty in estimating the cost of ill will.

Managing to Reduce Inventory Cost

It is important to keep all costs of operations at the lowest practicable levels. Inventory-related costs are certainly no exception to this objective. Often companies can work to reduce the need for inventory and thereby reduce some of the costs we have mentioned. Companies that have very reliable suppliers and suppliers who can deliver in quick response to an order can operate with lower inventory. Companies that work in close partnership with their major customers may share data on the customer's purchasing plans so that forecasts are more accurate and lower safety stock levels are required. If a company can shorten its manufacturing cycle so it can respond quickly to customer demand, it needs to hold less inventory to cover customer orders until it can make or buy more. Some companies purchase in large quantities because the cost to place and receive an order is so high that they want to spread this cost over many units. Or companies that make items may produce in large quantities because the setup cost is high. If these companies work to reduce the order or setup cost, they can buy or produce smaller amounts more frequently, so

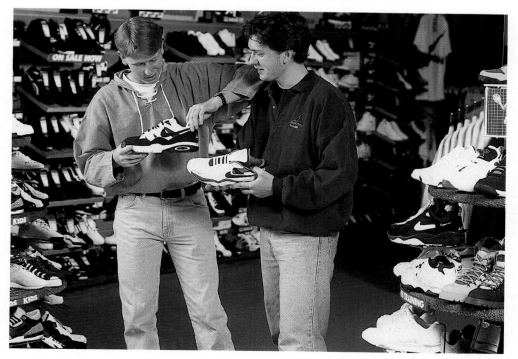

Bachmann/Stock, Boston

Managers at Nike have been able to keep inventory costs low with an inventory system dubbed "Futures." Nike requires retailers to place 80% of their orders 6 to 8 months in advance. In return, Nike offers a 10% discount. Given such specific order information and so much lead time, Nike doesn't have to maintain inventory to protect against uncertainty of demand. Key to the whole system is that customers want Nike shoes. If Nikes weren't such hot products, "Futures" would be less likely to work.

that inventory levels and costs will be lower. If a company can develop flexibility in its production rate, so that it can produce at least some items at the rate of demand, then it can serve its customers without accumulating inventory.

It could be to both the buying and selling companies' advantage to have more frequent, smaller deliveries. With monthly deliveries the supplier would need the capital and a large amount of warehouse space to accumulate a month's supply of an item. Then, when the delivery was made, the buying company would need a large amount of space to hold the item and more capital to pay for a month's supply. The buying company probably does not need a large amount at one time. More likely it uses some of the item every day. You can see why some companies are forming long-term partnerships with their suppliers, as discussed in Chapter 12.

Companies should seek ways, such as those discussed above, to keep inventories low and should implement all that are cost-justified. They should also work to reduce the cost for all factors affected by inventory, such as continuously working to improve the setup cost.

The most basic inventory model is discussed in the following section to show some of the costs that are considered and how they are traded off.

THE BASIC ECONOMIC ORDER QUANTITY MODEL

Since some costs increase as inventory increases and others decrease, the decision as to the best size of an order is seldom obvious. The best lot size will result in adequate inventory to reduce some costs, yet will not be so large that it results in needless expenses for holding inventory. A compromise must be made between conflicting costs. The *economic order quantity (EOQ)* model provides assistance in reaching a decision when the conditions are appropriate for its use.

The basic EOQ model is applicable to a procurement situation in which an item is purchased from another company. This EOQ model is based on several conditions or assumptions:

1. The use rate is uniform and known (that is, constant demand).
2. The item cost does not vary with the order size (that is, no quantity discounts).
3. All the order is delivered at the same time (that is, no back-order conditions).
4. The lead time is known well enough that an order can be timed to arrive when inventory is exhausted (that is, minimum inventory is zero, but the next order arrives when the balance reaches zero so that no sales are missed).
5. The cost to place and receive an order is the same regardless of the amount ordered.
6. The cost of holding inventory is a linear function of the number of items held (that is, no economies of scale in holding cost). When the impact on quality, obsolescence, and other factors associated with having a larger number of units on hand are included, the "holding cost" may increase at a rate that is greater than a linear function of the lot size. This matter will be discussed further after we develop the traditional model based on these six assumptions.

Under these assumptions the problem is deterministic—that is, there is no uncertainty or probability to consider—when these conditions are met. Some of these assumptions differ from the typical real-world situation. Recall from our discussion of decision making in Supplement E that the modeling process involves simplifying actual situations as long as the essential characteristics are included. The basic EOQ model is oversimplified for some situations, but it is used successfully by many firms with only a few embellishments, which are discussed later. First we develop the basic formula.

The basic EOQ model is a mathematical model that uses symbols to represent relevant variables. These symbols and symbols for other models in the chapter are defined as they are introduced. Some are repeated to remind you of what they stand for, and all are tabulated in the chapter summary.

Total Relevant Inventory Cost

The objective of the EOQ is to minimize the total annual cost of inventory factors for the item under consideration. These costs can be clarified by a graphical model of inventory levels over time, as in Figure 13.1. Notice that every triangle is the same shape. The diagonal lines all have the same slope because the use rate is considered to be the same over time (assumption 1). The inventory level goes to zero at the end of each cycle because of the assumption that shipments can be timed to arrive at just this moment (assumption 4). An order will be placed when the inventory level reaches the reorder level (RL), so the inventory is exhausted at the end of the lead time (LT). The reorder level for this problem is the use rate times the lead time, expressed as a fraction of a year (the unit of time being used). That is, $RL = D_a \times LT$ if the lead time is expressed as a fraction of a year. The heights of all the triangles are the same because the orders that arrive should all be the same size, since the entire shipment arrives each time and all other conditions are assumed to be the same throughout all the cycles. Figure 13.1 illustrates a fixed-quantity inventory system, so called because the same amount is ordered each time. It also represents a fixed-interval system; because the demand is the same each cycle, orders will be needed at the same intervals.

Knowing how the order size affects the inventory level enables us to write an equation for inventory costs in terms of the order size Q. Some time base must be established over which we wish to consider cost, so we consider the cost per year. If we minimize the average inventory costs for the typical year, we have minimized inventory costs. The average inventory is the average height of a triangle, or one-half its total height. Average inventory for the case is $Q/2$. The cost to hold inventory for a year is the average number of items held times the cost to hold an item for a year *(H)*, or $Q/2 \times H$. The average ordering costs are the number of cycles per year times the cost incurred for each order. If we must buy D_a units, the annual demand, during

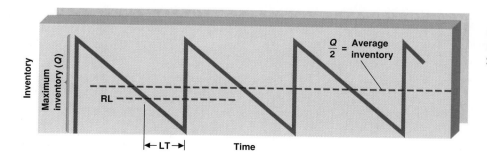

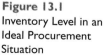

Figure 13.1
Inventory Level in an Ideal Procurement Situation

the year and Q units each time we buy, then we will have to place D_a/Q orders and the annual order cost will be $D_a/Q \times S$, where S is the cost to place and receive one order. The cost of the items is assumed to be constant regardless of the amount we purchase each time we order (assumption 2), so it can be excluded from consideration. Costs that are affected by the lot-size decisions, the relevant costs, are the order-related and *holding costs*. The total annual relevant costs, or TC, are determined by equation 13.1:

$$\text{TC} = \frac{Q}{2} \times H + \frac{D_a}{Q} \times S \qquad \qquad \text{[13.1]}$$

To review the symbols: Q = quantity ordered each time an order is placed
H = increase in cost from holding one more unit for a year ($H = h \times C$, where h is the holding cost as a percentage and C is the cost of a unit)
D_a = annual demand, or number of units used in a year
S = stocking cost, or additional costs incurred by placing and receiving one more order

The total annual relevant costs equal the average annual inventory times the marginal cost to hold an item for a year plus the number of orders placed per year times the marginal cost to place and receive an order. This equation shows how inventory costs are related to order size. The total cost and its two major components are shown graphically in Figure 13.2. Our objective is to find the EOQ, the value of Q, that will result in a minimum total annual relevant cost, TC.

Consider a marginal approach to the problem. Assume that we are considering adding to the order quantity at some point to the left of the minimum cost shown in Figure 13.2. If we increase the order quantity, say from A_1 to A_2, the holding cost will increase by ΔH_A and the order cost will decrease by ΔO_A. The decrease in order costs is greater than the increase in the holding cost, so there is a net reduction in TC.

If the order quantity were to the right of the EOQ, say at B_1, we might consider increasing it to B_2. The result would be an increase in holding costs larger than the decrease in order cost, or a net increase in costs. Somewhere between points A_1 and B_1 is the ideal order quantity. Moving from A_1 to the right reduced cost. We should

Figure 13.2
Inventory Costs vs.
Order Quantity

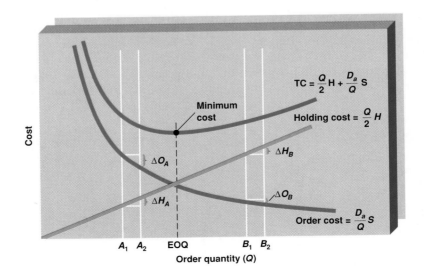

continue increasing Q from A_1 as long as costs are reduced but stop before we get to the place where they increase. Costs will then be minimized. The minimum is reached when the slope of the TC line is horizontal—when it has stopped coming down but has not yet begun to rise, in other words where the derivative of TC with respect to Q is zero. If we set the slope (the derivative) equal to zero (a horizontal line has a slope of zero) and solve for Q, we find the Q that minimizes costs, that is, the economic order quantity (EOQ).[1] Two expressions for the EOQ are shown in equation 13.2. They provide expression for the amount of an item one should order each time if the assumptions mentioned above are approximately true.

$$\text{EOQ} = \sqrt{\frac{2D_a S}{H}} \quad \text{or} \quad \text{EOQ} = \sqrt{\frac{2D_a S}{C \times h}} \qquad [13.2]$$

Notice that under the radical is two times the *annual* demand times the order cost divided by the *annual* holding cost. *Demand and holding cost must be expressed for identical time bases.* Monthly demand over annual holding cost, for example, will give the wrong answer. Monthly demand over monthly holding cost, however, would be correct.

Considerations for Applying the EOQ

The EOQ formula is useful as a conceptual model. It illustrates the general direction of how some relevant costs are affected by the order size. It does not provide an exact answer for at least two reasons. The six assumptions we presented earlier as the basis for the model probably will not all be accurate in most actual situations and the cost figures that a company would substitute into the formula would be approximate estimates at best. In most cases the use rate is a forecast that also is uncertain. Therefore the solution to the formula should be considered as an approximate answer. If, however, all the assumptions used in developing the model are assumed to be true then the annual holding cost as provided by the formula will be equal to the annual ordering costs.

In applying the EOQ model it may be difficult to estimate S, the incremental cost that would result from placing and receiving one more order. Usually a company can handle some increase in the number of orders without adding to its staff. At some level of increase, however, it would need additional employees to order, unload, and move items to the proper locations. One desires to estimate the average *increase* in cost per order over a series of increases in order activity that reflect a change in cost. This is different from the average cost per order because any fixed portion of the costs is not relevant since it will be paid regardless of the order-size decision.

---

[1]$TC = \dfrac{Q}{2} H + \dfrac{D_a}{Q} S$

Taking the derivative with respect to Q yields

$$\text{Slope} = \frac{d\text{TC}}{dQ} = \frac{H}{2} - \frac{D_a S}{Q^2}$$

Setting the slope equal to zero and solving for Q yield

$$\frac{H}{2} = \frac{D_a S}{Q^2} \quad \text{so} \quad Q^2 = \frac{2D_a S}{H}$$

Therefore, the minimum-cost Q or $\text{EOQ} = \sqrt{\dfrac{2D_a S}{H}}$

EXAMPLE OF ORDER QUANTITY DETERMINATION

Veneer Furniture Company handles several lines of furniture, one of which is the popular Layback Model T chair, which the company purchases from a plant only 10 miles from the store. Since the source is so near, Veneer has not bothered to stock a large number of chairs in its warehouse. Instead, it sends its truck to "pick up a few" when there are none on the showroom floor. Slim Veneer, the owner, has observed that many times when he needs his truck to make a delivery, it is tied up making trips to the Layback plant, and he suspects his ordering practices may not be optimal. He has decided to determine by use of the EOQ model the best quantity to obtain in each order.

Mr. Veneer has determined from past invoices that he has sold about 200 chairs during each of the past 2 years at a fairly uniform rate, and he expects to continue at that rate. He has estimated that preparation of an order and payment for the driver and truck and the invoice and other variable costs associated with each order are about $10, and it costs him about 1.5 percent per month, or 18 percent per year, to hold items in stock. His cost for the chair is $87, so it costs him $0.18 \times \$87 = \$15.66$ to hold a chair for 1 year. (Of course, a chair does not stay in stock that long, but Slim uses annual use rates, and the holding cost must be based on the same unit of time as the use rate. He could use the monthly use rate and the cost to hold a chair for 1 month. Any other time base could be used, as long as it was used for both the use rate and the cost to hold an item.) Veneer's calculations show that

$$EOQ = \sqrt{\frac{2D_aS}{H}} = \sqrt{\frac{2(200)(10)}{15.66}}$$

$$= \sqrt{255.43} = 15.98 \text{ units}$$

He has therefore told the buyer that each time she orders Layback chairs she should order 16 of them.

The unit holding cost, *H,* or average increase in cost to add one unit to the order size, must also be estimated. A company might increase the size of its orders by several units without noticing any change in the costs associated with holding units—other than perhaps the cost of the invested funds. However, a company that purchases its independent-demand items in less-frequent large lots will have higher inventory holding costs than a company that operates with more-frequent small lots. One would attempt to estimate the average increase in cost per unit of inventory held.

The assumption that inventory holding cost increases linearly as the order size is increased is also questionable. A company that orders small lots would probably have no obsolescence costs because it can adjust its purchases as consumer preferences shift. A company that purchases in large quantities would probably have large obsolescence costs, particularly in a dynamic, technology-driven market. It is apparent that some judgment and approximations are necessary in adapting the EOQ concept to an actual situation.

THE TRADITIONAL PRODUCTION LOT-SIZE MODEL

The general concept developed for the EOQ can be adapted to some situations where the independent-demand item is produced internally by the company rather than purchased from some supplier. It can also be applied for dependent-demand items that are used at a fairly uniform rate. In the production situation we wish to determine the economic production lot size, or EPL.

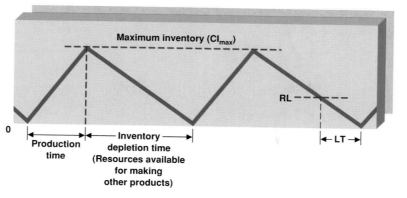

Figure 13.3
Inventory Level vs. Time for the Production Situation

For this model we change the assumption that the entire order arrives at the same time (assumption 3) as it would if it arrived in a shipment from a supplier. Instead assume that the order is produced internally or will be supplied at some uniform rate p. Naturally, the production rate p must be greater than the demand rate d, or no inventory will be accumulated. For the production situation, the graphical model of inventory level versus time also is a series of triangles, but the inventory replenishment portion of a cycle is not vertical (see Figure 13.3). Instead of building up instantaneously, inventory builds at the production rate minus the use rate $p - d$. If the company produces at a rate of 100 units each day and sells at a rate of 20 units per day, there will be $100 - 20 = 80$ units per day remaining to add to the inventory. To maintain consistent units of measure, the production rate and the use rate must be expressed as units per same time period. The production rate and use rate can be expressed as units per year, even though the production process would rarely be run continuously for a year.

The time that the process must run to produce Q units is Q/p. For example, to produce 500 units at a rate of 100 per day, the process is run $500/100 = 5$ days. Alternatively, using years as the measure of time, assume the production rate is 25,000 units per year (250 production days per year × 100 units per day). It would require $500/25{,}000 = 0.02$ year to produce 500 units at that rate. The production time is the same amount, 0.02 year × 250 workdays per year = 5 workdays.

The production process can be run for Q/p years to replenish inventory of one item, then the production equipment can be set up and run for some other product or products while the inventory of the first item is being depleted. In this way, the same equipment is used to produce several products such as in batch manufacturing. Our objective is to find the best quantity of a product to produce each time the setup cost is incurred. Each product probably will have a different setup cost and production rate and thus its own economic production quantity.

Examining one cycle of inventory replenishment and depletion (Figure 13.4), we see that CI_{max}, the maximum level of cycle inventory that builds up and is depleted over time, occurs at a time Q/p after inventory beings to accumulate. We find the maximum cycle inventory by multiplying the inventory accumulation rate, $p - d$, by the time inventory is accumulated:

$$CI_{max} = \frac{Q}{p} (p - d) = Q(1 - d/p) \qquad [13.3]$$

where p = production rate, such as units produced per week
d = demand rate, such as units used per week

Figure 13.4
One Cycle of Inventory Replenishment and Depletion for an Item

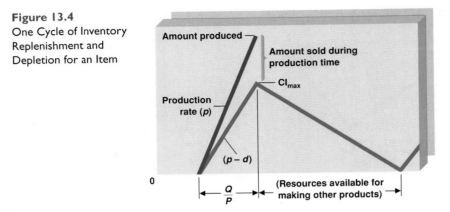

Note: For the ratio to be correct both p and d must be expressed for the same time period, such as per day, per week, and so on.

The maximum cycle inventory will be the production lot Q times the fraction $(1 - d/p)$ that represents production not sold. Since d/p is the fraction of production that is sold, $1 - d/p$ must be stored. Since only the fraction $1 - d/p$ of the production lot must be stored, the holding cost will be $Q(1 - d/p)/2 \times H$. The total relevant cost equation for the production situation is like equation 13.1, except that the first Q is multiplied by $(1 - d/p)$:

$$\text{TC} = \frac{Q(1 - d/p)}{2} H + \frac{D_a}{Q} S \qquad \text{[13.4]}$$

where S for this production model = the costs incurred to initiate a production order (setup, production control, and others). Companies should work continuously to reduce S.

Calculus can be used to derive an expression for the *economic production lot (EPL)*, resulting in equation 13.5. This expression is sometimes called the *economic production quantity.*

$$\text{EPL} = \sqrt{\frac{2D_a S}{H(1 - d/p)}} \qquad \text{or} \qquad \text{EPL} = \sqrt{\frac{2D_a S}{H(1 - D_a/P)}} \qquad \text{[13.5]}$$

where P is the production rate expressed as units per year and the other symbols are as defined previously

Alternatively, one could reason that since some material is being sold while the lot is being produced, the holding costs will be reduced. Only the fraction $1 - d/p$ must be held, so the holding cost can be multiplied by $1 - d/p$. Notice that equation 13.5 is identical to equation 13.2, except that the holding cost is multiplied by $1 - d/p$ or $1 - D_a/P$.

The Importance of Setup Reduction

The point was made in our earlier discussion that if the EOQ is used in purchasing situations, the ordering costs will equal the holding costs. This condition is also true for production situations. Under the assumptions of the model, the annual holding costs will equal the annual setup costs if the economic production lot is produced

A P P L I C A T I O N

EXAMPLE OF PRODUCTION LOT-SIZE MODEL

The Layback Chair Company sells to Veneer Furniture and many other retailers. The demand for the Layback Model T chair is relatively uniform at 15,000 per year. The company estimates that it costs $200 to set up all the equipment and paperwork for production of this chair. When the production facility is running the Model T, the production rate is 150 per day. Each chair costs the company $48.62 to produce, and the holding cost is estimated to be 24 percent per year, so $H = \$48.62 \times 0.24 = \$11.67$ to hold a chair in inventory for 1 year.

The production rate and the demand rate must be expressed on a common time base. Since the demand rate is already on an annual base, the production rate was converted to an annual base. The plant works 5 days a week for 50 weeks a year, so there are 250 workdays in its production year. The production in a year, if the process were run that long, would be 150 units per workday × 250 workdays per year, or 37,500 units per year. Use of equation 13.5 shows that

$$EPL = \sqrt{\frac{2D_aS}{H(1 - D_a/P)}}$$

$$= \sqrt{\frac{2[15,000(200)]}{11.67[1 - (15,000/37,500)]}}$$

$$= \sqrt{856,898} = 925.69 \text{ units}$$

The company should produce about 926 units each time it begins production of the Layback Model T. A production run will require 926/37,500 = 0.0247 year to produce (0.0247 × 250 workdays = 6.17 days). During the production run, 15,000/37,500 or 0.4 of the units produced will be sold, and 0.6 will be held in inventory. The maximum cycle inventory will be 926(0.6) or 556 units and the annual holding cost will be (556/2)($11.67) or $3,244.26. The annual setup cost will be (15,000/926)($200) = $3,239.74. Notice these two costs are approximately equal, as in the case of the economic order quantity determination.

---

at each setup. Therefore, efforts to reduce the cost per setup can pay off doubly. If a company reduces the cost per setup and operates with the appropriate production quantity for the reduced setup cost, it will also reduce the cost of holding inventory.

If the independent-demand item under consideration is an assembly of components, then S, the estimated setup costs that will result from initiating another lot, would include the incremental costs of all the setups that will be made at all the stages of production. If any of these operations are to be performed at *bottleneck* operations the setup cost estimates may be relatively large. A bottleneck is a resource whose capacity is less than or equal to the demand placed on it, that is, it limits the plant's output. The decision to have another setup here will reduce the percentage of the time the bottleneck operation is performing value-adding production, and therefore will reduce the plant's output. For nonbottleneck operations the setup cost is the average increase in cost that results from having another setup and may be relatively low.

Within the near term, setup costs may be considered a set amount that will result from a setup. However, companies should always look for ways to improve setup procedures to reduce the time and cost, particularly at bottlenecks because this will increase the plant's sales capacity. Also, setup requirements should be an important consideration in equipment selection and tooling design. When the setup cost is reduced, the setup cost line and the holding cost line will cross at a lower production lot size as shown by EPL_2 instead of EPL_1 in the assumed graph of costs presented in Figure 13.5. Use of this smaller EPL would result in a reduction of both the setup cost and holding cost, providing a double payoff for the setup improvement efforts.

Figure 13.5
The Effect of Setup
Reduction and Added
Lot-Size Costs on the
Basic EOQ Trade-off

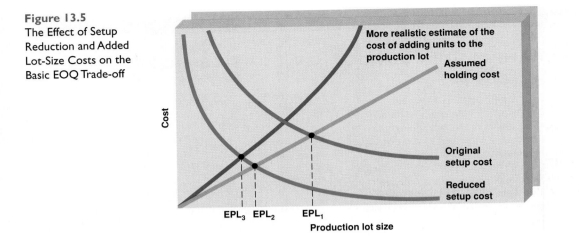

Estimating H, the incremental cost of adding one more unit to the production batch, may involve some complicating factors. The considerations so far have treated the holding cost as if it is a function of the production lot size. This assumption may be fairly accurate for the finished-goods inventory that result from production of a lot or receiving an order from a supplier. The production lot size does determine how many units will be added to finished goods when a production run is made. However, some of the holding cost for production of a lot results from the work-in-process (WIP) inventory as the lot is produced. WIP inventory is more a function of the transfer batch size than of the total production lot size. The *transfer batch* is the number of units that are accumulated at one step of production before they are moved to the next step. There is little WIP in repetitive manufacturing because as soon as a unit is processed at one step of production it is sent to the next. In a job shop the transfer batch often is the entire order, which is usually a small quantity. In batch manufacturing the transfer batch can range from one unit to the entire production batch. We will discuss this matter further.

A company that elects to use large transfer batches may require larger capacity materials-handling equipment, wider aisles, more space around processing equipment to hold containers of material waiting to be processed and material that has been through that processing step but waiting for the rest of the transfer batch to be processed so the batch can be transferred to the next step. The facility investment for this company will be higher than for a factory that transfers in small batches. Larger transfer batches move more slowly to subsequent production steps where quality problems often are discovered. Quality problems in larger batches usually mean that more defective units have been made and, since the problems are discovered later, there is less likelihood that the causes of the problems can be tracked down and solved. Consequently, it seems that the costs associated with larger transfer batches will be higher than a linear scale up of the costs that result from smaller batches. (Even though some of the costs related to having more units in a batch may not be the direct result of holding units, we will refer to these costs as holding costs or holding-related costs.) It is likely that the transfer batch size will be proportional to the production lot size. Under this assumption, the holding-related costs for large production batches is higher than a linear ratio of the holding costs for smaller production lots. When a nonlinear holding-related cost is used it shifts the production lot size to an even smaller quantity as shown by EPL$_3$ in Figure 13.5. Other considerations about production lots are discussed in later chapters where we discuss dependent demand, scheduling, and efforts to keep WIP low. The matter is introduced here because of the relation it has with selecting the amount to add to independent-demand or finished-goods inventory.

EVALUATING QUANTITY-DISCOUNT OPPORTUNITIES

One assumption of the most basic version of the EOQ model was that the cost of the item was not affected by the order size. *Quantity discounts* sometimes are offered for externally purchased items. In addition, economies of scale may result in different unit costs for different production lot sizes when items are produced internally. This section discusses selection of the economic order size when discounts (as in Table 13.1) are available.

A discount schedule that has *price breaks* at specified quantities results in steps in the total cost curve. The total annual relevant cost equation for this case includes the item costs and is

$$\text{TC} = \frac{Q}{2} H_i + \frac{D_a}{Q} S + D_a C_i \qquad \text{[13.6]}$$

where H_i = holding cost per unit that will be incurred for the particular Q being considered ($H_i = hC_i$)
C_i = unit price that must be paid if the item is purchased in the quantity being considered

Notice that C depends on the order quantity, and H is a percentage of C, so both change when we consider an order quantity that is in a different discount bracket. Calculus cannot be used to find the slope of a discontinuous curve, so we cannot obtain one equation that will always specify the minimum cost decision. To be completely sure that the minimum total cost has been found, it may be necessary to solve the TC equation several times, perhaps once for each possible item cost.

The ordering-cost part of equation 13.6 is the same as was developed previously for the first EOQ model. Since the holding cost is a percentage of the item cost, it will also be discontinuous. A graph of the relevant inventory cost as a function of order quantity is presented in Figure 13.6.

The total cost curve of Figure 13.6 is made by connecting portions of three different continuous curves. Each of these continuous curves (shown by a dashed line and the solid portion of the TC curve) is the TC curve that would result if the item cost remained constant over all quantities. The top line would result if all units cost C_1, the middle line if all units cost C_2, and so on. If we solved equation 13.2, the procurement EOQ model, using one cost, we would find the quantity that results in the

Table 13.1
A PRICE DISCOUNT SCHEDULE

QUANTITY	PRICE/UNIT
Less than Q_1	C_1
Q_1 and up to Q_2	C_2
Q_2 and above	C_3

Figure 13.6
Relevant Costs vs.
Order Quantity with
Price Breaks

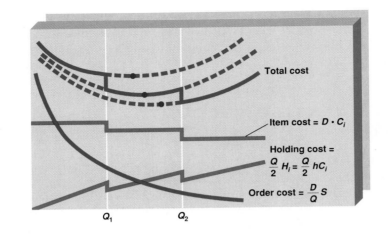

minimum holding cost plus ordering cost at this price. There are two problems with this quantity:

1. The resulting quantity may not be feasible; that is, we may not be permitted to purchase that quantity at the price used.
2. Even for a feasible minimum point on the curve, it may be more economical to purchase several more units and obtain a quantity discount. The savings in item cost achieved by purchasing a few more units and receiving a price break may more than offset the additional holding cost for a few extra units.

The procedure for finding the best order quantity in this type of situation is as follows:

1. Consider the lowest price, and solve the basic EOQ formula (equation 13.2) for the EOQ at this price. If the EOQ is feasible, this is the best quantity, so stop; otherwise go to step 2.
2. Solve for the EOQ for the next higher price. If this EOQ is feasible, proceed to step 4.
3. If the EOQ is not feasible, repeat step 2 until a feasible EOQ is found.
4. Compute the TC (use equation 13.6) for the feasible EOQ and for all the greater quantities where the price breaks occur. Select the quantity with the lowest TC.

Figure 13.7 illustrates the possible relationships that may exist between the total costs where the slope is horizontal and where price breaks occur. The price-break quantity is indicated by the vertical dashed line.

Figure 13.7*a* shows the EOQ determined by use of the lowest item cost. Since this EOQ is feasible, it is the lowest total cost, because all points on the TC curve for the next higher item cost will be higher.

Figures 13.7*b* and *c* show two relationships that can exist when some item cost other than the lowest one in the price schedule is being considered. In Figure 13.7*b*, the reduction in total cost due to purchasing at the next higher price break is not sufficient to overcome the holding costs that are increased because more inventory is purchased. Figure 13.7*c* shows a case in which purchasing more will achieve a quantity discount that reduces the item cost more than the increase in the holding cost. Any price-break quantities beyond the next higher one should be evaluated.

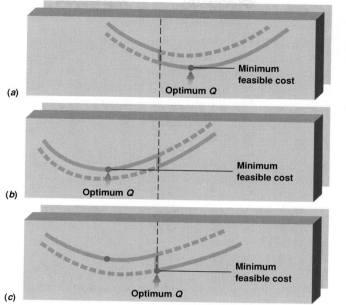

Figure 13.7
Possible Total Cost
Curve Relationships
When Price Breaks
Are Available

APPLICATION

EXAMPLE OF PRICE-BREAK ORDER QUANTITY

The Eagle Mountain Hospital uses disposable surgical packages for many routine operations rather than sterilizing and packaging the necessary bandages and instruments. It uses approximately 100 Surg Pac units each month. Elective surgery is scheduled for times when the schedule for other surgery is low, so that demand for Surg Pacs is fairly uniform. Each Surg Pac costs $35 in quantities of less than 75 and $32.50 if purchased in quantities of 75 or more. The hospital controller estimates that it costs $8 to process and receive an order. The cost of holding inventory is estimated to be 12% of the purchase price per year.

Karla Karmikel, the purchasing agent, examined the price schedule and performed the following analysis:

Step 1. If Surg Pacs are purchased at the lowest price, $32.50, the holding cost per unit-year, H, will be $0.12 \times \$32.50 = \$3.90$, so for this price

$$EOQ(\$32.50) = \sqrt{\frac{2D_a S}{H}} = \sqrt{\frac{2(1,200)(8)}{3.90}}$$
$$= \sqrt{4,923.08} = 70.16 \text{ or } 70$$

This quantity is not feasible. The hospital would not receive the lowest price if it purchased 70 packs each time.

Step 2. If Surg Pacs are purchased at $35 each, the holding cost will be $0.12 \times \$35 = \$4.20$ per unit-year.

$$EOQ(\$35) = \sqrt{\frac{2D_a S}{H}} = \sqrt{\frac{2(1,200)(8)}{4.20}}$$
$$= \sqrt{4,571.43} = 67.61 \text{ or } 68$$

This is a feasible order quantity, but another step will determine if it is the best. The hospital will achieve a sizable savings on the item cost if it purchases 75 units in each order.

Ms. Karmikel used the TC equation (equation 13.6) to evaluate this possibility and found the following total annual cost if 68 is used as the order quantity.

$$TC_{68} = \frac{68}{2}(\$4.20) + \frac{1,200}{68}(\$8.00)$$
$$+ 1,200(\$35.00) = \$42,283.98$$

If the hospital buys the Surg Pacs in quantities of 75, the total annual cost will be

$$TC_{75} = \frac{75}{2}(\$3.90) + \frac{1,200}{75}(\$8.00)$$
$$+ 1,200(\$32.50) = \$39,274.25$$

This price-break example for Surg Pacs was like the one illustrated in Figure 13.7c. It is more economical to purchase an amount above the point on the solid TC line where the slope is horizontal. Ms. Karmikel made a notation on the Surg Pac inventory record card that the proper order quantity was 75.

DETERMINING THE REORDER LEVEL

The previous models have been developed under the assumption of a deterministic use rate. That assumption was stated, and the illustrations showed that the reorder level was established so that the inventory level would reach zero just as the new material began to arrive. With a known use rate and lead time, the reorder level would be set equal to the use rate d (in units per time period) times LT, the number of these time periods in the lead time.

$$RL = d \times LT \qquad\qquad \text{[13.7]}$$

For example, if a company uses exactly 20 units of a particular component each day and the replenishment lead time is known to be 3 days, the RL for this component is $20 \times 3 = 60$ units.

The reorder level refers to the number of units on hand and on order, rather than to just the amount of inventory on hand. In many instances no orders are outstanding when the reorder level is reached, so the reorder level is often thought of as referring to only the number of units on hand. This misconception may cause no problem; but in some instances, the reorder level may be greater than the maximum inventory, and this could cause some confusion. For example, the lead time could be long, causing the reorder level to be very high. Also the order cost may be low in comparison to the holding cost, causing the order quantity to be small. In instances where one or more orders are outstanding when the reorder level is reached, it is important to remember that the reorder level refers to the number of units on hand *plus* those on order.

In the following section we will deal with probabilistic demand. When we do not know the exact demand rate and lead time, there is a chance that the amount demanded during the lead time will be greater than the reorder level unless we increase the reorder level beyond the amount expressed by equation 13.7 (above). The additional amount that is added to the reorder level is sometimes referred to as safety stock.

SAFETY STOCK

One reason for inventory is to allow production or procurement in economic lot sizes. Previous discussions in this chapter have dealt with lot sizing under a variety of conditions. The lot size, in effect, determines the *cycle stock,* or stock that is intended to be depleted and replenished, then depleted and replenished again through many cycles.

Another reason for inventory is to protect against uncertainty of demand. In previous inventory discussions, we assumed that demand and lead times were known (deterministic) and that reorders were timed so that replenishment stock arrived just as the previous order was exhausted. Usually one does not know precisely the number of units that will be demanded each day during the lead time. Also the duration of lead times may have unexplained or unexpected variation.

Demand can be thought of as a probabilistic variable with some expected amount of demand during a period of time and unexplained variation about the expected value. If we could replenish inventory on a moment's notice, there would be no reason to be concerned about demand uncertainty. Whenever inventory reached zero, we would restock. With some lead time between the placement of an

Errors in stocking too much or too little inventory have always been a problem, but the competitive world that businesses face heightens the problem. Today, there is less room for error.

Larry Lawfer/Picture Cube

order and its arrival, however, there is a chance that demand will be greater than we expected and we will incur a loss due to stockout. When stockout costs are high and demand is very unpredictable, the financial risk is sizable. For example, Compaq, the leading producer of PCs estimated that in 1994 it missed between $500 million and $1 billion in sales because it did not have the right items when and where the customer wanted to buy them. Many companies are working to develop quicker, more-flexible means of restocking quickly enough to prevent missing sales. Some companies (such as the Allen-Bradley electrical contactor and relay plant, discussed in Chapter 7) can produce some items so quickly that they make to order instead of trying to stock enough of each of these finished items so they can cover the levels of demand that might occur. Motorola's custom pager plant in Boynton Beach, Florida, takes orders for the pocket-size units by phone or E-mail. The data is digitized, pick-and-place robots select the proper components, and humans assemble the units, often within 80 minutes.

When lead times are longer *safety stock* or *buffer stock* can be used as another means of protecting against stockout. Here we discuss some considerations about selecting safety stock levels when it is to be used.

Safety stock is the average amount on hand when replenishment items arrive. Sometimes demand during the lead time is less than expected, and extra stock is on hand. Sometimes demand is greater than expected, and some of the safety stock is used. Safety stock can be thought of as remaining in inventory all year, on the average. Figure 13.8 illustrates inventory level over time when safety stock is present.

Safety stock (SS) is established simply by raising the reorder level above the expected lead-time demand. For probabilistic demand during lead time, the reorder level (RL) is given by equation 13.8, where *d* represents the mean demand per unit of time (the time units are consistent with the units for lead time, LT).

$$\text{RL} = (d \times \text{LT}) + \text{SS} \qquad \text{[13.8]}$$

Figure 13.8
Inventory Level When
Safety Stock Is Present

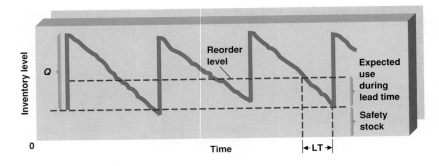

For example, an office supply company may try to maintain a safety stock or minimum inventory of 25 reams of 25 percent cotton cream stationery. Suppose that demand for this product averages 5 reams per day and the usual replenishment lead time is 6 business days. In these circumstances RL = (5 reams/day × 6 days) + 25 reams = 55 reams.

Factors Affecting Safety Stock Level

The best amount of safety stock to carry depends on the situation and the cost of carrying safety stock should be compared to the benefits it provides. All other things being equal, the following conditions tend to encourage higher levels of safety stock:

- The cost or loss due to stockout is high.
- The cost of carrying safety stock is low.
- The variability or uncertainty of demand is high due to forecast inaccuracy.
- The number of annual exposures to the risk of stockout is great because of numerous orders of small amounts.

A rigorous analysis of inventory costs would include consideration of the interrelationship of order quantity and stockout, solving simultaneous equations to obtain the optimum value for the order quantity and safety stock. Several texts and many actual applications ignore the interrelation, and so do we. We determine the EOQ by use of the equations previously developed and then determine the best safety stock level, given the order quantity we have found.

Methods of Determining the Safety Stock Level

When demand is probabilistic, inventory may reach its reorder level sooner or later than expected. The cycle time between replenishments will no longer be constant. There is no stockout risk involved with demand fluctuations between the time of maximum inventory and the time the inventory balance reaches the reorder level. The risk occurs after the reorder level has been reached. Demand during the lead time may turn out to be less than, equal to, or greater than the reorder level. These conditions are illustrated in Figure 13.9.

The objective of establishing safety stock is to define a reasonable maximum level of demand during lead time that will be covered by inventory. We shall discuss three methods.

INTUITIVE RULE OF THUMB Sometimes inventory managers or higher-level managers arbitrarily set ratios to guide the establishment of reorder points and safety

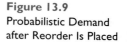

Figure 13.9
Probabilistic Demand
after Reorder Is Placed

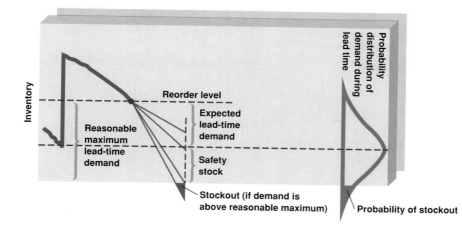

stocks. They may order whenever the on-hand quantity is twice (or 1.5 times, 1.2 times, or some such amount) the average use during a lead time. This method recognizes that lead time may be longer than expected, demand may be higher than expected, or both. The method does not, however, formally consider probabilities of stockout, cost of inventory, or cost of stockout. Examination of past back orders or canceled orders as a percentage of mean lead-time demand gives some indication of demand variation or risk of stockout for various reorder levels. The objective is to establish a reorder level at some "reasonable maximum" level of lead-time demand without identifying probability or stockout costs.

SERVICE LEVEL VS. HOLDING COST   The *service level* is a measure of how effective a company is at supplying demanded goods from its stock on hand (that is, how well it prevents lost sales and back orders). There are several methods of expressing a quantitative measure of service level. We use the probability of covering the demand that occurs during the inventory replenishment lead time. This is also the probability that we will not run out of stock during the inventory cycle.

To implement a policy specifying some service level, one must have information concerning the probability of various levels of demand during lead time. Often the quantity of an item demanded during the lead time varies from its expected value. Some of this variation may be caused by fluctuations in the length of the lead time and some by variation of the demand rate about its mean. Records from a number of previous reorder cycles can be examined to determine the number of units demanded between the time a replenishment order was placed and the time that material arrived. Let us call this variable *lead-time demand* or D_L. A frequency or probability distribution for lead-time demand can be constructed as in Figure 13.10. Lead-time demand may be expressed as discrete or continuous units, but Figure 13.10 illustrates a discrete distribution, and the relationships among safety stock, reorder level, and the probability of stockout are shown.

In setting service levels, however, we are not really interested in the probability that a particular value of lead-time demand will occur. Rather, we are interested in the probability that lead-time demand will be less than or equal to some particular level. Often it is easier to find the smaller probability of a stockout for a given reorder level. A greater-than cumulative probability distribution can be constructed by adding the probabilities in the right tail of the distribution and subtracting this total from 1 to determine the service level that would result from possible reorder levels.

Figure 13.10
A Probability
Distribution for
Demand during Lead
Time

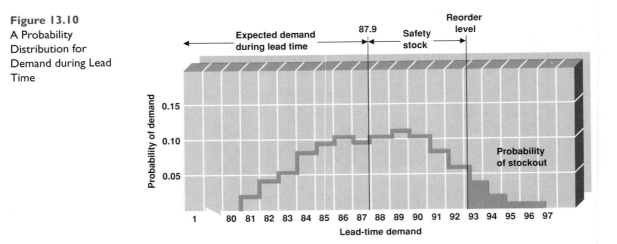

The shaded area in the right tail of Figure 13.10 corresponds to the probability of a stockout for a given reorder level. It can be computed for various reorder levels and plotted as a greater-than cumulative probability distribution. Figure 13.11 shows this type of distribution as a smooth curve, which would result from a continuous variable or from drawing a smooth curve through midpoints of the steps in a discrete cumulative distribution. The ordinate of Figure 13.11 has been provided with two scales: one showing the probability of stockout and one showing service level. Notice that the probability of stockout declines very rapidly near the middle. The service level can be increased from 0.70 to 0.80 by adding only 25 units to the reorder level. But an additional 55 units are necessary to increase the service level by another 0.10 to 0.90. Greater increments in the reorder level, causing greater increases in inventory holding costs, are required for each equal-sized increment to the service level as the service level is increased beyond 0.50.

Figure 13.11
A Greater-Than
Cumulative Probability
Distribution of Lead-
Time Demand

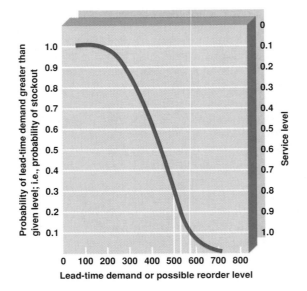

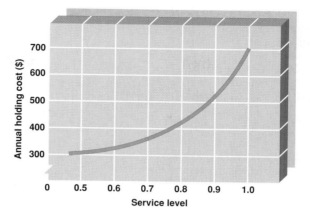

Figure 13.12
Holding Cost vs. Service Level

The total cost of holding inventory can be plotted as a function of the service level a company might consider providing. An example of this type of graph is shown in Figure 13.12. Managers may find a graphical presentation such as Figure 13.12 very helpful in establishing a service-level policy. They may be willing to hold a large inventory and provide a high service level if funds are rather plentiful and competition is fierce. They may elect to reduce service levels if competitive pressures are not as great and if funds are needed for other purposes. The service-level policy compares the percentage of demand that is met from inventory with the cost of holding inventory. It does not explicitly consider the cost of stockout. Some implicit value of stockout, however, can be inferred from the holding cost a company is willing to pay to prevent stockout.

APPLICATION

EXAMPLE OF SETTING A REORDER LEVEL ON THE BASIS OF AN EMPIRICAL PROBABILITY DISTRIBUTION

Earlier we saw how Karla Karmikel at Eagle Mountain Hospital determined the most economical number of disposable surgical packs to buy in each order. Now suppose that Ms. Karmikel wishes to determine the appropriate reorder level when there is variation in the number of units required during a lead time. Ordinarily the lead time is 4 days, but it has varied from 2 to 7 days, and use per day has varied from 0 to 10 units. Ms. Karmikel has reviewed data for the past 25 orders and has found considerable variation in the number of Surg Pac units used between the time the order was placed and the time it was received (that is, the lead-time demand).

A frequency count for lead-time demand for Surg Pacs is shown in Table 13.2. These data are plotted in a combined frequency distribution and probability

distribution, shown in Figure 13.13. The variable of primary interest is the probability that the number of Surg Pacs required during the lead time will be greater than some specified quantity. This probability will indicate the likelihood that the lead-time demand will be greater than each reorder level that may be selected. The desired probabilities are provided by a greater-than cumulative probability distribution such as that shown in Figure 13.14. These probabilities are found by accumulating probabilities beginning at the right tail of the probability distribution for demand during lead time (from the right-hand column of Table 13.2).

It has been agreed at meetings between the director of pharmacy, the director of materials, and the medical staff that a 95 percent service level is adequate for disposal of Surg Pacs. The operating room staff can prepare nondisposible kits in the event of a stockout. Therefore, Ms. Karmikel has selected 30 units as the reorder level that appears to be sufficient to cover 95 percent of the units demanded during lead time. The expected demand during lead time is 17 units, so the safety stock from this kit is $30 - 17 = 13$ units.

Table 13.2
LEAD-TIME DEMAND FOR SURG PACS AT EAGLE MOUNTAIN HOSPITAL

POSSIBLE LEVELS OF DEMAND (K)	FREQUENCY OF OCCURRENCE	PROBABILITY	CUMULATIVE PROBABILITY $P(D > K)$
6		0.00	1.00
7	1	0.04	0.96
8		0.00	0.96
9	1	0.04	0.92
10	11	0.08	0.84
11		0.00	0.84
12	1	0.04	0.80
13		0.00	0.80
14	11	0.08	0.72
15	111	0.12	0.60
16	1111	0.16	0.44
17	111	0.12	0.32
18	11	0.08	0.24
19	1	0.04	0.20
20		0.00	0.20
21		0.00	0.20
22	1	0.04	0.16
23	1	0.04	0.12
24		0.00	0.12
25		0.00	0.12
26	1	0.04	0.08
27		0.00	0.08
28		0.00	0.08
29		0.00	0.08
30	1	0.04	0.04
31		0.00	0.04
32	1	0.04	0.00
33		0.00	0.00
	25	1.00	

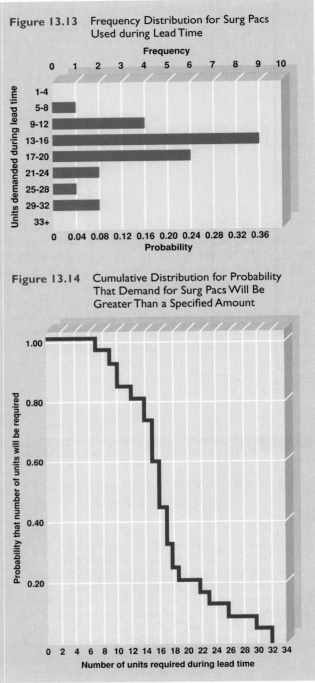

Figure 13.13 Frequency Distribution for Surg Pacs Used during Lead Time

Figure 13.14 Cumulative Distribution for Probability That Demand for Surg Pacs Will Be Greater Than a Specified Amount

EXPLICIT TRADE-OFF OF STOCKOUT COST We have seen that holding costs climb at ever-increasing rates as the service level is increased (see Figure 13.12). Attempting to cover all possible levels of lead-time demand can be a very expensive objective. At some point (the reasonable maximum demand) it may be less expensive to allow some stockouts to occur, at least for most products. A rational business exec-

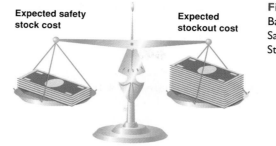

Expected safety
stock cost

Expected
stockout cost

Figure 13.15
Balancing Costs of
Safety Stock and
Stockout

utive will raise the safety stock level as long as the expected cost of carrying safety stock is less than the expected opportunity cost of stockout. The problem becomes one of determining the safety stock level that balances the expected cost of carrying safety stock with the expected cost of not having enough stock (Figure 13.15).

We can find the reorder level at which these costs are in balance by marginal analysis. The marginal cost of adding another unit to safety stock, H, is assumed to be a constant. The marginal gain from adding safety stock—the expected reduction in stockout cost—is a variable we can change by varying the reorder level. As the reorder level is raised, the probability of stockout, and hence its expected cost, is reduced.

The expected cost of stockout in a year requires some explanation. A stockout will occur if demand is any value greater than the value of the last unit added to the reorder level. In one lead time the probability of a stockout is $P(D_L)$, the probability that demand will be greater than the reorder level. This probability can be obtained from a cumulative probability distribution of lead-time demand, as shown in Figure 13.11. Each time a stockout occurs, we incur a cost of C_S such as the cost of an expedited shipment. Other models have been developed that deal with costs that are related to the magnitude and duration of the shortage. So the expected stockout cost per cycle is $P(D_L) \times C_S$. Since there are D_a/Q cycles per year, we must multiply the expected cost per cycle by D_a/Q to get the expected annual stockout cost.

The expected annual stockout cost for a given reorder level, $P(D_L) \times C_S \times D_a/Q$, declines as the reorder level is increased, because $P(D_L)$, the probability of stockout, is reduced as we add safety stock. Safety stock should be added until the holding cost from adding the last unit of safety stock is equal to the expected gain from adding the last unit. These cost relationships are illustrated in Figure 13.16.

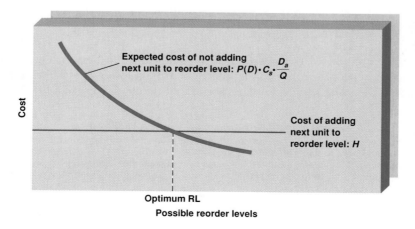

Figure 13.16
Costs Relevant to
Safety Stock

Cost

Expected cost of not adding
next unit to reorder level: $P(D) \cdot C_s \cdot \dfrac{D_a}{Q}$

Cost of adding
next unit to
reorder level: H

Optimum RL

Possible reorder levels

The two costs are equal when

$$H = P(D_L) C_S \times \frac{D_a}{Q}$$

Solving this expression for $P(D_L)$, we find $P(D_L)^*$, the probability of stockout at the "optimal" reorder level:

$$P(D_L)^* = \frac{H}{C_s} \times \frac{Q}{D_a} \qquad\qquad \textbf{[13.9]}$$

Equation 13.9 gives the probability of stockout for the optimal reorder level,[2] given the order quantity Q. One can then read the optimal reorder level from an empirical probability distribution for lead-time demand, such as Figure 13.11, if an empirical distribution is appropriate and has been developed.

If the lead-time demand fits a known probability distribution, the reorder level can be found with the aid of probability tables for the appropriate distribution. For example, assume that lead-time demand is normally distributed with a mean of 300 and a standard deviation of 100. Assume the optimal $P(D_L)$ is found to be 0.05; that is, we desire a 95 percent service level. A table giving the area under a standardized normal distribution (that is, a "Z distribution") can be used to determine the appropriate reorder level. Reference to a standardized normal probability table, as provided in Appendix I, reveals that 0.95 of the area under the curve lies to the left of $Z = +1.645$. That is, we must add $1.645\sigma_L$ to the mean of a normal distribution. So, for our problem, the reorder level we seek is RL = 300 + 1.645(100) = 465 units. In general, if lead-time demand is normally distributed, the reorder level can be found by

$$RL = \bar{D}_L + Z\sigma_L \qquad\qquad \textbf{[13.10]}$$

where D_L = average lead-time demand, or $\bar{d} \times LT$
  Z = the deviation in a standardized normal distribution
  σ_L = standard deviation of lead-time demand (this must be appropriate for the length of the lead time)

The expected use during the lead time is $\bar{D}_L$, so $Z\sigma_L$ is the safety stock. The standard deviation of lead-time demand must be measured over the lead time or adjusted to its length. If it is assumed that the demand in one period is independent of demand in the other periods and if the lead time is constant, then

$$\sigma_L = \sqrt{LT \times \sigma_p^2} \qquad\qquad \textbf{[13.11]}$$

where LT = number of periods in lead time
  σ_p = standard deviation of demand per period

Equation 13.11 shows that if the lead time can be shortened, such as by EDI or quick response from supplier-partners, then a lower safety stock can be used to provide the same service level. Suppose that demand averaged 40 units per week with a

---

[2]The order quantity and reorder level are interrelated. A large order quantity causes fewer replenishment cycles with fewer exposures to stockout, so the reorder level can be reduced, and vice versa. Theoretically, we would have to find simultaneous solutions to equations for Q and RL to find their optimal values. The values of D_a, S, and H are only estimates, and the value of the EOQ will be approximate whether or not an adjustment is made for the expected stockout cost. Consequently, as often is done, we disregard the interrelationship between Q and RL. We solve for the EOQ, ignoring its effect on stockout cost, and then we find the best reorder level for this value of Q.

ESTABLISHING A SAFETY STOCK LEVEL (REORDER LEVEL) WITH EXPLICIT STOCKOUT COST

The Celestial Grocery Coop distributes Jolly Red Giant red beans and wishes to establish a fixed-quantity inventory system for the product. Lead time to obtain these red beans from the Red Giant Company averages 1 week. Examination of past orders shows that demand has been fairly uniform and that lead-time demand has been normally distributed, with a mean of 320 cases and a standard deviation of 40 cases. Since demand averages 320 every week, annual demand is 16,640 cases. The company estimates that the order cost is $14.00, holding cost is $1.68 per year per case, and stockout cost is $2.00 per case.

The order quantity is

$$EOQ = \sqrt{\frac{2D_aS}{H}} = \sqrt{\frac{2(16,640)(14)}{1.68}}$$

$$= \sqrt{277,333.33} = 526.62$$

The company should order 527 cases each time, a quantity that would result in 31.6 cycles per year (16,640/527 = 31.6).

The remaining question is, What level of inventory should be on hand when the order is placed? The optimum probability of stockout in a reorder cycle can be found from equation 13.9:

$$P(D_L)^* = \frac{H}{C_s} \times \frac{Q}{D_a} = \frac{1.68}{2} \times \frac{527}{16,640} = 0.0266$$

A reasonable maximum demand is one that will be exceeded only 2.66 percent of the time. Referring to a normal probability table, we find that 97.34 percent of the area under the curve lies below a Z of 1.93. Therefore, the optimum reorder level is

$$RL = \bar{D}_L + Z\sigma_L = 320 + 1.93(40) = 397$$

The safety stock provided by this reorder level is 397 − 320 = 77 cases. As a result of these calculations, Celestial has established the following as its inventory policy for Red Giant beans: Order 527 cases every time the inventory level reaches 397 cases.

We can approximate the annual holding cost by assuming that the average inventory will include all the safety stock and half of the cycle stock. The annual holding cost will be ($1.68 per case) × [77 + (527/2)] = 1.68(340.5) = $572.04. This amount will not be equal to the annual ordering cost because it includes the cost of holding safety stock. The order-quantity formula makes the ordering cost equal to the cost of holding only the average cycle stock. The annual ordering cost will be ($14 per order) × (31.6 orders per year) = $442.40.

standard deviation, measured on a weekly basis, of 10 units. If the lead time were constant at 3 weeks, then σ_L would be found by equation 13.11:

$$\sigma_L = \sqrt{3(10^2)} = \sqrt{300} = 17.32$$

and

$$\bar{D}_L = 3(40) = 120$$

So for a 0.98 service level $Z = 2.05$ and $RL = \bar{D}_L + Z\sigma_L = 120 + 2.05(17.32) = 156$ units.

USING COMPUTERS TO MANAGE INDEPENDENT INVENTORY

You probably have noticed that in some grocery or department stores part of the labeling on products is scanned by some type of bar code reader at the checkout counter. Data indicating the item identification and quantity sold are recorded by this procedure and stored in an electronic memory. These data can be fed to a computer system to update the stock level and use rate for the item. In other stores, when an item is sold, the clerk removes the part of the price tag that contains the item identification. These tags are later read, and the data are fed to a computer. In yet other companies, the item identification and quantity sold are read from sales slips and keyed into a computer. In a factory or warehouse, shipping reports or inventory removal cards may be used as the source of data on stock removal. Receiving reports will indicate additions to the inventory by suppliers, and completed production orders will indicate additions to the inventory by production within the factory. You can see, then, that there are numerous ways to report data on inventory additions or withdrawals and to supply these data to a computer.

Computers can use data on receipts and withdrawals to maintain the amount of stock on hand for all the inventory items controlled by the computer system. Computer companies and commercial software companies offer software packages that will keep track of the on-hand balance and perform other functions, such as reporting items that are below their reorder levels and recommending the economic quantity to buy or produce. The computer may print a list each day, showing the items that need to be replenished. Sometimes a preferred vendor identification for each

Marriott Hotels use computers to monitor occupancy patterns for all their hotels. Armed with information on room usage, Marriott can attract and accommodate convention and other business clientele. They are also able to offer discounted prices for rooms at off times, when the rooms would otherwise be empty.

Andrea Pistolesi/The Image Bank

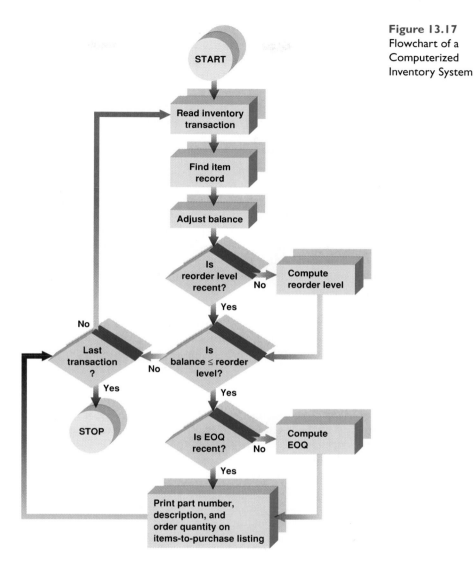

Figure 13.17
Flowchart of a
Computerized
Inventory System

item is stored in the data base, so the computer can automatically prepare the purchase orders to be sent or EDI can be used to automatically transmit orders.

Some software packages for managing independent-demand inventory use the basic theory presented in this chapter and are appropriate for items that have a relatively uniform demand rate. Figure 13.17 shows a simplified flowchart for an independent-demand inventory system to provide an overview of the decisions and calculations that might be made in such a system. Use history can be employed to calculate a forecast of the expected annual demand. Estimates of the holding cost, setup cost, or order cost for each item can be stored in the data base, from which order quantity recommendations can be calculated. The reorder level for each item can be stored in the data base, but often only the lead time and the desired service level are stored. The program can compute the reorder level on the basis of current estimates of the average use rate and a calculated standard deviation or mean absolute deviation (MAD) of forecast errors. This type of system maintains a large amount of data and performs numerous calculations to assist inventory managers. Of course, the system only makes recommendations, which can be overridden or implemented according to the decisions of the appropriate person.

SUMMARY

Inventory can be an important resource to assist a company in its competitive strategy by enabling the company to serve its customers more quickly. Inventory can also help protect a company against unpredicted surges in demand. Companies have tended to buy or produce large lots to spread the costs associated with a setup over more units and thus reduce the cost per unit. Large lots, however, can result in large inventories and significant costs to hold them and reduce flexibility. Since inventory can have advantages and will protect a company from its mistakes or from uncertainty, there has been a tendency for many companies to hold more inventory than they need. Instead of doing the hard work of solving problems, some companies just held extra inventory to protect themselves from error. Recession and tough competition have caused many of these companies to reconsider the question of how much inventory is needed.

Companies have worked to reduce setup costs and to build relationships with their suppliers so that the company can depend on faster resupply of materials. The result has been significant in many instances. Companies have had to improve their quality because they did not have excess material available just in case. Companies are working to be more flexible so that they can respond to demand without holding so much inventory. It is important to reduce the reasons for having inventory in addition to managing inventory wisely.

The basic EOQ model (that is, $\sqrt{2D_aS/H}$) assumes uniform use, a fixed cost to process each order, no quantity discounts, the entire order arriving at just the right time to prevent stockout, and a fixed cost per period to hold a unit of an item. The symbols used in this model and in other parts of the chapter are summarized in Table 13.3. Adjustments to deal with quantity discounts and production over time (instead of procurement) were discussed. Increasing the reorder level above the expected demand during lead time will provide some safety stock for protection from variability in demand (that is, $RL = \bar{d} \times LT + SS$). If demand during the lead time fits a known probability distribution, we can use a table of probabilities for that distribution to determine the probabilities of meeting demand during lead time from stock for alternative reorder levels. This approach provides a way of setting reorder levels. An arbitrary ratio and explicit modeling with stockout costs taken into account are two other approaches to determining reorder levels.

The models presented in this chapter are very basic but still appropriate when the assumptions are satisfied. These models, together with the ideas on dependent-demand inventory presented in the next chapter, are used by many companies to manage inventories. Some companies are moving to an approach to inventory called "just-in-time" production so that goods do not sit in inventory very long. Just-in-time manufacturing is discussed in Chapter 16.

Table 13.3
SYMBOLS USED FOR RELEVANT VARIABLES IN INVENTORY MODELS

VARIABLE	SYMBOL	DESCRIPTION OR UNIT OF MEASURE
Lot size or order quantity	Q	Units per order or dollar value per order, depending on units used to measure demand
Economic order quantity	EOQ	The quantity to purchase that minimizes total relevant cost
Economic production lot	EPL	The quantity to produce that minimizes total relevant cost
Annual use	D_a	The number of units of an item to be used or sold during a year
Use rate	d	The number of units used or sold per unit of time less than a year, such as per day, per week, or per month
Mean use rate	$\bar{d}$	The mean value of d when it is a random variable
Item cost	C	Cost of a unit in dollars
Holding cost	H	Dollars per year to hold one unit (the sum of all the costs that increase as inventory is increased)
Fractional holding cost	h	Annual holding cost as a decimal fraction of item cost; therefore $H = C \times h$
Order cost or setup cost	S	Dollars per order initiated, whether ordered from an external supplier or from the production department within the ordering company (the sum of all order-related costs)
Production rate	p	Units produced per time period
Annual production rate	P	The number of units that would be produced if the production process were run continually for a year
Reorder level	RL	The level of inventory that signals that an order should be placed (number of units on hand and on order)
Lead time	LT	The time between recognition that an order should be placed and the time it arrives
Lead-time use or demand	D_L	The number of units demanded during the replenishment lead time
Mean lead-time use	$\bar{D}_L$	The expected value of D_L: $\bar{D}_L = \bar{d} \times LT$
Probability of lead-time demand	$P(D_L)$	Probability that variable demand will be greater than a specified amount during the lead time
Maximum cycle inventory	CI_{max}	The maximum number of units added to inventory when a production lot is run
Stockout cost	C_S	The cost incurred for a period in which demand exceeds supply
Standard deviation of demand per period	σ_p	The standard deviation of the distribution of units demanded per period
Standard deviation of lead-time demand	σ_L	The standard deviation of the distribution of units demanded per lead time

KEY TERMS

Reorder level (reorder point)
Relevant costs
Setup costs
Stockout costs
Economic order quantity (EOQ)

Holding costs
Economic production lot (EPL)
Bottleneck
Transfer batch
Quantity discounts

Price breaks
Cycle stock
Safety stock (buffer stock)
Service level
Lead-time demand (D_L)

DEMONSTRATION PROBLEMS

Problem

Battery Wholesale, Inc., purchases batteries for $14 each, and it costs $11 to process an order. The company sells about 12,000 of a particular type of battery per year at a uniform rate. The company is open 5 days a week for 52 weeks per year with the exception of six holidays a year. The order lead time is 3 days, and the company wants to have an average of 2 days' sales on hand as safety stock when a new order is scheduled to arrive. The holding cost is estimated to be 24 percent of the item cost per year.

(a) Determine the EOQ.
(b) Determine the expected level of the maximum inventory.
(c) Determine the reorder level.
(d) Determine the average inventory level.
(e) Determine the average annual cost to hold inventory.

Solution

(a)

$$\text{EOQ} = \sqrt{\frac{2D_a S}{H}} = \sqrt{\frac{2(12,000)(\$11)}{0.24(\$14)}}$$

$$= 280.3 \text{ or } 280$$

(b) The average sales per day is $12,000/[(52 \times 5) - 6] = 47.24$. The company wants an average of 2 days' sales or 94.48 units in safety stock when an order arrives, so the maximum inventory should average $280 + 94.48 = 374.48$ or 374.

(c) Using equation 13.8, we get

$$\text{RL} = (\bar{d} \times \text{LT}) + \text{SS} = (3 \times 47.24) + 94.48$$

$$= 236.2 \text{ or } 236$$

(d) The average inventory level is ½ (maximum + minimum) = ½ (374 + 94) = 234. Another way to find the average inventory is ½ (cycle stock) + safety stock = ½ (280) + 94 = 140 + 94 = 234.

(e) The annual cost to hold inventory is the cost to hold a unit for a year times the average inventory level, or 0.24($14)(234 units) = $786.24.

Problem

Postal Posts, Inc., produces and sells cedar mailbox posts to a broad market in the Western states. Demand is fairly uniform at 10,000 posts per year. The company can produce 75 posts per day, and there are 242 production days in a year. The setup cost for the production equipment is $100, and the holding cost for a post is $2 per year.

(a) How many posts should be produced in each production run?

(b) What will be the maximum inventory level if the company tries to have a minimum of 300 posts in inventory?

Solution

(a)

$$\text{EPL} = \sqrt{\frac{2D_a S}{H(1 - D_a/P)}} = \sqrt{\frac{2(10,000)(100)}{2\{1 - 10,000/[242(75)]\}}}$$

$$= \sqrt{2,226,993.9}$$

$$= 1,492$$

(b) Production of this amount will take $1,492 \div 75 = 19.89$ days. During this time the company will sell $19.89 (10,000 \div 242) = 822$ posts, so the inventory will build up by $1,492 - 822 = 670$. If the inventory is 300 when production is initiated, the inventory level will reach a maximum of 970.

DISCUSSION QUESTIONS

1. What are some of the costs that increase with the size of inventory?
2. What are some of the costs that may decrease as inventory is increased?
3. What basic assumptions underlie development of the most basic (procurement version) EOQ model?
4. Which of these assumptions is changed if the item is produced internally?
5. Why is it important to analyze setup procedures and costs in order to seek all reasonable ways to keep setup costs low?
6. How is the most basic model adapted when demand is not deterministic?
7. Why can fixed cost be ignored in developing the EOQ?
8. Changes in what four general conditions might cause a company to increase its safety stock?
9. Describe briefly three methods that may be used to establish the amount of safety stock a company carries.
10. What is a service level?
11. Why is it difficult to determine an accurate estimate of stockout cost?

PROBLEMS

1. Extended Play Stereo, Inc., sells 750 Super Power amplifiers per year and expects sales to continue at that rate. The holding cost is 22 percent of the unit cost per year, and the amplifiers cost $180 each. The cost to process a purchase order is $15.
   a. What is the EOQ?
   b. How much will the company spend each year to order and hold Super Power amplifiers?

2. Suppose that Extended Play Stereo opens a second outlet but continues to use one central purchasing location. The holding cost, order cost, and item cost remain the same as in problem 1, but the annual demand doubles to 1,500 units per year.
   a. What will be the new EOQ? How much has it increased from the EOQ of problem 1?
   b. How much will the company spend each year to order and hold this model of amplifier with the higher level of demand?
   c. Do economies of scale apply to inventory under some conditions?

3. Each year the Yellowstone Company purchases 20,000 of an item that costs $16 per unit. The cost of placing an order is $12, and the cost to hold the item for 1 year is 24 percent of the unit cost.
   a. Determine the economic order quantity.
   b. Compute the average inventory level, assuming that the minimum inventory level is zero.
   c. Determine the total annual ordering and holding costs for the item if the EOQ is used.

4. Suppose the Yellowstone Company discussed in problem 3 uses an order quantity of 300 units and maintains a minimum inventory of 50 units.
   a. Determine the average inventory level.
   b. Determine the total annual ordering and holding costs for the item if the order quantity is 300 and the minimum inventory is 50 units.
   c. How much of the difference in total cost is caused by changing from the EOQ found in problem 3 to the order quantity of 300?

5. The Twin Rivers Driving Range has a fairly uniform business all year. About 20 dozen golf balls are lost, stolen, or damaged beyond use each of the 52 weeks of operation. The balls cost $5 a dozen to purchase. The cost to hold inventory is 1.5 percent per month, and the cost to place a purchase order is $7. The driving range needs a minimum of 200 dozen balls in inventory, and the replenishment lead time is 3 weeks.
   a. How many balls should this organization buy each time it buys?
   b. What is the reorder level for balls?
   c. Discuss methods of determining when the reorder level is reached. It costs about $12 to count the balls on hand—a job that must be done when the range is not in operation. What methods could be used to manage the inventory?

6. Pamona Electronics sells about 350 of a particular model of video cassette recorder (VCR) each year. The item costs $425, and the holding cost is 26 percent per year. The cost to process an order is $60.
   a. How many of the VCRs should Pamona order each time it buys them?
   b. What will be the annual ordering and holding costs if the company decides to keep a safety stock of 4 units?

7. The Domino Taxi company uses 200,000 gallons of gasoline per year at a consistent rate. It costs $40 to have the truck come to the garage and deliver gasoline and to process the orders, invoices, and checks associated with each delivery. Evaporation losses and other storage costs are $0.015 per gallon per month.
   a. How much gasoline should the company purchase with each order?
   b. What is the penalty if the company's tank will hold only 8,000 gallons, so that the company can purchase only 7,500 gallons at each order?
   c. Should the company spend $3,000 to have an additional storage tank installed?

8. The Green Mountain Mower Company produces assorted lawn implements. Storage of a stack of housings for 20-inch lawn mowers requires 4 square feet of floor space in the warehouse, but they can be stacked 45 to a stack. The cost of warehouse space including operating expenses is estimated to be $5.40 per square foot per year. The insurance on the materials in the warehouse costs 0.80 percent of the average inven-

tory value, and taxes are 2 percent of the average annual value in inventory. The cost of working capital invested in inventory is 20 percent per year. Each lawn mower housing costs approximately $4.27 to produce. The use rate for the housings is 36,000 per year. The production rate is 5,000 housings per month, and the setup cost is $100 per run. The company maintains a safety stock of 400 units.

   a. Find the economic production quantity for 20-inch mower housings.

   b. Find the average inventory level.

   c. What are the annual setup and holding costs for this item?

9. Suppose the Green Mountain Mower Company is successful in reducing its cost per setup to $25.

   a. What will be the new EPL?

   b. Find the average inventory level.

   c. What are the annual setup and holding costs?

10. Kincaid Memorial Hospital uses 100 syringes of a particular style each day, 365 days per year. The distributor of this product offers the following price schedule.

QUANTITY	PRICE/UNIT
0–999	$1.00
1,000–2,499	0.80
2,500 or more	0.70

The cost to hold an item in inventory for a year is estimated to be 30 percent of its cost, and the order cost for this item is estimated to be $15 per order. Determine the most economical quantity to buy each time this syringe is purchased. Assume the minimum inventory is zero.

11. The Williams Manufacturing Company uses an average of 250 model 178A relays per week at an approximately uniform rate throughout all 52 weeks of the year. The average cost of processing a purchase order is $25. The holding cost for one model 178A relay is approximately $0.10 per week. The supplier has offered two types of delivery plans to Williams: *(a)* He will deliver all the order in one shipment, or *(b)* for an additional $75 per order, he will deliver the order daily at an average rate of 300 per week until the order quantity is completed. Under plan *b,* the order quantity must be an even multiple of 300. Determine the most economical procurement option and the quantity that should be ordered. What is the total annual cost for each plan?

12. Shenandoah Textile Mills produces a special weave of cloth for pajamas, which is demanded at a relatively uniform rate of 180,000 yards per year (250 days). The production process can be set up at a cost of $150 and produces the cloth at a rate of 3,000 yards per day. The holding cost for 1 yard of this cloth is estimated to be $0.40 per year.

   a. Compute the economic production lot.

   b. How long must the process run to produce this quantity?

   c. What will the maximum inventory level be, assuming that the inventory is zero when the process is initiated?

13. Durango Castings has a long-term contract to deliver 1,450 pump housings per week, 52 weeks of the year. The company has a high-capacity machine that can produce these castings at a rate of 4,500 units per week. It costs $250 to set up this machine, and each unit produced by this method costs $21.50. The holding cost is 24 percent per year.

   a. Determine the EPL.

   b. Determine the total annual setup and holding costs if the company operates with this EPL.

14. Durango Castings, mentioned in problem 13, has a lower-capacity machine that will make the pump housing at a rate of 1,600 per week. It cost only $140 to set up this machine, but it is estimated that each unit produced by it will cost approximately $21.60. Since the pump housing contract will require most of the capacity of this lower-capacity machine, it has been decided that if the housings are run on this machine, the machine will be dedicated to the contract so the setup cost will be paid only once for the 3-year contract. As in problem 13, the holding cost is 24 percent per year.

    a. Determine the total annual cost of setup and additional production cost, and compare it to the costs found for problem 13.

    b. What other factors should be considered?

    c. Is this machine a lower-cost option than the high-capacity machine?

15. The Whacko Brass Company produces brass door knockers, among other things. The company expects next year's demand for door knockers to be 18,000 units at a uniform rate. It costs $125 to set up the equipment to produce the door knockers, and the production rate is 5,000 per month. The company's accountant estimates that it costs $0.30 per year to hold a door knocker in inventory.

    a. How many knockers should the company produce each time it initiates production of the product?

    b. It takes 3 weeks from the time the warehouse orders more knockers until finished knockers begin to arrive. At what inventory level should the company release production orders if it desires 1.5 times the average lead-time use to be designated as safety stock?

16. Not Knots, Inc., produces a variety of wood furniture. The production rate for one model of bookcase is 24 units per day (250 workdays per year). The sales rate for this case is 7 units per day. The setup cost for the equipment used to make the case is $72, and the cost to hold a case for a year is $18.

    a. Determine the economic production lot.

    b. Estimate to the nearest integer the average level of the maximum inventory if the company tries to have 10 units on hand when the first units in a new production run begin to be completed.

17. Super Sport Shoes, Inc., sells a special shoestring at a uniform rate of 2,400 pairs per year. The order cost is $10, and the holding cost is 20 percent of the unit cost. For less than 1,000 pairs, each pair of strings costs $0.22; from 1,000 to 1,499 pairs, each pair costs $0.20; and for 1,500 pairs or more, the cost is $0.18 per pair. What is the EOQ for this item?

18. Gemtronics Corporation produces electrical components for appliance and automotive industries. Previous daily demand for part XK202 has shown little seasonal variation, but has been normally distributed with a mean of 600 per day and a standard deviation of 100. The company works 250 days per year. A lead time of 10 days is required to schedule, wait for an available machine, and set up for a production run. The cost to initiate a production run is approximately $225, and the production rate for part XK202 is 3,000 per day. The holding cost for each unit of this product is $0.25 per year.

    a. Compute the optimal production quantity for this item.

    b. Compute a reorder level that will provide a 0.96 probability of meeting customer demand during the lead time.

19. Alien Auto Co. distributes parts for foreign cars in a large Midwestern city. Demand for a particular size of oil filter has been uniform. The lead time to obtain the filters is 1 month, and the average use rate is 500 per month. The lead-time use is normally distributed with a standard deviation of 70 units. Order cost is $12, and holding cost is $0.30 a year per filter. The estimated cost of a stockout is $10.

    a. What is the EOQ?

    b. How many orders per year will be placed at this EOQ?

    c. What is the optimum probability of a stockout?

    d. What is the optimum reorder level?

    e. How much will Alien Auto spend per year to hold inventory on this filter if it implements the values you determined above?

20. a. How much would Alien Auto spend each year to hold inventory if it tried to stock enough oil filters to give a 90 percent service level? 95 percent? 97 percent? 99 percent? 99.9 percent?

    b. Draw a graph of service level versus annual inventory cost.

    c. Where would you set the level? Discuss your reason.

21. Eleanor's Bike Shop sells an average of 8 bikes per week of a particular model. The weekly demand for this bike is normally distributed with a standard deviation of 3. The cost to process an order is $10, and the cost to hold a bike of this model in stock for a year is $22. In approximately 50 percent of the cases in which the company is out of stock and demand occurs, the sale will be lost, so the company misses only one sale. The average profit on a sale of this model is $50 per unit. The lead time to obtain this bicycle is 3 weeks.

    a. Find the economic order quantity.

    b. Find the optimal probability of stockout during the lead time.

    c. Find the optimal reorder level.

    d. Explain why the reorder level is greater than the order quantity.

BIBLIOGRAPHY

Allegri, Theodore H. Sr. *Materials Management Handbook.* New York: McGraw-Hill, 1991.

Bowersox, Donald J. *Logistical Excellence.* Englewood Cliffs, N.J.: Prentice-Hall, 1991.

————, **David J. Closs, and Omar K. Helferich.** *Logistical Management: A Systems Integration of Physical Distribution, Manufacturing Support, and Materials Procurement.* 3d ed. New York: Macmillan, 1986.

Green, James H., ed. *Production and Inventory Control Handbook.* 2d ed. New York: McGraw-Hill, 1987.

Lambert, Douglas M., and James R. Stock. *Strategic Logistics Management.* 3d ed. Homewood, Ill.: Irwin, 1992.

Production and Inventory Management (journal). Falls Church, Va.: American Production and Inventory Control Society.

Schonberger, Richard J., and Marc J. Schniederjans. "Reinventing Inventory Control." *Interfaces 14*, no. 3 (May–June 1984): 76–83.

Smith, Spencer B. *Computer-Based Production and Inventory Control.* Englewood Cliffs, N.J.: Prentice-Hall, 1989.

Tersine, Richard J. *Principles of Inventory and Materials Management.* 4th ed. Englewood Cliffs, N.J.: Prentice-Hall, 1993.

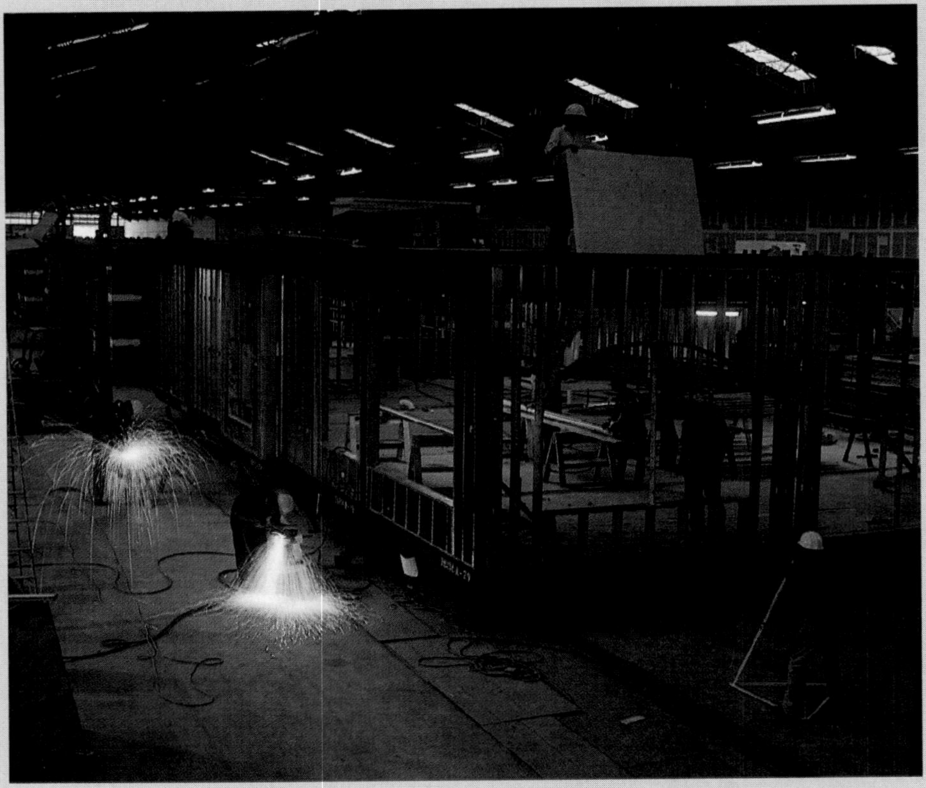

MANAGING DEPENDENT-DEMAND ITEMS AND CAPACITY

CHAPTER 14

Dependent-demand items are those that become part of some higher-level assembly (sometimes called a *parent item*) or set of items that are used together and eventually become part of an independent-demand item. They may be such items as raw materials that are further processed to become a component, components that are assembled into a subassembly, or subassemblies that go through a final assembly operation to become an *end item*. Some dependent-demand items may not be processed further or actually assembled to others, such as a collection of items that are shipped together like a set of dishes or a kit that includes a product, assembly instructions, owner's manual, and packaging materials. Once a company has determined the quantity of end items it wishes to make, it can calculate how many of each dependent item it will need. The quantities in the master production schedule can be multiplied by the appropriate number to calculate how many of each component or how much material to make components will be needed.

There is little uncertainty in these types of calculations. A bicycle manufacturer knows that it needs exactly 1,000 tires and exactly 500 handlebars if it wishes to make 500 of a particular model bicycle. Any uncertainty about quantities should have been addressed at the end-item level when the company decided how low to allow its inventory of that model bicycle to fall before beginning the production cycle to make more. This issue was discussed in Chapter 13 when we dealt with safety stock and reorder levels that would provide a desired service level for the end items, that is, independent-demand items.

In this chapter we primarily discuss *material requirements planning (MRP),* an information system used to plan the materials that are required to produce the quantities and items specified in the master production schedule. As we said earlier, both capacity and materials must be available before production can be started. Rough-cut capacity planning (discussed in Chapter 11) can be used to see whether the master production schedule seems reasonable for the key work centers. Once materials plans are refined and the company has more information on materials availability, the capacity plans can be further refined. The latter part of the chapter discusses capacity requirements planning, which is a more-detailed look at capacity needs.

Not all dependent-demand items will be managed by MRP. Items used in a constant stream at a relatively uniform rate may be managed with an inventory system such as we discussed for independent-demand items. Individually planning the amount of inexpensive items or C items, such as nuts and bolts, may not be justified. A simple two-bin system may be adequate for these. But for many items, particularly A items, most B items, and any other expensive items, it would be very wasteful to carry excessive amounts just to be sure there was enough to carry out the production schedule. MRP is particularly useful in managing the availability of these types of items.

MATERIAL REQUIREMENTS PLANNING

The abbreviation MRP may be used at times to refer to any one of three separate but related aspects of manufacturing planning and control. MRP may refer to the basic calculations used to determine component requirements from end-item requirements. It may also refer to a broader information system that uses the dependence relationship to plan and control manufacturing operations. An even broader information system, with the abbreviation MRP II, that examines requirements for human and financial resources also uses these initials. Before we proceed, let's look further at these three facets of MRP.

The MRP Technique—A Requirements Calculator

Early in its history, the MRP technique was used for its most limited capability. In its most basic form, MRP is a technique of working backward from the scheduled quantities and need dates for end items specified in a master production schedule to determine the requirements for components needed to meet the master production

HOW MANAGING DEPENDENT-DEMAND ITEMS CAN HELP ADD VALUE FOR CUSTOMERS

If value is to be achieved, all resources must be managed wisely. Excessive amounts of dependent-demand items would cause excessive costs and reduce profits or increase prices. The unavailability of any item, however, can mean that products cannot be produced and degrade a company's dependability and customer service. Selection of appropriate suppliers, maintenance of good supplier relations, and communication of accurate material needs help a company obtain high quality and value in its inputs so it can provide value to its customers. Production with good quality of the right quantities at the right times helps provide reliable service and helps keep costs for work in process and finished goods low so that value is improved.

schedule. The technique determines what components are needed, how many are needed, when they are needed, and when they should be ordered so that they are likely to be available as needed. If a company has several products made of numerous components, the number of data values and the calculations that must be performed to use the technique become unwieldy without a computer. MRP usually is a computer system that, as the name implies, plans when materials (and other components) will be required. MRP was originally perceived primarily as an inventory control tool, providing reports that specify how many components should be ordered, when they should be ordered, and when they should be completed. When we refer in this book to the technique of calculating the requirements for components from plans to make the parent items, the terms *MRP technique* or *requirements calculation* will be used. This limited use of the term *MRP technique*—which is sometimes referred to as an "order launch and hope" approach to managing inventory—does not include the use of feedback for tracking the actual progress of orders or for the readjustment of orders in response to actual performance.

Closed-Loop MRP—An Information System for Planning and Control

The logic of the MRP technique has made possible expanded computer systems that provide information for planning and controlling both the materials and the capacity required to manufacture products. The MRP logic has been extended, and it now serves as the key component in an information system for planning and controlling production operations and purchasing. Managers have found that the information provided by MRP can be useful in scheduling because it indicates the relative priorities of shop orders and purchase orders. The system uses lead-time estimates to determine the dates on which each level of assembly should be started in order to meet the scheduled completion date for the end product. The *start date* is the time when an order for the item should be released to the internal production shop or to some external vendor. The start date for one level of assembly is also the *need date* for all components of this assembly. A schedule is valid if the stated date on which the items are actually to be completed coincides with the need dates for all the items. When MRP is updated to show the delivery dates quoted by vendors, it shows if production operations can be performed as scheduled. Schedulers can use this information to expedite orders to keep parts on schedule or to deexpedite orders that will not be needed until later than originally expected. MRP is the basic foundation for *production activity control* or *shop-floor control,* for vendor follow-up systems, and for detailed capacity requirements planning, which is discussed later in this chapter. When MRP is extended to include feedback from and control of vendor orders and production operations, it is called *closed-loop MRP.* It is one of the tools that, when properly applied, can help managers achieve effective manufacturing control.[1]

MRP II—Manufacturing Resource Planning

The information available from closed-loop MRP helps companies develop realistic plans and improves their performance in achieving those plans. When it seems likely that a company will accomplish its production plan, the production plan and the information available from a closed-loop MRP system can be used to plan and coordinate resources other than materials and capacity. With valid projections of what materials and components will be purchased and when, the company can develop its purchasing commitments and a projected purchasing budget. The labor-hours projected in the capacity plan for each work center can be summed to develop personnel needs and labor budgets. Inventory budgets can be developed by multiplying the projected on-hand balance of each item by the item's cost and totaling these.

When the capabilities of closed-loop MRP are extended to provide information on financial resources in a manufacturing company, the system is sometimes called *manufacturing resource planning,* or *MRP II.* Manufacturing resource planning is a means of simulating to provide information on the use of resources for various assumed plans. Information about inventory investment levels, plant expansion needs, and work force requirements is useful for coordinating marketing, finance, engineering, and manufacturing efforts to achieve the company's overall business plan.

The Focus Is Manufacturing Planning and Control

The major consideration of this chapter is planning and controlling the purchase and production of dependent-demand items. Consequently, the broader use of the MRP technique, such as in MRP or MRP II, is discussed from the standpoint of its capabilities as a manufacturing planning and control system. The basic MRP technique is reviewed to explain how it calculates component requirements. Also discussed is how this information is used in managing the inventory of dependent items and in managing the capacity needed to produce these items. With this focus, only a few issues relating to resources outside the manufacturing function are considered. It is important to recognize, however, that information from MRP can be integrated with additional modules to help coordinate the activities in manufacturing with those of other parts of the company.

A GENERAL OVERVIEW OF MRP

MRP is a set of computer programs that are run periodically, usually once a week, to incorporate the latest schedule of production requirements, new information about current conditions, and updated schedules for component receipts. For the discussion in this chapter, we assume that current information is input and that the program is run each week to update the files and provide planning information. The

---

[1]George W. Plossl, *Production and Inventory Control: Applications* (Atlanta: George Plossl Educational Services, 1983), p. 84.

programs must be supported by accurate data in the numerous files if MRP is to operate correctly. Various types of information can be supplied by an MRP run. But basically MRP performs three important functions:

1. **Order planning and control:** when to release orders and for what quantity
2. **Priority planning and control:** how the expected date of availability compares to the need date for each item
3. **Provision of a basis** for planning capacity requirements and development of broad business plans

Although MRP can be used in a variety of settings, such as distribution operations, job shops, and process industries, it is applicable primarily to companies that perform fabrication and assembly of standard products.

Figure 14.1 is a flowchart that provides a general overview of MRP as a means of coordinating and controlling purchasing activities to support manufacturing as well

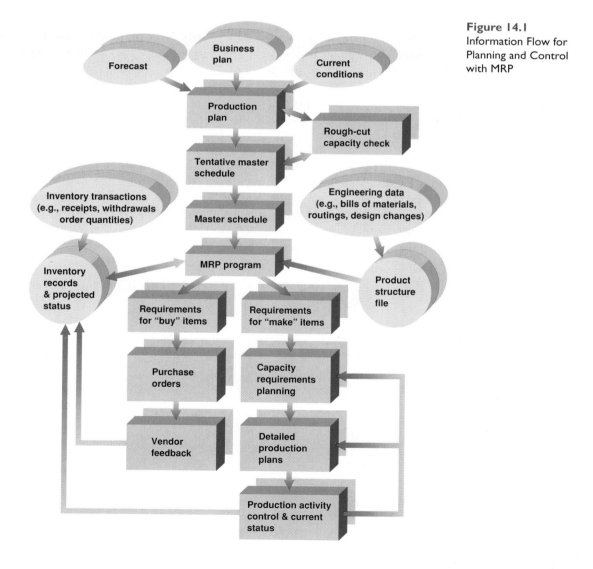

Figure 14.1
Information Flow for Planning and Control with MRP

as the material requirements and capacity requirements within manufacturing. The MRP program that performs the requirements calculations of the MRP technique is the central focus of the initial input plans and the feedback loops. The flowchart also shows the types of information developed from these calculations and some of the files that must be accurately maintained to make the system work properly.

Top-level executives develop the business plan, which considers the coordinated overall operation of all functions in the company. The production plan represents manufacturing's responsibility in carrying out the business plan and states the number of units of each product family to be produced during each general time block, often a month, throughout the planning horizon. Development of an appropriate production plan, or aggregate plan, was discussed in Chapter 11. Notice that the plan is checked for its impact on capacity to ensure that the plan makes reasonable use of capacity.

Schedulers under the direction of middle managers develop a more-detailed plan by converting the production plan into a master schedule that states the specific products to be produced in more-specific time periods, such as each week, for a horizon that typically extends for a year or more. The master schedule is the basic input that drives the rest of the system. The MRP program develops even more-detailed plans by determining which specific components of all end items in the master schedule will have to be purchased or produced and when the orders to initiate these activities should be released. Planning of the material requirements by the program follows the logic represented by the questions in Table 14.1.

When purchase orders are released to vendors, a delivery date is established. This information and information from follow-up contacts to vendors are fed back to provide the projected inventory status for these items. (We have assumed that the latest week's data are input and the program is run each week.) Similarly, information is fed back on the status or actual completion of orders for items to be produced internally. Feedback such as this brings actual progress into the new plans and is what "closes the loop" in closed-loop MRP. New plans are therefore based on updated information of actual conditions and the latest projection of future conditions. Such plans are likely to be more accurate than plans made without feedback information on actual conditions. The kinds of information obtained from an MRP run include:

What orders should be placed

What open orders should be expedited or deexpedited (indicates priorities)

Table 14.1
QUESTIONS ADDRESSED IN MRP PROCESSING

QUESTIONS	REMARKS
A. What do we want to produce and when?	Input to the MRP program through the master production schedule
B. What components are required to make it, and how many does it take?	Provided by the bill of materials
C. How many are already scheduled to be available in each future period?	Obtained from the inventory status file
D. How many more do we need to obtain for each future period?	Subtract C from B, if B is larger
E. When do we need to order these amounts so that they will be available when needed (not too early or too late)?	Move the order release time earlier in time by the production or procurement lead time for each item

What open orders should be canceled or suspended

What order releases are planned for the future

Information for load reports (capacity requirements planning)

It is apparent from this overview that MRP is useful in coordinating the numerous components that must be obtained and the numerous activities that must be performed to keep a manufacturing operation running efficiently. Let's now examine in greater detail how the MRP program develops its information and the files required to support this program. Later in the chapter we will consider some variations from the basic presentation. We will also see how MRP information is used to coordinate requirements for materials with requirements for production capacity.

INPUTS AND OUTPUTS OF MRP

In the following section we discuss in more detail the master production schedule that drives the MRP program and the two files needed to support MRP. We also describe the processing performed by an MRP program to update the inventory status file and to determine what orders for components should be planned.

The Master Production Schedule

Development of a good master schedule is a key ingredient in manufacturing planning and control. Both productive *capacity* and *materials* must be available before the production process can begin. Companies must also make efficient use of both these valuable resources. The objective of aggregate planning or rough-cut capacity evaluation is to ensure that the company has developed a master schedule that efficiently utilizes the company's capacity, yet one that can be realistically achieved within the capacity limitations of the company and its vendors. After a good master schedule is developed, MRP can be used to ensure that all the necessary materials will be available so that the master schedule can be achieved. The master schedule is the driving input to MRP that tells the program what the company intends to produce.

The *master production schedule (MPS)* is a series of time-phased quantities for each item that a company produces, indicating how many are to be produced and when. The time period in which the quantity of an item appears means that this quantity is to be completed through the final operation in that particular period. Figure 14.2 shows a portion of the master schedule for the Stowell Company, a manufacturer of office furniture and equipment. This master schedule shows plans based on time blocks, or time *"buckets,"* equal to 1 week. It indicates, for example, that the company plans to complete final assembly of 100 three-drawer files in week 7, 100 in week 10, and 100 in week 12. These quantities must be moved earlier (that is, offset) by the

Item		Week number											
		1	2	3	4	5	6	7	8	9	10	11	12
001	3-drawer file							100			100		100
005	4-drawer file				60			60	120		60		
007	desk						150			150		90	

Figure 14.2
Portion of the Master Schedule for Stowell Company

Figure 14.3
Mixture of Orders and
Forecast Demand in a
Master Schedule

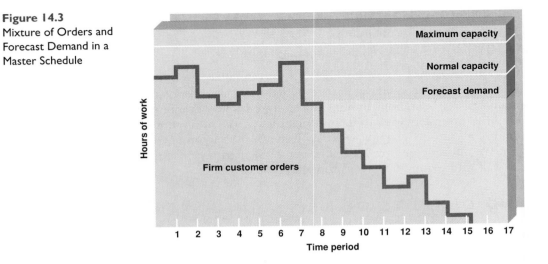

amount of the lead time to determine when the next-lower-level components are required so the assembly operation can begin. Offsetting is discussed again later in the chapter and is further illustrated at the top of Figure 14.7.

The information contained in a master schedule may include both plans to produce items that have already been ordered by customers and plans to produce items for forecast sales. Usually the sold orders are in the near portion of the planning horizon, as illustrated in Figure 14.3. The company must forecast probable sales so that future plans can be made. As actual orders arrive, they replace some of the forecast sales. If actual orders exceed the forecast level of sales, deliveries of these orders must be delayed or capacity adjustments must be made by some means, such as working overtime or subcontracting some of the work. Materials ordered for future delivery might be "pulled in" earlier to supply these production needs.

A company has more flexibility in planning the portion of the master schedule that lies beyond some minimum planning horizon separated by a time fence, as discussed in Chapter 11. The near portion of a master schedule, just before it enters the time fence, must be stated in terms of specific product models that the company intends to produce so that MRP can recommend orders for the specific components that must be obtained. An approximate master schedule with larger time buckets (such as months) can serve as a type of aggregate plan for distant time periods in the planning horizon. It is disaggregated into specific products for the near portion of the planning horizon before those time buckets enter the time fence. The MRP program obtains information about which components are needed to make an item from the bill-of-materials file.

Bill-of-Materials File

The bill-of-materials file, also called the product structure file, must contain information that identifies all components required to make one of any end item or component that will be planned through use of the MRP program. A bill of materials for MRP processing must be more than just a list of all the required parts; it must be structured to reflect the sequence of steps necessary to produce the product. The bill of materials can be viewed as having a series of levels, each of which represents a stage in the manufacture of the end item. The highest level, or zero level, of the bill represents the final assembly or end product. The next level down might represent

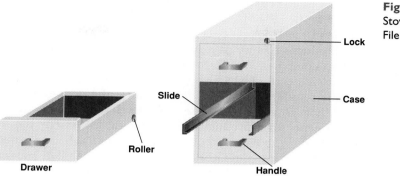

Figure 14.4
Stowell Three-Drawer
File Cabinet

the subassemblies that are combined to make the final assembly. The level below that might represent the parts needed to make the subassemblies, and the bottom level might represent raw materials from which the parts are made.

To facilitate MRP processing, each component at every level of the bill of materials must have a unique part number for its identification, even if the item is not held in inventory at this stage of assembly. The separate identifications enable the computer to find any parent item and to determine all the components needed to make it. Determining all the lower-level components needed to make a parent is called *exploding* the requirement by the bill of materials. The process can be reversed by imploding the bill to develop a *where-used listing*. A where-used list can be used to determine what products and orders cannot be made if some component is scrapped or will not be available on time.

Let us go through a product-structure breakdown for a relatively simple product, a three-drawer file cabinet produced by the Stowell Company, as shown in Figure 14.4. The *product structure tree* for the Stowell three-drawer file cabinet, without paint screws or other fasteners, is shown in Figure 14.5. The bill of materials for this prod-

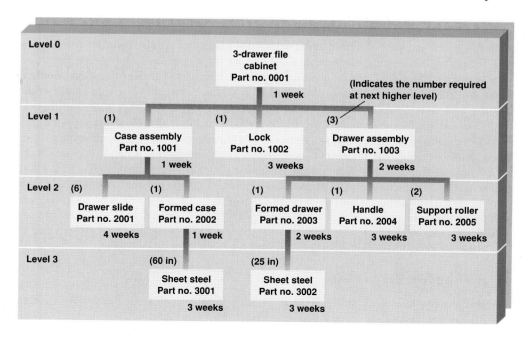

Figure 14.5
Product Structure Tree
for Three-Drawer File
Cabinet

uct, stating the components necessary to produce each level of the product, would be stored in the bill-of-materials file by the part numbers of the components, which are shown in each of the blocks in Figure 14.5.

Product structure data are stored as numerical data so they can be processed easily by a computer. Usually the product structure is stored in a series of *single-level bills of materials,* each of which contains a component's part number and a list of the part numbers and quantities of components at the next lower level. The computer must trace through a series of these single-level bills of materials to obtain the total list of components for a product that has several levels. The file may contain pointers to indicate the storage location of the bill for each component in order to link, or chain, the records and facilitate retrieval of a full bill of materials.

The series of single-level bills of materials for the three-drawer cabinet would contain the following data:

Numerical Listing	Description (not a part of the MRP processing)
0001	File cabinet
1001(1)	Case assembly
1002(1)	Lock
1003(3)	Drawer assembly
1001	Case assembly
2001(6)	Drawer slides
2002(1)	Formed case
1003	Drawer assembly
2003(1)	Formed drawer
2004(1)	Handle
2005(2)	Support rollers
2002	Formed case
3001(1)	Sheet steel
2003	Formed drawer
3002(1)	Sheet steel

These figures indicate that the completed file cabinet contains one case assembly, one lock, and three drawer assemblies. They also show that the cabinet case assembly contains six slide runners and one formed case. The lock has no lower-level components because it is a purchased component. A drawer assembly consists of a formed drawer, one handle, and two support rollers. The sheet steel from which the drawers and the case are formed would have the same part number if the same alloys of equal thickness, temper, and so on were used. The units of issue (such as square feet) would have to show the amounts of sheet steel required for each product made from it. Obviously, much work is required to develop the bill-of-materials file and accurately maintain all the records; moreover, the initial programming of this type of system is very demanding. The bill-of-materials file is updated when new products are added to the line, a product is redesigned, or a new production sequence is established. The file simply supplies information to the MRP program, and processing of the MRP program does not change it.

Inventory Status File

Data in the inventory status file can change greatly each time the MRP program is run, say each week. Much of the important information provided by MRP about

When manufacturing complex products that involve many components, inventory control is essential. If one part is missing, the whole system comes to a halt.

Spencer Grant/Picture Cube

what items should be ordered, how many should be ordered, and when orders should be released is developed in the inventory status file. The contents of this file are changed as the MRP program is run. Consequently, we discuss the processing logic of MRP as we discuss this file.

A brief overview will show where the inventory status file fits in MRP processing. The master schedule tells the MRP program what end items the company plans to make. The program then accesses the bill of materials to explode each item in each time period to see what components will be needed to produce this parent item. For every component needed in any time bucket, the MRP program must determine which of the following options exists:

1. The inventory on hand plus previously released orders will make a sufficient quantity of the item available when needed, so there is no need to produce it.

2. The inventory projected to be available will not be sufficient to cover the quantity required in some period, so an order should be released one lead time prior to this period.

Basically, the job of the inventory status file is to keep data about the projected use and receipts of each item and to determine the amount of inventory that will be available in each time bucket. If the projected available inventory is not adequate to meet the requirement in a period, the MRP program will recommend that the item be ordered.

The inventory status file should contain a record for every item to be controlled by the MRP system. The header, or item master, segment of each record will contain the part identification number, lead time, and perhaps other information such as an

Figure 14.6
Inventory Record for the Drawer Assembly for File Cabinets

Item: 1003 LT: 2 weeks Drawer assembly- file cabinet		Week										
		1	2	3	4	5	6	7	8	9	10	11
Gross requirements							300			300		300
Scheduled receipts			400									
On hand	20	20	420	420	420	420	120	120	120	−180	−180	−480
Net requirements										180		300
Planned order releases								180		300		

item description, list of vendors, and lot size. The inventory status segment of the record shows time-phased data indicating the planned inventory status in each time period throughout the planning horizon. Other data such as use-to-date, vendor delivery performance, and scrap rates may be stored in a third, subsidiary segment of the record.

Only the item master segment and the inventory status segment of the inventory status file are needed for MRP processing. Figure 14.6 shows a representative format for a printout of a *time-phased inventory status record*. The data in this example show the requirements and inventory plans for the drawer assembly used in the Stowell Company three-drawer file cabinet.

Figure 14.6 shows a time-phased inventory status record to illustrate the type of data that must be maintained for every item so that the MRP program can plan how much of the item should be ordered and when the order should be released to the vendor or to the production department. In this case weekly time buckets are used, as is usual for at least the early part of the planning horizon. Larger time blocks may be used in the later part of the horizon if the master schedule is constructed in that way. The actual record will usually show calendar dates rather than week numbers for the time periods.

GROSS REQUIREMENTS Numbers in the *"gross requirements"* row project use of the item in parent assemblies. In this case the company needs 300 drawers in week 6 to make the 100 three-drawer cabinets that are to be started in week 6 so they will be completed in week 7, as specified in the master schedule (Figure 14.2). An additional 300 drawers are to be started into assembly in week 9. Some convention must be used to specify when the requirements are withdrawn from inventory. We assume that the requirements occur during the week so that receipts at the beginning of the week are available to cover them, but they are withdrawn before the on-hand balance at the end of the week is calculated.

SCHEDULED RECIEPTS Numbers in the *"scheduled receipts"* row indicate when any previously released orders *(open orders)* are scheduled to be received and available for use. An order for 400 drawers is scheduled to be completed in week 2. We assume that receipt of the item occurs at the start of the week so that it is available in time to satisfy requirements during that time period.

ON HAND Numbers in the *"on-hand"* row indicate the number of units projected to be available at the end of each time period based on the current balance, projected requirements, and the scheduled receipts. The 20 at the beginning of this row indicates the current inventory of the item. At the end of week 0, which is the beginning of week 1, the company has 20 drawers. The number in any block of the "on-hand" row represents the number scheduled to be on hand at the end of that period. It is found by adding receipts for the period and subtracting requirements for the period from the amount on hand at the end of the previous period.

Some MRP programs show two subcategories (allocated and available) for the items that we show in the "on-hand" row. When an order is released to produce some higher-level item, such as an assembly, requisitions are released which authorize the appropriate work centers to withdraw the necessary components from the stockroom. Some components may not be withdrawn until several periods later, owing to queue time and work that must be completed on other items that will also go into the assembly. Although these items may still be in the stockroom, it would cause serious errors to consider that such items are available to cover other requirements. They are said to be *allocated.* That is, they have already been committed to cover requirements. For the format used in this chapter, the allocated items have been subtracted, and the on-hand balance is the number of units available to be allocated to requirements. It is assumed that a separate list is maintained to show the open requisitions or allocated stock. As long as the on-hand quantity in a period is positive, the company is said to have *coverage* for its requirements for that period.

In the first period that negative numbers begin to appear in the on-hand row, it means that the scheduled use of this component to produce items specified in the MPS will cause the currently planned availability of this component to run out in that period. It signals that something must be done at least one lead time prior to the first period with a negative on-hand quantity or there will not be enough of this component to produce the total quantities indicated in the MPS for the products that use this component. (The company will run out of coverage for its requirements of this item.)

If, before the next time the MRP program is run, an order is released to buy or make more of the component, the amount of the order will show up in the "scheduled receipts" row and will change the numbers in the projected "on-hand" row of the new printout. The previously negative number in this period will no longer be negative if the order is for at least the amount by which the on-hand number for this period was negative in the previous printout. The company will now have sufficient coverage for its requirements of this component through this period. (However, additional requirements may cause some negative numbers in more-distant future periods.) When negative numbers appear in the "on-hand" row it indicates what is referred to as net requirements.

NET REQUIREMENTS Any period in which there is insufficient coverage for the gross requirement is said to have a *net requirement* for the amount of the shortage. The printout format is usually set up so that in moving from left to right across the "on-hand" row, the beginning inventory and scheduled receipts will, in some period, be totally consumed by the gross requirements, and net requirements will begin to occur.

The net requirements begin to occur in the period when negative numbers begin to appear in the "on-hand" row. The net requirement in the first of these periods is equal to the amount by which the on-hand number is negative in this period. It indicates the minimum number of units that can be ordered to keep the on-hand number from becoming negative in that period. If the on-hand numbers become more negative in periods to the right of this first occurrence, the net requirement in a period is the difference in the negative on-hand balance shown for that period and the negative balance shown for the previous period. The net requirement for a period indicates the additional number of units that must be ordered at least one lead time before this period to keep the on-hand number from becoming negative again. A net requirement of 180 drawers is shown in period 9 of Figure 14.6. The figure 180 is found by the following calculation:

300	gross requirement for period 9
− 0	scheduled receipt for period 9
−120	on-hand at end of period 8
180	net requirement for period 9

The net requirement of 300 in period 11 is the difference between the −180 in period 10 and the −480 in period 11. (If, for some reason, there had been a scheduled receipt of 100 in this period, the on-hand number would have dropped by only 200 and the net requirement would have been only 200.)

PLANNED ORDER RELEASES Numbers in the "planned order releases" row indicate when orders should be placed to maintain coverage of the requirements for the item. (That is, to keep the on-hand number from becoming negative.) The time when the first order should be released is found by moving one lead time earlier than the earliest net requirement. (This procedure is called "*offsetting* by the lead time.") The earliest order must be large enough to cover the earliest net requirement. It may also include enough of the item to cover net requirements in a number of subsequent periods. For now, we consider that one order is planned for each period in which there is a net requirement. This procedure is called *lot-for-lot ordering*. Some other methods of lot sizing are discussed later in the chapter. The lead time to produce a drawer assembly is 2 weeks, so the order for the 180 drawer assemblies needed in week 9 should be planned for release in week 7, and the order for the 300 drawer assemblies needed in week 11 should be planned for release in week 9. Orders are usually placed at the first of the week in which they are to be released so that, assuming an accurate lead-time estimate has been used, they will be received at the start of the week and available for use before the gross requirement occurs, in midweek.

The inventory status file must be kept current for each run of the MRP program by posting all inventory transactions (receipts and withdrawals) against the inventory file for the appropriate item. The delivery dates and amounts actually stated by vendors in response to released purchase orders should be shown in the "scheduled receipts" row the next time the program is run. File maintenance entries should also be made to keep the lead time, scrap allowances, and other information accurate. It should be emphasized that MRP cannot develop correct data unless it receives correct information from the files and from its other inputs. MRP is a technique of coordinating the plans for all components with the plans to produce end items.

As it develops the projected inventory status of all items, the MRP program works level by level down through all products. The program must add all the gross requirements for an item within a time bucket before it subtracts the total of these gross requirements from the previous on-hand number to determine the projected quantity on hand or the net requirement for that time bucket. A common component can be used at different levels within the same end item or in multiple end items. A *low-level code* is sometimes stored in the inventory record of an item, to indicate the lowest level at which the item is used. This code signals the computer to continue accumulating gross requirements until it reaches the lowest level at which the item appears in

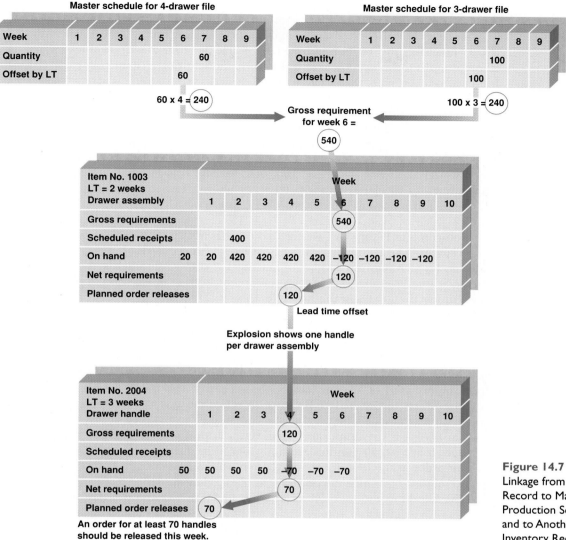

Figure 14.7
Linkage from Inventory Record to Master Production Schedule and to Another Inventory Record

any product. When the program has accumulated all the gross requirements for a period, it then can compute the balance on hand or the net requirement for that period.

A linkage is made between the parent item and its next-lower-level components as the program moves from one level to another. The planned order release date for the parent item tells when all components for the next lower level are needed, thus establishing the time bucket in which their gross requirements occur. The quantity of this gross requirement is determined by "exploding" the number of parent items to be ordered according to the bill of materials. Figure 14.7 shows the linkage between the master schedule and the inventory record for a parent item, and the linkage between the inventory record for the parent item and one of its components. Notice that the gross requirement for drawer assemblies comes from two sources in the master schedule: plans to begin production of three-drawer file cabinets in period 6 and plans to begin production of four-drawer file cabinets in period 6.

Since it takes three drawers to make a three-drawer cabinet, the 100 is multiplied by 3. Likewise, the 60 is multiplied by 4 for the four-drawer cabinets. The total requirements for drawers is 540. If this same model drawer (item 1003) were used in other products, such as a matching office desk, any requirements to make those products would also be accumulated in the gross requirements for drawers before the record for the drawer was processed further. By referring back to Figure 14.5 and considering only three-drawer cabinets, you will see that, while it was working at this level, the MRP program would also accumulate the gross requirements for locks (part no. 1002) and case assemblies for three-drawer cabinets (part no. 1001). (The program would also work with cases and locks for four-drawer cabinets.) We will not go through all the branches on the product structure tree because one branch will illustrate the linkage between records. Let's just trace through the linkages for the drawer.

Returning to Figure 14.7 we see that there is not enough coverage for the drawer requirement. The company will be short by 120 drawers, resulting in a net requirement and a planned order to begin making 120 drawers in week 4. A planned order release at one level makes a gross requirement in the same period at the next lower level (unless the item is at the lowest level on its branch of the product structure tree so the item is to be ordered instead of being made from components). Each time the MRP processing moves from one level to the next lower level, it multiplies by how many of the lower-level components are required to make one unit of the higher-level item (again, "exploding by the bill of materials"). Each drawer requires one handle so the MRP program would multiply by 1 in the explosion step and show a gross requirement of 120 for handles in week 4. If this model handle were used in other products in the master production schedule, the requirements from all uses would be accumulated before the netting step. The planned order release for 70 units in week 1 is very important. Basically, it is an *action message,* not just a planning message. If at least 70 handles are not ordered in the current week (remember also that we order at the first of the week) there will not be enough handles to cover the requirements to produce the products as planned in the MPS.

The handle is the lowest-level item on its branch of the product structure tree. This is where lot sizing can be done without causing instability in any lower-level requirements. Suppose the supplier for handles has a minimum order size of 300 handles. The company should release an order for 300 handles now. If the order is placed, the printout from the next MRP run would show 300 in the "scheduled receipts" in the period that had the −70 in the "on-hand" row. This would cause a positive "on-hand" amount of 230 where the −70 was, which would provide coverage for future requirements up to 230 units.

Again, MRP will link all planned order releases to every item required at the next lower level in the product structure tree. Refer back to the product structure tree in Figure 14.5. At the level that the MRP program accumulated the requirements for handles to make drawers it will also accumulate the requirements for support rollers (part no. 2005) and the formed metal drawers (part no. 2003) and for any other items shown at this level. If not enough formed drawers are already on hand or in process, a gross requirement for the sheet steel to make drawers will be generated.

MRP continues to link the planned order release at one level to the gross requirements at the next lower level until it has worked through all levels of the product's structure. Since it offsets by the planned lead time for each level, MRP develops a schedule of when to release orders for production or procurement of each compo-

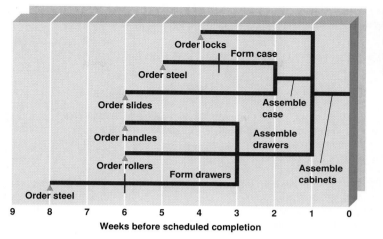

Figure 14.8
Time-Scaled Assembly Chart Showing Material Order Dates for Three-Drawer File Cabinets

nent. Thus MRP provides valuable scheduling information. The type of schedule developed by MRP can be visualized by turning the product structure tree on its side and plotting the lead time for each level on a time scale. Figure 14.8 displays an example of this type of information for the Stowell three-drawer file cabinet.

Outputs of MRP

A variety of reports can be constructed from the information made available by an MRP program.

PRIMARY REPORTS   The primary information for materials planning and control is of five general types:

1. Order release notices indicating the quantity of each item to order in the current time period
2. Planned orders (shown by the inventory status record for each item) indicating the quantity and timing of orders to be released in future time periods if the current master schedule is to be achieved
3. Revision notices indicating changes in quantity that should be made on open orders
4. Reschedule notices indicating which order due dates need to be changed and the dates to which they should be changed
5. Notices indicating any open orders that should be canceled or suspended because there is no longer a net requirement within the planning horizon.

WHAT-IF SIMULATION   MRP can also provide reports that can be used to determine feasible delivery dates for customer orders. When a potential customer order is entered into the master schedule for evaluation, the system backs up by the lead times and checks inventory availability at each level of the production process to see if sufficient lead time and materials are available to fill the order on time. When augmented by capacity requirements planning, the system will provide additional evaluation of whether the customer's requested delivery date is feasible. The company can evaluate alternative delivery dates, then select a reasonable date to quote to the potential customer.

MAKING GOOD MANAGEMENT BETTER WITH MRP II AT SKF ROLLER BEARINGS

One bearing manufacturer has excelled in combining a measure of science with the art of manufacturing management to improve productivity, profitability, and service to its customers.

The Roller Bearings Division of SKF Industries, Inc., produces spherical roller bearings for a wide range of applications in industries ranging from printing to mining and metalworking. This division also produces a specialized line of precision cylindrical roller bearings for traction motors that drive diesel electric locomotives. Historically, the bearings industry has been notorious for long lead times (up to 100 weeks or more during active business cycles), poor on-time delivery performance, and a general lack of responsiveness to changes in the economic environment. Unlike its competitors, SKF improved its performance significantly over the last few years through the implementation of a set of computer-supported planning and scheduling tools known as manufacturing resource planning (MRP II).

Since 1980, SKF's Hanover, PA, plant has achieved a 50% improvement in warehouse order fill rate. Past due customer orders are approximately one-eighth their former level, and raw material in inventory has been reduced dramatically as the purchasing and materials departments have gained the data they need to make informed decisions on what components are needed and when. The plant's work-in-process inventory, as measured by the number of days on hand, has declined by more than 15%, freeing valuable space on the factory floor.

In addition to the Hanover plant, the division operates a facility 50 miles away in Shippensburg, PA, that is one of its major suppliers of components. There are eight other divisions in the SKF Bearings Group, which is headquartered in King-of-Prussia, PA. The company also owns an Automotive Group, made up of McQuay-Norris, Inc., a leading supplier to original equipment manufacturers and the automotive aftermarket, and Eurasian Automotive Products, an importer and distributor of parts for foreign cars and motorcycles.

Employing more than 5,000 people at sixteen plants in nine states, SKF Industries is an affiliate of AB SKF, a diversified worldwide organization with headquarters in Gothenburg, Sweden. The parent company, founded in 1907, produced the world's first double-row self-aligning ball bearings.

SKF's Nice, Ball Bearings, and Specialty Bearings Divisions have also implemented MRP II systems, and the software developed in the Roller Bearings Division has been installed in plants in Brazil. Corporate management plans to convert all plants to MRP II eventually. Currently, the Hanover and Shippensburg plants have been certified as "Class A" users. Class A refers to operations that use the system as a game plan to run the business. They have material requirements planning, capacity planning and control, shop scheduling, and vendor scheduling tools in place. These users have also tied their financial systems into their operating system, and have developed simulation capabilities to test the "what-ifs" involved in planning and scheduling. Data in Class A systems must be at least 95% accurate for inventory records and routings, and bills of material must be at least 98% accurate.

The software used to run the division's system is IBM's RPS (requirements planning system) package, modified by the corporate systems staff into a data base format. From the day the basic software was installed, the division's DP staff has continually added enhancements that allow even greater control over their operations. Decisions on future system enhancements are made by a steering committee made up of division managers and the corporate information systems staff.

Benefits MRP II has brought to SKF are remarkable, even in "quality-of-worklife" areas that are difficult to quantify. Walt Baturka reflects, "The difference in the way managers spend their days around here now as compared to how it was in the late 70s is miraculous. The phones have stopped ringing a dozen times a day with angry calls from customers demanding to know where their orders are. We don't have to manage on a crisis basis anymore. We've got time for contemplation, philosophical discussions on the direction the division should take in the future, and improvements. And the understanding of the system filters down throughout the organization. I can go into the planning department and find young guys who've only been on the job for a year and a half talking about the first and second order effects of the changes in the master schedule and the production plan. You can't find that in just any company.

"Use of the system gives people an awareness of how the business functions and the impact of their actions out on the factory floor," Baturka continued. "In companies with 'informal' hip-pocket type systems, the planners don't really do anything. They can only create plans that no one has time to use. In fact, they usually don't even have a way of knowing whether their plans are being implemented or not."

Customer service, particularly in the area of OEM past due orders, has improved significantly at SKF because of the discipline the system demands. From 1980 to the present, the amount of backlog past due to original promise has shrunk from 16% to 2%, and past due to customer request has fallen from 26% to 5%. The plant's warehouse fill rate has risen from a low of 60% to over 90% today.

Improved inventory control has reaped similar benefits. The Hanover plant has been able to pare the dollar value of the raw materials in stock, including high-ticket items like tubing, bars, and forgings, by 68% with techniques including limiting access to the stockroom and maintaining accurate records of inventory transactions. The number of days of inventory on hand of raw material has been decreased from 144 to 60. Management has also been able to cut the combined value of their work in process and components by a total of 46%.

Perhaps the most dramatic changes the system has brought to the division are the new attitudes at every level of management. Many managers spent almost every day of their worklives "fighting fires"—expediting components to cover materials shortages—because they didn't have the tools needed to plan and reschedule effectively.

Source: Executive Reports Concerning Manufacturing Resource Planning. The Oliver Wight Companies, 5 Oliver Wight Drive, Essex Junction, Vt.

FINANCIAL INFORMATION   Other by-product information can be obtained from data developed through MRP. Planned purchasing expenditures and inventory budgets can be developed by multiplying the projected balances on hand by the appropriate item value and summing by period. Pegging reports, discussed later in this chapter, can be obtained to trace requirements for components to the end items of which they are a part.

ADDITIONAL EDITING CAPABILITIES   Secondary reports can be obtained from the system to indicate errors. Such messages indicate a wide variety of conditions such as alphabetic information in a numeric field, nonexistent part numbers or transaction codes, a number of digits too great for a field size, or indicated date for a requirement that is outside the planning horizon. This type of information is helpful in guarding against erroneous input that would degrade the data base stored in the supporting files and provide incorrect information to the organization.

The following Operations Management in Action box gives examples of some of the improvements that have been achieved through the capabilities that MRP provides.

OTHER APPLICATIONS OF THE REQUIREMENTS CALCULATION LOGIC

The time-phased inventory plan and the logic represented in it for calculating lots needed to cover future requirements can be used in applications other than planning dependent components. A time-phased inventory record, like the one illustrated in Figure 14.6, can be useful in planning orders for independent-demand items, particularly when the demand pattern is not uniform. This method uses the specific forecast for each future period, instead of assuming that the level of demand will be average, as the EOQ model did in the preceding chapter. Thus this independent-demand inventory method is forward-looking and suitable for nonuniform demand.

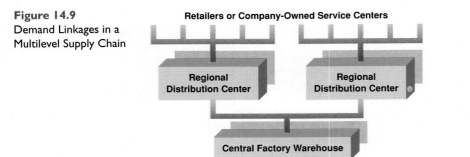

Figure 14.9
Demand Linkages in a
Multilevel Supply Chain

The inventory record displays the forecast future requirements, any scheduled receipts, and the resulting on-hand balance over time. A replenishment order is planned for one lead time before a period in which the on-hand balance is shown to drop below some established safety stock level. This application is referred to as *time-phased order point (TPOP)*. The amount to order may be determined by lot-for-lot ordering or some other lot-sizing algorithm, such as one of those we discuss later in this chapter.

Distribution Requirements Planning (DRP)

Another form of dependence between demands is found in the links within a supply chain. For example, the demand at a regional distribution center depends on the orders released by the local service centers or retailers it supplies. The demand at a central factory warehouse depends on the orders placed on it by the regional distribution centers it supplies. The links in this dependent-demand relationship are depicted in Figure 14.9.

The linkages between demands in a multilevel distribution network, or "supply chain," and the time-phased order point calculations mentioned above can be combined to provide a useful technique called *distribution requirements planning (DRP)*. DRP works best when all the links in the supply chain share information on their demand forecasts and available stocks. The concept can then be used to coordinate material needs and supply plans among the entire supply chain so that all links in the chain can serve their customers' anticipated needs while operating efficiently.

Figure 14.10 shows the time-phased inventory records for an item at a regional distribution center and at two of the local service centers that it supplies. Notice that, in this case, the "on-hand" row is computed differently than in the previous examples. The on-hand quantity includes planned order quantities in the periods in which they are scheduled to be received. The planned orders at the service centers become the gross requirements at the distribution center. The planned orders at the various regional distribution centers accumulate to become the gross requirements at the national distribution center. This discussion presents only a small portion of the complexity involved when numerous items from various factories are distributed through a multilevel network. It is intended only to show another useful application of the requirements planning logic discussed earlier.

SOME ADAPTATIONS IN USING MRP

The preceding discussion presented the basic concepts of MRP and showed how it converts the master schedule to net requirements and planned releases for compo-

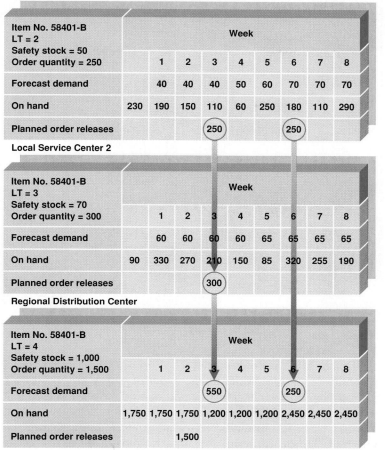

Figure 14.10
Time-Phased Inventory
in Distribution
Requirements Planning

nents. The example we used illustrated a master schedule for production of a finished product. Master schedules can also be developed at a level in the bill of materials below the finished product. Several other adaptations of the general approach to MRP presented thus far have been proposed and are in use. We now examine some of these deviations from the method we have described.

Master Scheduling at a Level Below Finished Product

Some companies make their products available in a wide variety of options—actually highly variable combinations of a few standard modules. An automobile manufacturer, for example, may have a limited product line: a four-door or a two-door body design. The car, however, can be purchased with a four-cylinder, six-cylinder, or V-6 engine; with no air conditioner, a standard air conditioner, or a deluxe air conditioner; with black bias-belted tires, whitewall bias-belted tires, black radial tires, or whitewall radial tires; with a four-speed or five-speed manual transmission or an automatic transmission; and any of ten colors. This company would have 2 body styles times 3 engine options times 3 air conditioner options times 4 tire options times 3 transmission options times 10 colors—or 2,160 unique combinations of its two basic cars. Think of how large this number would be in a more realistic situation where options include hubcaps, chrome trim, interior, radio, stereo, tape deck, and so on.

Rather than keeping an inventory of vehicles of particular colors, manufacturers can keep an inventory of different colors of paint. Vehicles can then be assembled and painted to order.

Jim Pickerell/FPG, International

To run MRP as we discussed it previously, this company would need to store and maintain 2,160 bills of materials, many of which are identical except for the paint color applied to the car. The company would have 2,160 finished products to forecast and would have a master schedule for this number of products. It would be almost impossible to know just how many red two-door cars with four-speed transmission and whitewall radials the company will sell during a particular time period—say, the period one procurement-plus-production lead time into the future. Actually, the company does not need to know that far ahead the exact combination in which its materials will be sold. It only needs to order the proper amounts of materials now. When these materials arrive, they must be processed into the proper number of optional modules—four-cylinder engines, six-cylinder engines, and so on. Production schedulers need to know only a few days in advance which combination of these options should be assembled to provide the finished product that the customer wants. The assembly of modules into finished products can be scheduled on a much shorter lead time than that required for the total sequence of procurement and production operations.

The auto company in our example could work with *modular bills of materials;* that is, it could maintain a bill of materials for each optional module and develop its master schedule in terms of modules. The number of bills of materials would be only 2 + 3 + 3 + 4 + 3 + 10, or 25 instead of 2,160. With this approach the company forecasts the number of cars it will sell, then breaks this total into the appropriate mix of options that its sales are expected to represent. The company would probably maintain an inventory of options to feed the production process, with some safety stock in case actual demand patterns were to differ from its forecasts.

To put this concept in simple terms, the company would not try to forecast the specific number of red cars that will be demanded and then maintain an inventory of these finished products. Rather it would purchase an inventory of red paint and use it on the appropriate cars as orders arrived or in accordance with a very short horizon forecast.

Regenerative MRP or Net Change MRP?

The previous discussion was written as though regenerative MRP was used. A *regenerative MRP* program constructs new data each time (usually each week) that MRP is run. Alternatively, a company might elect to use *net change MRP*. A net change MRP program revises only the data affected by the transactions that are put into it or by a new master schedule. Transactions may be entered into a net change MRP program frequently to reflect conditions as they change. Some systems are on-line and reflect current conditions by net change updating every time a transaction is entered.

Scrap Allowances

Suppose that the scrap rate at a particular starting operation averages about 5 percent of the units produced and that MRP processing shows that 100 of a particular component should be completed in a particular time bucket. It seems logical that 105 or more pieces of the raw material should be started into this operation to end up with the desired 100 components. Therefore, the bill-of-materials explosion could include multiplication by a factor such as $1/0.95$ to make an allowance for the usual scrap loss. When scrap history for a particular operation is available, some MRP systems include a provision for scrap shrinkage so that the user can elect this option.

Safety Stock

Make-to-stock companies often maintain safety stocks of finished goods to protect from uncertainty in their forecasts of independent demand. That is, they protect themselves from stockouts and missed sales. One might wonder about maintaining a safety stock of each dependent component the company uses so they will be unlikely to ever be out of stock. Several knowledgeable professionals recommend that safety stock usually not be maintained for subassemblies or items at levels in the bill of materials between the finished item and the basic purchased raw material or component. Safety stock of the purchased inputs will protect against uncertainty of supply and will permit making more intermediate subassemblies if they are needed.

There is no uncertainty in calculating the number of subassemblies needed to make the product or the number of components needed to make the subassemblies. If the on-hand balances are accurate the company will know how many good units it needs to complete. The scrap allowances mentioned above can be used to start extra units when the company needs a specified number of units and usually experiences some shrinkage due to rejected units at the production steps involved. The components needed to remake any extra units due to excessive scrap will probably be available in the safety stock maintained at the basic input level. Raising the reorder levels to provide safety stock at all levels in the bills of materials will distort the true quantity needed and the timing of orders.

Safety stock at the lowest levels in the bills of materials or basic input level is less expensive than maintaining inventories of intermediate-level items. Further, if these items are common components in multiple products, the inventory at this level gives more flexibility in that it can protect the availability of more than one assembly. Safety stock of a company's purchased inputs protects from uncertainty about a supplier's quality; that is, safety stock will protect from uncertainty in the quantity of usable units that will be delivered.

Safety Lead Time

When there is uncertainty about the supplier's delivery time, a company may elect to use safety lead time. Safety lead time is provided by releasing an order so it is expected to arrive ahead of when it is calculated to be needed. Safety lead time is appropriate in situations where a supplier's delivery time is erratic but the quality is good. Safety lead time is also a useful form of protection for make-to-order companies. They cannot use safety stocks of many components because they often do not know ahead of time what components they will need.

Companies monitor their suppliers' quality and delivery performance and try to resolve any problems. Many companies will provide assistance to help improve the quality from their supplier partners. Some companies prefer reliable lead-time quotations from their suppliers, even if the lead times are longer, instead of having shorter quoted lead times that sometimes are missed.

Lot Sizing

As it processes each level of components in a product, MRP develops a series of planned orders for procurement or production. Some order quantities may be so small that the setup or order cost will be spread over very few items, perhaps resulting in a sizable increase in the cost per unit. A question that should be examined is whether there is some economic lot size that should be purchased or produced. In production a minimum lot size is sometimes established, so that if a setup is made, at least a certain number of units will be produced. A minimum lot size can result in bringing in a sizable inventory for a small requirement in some period just prior to a series of periods with no requirements—which is counter to one benefit of MRP. Lot sizing at upper levels of the product structure can cause very drastic changes (nervousness) in the order sizes for lower-level components, particularly if the product is a complex one with a multilevel structure. Generally, recommendations in the literature caution against using algorithms that will recalculate lot sizes as the requirements listed in the master production schedule change slightly. This is particularly true for components at the upper level in the product structure. A company might evaluate its particular situation to compare the cost of nervousness to the cost of excessive orders. A company with a very stable master schedule over a reasonable horizon would have little impact from nervousness.

Lot sizing can be performed by a variety of methods. Four possibilities are:

1. A company may decide not to batch requirements but to release a separate order for each period's net requirement. This is called *lot-for-lot ordering.*

2. Requirements may be batched until they reach some arbitrary or theoretically developed minimum order size. If a requirement exceeds this minimum, the requirement will determine the order size.

3. The lot size may be determined by the *period order quantity (POQ)* technique. The POQ technique is a variation of the EOQ approach applied to requirements that occur, perhaps nonuniformly, over a series of periods. The average demand is used in the EOQ model to determine an approximate order size in units. This order size is then divided by the average demand per period, and the result is rounded to the nearest integer. This rounded value represents the number of periods' net requirements to be covered in each order. To illustrate, suppose that an item has the series of net requirements shown in Figure 14.11. These requirements would also be shown in the time-phased record of

Holding Cost = $0.10 per period   Order Cost = $30 or 30/0.10 = 300 part-periods

Figure 14.11
Lot-Size Calculation

Week	4	5	6	7	8	9	10	11
Requirement	100	225	250	125	100	140	60	400
Orders that would be released with POQ = 2	325		375		240		460	

MRP as the planned order releases one lead time earlier. The actual orders that would be released to cover these requirements if the POQ technique were used can be calculated as follows. The average demand per period is $1400/8 = 175$. The EOQ based on the average demand per period and the holding cost per period (remember the time base for the demand and the holding cost must be the same) is

$$EOQ = \sqrt{\frac{2(175)(\$30)}{\$0.10}} = 324$$

The number of average periods the EOQ will supply when rounded to the nearest integer is $324/175 = 1.85$ which rounds to 2. So the POQ policy for this situation is to order enough of the item each time to cover two periods' requirements. If period 4 were the first period in which there was a net requirement, the order for this period would cover periods 4 and 5. The order that is to arrive to cover period 6 would also include enough for period 7, and so on. The series of orders that would result from use of the POQ for this demand is also shown in Figure 14.11.

4. The lot size can be chosen to approximately balance ordering and holding costs. One method of doing this is the part-period algorithm, which is discussed below.

LOT SIZING BY THE PART-PERIOD ALGORITHM   The *part-period algorithm (PPA)* relatively simple approach to lot-size selection when a series of requirements, which are not necessarily uniform, are to be batched into orders so that the total cost will be near the minimum. The PPA does not guarantee the exact optimal solution, but it provides reasonably close solutions. The PPA is like the EOQ model in that it attempts to make the holding cost for a lot equal to the ordering cost for the lot, without dividing the amount required within a period into more than one shipment.

Unlike the EOQ model, the PPA may select a different quantity to be ordered each time an order is to be placed, since the requirements it batches are not uniform. Comparisons of the holding cost and order cost are simplified by expressing both in a unit of measure called part-periods, that is, the cost to hold one part for one time period. This unit of measure is arrived at by multiplying the number of parts on hand by the number of periods they must be held. It is assumed that there is no holding cost for the amount used in the period in which an order arrives. Each unit used in the next period must be held one part-period, and so on. The order cost is also expressed in part-periods to facilitate its comparison to the holding cost. The expression for the order cost in part-periods is arrived at by dividing the order cost by the cost to hold one part for one period.

USING THE PART-PERIOD ALGORITHM

It is one lead time (3 weeks) before a net requirement for rollers at the Stowell Company. Bill Bearson, an inventory planner, is using the PPA to determine the appropriate order quantities. For budgeting purposes, Bill has determined the orders that should be received during the next 2 months, assuming that the master schedule remains approximately the same. That is, Bill used the PPA to compute several future orders. Bill's calculations are shown below in Figure 14.12.

The calculations in Figure 14.12 are identified by steps. Each step works from left to right to develop the cumulative holding cost for an order (lot). The first order must be received in period 4 because there is a net requirement in that period.

Bill added requirements for future periods to this order until the cumulative holding cost exceeded the 300 part-period order cost. He then decided to end the horizon for the first order with the requirement for period 5. This causes the holding cost for the order (225 part-periods) to be nearer to 300 than it would be if another period's requirements were included in the order. (The holding cost would be 725 part-periods if the period 6 requirement were included.) Bill then started a new order horizon at period 6 and repeated this process. If the second order horizon is extended through period 8, the holding cost of 325 is closer to the 300 part-period order cost than the 125 holding cost that would result if the horizon were ended with period 7.

Figure 14.12 Lot-Size Calculations with the Part-Period Algorithm

Holding Cost = $0.10 per period				Order Cost = $30 or 30/0.10 = 300 part-periods				
Week	4	5	6	7	8	9	10	11
Requirement	100	225	250	125	100	140	60	400

Step 1 Develop 1st Lot

Holding Cost for Requirement since Order Received (Part-Periods)	100 x 0	225 x 1	250 x 2					
Cumulative Holding Cost for Order	0	225	725					

Step 2 Develop 2nd Lot

Holding Cost for Requirement since Order Received (Part-Periods)			250 x 0	125 x 1	100 x 2			
Cumulative Holding Cost for Order			0	125	325			

Step 3 Develop 3rd Lot

Holding Cost for Requirement since Order Received (Part-Periods)						140 x 0	60 x 1	400 x 2
Cumulative Holding Cost for Order						0	60	860

Period in Which Order Should Be Received	4		6		9		1
Order Quantity	325		475		200		?

The PPA assumes that an order will be scheduled in the first period in which there is a net requirement. The requirement for the next period is added to the order if the cost of holding these units until they are used is less than the cost of receiving them as a separate order. After the requirement for one period is added to the lot, the requirement for the period beyond it is considered. Requirements for future periods continue to be added to the lot until the total holding cost for the lot comes as close as possible to the order cost without dividing a period's requirement. A requirement is never divided; either it is batched into an order for some previous period, or it causes a new order to be received in its time period.

You can see that the orders are for different quantities and will provide materials for different time spans. The lot sizes change with varying requirements and depend on the demand patterns, unlike the equal lot sizes that result when the use rate is assumed to be the same during each period, as discussed in Chapter 13.

The part-period algorithm does not consider all possible groupings of requirements into lots and therefore does not always give the theoretical minimum-cost lot sizes. However, it is considered to be less expensive in terms of computer time than an optimization model, and it provides answers that usually are satisfactory.

CAPACITY REQUIREMENTS PLANNING

Managers' responsibilities include planning what is to be done and then organizing, directing, and controlling the execution of the plan. Managers often expend great amounts of time in planning, or they delegate planning activities to capable staff members. Time spent on planning can pay great dividends, since hundreds of people and vast sums of money may be involved in executing the plan. Good execution of a poor plan can lead to disaster, but even moderate execution of a good plan can bring success. The point is that if a company starts out with a poor plan, it expends resources doing the wrong thing; and it must then expend extra resources to correct its errors, or it can never achieve goals that should have been within reach.

Planning and controlling a company's productive capacity (plant, equipment, and people) is a vital responsibility of management. Capacity is a major expense in manufacturing companies. Managers must prudently plan and control the available capacity and its utilization if they are to help achieve the company's objectives for profitability and return on investment. If too much capacity is available, the company has heavy capital and operating expenses. If too little productive capacity is available, or if the proper amount is available but poorly utilized, a company cannot meet the level of demand that could be possible. In either case profitability will suffer.

Capacity requirements planning (CRP) is an effort to develop a match between the MRP schedule and the production capacity of a company. Capacity is the highest sustainable output rate of a unit, given a particular product mix, a specified level of equipment and labor, and a normal work schedule. Determination of the capacity of its work centers and the capacity requirements imposed on those work centers by a particular product mix enables a company to know what level of sales its production system can support. Thus the company is less likely to make sales commitments that are unrealistic or overly expensive to achieve. Capacity planning helps to avoid underutilization of capacity, which would prevent the company from achieving the highest return attainable from its investment in capacity. Capacity requirements planning also enables a company to anticipate production bottlenecks in some work centers in time to take corrective action.

To be accurate and effective, capacity requirements planning must be coordinated with material requirements planning. If materials are available but the capacity is inadequate, the schedule cannot be met and the company must pay to hold materials. If capacity is available but materials have not been obtained, the schedule cannot be met and the company is paying for unused capacity. A computer program that performs CRP can be run in conjunction with MRP. Working together, the MRP and CRP programs translate the master schedule to requirements for components and capacity, simulating the impact of the master schedule that provided the input for the MRP program. Until a reasonable master production schedule is developed through rough-cut capacity planning (discussed in Chapter 11), the expense of running MRP and CRP is not justified. CRP can be used to further refine the master production schedule after MRP has been run.

The output of MRP tells when planned orders should be released for every component and the quantity needed to support the master schedule. It also tells when open (already released) orders need to be completed to support the master schedule. This information is fed into a CRP module. The CRP module also requires a routing file, stating the sequence of operations that must be performed on each component to convert it into the next-higher-level item and the work center that is to perform each of these operations. The routing file, or a separate standard-time file, contains information about *production standards,* that is, the time required to perform each operation. The CRP module can then sum the production time required in each work center during each time period covered by the master schedule. This flow of information is shown in Figure 14.13. The output of CRP is a load profile for each work center, similar to the load profiles developed by rough-cut capacity planning. Load profiles based on the output of MRP and CRP, however, are more accurate than the profiles provided by rough-cut capacity planning. CRP considers all affected work centers, whereas rough-cut planning might consider only a few key centers. MRP subtracts available inventory to determine the actual net requirements, it takes into account the lot sizes that will be produced, and it adjusts for the lead time at each production stage. Thus by working with the output of MRP, CRP processes data that more accurately represent actual work requirements.

The load profiles produced by detailed CRP can then be used to refine the planning process to develop an improved master schedule or change the capacity that is made available. Management analysis of the load profiles might indicate any of a variety of conditions: (1) The capacity of the major work centers is effectively utilized, and no overloads exist. In this case no revisions to the plan are necessary. (2) Capacity is not sufficiently utilized in some work centers. Under this circumstance, managers may elect to revise the master schedule and "pull ahead" some work that was scheduled to be performed further into the future. Alternatively, they may elect to reduce capacity in these work centers. (3) Bottlenecks and overloads may exist in some work centers. Management can revise the master schedule to perform the work in later time periods if capacity will then be available, or it may expand capacity through overtime, additional personnel and equipment, subcontracting, and so on. (4) Some work centers are overloaded, and others are underloaded. Under these conditions managers might consider such options as shifting the routing on items where it is feasible so that these items will be worked on in underloaded rather than in overloaded work centers. Perhaps personnel can be transferred between work centers to adjust capacity to the anticipated load in those work centers. Alternatively, the master schedule can be revised so that portions of the schedule that cause overloads are planned to occur at other times. Also note that work that is not in the master

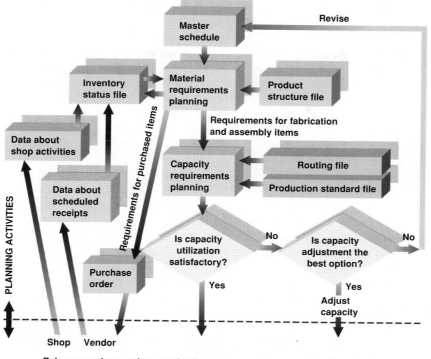

Figure 14.13
Flow of Information in Capacity Requirements Planning

schedule is sometimes called for—replacement of scrap, for instance, or rework, new products, or special operations requested by customers.

A technique known as *pegging* enables a planner to trace from a work load in a work center back through its higher-level assemblies to determine what end item in the master schedule caused the load. Often single-level pegging is used, which tells the immediately higher-level parent of a component. A series of single-level peg inquiries are required to trace work requirements to the production schedule for end items.

Use of the output from MRP to run CRP, which provides data that are fed back to refine the master schedule, creates a closed loop in the information flow for planning. The flow of feedback information from capacity requirements planning to the master production schedule is shown in Figure 14.13. Also shown is a path depicting the feedback of actual due dates for vendor orders, which will indicate the time bucket in which scheduled receipts will fall. CRP is a valuable step in establishing manufacturing control. It provides the information needed to adjust plans according to conditions within the production system. The feedback from CRP is based on anticipated conditions that are likely to occur as a result of the plan. Feedback from the other sources can be obtained during the execution phase of the production cycle, allowing the company to revise and refine plans further in response to current conditions. Control, as we have said, involves feedback about actual progress, detection of significant deviations from planned results, and corrective action when it seems desirable. The process of using feedback from actual results to revise the plans fed into MRP is called closed-loop MRP, a process mentioned early in this chapter. The use of MRP to assist in controlling progress during production is further discussed in Chapter 15, which deals with scheduling and control in manufacturing.

POTENTIAL BENEFITS FROM THE USE OF MRP

It has been said that MRP is a new way of managing a manufacturing operation. It has become more than just a way of calculating how much material to order and when. The technology involved in getting the program to run on a computer is only part of the challenge; it only makes possible the potential benefits of MRP. MRP can, in addition, lead to significant changes in the way many parts of the company operate.

MRP is not an automatic decision system; it is a decision support system or management information system. It provides timely and valuable information to *people* who make the decisions and who make a company run. We have seen many of the details of how basic MRP works. There are no complex and sophisticated mathematical models. The contribution of MRP is that it can perform the massive data processing required to plan every component in hundreds of products to be produced over a lengthy horizon. The availability of this information enables the many diverse elements of an organization to plan and operate with greater coordination and effectiveness. People who use MRP must fully understand it and the meaning of the data it provides before they can realize its full potential.

When it is properly developed and is implemented in an appropriate setting, MRP can provide numerous benefits to several parts of a company. Some of these benefits are listed below, with the part of a company that might most directly profit identified in each case. Most of these elements of the organization also must provide accurate information to the system to keep MRP operating properly.

1. *Inventory:* MRP provides information to better coordinate orders for components with plans for parent items so that the average amount of inventory for dependent-demand items (work in process and raw materials) can be reduced. The company can have only what is needed instead of plenty of everything.

2. *Production:* Human and capital resources (capacity) can be better utilized, because information from MRP will show the need to delay on some components if other necessary components are not available. Better delivery performance is possible because of more-accurate priority information. MRP can also improve work flow, resulting in reduced elapsed time between the start and finish of jobs.

3. *Sales:* MRP tells ahead of time if desired delivery dates appear achievable. It improves the company's ability to react to changes in customer orders, improves customer service by helping production meet assembly dates (keeping components on schedule and minimizing parts shortages), and helps cut delivery lead times.

4. *Engineering:* MRP helps plan the timing of design releases and changes and aids in their implementation.

5. *Planning:* MRP can simulate changes in the master schedule for evaluation, and it facilitates systems that provide a picture of equipment and facility requirements, work force planning, and procurement expenditures, based on a proposed master schedule.

6. *Purchasing:* MRP recommends changes (to expedite or deexpedite) in due dates for orders. The company can improve vendor relations because it knows the real priorities.

Charles Gupton/Stock, Boston

Black & Decker has seen many of the benefits of MRP. MRP has helped Black & Decker improve operations, reducing engineering change orders and inventory. Improved recordkeeping has meant Black & Decker has a lower inventory investment and still maintains better customer service.

7. *Scheduling:* MRP allows better scheduling through better knowledge of priorities.

8. *Finance:* MRP can facilitate better planning of cash-flow requirements. It can lead to identification of true capacity constraints, resulting in better capital investment decisions.

IMPLEMENTATION OF MRP

After reading about the potential benefits that can be achieved from MRP, you may wonder why it is not used by every manufacturing company. Remember, the benefits discussed are only *potential* benefits that can be gained from a *good* manufacturing control system that is *properly* installed and utilized. A basic MRP program does not provide all the benefits mentioned, such as capacity planning or production scheduling. It is expensive to develop, apply, and maintain an information system that would enable a company to reap all the potential benefits of MRP.

Moreover, not all installations are successful. The degree of potential improvement that can be realized from implementing MRP depends on the effectiveness with which production and inventory activities are planned and controlled before MRP is introduced. Ironically, many companies that could achieve great improvements through the use of MRP have had poorly run operations prior to MRP and consequently are less likely to have the commitment, teamwork, and discipline necessary to achieve the full potential of MRP. Companies that do not carefully plan and administer the implementation of MRP may conclude that the system does not work. The MRP package does nothing more than process the data provided by the organization and provide further information to the organization. The people within an organization must maintain accurate data and must use the output of the system effectively if MRP is to be successful. Just the fact that the computer processes the input data does not ensure that MRP's potential is being fully achieved.

Several suggestions for successful MRP implementation appear in the literature. Some of these are discussed below.

Management Commitment

Top-level managers and managers in all parts of the organization that will be affected by MRP must clearly recognize all the efforts needed to achieve this new way of managing their activities. These managers must fully support all the changes and must remain supportive of the new system.

User Involvement

A team of people will be responsible for the development and implementation of MRP. This team should include people from all parts of the company that will use the MRP system so that the system will reflect the particular needs of its users. The participation of users of the system in its development will make these people more familiar with the system, so they will know better how to use it effectively. Further, they are likely to become more committed as a result of being involved in the system's development.

Education and Training

If a system is to work, all the people who work with it must understand it and know how to use it—what information to provide and how to provide it; what information to ask for and how to obtain it. Beyond this, people must know what conditions in the operation are indicated by the messages provided by the system. Always, there is a need for good judgment and initiative to take the proper action to correct those things that need correcting and to leave alone those things that do not.

Selection of Packages

The potential user must decide whether to use net change or regenerative MRP. A regenerative system constructs new data each time (usually each week) that MRP is run. A net change system revises only the data affected by the transactions or schedules fed into it, which occurs as frequently as needed to reflect conditions as they change—perhaps daily or more often.

Several companies offer software packages that perform MRP. A company considering the use of MRP must decide whether to develop its own programs or to purchase and adapt some available package. Companies often opt to buy software because a great deal of time is required to develop these programs, and there is the possibility of making mistakes that will probably already have been corrected in a commercial package. It is likely that the company will have some existing systems or elements that it does not intend to change and that must interface with MRP. For example, the software package might need to be compatible with the company's computer, operating system, order entry system, inventory system, purchasing records, labor reporting, cost accounting, bill-of-materials processor, and master scheduling system.

Data Accuracy

For MRP to operate effectively, the company must have accurate records in the supporting files. All the bills of materials must be reviewed, updated, and structured so that they provide the data needed by MRP. Inventory records also must be reviewed, corrected, and entered into a computer file for access by MRP. After a system is installed, careful attention and discipline must always be exercised to ensure that all data used by the system are accurate. For example, if a clerk is supposed to enter a code 3, indicating that the item is purchased in hundreds, but instead enters a code 2, indicating that it is purchased in dozens, serious errors and material shortages are likely to occur. If a system gives erroneous data at times, people may develop informal methods of getting the data they need and may no longer bother to update their input into the formal system, since they no longer use it. The system could then become even less reliable and be a burden rather than a benefit. This is one reason why managers must remain supportive of the system and must apply the necessary effort to see that accurate and timely data are supplied to it.

Realistic Master Scheduling

A plan must be realistic if a company is to achieve it—whether the company uses MRP or any other system. The master schedule must not be management's fantasy about what the scheduler would like to achieve. If the master schedule overloads the capacity of a plant, MRP will not save the day. MRP can, however, be used to find the relative priorities of components so that the capacity can be most effectively utilized by signaling the proper jobs to be worked on.

Capacity requirements planning used in conjunction with MRP provides great potential. The company can develop plans (master schedules) that effectively utilize its capacity without bottlenecks or overloads. Thus MRP helps to achieve the plan as stated in the master schedule, through procurement and production of the proper components at the proper time. This is a great deal of what good production and inventory management is all about—planning and controlling to achieve wise use of resources.

SUMMARY

Demand for components that are used only to feed the production process—that is, dependent-demand items—occurs only when production of the parent assembly is performed. In many instances dependent demand is not uniform. Independent-demand inventory models assume relatively uniform use and often are not appropriate for dependent-demand situations. Requirements for such dependent items as intermediate-level assemblies, purchased components, and raw materials should not be forecast individually. Requirements should be determined from the master production schedule through material requirements planning (MRP). MRP calculates the requirements for dependent components by multiplying the number of parent items to be produced by the number of components per unit as specified in the bill of materials for the parent item. Timing of each requirement is determined by offsetting, that is, backing up in time from the scheduled completion for each stage of production by the time required to perform that production step.

MRP is usually run weekly but may be run more often, such as daily. The output of an MRP run can provide useful information for planning and controlling orders to suppliers or orders to the production floor. Information obtained from MRP is also useful in determining capacity requirements and in making plans for effective utilization of capacity.

Production of an item requires both the availability of the necessary components and the availability of adequate production capacity to perform the production operations. Thus capacity requirements must be planned in coordination with material requirements. Capacity requirements planning (CRP) attempts to match the master production schedule and the production capacity of a company. A computer program for CRP uses the output of MRP to make detailed projections of the load imposed on the production system so that overloads, underloads, or bottlenecks can be identified in time to take the necessary corrective action. CRP enables a company to plan for the efficient utilization of production capacity, and MRP enables it to execute those plans efficiently. These two packages (MRP and CRP) are valuable assets in achieving efficient use of resources and profitability in production operations.

MRP is a program that evaluates a master production schedule. In addition, it provides recommendations on when to release orders, tells when orders are really needed, and provides data for capacity requirements planning.

MRP requires accurate inventory status records for every component and an accurate bill of materials for every level of component, from the basic raw material through the end item. Implementation of MRP also requires commitment and continuous support from management, proper hardware and software packages, and full training of users and support personnel.

KEY TERMS

Parent item
End item
Material requirements
   planning (MRP)
Start date
Need date
Production activity control
Shop-floor control
Closed-loop MRP
Manufacturing resource
   planning (MRP II)
Master production
   schedule (MPS)
Time "buckets"
Exploding

Where-used listing
Product structure tree
Single-level bills of
   materials
Time-phased inventory
   status record
Gross requirements
Scheduled receipts
Open orders
On hand
Coverage
Net requirement
Offsetting
Lot-for-lot ordering
Low-level code

Time-phased order point
   (TPOP)
Distribution requirements
   planning (DRP)
Modular bills of materials
Regenerative MRP
Net change MRP
Period order quantity
   (POQ)
Part-period algorithm
   (PPA)
Capacity requirements
   planning (CRP)
Production standards
Pegging

DEMONSTRATION PROBLEMS

Problem

The Kangaroo Special BMX dirt bike is composed of nine major subassemblies: frame, seat assembly, rear wheel assembly, chain, front wheel assembly, fork, brake assembly, handlebar assembly, and pedal-crank assembly. The handlebar assembly consists of the handlebar, post, and two handlebar grips. The front wheel assembly consists of a tire, a tube, a rim, thirty-six spokes (20 mm), and a front hub assembly. The front hub assembly is composed of the front hub, two bearings, two bearing retainers, an axle, and four axle nuts. The pedal-crank assembly is composed of a crank, a sprocket, two bearings, a bearing retainer, a nut, and two pedals.

Construct a product structure tree, showing the entire composition of a Kangaroo Special one level below the end product, and extend the composition of the front wheel assembly as far as possible.

Solution

Kangaroo Special

| Frame | Seat assembly | Rear wheel assembly | Chain | Front wheel assembly | Fork | Brake assembly | Handlebar assembly | Pedal-crank assembly |

Front wheel assembly:
Tire | Tube | Front hub assembly | 36 Spokes (20 mm) | Rim

Front hub assembly:
Front hub | 2 Bearing retainers | Axle | 2 Bearings | 4 Axle nuts

Problem

The Neptune Co. produces two models of aeration systems for aquariums: the Junior *(J)* and the Senior *(S)*. The product structure trees for these products are shown below with the lead times to purchase or make each component shown in parentheses after the letter that stands for the component. The levels that the items would appear in the bill of materials are also indicated to the right for each level of product structure. The quantity of a component required to make one unit of the next-higher-level item is indicated to the left of the letter that stands for the component. The *J* requires one pump assembly *(A)* that attaches to one end of a low-capacity motor *(L)*. The *S* requires two pump assemblies *(A)*, one installed on each end of a higher-capacity motor *(H)*. Each pump assembly *(A)* consists of a purchased pump kit that includes all the hoses and attachments *(P)* and four brackets to attach the pump to the motor *(B)*.

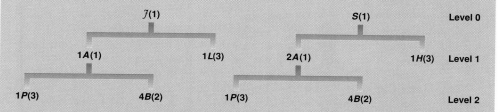

				Level 0
$J(1)$			$S(1)$	
$1A(1)$	$1L(3)$	$2A(1)$	$1H(3)$	Level 1
$1P(3)$	$4B(2)$	$1P(3)$	$4B(2)$	Level 2

The longest lead time through any branch on the product structure trees is for the pump kits. The execution time for procurement and production on this branch is $1 + 1 + 3 = 5$ weeks, so the company must complete plans for these products while the periods being planned are at least 6 weeks in the future. The master production schedule (MPS) for products *J* and *S* for weeks 6, 7, and 8 is shown below.

MASTER PRODUCTION SCHEDULE

PRODUCTS TO BE COMPLETED	WEEKS	6	7	8
Junior pump system (*J*)		150	180	160
Senior pump system (*S*)		85	80	85

The following are the "on-hand" balances and "scheduled receipts" for the components of the company's products:

COMPONENT	ON HAND	SCHEDULED RECEIPTS
L	100	200 in week 1
H	200	200 in week 1
A	100	50 in week 1
P	25	80 in week 2
B	400	400 in week 2

(*Note:* In many actual applications of MRP, the time-phased inventory records for finished products and components would show requirements in the early periods and sufficient scheduled receipts to cover these requirements. Gross requirements and most of the scheduled receipts in the early periods have been omitted from this problem and many of the problems in this chapter because they add numbers that might obscure the objective of illustrating how a set of requirements from the master production schedule is transmitted to all the levels of components of the products. One scheduled receipt is shown for each component to show how these affect the on-hand balance.)

(a) Develop the time-phased inventory records for all of the components (*L, H, A, P,* and *B*) showing the numbers that result from the master production schedule, on-hand balances, and scheduled receipts that were given.

(b) Is there any indication that the Neptune Co. should take any action this week?

Solution

(a) The first step is to back up by the 1-week lead time required to assemble the finished products (the level 0 items) to determine when the orders should be released to assemble *J* and *S*. This step determines when the level 1 components are required. The company will need components to begin making 150 *J*'s and 85 *S*'s in week 5. Since it takes only one *L* to make a *J* and the *L*'s are not used elsewhere, the company will need 150 *L*'s in week 5. Likewise, 85 *H*'s will be required in week 5.

Determining the requirements for component *A* is more involved. *A* is used in both products. Also, if more than one unit of a component at the next lower level is required to make an assembly, then the number of assemblies to be made must be multiplied by the appropriate number to determine how many of that lower-level component will be required. It takes 2 *A*'s to make each *S* so the company will need 2 × 85 = 170 *A*'s in week 5 to begin making *S*'s. It will need an additional 150 *A*'s in week 5 to begin making the 150 *J*'s, bringing the total requirement for *A*'s in week 5 to 170 + 150 = 320. The requirements for *L, H,* and *A* in weeks 6 and 7 are determined similarly. Once all the gross requirements at level 1 are determined, then the time-phased inventory records for *L*,

Figure 14.14
Relationships Between the MPS and Inventory Records

			Weeks into the future						
		1	2	3	4	5	6	7	8
Completion dates and quantities in the MPS	System J						150	180	160
	System S						85	80	85
Time periods in which orders to assemble these systems must be released (started)	System J					(150)	(180)	(160)		
	System S					(85)	(80)	(85)		

Therefore, the level 1 components (L, H, and A) will be required when the assembly operations are to start (as shown in the first three records below).

Component L
Lead time = 3 wks.

		1	2	3	4	5	6	7	8
Gross requirements						150	180	160		
Scheduled receipts		200								
On hand	100	300	300	300	300	150	−30	−190		
Net requirements							30	160		
Planned order releases			30	160						

Component H
Lead time = 3 wks.

		1	2	3	4	5	6	7	8
Gross requirements						85	80	85		
Scheduled receipts		200								
On hand	200	400	400	400	400	315	235	150		
Net requirements										
Planned order releases										

$$\{(150 \times 1)+ (85 \times 2)\} \quad \{(180 \times 1)+ (80 \times 2)\} \quad \{(160 \times 1)+ (85 \times 2)\}$$

Component A
Lead time = 1 wk.

		1	2	3	4	5	6	7	8
Gross requirements						320	340	330		
Scheduled receipts		50								
On hand	100	150	150	150	150	−170	−510	−840		
Net requirements						170	340	330		
Planned order releases			(170)	(340)	(330)					

Component P
Lead time = 3 wks.

		1	2	3	4	5	6	7	8
Gross requirements						170	340	330		
Scheduled receipts			80							
On hand	25	25	105	105	−65	−405	−735			
Net requirements					65	340	330			
Planned order releases		65	340	330						

"Action"

×4   ×4   ×4

Component B
Lead time = 2 wks.

		1	2	3	4	5	6	7	8
Gross requirements						680	1360	1320		
Scheduled receipts			400							
On hand	400	400	800	800	120	−1240	−2560			
Net requirements						1240	1320			
Planned order releases			1240	1320						

H, and *A* can be processed to determine if there are any planned order releases for these items. The time-phased records for these components and the others are shown in Figure 14.14. The company will need to plan and release orders for some *L*'s before week 3 in the future (week after next). The company does not need to order any *H*'s to carry out the MPS that has been processed. The company will have to make some *A*'s, so the records must be processed for the components required to make *A*'s to see if anything must be done to make sufficient supplies of the level 2 components available when needed.

Since the items at level 2 (components *P* and *B*) are components of *A*, they will be required only if the time-phased record indicates planned order release(s) to make *A*'s. The time-phased record for *A* shows planned order releases of 170, 340, and 330 in weeks 4, 5, and 6, respectively. Since each *A* requires one *P* there will be gross requirements for *P* of 170, 340, and 330 in the same weeks. Since each *A* requires four *B*'s the gross requirements for *B* are four times the number of *A*'s to be made. These gross requirements are also in weeks 4, 5, and 6, respectively. The time-phased inventory records for the items at level 2 (components *P* and *B*) can now be processed. The results are shown in the bottom two records in Figure 14.14. These records show that additional quantities of *P* and *B* will be needed to carry out the MPS.

(b) Notice that the planned order release for 65 *P*'s (pump kits) in week 1 is important. It is more than just a plan for the future. Plans for week 1 in the future are often called "action items" because they indicate things that must be done this week. Remember also that orders are to be released at the first of the week. This number indicates that Neptune's buyer responsible for pump kits must place an order for at least 65 pump kits right away. The buyer may place an order for more than 65 pumps if the Neptune Co. uses lot sizing for orders at this level in the bill of materials or if the pump supplier has some minimum order requirement that is greater than 65. A decision should be made regarding the order quantity and the order released soon.

DISCUSSION QUESTIONS

1. Why are dependent-demand items often managed by inventory systems that are different from those studied in Chapter 13?
2. What is the basic core of material requirements planning (MRP)?
3. What, if any, applications does MRP have beyond basic inventory control?
4. What is a master production schedule? How does it differ from a forecast? What is lead-time offsetting?
5. What basic information must be in the inventory status file? What additional information might a company want to maintain in this file?
6. Discuss some fears people might have about setting a planned lead time and not using safety stock in an MRP system.
7. Briefly describe the steps that MRP goes through in processing a master production schedule to obtain material requirements.
8. Why is data accuracy important for MRP?
9. Why do some companies develop their master production schedule for items below the end-item level in the product structure?
10. How do you distinguish between planned orders and open orders?
11. Is capacity requirements planning important? Give some reasons for your response.

12. What are pegged requirements?

13. Distinguish between net change and regenerative MRP systems.

PROBLEMS

1. A Double Pleasure popsicle is pictured below. Construct a product structure tree for a carton of 12 orange-flavored popsicles.

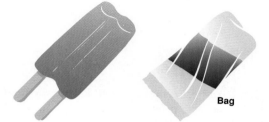

Bag

2. The Easy Roller Skate kit consists of the following: box, warranty, key, left skate, right skate. A skate consists of a strap, a heel plate assembly, and a left or right sole plate assembly. A heel plate assembly consists of the heel plate and a truck assembly. A truck assembly consists of two wheels and an axle assembly. An axle assembly consists of a fork, an axle, and two nuts. A sole plate assembly consists of a sole plate, two toe retainer clamps, a toe retainer adjustment bolt, and a truck assembly.

a. Draw a product structure tree for the Easy Roller Skate kit.

b. Construct a single-level bill of materials for the kit and each of its components.

3. The gross requirements, on-hand inventory, and scheduled receipts for steel tubing at the Kangaroo Bike Factory are indicated in the time-phased inventory status record below. Its lead time is 4 weeks. Complete the inventory status records, showing when planning orders should be placed. The company uses lot-for-lot ordering.

Steel tubing: LT = 4 weeks	Week									
	1	2	3	4	5	6	7	8	9	10
Gross requirements	100	300	250	200	300	150	300	250	100	150
Scheduled receipts	300		400							
On hand 150										
Net requirements										
Planned order releases										

4. The current on-hand balance, the gross requirements, and the scheduled receipts for part number R441 are indicated in the inventory status record shown below. Complete the time-phased inventory record. The company uses lot-for-lot ordering.

Item R441: LT = 3 weeks	Week									
	1	2	3	4	5	6	7	8	9	10
Gross requirements	75	55	90	120	75	65	30			
Scheduled receipts		150								
On hand 80										
Net requirements										
Planned order releases										

5. Given the product structure shown below, determine the quantity of each component that must be purchased or produced if there is no inventory of any component at present and the company has scheduled production of 75 units of product *A*.

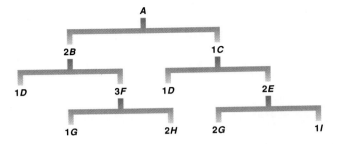

6. The product structure trees for products *A* and *F* are shown below. Part of the master schedule showing when the company will complete production operations for quantities of these products is shown in the table below. Find the gross requirements for item *B* throughout the first 12 weeks of the master schedule.

MASTER SCHEDULE

WEEK	1	2	3	4	5	6	7
Product *A*			200	150	250	160	250
Product *F*			80	180	125	200	210

WEEK	8	9	10	11	12	13	
Product *A*	300	325	300	225	180	150	
Product *F*	100	180	150	250	200	260	

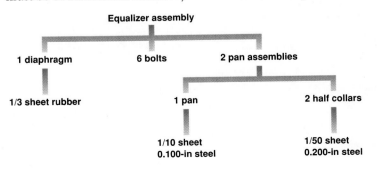

7. The Regular Regulator Company produces pressure regulators that are composed of two pan assemblies, a diaphragm, and six bolts. A pan assembly consists of a pan and two half collars. One sheet of rubber provides enough material for three diaphragms. One sheet of 0.100-in-thick steel is required for each 10 pans. One sheet of 0.200-in-thick steel is required for each 50 half collars. The product structure tree for the 16-mm equalizer is shown at the end of the problem. The company plans to make 300 of the 16-mm equalizers in a scheduled production run. How many of each component must be obtained if no inventory is available and no open orders are outstanding?

Equalizer assembly

1 diaphragm   6 bolts   2 pan assemblies

1/3 sheet rubber   1 pan   2 half collars

1/10 sheet   1/50 sheet
0.100-in steel   0.200-in steel

8. The lead time required to purchase or produce (from its immediately lower components) each component of the 16-mm equalizer is shown in parentheses below the component on the product structure tree that follows. How many components should be ordered, and when should they be ordered or started into each production operation, so that the company will complete 400 equalizers in week 10 (10 weeks in the future)? Disregard scrap allowances or any equalizers or components that are already on hand.

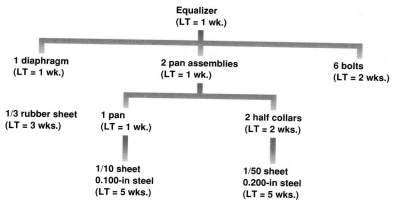

9. The Regular Regulator Company has on-hand inventory of some components for the equalizer shown in problem 8. The inventory levels and open orders for components of this equalizer are indicated below. The master schedule shows only one production lot for 400 equalizers to be completed in week 9. These 400 units are to be produced in addition to any inventory of the end item that may be available. Show the time-phased inventory status records for the pan assembly, pan, and 0.100-in steel for the next 8 weeks to support the production quantities in the master production schedule.

ITEM	ON HAND	SCHEDULED RECEIPTS OF OPEN ORDERS	ITEM	ON HAND	SCHEDULED RECEIPTS OF OPEN ORDERS
Pan assembly	0		0.100-in steel	10	30, week 3
Equalizer	250		Half collar	500	
Diaphragm	1,600	200, week 8	0.200-in steel	700	100, week 4
Rubber sheet	400		Bolts	3,200	
Pan	200				

10. The product structure tree for a drafting table (part *A*) is shown below. The number of an item required to make one unit of the item above it is indicated in front of the item. The lead time required to purchase an item or to produce it from the component(s) at the next lower level is indicated in parentheses following each item. The company uses lot-for-lot ordering and plans to complete 175 tables in week 7 and 250 in week 8. No other requirements for the table or its components are planned within this lead time. The on-hand balance and scheduled receipts values for the sides and legs are given in the table below the product structure tree. Construct time-phased inventory records for the side and the legs.

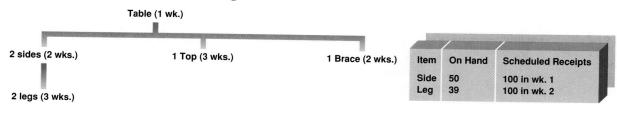

11. The product structure tree for a ceiling fan is shown below. The number of an item required to make one unit of the item above it is indicated in front of an item. The lead time required to purchase an item or to produce it from the component(s) at the next lower level is indicated in parentheses following each item. The company uses lot-for-lot ordering and plans to complete 600 fans in week 10 and 700 in week 11.

No other requirements for the fan or its components are planned within this lead time. The on-hand balance and scheduled receipts values for parts are given in the table below the product structure tree. Construct time-phased inventory records for the lamps and globes.

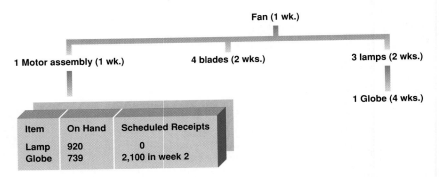

Item	On Hand	Scheduled Receipts
Lamp	920	0
Globe	739	2,100 in week 2

12. The product structure tree for a lawn sprinkler (part S) is shown below. The number of an item required to make one unit of the item above it is indicated in front of the letter representing an item. The lead time required to purchase an item or to produce it from the component(s) at the next lower level is indicated in parentheses following each item. The company uses lot-for-lot ordering and plans to complete 1,750 sprinklers in week 6 and 1,200 in week 8. No other requirements for the sprinkler or its components are planned within this lead time. The on-hand balance and scheduled receipts values for parts T, U, and V are given in the table below the product structure tree. Construct time-phased inventory records for parts T, U, and V.

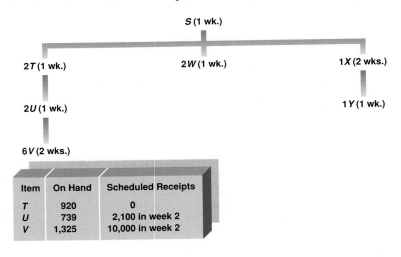

Item	On Hand	Scheduled Receipts
T	920	0
U	739	2,100 in week 2
V	1,325	10,000 in week 2

13. The structure of a product is shown in the tree diagram below, with the quantity required to make one unit of the higher-level item shown to the left of each item and the lead times in weeks indicated in parentheses. The company plans to complete production of 250 A's in week 8, 300 in week 9, and 300 in week 10. The company has

the quantities of the items on hand and on open orders as indicated in the table below.

ITEM	ON HAND	ORDERS SCHEDULED TO ARRIVE
B	500	500 in week 4
C	500	
D	200	1,000 in week 2
E	1,000	

Construct time-phased inventory records for items C and D. Use lot-for-lot ordering.

14. Refer to the product structures for products A and F presented in problem 6. The company has 500 units of B on hand, and 1,000 units are scheduled to be received in week 3. The master schedule shows that the company will complete the indicated quantities of end products during the scheduled weeks.

MASTER SCHEDULE

WEEK	1	2	3	4	5
Product A					
Product F					

WEEK	6	7	8	9	10
Product A			100	150	80
Product F		225	225	170	

Using the time-phased inventory record, show the gross requirements, net requirements, on-hand balance, scheduled receipts, and planned order releases for component B. Use lot-for-lot ordering.

15. The Crime Stopper Alarm Company produces two models, A and T, for which the product structures are shown at the end of this problem. The quantity required to make one of the next-higher-level items is shown to the left of an item, and the lead time in weeks for each procurement or production stage is indicated in parentheses on each diagram.

The company has on-hand balances and scheduled receipts as indicated below.

ITEM	ON HAND	SCHEDULED RECEIPTS
C	50	100 in week 2
D	1,000	
F	1,000	5,000 in week 2
G	500	
L	60	150 in week 1

A master schedule, indicating when final assembly of models *A* and *T* will begin, is shown below. Construct material requirement plans in the format of a time-phased inventory status record for components *C*, *L.*, *D*, and *F*. Use lot-for-lot ordering.

MASTER SCHEDULE

WEEK	1	2	3	4	5	6
Model *A*						
Model *T*						

WEEK	7	8	9	10	11
Model *A*		100	200	150	100
Model *T*		225	180	210	250

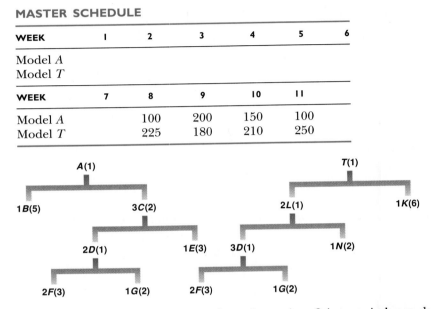

16. The net requirements for an item through a series of time periods are shown below. The setup cost for the item is $100 per order, and the holding cost is $0.25 per unit per period. Use the part-period algorithm to determine the orders into which these requirements should be batched.

Period	1	2	3	4	5	6	7	8	9	10
Requirement	200	150	100	200	100	100	150	200	150	200

17. Refer to the information in problem 16. Use the period order quantity technique to determine the size and timing of the planned order receipts.

18. Net requirements for item R557 during a series of time periods are shown below. The order cost for this item is $30 per order, and the holding cost is $0.10 per unit per period. Using the part-period algorithm, determine the timing and size of the orders that should be received.

Period	1	2	3	4	5	6	7	8	9
Requirement	50	200	50	250	0	0	100	100	300

19. Refer to the information in problem 18. Use the period order quantity technique to determine the size and timing of the planned order receipts.

20. For the data provided in problem 18, calculate the mean weekly requirements, and round to the nearest integer. Use this number as a uniform weekly requirement, and use the order cost and holding cost that were given in problem 18.
    a. From the EOQ formula determine the optimal order size for the item.
    b. Using the part-period algorithm, compute the sizes of orders that should be received with the same series of uniform requirements.
    c. Compare the results you obtained in parts *a* and *b* and explain any differences.

d. The average requirement per period in problem 18 is 117 units. Compare the number of periods that an order covers in the solution to problem 18 with the number of periods in the solution to part *b* of this problem.

COMPUTER-BASED PROBLEMS

MRP

Use a spreadsheet to set up the master production schedule for item *A* and the MRP inventory status records for all the dependent items. The needed data are given below.

MASTER SCHEDULE FOR ITEM *A*

WEEK	5	6	7	8
Begin Production	400	0	300	450

INVENTORY STATUS

ITEM	ON HAND	SCHEDULED RECEIPT
B	200	600(2), 400(4), 200(6)
C	300	100(1), 200(4), 100(7)
D	400	1,200(5)
E	2,000	5,000(3), 5,000(5), 5,000(8)
F	300	700(3)
G	200	1,000(3), 500(7)

Numbers in parentheses indicate week of receipt.

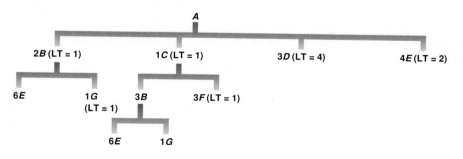

Bill of Materials

Make a printout of the MRP inventory records for each of the following cases:

a. The given master schedule and inventory status data.

b. Production for 300 units of *A* is added to week 6 for item *A*.

c. Item *A* production quantity of 300 units is moved up by 1 week from week 7 to week 6; the scheduled receipt for item *C* of 200 units in week 4 is delayed to week 5; and the on-hand inventory for item *E* is found to be only 1,700.

Suggested Steps for the MRP Assignment

The net requirement row of the inventory status record is set up in two stages. First, an intermediate row is set up by using the "on-hand" row. Then both the "on-hand" row and the intermediate row are used to set up the "net requirements" row. An example is shown below:

	A		B	C	D	E	F
21	Item:						
22	Week			1	2	3	4 . . .
23	Gross requirements						
24	Scheduled receipts						
25	On hand						
26	Net requirements						
27	Planned order releases						

Stage I

Set up the master schedule, bill-of-materials data, and on-hand inventory data at the top of the worksheet.

Stage II

1. Set up a status record as shown above.
2. Set up the needed formulas for the "on-hand" row.
3. In cell c26: @if(c25<0,−c25,0)
4. In cell d26: @if(d25>=0,0,@if(c25<=d25,0,@if(c25>0,−d25,c25−d25)))
5. Copy the formula in cell d26 into the corresponding cells of columns *E* through the last week in the inventory record.
6. Copy this typical status record as many times as the number of dependent items.

Stage III

Repeat the following for each item:
1. Enter a formula for the actual on-hand quantity (use the cell in column *B* for this). Then enter the scheduled receipt quantities.
2. For each item set up the "planned order" row of each item.
3. Set up the gross requirement formula for the dependent items. Repeat this step in the order of "low-level" code.

BIBLIOGRAPHY

Gallagher, Gerald R. "How to Develop a Realistic Master Schedule." *Management Review,* April 1980, pp. 19–25.

Greene, James H., ed. *Production and Inventory Control Handbook.* 2d ed. New York: McGraw-Hill, 1987.

Kanet, John J. "MRP 96: Time to Rethink Manufacturing Logistics." *Production and Inventory Management Journal,* 2d quarter 1988, pp. 57–61.

Lunn, Terry, and Susan A. Neff. *MRP: Integrating Material Requirements Planning and Modern Business.* Burr Ridge, Ill.: Irwin Professional Publications, 1992.

Mather, Hal F. "Reschedule the Reschedules You Just Rescheduled—Way of Life for MRP?" *Production and Inventory Management 18,* no. 1 (1st quarter 1977): 60–79.

McLeavey, Dennis W., and Seetharama L. Narasimhan. *Production and Inventory Control.* Boston: Allyn and Bacon, 1985.

Plossl, George W. *Production and Inventory Control: Applications.* Atlanta: George Plossl Educational Services, 1983.

Smith, Spencer B. *Computer-Based Production and Inventory Control.* Englewood Cliffs, N.J.: Prentice-Hall, 1989.

Vollmann, Thomas E., William L. Berry, and D. Clay Whybark. *Manufacturing Planning and Control Systems.* 3d ed. Homewood, Ill.: Irwin, 1992.

Wallace, Thomas F. *MRP II: Making It Happen.* 2d ed. Essex Junction, Vt.: Oliver Wight, 1990.

White, Edna M., John C. Anderson, Roger G. Schroeder, and Sharon E. Tupy. "A Study of the MRP Implementation Process." *Journal of Operations Management 2,* no. 3 (May 1982): 145–153.

Wight, Oliver W. *MRP II: Unlocking America's Productivity Potential.* Boston: CBI, 1984.

SCHEDULING AND CONTROLLING MANUFACTURING

CHAPTER 15

I n previous chapters we discussed several aspects of planning that establish the types of capabilities and amount of capacity that a company will have. Implementation of long- and intermediate-range plans establishes such things as fixed capacity, adjustable capacity, and relationships with suppliers. Actions taken to implement these plans are important, but they do not serve the customer—they only establish the capabilities to serve customers. In addition to these capabilities, activities based on short-range plans determine how well the customer is (or is not) served. It is the day-to-day work activities to effectively apply the capacity that has been made available that actually produce salable products. The series of plans that starts with very general long-range plans eventually leads to specific daily work activities. The ways in which some of the planning relates to operations are summarized in Table 15.1.

HOW SCHEDULING AND CONTROL CAN HELP ADD VALUE FOR CUSTOMERS

Scheduling of manufacturing operations to produce the right products at the times they are needed and controlling operations to keep items on schedule are important to provide dependable service to customers. Not overloading departments or letting jobs get behind schedule also helps reduce costs such as overtime premiums. Scheduling to keep jobs moving through operations can also hold down the cost of WIP inventory and help make production times short so the company can be more flexible and offer customers quicker service. Scheduling work so that it does not have to be done in a rush can also improve quality.

Efficient use of resources to provide the desired mix of items at the desired completion times depends upon how well production tasks are scheduled and controlled to achieve coordinated results. Control requires monitoring actual job progress and taking corrective action when it differs from the plan by more than an acceptable amount. This chapter discusses scheduling and controlling production in job shops, batch manufacturing, and repetitive, or continuous, production factories. Some characteristics of these types of factories are summarized in Table 15.2. We look further at each type of factory, but first let's examine the objectives that companies try to achieve in production scheduling and production control.

OBJECTIVES IN SCHEDULING AND CONTROL

A great deal of research has been done and continues to be done on production scheduling problems. Relatively small hypothetical problems are very challenging, even when conditions are assumed to be static. Researchers may take weeks or months to develop approximate solution methods for these problems. Most actual manufacturing companies face larger problems, and the conditions are dynamic, in that numerous new orders may be received and some orders may be canceled before the processing on a set of orders is completed. Observers have pointed out that in

Table 15.1
ELEMENTS OF PLANS THAT RELATE TO SCHEDULING

	LONG RANGE	**INTERMEDIATE RANGE**	**SHORT RANGE**
Focus of plans related to operations scheduling	Fixed capacity	Adjustable capacity	Scheduling and dispatching
Example decisions	What products, locations from which to operate, facility design, mission for each location, process and equipment selection	Use of inventory, work force, subcontracting (make-or-buy), production rate (shifts and work hours), long-term supplier agreements for materials	Lot size (how many), which jobs to run, in what sequence, should alternative routing be used, schedules for specific materials deliveries

Table 15.2
SOME GENERAL CHARACTERISTICS OF THREE FACTORY TYPES

CHARACTERISTIC	JOB SHOP	BATCH	REPETITIVE
Mission	Sells capacity and skills	Sells variety of products that use the same processes	Sells one or few products
Item flow	Few or no dominant paths	One or few dominant paths	Single-flow path
Bottlenecks	Shift frequently	Shift less frequently	Stationary
Equipment selection	General-purpose, flexible	Some focus but must accommodate various models of products	Specialized equipment for high volume
Run length	Short	Moderate	Long
Setup cost	Low	Medium	High
Labor content	High	Medium	Low
Scope of direct jobs	Broad	Moderate	Often narrow
Controller of work pace	Worker and foreman	Worker, foreman, and supervisor	Equipment and process design
Raw material inventory	Low	Moderate	Varies
In-process inventory	High	Medium	Low
Finished-goods inventory	Low or none	Varies	Often high
Suppliers	Uses variety of suppliers frequently	Uses fewer suppliers fairly consistently	May use suppliers consistently over long term
Worker information required for jobs	Typically new instructions for each job	Workers trained for each type of product	Limited requirements unless product design changed
Scheduling	Uncertain, frequent changes	Varies, frequent expediting	Inflexible, sequence and timing often designed into process
Challenges	Estimating, loading, fast response to bottlenecks	Balancing process stages	Productivity improvement, avoiding down time, process control
Response to reduced demand	Lays off some workers in affected department	Reduces some workers and rebalances work	Works shorter weeks or shifts

Source: Adapted from Robert H. Hayes and Steven C. Wheelwright, *Restoring Our Competitive Edge: Competing through Manufacturing* (New York: Wiley, 1984), pp. 180–182.

actual businesses the criteria for what constitutes a good schedule may be somewhat vague and may change over time. For example, not all jobs may be evaluated by the same criteria. Some customers may complain more than others or may complain to higher officials, so their jobs receive more attention. Some orders may have a greater potential than others to lead to desired future business, and some may be for a type of work that the company is not as interested in pursuing. In addition, the number of possible schedules is so great and the number of factors that may be impacted by the job schedule or sequence is so large that it may be almost impossible to evaluate the impact of scheduling decisions on the criteria—even if the criteria are well defined and communicated.

The following two goals summarize the criteria for many companies: (1) Meet customer delivery dates or inventory replenishment dates, so that the specified level of customer service will be maintained. (2) In doing this, use no more resources than are cost-justified.

The use of only the necessary resources may be expressed in other, but closely related, criteria for good scheduling and control. A goal might be to minimize the throughput time from the first operation through the last with no unjustified delays. This goal minimizes the unjustified work-in-process (WIP) inventory and the space required to hold it. (It also reduces the complexity of tracking jobs, recording data, and *dispatching,* i.e., determining which jobs have the highest priorities to be worked on, because there are very few in the plant at any time.) Financial measurements such as return on investment encourage companies to achieve the product flow with very little excess equipment, with no more than the justified work force, and with little expense for overtime pay. Part of the difficulty in dealing with this problem is that the resources are interchangeable to some degree. More equipment and more employees will often allow quicker throughput. A larger work force will reduce the amount of overtime cost, or more overtime pay can enable a company to operate with a smaller work force. The company must try to find the proper mix of resources to use, often under the dynamic conditions mentioned earlier.

If too much WIP is accumulating, a company may elect to use overtime. If lead times for customer deliveries are becoming too long, the company may purchase more equipment and/or add workers. Generally, the criteria mentioned above are related to the way companies behave, although it may be difficult to determine and measure the exact linkage between decisions and some measures of performance.

Manufactured products often are assemblies of many parts and subassemblies, many of which may be produced at different factories owned by the manufacturing company and by its suppliers. Obviously, much data must be collected and analyzed to plan, monitor, and coordinate the work that is done in a manufacturing operation and to coordinate the procurement activities that are required. An effective information system is essential to good production planning and control.

INFORMATION SYSTEM LINKAGES FOR PRODUCTION PLANNING AND CONTROL

Good production control depends on

1. Formulating a good plan and schedule for each job, one that recognizes the needs of other jobs that must use the same facilities

2. Communicating these plans to all who must help carry them out

3. Obtaining communication about the actual progress of each job and about the composite situation

4. Revising the plans and schedules whenever the situation makes improvement desirable or necessary (This is really a return to step 1.)

It is apparent that good production control involves good communication, that is, the efficient collection and transmittal of data. The production control group serves as the nerve network of a production system, sending signals to evoke action and sensing the results and need for further action.

Updated data must be maintained and reports prepared showing the status of jobs and the work loads in the various work centers. Scheduled arrivals of raw materials and purchased components should also be monitored and maintained. Data can be updated manually in small factories, but computers provide information faster and require less effort to analyze the data and prepare reports.

The massive amount of data accumulated in tracking the numerous parts of all jobs makes automatic data processing essential to sizable shops, if timely reports are to be available. Networks of computer terminals can help to coordinate widely dispersed work centers, inspection stations, purchasing offices, and stockrooms. An interactive system such as this makes possible data entry and inquiry from multiple locations. It is desirable to use a common data base to coordinate all the organizational elements. Commercial software packages that link many applications into a common data base are available through computer manufacturers and software houses. These packages often integrate other applications as well as production control activities. For example, sales information is related to the use of inventory, inventory withdrawal is tracked to see when production should occur, production activities result in material requirements, and materials procurement affects accounts payable. Labor hours are reported to track work performed on jobs, and these same data can be used for payroll preparation. Clearly companies are interrelated networks of transactions, and tracking production activities is an important part of this network in a manufacturing company. Figure 15.1 shows some of the information that flows between applications that are linked in an integrated information system.

Computer systems can use a variety of methods for data entry, such as terminals and bar code scanners, at various stations. Terminals can be placed at various locations in the plant so that timely data can be reported to a memory unit that is accessed by the computer when the update calculations are made. A worker provides data at the terminal each time an operation on a work order is begun or completed. The data terminal can automatically read a great many data. An internal clock records the start or stop time. A scan of a magnetic strip or bar code can be used to record the employee's identification from a badge and the job number from a route sheet or work order. The employee may need to key in only the number of good units completed and perhaps the number of defective units. Feedback may be needed from several or all work centers to track all jobs and update their progress when materials can take a variety of paths through the factory.

SCHEDULING AND CONTROL NEEDS VARY AMONG MANUFACTURING TYPES

The types and amount of scheduling and production control efforts vary among the three types of factories we consider. Each factory type has different characteristics for the work mix that it must schedule and control, as shown below.

Repetitive: Must deal with repetition of a few familiar jobs since it produces a standard product in relatively high volume

Figure 15.1
Information Flow
Between Some
Applications in an
Integrated System

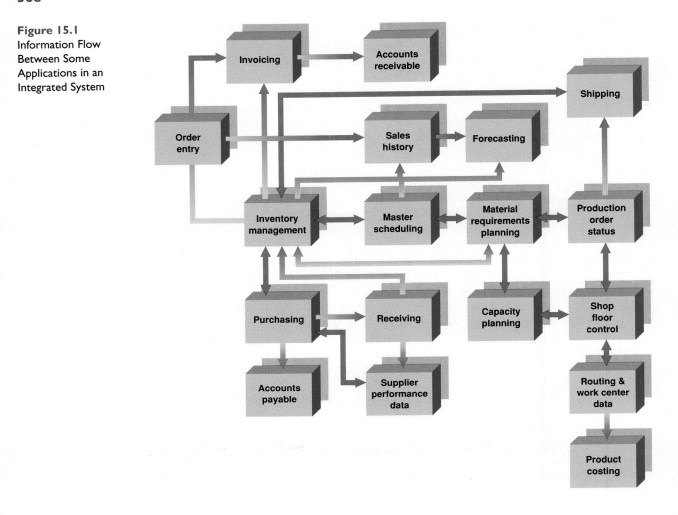

Batch: Must deal with a recurring variety of familiar jobs since it makes a variety of standard products by switching from one to another

Job shop: Must deal with an ever-changing mix of unfamiliar jobs since it bids on custom products and may seldom repeat production of the same item

Repetitive manufacturing processes the same product or similar products through the same series of steps. Process planning is very important because so many items will be run through the routing that is developed. A considerable effort should be put into process engineering when the factory is designed. Usually the routing is built into a production line, so instructions on where to move items are not required. That is, the route sheet is built into the plant. The *cycle time* for a production line (that is, the time between successive items produced on the line) is also designed into the line in many cases. It may be possible to change the cycle time and rebalance the line if it involves only manual assembly operations. Often, however, the fabrication steps are performed by machines for which the process times are difficult to vary. The availability of flexible automation in the future can increase flexibility in

A custom furniture maker is an example of a job shop. Each order is made to meet the specific requirements and individual tastes of the customer.

J. T. Miller/The Stock Market

some applications. Frequently, the amount of output of a particular item is changed by varying the number of hours the facility is run. The facility may work a 4-, 5-, or 6-day week, and so on, or the facility may be run for one, two, or three shifts a day.

A batch manufacturing factory is generally more complex to schedule and control than a repetitive facility of the same size. There are a wider variety of standard items to plan, so job planning and routing require more work. Each batch may flow through a different routing but must compete with other jobs for use of some work centers. Much of the complexity arises in determining the relative priority of the jobs because the mix of items at each work center may change frequently. Each type of product is more familiar to workers than in a job shop. The time estimates can be refined over time to become very accurate, and various schedules can be tried and improved. Although there are more bills of materials, part numbers, and routings than in a repetitive manufacturing factory, the personnel can become familiar with these.

Job shop production usually involves the greatest complexity. A great deal of work must be done in job planning since such companies must plan each job that is bid in order to provide a safe estimate of the cost, yet a competitive price to the customer. Since the jobs have not been produced before, the company may go to considerable effort to find suppliers for the materials needed for jobs that are awarded to the company. Each schedule is a new problem because it is a new mix of tasks and amounts of work. The estimates of the amount of work to be done may be inaccurate because in many instances the jobs have not been produced before. Tracking work may also be more difficult because the bills of materials, routings, and part identification numbers are unfamiliar. It is less likely that this type of plant will use as much automation in data entry to capture data on the items' movement.

The discussion above offers a brief overview of some activities related to production scheduling and control. We discuss some of these further as we focus on each of the three types of factories. First we discuss preproduction planning, which applies to some degree to all three factory types.

PREPRODUCTION PLANNING AND COST ESTIMATION

Detailed planning of the best way to produce each item that goes into a product is important in job shops, batch, and continuous, or repetitive, manufacturing factories. It can lead to better products and lower-cost production. Estimating the amount of time required to make items and their cost is an important part of the *preproduction planning.*

Job shops must estimate work requirements most often because they usually prepare a bid on each item for which a customer requests a quotation. These estimates must be accurate. If a bid is too high, the job shop will not be awarded the contract. If the bid is too low, the job shop may receive the contract but lose money on the work. Companies, such as batch or repetitive manufacturers, that produce standard products also must estimate product cost by a similar procedure to determine the feasibility of beginning production of an item. Estimates of the time to perform each production step are used to estimate the labor cost and to determine the investment in production capacity that will be required for a given output. Also companies with standard products may prepare new cost estimates from time to time as internal improvements are made or as prices change, to reevaluate their make-or-buy decisions.

People involved in estimation study the blueprints and specifications for the end item and its components. The cost of each item shown on the bill of materials for the product (such as the one shown in Table 15.3) must be determined. Each component of the end item must be purchased or manufactured, so make-or-buy decisions must be made—perhaps by requesting bids from suppliers and comparing them to estimated costs. The purchasing department obtains prices of all items to be purchased and the raw materials for all items to be manufactured.

For all items to be manufactured, it is necessary to estimate the labor-hours required for all operations required to convert the raw materials into the finished components and to assemble the components into the finished product. The time for inspection or other quality-control activities may also be included. Sometimes route sheets or crude approximations are prepared. A *route sheet,* or *operations sheet,* is a document listing the routing or the sequence of operations through which an object must pass as it is produced. An example of a route sheet is provided in Table 15.4. If the cost per labor-hour is different in some work centers, this difference must be taken into account in the estimate. The labor-hours are multiplied by the appropriate wage rates to arrive at the direct labor cost.

A completed cost estimate has several components. Direct labor costs, developed by the procedure described, direct prices of materials to be purchased, and the cost of raw materials that will be used from stock are added to find the direct cost estimate. Overhead expenses (sometimes called burden or administrative expenses) and a target profit are added if the estimate is to become a quote on a make-to-order

Table 15.3
EXAMPLE OF BILL OF MATERIALS

DATE 12/11/95   INDENTED BILL OF MATERIAL

ITEM 99001   UM EA   I/T 1   SPRAY UNIT
                              S-NO. 02010100000000000000 ENG. DRAWING
RELATIVE   COMPONENT   QTY   1   SBQ   1.000
LEVEL   ITEM NUMBER   QTY PER   UM IT FROM / TO   DESCRIPTION-TRUNC.

RELATIVE LEVEL		COMPONENT ITEM NUMBER	QTY PER	UM	IT FROM / TO	DESCRIPTION-TRUNC.
1		03590-F3	FEATURE 03	NON-REQD		SWITCH FEATURE
.2	0-01	03590	1.000	EA	4	AUTO SWITCH
1		03591-F1	FEATURE 01	REQUIRED		WHEEL FEATURE
.2	0-02	03591-10	2.000	EA	4	WHEEL 12 IN DIA
1		27006-F2	FEATURE 02	REQUIRED		TANK SIZE FEATURE
.2	0-01	26006-20	1.000	EA	1	TANK 8 BY 12 INCHES
..3		03426	1.000	EA	4	TUBE 8 IN DIA
..3		27006-00	1.000	EA	4	TANK TOP 8 INCHES
..3		27006-70	1.000	EA	4	TANK BOTTOM 8 INCHE
1		27009-PH	1.000	EA	0	FINAL ASSEMBLY GROU
.2		03424	1.000	EA	1	TREADLE ASSEMBLY
..3		03421	1.000	EA	4	HINGE ARM
..3		03422	2.000	EA	4	LEVER ARM
..3		03423	1.000	EA	4	TREADLE
..3		03592	2.000	EA	4	PIN 1 1/2 INCH
.2		03428	2.000	EA	2	STAND
..3		99465-RM	6.000	FT	3	SHEET METAL STRIP
.2		03443	2.000	EA	2	MOTOR SUPPORT
..3		99910-RM	3.280	LB	3	IRON PLATE 1/4 IN
.2		27005-A	1.000	EA	1	PUMP ASSEMBLY
..3		27000-02	1.000	EA	4	COMPRESSOR
..3		27003-20	1.000	EA	4	PUMP MOTOR
..3		33480-A	1.000	EA	4	CONTROL BOX
.2		27007-A1	1.000	EA	4	BASE ASSEMBLY
.2		34250-A	1.000	EA	1	TANK COVER ASSEMBLY
..3		03425	1.000	EA	4	COVER
..3		03592	2.000	EA	4	PIN 1 1/2 INCH

Source: Reprinted by permission of MAPICS, 12/11/95 by International Business Machines Corporation.

Table 15.4
EXAMPLE OF AN OPERATIONS SHEET OR ROUTE SHEET

DATE 12/06/95   ROUTING OPERATIONS

ITEM   03428   STAND

	M				-----RUN-----		---SETUP---		OP	
OPER	S	DESCRIPTION	TBC	MACH	LABOR	TIME	CREW	ST	FAC
0010		CUT TO LENGTHS	P	24.00	24.00	.20	1	10	AA001
0020		SHAPE LEGS	P	8.00	8.00	.30	1	10	RS075
0030		SHAPE TOP	P	48.00	48.00	.30	1	10	RS075
0040		WELD	P	.00	10.00	.00	1	10	WL085
0050		PRIME PAINT	P	.00	25.00	.00	1	10	PT065
0060		FINISH PAINT	P	.00	20.00	.00	1	10	PT065

Source: Reprinted by permission of MAPICS, 12/6/95 by International Business Machines Corporation.

Figure 15.2
Schematic Overview of
the Pre-bid Estimating
Procedure for a Job
Shop

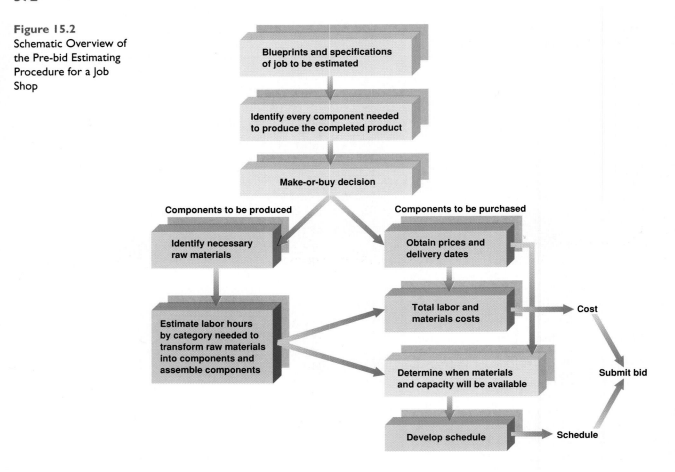

item. Often a delivery lead time is also developed and included in quotations for this type of work. A schematic of this procedure for a job shop is shown in Figure 15.2.

After jobs are planned, any necessary materials and components are ordered. The planned work activities to produce the item are scheduled to occur at the appropriate time when both the capacity and the materials will be available. We now discuss scheduling and controlling in each of the three types of factories, beginning with repetitive, or continuous, manufacturing and following with batch manufacturing and job shops.

PRODUCTION CONTROL FOR REPETITIVE MANUFACTURING

Repetitive, or continuous, manufacturing is characterized by long runs of identical or similar discrete items through the same sequence of processing steps. Equipment or work stations are placed near one another along a production line or assembly line for efficient materials handling. This layout also simplifies the coordination of various stations. Repetitive production faces a simpler production scheduling and control problem than a batch or job shop manufacturing factory. The routings are fixed, so planning each individual job and preparing individual route sheets are not necessary. The processing steps, routing, and work methods are primarily planned when the production system is designed—hence the need for good manufacturing engineering when the system is designed. The waiting time between operations and the WIP inventory are both minimal, so there usually are no queues of different kinds of jobs waiting at a work center, priorities do not have to be determined, and dispatching at each work center is not necessary.

Individual parts are not scheduled and tracked unit by unit in this type of production. A particular door for a 12-cubic-foot refrigerator will fit any refrigerator of that model, so it is not important to complete a particular door just when a particular refrigerator is completed. The important thing is to complete doors for this model at the same rate at which the refrigerators are being produced. More realistically, every component of the refrigerator must be completed at a rate proportional to the quantity of the component used in the refrigerator. Repetitive manufacturing often uses *rate-based schedules,* such as simply indicating that production is to be at a rate of 225 units per day for the next 2 weeks. This is an application of "flow control," in contrast to "job control" used in a job shop.

Control of this type of factory is simplest when only one product is produced. Consider a simple example of a five-station production line that performs all the work on the input material to make a finished product, product *A*. There are no other uses of the partially completed items, so each stage in the line feeds only the next downstream stage. Assume that the market demand exceeds the capacity of the line so that the constraint on production (called a *bottleneck*) is internal. The times required at each operation are shown in Figure 15.3, so we see that the third stage is the bottleneck, that is, it limits the output of the system. The stages downstream from this bottleneck receive work at the rate at which the bottleneck produces, if we keep the bottleneck running. If material is fed into the line faster than the processing rate of the bottleneck, the result will be an accumulation of WIP inventory in front of the bottleneck and at the second station, if material is fed in greater excess. This action does not increase the output of the line, but it does add to the cost of partially processed inventory and the need for space to keep it. This situation also requires a longer throughput time to get the average item through the line because some of the items are delayed in the queues.

A small amount of inventory may be intentionally maintained in front of the bottleneck in case, for some reason such as machine breakdown or employee absence, some upstream work station falls behind in feeding the bottleneck. Work should then be released to the *starting work station* ("gateway") only at the rate at which it flows out of the bottleneck, to prevent buildup of unjustified WIP. Coordinating this line requires monitoring the output rate at the bottleneck and releasing (dispatching) work at the starting work station at that rate. This action will serve customer demand to the extent possible with the currently available capacity of the company. A company in this situation probably would try to increase production at the bottleneck (perhaps through methods improvements or installing higher-capacity equipment)

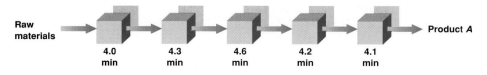

Figure 15.3
A Simple Five-Station Production Line

Raw materials → 4.0 min → 4.3 min → 4.6 min → 4.2 min → 4.1 min → Product *A*

Here at the GE Appliance Home Laundry plant in Louisville, Kentucky, assembly-line employees install wire-harness to the backsplash of clothes washers. Completed backsplashes continue on to a new part of the assembly line to be added to the apron of the washer. As with refrigerator doors mentioned in the text, the backsplashes will fit any washer of the same model, so the important thing is to schedule backsplashes and washer aprons for the same model at a proportional rate.

GE Appliances, photo by Ted Wathen/Quadrant

and to ensure that equipment there was well maintained (so it did not break, because lost production there is lost sales). The company might also explore ways to subcontract part of the bottleneck operation.

Tracking items through this type of facility is not difficult because all items follow a common routing. It might be necessary to count only the items that come off the line at the last operation and any items scrapped at any other station to know how many items were worked on at each station. Alternatively, scanners (maybe bar code) can be installed along the line to record how many pass between the stations, or item counts can be reported manually at each station. The amount by which the inventory level of each component should be reduced could be determined by *backflushing* or *post-deducting*, that is, multiplying the number of items finished by the quantities in the bill of materials and adding the amounts in any items that were scrapped along the line.

This example is very simplified, but it illustrates scheduling to use the available capacity to serve customer demand to the extent possible while not wasting resources anywhere in the system. If the product were composed of several components, there would be a line for each. The rates of output for the lines would be synchronized to produce the necessary quantities of each component.

The basic ideas in this example apply to more complicated settings such as batch and job shop manufacturing. In those types of factories it is more complicated to collect information on all items and work centers, to find the constraints, and to evaluate the many combinations of variables that might be used to accomplish the objective. We discuss some of these later. First, let's consider another possible variable in the example we just discussed.

If the constraint for the company above were market demand, several options might be available, depending on how much the capacity exceeds demand. The company might be satisfied to run 7-hour shifts or to run one or two shifts per day. It might operate with 4-day weeks with the employees assigned to other activities when the line is not being run. If there is much extra capacity, probably the company will seek at least one other product that would use the same production resources. Assume that the demand for product *A* declined, and the company has decided to produce product *A* and product *B*.

Another dimension of complexity and analysis has been introduced. The company must build an inventory of finished *A*'s to supply customers while the company is producing *B*'s, and vice versa. A question arises regarding how much product *A* should be produced before shifting to production of *B* and how much *B* to make before shifting back to *A*. Setups are now a factor, and setup time may be a problem that has to be considered. For example, assume that the number of units to be produced in each production run was determined by use of the economic production lot (EPL) model discussed when we considered lot sizes in Chapter 13. The EPL model considers a trade-off of only the setup *cost* against all the costs that are increased by adding units to the lot size (if we use a more realistic cost rather than considering only the holding cost in this category). This model, however, does not consider setup *time*. It is possible that the actual run time would use almost all the production capacity, leaving insufficient time for the setups required if the items were produced in the quantities recommended by the EPL model. The company might have to increase the lot sizes so that fewer setups would be required. Alternatively, the company might miss some production (and hence some sales) by performing more setups and producing in lot sizes that would keep inventory costs lower. This is an example of the reasons why setup time reduction is important. Obviously, even with only two products, the situation can become complicated. But companies must find acceptable solutions to such problems. No one model or set of models gives *the solution* for the many situations that companies can encounter. The specific set of products, the company's capacity, and the demand patterns that a particular company is facing must be considered. The idea of having more than one product to produce from the same resources leads us to a discussion of batch manufacturing.

PRODUCTION CONTROL FOR BATCH MANUFACTURING

Most companies face situations more complex than one product made on one production line, such as the one we initially discussed for repetitive manufacturing. There is a continuum of possibilities, ranging from a factory that produces only one product on a continuous basis to a job shop that has numerous orders in process at any given time, each for only one or a few of a custom product that it will never make again in the future. Most companies fall somewhere between these two extremes. Batch manufacturers make a variety of standard products. Unlike products in repetitive manufacturing, these products do not follow a common routing, but they do share some of the same work centers and machines. Usually there are several batches (or shop orders) on the shop floor at one time, each for a different part of several end items. Each of these orders travels through its own routing, and at some work stations it will compete for use of the common resources. Production control employees must track the orders and determine which order should be processed next, when capacity becomes available.

Food freshness and cleanliness standards are important issues in planning a frozen food production line. Here Stouffers' employees weigh beef and noodles, the makings for beef stroganoff.

Arthur D'Arazien/The Image Bank

These factories deal with a set of standard products with which their employees are somewhat familiar. Job planning is more frequent than in a repetitive manufacturing factory but not as frequent as in a job shop. Routings and instructions can be reused each time production of a particular item is repeated. Since the same jobs are repeated, the production methods and the accuracy of the estimates for standard times can be improved over time. The facility usually cannot be laid out to fit any one item exactly because not all items have common flow patterns. At least part of the plant can be arranged in manufacturing cells (discussed in Chapter 6 when we considered layout of the operations systems) where patterns of similar flow are found. Often, however, part of or all the factory may be laid out by function, as a job shop is, so information may have to be collected in many places and compared to the appropriate job routings and schedules to see how the jobs are progressing relative to their plans.

Just as with the simple production line we discussed first, the general goal is to ship products at the rate permitted by the capacity (assuming the constraints are internal) and to use resources wisely, otherwise the company should ship in accordance with demand. To achieve this goal requires that the company identify the bottleneck(s) and schedule work into the factory ("load the factory") in an amount no greater than the capacity of the bottleneck(s), to keep from building excess WIP inventory. Then production control personnel and shop supervisors must practice shop-floor control to coordinate the work in the work centers, so that this scheduled rate of flow is achieved. There is a tendency in many factories to keep equipment and people busy if possible. This may only accumulate work in process (WIP) in front of the slower or more heavily loaded work centers. Excessive WIP increases inventory cost, clutters the shop and requires more shop space, makes determining job priorities more difficult, creates long lead times, reduces flexibility, and causes poor customer service.

Scheduling and controlling to achieve a flow of orders through a batch shop may be done by at least three methods. Some companies use closed-loop MRP (material requirements planning), which we discuss in this section. Some companies use a pull method of just-in-time (JIT) manufacturing, which is presented in the next chapter. Others use approaches that we discuss later in this chapter when we discuss job shop production control.

Shop Loading with MRP

Earlier we discussed capacity planning with MRP. The purpose of rough-cut capacity planning (RCCP) is to look at the work load that a tentative master production schedule will place on each of the key work centers. This procedure is analogous to finding any bottlenecks that would prevent the scheduled flow of work. Use of RCCP in the production planning process while periods are a considerable time ahead of the time fence allows a company to identify work centers that might have serious capacity constraints which could impede the work flow being considered. The company can then reduce the schedule and/or increase the capacity of these work centers. This planning helps develop a master production schedule that is feasible and will use resources wisely. Some companies use detailed capacity requirements planning to further evaluate constraints after MRP has been run to see how many components must be produced and when they will be needed. The next challenge is to exercise production activity control that will implement the master production schedule.

Production Activity Control with MRP

Development of a good schedule or plan is only the first step in effective use of resources to provide quality goods or services on time. Control to ensure that actual activities are consistent with a good plan is also vital if the plan is to become a reality. *Production activity control* is the activities performed to make the actual work loads at the work centers consistent with the current conditions and plans. Production activity control has two main components: input/output control and priority control.

INPUT/OUTPUT CONTROL   *Input/output control* is used to control the size of the queues in front of work centers, thereby helping to control manufacturing lead times. Consider what is referred to as a "push system" of linking work centers. When a batch of items is completed at one work center, it is pushed to the next work center, where it waits in a queue until it is selected to be worked at that work center. Input/output control is important because it is a form of queue control, and a great portion of the time that a job spends in a plant may be spent waiting in queues. In some job shops and batch manufacturing factories queue time may consume as much as 80 to 95 percent of the total time a job spends in the factory.

The components of the total time that a job spends in a factory are shown in Figure 15.4. The time a job spends waiting to be moved and the time it spends being

| Move time | Queue time | Setup time | Run time |

Figure 15.4
Components of Lead Time

moved are functions of such factors as the type of materials-handling equipment used, the number of employees assigned to materials handling, and how the work centers are arranged in relation to each other. This time is relatively fixed by the physical facilities and is influenced very little by the scheduling and controlling activities. The run time includes such operations as inspections as well as other work operations. Run time is a function of the processing technology rather than of the schedule. Sometimes run time is reduced over the long term by improvements in technology or the effect of the learning curve (which we discuss at the end of the chapter). Setup times can also be improved over time if a company tries. At the time any given order is released, however, a set amount of time should be allowed for the setup.

The lead-time component that is most influenced by control activities is the queue, that is, the amount of work that builds up in front of a work center. With a given capacity, the work center can perform only a set amount of work per hour or day. If work flows to the center faster than this, without a change in capacity, it will only cause the queue to become longer and make the average queue time greater. The time spent in the queue is the major component of lead time that can be influenced or controlled.

Manufacturing lead times (and thus queue times) have an important impact on both the firm's ability to meet its planned schedules and its work-in-process (WIP) inventory levels. When plans to produce an assembly are developed, the start times for the components are established by backing up by some planned lead time so they will all be completed at the time when the assembly operation is to begin. Each component, therefore, will be started at some planned lead time before the assembly is to begin. The assembly cannot be made on schedule if the actual lead times for all components are not equal to the planned lead times. Some components would be completed early and would then be delayed as excess WIP, while other components would be completed late and would delay the entire job of which they are a part. Queues should be controlled within some consistent bounds so that actual lead times are very close to the planned lead times.

Small queues in front of the proper work centers can help improve operations. If a work center has several workers with a range of skill levels, a queue might provide an assortment from which to select an appropriate job when a worker becomes available. A queue also provides a buffer that keeps a work center from running out of work if the arrival of another job cannot be timed to occur just before a current job is completed. This type of protection is important at a bottleneck, since time lost there reduces the output of the total plant. Keeping the other, quicker, work centers busy may not be desirable, however. It may just lead to more WIP in front of the slower work centers.

Companies have had a tendency to allow queues to become too large. If large queues form, the investment in WIP becomes excessive and extra shop space is required to hold it. The complexity of determining which job to work on next increases immensely when jobs are allowed to pile up. The lead times to respond to customer demand can become so long that a make-to-order company's competitiveness is affected, and contracts may be lost. With the extra queue time, it takes much longer for jobs to flow through a shop, so quality problems are discovered after more defects are made and quality problems are more serious. A make-to-stock company has to work in response to a longer-term forecast, which will be less accurate. More safety stock may therefore be required, causing an even higher investment in inventory. If the amount of work assigned to the work center is significantly less than the capacity, the queue will shrink, and the work center may even run out of work. In this

Figure 15.5
Input/Output Control Report (Hours of Work for Work Center 16)

Week ending		5/31	6/7	6/14	6/21	6/28
Planned input		320	310	315	325	310
Actual input		325	320	310	330	320
Cumulative input deviation		+5	+15	+10	+15	+25
Planned output		320	320	320	320	320
Actual output		310	325	310	300	320
Cumulative output deviation		–10	–5	–15	–35	–35
Actual backlog	60	75	70	70	100	100

(Amounts are in standard hours of work)

case, it may be desirable to temporarily utilize some workers from that center for other work assignments.

Input/output control is used to monitor and control the amount of work in a queue at a work center so that queue times are more consistent and predictable. The actual output, in standard hours of work, that flows from a work center is the demonstrated actual capacity of the center. If this capacity differs from the planned amount of work over a few scheduling periods, the problem needs to be investigated. If the work that flows to the work center is greater than the actual output, the queue in front of the center will grow. Either the rate of releasing work to the center must be slowed, or capacity must be increased through such measures as overtime, additional personnel, subcontracting, or rerouting the work to an alternative work center. Otherwise, some of the problems mentioned above will occur.

An input/output control report like Figure 15.5 can be used to see whether actual results are in reasonable agreement with the plan and to show the impact of a plan on the queue at a work center. The relationship between the actual flow to a center and the actual flow out determines the growth or shrinkage of the queue. The numbers in the "cumulative input" and "cumulative output" rows are computed by subtracting the planned amount for a week from the actual amount for the week and adding the result to the cumulative deviation for the prior week. The actual backlog numbers refer to the backlog at the end of a week and are computed by starting with the prior week's actual backlog and then adding the actual input during the week and subtracting the actual output during the week. Input/output reports might be maintained to monitor the gateway or starting work centers, because the output of these centers determines the input to subsequent centers and the entire factory. If the capacity of some downstream work center (a bottleneck) is less than that of the gateway work center, the input at the gateway can be geared to the output at the bottleneck to prevent excessive WIP. Capacity at any work center should be adjusted, if practicable, to keep queues from becoming large, because coordinated plans can be wrecked by unplanned delays at any work center through which one part of an assembly passes. Effective input/output control should keep the average actual lead time equal to the lead-time offsets used when the schedules were made.

The relationship between actual lead times and the planned lead time is shown in Figure 15.6. The actual lead times will not all be of exactly the same duration. They will vary about some mean, but their average durations should be equal to the planned duration. Even when the average of the actual lead times is equal to the planned lead time, there can be problems in completing all components of a job on time, unless priority control is also used.

Figure 15.6
Relationship of Actual
and Planned Lead Times

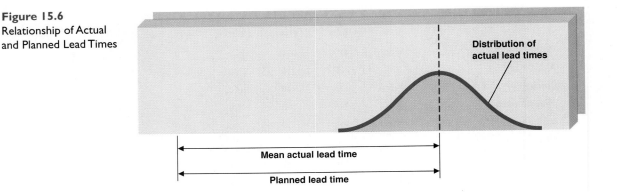

Distribution of
actual lead times

Mean actual lead time

Planned lead time

PRIORITY CONTROL *Priority control* is concerned with dispatching or determining which job in the queue will be selected for work when capacity within a work center becomes available. It is intended to answer the question of which item a worker should work on next when he or she finishes an item. Figure 15.6, which shows a symmetric distribution of actual lead times, indicates that about half the jobs will finish ahead of the average lead time and about half will take longer than the average lead time at a given work center. With effective queue control, the average actual lead time will approximate what was planned. Without effective priority control, however, half the items could be completed too early and have to wait as excess WIP, while the other half could be completed too late. An objective of priority control is to see that the jobs that are behind schedule go to the front of the queue and therefore take less than the average time at that work center. Jobs that are ahead of schedule are placed in the queue behind the late jobs and become the jobs that spend more than the average time in the queue. The result is that all jobs will finish closer to the planned time than they otherwise would.

If late delivery of materials, absenteeism, rework, or anything else causes a job to arrive at a work center late, it will be given priority and will not stay in the queue long. It will be worked ahead of jobs that arrive at the work center earlier than planned, owing to such factors as lack of other jobs at an upstream work center or early delivery of material. In this way, jobs finish closer to the planned dates that were established in coordination with other dependent items that are part of the same product. To implement this priority criterion, a company simply has to develop its daily *dispatch lists* (that is, work schedules) for each work center, listing jobs for that operation in order of their due dates. Jobs that are due first will experience very short queue times, and the other jobs will be worked in the order in which they are needed. If input/output control is effective in keeping the average lead time equal to the planned amount, then jobs will flow through the plant at the planned rate. This indicates that the capacity is adequate. Priority control allocates the capacity to jobs in the order of their need, so that the right jobs flow through the work centers. These control efforts help make the plans materialize so that the detailed activities in the factory support accomplishment of the company's overall longer-term strategic goals.

When an item is completed or almost completed at one work center, the shop-floor control system should add it to the dispatch list for the next downstream work center. The number of standard hours associated with each completed operation should be added to the actual output of the appropriate work centers, so that the input/output report is accurately updated. A labor reporting system should also track the actual labor-hours on the job. Actual hours can be compared to the estimated

standard hours to determine the efficiency at each work center, so that future estimates can be more accurate. Each time a component or subassembly of an end item
is completed, it affects the number of these items on hand. The number of available
items, in turn, affects the netting process when MRP is run and can affect the priorities of other shop orders. For example, a scrap rate might be lower than anticipated,
and more of an item might become available than was originally planned for a scheduled receipt. An order to produce a few of these items in a later period might no
longer be needed, and the order's priority would become very low. Overshipments or
undershipments from suppliers also can affect the inventory level, thereby changing
priorities on the shop floor. Figure 15.7 shows the flow of information in coordinat-

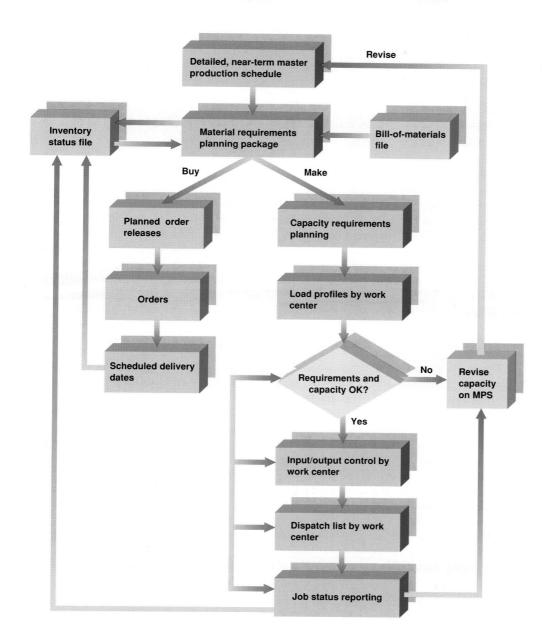

Figure 15.7
Information Flow for
Shop-Floor Control

ing shop-floor operations with MRP. The feedback of information into the earlier steps of the flowchart illustrates closed-loop MRP.

Further Consideration of Dispatching Decisions

In our discussion of priority control we mentioned that jobs are sequenced according to the operation due date. This general rule of thumb for selecting the order to work on jobs is commonly used with dependent items because it helps make the actual lead time closer to the planned lead time. This increases the likelihood that all components of an assembly will be finished at about the same time so the assembly can be made. Many other criteria such as the shortest processing time or first-come-first-served have been proposed for selecting the sequence in which jobs will be performed. Frequently some general heuristic (or rule of thumb) is used as a guideline, because determining a mathematically optimal sequence of jobs is a complex task. We discuss dispatching rules or sequencing rules further when we consider job shop production control.

JOB SHOP SCHEDULING AND PRODUCTION CONTROL

Most job shops bid competitively for a large percentage of the jobs they receive. Much of the planning for a job must be performed before a bid is submitted, so that the bid will be accurate enough to get profitable jobs. Consequently, much of the job planning (such as production methods, routing, and materials sourcing) will already have been performed for the jobs that such a company is awarded. The bid will usually include a delivery time stating how long after receipt of the order the item will be delivered. These delivery-time estimates are based on the work backlog for the work centers that must perform work on the particular job quoted. Therefore it is important that job shops keep accurate backlog reports or load reports of the work that they have already contracted to perform.

Backlog or Load Charts and Reports

Companies strive to develop accurate, achievable schedules that smoothly utilize available capacity. Effectively utilizing each department's capacity depends on accurate information regarding the available capacity throughout the planning horizon and an accurate backlog of committed work load. A load report, also called a backlog report, for a work center can be manually prepared, or it can be obtained from a computerized system such as MRP. A sample load report is shown in Figure 15.8. Capacity is available in week 3 and beyond. A job requiring 20 hours or less of production time in work center 16 could be loaded into week 3 if the materials will be available and if its earlier production steps can be completed in time. A job requiring more than 20 hours would require overtime, or it could be scheduled to be completed sometime after week 3. A bar chart with a vertical or horizontal bar for each week's load can be used to indicate the load shown in a load report. Figure 15.9 displays graphically the information in Figure 15.8.

Job shops have difficulty building a uniform schedule for each work center. On the average, they must quote on several jobs to be awarded one. But this "hit ratio" is not a consistent percentage of the work hours quoted. A company may receive a higher than average percentage of some types of jobs and temporarily overload some

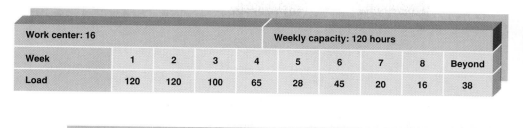

Work center: 16				Weekly capacity: 120 hours				
Week	1	2	3	4	5	6	7	8	Beyond
Load	120	120	100	65	28	45	20	16	38

Figure 15.8
A Backlog or
Load Report

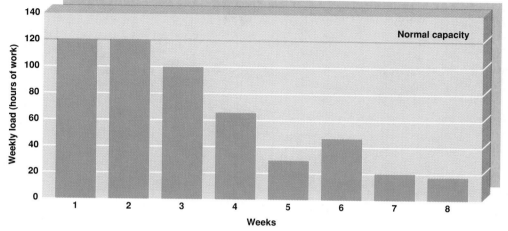

Figure 15.9
A Graphical
Backlog Report

of its work centers, requiring overtime work, subcontracting, delayed deliveries, or other measures. At other times insufficient work will be received to load the shops fully. Some future jobs may be worked early, or there may be idle time or layoffs. The persons who make quotations must try to balance the amount of work quoted and the flexibility in delivery times quoted, so there can be some adjustment of when the work is loaded into the shop if a contract for the work is received. When a contract is received, materials must be obtained and the work must be scheduled and coordinated through all the appropriate steps.

Jumbled Flow in a Job Shop

The contracts awarded to a job shop usually represent an ever-changing mix of jobs. These jobs will be routed through the appropriate series of work stations to perform the necessary operations. At any one time, a sizable job shop might have dozens of jobs in process. Many of these jobs could have hundreds of parts at various stages of completion scattered through a dozen or more work centers. Many jobs will be waiting at work stations to be worked on while work is progressing on other jobs. The flow path of a particular part is determined by the sequence of operations required to convert its raw materials into the desired item. When an item leaves one work station, it might be moved to almost any other work station in the factory. A job shop can be visualized as a set of work stations with waiting lines, or queues, in front of them and a set of nearly random flow paths connecting the work stations. This arrangement is shown in Figure 15.10. Most actual shops have many more work stations than are shown in the figure. Obviously, no one person can track and coordinate all the parts of jobs as they flow through such an extensive array of activities and so many possible paths. Job shops, therefore, normally have a production control

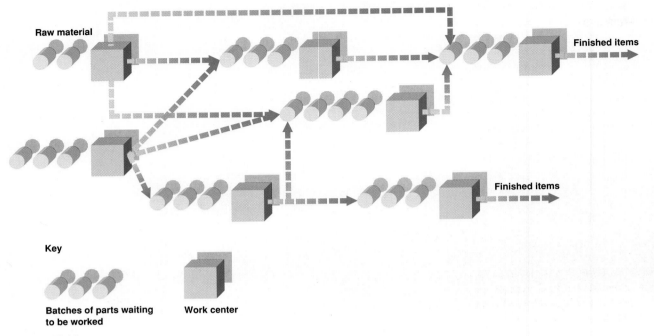

Key

Batches of parts waiting to be worked

Work center

Figure 15.10
Sketch of the Flow in a Job Shop

group to assist management. Production control is usually a staff function that does not directly supervise workers but advises direct-line supervisors.

Scheduling and Controlling Contracts

Scheduling and controlling a contract as it is processed through facilities with perhaps dozens of other contracts involves several organizational components. Numerous activities involved in processing one order occur simultaneously with the activities involved in other orders at various stages of processing. The sequence of activities in processing one order, from receiving the order to shipping the item, is outlined below. (Many of these activities are also shown schematically and numbered in sequence in Figure 15.11.)

The customer places an order with sales. Sales notifies production control to proceed with the job. Production control performs the detailed planning by preparing a route sheet for every component to be produced. Requisitions are prepared for all raw materials and purchased components and sent to purchasing. Move tickets may be prepared to instruct materials-handling personnel to move the items to the appropriate next operation after each step of processing is completed. If any special tooling is required, it must be specified and requisitioned to be produced by an internal or external tool-and-die shop. Requisitions for externally produced tooling are sent to purchasing. The route sheets, blueprints, special instructions or specifications, and move tickets make up what is sometimes called a "traveler package," which is sent to scheduling.

Scheduling is performed in two stages. The first is called loading. Loading is assigning to a particular work center the task to be performed during some gross scheduling period, such as a week. Some desired completion date, however, is usually assigned to each task. Loading of work centers depends on the open (available) capacity in the load report and the expected availability of the material for the job. If material is available early, it may be held in a material control area until the period in which the job is to be released to the work center. The jobs loaded to a work center are considered to form a waiting line, or queue, of waiting jobs, even though some jobs may not be present physically.

The second stage of scheduling is dispatching. Dispatching is sequencing the tasks that are waiting to be worked on at a work center and releasing them to be performed at a particular time by a specific machine. Dispatching decisions depend on many factors and frequently are made a short time before dispatching is begun, so that the current status of these factors can be taken into account.

The planned hours in a task are removed from the backlog, or load, when a work center completes the task. Dispatchers can obtain this feedback by talking with the supervisors of the work centers or by collecting move tickets showing that the item has left the work centers. Sometimes computerized information systems are used; dispatch lists with completed tasks marked off can be returned to a collection point for data entry, or terminals are located on the shop floor so that workers can key in or bar code scan the completion of assignments.

Completed parts or subassemblies are usually held in a material control area until all components of a job are completed. After final assembly operations are performed, the job is inspected and shipped to the customer. Naturally, cost data are collected during production. The customer will be invoiced for the contract price of the job, which the company hopes is greater than the total cost.

Figure 15.11

Overview of Production Control and Other Activities That Must Be Considered to Produce a Product

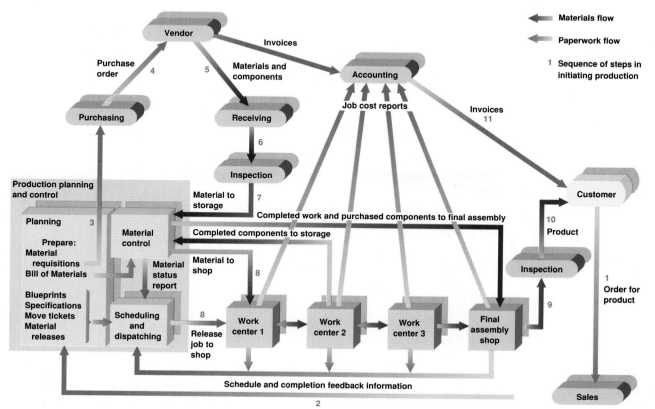

Forward and Backward Scheduling

As we mentioned, the jobs that are received must be scheduled for the necessary amounts of work in all work centers on the route sheet. The scheduler or a scheduling program looks for available capacity in the backlog of the work center at a time when the materials are available and have been processed up to that stage. The backlog report shown in Figure 15.8 is a valuable tool in this process. It is important that the backlog or load report be accurate. This report must be updated each time work is scheduled, rescheduled, or canceled for a work center. Another format for displaying the load in a factory or in a work center is the Gantt load chart. This chart is particularly useful if there are several dissimilar types of equipment in a work center and the desire is to see where there is open capacity on each. Figure 15.12 shows an example of this type of chart.

Another form of time-phased bar chart is useful for displaying the schedule and for tracking progress on all components of a job. The *Gantt schedule chart* focuses on the activity sequence and timing for various components of a job (as opposed to showing the amount of work scheduled on each type of resource, as the load chart does). The Gantt schedule chart can also be used to monitor the actual progress of a job in relation to the plan. Figure 15.13 provides an example of a Gantt schedule for a custom refrigerated locker. A bar is used to represent subtasks within the total job. The location of each bar indicates the time at which each subtask is scheduled to be performed. Additional information can be included to indicate the planned production hours, say, at the top of the bar. The chart can be marked to indicate actual progress of the job as feedback is obtained from the shops. The chart gives a graphic overview of the job's status, suggesting where corrective action may be desired. The brackets show when a task is scheduled to occur. A solid bar shows the extent of actual progress. The current date pointer at the bottom of the chart indicates that progress on the stand is ahead of schedule and receipt of the compressor is behind schedule.

Computers can display the same types of information on a screen or a printed graph. Other devices display schedules using string, plastic, or metal strips to represent the bars. The later types of devices must be updated manually to show the status of jobs.

The completion date for a job can result from either of two basic approaches to scheduling or from some combination of the two. The first major approach is called *backward scheduling*. In this case the potential customer specifies a required delivery date, and the scheduler works backward from the required delivery to determine when (or at least the latest time at which) the necessary production tasks must occur. Backward scheduling was discussed as the scheduling performed in material require-

Figure 15.12
A Gantt Load Chart

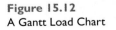

Work center: 16							
Week	1	2	3	4	5	6	
Machine 1	Job A		Job B				
Machine 2	Job C	Job D					
Machine 3	Job E						
Machine 4	Job F						

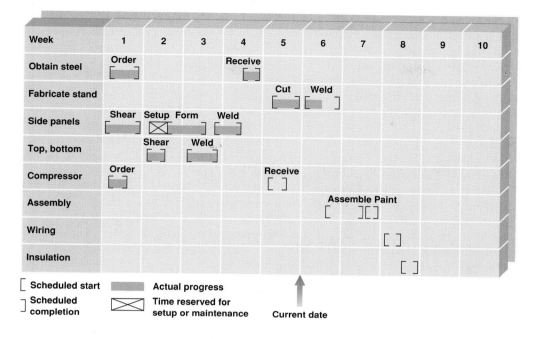

Figure 15.13
A Gantt Schedule Chart

ments planning where the planned lead time is subtracted from the period in which an item is needed to determine the planned order release time.

If each task can be fitted into the available capacity (total capacity minus the backlog of work already under contract) in some period before its latest allowable date, the requested delivery date can probably be met. If the backlog of contracted work is too great to allow the requested delivery, the job shop must decide whether to quote a late delivery or plan to increase its capacity if it is awarded the job on the basis of the requested date.

The second basic approach is *forward scheduling*. In this approach, each task is scheduled to occur at the earliest time that the necessary material will be on hand and capacity will be available. The earliest completion date, assuming everything goes as planned, could be quoted to the potential customer. Considerable time is usually added between operations to allow for movement to the next work center and for queue time. Part of the challenge to achieving rapid throughput is scheduling so that capacity will be available shortly after the job arrives at a work center, so it does not have to wait long. Normally some queues occur.

After jobs have been scheduled, production control personnel release the jobs to the starting work center on the routing at the appropriate time (assuming that capacity and materials are available). Releasing the job to a work center that is overloaded will not accomplish any additional productive work. As jobs flow through their routing, they enter queues along with other jobs that are also scheduled to use the capacity of that work center. At this point dispatching or sequencing decisions must be made.

Job Sequencing (Assigning Priorities)

The question of *job sequencing* has received much attention in research and analysis. Enumeration of all possible sequences rapidly becomes an overwhelming combinatorial problem, even when the number of jobs and work centers is small. Consider a very simple problem of n jobs to be sequenced for processing on one machine (that is, the $n/1$ sequencing problem). There are n jobs that could be selected to be first, $n-1$ jobs left for the second place, $n-2$ left for third place, and so on, leading to $n!$ possible sequences. If we had 10 jobs to sequence, that would be $10! = 3,628,800$ possible sequences. If you could evaluate 1,000 in a minute, it would take more than 60 hours to determine the best sequence by enumerating all of them. During this time some jobs could be run even if they were only in a "good" rather than optimal sequence. During this time new jobs would also be received, and some of the other jobs could be canceled. Imagine trying to enumerate all possible sequences of 100 jobs across 10 work centers and then determine the cost of each possible sequence!

Despite the large number of possible sequences, it has been shown that the $n/1$ problem (n jobs to be processed through one machine) can be optimized. If the criterion is to minimize average flow time or average job lateness, the job sequence should begin with the shortest processing time and progress in order of increasing processing time. Flow time is the total time a job spends in the shop, either waiting or being processed. Job lateness is the actual delivery date minus the due date, and it can be positive or negative. This solution is suitable if there is no significant difference in job priorities or their-in-process inventory cost and if the setup costs are independent of sequence. Average job lateness may be a poor criterion when the jobs are parts of an assembly. Having some early and some late can make the average lateness zero, but the assembly cannot be put together until all the parts are finished. Some heuristics, therefore, focus on the due date.

Determining an optimal sequence to process jobs through several machines or work centers when there is no consistent flow pattern is impractical in many instances. Consequently, researchers and practitioners use heuristics or rules of thumb to establish job priorities that set their sequence. A widely used rule is to first run the job that has the least amount of slack per operation and to sequence the jobs in order of increasing slack per operation. The slack per operation is found by equation 15.1:

$$\text{Slack per operation} = \frac{\left(\begin{array}{c}\text{available work time}\\\text{until delivery date}\end{array}\right) - \left(\begin{array}{c}\text{total estimated}\\\text{processing time}\end{array}\right)}{\text{number of remaining operations}} \qquad [15.1]$$

Another method used by some companies to establish the relative priorities of jobs waiting at a work center is called the *critical ratio*. The critical ratio (CR) is the ratio of the time left until the job's due date to the expected elapsed time for the job to be processed through the remaining work centers to its completion.

$$\text{CR} = \frac{\text{due date} - \text{today's date}}{\text{days required to complete job}} \qquad [15.2]$$

If the ratio is less than 1, the job is behind schedule and should receive special attention. Sequencing jobs at a work center in order of increasing critical ratio is intended to use the capacity in order of greatest need first.

To illustrate the use of the slack per operation and the critical ratio as dispatching rules refer to Table 15.5. It is assumed that today's date is shop day 203. Since job C is due to be completed on shop day 218 it has $218 - 203 = 15$ days remaining. Job Y was due yesterday (shop day 202) so it has $202 - 203 = -1$ day remaining. If the jobs

Table 15.5
CONDITIONS AND JOBS WAITING AT WORK CENTER 33 ON SHOP DAY 203

JOB	DUE DATE (IN SHOP DAYS*)	PROCESSING TIME AT THIS WORK CENTER (DAYS)	PROCESSING TIME AT ALL REMAINING OPERATIONS (DAYS)	NUMBER OF REMAINING OPERATIONS	CRITICAL RATIO	SLACK PER OPERATION
C	218	4	8	5	$15/8 = 1.88$	$(15 - 8)/5 = 1.4$
E	209	0.5	4	1	$6/4 = 1.5$	$(6 - 4)/1 = 2$
H	216	2	2	2	$13/2 = 6.5$	$(13 - 2)/2 = 5.5$
J	220	3	5	3	$17/5 = 3.4$	$(17 - 5)/3 = 4$
Y	202	1	1	1	$-1/1 = -1$	$(-1 - 1)/1 = -2$

*Shop days = workdays. Today's date is shop day 203.

were performed in the order of increasing slack per operation the sequence would be Y, C, E, J, H. If the jobs were performed in the order of increasing critical ratio the sequence would be Y, E, C, J, H. Both of these rules consider the time until the due date and would call for job Y, which is behind schedule, to be performed first.

Various *dispatching rules* have been evaluated by simulation to see which perform best according to some criterion. One rule that frequently is shown to minimize the number of late jobs is the shortest-processing-time (SPT) rule. This rule simply dispatches the queue of jobs at each work station in the order of their estimated processing time. The jobs in Table 15.5 would be placed in the sequence of E, Y, H, J, C. Notice that job E would be worked first even though job Y is already 1 day late. Also consider that as new jobs continue to arrive, the shorter ones will be worked and a lengthy job may be delayed indefinitely. The longest job would not be worked unless the work center ran out of alternatives. The longer jobs, however, might represent more inventory cost for keeping them in the queue and more delayed profit for delaying them. Consequently, modifications of this rule have been developed. In view of the difficulties, it is doubtful that one simple rule will correctly solve all the problems that can arise. For example, in a shop with a dominant flow path, good results were obtained by using the SPT rule in the early work stations and the critical ratio for the latter stages.[1] Considerable research is still being done on the job shop scheduling problem.

An optimal solution has been found for the situation in which all jobs flow through two work centers in the same order. The procedure to sequence jobs optimally in this case is often called Johnson's rule, after its developer.

JOHNSON'S RULE   Consider the situation of two work centers, say, machine 1 and machine 2, where all jobs flow from the first to the second. If the objective is to minimize idle time and the time from the beginning of the first job until the finish of the last job, scheduling can be optimized by the use of Johnson's rule.[2] The method is suitable when the in-process inventory cost and setup cost are independent of sequence.

[1] R. Lawrence LaForge and Samir Barman, "Performance of Simple Priority Rule Combinations in a Flow-Dominant Shop," *Production and Inventory Management Journal*, 3d quarter 1989, pp. 1–4.
[2] S. M. Johnson, "Optimal Two- and Three-Stage Production Schedules with Setup Times Included," *Naval Research Logistics Quarterly*, March 1954, pp. 61–68.

JOB SEQUENCING BY JOHNSON'S RULE

Stan's Furniture Refinishers has five items of furniture to sand and varnish the next day. The times for these two operations are shown in Table 15.6. Stan supervises all refinishing and does not go home until the last operation is finished. Find the sequence that will minimize the time from the beginning of the first item until the finish of the last (that is, minimize the total flow time).

Table 15.6
HOURS REQUIRED TO SAND AND VARNISH FIVE ITEMS OF FURNITURE: FIRST STEP IN JOB SEQUENCING BY JOHNSON'S RULE

ITEM	SANDING TIME (HOURS)	VARNISH TIME (HOURS)
A	2.25	1.25
B	2.00	2.25
C	1.00	2.00
D	2.50	2.00
E	1.75	1.75

The shortest time for all the tasks is sanding item C. Since this time is for the first task, job C is placed first in the sequence (Table 15.7).

Table 15.7
SECOND STEP IN JOB SEQUENCING BY JOHNSON'S RULE

SEQUENCE

1st	2d	3d	4th	5th
C				

Item C is eliminated from further consideration. The shortest remaining time is 1.25 hours for varnishing item A. Since this is for the last task, item A is placed last in the sequence (Table 15.8).

Table 15.8
THIRD STEP IN JOB SEQUENCING BY JOHNSON'S RULE

SEQUENCE

1st	2d	3d	4th	5th
C				A

Item A is eliminated. The shortest remaining time is 1.75 hours for item E. Whether E is performed second or fourth will not change the total flow time. It is arbitrarily placed as early as possible (Table 15.9), but the fourth slot would also be permissible.

Table 15.9
FOURTH STEP IN JOB SEQUENCING BY JOHNSON'S RULE

SEQUENCE

1st	2d	3d	4th	5th
C	E			A

Jobs B and D remain and are tied for minimum time for a task. The 2-hour time for job B at the first stage favors putting it early, and at the second stage for job D favors putting it late. The completed sequence is shown in Figure 15.14. Notice that Stan will have to work 10.75 hours to be present while all the work is done.

Figure 15.14   Minimum Flow Time Solution by Johnson's Rule

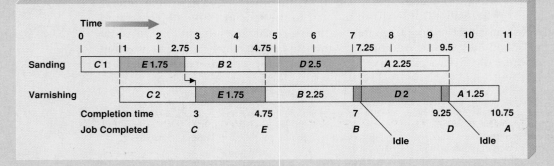

Johnson's rule consists of the following four steps:

1. List the processing times (including setup) for all jobs in both production stages.

2. From the unscheduled jobs, select the job with the shortest time in either stage.

3. If the shortest time is for the first processing stage, put the job as early as possible in the unfilled portion of the job sequence. If the shortest time is for the second processing stage, put the job as late as possible in the unfilled portion of the job sequence. If the time on the first stage for one job equals the time on the second stage for some other job, fill the earliest slot with the job having this amount of time for the first stage and fill the latest slot with the job having this amount of time for the second stage. If a job has the same time for both stages, it can be placed arbitrarily at the earlier or later end of the unfilled sequence.

4. Delete the job selected in step 2, and repeat the steps until all jobs have been sequenced.

Johnson's rule has been adapted to the three-machine problem in some instances. No simple optimization algorithms are available for problems of greater size, although many jobs in job shops require work at more than three work centers. In any case, there are other factors to be taken into consideration besides the minimum flow time.

Many schedule-related factors, mentioned earlier in this chapter and elsewhere in the book, depend on the times required to perform tasks. Some examples are capacity and staffing requirements, the cycle time for a production line (determined by the bottleneck), determination of the best sequence for jobs, and synchronization of the output rates of lines or cells. The time required to perform tasks may change as individuals, improvement teams, and companies work to develop better ways to work and become more competitive. Decisions based on times for jobs should be reevaluated occasionally. The reduction of task times over extended periods is often referred to as a learning-curve or improvement-curve effect.

LEARNING CURVES: PLANNING FOR IMPROVEMENT OVER TIME

When a sizable volume is produced, the direct labor-hours required to produce a unit may decrease markedly as more and more units are produced. This reduction frequently is sizable enough that it should be taken into account in scheduling delivery rates and in planning capacity utilization.

Normally, one would expect the second unit to require less time than the first, because considerable study and thought may be involved in producing the first unit. However, in some industries, such as those that produce aircraft, data processing equipment, and large machines, the reduction has been found to continue for hundreds and even thousands of units. This phenomenon is called a *learning curve,* or sometimes an improvement curve, a progress curve, or a manufacturing progress function.

A learning curve is a graph or equation that expresses the expected *rate of improvement* in productivity as more units are produced. The term *learning* suggests that the reduction in production time occurs because of improved dexterity of workers over time as their skills improve. Actually, increased skill may account for little of the improvement. Employee suggestions for improved work methods, designs for new tooling to assist in performing work, revision of the material or redesign of the product to make production easier, or other innovative work methods and technological improvements may account for much of the reduced production time. Unit production times may be improved in a few large steps or through a collection of numerous small steps. Therefore, the progress or "learning effect" may be somewhat erratic rather than a smooth progression. Given a particular industry and type of product, however, a rather consistent average relationship between the unit production time and the number of units produced has sometimes been found. The direct labor-hours per unit may be reduced by a fairly consistent percentage each time the cumulative number of units produced is doubled. For instance, with an 80 percent learning curve, the 2d unit requires 80 percent of the direct labor-hours required to produce the 1st unit. The 4th unit requires 80 percent of the time required to produce the 2d. The 100th unit requires 80 percent of the direct labor-hours required to produce the 50th unit, and so on. An 80 percent curve represents a faster improvement rate than a 90 percent curve, and so on, as can be seen in Table 15.10 and Figure 15.15.

A mathematical expression frequently used to describe the learning curve is

$$Y_n = (Y_1) n^R \qquad\qquad\qquad\qquad \text{[15.3]}$$

where Y_n = direct hours required to produce nth unit
Y_1 = direct hours required to produce 1st unit
n = number of unit for which time is estimated
R = logarithm of the ratio of production time for a doubled-quantity unit to production time for the base unit divided by log 2

The exponent R is the ratio of two logarithms and can be computed with base-10 logarithms or natural logarithms, as long as both the numerator and the denominator have the same base.

Let us illustrate the use of equation 15.3 with an example. Suppose that a computer manufacturer has experienced an 85 percent learning curve for similar products and expects this same learning rate to apply to a new model. Say it took 3,000 hours to produce the 1st unit and the company wants to estimate how many hours the 50th unit will take. For this problem

$$R = \frac{\log 0.85}{\log 2} = \frac{0.92942 - 1}{0.30103} = \frac{-0.07058}{0.30103} = -0.23446$$

$$Y_{50} = 3{,}000 \times 50^{-0.23446}$$

$$= 3{,}000 \times 0.39963 = 1{,}198.9 \text{ hours}$$

The 50th unit therefore is estimated to take about 1,200 hours.

Equation 15.3 is an exponential equation. When this type of curve is plotted on arithmetic-scale coordinates, the rate of reduction in direct hours declines as more units are produced. Table 15.10 gives the hours required for doubled-quantity units for a 90 percent and an 80 percent learning curve. Figure 15.15 shows four learning curves plotted on arithmetic scales. A learning curve as expressed by equation 15.3 is a straight line when it is plotted on logarithmic-scaled ("log-log") paper. Figure 15.16 shows the same four learning curves plotted on logarithmic paper.

Table 15.10
DIRECT LABOR-HOURS REQUIRED TO PRODUCE DOUBLED-QUANTITY UNITS FOR 90 AND 80 PERCENT LEARNING CURVES

CUMULATIVE UNITS	Direct Labor Hours	
	80% SLOPE	90% SLOPE
1	100.00	100.00
2	80.00	90.00
4	64.00	81.00
8	51.20	72.90
16	40.96	65.61
32	32.77	59.05
64	26.21	53.14
128	20.97	47.83
256	16.78	43.05
512	13.42	38.74
1,024	10.74	34.87
2,048	8.59	31.38
4,096	6.87	28.24
8,192	5.50	25.42
16,384	4.40	22.88
32,768	3.52	20.59
65,536	2.81	18.53

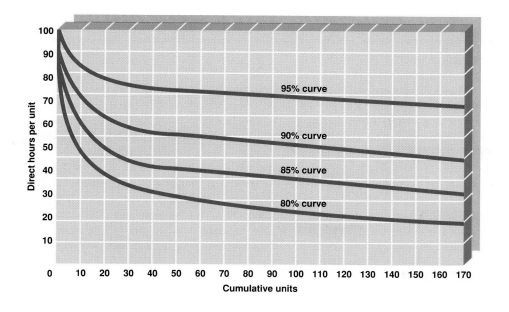

Figure 15.15
Learning Curves on Arithmetic-Scale Graph

The rates of improvement shown in Figures 15.15 and 15.16 are among the range of curves that appear most frequently. (Appendix II provides the expected time and cumulative expected time for specific numbers of units.) Most industries strive to improve productivity, for obvious reasons. Governments record and study

Figure 15.16
Learning Curves on
Logarithmic-Scale Graph

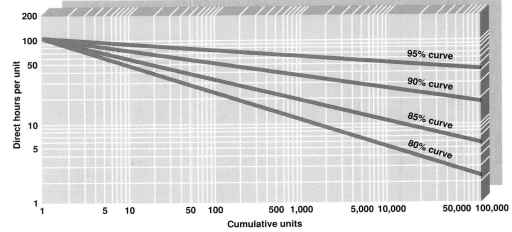

the changes in productivity on a national scale. At the grass-roots level, learning curves show a company how much productivity improvement it has achieved. After a company has an estimate of its usual rate of improvement, this information can be used in planning. The learning-curve effect may be taken into account in capacity planning, scheduling, or pricing for large-volume production. It also may be used in purchasing large quantities as a means of persuading potential suppliers to offer discounts for purchases of a large quantity over an extended time.

SUMMARY

Efficient use of resources to provide the desired mix of products at the desired completion times depends on how well production tasks are scheduled and controlled. The three factory types (repetitive, batch, and job shop manufacturing) deal with the same general steps, but sometimes in different ways. Four major steps they perform are planning the jobs, scheduling jobs, releasing and dispatching jobs to keep them on schedule, and tracking jobs and updating status information. All three types of factories must estimate costs to bid on jobs, to reach make-or-buy decisions, or to control costs.

Repetitive manufacturers deal with a narrow variety of standard products. Scheduling often is based on rates of output that can be paced by market demand or the constraining (bottleneck) production step. Output can be adjusted by varying the number of hours that the system is operated.

Batch manufacturers deal with standard products that may not follow entirely common flow paths. They may share many of the same production resources. Loading the plant without overloading any work centers helps prevent bottlenecks. Input/output analysis keeps the flow of jobs at the right rate. Priority control helps ensure that the right jobs flow.

Job shops try to prevent bottlenecks by monitoring the backlogs for work centers and by staffing the work centers and quoting deliveries that will not overload the work centers. A wide variety of dispatching rules have been investigated to determine which are better for keeping the right jobs flowing in job shop environments. The least slack per operation and the critical ratio are two rules commonly used to sequence jobs. Optimization of dispatching can be achieved only with respect to a few criteria and only for small problems. Johnson's rule will minimize flow time and average job lateness when there are only two work stations and all jobs must flow through the first and then the second.

Capacity and scheduling decisions require estimates of the time required to perform tasks. The times to perform certain types of jobs have been found to improve over extended periods in certain situations, because of the learning-curve effect. Learning curves can be used to estimate improvements in job times and the cumulative production time required to produce large numbers of an item.

KEY TERMS

Dispatching	Backflushing or post-	Forward scheduling
Cycle time	deducting	Job sequencing
Preproduction planning	Production activity control	Critical ratio
Route sheet or operations	Input/output control	Dispatching rules
sheet	Priority control	Learning curve
Rate-based schedule	Dispatch list	Rate of improvement
Bottleneck	Gantt schedule chart	
Starting work station	Backward scheduling	

DEMONSTRATION PROBLEM

Problem

Five jobs are to be run—first on process I, then on process II. The jobs are listed in the following table with their time requirements on the two processes.
(a) Sequence the jobs by Johnson's method so that the total flow time and idle time will be minimized.
(b) Show the sequence and durations on a bar chart, and indicate how long after the start of the first job until each job will be completed.

	Time (Hours)	
JOB	**PROCESS I**	**PROCESS II**
A	0.6	1.3
B	1.5	1.9
C	3.1	0.9
D	1.2	1.6
E	2.2	1.8

Solution

The shortest time in either column of the table is 0.6 for job *A*. Since this time is on the first process, job *A* should be done first. The shortest time for any of the remaining jobs is 0.9 for job *C*. Since this time is on the second process, job *C* should be done last. The shortest time of the remaining jobs is 1.2 for job *D*. Since this time is on the first process, job *D* should be done as early as possible in the remaining openings, so it will be done just after job *A*. The shortest of the remaining times is 1.5 for job *B*. Since this time is on the first process, *B* will be placed as early as possible so it will be just behind *D*, in third place. Job *E* fills the remaining slot in fourth place.

A Gantt chart showing this schedule for the two processes is shown below.

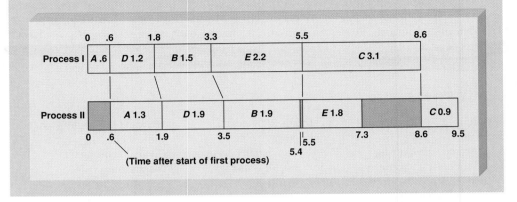

DISCUSSION QUESTIONS

1. Why is it difficult to select one criterion that will ensure optimum performance of a production system?

2. Briefly describe the steps in estimating the cost and delivery dates for job shop work.

3. What is a backlog report?

4. Why should production control bother to keep track of the amount of work that has been completed?

5. Is the production control organization usually a line organization or a staff organization?

6. What is dispatching? Describe a few rules of thumb (heuristics) that may be used in dispatching.

7. What problems could result if a company's dispatching rules were always to work on the item with the shortest processing time? To work on the item with the longest processing time?

8. **a.** Discuss the objectives of input/output control.
   b. How can input and output be properly controlled and delivery performance still be mediocre?

9. Why is it necessary to continually replan priorities in a production system?

PROBLEMS

1. The jobs listed in the first column of the accompanying table are waiting at work center 16. The shop works 16 hours per day.
   a. Arrange the jobs in priority sequence according to the lowest average slack per operation given by equation 15.1.

b. Arrange the jobs in sequence for work center 16 according to the critical ratio given by equation 15.2.

JOB	ESTIMATED PROCESSING TIME AT WORK CENTER 16 (HOURS)	WORKDAYS UNTIL JOB DELIVERY DATE	TOTAL ESTIMATED PROCESSING TIME REQUIRED INCLUDING WORK CENTER 16 (HOURS)	NUMBER OF REMAINING OPERATIONS INCLUDING WORK CENTER 16
A	12	18	160	3
B	28	14	120	4
C	17	20	270	2
D	6	10	91	3
E	21	9	118	5

2. The jobs listed in the following table are waiting at work center 41. The shop works 8 hours per day.

    a. Arrange the jobs in sequence for work center 41 according to the shortest-processing-time rule.

    b. Arrange the jobs according to the lowest average slack per operation (equation 15.1).

JOB	ESTIMATED PROCESSING TIME AT WORK CENTER 41 (HOURS)	WORKDAYS UNTIL JOB DELIVERY DATE	TOTAL ESTIMATED PROCESSING TIME REQUIRED INCLUDING WORK CENTER 41 (HOURS)	NUMBER OF REMAINING OPERATIONS INCLUDING WORK CENTER 41
A	5	3	13	1
B	6	10	35	4
C	8	12	45	5
D	4	6	13	3
E	3	8	25	4
F	9	8	20	2

3. The jobs listed in the first column of the following table are waiting at work center 4. The shop normally works 8 hours a day.

    a. List the sequence in which the jobs would be done according to the shortest-processing-time rule.

    b. In what order would the jobs be sequenced according to the lowest average slack per operation?

    c. Is there a problem with the scheduling of one job, and if so, what would you do about it?

JOB	ESTIMATED PROCESSING TIME AT WORK CENTER 4 (HOURS)	WORKDAYS UNTIL JOB DELIVERY DATE	TOTAL ESTIMATED PROCESSING TIME REQUIRED INCLUDING WORK CENTER 4 (HOURS)	NUMBER OF REMAINING OPERATIONS INCLUDING WORK CENTER 4
A	6	9	38	3
B	3	6	8	2
C	22	20	106	6
D	5	5	42	4
E	6	7	9	3
F	10	5	20	4

4. It is the start of work on Monday morning. The jobs listed above are the queue of work waiting to be done at work center 6, which is a single machine that is one of the bottlenecks in the shop. The shop normally works 8 hours a day. Sequence the jobs according to the critical ratio. If no more jobs arrive at the work center this week, what will you do about planning the work of this machine during the latter part of the week?

JOB	DAYS REMAINING	PROCESS TIME AT WORK CENTER 6 (STANDARD HOURS)	PROCESS TIME AT SUBSEQUENT STATIONS (STANDARD HOURS)
A	16	8	10
B	14	3	7
C	19	15	13
D	7	6	3
E	4	12	12

5. Work center 403 is the starting work center for four relatively simple jobs whose route sheets are shown in the following four tables.

Route Sheet: Job A		Due Date: Shop Day 174	
OPERATION	WORK CENTER	PROCESSING TIME (STANDARD HOURS)	SCHEDULED START (SHOP DAY)
10	403 lathes	16	166
20	406 mills	19	169
30	409 assembly	3	172

Route Sheet: Job B		Due Date: Shop Day 176	
OPERATION	WORK CENTER	PROCESSING TIME (STANDARD HOURS)	SCHEDULED START (SHOP DAY)
10	403 lathes	6	168
20	406 mills	22	169
30	408 drills	3	173
40	409 assembly	6	174

Route Sheet: Job C		Due Date: Shop Day 175	
OPERATION	WORK CENTER	PROCESSING TIME (STANDARD HOURS)	SCHEDULED START (SHOP DAY)
10	403 lathes	5	167
20	407 welding	6	169
30	406 mills	17	171
40	409 assembly	4	174

Route Sheet: Job D		Due Date: Shop Day 174	
OPERATION	WORK CENTER	PROCESSING TIME (STANDARD HOURS)	SCHEDULED START (SHOP DAY)
10	403 lathes	22	167
20	407 welding	12	172

Sequence the jobs according to:

a. The shortest processing time at the current work center
b. The shortest processing time at the next work center
c. The shortest remaining (also total, in this case) processing time
d. The longest processing time at the work center
e. The longest remaining processing time

6. Today is shop day 167, and the backlogs already in queue at each of the work centers through which each of the jobs in problem 5 must flow are presented in the following table.

WORK CENTER	BACKLOG CURRENTLY IN QUEUE	CAPACITY
403	98	80
406	60	80
407	40	40
408	35	40
409	90	80

a. Sequence the jobs from problem 5 in order of the scheduled start date at work center 403.
b. Sequence these jobs in order of the job due date.
c. Sequence these jobs in order of the smallest backlog at the next operation after work center 403.

7. Bondum Auto Body Shop has five cars that must have fenders straightened and be repainted. Mr. Bondum must be present while the work is being done, although the person who straightens fenders can work independently of the painter.

CAR	HOURS OF STRAIGHTENING REQUIRED	HOURS OF PAINTING REQUIRED
A	1.0	1.4
B	2.5	1.7
C	2.5	1.5
D	1.6	2.0
E	2.0	1.1

a. Sequence the cars so that Mr. Bondum's workday will be as short as possible.
b. How long will Mr. Bondum's workday be if he comes to work when the straightener begins and leaves when the painter leaves?
c. How long must the fender repairer work during the day?
d. When should the painter come to work and how long must she work if she begins as soon as the first job is available?

8. Five jobs are to be run on two processes, all in the sequence of first process 1, then process 2. The duration (in hours) of the operations is indicated in the table below.

JOB	TIME, PROCESS 1	TIME, PROCESS 2
A	3.0	1.2
B	2.0	2.5
C	1.0	1.6
D	3.0	3.0
E	3.5	1.5

   a. Sequence the jobs according to Johnson's rule.
   b. Use a Gantt chart to show how long after the start of the first job on process 1 each job will be completed on process 2.

9. Morris Machine Shop has four jobs waiting to be run on the milling machine, and three of them must then go to the drill press for the next operation before they are completed. There is an operator for each machine. Times for the two processes are shown below.

JOB	MILLING TIME (HOURS)	DRILLING TIME (HOURS)
A	2.4	2.10
B	2.5	1.5
C	2.1	0.00
D	1.7	2.2

   a. Sequence the jobs so that all will be completed in the minimum time.
   b. How long will the milling machine be operated to do these jobs?
   c. If the drill press operator and the milling machine operator can be scheduled to work at different times, how long after the milling machine operator begins should the drill press operator arrive?
   d. How long will the drill press operator need to work to complete these jobs in 1 day?

10. Given below is the input part of an input/output control report.

Planned input	400	400	400	400	400	400
Actual input	317	416	420	331	489	316
Cumulative input deviation						

   a. Compute the cumulative deviations in input.
   b. What is the minimum queue this work center could start with and not run out of work?
   c. How much capacity should the work center have on average to keep the average queue at this work center at its starting level?

11. Given below is a partially completed input/output control report for a certain work center.

Planned input	420	420	420	420	420	420
Actual input	400	450	440	465		
Cumulative input deviation						

Planned output	420	420	420	420	420	420
Actual output	416	402	425	420		
Cumulative output deviation						

a. Compute the remainder of the table for the first 4 weeks.
b. What problem appears to exist?
c. What corrective actions can you suggest?

12. The Silver Bullet Aircraft Company has just produced the first of its model R-80 airplanes, which required 36,500 direct labor-hours. The company has experienced a 90 percent learning curve for similar aircraft it has produced in the past. (Use Appendix II.)
a. How long will the 10th airplane take?
b. The 25th?
c. The 100th?

13. Remelt Inc. refines basic metals for recycling. Currently it requires 26 labor-hours per 10-ton batch to recover a particular alloy. Since a large percentage of the labor time during production is required for the operator to tend the furnace while it raises the alloy to the melting temperature, the company scheduler feels that this portion of the time cannot be reduced. He thinks that they might achieve a 95 percent improvement rate.
a. If the company can achieve a 95 percent improvement rate, how many labor-hours will be required to produce the 100th batch?
b. The 1,000th?

14. Steadman Electronics is introducing a remote pager model. The company works at continuous improvement and has achieved a 90 percent improvement rate on similar small electronic devices, so a 90 percent improvement rate is expected with the new pager. It is estimated that initial production of the pager will require about 28 minutes per unit.
a. How many cumulative hours of work would be expected to produce the first 1,000 units?
b. How many additional hours will be expected to produce the second 1,000 units?
c. What will be expected as the average minutes per unit when the company has produced 2,500 units?
d. What will be expected as the average minutes per unit when the company has produced the 5,000th unit?

15. The Pear Computer Company produces computers for home and small business applications. The first of its new model TLC-10 computers required 5.6 labor-hours to complete. The company has experienced an 85 percent learning curve on its past models and expects this learning rate to apply to the TLC-10 as well. In the next 6 months the company plans to produce a total of 5,000 computers. How many employees will be required if each employee can contribute 1,000 production-hours during the 6-month period?

16. The Adams Company has just completed development of a new leaf blower. The first one required 47 minutes to produce, and it is estimated that the company will have a 95 percent improvement rate.
a. Estimate the time required to produce the 1,000th, 2,000th, and 5,000th units.
b. Estimate the cumulative time required to make the first 1,000 units. The first 2,000 units. The first 5,000 units.

17. A landscaping contractor has received a contract to plant shrubs for a new subdivision in a nearby city. He intends to send one of his supervisors, who will employ a crew of workers in that city to perform the work.

The subdivision contains 30 houses with basically similar landscape plans. She has been asked to bid on performing the landscaping services for 5, 10, 15, 20, 25, and 30 houses. She knows from experience that she can expect a 95 percent learning curve. She also estimates that the first house will require 28 hours.

a. How much total time will the first 5 houses require?

b. How much total time will the last 5 houses require if 30 are landscaped?

c. What will be the average number of hours per house if all 30 houses are landscaped and a 95 percent learning curve is appropriate?

18. Congratulations, you own a job shop manufacturing company. Your company has been requested to quote on a simple assembly: a special-size metal door for McCall Enterprises. The door assembly consists of the door, the frame, two hinges, and a latch. The door must go to shop 5 for 1 hour and then to shop 9 for 2 hours. The frame must go to shop 2 for 0.5 hour and then to shop 6 for 1 hour. After the above processing, both the door and the doorframe must go to the paint shop for 1 hour of labor and 4 hours of drying time. Next the components must go for 1 hour to assembly, where the hinges and latch are installed and a pasteboard protective crate is strapped around the assembly.

Raw material for the door and the frame can be obtained with 2 days' lead time. Backlog data for the four shops involved in this job are shown below. Assume adequate time is available in the paint and assembly shops.

In the past few days you have quoted jobs that, *if* they are awarded to you, will require you to use all available capacity in all the shops and a 10-hour overload in shop 9 for the next 4 weeks.

Backlog Reports

Shop 5						Capacity 40 hours/week	
Week	1	2	3	4	5	6	7
Load	50	35	28	32	20	10	6

Shop 9						Capacity 80 hours/week	
Week	1	2	3	4	5	6	7
Load	100	80	70	50	40	20	16

Shop 2						Capacity 40 hours/week	
Week	1	2	3	4	5	6	7
Load	25	20	18	22	10	5	0

Shop 6						Capacity 40 hours/week	
Week	1	2	3	4	5	6	7
Load	16	25	40	40	25	16	2

a. When can you deliver the doors to McCall Enterprises? Should you quote a little later delivery just in case some of the outstanding quotes are awarded to your company and use some of the available capacity? Remember, a later delivery date may reduce your chance of being awarded the contract.

b. Should you quote a price that would include overtime pay, just in case the outstanding quotes are awarded to you and use the available capacity?

c. Does it concern you that you have people on the payroll in shops 2 and 6 and do not have sufficient work in those shops to utilize their capacity fully? What are you going to do about this situation?

COMPUTER-BASED PROBLEM

LEARNING CURVE

Dan Paramesh of Hugo Optical Equipment Company is developing a production plan for the assembly of special survey equipment for offshore oil exploration. The contract calls for the following shipping schedule:

MONTH	SHIPPING SCHEDULE
1	100
2	150
3	175
4	200
5	250
6	250
7	250
	1,375

The first survey equipment was assembled in 755 standard hours. In the past, for similar products, Hugo has experienced learning curve rates in the range of 95 to 70 percent. The expected learning rate for this contract is 95 percent. Better learning rates may be achieved with additional training and investment in automation.

Find the number of workers needed for each month for learning rates of 95, 90, 85, 80, 75, and 70 percent. Compute the total labor cost for each learning rate. Compute the labor cost savings for each 5 percent improvement in the learning rate. What learning rate should Dan try to achieve? Explain.

Each worker works 180 hours per month for $15 per hour.

Hints

1. The cumulative total labor hours ΣY_n can be approximated with the following formula:

$$\Sigma Y_n = \frac{Y_1 * n^{(1 + R)}}{(1 + R)}$$

2. With Lotus 1-2-3, use the Data Table 1 command to find and display the labor cost for the various learning rates.

BIBLIOGRAPHY

Ashton, J. E., M. D. Johnson, and F. X. Cook. "Shop Floor Control in a System Job Shop: Definitely Not MRP." *Production and Inventory Management Journal,* 2d quarter 1990, pp. 27–31.

Conway, Richard W., William L. Maxwell, and Louis W. Miller. *Theory of Scheduling.* Reading, Mass.: Addison-Wesley, 1967.

Graves, Stephen C. "A Review of Production Scheduling." *Operations Research,* July–August 1981, pp. 646–675.

Greene, James H., ed. *Production and Inventory Control Handbook.* 2d ed. New York: McGraw-Hill, 1987.

Hayes, Robert H., and Steven C. Wheelwright. *Restoring Our Competitive Edge: Competing through Manufacturing.* New York: Wiley, 1984.

LaForge, R. Lawrence, and Samir Barman. "Performance of Simple Priority Rule Combinations in a Flow-Dominant Shop." *Production and Inventory Management Journal,* 3d quarter 1989, pp. 1–4.

McLeavey, Dennis W., and Seetharama L. Narasimhan. *Production and Inventory Control.* Boston: Allyn and Bacon, 1985.

Mather, Hal, and George W. Plossl. "Priority Fixation versus Throughput Planning." *Production and Inventory Management,* 3d quarter 1978, pp. 27–50.

Melnyk, Steven A., and Phillip L. Carter. *Production Activity Control.* Homewood, Ill.: Business One Irwin, 1987.

Plossl, George W. *Production and Inventory Control: Applications.* Atlanta: George W. Plossl Educational Services, 1983.

Smith, Spencer B. *Computer Based Production and Inventory Control.* Englewood Cliffs, N.J.: Prentice-Hall, 1989.

Umble, M. Michael, and M. L. Srikanth. *Synchronous Manufacturing: Principles of World Class Excellence.* Cincinnati, Ohio: South-Western, 1990.

Vollman, Thomas E., William L. Berry, and D. Clay Whybark. *Manufacturing Planning and Control.* 3d ed. Homewood, Ill.: Irwin, 1992.

THE JUST-IN-TIME PHILOSOPHY OF SEEKING EXCELLENCE

CHAPTER **16**

ust-in-time (JIT) is a philosophy of improvement through aggressively discovering and resolving any problems or weaknesses that impede the organization's effectiveness and efficiency. Basically, it seeks to eliminate all waste within the organization, including the waste of underutilizing the talents, skills, and potential of its employees. Anything that does not contribute to adding value for an internal or external customer is considered waste. The philosophy originated in manufacturing operations, but its concepts have been applied in other areas such as administrative work, services, and distribution. JIT can be very effective and powerful as a means of improvement. Consider, for example, some results of Harley-Davidson's experience with the concept.

Harley-Davidson, an 80-year-old U.S. motorcycle manufacturer, suffered such staggering losses in 1981 and 1982 that the future of the company was seriously in question. Some of the external problems were Honda, Suzuki, Kawasaki, and Yamaha—four Japanese competitors that had taken most of the market. Harley-Davidson's major internal problem was an overpriced product that received numerous customer complaints about quality—a result of what seemed to be a long series of quick fixes to help the company get along. Between 1982 and 1986, the firm made significant improvements. Inventory turnovers increased from less than 7 to about 20 a year. Productivity per employee rose about 50 percent. Rework costs were reduced by 80 percent, and warranty costs were down by 46 percent. The motorcycle part of the company has been profitable since 1983. The reason for this dramatic turnaround is a companywide effort based on the just-in-time (JIT) manufacturing philosophy.

Other U.S. companies, too, have achieved spectacular improvements in their performance through JIT. A review of implementation successes in five companies showed an average lead-time reduction of 90 percent. Inventory was reduced by 35 to 73 percent, and changeover times were reduced by 75 to 94 percent. The cost of purchased materials was reduced 6 to 11 percent, and the cost of quality was reduced by 26 to 63 percent.[1] Even the lower ends of the ranges are impressive! Similar results have been achieved in Japan, where the concept was first applied, and in other Asian countries, Europe, and Australia.

Successful companies develop and implement strategies that will give them a distinct competitive advantage. A company that improves performance as much as those cited above certainly will gain a competitive advantage, unless its competitors also make dramatic improvements. Improvements of this sort in a competitor can certainly spell disaster for a company that has not matched the competitor's efforts. In Chapter 2 we discussed how companies seek competitive advantages by emphasizing some performance characteristics—flexibility and quick responsiveness, cost efficiency, quality, or dependability and service. It was mentioned that through JIT, Japanese manufacturers have been able to occupy more of the pyramid that represents mixtures of these various performance characteristics. That is, they exhibit competitive performance that is rich in all these characteristics. The results reported above show that U.S. manufacturers are also able to use JIT to achieve this kind of performance.

In this chapter we briefly introduce the origin of the JIT philosophy. We will then review in more detail some of the elements or techniques of JIT and how they work together to achieve remarkable results such as those mentioned above. One of the wastes that JIT seeks to eliminate is any delays or interruptions that cause an accumulation of paperwork or unnecessary inventory. In manufacturing applications, the reduction of work-in-process inventory, or WIP, is one of the more noticeable results of JIT. This characteristic led some persons to think incorrectly of JIT as only an inventory reduction program. JIT is a much broader philosophy that leads to smoother flow so that much less WIP occurs. At the end of the chapter we will discuss the theory of constraints (TOC), which is another philosophy that had its origin in manufacturing and can be used to reduce waste and achieve a smoother flow of transactions in manufacturing and other settings. We will review some of the principles of optimized production technology (OPT), which is the term used for the basic ideas from which TOC has developed.

---

[1]Martin P. Edelman, "Embracing of JIT by the Masses: Far Better than MRP II and for Good Reason," *1987 APICS Conference Proceedings*, p. 405.

ORIGINS OF JIT

Henry Ford, with his application of the assembly line, was one of the first to achieve just-in-time manufacturing. Ford worked to reduce manufacturing time in order to produce a small, simple, reliable car that many could afford. By 1926 the company could remove raw material from the earth, ship it to the factory, convert it into an automobile, and deliver it to the customer in a span of 81 hours. His company reduced the price of the car by 40 percent between 1908 and 1924. The early production methods did not offer much variety, however. It is said of the early Model T that customers could have any color they wanted as long as it was black. Many companies have applied some of the accomplishments that Ford developed. However, in developing more product variety, most employed much more inventory than was necessary.

After World War II, Japanese industrialists worked to restore the industrial base for the economy and needed great efficiency in their production methods. Their efforts, particularly at Toyota Motor Company, to apply and improve on the existing production methods while offering significant product variety, led to what has become the JIT philosophy. Through research and application over some 30 years, the Toyota Motor Company, Ltd., developed a very effective method of manufacturing that was well suited to its needs and environment. For the first two decades after World War II, Japan had to work hard to improve performance and to overcome an image of poor quality if its goods were to become competitive in the world marketplace. Quality was, and still is, accorded high priority by Toyota and other Japanese companies. With Japan's high population density, space is scarce and industrial prop-

Farrell Grehan/FPG, International

Saturn is one of the companies that has used the just-in-time philosophy to its advantage. The factory in Spring Hill, Tennessee (see photo in Chapter 12) was built with 101 doors so that parts and equipment could be quickly delivered directly to the factory floor. But it is the support of Saturn employees on the factory floor that has been the key to JIT's success.

erty is expensive, so plants and warehouses have to be compact and efficient. The country also has few natural resources, so its people have always had to use resources wisely, and any form of waste is abhorred.

JIT: A Comprehensive Philosophy

Some facets of the management practices Toyota developed are ideologically related to Japan's unique customs, culture, and labor-management relations. Nevertheless, most of the philosophy and many elements of the Toyota production system have been adapted to other companies and cultures. The concepts have been applied successfully in many companies throughout the world. Adaptations of the general philosophy in the United States have been called just-in-time (JIT) manufacturing, manufacturing excellence, world-class manufacturing, and several other names. The most frequently used title is *just-in-time manufacturing* because the most noticeable characteristic is operating with very low work-in-process (WIP) inventory and often with low finished-goods inventory. Products are assembled just before they are sold, subassemblies are made just before the products are assembled, and components are fabricated just before the subassemblies are made—so WIP inventory is low and production lead times are short. To operate with these low inventories, the companies must be excellent in other areas. They must have consistently high quality throughout the organizations. To achieve this quality and coordination, they must have the participation and cooperation of all employees. So JIT manufacturing or manufacturing excellence is a broad philosophy of continuous improvement that includes three mutually supportive components. The three components, which have been referred to as the productivity triad, are

1. People involvement

2. Total quality control

3. JIT flow (that is, production of goods shortly before they are needed, to keep inventories low)

We discuss the first two categories of effort rather briefly and discuss the third category of JIT production techniques in more detail, because in this chapter we are focusing primarily on scheduling and controlling production. Quality control and people involvement are discussed in other chapters. Keep in mind that all three of these categories are interrelated and mutually supportive.

HOW JUST-IN-TIME MANUFACTURING CAN HELP ADD VALUE FOR CUSTOMERS

JIT manufacturing includes a commitment to total quality which increases the value customers receive. JIT includes people involvement which gains the advantage of the talents of many employees to reduce waste and improve performance. The improved motivation and the power of numerous employee suggestions can reduce costs and improve quality and responsiveness. Reduced WIP can improve quality, reduce costs, cut the lead time to serve customers, and make the company more flexible. JIT also involves preventive maintenance, which can improve the dependability of operations.

PEOPLE INVOLVEMENT

Probably all management efforts have some behavioral aspects, because management is working through other people to accomplish the organization's objectives. Management plans and decisions only lay the groundwork. It is the resulting human behavior that determines a company's success or failure. Such terms as *zero inventory* and *stockless production* have given some people the impression that JIT is only an inventory program. JIT has a strong human resources management component that must be recognized if the technical component is to be fully successful. Much of the success of JIT can be traced to the fact that companies that use it train their employees to have the appropriate skills, give them responsibility, and coordinate and motivate them.

The JIT philosophy of continuous improvement and minimization of waste considers waste to be any activity that does not add value to the product or serve the customer in some way. One form of waste that is inconspicuous and difficult to combat is the underutilization of human talent. JIT seeks to utilize more fully the creative talents of employees, suppliers, subcontractors, and others who may contribute to the company's improvement.

Teamwork

Successful *people involvement* stems from a culture of open trust and teamwork in which people interact to recognize, define, and solve problems. Sometimes it is mistakenly assumed that this component is just another program, such as a suggestion program or a quality circle program. People involvement can include these programs and others, such as ad hoc project teams that focus on specific improvement targets and semiautonomous work teams whose membership seldom changes. The involvement component of JIT is much broader than a program or two; it is a management style and a permanent companywide attitude of teamwork, so that each person works to improve the company. People are encouraged to suggest ways to improve methods. Suggestions are quickly and fairly considered, and the companies are open to trying something new that seems like a worthwhile improvement.

Discipline

This open, improvement-driven atmosphere does not mean, however, that any employee is free to work by any method he or she chooses to try. Usually there is a standard way each job is to be done. If an improvement is suggested and approved, a new standard procedure will be adopted. This standardization prevents variations in products or services which can cause defects. Defects occur because some variation has been introduced into a material or procedure that normally produces good results. When an efficient procedure that results in good quality is established, it is to be followed until a better way is tested and approved. You can see that creativity and openness to change are needed, but it is creativity in conjunction with teamwork and discipline that achieves consistent good quality and leads to improvements.

Supplier Partnerships

The JIT philosophy may extend beyond the walls of the company applying JIT, to include its suppliers. It has an impact on the entire logistics system, or "supply chain." Since the JIT company does not maintain large inventories, it must have very reliable suppliers of high-quality inputs. Often JIT companies seek to develop a very close *supplier partnership* with one or a few suppliers for each of its major purchased items. Xerox, for example, pared its supplier list from about 5,000 to less than 500. By placing a bigger percentage of its business with its best suppliers, the company can improve its quality and the reliability of receiving items. The partnership is a long-term agreement so the companies can develop a smooth working relationship. The desire is for the supplier to become an extension of the company so that the supply chain is a seamless organization that works to serve the ultimate customer better than any competing supply chain could. The JIT company can also benefit from the supplier's expertise by having supplier representatives participate is the design phase of new products and recommend improvements.

It can be beneficial to a supplier to work in such a relationship, particularly with a high-volume manufacturer. When a company reduces the number of suppliers for an item, the volume of purchases from the remaining supplier or suppliers can increase dramatically. Davidson Rubber Company, for example, which produces padded vinyl products such as dash panels and armrests for automobiles, would have little demand for those products directly from individual customers. Yet Davidson is a JIT supplier for approximately 45 percent of the armrests used by North American automobile producers. Davidson will prosper in the future as its current customers gain a larger share of the market or as its performance capabilities become preferred by other automobile producers.

The partners in a supplier partnership may even agree to share cost information. The purchasing company must be assured that it is not paying too much since it may choose not to shop for the best price. It also must respect the right of the supplier to make a fair profit and should help the supplier keep its costs low. The purchasing manager for the Ocean Spray Cranberries plant in Middleboro, Massachusetts, pointed out that a company only kids itself if it simply has its suppliers hold inventory for it, because "their costs will become your costs." A supplier-buyer team reduced the new-label cycle time from 30 to 7 days and lead times from 40 to 10 days. It reduced the inventories at the plant by more than $130,000. The team's program is now being adapted at the company's other drink-production plants.

The supplier can also benefit when new products are introduced by its partner. The company may provide a respected supplier with a contract stating quality specifications and a target price. The supplier can retain the contract for as long as it meets these conditions and provides on-time delivery. The item's price has to provide a reasonable profit for both companies if the relationship is to be mutually beneficial in the long run. The purchasing company may provide assistance to improve the supplier's productivity or quality. The purchaser is also likely to share its future production plans and schedules with suppliers so the suppliers can plan their levels of business, budgets, and capacity requirements and make appropriate arrangements with their own suppliers. Obviously, participation and teamwork are necessary if the JIT philosophy is to work well.

The cooperation between the supplier partners may even extend to a relationship called *JIT II*. In this concept a representative of the supplier is housed at the purchaser's business and is authorized to place orders with the supplier (his or her own company) when the purchaser needs to be restocked. Such an agreement means there is a great deal of trust on the part of the purchaser but it facilitates a close working relationship that can be very effective. The supplier has to be willing to pay the salary of an employee that is spending a great deal of time servicing a customer. Naturally, the volume of business must be large for a JIT II agreement to be practical.

TOTAL QUALITY CONTROL

Quality Is Everybody's Job

One interpretation of the term *total quality control* is that the achievement and improvement of quality in a JIT company involve every department and every employee in the company. The quality of a product or service is its ability to serve the company's ultimate customer satisfactorily. Quality-related activities begin with the efforts of the marketing staff to learn the customers' needs and desires. Then further efforts are needed to define the features and capabilities that a product must have to serve those needs. Employees in research, product development, and engineering work to design a product that can be produced economically and reliably and that has the desired features and capabilities. Process design and plant engineering personnel work to develop processes, equipment, and human tasks that will produce the product consistently and economically. Purchasing and quality control personnel work to obtain reliable suppliers who will provide the necessary quality in materials and other supplies. Personnel staff and managers work to train and motivate employees to devote their efforts to the task of making the items efficiently and correctly. Maintenance works to see that the capabilities of the processes remain at least adequate. All employees should seek ways to serve the final customer better so that the company can remain competitive.

The Immediate Customer

JIT companies often have a broad definition of who "the customer" is. An employee in a non-JIT company might say that the customer is a person outside the company who buys and uses the product. JIT plants add to this definition the concept that each employee has an *immediate customer,* who is the next person, inside or outside the company, who uses or further processes the item or information. If each worker sends only good items to his or her immediate customer, defective products will not be produced.

Quality at the Source

Each employee is given responsibility for quality at his or her work station. Employees are trained in quality principles and testing procedures. Often they inspect their own work to ensure that they do not send defective items to their immediate customers. Where it is practical to do so, testing is made automatic, in order to eliminate human variability and subjectivity and to reduce labor cost. Often there are no separate departments for rework—each employee corrects his or her own mistakes. In this way the employee learns what defects are occurring and what is causing them and can develop methods to prevent such problems. This procedure provides immediate feedback on problems and makes employees truly responsible for quality. At Harley-Davidson, for example, the workers are trained in statistical process control and are expected to measure their products and update the control charts. The program is called "Statistical Operator Control" to emphasize that the operator does the controlling.

Sometimes a defective element is more easily detected by the immediate customer than by the person who is responsible for it. A part, for example, may not fit into an assembly if it is improperly made. A procedure called *jidoka* is often brought into play. Any employee who senses that a process is producing defects or is about to go out of proper specification has the authority and the responsibility to stop the process. The philosophy is that it is better to make nothing than to make it incorrectly. If something is wrong, stop and fix it. The objective is to make things right the first time. At NUMMI in Fremont, California, and at other assembly-line operations, the workers on the assembly line can stop the process if they have a problem or spot a problem that needs to be fixed.

A Culture, Not a Program

Another view of total quality is that it is total in terms of time—it never ends. There is never a level of quality that is "good enough" that people can stop looking for ways to make it better. Companies continue to look for incremental product improvements and process refinements. One objective is to reduce variability in processes and in parts because, as we mentioned earlier, variation is what allows results to deviate from the target quality level. Hewlett-Packard has a six-sigma program that means they aim to reduce the variability of their processes to less than half the allowable range within the product specifications. (This means the process capability index would be at least two.)

The total quality effort extends to suppliers. When a supplier's quality reaches a consistently high level, the supplier is certified and the parts he or she delivers then need not go through a receiving inspection. If the purchasing company has to inspect, say, 10,000 items on average to find a defective one, it is just too expensive to look for them. A separate inspection is a non-value-adding operation that is one of the wastes that the JIT philosophy seeks to prevent. The parts can possibly be checked visually or automatically as they are being processed. Total quality is a consistent, pervasive, and continuing activity.

JIT FLOW PROVIDES ADVANTAGES

Insidious Excessive Queues

A queue in front of a work center is often seen as having certain desirable effects, such as ensuring that the work center and those downstream from it will not run out of work unless there is a lengthy work stoppage at some upstream work center. Queues can make a variety of jobs available so that one can be selected to match the skills of an available worker. Apparently, by focusing on the advantages rather than the disadvantages of work-in-process (WIP) inventories, many companies have tended to rely on WIP to bail them out in case something goes wrong. Instead of managing carefully to prevent things from going wrong, many companies have accumulated excess inventories for protection. Ironically, such inventories hide problems so well that the problems may never be discovered and solved. When items wait in queues for a long time before they are processed further, a company can produce great amounts of scrap before it is discovered. Once the scrap is detected, it is less likely that anyone can recall precisely which machine, tooling, settings, raw material, and so on were being used. It is therefore unlikely that the cause of the problem will be found and corrected. If items are quickly run through subsequent processes and inspections, defects are discovered before many defects are made. The problem-causing process may still be running. At any rate, it is more likely that the problem can be traced, and problems must be identified before they can be solved.

Dell Computer Corp. builds custom computers and software packages for mail-order clients. Because they don't hold a lot of inventory, they are able to build new technology into their computers while other companies are still selling the computers left in stock. For example, when Intel Corporation came out with the Pentium chip, Dell was quickly able to offer it in their computers. When the chip was found to be flawed, they were again able to quickly change to the replacement chip.

Bob Daemmrich/Stock, Boston

Queues Are a Waste that JIT Fights

When queues are long, the cost of holding the WIP becomes high and the time required for a job to flow through all the required work centers becomes excessive. Make-to-order manufacturers are at a disadvantage if they allow customer response times to become long. Make-to-stock manufacturers must maintain more finished goods to serve customers if their factories are slow to respond to changes in demand. Also they must forecast demand further into the future, increasing the uncertainty of their forecasts. More safety stock is therefore required, so that the cost of inventory is increased still further.

Instead of paying for excessive inventories, companies can work to prevent some of the problems they use inventories to protect them from. Often the cost of this work is less than the cost of holding the inventory. In addition, the companies can gain the competitive advantages of quick responsiveness and, as mentioned above, quality levels can be improved. We now examine elements of the JIT production method so that we may better understand how it keeps queues low and provides some of these advantages.

ELEMENTS THAT SUPPORT JIT FLOW

A major objective of JIT is to have only the right item at the right place at the right time; or, to say it another way, to purchase and produce items only a short time before they are needed so that work-in-process inventory is kept very low. The practice reduces not only working capital requirements but also the need for floor space, and it shortens the flow-through time because material spends very little time in queues. Numerous other benefits occur where this practice is successfully employed. JIT has received so much attention in the past few years because it is believed to be a major contributor to the success of many Japanese repetitive manufacturers.

Limited Variety within a Factory (Focused Factories)

A JIT factory is expected to be able to assemble most of its products just before they are shipped. In order to respond quickly, JIT factories in repetitive or batch manufacturing businesses often maintain at least some inventory of the subassemblies and other components that go into the product so they can begin assembly while more component and subassemblies are made. The factory would also need some inventory of the inputs required to make components so workers can begin making components to replace those being used while suppliers are making and shipping more inputs. If a factory offered a wide variety of products and options it would need a massive inventory just to have some of every component or material that it might need. Consequently, JIT factories for repetitive or batch manufacturing businesses often are *focused factories*. That is, the scope of their products tends to be a narrower variety of compatible products. Sometimes they use common components in multiple products. These businesses may make some features standard rather than optional, which makes their product more desirable and helps standardize more of their work. Job shops that operate with the JIT philosophy may use many of the elements we will discuss below, but they cannot maintain component inventories since they usually do not define the final product and therefore do not know all the components they may need.

Many advantages of JIT can also be achieved by low-volume or intermediate-volume manufacturers. The following are some of the important elements frequently found where JIT production methods are used:

1. A set, uniform production rate and mixed-model assembly
2. A pull method of coordinating work centers
3. Purchasing and producing in small lots
4. Quick, inexpensive setups
5. Multiskilled workers and flexible facilities
6. High quality levels
7. Effective preventive maintenance
8. Continual work to improve

Uniform Production Rate

An objective of JIT is to achieve a smooth flow of materials from the company's suppliers to the company's customers with no delays or interruptions beyond the very minimum required by the production processes. Any unnecessary delays or in-process inventory is considered waste, so the work-in-process inventory is kept to a minimum. Inside the plant the objective is to achieve a smooth, synchronized flow of small lots of material at a uniform rate. Since there is no extra inventory in the system, it is not possible occasionally to withdraw and assemble a large lot of material. If there were enough inventory to produce an occasional large lot, but small lots usually were produced, the result would be undesired excess inventory. The JIT system works best when the production schedules are kept level. When production levels must be changed, they are scaled up or down in small steps.

Several Japanese manufacturers who use JIT production methods set their production rate for the month equal to the expected demand rate for the month and hold daily production rates at this monthly rate. Instead of making one product for an extended period and then shifting to another product, they use a technique called *mixed-model assembly*. Each day a mix of the models is produced in short repetitive sequences, so that each model is frequently repeated in proportion to its relative demand. The work load in each work center remains uniform within a day and for each day of the month, so neither workers nor work tasks have to be reassigned. Suppose that three models of refrigerators—*A*, *B*, and *C*—are to be produced and that the expected demand for the three models during the next month is 3,000, 2,000, and 1,000 units, respectively. The three models might be produced on the assembly line in the sequence *A, B, A, B, A, C*. Repetition of this sequence throughout the month will make a uniform work content for all the jobs on the assembly line, even if the work required to assemble a model *A* is above average and the work required to assemble the other models is below average. Such a repetitive cycle also causes a uniform work load for the work centers that feed the final assembly line, even if model *C* has components that are not used in any of the other models.

Pull versus Push Method of Coordinating Work Centers

Coordinating fabrication and assembly operations through all the work centers that feed the final assembly line can be complex if a variety of models are being produced on the line, particularly if the product mix is frequently changed. There are two basic approaches to coordinating the feeding of work centers: the push method and the pull method. The *push method* is like the production control method described in Chapter 15 for the job shop. The production control group schedules the necessary quantities of raw material to produce all components of the desired quantities of final assemblies, and the materials are released for work at the starting work centers at the appropriate times. When work is completed at one work center (WC), the parts are pushed to the next WC, where they wait until that WC is ready to work on them. Eventually the appropriate components and subassemblies reach the final assembly operation and are assembled into the intended product.

When a repetitive factory uses the *pull method*, each WC holds some designated number of standard containers of each component or subassembly it produces. A WC does not produce any more unless a full container is pulled away (with appropriate authorization) by some downstream WC. (The authorization comes through the kanban system, which we discuss a little later.) Then the WC works only to replace the number of items pulled. This procedure limits the amount of inventory that accumulates between each pair of using and supplying WCs. It also serves to authorize each WC to produce only what is being used by the downstream WC. The chain reaction of these linkages makes each WC produce only the items required to feed the final assembly operation and in the amounts needed.

With this method of coordinating WCs, the major scheduling and control activities consist of planning the production rate, setting the number of containers authorized between supplying and using WCs, and ensuring that suppliers are informed of the planned amounts of purchased items required to feed the processes. An overview of the pull system is shown in Figure 16.1. The planning procedure under the pull system is much like planning under MRP. In fact, many JIT manufacturers use MRP to plan materials requirements. Many companies develop production schedules in terms of build rates (such as a specific number of units per day) for the appropriate number of each type of product, so the forecast demand mix is made using mixed-model assembly. Efforts are made to hold the production rate and mix constant for some horizon, often 1 month but perhaps as long as 3 months. The master schedule

Figure 16.1
Integration of MRP
and the JIT Pull System

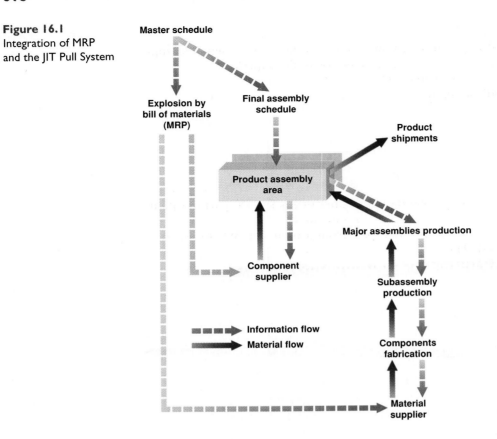

is exploded by the bill of materials to obtain the requirements for purchased materials and components. This plan is communicated to suppliers, as shown by the red dashed arrows to suppliers in Figure 16.1. This shared information permits vendors to coordinate their work with that of their suppliers and to plan capacity levels. The vendors do not ship according to this anticipated production rate. They are linked to the actual production pace by the pull method, just as the internal work centers (WCs) are. This system keeps in-process inventory very low in a focused factory, that is, one that has a limited product line. Otherwise, significant amounts of WIP inventory might be required so that any WC could provide any item that might be pulled by its user WCs.

MRP ADAPTATIONS FOR JIT The requirements planning logic of MRP is useful to explode the bills of materials and determine the amount of input items needed so that materials and components can be ordered from suppliers at the appropriate lead times. Many fewer levels are found in the bills of materials for JIT production because intermediate levels are not produced and held. An objective is to eliminate inventory at intermediate levels. The rapid throughput times achieved when delays are eliminated between the production steps often cause another change in MRP applications. The lead-time offset for many operations may be set to zero because the duration required for the work has been reduced to the extent that the lead time will not require the prior operation to be performed in an earlier time bucket. The shop-floor control part of an MRP package may not be used by repetitive factories because these functions are performed by the pull system and the use of kanbans.

The Kanban System

The *kanban system* is a simple information system used by a WC to signal its supplier WC to send a container of an item and to authorize the supplier WC to make another container of that particular item. The name comes from the Japanese word *kanban,* which means "card" or "sign." Originally a card was used to signal the supplying work center. A WC can use any of a variety of methods to trigger resupply by its supplier WC. For example, a flashing light, the empty container itself, or a message on a computer terminal can communicate a request for more material. We discuss the two-card kanban system to provide some detail about how it is used in linking work centers.

In the two-card kanban system, one type of card, called a *production card,* or *P-card,* authorizes a WC to make one standard container of a particular part specified on the card. The second type of card, called a *move card,* or *M-card,* authorizes the movement of one container of the specified part from a particular WC to another WC as specified on the card. These cards are ordinarily recirculated and new cards are issued only when production of an item is to be started or changed significantly. The circulation of a move card is illustrated in Figure 16.2. The production card circulates repeatedly between the outbound material location at a WC and the work area where the item is produced. Similar card transactions link the supplier WC shown in Figure 16.2 and the WCs that supply it. The user WC will also be linked to one or more WCs that it supplies. A series of these linkages connects the final assembly operation with the WC that performs the first operations in making the product. Often, even the raw material vendor is linked with the starting operation through a kanban signal. Kanbans picked up when one delivery is made authorize the vendor to make specified items and deliver them on the next delivery.

The kanban system can be a very simple, inexpensive, and effective method of coordinating work centers and vendors. The organization must be well disciplined so that there is always an authorizing kanban with every container, ensuring that only the appropriate items are produced and excessive inventory does not build up. There is also the opposite danger—that some WC might run out of material and cause work to stop at all subsequent WCs. If this or any other pull method is to work well with

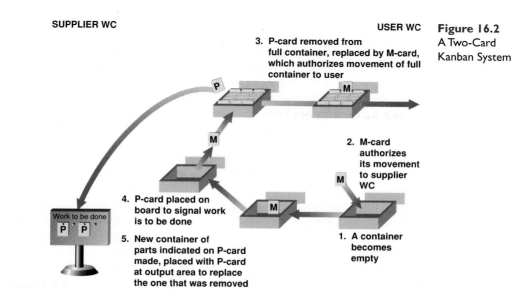

SUPPLIER WC   **USER WC**

Figure 16.2
A Two-Card Kanban System

3. P-card removed from full container, replaced by M-card, which authorizes movement of full container to user

2. M-card authorizes its movement to supplier WC

4. P-card placed on board to signal work is to be done

1. A container becomes empty

5. New container of parts indicated on P-card made, placed with P-card at output area to replace the one that was removed

Work to be done

Kanban cards, like this one for a Toyota manufacturing division in the United States, carry important information that communicates to people on the production line what needs to be done.

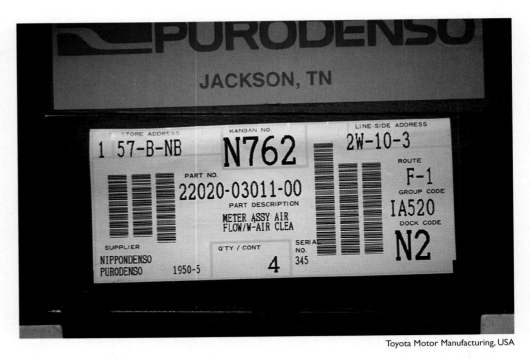

Toyota Motor Manufacturing, USA

small inventories, there must be no problems to disrupt production; because there simply is not enough inventory to keep the plant running while a problem is corrected. A uniform production rate and the elements of JIT discussed in the following sections interact to make JIT and the kanban signal system work together effectively.

Production and Procurement in Small Lots

PRODUCTION LOTS AND TRANSFER BATCHES With the pull system a supplier WC is signaled to make each day only what its user WCs have used in a day and no additional inventory is introduced into the system. Another factor helps keep work-in-process inventory low. The items that are produced are conveyed and controlled in small containers that hold perhaps less than 1 hour's production. In a high-volume factory this splits the day's production into small batches (transfer batches), each controlled with a kanban card. With small batches, a batch is not detained long at any step of production, while the units in the batch are processed, before it is moved to the next step. Thus, the amount of material waiting (WIP) at any stage of production is relatively low.

When multiple containers are in circulation between a supplier WC and a user WC, there is some flexibility in the size of the production lot. The supplier WC may accumulate multiple kanbans for the same item before the equipment is set up and the item is made. The production lot size may vary depending on the WC's requirement to make other items, the time lost to make the setup, or other factors.

Small containers provide other advantages because they can be handled manually or with light capacity materials-handling equipment (reduced capital investment in equipment and floor space). The containers are sometimes compared to egg cartons because they are divided into compartments for each part. This protects the parts, makes them easy to grasp as they are used from the container, and makes the container hold only the specified amount.

MINIMUM FEASIBLE LOT SIZE   One effort that is part of JIT and that makes small lot sizes feasible is to reduce the setup time so that very little production time is lost by having a setup. Quick setups also may help reduce any time-related cost of setups, with the result that the conceptual trade-off we considered in discussing the economic production lot (EPL) in Chapter 12 supports having smaller production lots. In some cases the incremental cost for having an additional setup on a machine may be negligible (e.g., when salaried workers perform their own setups) as long as the nonproductive time caused by having the setups does not restrict the output below the needed amount. Because of this reasoning and the additional advantages of keeping WIP low, companies prefer to run very small production lots. In some cases, however, the time lost to perform setups would block out some of the required run time if the company sets up frequently in order to run very small lots. In such cases a company may wish to determine the *minimum feasible lot size (MFL)* for items produced on the same machine or process.

The first step to find the MFL is to subtract the required processing time from the time a machine is available in a day or a week to determine the remaining time that can be used for setups. Then this time is allocated to the products that are to be run on the machine in proportion to the importance of keeping their lot size small, or some other basis. In the following example each item is allocated an equal share of the available setup time.

Consider the following scenario. Three items, A, B, and C, are run on the same machine. The process time (in seconds) to make one unit of each item is given in Table 16.1. The near portion of the master production schedule has been frozen and the average daily requirements for each item are also shown in Table 16.1. At the current stage of the company's progress in setup improvement, it requires 15 minutes to change from production of one of these items to any other.

The machine is assumed to be available for 420 minutes (or $420 \times 60 = 25,200$ seconds) per day and any maintenance is performed after the normal shift. As shown in Table 16.1, the total run time required per day is 20,010 seconds, which leaves $25,200 - 20,010 = 5,190$ seconds for setups. Each setup takes 15 minutes or 900 seconds. The machine can therefore have $5,190/900 = 5.77$ or five setups per day without having any work performed on overtime. Five setups will allow production of six lots per day, if the first item run on the machine each day is the same item it was producing at the end of the previous day. Therefore, in a day the machine can produce two lots of each item with each lot equal to half a day's requirement. For A the lot would be 230, for B it would be 105, and for C it would be 40.

Table 16.1

DATA FOR DETERMINING THE MINIMUM FEASIBLE LOT
SIZES FOR ITEMS RUN ON A MACHINE

ITEM	PROCESSING TIME/UNIT (SECONDS)	AVERAGE DEMAND (UNITS/DAY)	DAILY PROCESSING TIME (SECONDS)
A	28	460	12,880
B	13	210	2,730
C	55	80	4,400
			Total 20,010

DELIVERY LOTS   With small production lots, only small amounts of incoming raw materials and components to go into subassemblies are needed at a time. Supplier deliveries therefore also come in small lots and at frequent intervals. Some suppliers of high-volume items make deliveries four or more times per day, and obviously it is desirable for such suppliers to be located close to the plant.

In some cases, the supplier is tied into its customer plant's computer scheduling system and receives printouts of the production schedule to aid in the supplier's planning. The supplier may actually stack the items according to the sequence in which they will be used. For example, automobile seats may be stacked in sequence according to the colors, fabrics, and models that will be assembled that day.

In general, the supplier and the purchasing company have a long-term relationship of mutual support and respect. Each realizes that its future depends on working smoothly with the other. The supplier works to provide good quality and achieve on-time deliveries, and these efforts improve the chances of success for both companies. Suppliers who provide very high quality are certified and are permitted to deliver their items to the points of use in the factory, instead of having them first go through a receiving inspection.

Quick, Inexpensive Setups

One element that is necessary to make production in small lots work well is the achievement of quick, inexpensive setups, since setups occur often. The traditional approach has been to say that since setups are expensive and delay production, it is better to run large lots and keep setups to a minimum. Yet with infrequent setups, workers never become skilled at them, so setups remain expensive. The JIT philosophy is that if the company has frequent setups, the workers will get good at setups.

SETUP REDUCTION EFFORTS   A company may provide training in *setup reduction* techniques and have individuals or teams of workers improve the setups in their work areas. Specialists and tool designers may also be available for assistance. A general approach is to standardize the equipment and setup procedures and to move much of the work to external setup steps (those that can be performed before production must be stopped and the machine turned off to complete the setup). All tools and supplies must be at the machine, and the setup people must be ready before the machine is stopped for the internal steps. The internal steps are to be minimized and standardized. Quick-release clamps may be used instead of bolts to attach devices that must be removed and replaced. If bolts are required, as many as possible will call for the same size wrench. A wrench of this size is made part of the standard setup tool kit or is kept at every machine where it is used. Preset templates may be used to reduce the time required to adjust tooling. A setup person or team may practice a setup routine the way an athletic team practices its plays. They may videotape the procedure, critique it, and practice the improved procedure while they look for ways to improve it further. At a Japanese plant the author visited, a die change on an injection molding machine—a change that would take more than 1 hour in some plants—was completed in 50 seconds.

Multiskilled Workers and Flexible Facilities

A WC may be called upon to make first one item, then a different item. One or more workers in a WC may be available at the time the WC is called on to produce a replacement container of any item the WC supplies. The workers must be capable of performing any operation that is required so that production will not be delayed. Many of the Japanese plants that use JIT have much of their work force on lifetime employment. The company and these employees work to develop a variety of skills to serve any production function the company needs. These *multiskilled workers* are among their firms' most valuable assets.

The WCs in JIT plants often are arranged in cells to facilitate efficient production of the items made at each WC. Since repetitive manufacturers make the same product often, probably daily, the products follow the same flow paths repeatedly. Instead of stationing equipment in functional departments, where all equipment that performs the same function is located in the same area (which would require long material movements), the equipment may be distributed to cells. A *cell* is a close grouping of different types of equipment, each of which performs an operation in a frequently repeated series of operations. Cells are beneficial where the same item is made in large numbers or a family of items that require the same series of operations is made frequently. The headlight assemblies for several models of automobiles, for example, may all require the same series of operations. A cell may be arranged so that it can be used to make headlight assemblies for one model of car for a while and then make headlight assemblies for another model. Cells were discussed further in Chapter 6, where more details on the design of operations facilities were presented.

Since very little WIP is present, the machines can be placed near each other. If possible, the machines are placed in the order in which they are used to make the item. If the items are small or the containers of items are light, they can be manually handled from one process to another. This arrangement permits low investment in materials-handling equipment, low materials-handling cost, and quick throughput. It also facilitates close coordination of workers without the need to transmit information through a central production control area. In lieu of all the handling required to pass items along, a multiskilled worker may step from one machine to the next and perform several or all the steps needed to make the item. This practice further reduces handling and coordination problems and enlarges the worker's job.

High Quality Levels

High quality is required for JIT to work well. Since there is no excess inventory of items, it is not possible for a company to sort through reserves and find enough good items to keep subsequent processes going if one process begins making defective items. There could be frequent disruptions to the JIT flow if quality is not kept consistently high. It is possible to have high quality without using JIT, but it would be difficult to have JIT without high quality.

JIT methods help a company maintain good quality levels. With low WIP inventory, items flow to subsequent operations more quickly, so defective items will be discovered at subsequent work stations soon and the process will be stopped and corrected before many defectives have been produced. Since small containers of parts are made and pulled to the next work center only as needed, the parts may have been made only hours or minutes before the defective ones are discovered. The worker who made the items can be identified and will probably recall which machine and tooling were used, what the machine settings were, what batch of raw material was used, and so on. Workers have a good chance of finding out what went wrong and correcting it before much scrap is made or many items have to be reworked. If one WC is making defects, the downstream WCs will soon be out of material so they will probably be stopped, and several people may be available to help solve the problem. It is important that these investigations be conducted in a positive way. The purpose is not to find someone to blame and reprimand. Some Japanese firms look at a defect as a treasure because it can reveal a way to improve the production system. That is the positive approach that a company should encourage to gain full cooperation in improving quality. Workers and managers are on the same team, trying to improve the system. The effect of this self-stopping, quick diagnosis, and rapid correction is to ensure that very few defective items are produced. If large lots were produced, it might be a long time before problems were discovered. Not only would more defects be produced, but it would be more difficult to determine exactly when the defects occurred and therefore more difficult to determine their cause.

Effective Preventive Maintenance

Equipment must be kept in excellent working condition to enhance quality and to make the production system reliable. As we have mentioned, one means of achieving good quality consistently is to reduce any sources of variation in the processing which might seriously degrade quality. Equipment must be adequately maintained to prevent variability in its performance. Few equipment breakdowns can be tolerated in a production facility that maintains very little extra inventory to keep it operating while a machine is repaired. Breakdown of one machine can stop the entire plant if it is the only machine that can make a part that goes into every product. Thus it is imperative that equipment be kept in proper working condition. Workers take pride in maintaining their equipment, and they learn to repair some equipment problems themselves. If a machine is not operating, workers cannot continue to produce parts, so they spend the time repairing or helping to repair the machine. A set of records about each machine is kept, telling what needs to be done to maintain the machine and how often, when the machine was last repaired, and what was done. Equipment is treated with respect because there is little inventory to operate with while a machine is being repaired and employees feel a vested interest in avoiding breakdowns. (Maintenance is discussed further in Supplement G.)

Continuous Improvement

The JIT philosophy carries with it an objective of *continuous improvement*. The goal is to be getting better, and the way to measure a plant's performance is to see how little WIP it requires to operate. Since inventory protects a plant in case of problems, in essence it hides the problems, so they go unnoticed and unsolved. Problems must be found before they can be solved, and the way to find them is to drain off some WIP inventory. The amount of inventory in the production system is the sum of that which circulates between each pair of WCs. The inventory at a pair of WCs is limited by the number of kanbans that authorize containers of WIP to circulate between the two WCs. When the system is operating smoothly, a manager may remove a kanban or two to reduce the number of containers of inventory at this stage in the system. If the process still runs smoothly, the manager may remove another card. When a problem appears, it represents an opportunity to improve the production system. A setup may take too long, or a production rate may be too slow at one step in the system. Once a problem is identified, the last kanban that was removed will be replaced to restore smooth operation, and workers can begin to seek a solution to the problem that was identified. The participative efforts of workers are called upon in these and other improvement activities as the company strives to improve quality, reduce inventories, and achieve more efficient operations.

OPERATIONS MANAGEMENT IN ACTION

TEAMWORK³ AT TEAM MOBILITE

Although there's no universal teamwork formula, Mobilite's shared goals and values reflect a sincere commitment to this objective. Considerable teamwork efforts helped the company make great strides toward world-class manufacturing during the past several years.

When Mobilite began its continuous improvement transition in 1985, the Orlando, Fla. plant had serious competitive problems and was losing money. Management needed to reduce product cost by about 20 percent. Sales annually rose about 100 percent during the 1982–85 period. Other challenges, which probably hastened cultural change: a 50 percent annual employee turnover, negligence in meeting customer needs, and many product quality problems.

Interrelated Challenges, Solutions

Struggling to manage rapid growth with little time to focus on efficiency, Mobilite people faced daily struggles:

- Too many different bed configurations made accurate production forecasting impossible.
- Inventory consumed about 25 percent of available plant floor space.
- Shipping costs escalated because of less-than-truckload shipments.
- Small purchase order quantities were caused by an urgent directive to get parts in the door.
- High defect rates resulted from an unstable work force.

In 1985, Mobilite launched its continuous improvement program, beginning with the establishment of a new management team. The team was charged with implementation of a JIT inventory system, Total Employee Involvement, and Quality Function Deployment ("Teamwork³" drawn from this three-way approach). Understanding that business survival came first, the three aspects were addressed in that order.

Plantwide Teamwork

A lean work force coupled with a flat organizational structure enabled Mobilite to avoid the functional silos so typical of many bureaucratic corporations. With the management team leading the way, teams sprang up at the plant floor level to pursue a continuous improvement strategy.

Three focused factories evolved, producing chairs, home health care beds, and nursing home beds. Within each focused factory, teams work closely with their

> **About Mobilite**
>
> Invacare, including the Mobilite Division, is the world's largest manufacturer of home health care beds and wheelchairs. Other Invacare business units manufacture various health care products.
>
> Products from the Mobilite plant are shipped to and distributed from a network of 30 Invacare warehouses. Invacare handles marketing and sales.

customers and suppliers. For example, the fabrication team is supplied by the external supplier of the raw material and serves the weld team. The weld team serves the powder coat line, which serves assembly. Next come the customers in packing and loading, followed by the external customers. At each step, everyone has a thorough understanding of who their customers and suppliers are.

Team members cross-train to perform other jobs, gaining an appreciation for the work others do and of the production cycle. Teams meet each morning to review performance and assignments. Their representatives also participate in the interview process and make their own employment decisions.

Continuing Improvements

Each team area has an "idea board." Individuals or teams write improvement suggestions on "I have an idea" cards which are posted on the idea board. Supervisors respond to the suggestions within 48 hours. Employees who make suggestions are recognized in the company newsletter, at luncheons, and so forth. There is no formal monetary award program yet for suggestions. During the first 5 months of the program, employees made an average 2.3 suggestions apiece.

Mobilite, which is non-union, believes that employees benefit from process improvements through enhanced security and job challenge. Production teams helped to develop the performance evaluation system which was revised to recognize employees' improvement efforts. The reviews focus on an employee's efforts toward satisfying the customer and continuous improvement.

Training is on a "need to use" basis. Each employee received an average of 23 hours' training in 1989, with a goal of increasing to at least 40 hours. A 1-day orientation program for new employees changed to focus on commitment, continuous improvement, and world-class manufacturing.

Human resource improvements contributed to significant reductions in turnover. The 50 percent turnover rate in 1987 decreased to 22 percent in 1989. Employment standards were raised to ensure that newly hired individuals can be trained in world-class principles. The new turnover goal is 10 percent, which is considered good in an extremely transient area.

Product Simplification

Enabling many other improvements, product simplification claims high priority. With the many product configurations, Mobilite's 1985 inventory was huge. It eclipsed efforts to develop efficient product flow paths. Management decided to discontinue several product variations. The remaining bed accounted for 98 percent of sales.

Three models of electric controls were available from numerous suppliers. A low-voltage control would satisfy all customers but it was more expensive. By consolidating all of the purchases to the low-voltage supplier, Mobilite achieved a price that would reduce annual expenses for the item. This step reduced the number of models again by one-half. By further standardizing the beds early in the fabrication stage, the company decreased bed models by 50 percent again.

The company tries to fix the production schedule for 30-day segments. The stages prior to assembly are triggered by pull from assembly. An MRP system primarily assists "B" and "C" item planning. "A" items are planned manually.

Focus and Flow

With the complexity reduction yielding reduced numbers of components in stock, the company decreased parts storage racks by 77 percent. The "new" space accommodates the focused factory arrangement, with room for point-of-use storage and efficient product flow.

Better coordination and control by sight is the norm. Part shortages are infrequent and it is easier to uncover quality problems. Productivity zoomed: labor cost per equivalent unit decreased by 49 percent from 1985 to 1989.

Supplier and Shipper Programs

Mobilite's supplier base decreased by 35 percent. Long-term supplier relationships were developed and costs declined as a result.

A noteworthy example is with bed motors and controls, which are "A" items. Each Wednesday finds Mobilite people determining the next week's requirements and faxing a release against an annual purchase order to a motor supplier. They also fax a release to a controls supplier—nearby the motor supplier. The shipper makes a milk run to load at the motor supplier on Friday morning and at the control supplier on Friday afternoon. On Monday morning the shipper's truck unhooks from the trailer of motors and controls at the Mobilite plant and hooks to a trailer of finished products to pull to a warehouse on the way back. This program supports Mobilite's JIT concept and yields 52 inventory turns on motors and 26 turns on controls. These items are the two highest dollar-volume purchases. A similar arrangement works with all other supplier parts.

Mobilite seeks suppliers' advice in product design. A computerized Supplier Information Network (SIN) displays delivery and quality performance. Objectives include JIT supplier payments to gain trade discounts and on-line supplier links with Mobilite's production schedule. These efforts assist Mobilite's 20-turns-per-year performance; the goal is 26 turns for 1990.

Building Quality Capability

In 1985, fourteen inspectors checked every product before shipment. Defects were corrected but root causes rarely surfaced. Now there is one quality auditor who checks the process but not the product.

Quality responsibility rests with departments making the products. Quality personnel are available as a resource to develop procedures and to train production employees. Every employee inspects his or her operation and is empowered to stop production if the situation warrants this step. Production employees, on a rotating basis, randomly audit the quality of outgoing products against a checksheet developed by various team representatives. Employees conduct telephone surveys of customers to obtain feedback on customer preferences and product performance. Information from returned products is fed to production and design.

Mobilite initially trained all employees in statistical process control (SPC) but believes that it was a mistake. Now they train people who can *apply* SPC. Lead and setup people are trained in process capability studies. Machine operators learn to do their own setups and maintenance. Variable control charts are used in areas such as fabrication. Scrap has decreased by 96 percent in the last 5 years.

Fueling their progress: Mobilite managers believe that they still have many improvements to make. Encouragement comes from their employees' understanding of the company's core values and their continuous improvement teamwork.

Source: James B. Dilworth, *Target,* The Association for Manufacturing Excellence, Winter 1990, pp. 51–53.

It is apparent that the JIT approach to repetitive manufacturing can be a very powerful competitive weapon. It achieves a synchronized flow of the desired product mix with very little in-process inventory. It enables quality to be more easily improved and provides greater plant flexibility. Less plant floor space and a lower plant investment are required. JIT further improves a company's competitiveness by speeding up product throughput so the company is quicker to introduce product innovations or to respond to customer demand. The JIT philosophy and many of its elements can be applied in job shops and intermediate-volume manufacturing companies. Certainly all companies can benefit from an emphasis on quality, participation, and teamwork. Some JIT elements must be adapted if they are to be applied in job shops. The concept of a uniform work load still applies, but naturally it will not be a uniform level of a repeating mix of standard products in a job shop setting. The number of hours of work is kept level. Large queues of WIP can be prevented in a job shop by not sending work to a work center until it has capacity available and pulls the work there. Many of these factories already use small lot sizes, and this fact makes setup time reduction important for them. Effective preventive maintenance and quality programs are also important in job shop factories, just as in others. Even service companies can apply many of these concepts. No wonder a growing number of companies are completely or partially run by the JIT concept (see box).

Nonmanufacturing Applications of Just-in-Time

The JIT concepts of reducing delays in processes can be applied to the handling of paperwork or other transactions in administrative activities such as order entry, scheduling, accounting, and billing. In addition to manufacturing, they have been applied in services, publishing, and distribution.

A recommended approach to applying JIT is to first study the work and eliminate any steps that do not add value. Table 16.2 lists some of the activities that often add little value in manufacturing and the corresponding activities in administrative work that should be examined carefully for possible elimination or improvement. Sometimes the work steps can be standardized to reduce the variability that can cause imbalances that lead to delays and overloads in the flow. Standardization of work facilitates cross-training workers so they can be assigned to areas where the demand is greatest. In some cases multiskilled (cross-trained) workers enable a company to

Table 16.2

CORRESPONDING ACTIVITIES IN MANUFACTURING AND ADMINISTRATIVE WORK WITH LOW VALUE-ADDING POTENTIAL

MANUFACTURING ACTIVITY	ADMINISTRATIVE ACTIVITY
Storing	Batching, filing
Moving	Mailing, transmitting
Expediting	Rush ordering
Scheduling, dispatching	Routing, prioritizing
Inspecting	Proofing

Source: Adapted from Thomas J. Billesback and Marc J. Schniederjans, "Applicability of Just-In-Time Techniques in Administration," *Production and Inventory Management Journal,* 3d quarter 1989, p. 41. Reprinted with the permission of APICS, Inc.

group work into cells, so that the workers perform enlarged jobs and flexibility is enhanced.

The JIT philosophy can sometimes be applied in distribution settings. The amount of inventory required to provide a certain level of service protection can be reduced if the inventory is held in a form that provides the greatest flexibility. Some items, for example, may be supplied to different retailers in differently labeled packages or they may be packaged in different quantities—such as singles, four-packs, and so forth. More total inventory is required if the product is packaged at the factory and the distribution center(s) maintains an inventory of each brand and/or package size. Instead the packaging may be stored more compactly in its collapsed form and a supply of the product maintained. Packaging is then done at the distribution center as inventory needs appear or as orders are received. Another example of this concept is storing in a "knocked-down" form various sizes of spools for wire. One very large spool of wire can then be sold in 100-, 250-, 500-foot spools or other lengths. Other products might be stored in bulk and packaged in the sizes needed after the orders are received. This type of application provides more flexibility in serving the local demands and it makes the distribution centers a value-adding link in the supply chain.

We have discussed many elements and applications of the just-in-time philosophy. It is a very comprehensive approach to reducing waste and seeking excellence. We will now discuss another approach to accomplishing these goals. The remainder of the chapter discusses a concept called the theory of constraints (TOC), which is the extension of earlier work called optimized production technology (OPT).

THEORY OF CONSTRAINTS (TOC)

Theory of constraints (TOC) was developed in Israel during the 1970s as a means of increasing the output of a factory whose capacity constraints prevented it from fully meeting demand. Much of the early material on this concept refer to it as *optimized production technology (OPT)*. The technology, which has been applied in the United States and several other countries, can be supported by a software package that incorporates many of the principles we will discuss. The principles behind the software can be applied without the software. We discuss some of these ideas in the remainder of the chapter. We use the term TOC since it is more recent and is used in much of the literature.

An objective of TOC is to maximize utilization of the bottlenecks. TOC seeks also to keep WIP inventory low by synchronizing the flow of items through a factory, just as JIT does. The methods of achieving this objective, however, are different. TOC does not rely on having a uniform mix of products that are made at a uniform rate over time. Wide swings in the product mix over time could, however, cause a shift in the location of bottlenecks, which would require a reanalysis of the plant. TOC does not rely on having downstream work stations pull items from feeding stations to make their rates of flow equal to the rate of use in the final assembly schedule. Instead, it develops coordinated schedules to synchronize the flows of dependent items so the flow rates are matched to the production rate at the bottleneck.

It is assumed that the plant makes assembled products instead of, or in addition to, selling individual components and that demand exceeds the capacity of the plant. Certain critical work stations, or *bottlenecks,* will limit the production rate of some components of the product(s). Since the product(s) must contain these components, the bottlenecks actually limit the rate at which salable products can be made. Hence the bottlenecks limit the sales revenue of the plant. The number of all other components needed is determined by the number of components that must flow through the bottlenecks. Use of the nonbottleneck resources beyond the amount required to match the bottleneck-produced items will produce needless WIP. A large part of the TOC logic is directed at identifying bottlenecks, ensuring that these resources are fully utilized, and scheduling use of the nonbottlenecks in synchronization with the bottlenecks (that is, the rate at which the plant is capable of making complete, salable products).

Much of the TOC logic, termed *thoughtware* by Dr. Eli Goldratt, one of its originators, is summarized in nine principles that many companies can apply. Some companies use algorithms that apply these principles in their production planning and control software. The following material presents the nine TOC principles and provides a brief discussion of how they might be applied.

The TOC Principles

1. Balance flow, not capacity. It is more important to synchronize the flow of items than to make sure that the capacities of the equipment are equal.

2. Utilization of a nonbottleneck is determined by some other constraint in the system, not by its own potential. Since the items run on a nonbottleneck must be assembled with items made at bottlenecks, the bottlenecks determine how many items should be run on the nonbottlenecks.

3. Utilization and activation of a resource are not synonymous. *Activation* is the time spent running units on a machine or other resource whether they are needed or not. Making parts that cannot be used, just to keep the resource busy, is not utilizing the resource. *Utilization* is running the resource in accordance with the rate at the bottleneck.

4. An hour lost on a bottleneck is an hour lost for the total system. A company should be careful to keep the bottlenecks running efficiently because they determine the amount of salable product that can be made.

5. An hour saved at a nonbottleneck is a mirage. Nonbottlenecks have extra capacity, so saving an hour there just adds to the extra capacity.

6. Bottleneck's govern both throughput and inventories. Inventories (particularly WIP) are a function of the amount necessary to keep the bottlenecks utilized.

7. The transfer batch size may not, and many times should not, be equal to the process batch. Sometimes it is desirable to split a production lot and move some of it to the next machine, so it can begin processing before the entire run is completed on the earlier operation.

8. The process batch should be variable, not fixed. The number of items run per batch at one operation may differ from other operations and may be different the next time the item is made. Batch size depends on such variables as demand and the time available for additional setups.

9. Schedules should be established by looking at all the constraints simultaneously. Lead times are a result of the schedule and cannot be predetermined. Lead times are a function of the lot size, transfer batch, priority, and other factors. They should not be assumed to be fixed.

Application of TOC Principles

Application of the principles presented above involves three general steps: (1) A company must identify its bottlenecks. (2) Then it must schedule and operate to see that the bottlenecks are fully utilized. (3) It should schedule the nonbottleneck operations so they keep the bottleneck operations well supplied while holding WIP inventory low.

IDENTIFY BOTTLENECKS   A company that has been operating with the product mix it intends to run probably knows where the bottlenecks are. The bottlenecks will have the largest queues if demand exceeds capacity; otherwise they will be the busiest work centers. If the product mix has not been run previously, a company can multiply its forecast monthly demand by the number of each component specified in the bills of materials to see how many of each component must be produced. These quantities are then multiplied by the standard hours of work per unit that must be performed at each operation required in the item's production routing. The total work per month at each work center is then summed and compared with the work center's capacity. The work centers can be arranged in descending order of capacity load. The centers with the highest percentages of load are the bottlenecks. If these bottlenecks are overloaded or almost fully loaded, alternative routings for the items that flow through these centers should be identified, to see if their use is advisable.

This step helps divide the factory into critical resources and noncritical resources. The factory can be represented as a network of linked work centers. Figure 16.3 shows a simplified network with the operations required to make various products sequenced from the bottom to the top of the figure. *Critical resources* are the bottleneck operations and all operations that are fed by a bottleneck operation. The critical resource portion of the network, therefore, consists of the bottlenecks and the operations that follow them, all the way through the final assembly operation. The critical resource network is shown at the top of Figure 16.3. The remainder of the network consists of noncritical resources.

SCHEDULE THE CRITICAL RESOURCES   Finite forward scheduling is applied to the critical resources—the part of the network where there is a capacity constraint—to load the bottlenecks to 100 percent capacity. That is, the load report for the bottleneck should be examined for each forward period until capacity is found to run the job. Relatively large lot sizes are run on the bottlenecks to save setup time and provide more run time. The bottleneck operations should be kept running to the greatest practicable extent. They may be staffed to run during lunch and coffee breaks, because they limit the output of the entire plant. Preventive maintenance is more important for this equipment than for other equipment, and repair of any breakdown is given very high priority. The schedule for the noncritical portion of the network is then established to get the parts to the critical operations slightly before the times at which they are scheduled to be run.

SCHEDULE THE NONCRITICAL RESOURCES   The objective in scheduling the noncritical resources is to synchronize their operations with the time at which operations must occur on the critical resources. The noncritical resources have excess capacity and hence more flexibility in scheduling. Items that will flow to the critical resources are backed up by a lead time to determine when the noncritical operations should occur (backward scheduling). The lead times can depend on the lot size rather than on some preestablished fixed estimate. The lots may be split (that is, the

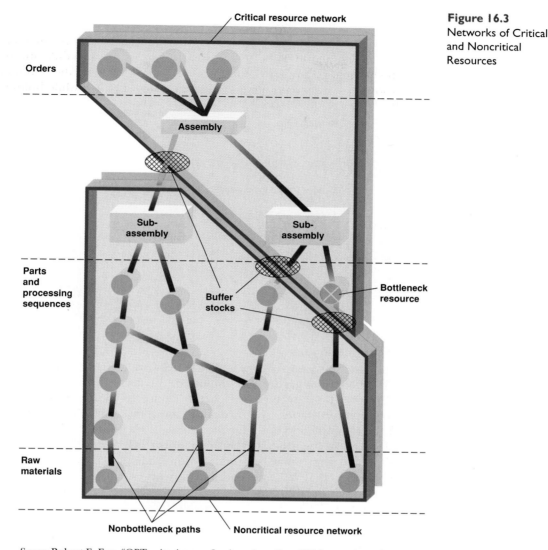

Source: Robert E. Fox, "OPT—An Answer for America—Part IV," *Inventories and Production,* March–April 1983, p. 20.

transfer batch may differ from the process batch). This practice can significantly reduce the lead times from what they would be if each operation had to wait until the prior operation had processed the entire lot before production could begin. For example, assume that a production lot of 300 units were to be processed through three work centers having no queues to delay it. Assume that the work operations to be performed on each unit take 1 minute at each work center. There would be 300 minutes of processing time at each work center. If the transfer batch were the entire lot, the entire lot would be held at each work center for 5 hours (that is, 300 minutes of processing time) before being moved to the next work center. The times for the movement of a transfer batch of 300 are shown at the top of Figure 16.4. If the production lot were split into three transfer batches of 100 units, the second work center could begin its work after only 100 minutes, or 200 minutes earlier. It would com-

Figure 16.4
The Effect of Lot Splitting on the Starting and Completion Times at Subsequent Work Stations

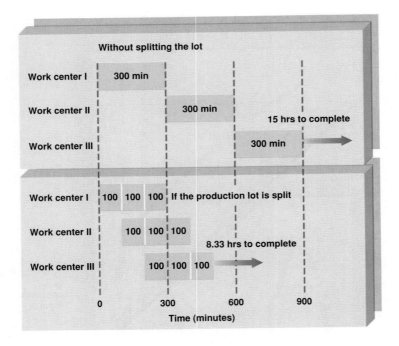

plete its work 200 minutes earlier. The third work center could begin and complete its work 400 minutes earlier. The timing for the faster throughput with smaller transfer batches is shown in the lower part of Figure 16.4. Since the work flows through the work centers faster, the work-in-process inventory is lower. The difference between the completion times for the two methods would be much greater if the production lot had to be processed through more work centers.

Additional setups may be scheduled on some noncritical operations to keep the lot sizes small so that WIP and lead times are also small. The extra setups are not considered to result in additional cost because these resources have excess capacity. The number of setups is not increased enough to use all of the extra capacity. Thus there is safety capacity on the noncritical resources to permit catching up in the event of a delay or other schedule disruption. The objective is to get a smooth flow of product, uniform utilization of capacity, and a fairly uniform level of safety capacity on the noncritical resources. This step determines the dispatch lists for the noncritical resources and material requirements for the starting operations so that supplier deliveries can be scheduled.

The safety capacity in the noncritical portion of the production system provides some protection against late materials, absent workers, machine breakdowns, and the like. These resources will eventually catch up to the critical resources if they happen to fall behind. The bottlenecks, however, would lack a supply of parts to process until the noncritical resource got going again—unless additional protection were provided. For this reason, a *buffer inventory,* or safety stock, of a few days' WIP is maintained where parts feed into the critical portion of the production system. This buffer inventory is shown in Figure 16.3.

IMPROVING THE SYSTEM The philosophy of continual improvement and efforts to involve employees and suppliers in productivity and quality improvements can be used in a TOC plant, just as in a JIT plant. As the reliability of the system improves and the variability of the flow rates into the critical resources is reduced, the amount of buffer inventory can be reduced. Suppose, for example, that management had established a policy of having an average of 3 days' buffer inventory. That is, jobs were scheduled to arrive at these locations 3 days ahead of the time they were scheduled to be run. Suppose records showed that no job arrived later than 2 days before it was needed (1 day later than it was scheduled to arrive). Management might then decide to reduce the buffer stock to, say, 2 days' or even 1 day's inventory.

This discussion provides some understanding of how TOC principles can be used. The TOC approach differs from JIT in its focus on scheduling. TOC schedules are based on fully utilized capacity at the bottlenecks. JIT operations are based on the final assembly schedule, implying that assembly will be treated as the internal bottleneck and that sufficient capacity will be available at all the other work centers. In JIT, the final assembly schedule should be checked against capacity if there is a danger of exceeding it. Some of the TOC ideas appear to be very useful when the product mix and level of demand change considerably.

The productivity of working capital has also been greatly improved because of the reduced investment in WIP and because of the rapid rate at which jobs are completed, so that payments can be received more quickly. It is apparent that benefits accrue to companies that can achieve some of the goals we discussed regarding TOC and earlier in our discussion of the JIT philosophy.

SUMMARY

JIT manufacturing is a broad philosophy of seeking excellence and eliminating waste. It includes people involvement, total quality control, and JIT throughput or flow to make items just before they are needed in order to eliminate the waste associated with queues.

Excessive queues result directly in unnecessary cost for holding WIP inventory. Beyond that, queues require space and require materials to be moved longer distances. Efforts to produce in small lots so that queues are smaller can help make quality improvement efforts more successful. This chapter discussed some of the ways companies are working to keep queues small.

Another method of reducing queues was discussed. TOC focuses on bottlenecks because that is where excess queues will form if a company seeks to make full use of all its work centers. Its goal is to have queues only ahead of the critical resources and to have them no larger than is necessary to protect the critical resources.

KEY TERMS

Just-in-time (JIT)
  manufacturing
People involvement
Supplier partnerships
Total quality control
Immediate customer
Jidoka
Focused factory
Mixed-model assembly
Push method

Pull method
Kanban system
Production card (P-card)
Move card (M-card)
Minimum feasible lot size
  (MFL)
Setup reduction
Multiskilled workers
Cell
Continuous improvement

Theory of constraints
  (TOC)
Optimized production
  technology (OPT)
Bottlenecks
Activation
Utilization
Critical resources
Buffer inventory

DISCUSSION QUESTIONS

1. Briefly distinguish between JIT manufacturing and JIT flow.

2. What are the three major components of JIT manufacturing?

3. Name the elements that work together to make JIT flow occur so effectively in repetitive manufacturing.

4. Compare the push and the pull methods of coordinating work at work stations.

5. How do small lots contribute to high quality? To flexibility? To cost efficiency?

6. Why is preventive maintenance important in JIT production?

7. Single-minute exchange of dies (SMED) is a coveted goal of many JIT factories. Why are quick changeovers considered one of the pillars of JIT?

8. Generally describe some setup reduction ideas that a manufacturing company might apply.

9. What is jidoka? What messages about human resources management and the relative importance of output versus quality are conveyed by the use of jidoka?

10. In what ways does the role of purchasing change when a company shifts to JIT manufacturing?

11. Describe the difference between the JIT and the TOC scheduling processes. What are the focus and primary goal of each?

12. Describe the three phases of TOC scheduling.

13. Describe some situation in which TOC scheduling principles are applied or could be applied in a service operation.

PROBLEMS

1. The company mentioned in the chapter with the discussion of the minimum feasible lot size has been working for continuous improvement. The setup time has been reduced to 12 minutes to change from running one of the items considered earlier to running any of the others. Also the processing time for item *A* has been reduced. Data for determining the MFL is given in the table below. The machine is still available 420 minutes per day. Determine the lot sizes for the current situation if the available setup time is allocated evenly to the three products. The company does not need to start each day running the same item (i.e., there does not need to be a setup at the start or the end of a day).

ITEM	PROCESSING TIME/UNIT (SECONDS)	AVERAGE DEMAND (UNITS/DAY)
A	25	460
B	13	210
C	55	80

2. A company runs three items on the same machine. Demand and processing time for the three items are given in the table below. Setup time to change from production of any item to any other is 16 minutes. The machine is available for 420 minutes a day. The company wishes to start each day with the same item and run the same sequence

each day (i.e., the number of setups each day will equal the number of lots to be run). Determine the lot sizes to run if the setup time is allocated evenly to each item.

ITEM	PROCESSING TIME/UNIT (SECONDS)	AVERAGE DEMAND (UNITS/DAY)
R	10	900
S	6	450
T	15	200

3. A company runs three items on the same machine. Demand and processing time for the three items are given in the table below. Setup time to change from production of any of the items to any other is 20 minutes. The machine is available for 420 minutes a day. The company wishes to start each day with the same item and run the same sequence each day (i.e., the number of setups each day will equal the number of lots to be run). Determine the lot sizes to run if the setup time is allocated to each item in approximate proportion to the number of units of the item to be produced each day.

ITEM	PROCESSING TIME/UNIT (SECONDS)	AVERAGE DEMAND (UNITS/DAY)
X	11	750
Y	12	500
Z	14	250

4. A company runs four items on the same machine. Demand and processing time for the four items are given in the table below. Setup time to prepare the machine for production of each of the items is also given in the table. The machine is available for two shifts or 840 minutes a day. The company wishes to start each day with the same item and run the same sequence each day (i.e., the number of setups each day will equal the number of lots to be run). Determine the number of times the company can run through the sequence of the four items in a day.

ITEM	PROCESSING TIME/UNIT (SECONDS)	AVERAGE DEMAND (UNITS/DAY)	SETUP TIME TO RUN THE ITEM (MINUTES)
M	18	400	12
N	15	700	15
O	12	500	8
P	20	300	12

BIBLIOGRAPHY

Billesback, Thomas J., and Marc J. Schniederjans. "Applicability of Just-in-Time Techniques in Administration." *Production and Inventory Management Journal,* 3d quarter 1989, pp. 40–44.

Dilworth, James B. "Strategic and Tactical Issues in Just-in-Time Manufacturing." *Proceedings of the 1985 Conference.* Wheeling, Ill.: Association for Manufacturing Excellence, 1986.

Fry, Timothy D., and James F. Cox. "Manufacturing Performance: Local versus Global Measures." *Production and Inventory Management Journal,* 2d quarter 1989, pp. 52–56.

Goldratt, Eliyahu M., and Jeff Fox. *The Goal: Excellence in Manufacturing.* 2d rev. ed. Croton-on-Hudson, N.Y.: North River Press, 1992.

Hahn, Chan K., Peter Pinto, and Daniel Bragg. "Just-in-Time Production and Purchasing." *Journal of Purchasing and Materials Management,* Fall 1983, pp. 2–10.

Hall, Robert W. *Attaining Manufacturing Excellence.* Homewood, Ill.: Dow Jones-Irwin, 1987.

————, **and Jinichiro Nakane.** "Developing Flexibility for Excellence in Manufacturing: Summary Results of a Japanese-American Study." *Target,* Summer 1988, pp. 15–22.

Helms, Marilyn M. "Communication: The Key to JIT Success." *Production and Inventory Management Journal,* 2d quarter 1990, pp. 18–21.

Jacobs, F. Robert. "OPT Uncovered: Concepts behind the System." *Industrial Engineering 16,* no. 10 (October 1984): 32–41.

Kenney, Martin, and Richard Florida. *Beyond Mass Production: The Japanese System and Its Transfer to the U.S.* New York: Oxford University Press, 1993.

Krupp, James A. G. "JIT in Distribution and Warehousing." *Production and Inventory Management Journal,* 2d quarter 1991, pp. 18–21.

McLeod, Alan H. "Partnership Triangle to an Effective Supplier Certification Program." *Just-in-Time/Quality Conference Proceedings.* Falls Church, Va.: American Production and Inventory Control Society, 1987, pp. 104–107.

Moden, Yasuhiro. *Toyota Production System: Practical Approach to Production Management.* Atlanta: Industrial Engineering and Management Press, 1983.

Reid, Peter C. *Well Made in America: Lessons from Harley-Davidson on Being the Best.* New York: McGraw-Hill, 1990.

Ritzman, L. P., B. E. King, and L. J. Krajewski. "Manufacturing Performance—Pulling the Right Levers." *Harvard Business Review,* March–April 1984, pp. 143–152.

Sandras, William A., Jr. *Just-in-Time—Making It Happen: Unleashing the Power of Continuous Improvement.* Essex Junction, Vt.: Oliver Wight Ltd., 1989.

Schonberger, Richard J. *World Class Manufacturing: The Lessons of Simplicity Applied.* New York: Free Press, 1986.

————. "Frugal Manufacturing. "*Harvard Business Review,* November–December 1987.

Sepehri, Mehran. *Just-in-Time, Not Just in Japan: Case Studies of American Pioneers in JIT Implementation.* Falls Church, Va.: American Production and Inventory Control Society, 1986.

Shingo Shigeo. *Study of Toyota Production System from Industrial Engineering Viewpoint.* Tokyo: Japan Management Association, 1981.

Srikanth, Mokshagundam L., and Harold E. Cavallaro, Jr. *Regaining Competitiveness: Putting the Goal to Work.* 2d rev. ed. Great Barrington, Mass.: North River Press, 1993.

Stundza, Tom. "Suppliers Clip Costs from Their Customers' Stockpiles." *Purchasing,* November 4, 1994, pp. 28–29.

Target (quarterly journal). Wheeling, Ill.: Association for Manufacturing Excellence. All issues.

Wantuck, Kenneth A. *Just-in-Time for America.* Milwaukee: The Forum, Ltd., 1989.

TOTAL PRODUCTIVE MAINTENANCE

SUPPLEMENT

G

Companies that work for continuous improvement seek ways to improve their processes. Often this means that any equipment used in their processes must also be improved to upgrade its performance and to keep problems from interrupting service. Customer satisfaction and competitiveness will not be high if equipment failures make deliveries late or equipment works so poorly that quality is inferior. In the past, some companies looked upon maintenance just from the standpoint of cost. Some operated on the principle of fix it when it breaks and then run it until it breaks again. Most companies, however, have recognized that an ounce of wisely applied prevention is worth a pound of cure and employ preventive maintenance (PM) to reduce equipment problems. This routine maintenance helps reduce equipment variability that degrades quality; reduce failures, down time, and repair costs; and make equipment last longer.

A growing number of companies have recognized that a sound maintenance program supports competitiveness and profits and have moved beyond focusing on minimizing the costs of maintenance and repair. A company whose equipment produces better results with very little unscheduled down time can outperform a company with unreliable equipment that turns out mediocre results. The company with better performance may spend more on its equipment, but it is more likely to also have higher revenues and profits and to gain market share over the other type of company. This simple comparison illustrates some of the ideas behind total productive maintenance. *Total productive maintenance* is a systematic approach to involving all employees in improving the performance of equipment so that it performs better work and does so with higher reliability. Total productive maintenance is one of the areas in which excellent companies apply employee participation. All employees (that is why it is called "total") are encouraged to improve their knowledge of the equipment they use in their work and to apply this knowledge to improve the ways the equipment can support excellent performance. Equipment operators may perform routine maintenance on their equipment to keep it operating reliably. Employees also seek other ways to increase reliability, reduce variability in performance, improve safety, or develop other benefits.

This supplement overviews many of the matters that often are evaluated in reaching management decisions about maintenance. Some of these evaluations traditionally have been phrased in terms of cost trade-offs. It is important to recognize that with a total-productive view of maintenance, some of these costs represent more than the out-of-pocket charges that result from equipment repair and equipment failure. Cost considerations should also include the opportunity costs associated with damaged competitiveness when equipment degradation prevents excellent customer service. It is probably not possible to establish precise costs for consideration in such trade-offs, but they provide a conceptual basis for evaluating some of the issues involved in managing maintenance.

MANAGING MAINTENANCE ACTIVITIES

In many respects, managing maintenance activities is like managing some of the other operations. Preventive maintenance efforts are recurring efforts that are performed at scheduled times. *Preventive maintenance (PM)* consists of maintenance activities performed before equipment breaks, with the intent of keeping it operating acceptably and reducing the likelihood that it will break down. PM includes:

1. Periodic inspection and record keeping to assess the condition of facilities and equipment so breakdowns can be avoided.
2. Adequate lubricating, painting, cleaning, and adjusting to maintain operating conditions.
3. Periodic repetitive servicing, repair, or overhauls, even though no breakdown has occurred.
4. A branch of preventive maintenance called *predictive maintenance* uses sensors installed on equipment and technical data from equipment to determine when the performance of equipment is about to degrade too far or when it is about to break down. With this forewarning, the needed parts can be obtained and the machine repaired on an organized schedule.

The first three of these activities are much like provision of a standardized service or production of a standardized product on a recurring basis. In total productive maintenance, routine activities such as these, particularly items 1 and 2, often are transferred to machine operators and their supervisors. One of the objectives is to move responsibility for routine maintenance close to the need for the work.

Managing remedial maintenance, however, is more like managing a custom production or a special project than a standard operation. *Remedial maintenance* consists of efforts to restore facilities and equipment to an acceptable operating condition after a breakdown has occurred. Usually equipment fails when it is being used so it is likely that some work is being delayed while the equipment is broken, unless backup equipment is available. Remedial maintenance, therefore, is often performed under expedited conditions to reduce down time. The problem must be diagnosed and all the necessary tools, equipment, and replacement parts must be obtained if they are not already on hand. People with the appropriate skills must also be available. Sometimes there may be multiple demands and priorities must be established for the jobs to be done. At other times there may be no remedial work to do and the maintenance staff may work on equipment improvements, preventive maintenance, or training production personnel to perform the routine maintenance procedures.

Companies that use much equipment usually have some organizational unit designated to be in charge of coordinating maintenance. Such a unit would retain repair manuals, diagrams, and histories of the maintenance that has been performed on the equipment. Maintenance histories are an important source of data about how reliable each machine is, which parts fail and how often. These data help in determining staffing needs, the types of skills that are needed, and what repair parts to keep in stock. This organization would employ maintenance specialists who would handle complex PM and most remedial work and/or coordinate the efforts of suppliers who provide this type of work when it is required.

Some considerations discussed in earlier chapters regarding inventory also apply to maintenance operations. An inventory of repair parts may be maintained to reduce the lead time before repairs can begin. Information from equipment vendors and from past repair records may be used to help forecast the reliability of various components and equipment in the operations system. The costs of down time (lost production and customer ill will) are similar to stockout costs. The savings to be achieved by reducing repair lead time must be evaluated and compared with the cost of keeping parts in inventory. This information can be used to determine the items and amounts that should be held as inventory of repair parts. Spare-parts inventories are subject to costs for obsolescence, taxes and insurance, costs of invested capital, and other costs, as are any other types of inventories. Some multidivision companies achieve savings by analyzing parts usage and stocking only the more frequently used

OPERATIONS MANAGEMENT IN ACTION

DISNEY WORLD MAINTENANCE

Maintenance is critical to theme parks, and at Disney World it gets high-profile attention from management although most of it is kept hidden from guests. What a guest is most likely to see, and remark on, is the cleanliness. A fallen gum wrapper is immediately whisked up by the closest Disney employee—of any rank.

Although Disney World has a $20 million maintenance manpower budget, 2,000 full-time maintenance workers, and a maintenance software package second to none, that spirit is the key to breaking down the fences between functional turfs. This spirit comes from the Walt Disney management principles which the master himself enunciated in 1966:

1. Quality will win out.
2. Give the public everything you can give them.
3. Keep the place clean.
4. Keep the place friendly.

The last principle translated to employment atmosphere means to take your job seriously but don't take yourself seriously. Have fun at work.

The Disney maintenance force is represented by ten craft unions. The potential for turf squabbles is ever present, but the means for keeping it in check is that *executives establish pride in the work itself and set examples.* The executive snapping up a gum wrapper is part of that. Pride is cultivated, starting with signs in maintenance saying that under this roof are the world's finest craftsmen. Shoddy work is not part of anyone's expectations.

Essential to this pride is a sense of the importance of any work, including the smallest details. For instance, the gold inlay on the manes of carousel horses is not false; it is the 24-carat real thing. A guest will probably never know. The workers do. In the Disney setting, this carries the motivation behind the scenes.

The operational readiness rate of Disney equipment is 99.4 percent, and they target still better. The biggest Pareto items causing down time are weather-related, so improving this performance requires improved weatherproofing of equipment designs.

The computer system is Disney-conceived and Disney-programmed. The on-line system handles a 24-month history on 38,000 items of equipment. There are 60,000 variable-time job orders per month in addition to the 130,000 fixed-time PMs on the schedule. The program does a failure-code analysis to assist with predictive maintenance.

Other programs are used for special projects. For instance, Disney has a huge number of two-way radios on-site. Radio failures and repairs are being simulated to better establish maintenance cycles for radios, and to determine how many radio maintenance locations should be on the premises.

Disney redesigns troublesome parts. They are on their sixth or seventh generation of soft-drink dispenser heads to stretch the times between failures. An ordinary commercial design has a failure rate of "500 percent per year or more" under the special stress of Disney World use.

Most of the routine maintenance at Disney World takes place at night. The day shift mans underground shops near equipment for which they are responsible. Unless there is an emergency, these shops are busy making spare parts or revised parts. A great deal of Disney equipment uses unique design parts.

Disney provides a generous budget for maintenance. A manufacturer of cost competitive products is apt to feel that they cannot afford to copy Disney. They probably cannot afford the same elegance of system and the "imagineering talent," but everyone can afford the Disney management attitude. That costs nothing but the effort to develop it, which is considerable.

Source: Robert W. Hall, "Total Productive Maintenance—Essential to Maintenance Progress," *Target 3*, no. 3 (Fall 1987): 10. Courtesy of The Association for Manufacturing Excellence.

spares at all locations where they are used. Less frequently used items may be stocked at only one location but can be rapidly sent to any location where they may be needed. Some replacement parts, such as parts for a nuclear power plant, are very expensive and require a long lead time to obtain. Several companies may cooperate to purchase and hold one spare of such an item. If a company needs the part, it uses the available spare and purchases another to replace it.

The quality of maintenance work must be ensured if equipment is to be kept running properly. The material on quality in Chapters 3 and 10 applies also to maintenance management (see box).

BASIC MAINTENANCE DECISIONS

Centralized versus Decentralized Maintenance

Some companies choose to have one large maintenance department; others have a small maintenance department for each part of the company. Individual or *decentralized maintenance* departments may be justified if each part of the company needs a different special skill, special equipment, or very rapid response. However, the work load is more easily distributed with a *centralized maintenance* department.

Contract versus In-House Maintenance

Some companies do not have enough equipment to justify the expense of a maintenance department. A company with one or two automobiles would not employ a full-time mechanic to repair and service them. Many companies with large fleets of vehicles, however, have their own service garages. Some companies that have their own maintenance departments with facilities to do repair work still use outside contract workers for some of their maintenance. Occasional highly specialized or seasonal maintenance work may be contracted.

Standby Equipment

Sometimes older machines are not sold when they are replaced but are held as *standby equipment* for occasional use in production. Also newer equipment may be purchased to provide redundancy so that the reliability of the production system is enhanced. One issue related to maintenance is the number of standby machines a company should have. The need for extra equipment depends on many factors, such as the reliability of each piece of equipment, the time required to perform a repair, the waiting time to begin a repair, the percentage of time scheduled for production operations, and the cost of lost production time.

Repair versus Replacement

When a machine breaks down, the best course of action is not always obvious. If equipment is due to be replaced before long, it may be better to replace it than to invest additional money in repairing it. The cash flows required to repair and keep currently owned equipment may be compared with the cash flows required for the best alternative replacement equipment.

Individual versus Group Replacement

Some items are used in large quantities—light bulbs, for instance. The saving in labor costs to replace all the bulbs in one section of a building at the same time may more than offset the cost of the good bulbs that are removed. Decisions must also be reached regarding the frequency of replacement.

Amount of Maintenance Capacity

The amount of maintenance capacity a company should have is related to many other issues. The amount and type of equipment to be maintained and the extent to which contract maintenance is used are two basic factors that affect the size of the in-house force. The frequency of requirements for service and the cost of lost production time also are important determinants of the proper capacity.

Insight into the question of capacity can sometimes be gained through simulation (discussed in Supplement H) and queuing theory, which is introduced here and discussed further in the next chapter. All machines in a facility represent a population from which demands for service may arrive at the maintenance department. The cost of down time (which includes an estimated cost for the damage to competitiveness) while the equipment is waiting and being serviced is compared to the cost of maintenance capacity sufficient to provide rapid repair. A balance between these costs should be reached. We will consider a traditional approach that minimizes the sum of these costs.

Suppose that a group of machines is large enough to make the probability of an arrival constant and that the interarrival times and service times are distributed according to a negative exponential distribution (Poisson arrival rates). Suppose that the machines break down at a mean rate λ of 0.8 per week. One worker can repair one per week ($\mu = 1$ per week), and the equipment is such that repair time is reduced proportionally as more workers are available, up to a maximum of four. Beyond that number of workers, a second channel in the queuing system is opened. Maintenance workers are paid $500 per week, and idle machine time is valued at $1,500 per week. Assume the cost of additional tools is negligible. How many workers should be employed?

If one worker is employed, the cost of tending the facility will be $500. The cost of idle time can be found from queuing formulas. The mean number of broken machines in the system (being repaired and waiting to be repaired) is given by

$$L_s = \frac{\lambda}{\mu - \lambda} = \frac{0.8}{1 - 0.8} = 4$$

The total cost with one repair worker would be $1(\$500) + 4(\$1,500) = \$6,500$ per week. Two workers would raise the service rate to two machines per week, so

$$L_s = \frac{0.8}{2 - 0.8} = \frac{0.8}{1.2} = 0.6667$$

The total cost would be $2(\$500) + 0.6667(\$1,500) = \$2,000$ per week.

Three workers would raise the service rate to three machines per week.

$$L_s = \frac{0.8}{3 - 0.8} = 0.3636$$

The total cost would be $3(\$500) + 0.3636(\$1,500) = \$2,045.40$ per week. The number of workers that will minimize the expected costs is two. The company might consider that it is worth the additional \$45.40 per week to operate with three maintenance workers for this group of machines to reduce the likelihood of numerous machines being inoperable.

Preventive Maintenance versus Remedial Repair

Should a company spend most of its time on minor tune-ups and preventive work, or should it just wait until something breaks and then fix it? The answer to this question depends on several factors, including the relative cost of prevention versus the cost of repair. Probably the best level of prevention is somewhere between none and the maximum possible. Rebuilding equipment every evening or every weekend would be excessively expensive and it probably would reduce the equipment's reliability below what it might be with less rework. Mechanical parts often have to "run in" and electronic parts have to "burn in" before they work their best. The failure rate often is higher just after a repair than it is during the midlife of the device. Then reliability degrades (the failure rate increases) as wear and age take their toll. The cost of preventive efforts and the costs of down time and repair may be considered to have the general relationship shown in Figure G.1 in many cases.

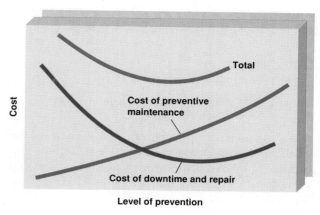

Figure G.1 Cost of Preventive Maintenance vs. Cost of Repair

EVALUATION OF PREVENTIVE MAINTENANCE POLICIES

The absence of preventive maintenance can be expensive because of down time and because the cost of repairs may be more expensive than preventive action. Too much preventive maintenance, however, may be excessively expensive. A balance between the two extremes sometimes can be found by modeling the costs.

Assume that M identical machines are used for a process and that the average cost of a preventive maintenance service is C_p. The cost of a major repair if the machine is run until breakdown is C_R. (Naturally C_R will be greater than C_p, or we would not be interested in preventing breakdowns.) Let P_i be the probability that the machine will break down in the ith period after it has been serviced.

The mean time between failures (MTBF) will be

$$\text{MTBF} = \sum_{i=1}^{n} iP_i$$

where $n =$ the longest number of periods that a machine will go without failure

The expected total cost per period of not providing preventive maintenance will be

$$\text{TC (no preventive maintenance)} = \frac{C_R M}{\displaystyle\sum_{i=1}^{n} iP_i}$$

To begin, let us calculate the cost of routine preventive maintenance every period. Part of this cost will be $C_P \times M$ to perform the preventive service. In addition, some number of machines B_1 will break down during the first period after preventive service and be repaired. So $B_1 = M \times P_1$, where P_1 equals the probability that a machine will break down in the first period after it is serviced. The cost of repairing breakdowns if machines are serviced every period will be $C_R B_1$, so

$$\text{TC}(1) = C_P M + C_R B_1 = C_P M + C_R M P_1$$

where TC(1) = the total cost if machines are serviced every period

We can extend this type of analysis to consider repairing machines every j periods. Let B_j equal the number of breakdowns between preventive services when these services are performed every jth period. Recall that P_i equals the probability that a machine will break down in the ith period after it is serviced. Then

$$B_2 = M(P_1 + P_2) + B_1 P_1$$

where B_2 is the number of machines expected to break down between servicing if preventive service is performed every two periods, $M(P_1 + P_2)$ is the expected number of breakdowns during the two periods for the M originally functioning machines, and $B_1 P_1$ is the number of machines expected to be repaired during the first period and to break down during the second period. Likewise, $M(P_1 + P_2 + P_3)$ is the expected number of the originally functioning M machines that will break down if there are three periods between preventive servicing. Therefore,

$$B_3 = M(P_1 + P_2 + P_3) + B_2 P_1 + B_1 P_2$$

In general,

$$B_j = M(P_1 + P_2 + \ldots + P_j) + B_{j-1}P_1 + B_{j-2}P_2 + \ldots + B_1 P_{j-1}$$

and the total cost for j periods if the machines are repaired every j periods is

$$\text{TC}(j) = C_P M + C_R B_j$$

The average total cost per period for this policy will be $\text{TC}(j)/j$.

We have examined the type of analysis that may be used to determine preventive maintenance frequency when the PM cost is compared with the cost of repairing a breakdown. But consideration should be given to other factors as well. Since breakdowns cannot be scheduled, they usually disrupt productive activities and cause additional expenses for

rescheduling and expediting work. Breakdowns also cause delivery dates to be missed, resulting in customer ill will.

Preventive activities usually can be scheduled to occur when equipment is not normally in operation (such as evening shifts or weekends). We shall see in the discussion of queuing in Chapter 17 that random occurrences of demand make the queuing situation more difficult and cause poorer use of capacity than can be achieved with scheduled arrivals. Thus the use of maintenance personnel can be made more efficient in scheduled preventive activities than in unscheduled remedial activities. It is apparent that in analyzing preventive versus remedial maintenance, factors other than the direct cost of each type of activity should be considered.

PREDICTIVE MAINTENANCE

Preventive maintenance is intended to prevent breakdowns, particularly catastrophic ones that cause secondary damage to other parts. Routine inspection and replacement of certain parts through preventive maintenance often require that the machine be taken out of service, and parts may be replaced if they seem likely to need replacement before the next scheduled preventive work on the machine. Rather than performing this periodic maintenance work at set intervals, some companies have a program of predictive maintenance. Predictive maintenance is a program of periodically monitoring equipment and tracking certain measures of its performance. Problems are detected while the machine is still performing satisfactorily, and a failure can be predicted before it occurs. Sometimes the proper replacement parts can be obtained and the appropriate maintenance work can be scheduled to occur when the machine is not scheduled to be used. This reduces the cost of expediting parts shipments, overtime costs for maintenance labor, and the number of delayed jobs that were scheduled to be run while the machine is down.

Predictive maintenance is more feasible today because of technology that is available for equipment surveillance and diagnosis of problems while the machines are still running. The condition of a machine can be monitored by several means. Critical monitor points on equipment are identified. Sensors may be installed, or periodic readings may be taken with portable units to measure the temper-

ANALYZING COSTS OF MAINTENANCE VERSUS REPAIR

T he Delsoni Laundromat chain has 50 identical coin-operated machines in its facilities throughout the city. The cost of preventive servicing C_P is $20, and the cost of repair after a breakdown C_R is $100. The company seeks the minimum-cost preventive servicing frequency and has collected the data on breakdown probabilities in Table G.1.

The mean time between failures is 5.4 months, and the expected cost with no preventive maintenance would be $100 \times {}^{50}\!/_{5.4} = \$925.93$ per month. The following calculations show B_j, the expected number of breakdowns between preventive maintenance intervals, for the possible intervals that may be considered. The costs of various preventive maintenance intervals are summarized in Table G.2.

$B_1 = MP_1 = 50(0.10) = 5$

$B_2 = M(P_1 + P_2) + B_1P_1 = 50(0.10 + 0.05) + 5(0.10) = 8$

$B_3 = 50(0.10 + 0.05 + 0.05) + 8(0.10) + 5(0.05) = 11.05$

$B_4 = 50(0.10 + 0.05 + 0.05 + 0.10) + 11.05(0.10) + 8(0.05) + 5(0.05) = 16.75$

$B_5 = 50(0.10 + 0.05 + 0.05 + 0.10 + 0.15) + 16.75(0.10) + 11.05(0.05) + 8(0.05) + 5(0.10) = 25.63$

$B_6 = 50(0.6) + 25.63(0.1) + 16.75(0.05) + 11.05(0.05) + 8(0.1) + 5(0.15) = 35.5$

$B_7 = 50(0.8) + 35.5(0.1) + 25.63(0.05) + 16.75(0.05) + 11.05(0.10) + 8(0.15) + 5(0.15) = 48.72$

$B_8 = 50(1) + 48.72(0.1) + 35.5(0.05) + 25.63(0.05) + 16.75(0.1) + 11.05(0.15) + 8(0.15) + 5(0.2) = 63.46$

A policy of performing preventive maintenance every 4 months results in the lowest average cost, about $669. This amount is $257 per month less than the $926 expected cost without preventive maintenance. This policy would reduce costs by $({}^{257}\!/_{926})\, 100 = 27.75$ percent below the cost of repairing the machines only when they break down.

Table G.1
PROBABILITIES OF WASHING MACHINE BREAKDOWN, BY MONTH

MONTHS AFTER SERVICING THAT BREAKDOWN OCCURS i	PROBABILITY THAT BREAKDOWN WILL OCCUR P_i	iP_i
1	0.10	0.10
2	0.05	0.10
3	0.05	0.15
4	0.10	0.40
5	0.15	0.75
6	0.15	0.90
7	0.20	1.40
8	0.20	1.60
	1.00	5.40

Table G.2
COST OF ALTERNATIVE PREVENTIVE MAINTENANCE INTERVALS

(1) NUMBER OF MONTHS BETWEEN PREVENTIVE SERVICES j	(2) B_j EXPECTED NUMBER OF BREAKDOWNS IN j MONTHS	(3) EXPECTED COST PER MONTH TO REPAIR BREAKDOWNS $C_R \times B_j/j$	(4) COST PER MONTH FOR PREVENTIVE SERVICE EVERY j MONTHS $C_P(M)/j$	(5) TOTAL EXPECTED COST PER MONTH OF PREVENTIVE MAINTENANCE AND REPAIR (3) + (4)
1	5.00	$500.00	$1,000.00	$1,500.00
2	8.00	400.00	500.00	900.00
3	11.05	368.33	333.33	701.66
4	16.75	418.75	250.00	668.75
5	25.63	512.60	200.00	712.60
6	35.50	591.67	166.67	758.34
7	48.72	696.00	142.86	838.86
8	63.46	793.25	125.00	918.25

ature or vibration. Vibration sensors and ultrasonic sensors are used to feed data into a computer for analysis. Trends away from normal vibration patterns, which were recorded when the machine was working properly, are analyzed to determine where a problem is developing and when it will become serious. Infrared imaging can detect areas that are unusually warm—another indication of a trouble spot.

Small particles are torn away as parts wear. Laboratory analysis of particles in the lubricants from a machine can reveal the amount of wear that has occurred and the type of material that has worn. This wear particle analysis can be used to detect signals that trouble is on the way and that repair work should be planned. Fiber optics can be used to examine some parts of equipment without disassembling it, so that the seriousness of problems can sometimes be determined before the machine has to be stopped.

A program of this type prevents unplanned down time that disrupts production schedules, idles the work force, and degrades overall customer service. The maintenance department does not have to wait until equipment is disassembled to determine what parts are needed and how many workers with what skills will be required to repair it. Machines often are out of service for a shorter time because much of the diagnostic work has already been done and the necessary parts and people are already available. Companies can keep a smaller supply of repair parts if it is possible to predict ahead of time when the parts will be needed. There are several benefits to predictive maintenance, and the concept will improve as technology develops and more people learn to apply it.

SUMMARY

Maintenance activities affect the competitiveness and performance of operations in several ways. There is a direct cost for conducting preventive and/or remedial maintenance work. Maintenance also affects the reliability of the operations system by varying the percentage of its capacity that is productive. Breakdowns often cause inefficiencies in rescheduling and expediting delayed work as well as the cost of ill will if deliveries are delayed. Care and maintenance of equipment affect the lifetime and salvage value of equipment, thereby having an impact on the rate of return earned on the invested funds. Many companies are moving to total productive maintenance by involving all employees in improving equipment performance.

In evaluating maintenance policies a company may consider several options and trade-offs, among them (1) centralized versus decentralized maintenance; (2) the use of contract versus in-house maintenance; (3) the number of standby machines to hold; (4) repair versus replacement of defective equipment; (5) individual versus group replacement, when large numbers of similar items are employed in an operation; (6) the amount of maintenance capacity that should be kept available; and (7) the extent to which preventive and remedial maintenance should be used.

KEY TERMS

Total productive maintenance
Preventive maintenance (PM)

Predictive maintenance
Remedial maintenance
Decentralized maintenance

Centralized maintenance
Standby equipment

DISCUSSION QUESTIONS

1. Discuss the difference between preventive and remedial maintenance. Give examples of each.
2. How might managing a maintenance operation incorporate some features of managing both a job shop and a make-to-stock operation at the same time?
3. What is predictive maintenance?
4. What are some of the advantages of a predictive maintenance program?

PROBLEM

1. The Ecstasy Inn motel has 100 television sets in its rooms. The manager has an opportunity to sign a maintenance contract that calls for an annual payment of $12 per television set. The contract will provide preventive maintenance and adjustments to the sets at 6-month intervals. Currently the average repair cost is $25 each time a set is repaired or adjusted. The probabilities of breakdown at various intervals after a repair are given in the following table.
   a. Should the manager purchase the maintenance service as offered at 6-month intervals?
   b. Should he attempt to obtain service at other intervals?

MONTH	PROBABILITY	MONTH	PROBABILITY
1	0.12	6	0.08
2	0.08	7	0.08
3	0.08	8	0.11
4	0.08	9	0.13
5	0.08	10	0.16

COMPUTER-BASED PROBLEM

MAINTENANCE MANAGEMENT

Safeway Rentals has a fleet of 30 rental cars. It is in the process of reviewing its preventive maintenance program. The cost of performing preventive maintenance is $25 per car. The probability distribution for breakdown after a preventive maintenance is given in the following table.

The average cost of repair in case of a breakdown is $250. Analyze the data and determine whether it is economical to continue the preventive maintenance program. If so, what should be the frequency of preventive maintenance?

MONTH	P_i	MONTH	P_i
1	0.02	7	0.15
2	0.04	8	0.20
3	0.05	9	0.15
4	0.10	10	0.05
5	0.10	11	0.03
6	0.10	12	0.01

BIBLIOGRAPHY

Dowst, Somerby. "MRO and JIT: How the Pros Pull Them Together." *Purchasing 100,* no. 10 (May 22, 1986): 62–68.

Hall, David. "Failure Prediction Is Essential Key to Increased Uptime, Spares Control." *Pulp and Paper 61,* no. 9 (September 1987): 111–114.

Hall, Robert W. "Total Productive Maintenance—Essential to Maintain Progress." *Target 3,* no. 3 (Fall 1987): 4–11.

Hora, Michael E. "The Unglamorous Game of Managing Maintenance." *Business Horizons 30,* no. 3 (May–June 1987): 67–75.

Katzel, Jeanine. "Maintenance Management Software." *Plant Engineering 41,* no. 12 (June 18, 1987): 124–170.

Mann, Lawrence, Jr. *Maintenance Management.* Rev. ed. Lexington, Mass.: Lexington Books, 1983.

Mobley, R. Keith. *An Introduction to Predictive Maintenance.* New York: Van Nostrand Reinhold, 1990.

Nolden, Carol. "Predictive Maintenance: Route to Zero Unplanned Downtime." *Plant Engineering 41,* no. 4 (February 1987): 38–43.

———. "Plant Maintenance Costs: How Do They Measure Up?" *Plant Engineering 41,* no. 14 (July 23, 1987): 38–42.

Peele, Timothy T., and Robert L. Chapman. "Designing a Maintenance Training Program . . . that Gets the Job Done and Saves Money." *Plant Engineering 41,* no. 15 (August 13, 1987): 52–55.

Tomlingson, Paul D. "Organizing for Productive Maintenance." *Production Engineering 34,* no. 10 (October 1987): 38–40.

Tonkin, Lea A. P. "Total Productive Maintenance: Fixing Problems before Fate Happens." *Target* (January–February 1995): 46–47.

THE NATURE AND SCHEDULING OF SERVICES

CHAPTER 17

This book provides three chapters that primarily discuss issues and challenges involved in scheduling the use of resources to serve customer needs. Each of these chapters focuses on scheduling in a particular setting. The three settings of manufacturing (presented in Chapter 15), services (discussed in this chapter), and projects (discussed in the next chapter) are useful divisions that provide insight into the origin, objectives, and techniques often used in scheduling. Keep in mind, however, that a particular concept or technique often is not limited to the setting in which it is introduced. For example, the Gantt chart introduced with the discussion of manufacturing in Chapter 15, can also be applied in services and in projects. The concepts of project management and network scheduling methods that are introduced in the next chapter can be employed in managing projects in services and in manufacturing.

It was pointed out in Chapter 15 that excessive queues or WIP (work in process) can form in manufacturing and cause several undesirable effects. Chapter 16 reviewed some of the ways that manufacturing organizations try to prevent delays and manage bottlenecks that can cause these queues, or pockets of inventory. Recall that some service applications of JIT concepts were presented in that discussion. Services are in some ways a further extension of the idea of operating with reduced inventory. Businesses cannot store in inventory the service component of the value they provide so that it will be available quickly when demand occurs. Since service is the major output of a service business, they cannot advantageously use inventory of their output in this way. Customers often are present during the service-delivery process, so one might think of customers that are being served as work in process. A company does not want undesirable delays or inefficiencies in the flow of work that would cause customer delays, or excessive WIP, and directly impair customer satisfaction. Of course, there are exceptions to this analogy. Patients in a hospital should not be rushed to leave the facility too soon. Hotels and motels also like to have high occupancies. The point is that it is desirable to have customers feel they are served expeditiously.

This chapter discusses scheduling so that a satisfactory flow of work can be provided in services. Before moving to the details of scheduling services, however, we will overview the general nature of services and why scheduling in this setting often differs from scheduling in a manufacturing setting.

WHAT'S DIFFERENT ABOUT SERVICES?

Basically, a service is an intangible analysis or action performed for someone, as opposed to a tangible object, such as a manufactured product. Figure 17.1 illustrates a source of some differences between services and manufacturing and the ways they are managed. Generally, there is a more direct link between the employees' work and the customer of a service. The manager of a service business plans and directs employee actions that directly serve the customer. A manufacturing manager plans and directs employee actions to produce a product that serves customers' needs. The existence of the intermediate product between the employees' efforts and the consumer enables manufacturing operations to be managed differently from services.

Four general differences between services and manufacturing were discussed in Chapter 1, and they are reviewed here:

1. The intangible nature of services makes it difficult to measure the output of a service business as explicitly as manufactured output can be measured.

2. The quality of services is more difficult to specify and measure objectively.

3. Contact between a customer and a service provider is more likely, and often the customer is a participant in the service process.

4. Services cannot be stored ahead of time for later consumption, even though facilitating goods, such as repair parts, can be stored.

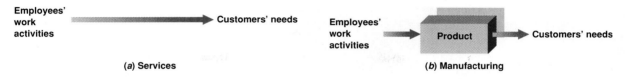

Figure 17.1
Relationship Between
Employees' Work and
Customers

These four general differences between services and manufacturing, and possibly several others, affect the way services must be managed. The following briefly outlines some ways in which these differences affect the development and operation of a service delivery system.

DEFINITION OF THE CUSTOMER AND THE SERVICE PRODUCT

To determine the appropriate features of a service delivery system, a business must decide what service will be provided, where, and to whom. Thus the design of the service delivery system and the way it is operated are determined by the initial strategic phase of market definition. In this phase a service company identifies a target market (a set of people with a given set of demographic characteristics) and identifies a set of needs among those people which the company will seek to satisfy. The company wants to find a market niche and position itself with distinguishing features that will appeal to this group. One factor that may complicate the process is that in some cases the consumers of a service are not the ones who make the decision to purchase it. Radio and television stations, for example, design program material to appeal to listeners who are their "consumers." Yet the stations' revenues come from other paying clients—advertisers or sponsors. As a similar example with a more physical consumer benefit, consider the French service company of Jean-Claude Decaux. This company erects and maintains bus stop shelters at no charge to the bus companies or the users. It gains its revenues by leasing advertising space on the shelters. This might be considered an advertising company with a very utilitarian form of outdoor billboard. Our discussion illustrates that determining the market for a service sometimes is not so straightforward as finding the needs of the persons who must pay the bills.

HOW THE SCHEDULING OF SERVICES CAN HELP ADD VALUE FOR CUSTOMERS

Services cannot use inventory of their output so they have to balance the cost of extra capacity against the delays in customer service caused by lack of reserve capacity. Success in leveling the demand enables the provision of better service without the cost of larger amounts of capacity. Costs sometimes can be reduced by separating the back office operations so they can be run more efficiently. Quality can be improved by assigning employees with good "people skills" to front office operations. Service can be provided with fewer delays or with less cost for capacity if random variations in the customer arrival patterns or service times can be reduced.

United Parcel Service (UPS) has long been interested in providing quality service. It's just that it wasn't until recently that it understood that speedy delivery wasn't customers' first priority. UPS drivers are often the only personal contact customers have with the company, and customers want drivers to have the time to answer questions and provide shipping information. Time is now built into each driver's day to allow for conversations with customers.

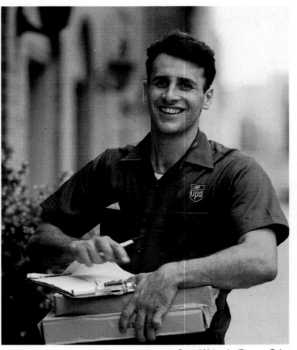

Steve Weinrebe/Picture Cube

The Product, or Service Package

After a target market is defined, the second step is to define the "product"—a *service concept* or *service package*—that the customer is to receive. What do customers want from the business, and how does the business see that it is provided? The business must identify what the consumer will experience at all stages of the service encounter. Since a service is primarily an intangible act rather than a physical object, it is difficult for a service business to demonstrate its product before the sale, as many manufactured products can be demonstrated. The consumer cannot be so sure, before the fact, of the quality he or she will receive. A potential customer may seek recommendations from satisfied or dissatisfied customers. Customers often must judge quality during a service or after it is provided. Judgments of quality may be based on a set of implicit psychological benefits as well as the more explicit physical benefits that the customer may receive. A client of an exercise program, for example, may receive feelings of pride, confidence, and well-being, in addition to the physical changes in muscle tone, body dimensions, and percentage of body fat. Hotel and motel customers seek more than just a room in which to spend the night. They expect efforts to ensure privacy, comfort, cleanliness, courtesy, and security from fire, burglary, or disturbances.

The design of the package of services a customer receives should address every aspect of the customer's service encounter. This means the service company should take every opportunity to demonstrate its commitment to and skill at providing high-quality service. For example, consider a fine restaurant. The service encounter includes the telephone call by the customer to make reservations. The call should be pleasant and should verify all the pertinent facts such as the name, number of persons, date, time, and so forth, so that there is no chance of error. The actions of the parking attendant, host or hostess, coat check attendant, waiter or waitress, and any other persons involved should be pleasant and efficient. Naturally, the art of food preparation is important, and all the details of preparing fine meals must be recognized. Even the details of washing silverware, dishes, and so on, and the care of the linens are important. The appearance of the building, the grounds, the rest rooms, and the parking facility all enter into the customer's perception of the service encounter. Once all of the elements of a high-quality service encounter have been identified, the staff should be instructed in the parts they play in providing a high-quality service encounter. Training helps ensure that all participants have the appropriate knowledge and skills. Continual efforts must be made to ensure that the organization consistently performs up to the standards.

In defining a service package a company can often benefit from customer input. Airline customers naturally expect more than just the right to occupy an assigned seat on a particular flight. They want and expect a pleasant travel experience. But a company has to be more specific about its customer's expectations if it is to meet those expectations through its employees. British Airways conducted market research to determine what factors people consider most important in their flying experiences and how the airline compared to others with regard to these measures. Four factors stood out above the rest as critically important. First, customers expect that employees are genuinely interested in them and will show care and concern. Second, employees should have the skills and knowledge necessary to provide the services and solve problems. Third, customers expected spontaneity (the frontline people have authority to solve problems that do not fit standard procedures, that is, they are not bound by bureaucracy when they need to act). The fourth factor is called recovery (someone will go out of his or her way to make amends to the customer when something goes wrong).

Airline passengers certainly cannot control the system once they agree to travel with an airline. Many are not familiar with airplanes, airports, and schedules—particularly when something changes from the usual. These factors suggest that passengers expect airline employees to look out for the customers' interests and keep them from being victims of the system. There are often numerous subtle ways that service providers affect customers and therefore numerous opportunities to show exceptional service.

Since services embody so many implicit benefits, it is difficult to know how much service has been provided and to judge the quality of those efforts. An objective in operating the service delivery system is to maximize the perceived benefits to the consumer in relation to the cost of providing the service. Achievement of this objective will gain the maximum customer satisfaction and the maximum strategic advantage.

Marketing and Operations Overlap

The challenges we have discussed probably seem to relate as much to marketing efforts as to operations, if not more. This is precisely the point, and it is a very important point: These matters are the concern of both marketing and operations, and they cannot be totally separated. There may be a great deal of overlap among functions in many business matters. The marketing and operations elements of the service delivery system overlap to a great extent in service businesses. In some service businesses the marketing function is organizationally part of the operations division.

Since services cannot be stored, they often are produced while the customer is present. That is, the services are delivered as they are produced. In essence, the manager of such a business is simultaneously managing the marketing channel (channel of distribution) and the production system that produces the service. Having recognized that it also has an important impact on marketing success, let us focus on the service delivery system.

DEFINING THE SERVICE DELIVERY SYSTEM

After a service package has been specified for a target market, a company can more fully determine and define the requirements of a service delivery system. It is beyond the scope of this book to describe the specific characteristics of each type of service business. The general characteristics and requirements of service businesses, however, can be categorized according to several schemes.

A Service Characteristics Matrix

We use a 2-by-2 matrix to delineate some of the characteristics and requirements of different service delivery systems. This matrix divides services into four groups or quadrants, with the complexity of the service as one dimension and the degree of service customization as the other. Figure 17.2 shows a matrix of this type with several services listed in each of the four quadrants. The complexity of the service represents the degree of knowledge and skill or capital investment that the service provider must possess in relation to the amount that the typical consumer might have. The consumer might be able to do an acceptable job of providing many of the services on the right side of the matrix, but would require some practice and would be slow. Many of the less complex services on the right side of the matrix are primarily conveniences that save consumers time and effort.

Figure 17.2
Matrix of Service
Characteristics

Complexity of Service Provided

	High	Low
Custom	**I** Physician Attorney Dentist Optometrist Auto repair Appliance repair Air charter	**II** Beauty and hair care Lawn care House painting Wallpapering Moving company Restaurant Taxi
Standard	**III** Radio and television Movie Zoo Museum Long-distance call School Routine auto tune-up Symphony orchestra Airline	**IV** Trash collection Fast food Car wash Car rental Dry cleaning Storage Retail Bus

Degree of Customization

Services on the left side of the matrix require a great deal more training and/or capital investment to perform because the services are more complex to perform and require knowledge or equipment that cannot be readily obtained by the typical consumer. Services in the upper half of the matrix are more customized or personalized in that they are designed specifically for the individual needs of a particular consumer. The services in the lower half of the matrix are more standardized in that the same service will be received by many consumers. In fact, many of the services in quadrant III (radio, television, school, symphony orchestra, and movies) are delivered to large numbers of people simultaneously.

Since workers in many services are likely to have contact with customers, businesses in all four quadrants of the matrix select employees who are warm and courteous and have good interpersonal skills for the jobs that entail significant contact with customers. Many of the service businesses in quadrants II and IV can train their own employees in the necessary skills. Companies in quadrant IV are more likely to develop procedures and to train employees for reliable, consistent service encounters. Workers in quadrant II need to have broader skills and be more flexible in response to the directions of the consumer. The work involved in many of the services in quadrant I require extensive professional training that must be obtained outside the business. Problem-solving and advisory activities often are an important part of these services, so their employees must have good perception of conditions and good diagnostic abilities. Investment in facilities and equipment is often significant for services in quadrant III. The amount of special training for employees in these businesses may also be high, but economies of scale help reduce the cost to each consumer. These businesses must interpret the needs of people and offer the appropriate mix of services if they want to attract large numbers of customers.

Each Service Must Address Numerous Issues

Beyond the skill required to deliver the service package and the extent to which the service will be standardized, numerous factors have an effect on the delivery system's design, staffing, and operation. Seemingly countless questions must be addressed. What is the best location and exterior appearance? What is the best interior arrangement or layout? What types of procedures are required to provide the service package? Where can equipment and technology be used to greatest advantage? What are the appropriate roles of employees and of customers? How can quality be stimulated, measured, controlled, and rewarded? How much flexibility of capacity and volume is needed, and how can it best be obtained? How many skills and how much versatility are required for personalization of services? What are the overall costs and how can they be controlled? How do customers perceive the benefits, quality, cost, and responsiveness of the service package in comparison with the services provided by competitors? How can demand be managed, and how can the supply of services be controlled? The intent is not to address all these questions but to show many of the kinds of questions that businesses must address. The last two questions on how to manage demand and supply are directly related to scheduling and are addressed later in the chapter. It is significant that the question of managing demand is closely related to marketing activities, and the question of how to manage the supply (that is, capacity) of the service delivery system is more typically an operations management issue. Here we see one of the many ways that marketing and operations aspects are interrelated.

Customers come to bookstores to buy books, but the popularity of coffee bars in bookstores implies that intangible aspects of the book-buying process, such as relaxing in an atmosphere conducive to thinking, are important parts of the service package. This is a Barnes & Noble bookstore located in Manhattan.

Left, Bernard Boutrit/Woodfin Camp; right, Barnes & Noble

UNIQUE CHALLENGES IN MANAGING THE SERVICE DELIVERY SYSTEM

Some of the major challenges that differentiate the management of a service delivery system from management of a manufacturing operation stem from two of the general differences between services and manufacturing mentioned earlier. First, service operations generally have more direct involvement with the customer than do manufacturing operations. Second, manufacturing operations can often store their output to have it available in inventory when requested, whereas pure services generally are created as they are provided. These two differences greatly affect the ways in which service operations must operate and therefore the ways in which managers must plan and direct these operations. Let us now consider some of the implications of these two major differences.

Customer Involvement

Traditionally, one tends to think of services as being more custom-designed and involving more personal contact with the customer in order to assess his or her specific needs and desires. This *customer involvement* or *contact* has an impact on the way the service operation can be run.

LACK OF STANDARDIZATION AFFECTS EFFICIENCY Customer contact and involvement affect the degree to which service operations can be standardized and specified for efficiency. Customer involvement provides an opportunity for special requests and instructions to be issued by the customer, which tends to disrupt routine procedures and the efficiency with which services can be provided. In addition, variability in customer preferences makes it difficult to set standards for staffing and predict how much time it will take to serve a given number of customers. Sometimes the customer is in a hurry and service seems slow. At other times, the customer may have time to waste and may feel rushed by the same speed of service.

CAPACITY CAN BE LOST IN PROVIDING NONSERVICE AMENITIES Social relationships are involved so customer contact cannot be strictly limited to the time needed to deliver the actual service—if the provider is to avoid appearing abrupt or rude. Customers often expect a certain amount of conversation—to obtain information, but also to overcome loneliness or have an opportunity to share their interests and concerns. Some may want to discuss pets, grandchildren, sports, or politics and others may just want to be left alone.

PERCEPTION OF QUALITY IS SUBJECTIVE The pure service component of a service operation's output is intangible, and objective measurements of its quality are difficult to obtain. Quality is closely related to the customer's perception of satisfactory service. Customers who feel that they were not treated as important or that their requests were not adequately responded to are not likely to feel satisfied. These customers will tend to rate the service low on quality, even though they may actually have received the same amount of pure service as some other customer—or more. Thus operations employees who work in the areas where customer contact occurs must have sensitivity and customer-relations skills as well as the skills required to provide services. They must be skilled at interpreting what the customer really wants.

DEGREE OF CUSTOMER INVOLVEMENT AFFECTS EFFICIENCY Not all service businesses experience the same degree of customer involvement. Table 17.1 lists some examples of nonmanufacturing operations classified according to whether the customer has high, moderate, or low contact with the system. Also some parts of a business's operations function may experience more customer contact than others.

The degree of customer contact often makes a big difference to the way in which an operation can be run. In fact, Richard Chase contends that the degree to which an operation can achieve efficiency is directly related to the extent of customer contact. Table 17.2, which contrasts high- and low-contact operations, demonstrates the basis of that contention.

MINIMIZING THE EFFECTS OF CUSTOMER CONTACT Operations have a variety of methods to achieve efficiency and still provide the customer with good service. One way in which operations limit disruption from customer contact, such as unusual requests and changes in customer instructions, is to standardize the services they offer. A limited-menu or fast food restaurant is an example of standardization as well

Table 17.1
DEGREE OF CUSTOMER CONTACT IN VARIOUS OPERATIONS

LOW CONTACT	MODERATE CONTACT	HIGH CONTACT
Mail service	Restaurant	Counseling service
Freight truck line	Motel	Dental care
Mail-order store	Self-service gas station	Personal transportation
	Discount store	Full-service retail store

Table 17.2
MAJOR DESIGN CONSIDERATIONS IN HIGH- AND LOW-CONTACT SYSTEMS

DECISION	HIGH-CONTACT SYSTEM	LOW-CONTACT SYSTEM
Facility location	Operations must be near the customer.	Operations may be placed near supply, transportation, or labor.
Facility layout	Facility should accommodate the customer's physical and psychological needs and expectations.	Facility should enhance production.
Product design	Environment as well as the physical product define the nature of the service.	Customer is not in the service environment so the product can be defined by fewer attributes.
Process design	Stages of production have a direct immediate effect on the customer.	Customer is not involved in the majority of processing steps.
Scheduling	Customer is in the production schedule and must be accommodated.	Customer is concerned mainly with completion dates.
Production planning	Orders cannot be stored, so smoothing production flow will result in loss of business.	Both backlogging and production smoothing are possible.
Worker skills	Direct work force comprises a major part of the service product and so must be able to interact well with the public.	Direct work force need have only technical skills.
Quality control	Quality standards are often in the eye of the beholder and hence variable.	Quality standards are generally measurable and hence fixed.
Time standards	Service time depends on customer needs, and therefore time standards are inherently loose.	Work is performed on customer surrogates (for example, forms), and time standards can be tight.
Wage payment	Variable output requires time-based wage systems.	"Fixable" output permits output-based wage systems.
Capacity planning	To avoid lost sales, capacity must be set to match peak demand.	Storable output permits setting capacity at some average demand level.
Forecasting	Forecasts are short-term, time-oriented.	Forecasts are long-term, output-oriented.

Source: Richard B. Chase, "Where Does the Customer Fit in a Service Operation?" *Harvard Business Review,* November–December 1978, p. 139. Copyright © 1978 by the President and Fellows of Harvard College; all rights reserved.

as of other strategies for running a service operation efficiently that are discussed later. Some service businesses limit customer contact by automating parts of their operations, such as the use of automatic tellers at a bank. This method not only reduces labor costs but also limits the customers' options to a particular set of standard transactions.

Table 17.3
SOME OPERATIONS WITH FRONT AND BACK OFFICES

OPERATION	FRONT OFFICE	BACK OFFICE
Bank	Tellers, loan officers	Posting clerks, encoders
Stock brokerage office	Brokers	Transaction clerks, keypunch operators
Restaurant	Hostesses, waiters	Chefs, cooks, dishwashers
Library	Reference desk	Purchasing, reshelving
Auto shop	Service writers	Mechanics
Laundry	Pickup counter	Pressers, folders

A common strategy to improve the overall efficiency of an operation is to keep separate from customers those portions of the operation that do not require direct customer contact. In a hotel, for example, it is better for the cleaning staff to straighten up the guests' rooms when the guests are absent. Not only does this avoid disturbing the guests, but also the lack of contact permits the employees to clean efficiently according to a prescribed procedure, rather than acting as personal servants and following the individual instructions and preferences of the guests. There is a *front office* operation—involving such functions as the registration clerk, bell captain, and cashier—that is intended to interact with the guests and to provide a friendly personal atmosphere. Workers in the *back office* operations, such as cleaning and maintenance people, primarily take their directions from the hotel staff rather than from the guests, although they also contribute to the guests' service. There are numerous other services that have some parts of their operation separated from contact with the public so these parts can run with little direction or interruption from the customer. Table 17.3 provides further examples of some operations that have both front and back offices.

Other advantages can result from separating the front office operation from the back office. Since the front office must provide the customer interface, it needs to be located in convenient, but often more expensive, high-traffic areas. The amount of this expensive real estate that is needed can be reduced by placing all noncontact operations in less expensive areas, and sometimes these operations can be consolidated for economies of scale. Customer-contact areas need to be designed for customer appeal, and employees there need to be more oriented to good customer relations; however, facility arrangement and employees in the low-contact areas can be more oriented to efficiency. Capacity in the customer-contact area must be kept consistently high or scaled up and down in anticipation of the demand profile if customers are not to be kept waiting. Capacity in the noncontact areas can be kept at a more uniform level, even though demand may vary, and this capacity can be more fully utilized.

Separation of the back office operation from the front, coupled with modern information technology and international overnight package delivery, makes it possible to locate the back office at a considerable distance from the customer and in some instances in other countries. Offshore operations are used for such activities as data entry in processing payments on magazine subscriptions and credit cards and for preparing mass mailings. Interesting examples of a remote operation separated from its customers are provided in the following boxes.

OPERATIONS MANAGEMENT IN ACTION

INFORMATION TECHNOLOGY SUPPORTS SEPARATION OF OPERATIONS

Tata Software Consulting, headquartered in Bombay, India, develops software for an international market. Tata considers that the client understands its business, and Tata is to apply information technology to fit the client's business needs. A small portion of the staff is required to gather information on the customer's business and to define the system requirements. Software is coded in India and can be delivered on diskette or data communication links to the client's equipment. Worldwide networks are available for machine-to-machine linkages. This type of operation requires personnel with a variety of speaking and computer languages. The company also must maintain a variety of computer equipment from different manufacturers so that software can be tested as it is developed at the remote site. The method of conducting business provides a combination of a broad market base and very cost-effective operations. It is an interesting example of exporting services.

OPERATIONS MANAGEMENT IN ACTION

INFORMATION TECHNOLOGY TO THE AID OF HEALTH CARE

Health care organizations and agencies face a challenge to provide quality services at lower cost. A combination of video and communications technology has been developed to provide "telemedicine" or practicing medicine by wire. Medical images can be transmitted over wires to permit specialists at remote locations to make diagnoses or confer about treatment. This technology can allow more persons to have access to better health care and can reduce the travel time for the physician and/or the patients.

Twenty states have worked to develop more than seventy networks for the exchange of medical information. The University of California at San Francisco is linking five hospitals with fiber optics to cut interhospital delivery time from several hours to a few minutes. The information superhighway will allow telemedicine services to even more areas in the United States.

Telemedicine is also facilitating the export of more medical services. For example, a team of seventy radiologists at Massachusetts General Hospital has X-ray images wired from their telemedicine center in Riyadh, Saudi Arabia. The team can examine patients and confer about treatment needs.

Source: "The Doctor Will See You Now—Just Not in Person," *Business Week,* October 3, 1994, p. 117.

Limited Ability to Hold Services in Inventory

A second major difference that affects services, as we mentioned earlier, is the general inability to hold output in inventory. Some services can perform part of their work in anticipation of demand and, in essence, hold it. Wholesale and retail operations, for example, can perform the services of purchasing, distributing, packaging, and placing items for display before actual customer demand occurs. The transfer-of-ownership portion of their service occurs only after demand. The prior service activities the company performed can be held until the goods are sold. For many other services, the capacity to provide service is lost if it is not used. If an airplane takes off with empty seats, that capacity is lost and can never be recovered. Empty seats at one showing of a movie will not be balanced by turnaway crowds the next evening.

This perishable nature of some services makes good forecasting very important for service companies. Companies that deal in tangible items can hold inventory, such as safety stock, in case demand is greater than expected. If demand is less than expected, the items can be held a few more periods until they sell. Forecasts of the quantity and pattern of demand are important for planning service capacity. Estimates of changes in the demand pattern, even in time blocks as short as 10 minutes, may be helpful for detailed planning, such as assignment of the number of tellers in a bank or the number of employees in a restaurant.

The pattern of demand variations over a longer term can also have a significant influence on the planning of efficient service operations. Many goods-producing operations can use inventory to decouple their production activities from fluctuations in demand so that production can proceed at a more uniform and economical rate. Scheduling and coordinating problems can thus be reduced, and operating expenses can be lower than they would be if manufacturing had to respond instantly to fluctuating demand. Capital investment can be lower and capacity will be more fully utilized throughout the year if a goods producer can accumulate inventory to serve peak demand rather than being required to have sufficient capacity to produce at the peak demand rate.

Service operations are also more efficient to the extent that they can operate at a uniform level. Level operations would enable the company to serve the same amount of business annually with lower peak capacity, and the fixed capacity would be more fully utilized to spread the investment cost over more units of service. However, services rarely can achieve uniform utilization of their capacity—unless they operate *by appointment only.* When the operation cannot achieve a demand rate that matches its desired capacity level, its objective usually becomes one of developing a capacity profile that matches its demand profile, to the extent that this is feasible and economically viable. Let's now review some ways in which services attempt to develop more-uniform demand patterns and to vary their capacity so they can serve nonuniform demand patterns more efficiently.

STRATEGIES FOR INFLUENCING DEMAND PATTERNS

Sometimes, through pricing or other policies, a business can influence the times at which demand occurs or service is provided so that the effect is a somewhat more-uniform and manageable rate of service. We look at four common strategies that serve to some degree to shape the demand pattern so that capacity can be more uniformly utilized.

Maintenance of a Fixed Schedule

Some services, such as most of those in quadrant III of Figure 17.2, can fix a schedule of the times at which their services are available. Most commercial airplanes do not fly whenever the customer decides to go somewhere. Instead the customer travels at the scheduled time of flight. Fixed scheduling is involved in many commercial airline, bus, rail, and shipping operations. The time of departure and expected duration of the trip are established and publicized. Demand occurs as people purchase tickets to use some of the previously scheduled transportation capacity. More cars can be added to a train to make the capacity more flexible. Larger planes or buses may be allocated to the routes over which demand is highest.

Airlines face the problem of having their capacity already filled when a customer requests a ticket. Rather than wait for another of the airline's scheduled flights, the customer may switch to another airline.

Use of an Appointment System

Some services, many of which are in the upper half of the matrix in Figure 17.2, are provided by appointment. Dentists, for example, set appointments for routine patient care and allow some time for emergency care. The appointments smooth out the utilization of the dentist and his or her staff rather than having a waiting room full of people who arrived at a time convenient for them.

Use of an appointment system permits demand to be moved into available time. The delay between a request for an appointment and the time of the appointment may depend on the backlog or queue of waiting work. The following strategy is similar, except that no appointment is made.

Delayed Delivery

We do not need an appointment to take a watch or small appliance in for repairs and sometimes have no appointment to get an automobile repaired. The air conditioner repair technician may not get to your house for several days if you call in July, yet in October repair service may be available in a short time. The lead time between a request for service and its delivery depends on the amount of work waiting to be performed. Each request for service waits its turn through the backlog or queue of service requests. Delaying jobs until capacity becomes available serves to make the work load more uniform. Of course, even with the use of overtime or part-time employees, the demand rate may still be so great that some work must be delayed. Routine work may be set aside to make capacity available for rush jobs. This procedure is the equivalent of developing dispatching rules in a manufacturing operation.

Providing Economic Incentives for Off-Peak Demand

Some operations have a heavy capital investment in the capacity they must have to provide their services. The unit cost of capacity that is used only occasionally for peak demand periods is very high. These operations try to keep the demand as uniform as possible by use of economic inducements. Telephone companies, for example, provide discounts for long-distance calls that are made during the off-peak hours. Electric utilities may try to discourage erratic consumption with high peaks by charging rates that are based on the customer's maximum rate of use as well as on the total amount of energy that the customer consumed. But at best such strategies are only partially successful. Nonuniform demand persists.

STRATEGIES FOR COPING WITH NONUNIFORM DEMAND

Staggered Work-Shift Schedules

In spite of their attempts to promote *off-peak demand* through economic incentives, many operations still experience highly nonuniform demand patterns. Tele-

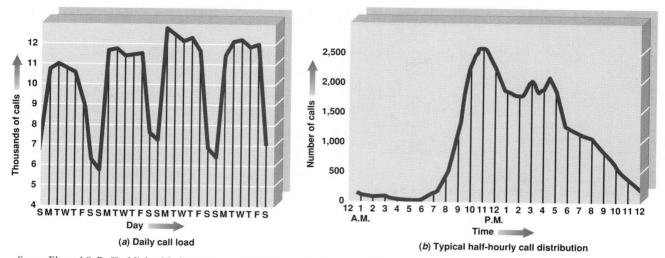

Source: Elwood S. Buffa, Michael J. Cosgrove, and Bill J. Luce, "An Integrated Workshift Scheduling System," *Decision Sciences,* October 1976, p. 622. *Decision Sciences* is published by the Decision Sciences Institute.

Figure 17.3
Distribution of Telephone Calls in Long Beach, California, January 1972

phone companies are a classic example. Most business calls are made during business hours, and many people consider it bad manners to make personal calls in the middle of the night. Consequently, the demand for telephone service is extremely nonuniform. Figure 17.3 shows how telephone calls in Long Beach, California, vary from day to day during a month and how nonuniformly the demand is distributed during a 24-hour period.

In the telephone business, price differentials are used not only to influence when calls are made but also to encourage direct dialing so that automated switching can be used almost exclusively. A certain portion of calls, however, will always be operator-assisted. The customer will be kept waiting if the operator staff is not adequate for the volume of business. Having a full-time staff sufficient to handle the peak daily demand volume would be prohibitively expensive.

Scheduling the availability of capacity to cover demand involves constructing work shifts so that the number of operators available at any time matches the demand profile. Willie Henderson and William Berry developed a heuristic method to assign work-shift times for telephone operators. The objective was to find the minimum number of operators required to meet demand that varies throughout the day. This study examined various patterns of assigning work shifts to operators so that the total worker-hours available at any time during the day was sufficient for the expected demand. They investigated the practices of varying the number of hours each employee was to work, varying the starting times of the first and second sessions, and varying the times of work breaks and the length of the idle session (often a lunch break) between the two major work sessions. The solution method involved linear programming and branch-and-bound logic.[1] Available alternatives (branches) were identified, and a reasonable solution (bound) was specified. As soon as a branch appeared to be nonoptimal, it was given no further consideration, thus saving time and computation.

[1]Willie B. Henderson and William L. Berry, "Determining Optimal Shift Schedules for Telephone Traffic Exchange Operators," *Decision Sciences,* January 1977, pp. 239–255.

OPERATIONS MANAGEMENT IN ACTION

HOW THE USPS COPES WITH NONUNIFORM DEMAND

The U.S. Postal Service (USPS), which is a gigantic materials-handling system, has a varying demand for its services. Extra demand occurs at such times as Mother's Day and Father's Day, during the Christmas season, and whenever large mailers send material through the mail.

The system has data going back many years on the volume of mail between bulk mail centers and area distribution centers, and it develops forecasts of demand in each area that are distributed to offices in the system. Whenever local variations are known, forecasts are adjusted by local offices. For example, a mail-order house might notify its local office of a large promotional mailing, or the Treasury Department might notify the office of mailings of Social Security or Veterans Administration retirement checks.

On the basis of these forecasts, the offices can assign additional equipment and have enough people on hand to handle the work.

Mail that is collected at post offices must be sent to area distribution centers, where it is sorted by zip code, packaged according to destination, and loaded on trucks that move it to its proper destination. In some instances sorting schedules have to be coordinated with airline flight schedules—and adjusted if flight schedules change.

Post offices have standards for how much mail can be processed by workers. Hand sorting can accommodate about 850 letters per hour. Mechanical sorting—having individuals key in zip code digits as pieces of mail move through small tracks—can handle about 1,800 per hour. Automatic OCR equipment can sort about 10,000 per hour. From such standards, offices can determine how many employees are needed. The offices have lists of part-time employees and relief clerks who can be called in. They can also call in regular employees who would otherwise be off-duty, or regular employees who can work overtime.

Mail is color-coded for the amount of time permitted before it must reach its destination, depending on the class of mail and the distance between its points of origin and destination. If the work load is above capacity, mail that is ahead of its required schedule is held while higher-priority mail is processed ahead of its normal delivery rate. Extra trucks are dispatched on routes when extra mail is to be moved between cities. If extra trucks are frequently used, a larger truck or an additional truck will be regularly scheduled.

Thus it can be seen that the postal system uses variable capacity in response to a forecast and the equivalent of buffer inventory to utilize its capacity efficiently and process mail on schedule.

Part-Time Staff

More flexibility to schedule and smooth the work demand is often available for those parts of a service where the customer is not present and the service is provided by working with some surrogate for the customer. For example, consider the back office operation in a bank, where the daily intake of checks drawn on other banks is encoded for processing. The customer is not present for this work, so it can be delayed or batched, but all checks that will be credited to the bank for a day must be completed by some deadline, say 10:30 P.M. The number of checks that will arrive in a day is a probabilistic variable that is forecast. If some checks are not processed because of insufficient staff, the bank will suffer an opportunity cost because it will not receive credit for the funds for an additional day. The bank will suffer another type of cost, however, if it overstaffs to ensure sufficient capacity. Often a part-time work force is scheduled to provide a capacity level that trades off these two risks and matches capacity to the distribution of forecast demand. This problem has been addressed by Vincent Mabert as an integer programming problem.[2] A later study, by Mabert and Charles Watts, used simulation (discussed in Supplement H at the end of

[2]Vincent A. Mabert, "A Case Study of Encoder Shift Scheduling under Uncertainty," *Management Science,* July 1979, pp. 623–631.

OPERATIONS MANAGEMENT IN ACTION

HOW A FAST FOOD RESTAURANT COPES WITH NONUNIFORM DEMAND

Some operations have large variations in their demand rates and cannot use inventory to smooth the work requirements. At Burger King, for example, the maximum shelf life of most of its products is 10 minutes, so this operation is extremely limited in how much production it can store in low-demand periods to sell when demand is high. A Burger King restaurant might produce 800 burgers per hour during the lunchtime rush, yet produce only 40 per hour before or after this period. In such restaurants, the design of the facility determines the peak capacity, and the store can be operated at various levels up to its peak capacity.

Customers place their orders at point-of-sale (POS) stations in the front of the store. The number of POS stations that should be open for a given level of demand is optimized by a computer simulation model. Orders are communicated to the production area by microphone or, in newer stores, by CRT. The production area maintains a flow rate of standard items (burgers and fries) for the level of demand and produces special-order items. In newer stores, production flows from the back of the store, where ingredients are stored, through the cooking area, then through the sandwich dress and

assembly area, to the front of the store where the fry pots and drink stations are located. Counter personnel collect the items to complete an order and deliver them to the customer at the POS stations. The number of employees needed at each of these work areas depends on the level of business.

Labor scheduling is, needless to say, a very important factor in managing a restaurant such as a Burger King. Payroll costs are close to overtaking food costs as the largest expense item. Operating with sufficient full-time staff to meet the peak demand would be prohibitively expensive, so part-time workers are employed. Burger King headquarters in Miami has a simulation model used to determine the staffing levels and job assignments that will best achieve the established service time standards for any level of demand a store might experience. The output of the model is documented in an easy-to-read format for restaurant managers to use. Savings resulting from this labor productivity program exceed 1 percent of the company's annual sales. And 1 percent of $2.5 billion is $25 million per year!

Source: Richard D. Filley, "Putting the Fast in Fast Foods: Burger King," *Industrial Engineering*, January 1983, pp. 44–47.

this chapter) to evaluate sets of shift schedules under the probabilistic demand patterns in order to select the one that appeared to be best.[3]

Let the Customer Select a Level of Service

The U.S. Postal Service provides an interesting example of a service that has little contact with the customer but instead performs its service by working with letters and other pieces of mail sent by customers (see box on page 664). This service does not try to smooth the profile of demand with which items are mailed. It does, however, offer incentives for flexibility that the customer permits in delivery time. Express mail or special delivery requires a premium fee; first-class mail takes priority over less-expensive classes of mail, which permits more flexibility about when they must be delivered.

Auxiliary Capacity or Subcontractors

The use of part-time employees is a common means of adjusting capacity to a higher-than-normal demand rate, particularly if the equivalent to inventory cannot be used. Consider the example of Burger King, presented in the above box. Also

[3]Vincent A. Mabert and Charles A. Watts, "A Simulation Analysis of Tour-Shift Construction Procedures," *Management Science*, May 1982, pp. 520–532.

notice that there is a front office for customer contact and a back office that is set up for efficiency. The back office area has a production line or flow line for production of standard components. Standard items are produced at a flow rate. The standard components are assembled in a versatile assemble-to-order area. Notice also that computer simulation (discussed in Supplement H) is used to analyze decisions about staffing levels and scheduling.

The facility capacity in a restaurant must be adequate for the number of customers who dine inside. But a drive-through service operation makes it possible to increase the volume of business to levels well above a given seating capacity. Services that can use on-call or part-time equipment as well as part-time workers are also less restricted by their facilities. A freight line, for example, can contract with independent truck owner-operators to move freight for it. A freight line's terminal may own a fleet of trucks to move some of the loads it ships. Beyond these, the dispatcher at each freight terminal keeps a list of trucks in the area that are waiting for a load to move and can call one when a load has to be moved. If there are not enough trucks on the list at a terminal and if that terminal is part of a large truck line, the terminal dispatcher will call the central dispatcher of the truck line to determine if any equipment is in the area or bound into the area that can haul the load. If this does not locate sufficient equipment, the local dispatcher may call local truck stops to find an available truck and driver that can be contracted. Independent owner-operators are looking for loads, and freight companies are looking for trucks. In some instances brokers match shippers in an area with truckers who are looking for a load to haul and charge a fee for this service. Such a means of expanding capacity is equivalent to subcontracting work in a manufacturing operation.

Multiskilled Floating Staff

Some services have a maximum capacity that is fixed by the facility, but they can still use part-time employees to scale up or down as some capacity changes appear to be in order. Also, as in the case of a hospital, it might be desirable to have some *floating capacity* that can be shifted from one department to another if the number of patients or the amount of nursing attention required in each department varies.

The scheduling of the nursing staff in a hospital involves assignment of nurses to shifts in various wards. There is considerable variation in the requirements for direct nursing care even though the census in a ward may remain fairly stable. The nursing care requirement depends on the proportion of patients who are designated as total-care, partial-care, or self-care patients. Nursing requirements in one ward are statistically independent of the requirements in other wards, so this type of demand can be served by a stable staff of nurses plus a *floating staff*. The floating staff is moved to the wards that have a high percentage of total-care patients (see box on page 667).

Customer Self-Service

One means of adjusting capacity to meet demand is to have the customer provide his or her own service. With this option, the service capacity arrives when the demand does. We are familiar with pump-your-own gasoline sales and self-service car washes. Customers at supermarkets and many department stores select most of their own merchandise. A wide variety of food service establishments permit customers to make their own salads, desserts, sandwiches, and so forth. Do-it-yourself picture framing and automatic teller machines are other examples of self-service as means of adjusting the capacity of the service delivery system to meet the level of demand.

OPERATIONS MANAGEMENT IN ACTION

HOW HARPER-GRACE HOSPITALS COPE WITH NONUNIFORM DEMAND

Harper-Grace Hospitals in Detroit (over 1,400 beds and 5,000 employees) have developed an effective and logical approach to scheduling nurses to the various work areas in the hospitals. Near the end of each shift, designated nurses evaluate the patients in each area according to the patients' requirements for nursing care, that is, the "care level." Care levels range from minimal care to intensive care. Management engineers and nurses have developed standards for the amount of work required to respond adequately to each care level. The care requirements for each area in the hospitals are added, and allowances are made for new admissions, discharges, and returns from surgery. About an hour before each shift begins, a scheduler (usually the shift supervisor) can determine how many nurses are required in each area and can then make appropriate assignments. This approach prevents the overassignment of nurses to an area—resulting in nurses distributing linens just to have something to do—or underassignment—resulting in nurses being overworked and frustrated because they cannot render the level of care they feel they should.

As outcomes of this scheduling approach, the hospital reported cost savings, an increase in quality of care for the patients, and improved job satisfaction for the nurses.

Source: Richard D. Filley, "Cost-Effective Patient Care: Harper-Grace Hospitals," *Industrial Engineering,* January 1983, pp. 48–52.

A Production-Line Equivalent

In a restaurant or a hospital, the customer is present and in most cases is aware of the work that is done in his or her behalf and whether the service is prompt. Some of the other services we have discussed, however, work with a surrogate for the customer. As long as the service involves working with some surrogate for the customer (that is, as long as it is a very low contact service), work on one item can be delayed

Self-serve salad bars save food service operations from complex scheduling problems at lunch time. Customers probably don't notice this. What they notice is that they can choose from a variety of fresh foods and get exactly what they want, without waiting in long lines.

B. Daemmrich/The Image Works

or moved ahead to smooth the use of capacity. The customer is not present and therefore is not offended by being ignored for a while or by having other work performed ahead of his or hers as long as the service is completed within a reasonable time. In some ways working with a surrogate is like having a buffer inventory to smooth the flow of work. This inventory equivalent can be used in the back office operations of some services, resulting in a flow that is much like that of a production line, especially if the volume is sufficient.

An example of such a situation is provided by the policy issue department of a moderate-size life insurance company. Several stages of work are involved. Some stages require manual and mental work, others require machine activities such as computer input and response. Some stages perform inspection or quality control operations, and others are equivalent to in-process inventory. Consider an insurance company that receives about 1,000 applications for insurance policies each week. Each application goes through the same steps of review and processing, so they flow along the same route. Table 17.4 describes the steps involved in processing an application, the time each application requires on average, and the number of persons employed at each stage. The equivalent of in-process inventory is held at stage 4. Inspections occur at stages 4 and 6.

The insurance example differs in some respects from an assembly line or production line. Policy applications do not move one at a time but in batches. Some may be held at one station or another, thus allowing applications to pass one another along the way. At one point the policies are held up to await a medical report, or perhaps more than one if the applicant appears to have some health problem. Each application is unique and must be "assembled" with the specific medical report for its client. A conventional manufacturing assembly line would have ordered materials ahead of time because the people who schedule the operations have specified the number of products of various types scheduled to be produced. Such planning is not possible with the processing of policy applications because at least one component (the medical examination) is made to order for each individual. The parts are not interchangeable in the processing of policies.

Table 17.4
PROCESSING STEPS FOR INSURANCE POLICY ISSUE

STAGE	NUMBER OF EMPLOYEES	PROCESSING	EXPECTED TIME PER UNIT (MINUTES)
1	2	Log in, check signatures, account for payment	4
2	1	Enter data into automated information system	2
3	2	Check previous insurance history and pull file if company has any records	4
4	2	Check application for medical examination data; hold until medical data arrive from examining physician	3
5	7	Underwriting	10–20
6	3	Check information on computer system to see that it is what underwriter has approved	5
7	2	Prepare policy by printing standard forms; attach riders and amendments	4
8	1	Prepare for mailing	1

The staffing at the stages in the policy issue department is adequate for the average level of demand. But policy applications do not flow in at a uniform rate. About half the applications arrive the first 2 days of the week and the next 2 days have low demand. The average week's work is distributed through the 5 days of the workweek at 25, 25, 15, 15, and 20 percent, respectively. This nonuniform demand is managed by flexibility in the skills and capacity of the department in addition to the ability to delay policy applications at any stage. During Mondays and Tuesdays persons normally assigned to stages 6, 7, and 8 can work parts of the day at the first few stages of the process. Thus work builds up at various stages of the system so that each employee has an adequate supply of work. The line is balanced by a temporary increase in its capacity where demand is high.

A Trade-off between Capacity and Service Delays

The degree to which demand fluctuates over time and the extent of uncertainty in demand affect how well companies can meet demand without having large amounts of standby capacity. Excess capacity results in extra costs and can affect customer satisfaction and competitiveness. However, long delays or waiting lines can occur if a company does not have enough extra capacity. Customers may refuse to wait, and business will be lost if capacity is too low. A balance between the amount of capacity and the level of demand must be maintained so that waiting is not excessive, yet capacity utilization is great enough that costs are reasonable. Waiting-line analysis or queuing theory provides some tools to explore this trade-off.

WAITING-LINE ANALYSIS

Several examples have been provided to illustrate some strategies service operations can use to try to match capacity to demand or to try to make demand more compatible with capacity. You will recognize that these strategies can also be used by many manufacturing operations. Make-to-stock companies can use finished-goods inventory in addition to these strategies. Job shops, like service operations, are limited to strategies that utilize the equivalent of in-process inventory or adjustments to demand and/or capacity. They can try to shift demand to make it more uniform, provide excess capacity, miss sales, or adjust the level of some flexible capacity to fit demand.

Not all scheduling problems can be solved by flexibility in scheduling the labor force. Some portion of capacity is "fixed capacity" provided by the facilities and equipment that are available on a permanent basis. Additions to facilities and equipment often require more lead time and are more difficult to reverse than employment agreements and assignments of working hours. Facilities impose an upper limit on capacity. The amount of capacity that should be made available depends on the expected rate of demand, its variability, and the promptness with which it is to be met.

Waiting-line or *queuing theory* is sometimes useful as a guide in determining the expected waiting time for an arriving patron and the average number of patrons who will be waiting for service. Queuing theory can provide information useful in determining the amount of capacity that is needed so that waiting times will be reasonable and the amount of space that should be provided for customers, objects, or jobs waiting for service.

The Structure of Queuing Systems

Queuing situations may occur in a variety of settings. Several examples are listed below:

Customers at the checkout counter of a grocery, discount, or department store

An accumulation of jobs to be processed at a work center

Patrons at bank teller windows

Computer jobs waiting to be run

Trucks at a loading dock

Vehicles at a highway toll booth

Cargo ships waiting for space at a pier

Airplanes circling while waiting to land

Broken machines waiting to be repaired

A list of patients the doctor is to see as he or she makes hospital rounds

Patients waiting in a dentist's office

A stack of reports and memoranda waiting to be typed

The basic structure of a simple *single-channel, single-phase* queuing system is shown at the top of Figure 17.4. Arrivals represent demand for use of the facility. They enter the system from some population of possible arrivals. If the service facility is already occupied (in use), the arrival waits in a queue until capacity in the service facility is available.

The system may contain more than one service facility that may be utilized through various flow patterns within the system. Parallel service facilities may be provided in a *multiple-channel* system so as to increase the service capacity. Servicing of arrivals may involve more than one stage of processing, so queues may form between these stages. The example at the bottom of Figure 17.4 depicts a combination of *multiple-phase* processing with a variety of sequences in which the service processing may occur. This structure resembles the flow between queues and work stations that might represent jobs in a job shop manufacturing system, design projects in an architect's office, patient flow in an outpatient clinic, or some similar situation.

In addition to a wide variety of system structures, several other parameters influence the performance of a queuing system. Some important variables are discussed below.

POPULATION SIZE The population from which arrivals come may be so small that the number of entities in the system may affect the probability of an arrival. In contrast, the population may be large enough to be assumed to be infinite.

ARRIVAL RATE The number of units arriving per time period, the *arrival rate,* may be constant or may be some deterministic or probabilistic variable. Usually arrivals occur randomly and are assumed to occur according to a Poisson or other discrete probability distribution.

QUEUE DISCIPLINE Arrivals may be selected from the queue to receive service according to one of many possible rules. Priorities may be assigned on the basis of the highest profit attainable, emergency needs, earliest due date, shortest processing

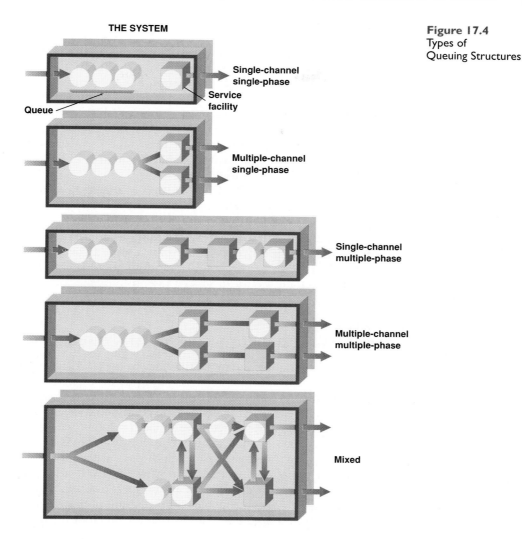

Figure 17.4
Types of
Queuing Structures

time, or some other logic. The most commonly assumed *queue discipline* and the one used in deriving basic queuing formulas is first come, first served.

BEHAVIOR OF ARRIVALS AT QUEUES In some circumstances, arrivals may balk (that is, not join the queue) if it is too long when they arrive. People may see a long line at a movie and decide to go elsewhere (balk). Or they may wait for a time, become impatient, and leave (renege). This behavior may not occur in other circumstances. Machines that break down join the queue of machines waiting to be repaired without choice.

SERVICE TIME The time required to provide service may vary considerably. Each repetition of a service may take precisely the same time as every other, as in an automatic car wash. *Service time* may be variable but predictable, or it may be random. Random service times may follow some empirical distribution or perhaps a normal, exponential, Erlang, or other theoretical distribution.

Development of Queues

A queue or waiting line forms because the short-term demand rate exceeds the short-term service rate, that is, whenever an arrival occurs and the server or servers are busy. If the interarrival times are known, it may be possible to schedule the availability of service capacity so that a queue does not form. Unless these times are constant or nearly constant, however, it may be very expensive to try to adapt capacity to them. When interarrival times are constant, queues can be prevented as long as the time between arrivals is greater than or equal to the service time. If either the interarrival times or the service times are probabilistic, an arrival may occur while the facility is occupied, causing a queue to develop.

Frequently the mean arrival rate λ (that is, the reciprocal of the mean interarrival time) is used to express the density of demand. The *service rate* μ (that is, the reciprocal of the mean service time) is used to express the system's capacity. If cars arrive at a bank's drive-in window every 5 minutes on average, then the mean arrival rate λ is 60 min/hr ÷ 5 = 12 cars per hour. If it takes an average of 3 minutes to serve a car, μ is 60 ÷ 3 = 20 cars per hour. In random queuing situations, the mean arrival rate must be less than the mean service rate, or a queue will continue to grow if the customers do not renege or balk.

Mathematical Solutions to Waiting Problems

The variety of waiting situations that may occur is so great that we cannot discuss them all here. But we consider a few situations to illustrate some formulas used in the analysis of waiting situations. It is important to recognize that the equations and figures presented below are for steady-state conditions, which assume that the distributions of arrival rates and service times remain stationary over time and that the system has operated long enough to be in equilibrium. That is, the effects of initial start-up conditions have been overcome, and the probability distributions of queue statistics have stabilized about their respective means. If λ is greater than μ, the system may never reach a steady state. In any event, the system may not remain in operation long enough to become stable. If an operation closes down for several breaks during the day, it may not be in equilibrium for much of the day. Simulation often is used to analyze situations that are not in equilibrium or that do not fit adequately the assumed condition of queuing theory. For instance, the probability distributions may not be described by standard theoretical distributions for which equations are available. Sometimes the mathematical complexity is overwhelming when the situation is very involved, as in the mixed structure in Figure 17.4.

Consider the simplest type of queue structure, with one service facility and a single queue from which arrivals are served on a first-come-first-served basis. These models are based on the assumption that arrivals are patient and will wait until service is received (no reneging). Arrivals come from an infinite population with an arrival rate described by a Poisson probability distribution. (Poisson arrival rates are associated with exponential interarrival times.) With a Poisson arrival rate, the probability of x units arriving in a given period is given by

$$P(x) = \frac{\lambda^x e^{-\lambda}}{x!} \qquad\qquad [17.1]$$

where λ is the mean rate of arrival and $e = 2.718$, the base of natural logarithms.

Other symbols we will use are given below:

μ = mean service rate (it is assumed that $\mu > \lambda$)

$\rho = \lambda/\mu$, utilization factor or traffic-intensity factor

P_n = probability that n units will be in the system (i.e., the service facility and the queue.)

L_s = mean number of units in the system

L_q = mean number of units in the queue

W_s = mean time a unit spends in the system

W_q = mean time a unit spends in the queue

The probability that the service facility will be in use is the *utilization factor* $\rho = \lambda/\mu$. The probability that no unit will be in the system is

$$P_0 = 1 - \frac{\lambda}{\mu} \tag{17.2}$$

which is the percentage of time that the facility will be idle. The probability of n units in the system is

$$P_n = \left(\frac{\lambda}{\mu}\right)^n P_0 = \left(\frac{\lambda}{\mu}\right)^n \left(1 - \frac{\lambda}{\mu}\right) \tag{17.3}$$

The mean number of units in the system is

$$L_s = \sum_0^\infty nP_n = \frac{\lambda}{\mu - \lambda} \tag{17.4}$$

The mean number of units waiting in the queue will be the mean number in the system minus the mean number being serviced:

$$L_q = L_s - \frac{\lambda}{\mu} = \frac{\lambda^2}{\mu(\mu - \lambda)} \tag{17.5}$$

The mean time each arrival spends in the system (waiting in the queue and being serviced) is

$$W_s = \frac{L_s}{\lambda} = \frac{1}{\mu - \lambda} \tag{17.6}$$

The mean time spent in only the queue W_q can be found by subtracting the mean service time from the mean time in the system:

$$W_q = W_s - \frac{1}{\mu} = \frac{\lambda}{\mu(\mu - \lambda)} \tag{17.7}$$

Equations 17.4 through 17.7 approach infinity as λ approaches μ; therefore these equations apply only if μ is greater than λ. The equations for P_0 and P_n apply only for $\mu \geq \lambda$. If arrival and service rates are random, we should not expect to get full utilization of a service facility without very long queues because λ/μ must be less than unity. Figure 17.5 shows the behavior of L_q and W_q for a system with Poisson arrival rate and Poisson service rate as the utilization factor ρ is increased toward 1. The abscissa of Figure 17.5 is expressed in terms of ρ, sometimes called the traffic factor, which is the ratio of λ to μ. This relationship makes very clear the kinds of waiting

Figure 17.5
Mean Queue Length and
Mean Waiting Time in
Queue for Poisson
Arrival Rate and Poisson
Service Rate Model

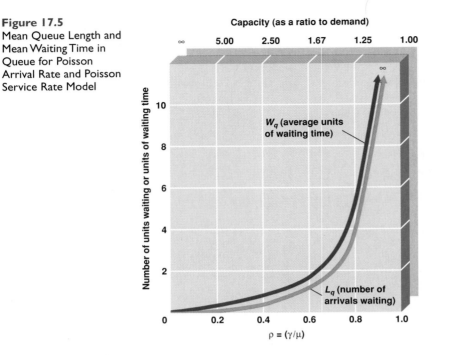

lines that can be expected given a particular level of capacity to serve a given arrival rate.

Queue statistics also can be developed for multiple-channel queuing systems. The equations for the mean wait, mean queue length, mean number of arrivals in the system, and so on, are more complicated and are not presented here. The behavior of the mean number in the system as a function of ρ is shown in Figure 17.6. The utilization factor ρ for multiple-channel systems is given by $\lambda/(s\mu)$, where s is the number of parallel channels.

Constant Service Time

When the service rate or the arrival rate is constant, the mean queue length or the mean waiting time will be reduced. For a single-channel system with Poisson arrivals and constant service time, the mean length of the queue L_{qc} and mean wait time in the queue W_{qc} are half what they are when both the arrival rate and service rate are Poisson-distributed.

$$L_{qc} = \frac{\lambda^2}{2\mu(\mu - \lambda)} \qquad \text{[17.8]}$$

$$W_{qc} = \frac{\lambda}{2\mu(\mu - \lambda)} \qquad \text{[17.9]}$$

The mean number in the system is the mean number in the queue plus the mean number in the service facility, or $L_{qc} + \lambda/\mu$. The mean wait in the system is the mean wait in the queue plus the service time, or $W_{qc} + 1/\mu$.

Figure 17.7 shows the number of units in the system as a function of ρ for both single- and multiple-channel systems when the service times are constant.

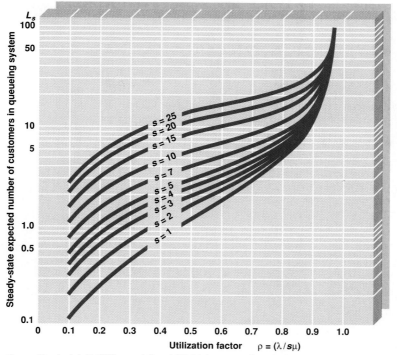

Figure 17.6
Values of L_s for Poisson Arrival Rates and Service Times

Source: Frederick S. Hiller and Gerald J. Lieberman, *Introduction to Operations Research,* 4th ed., 1986, p. 549. Reproduced with permission of McGraw-Hill, Inc.

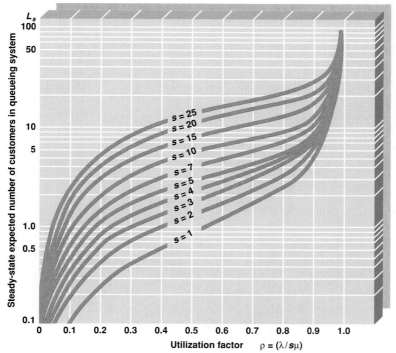

Figure 17.7
Values of L_s for Poisson Input and Constant Service Times

Source: Frederick S. Hiller and Gerald J. Lieberman, *Introduction to Operations Research,* 4th ed., 1986, p. 565. Reproduced with permission of McGraw-Hill, Inc.

· A P P L I C A T I O N ·

ANALYSIS OF A SINGLE-CHANNEL QUEUE

The Armstrong Wholesale Grocery Company owns a small distribution center in one of the cities it serves. The loading dock will accommodate only one truck to be loaded or unloaded. Company-owned trucks arrive according to a Poisson distribution with a mean rate of 3 trucks per day. At present the company employs a crew of 2 to load and unload the trucks, and the unloading rate is Poisson-distributed with a mean rate of 4 trucks per day. The company can employ additional persons in the loading crew and increase the average loading rate by 1 truck per day for each additional employee up to a maximum of 6 persons who can be utilized effectively in the process. The company estimates that the cost of an idle truck and driver is $40 per hour, and the company pays $12 per hour including fringe benefits for each employee in the loading crew.

Daniel Baker, who manages the distribution center, does not want to add any additional employees because he says the utilization of the current loading crew is very low. Actually, the utilization is

$$\rho = \frac{\lambda}{\mu} = \frac{3}{4} = 0.75$$

His quarterly bonus is based on the profit of the distribution center computed on the basis of its sales minus its costs. The truck costs and drivers are paid by the transportation center. The company's executive vice president says that the company, overall, would benefit by faster loading and unloading of trucks because the trucks spend too much time at the dock.

The mean wait in the system is

$$W_s = \frac{1}{\mu - \lambda} = \frac{1}{4 - 3} = 1 \text{ day}$$

The mean number of trucks waiting in the system is

$$L_s = \frac{\lambda}{\mu - \lambda} = \frac{3}{4 - 3} = 3 \text{ trucks}$$

The daily cost of delaying trucks plus the facility cost is:

Cost for trucks and drivers = 3 trucks × $40/hour
× 8 hours = $960

Cost for loading crew = 2 × $12/hour × 8 hours
= $ 192
$1,152

The executive vice president and his assistant prepared a table (Table 17.5) and had a meeting with the transportation manager and Dan. It was agreed at the meeting that Dan would hire 2 more employees to load and unload trucks. He could then try to reduce operating costs by finding additional duties for these people when trucks were not being loaded or unloaded, because the utilization of the crew would then be $\lambda/\mu = 3/6 = 0.5$.

Table 17.5
QUEUING ANALYSIS FOR ARMSTRONG WHOLESALE GROCERY COMPANY
(Arrival rate $\lambda = 3$ trucks per day)

(1) SIZE OF LOADING CREW	(2) MEAN LOADING RATE (μ)	(3) DAILY COST OF LOADING CREW	(4) MEAN NUMBER OF TRUCKS IN SYSTEM $L_s = \frac{\lambda}{\mu - \lambda}$	(5) DAILY COST OF IDLE TRUCKS $40(8)L_s$	(6) DAILY/COST OF IDLE TRUCKS PLUS LOADING CREW (3 + 5)
2	4	2($12/hr) (8 hrs) = $192	$\frac{3}{4-3} = 3.0$	$320 × 3 = $960	$1,152
3	5	3($12/hr) (8 hrs) = $288	$\frac{3}{5-3} = 1.5$	$320 × 1.5 = $480	$ 768
4	6	4($12/hr) (8 hrs) = $384	$\frac{3}{6-3} = 1.0$	$320 × 1 = $320	$ 704
5	7	5($12/hr) (8 hrs) = $480	$\frac{3}{7-3} = 0.75$	$320 × 0.75 = $240	$ 720
6	8	6($12/hr) (8 hrs) = $576	$\frac{3}{8-3} = 0.6$	$320 × 0.6 = $192	$ 768

Assume that a friend of yours is planning to construct an automatic car wash at a location he has selected. The traffic count and market study indicate that a mean arrival rate of 6 cars per hour can be expected. Assume that arrivals will be Poisson-distributed. Your friend can buy either of 2 automatic washers, one with a constant service time of 5 minutes (12 washes per hour) and a more expensive one with a constant service time of 4 minutes (15 washes per hour). He has established a criterion that the mean waiting time to get into the wash area should not be more than 2 minutes and will buy the slower machine if it meets this criterion. Which should he buy?

For the slower washer, the mean waiting time in the queue will be

$$W_{qc} = \frac{\lambda}{2\mu(\mu - \lambda)} = \frac{6}{2(12)(12 - 6)} = \frac{6}{24(6)} = 0.0417$$

0.0417 hour (60 minutes/hour) = 2.5 minutes

For the faster washer, the waiting time in the queue will be

$$W_{qc} = \frac{6}{2(15)(15 - 6)} = \frac{6}{30(9)} = 0.0222 \text{ hour}$$

0.0222 hour (60 minutes/hour) = 1.33 minutes

Therefore, your friend should buy the faster washing equipment.

Truncated Queues

The length of a queue may be limited by some factor such as the space allowed for waiting or the impatience of the customers after the queue has reached a certain length. When the queue is not allowed to reach its normal maximum length at times, the average queue length and average wait will be reduced. The utilization of the facility will therefore be less than what it would otherwise have been because some arrivals will be turned away.

Let N be the maximum number allowed in the system. Then[4]

$$P_0 = \frac{1 - \rho}{1 - \rho^{N+1}} \text{ for } \lambda \neq \mu \qquad \text{[17.10]}$$

and

$$P_n = P_0 \left(\frac{\lambda}{\mu} \right)^n \qquad \text{[17.11]}$$

The probability that the system will be full and business will be lost because of lack of capacity is P_N, and λP_N is the number of persons turned away per unit of time over which λ and μ are measured.[5] These calculations could be used to compute the expected cost of business lost because of a *truncated queue* owing to insufficient capacity or impatient customers.

By now it should be apparent that queuing theory is a complex subject. Formulas are available for solution of problems when the arrival patterns and service times follow certain theoretical distributions. Further, these formulas apply only in steady-state conditions, so that there are many queue situations that have no mathematical solu-

---

[4]Frank S. Budnick, Richard Mojena, and Thomas E. Vollman, *Principles of Operations Research for Management* (Homewood, Ill.: Irwin, 1977), p. 471.
[5]Ibid., p. 447.

THE EFFECT OF A TRUNCATED QUEUE

Sally Cook owns several Star Cook sandwich shops in the concourses of a large international airport. Sandwiches are prepared to order in a small kitchen behind the counter. The mean service rate for preparing and wrapping sandwiches and collecting money is 1 customer per minute. The distributions for the service and interarrival times are negative exponential. Customers arrive at an average rate of 0.75 per minute, or 45 per hour. Sally has noticed that the number of persons in the system almost never exceeds 4. Apparently travelers at the airport feel that their schedules will not permit their waiting through a longer line for a snack. Those with more time evidently go to a full-service restaurant farther down the concourse.

Sally thinks it will be more profitable to prepare sandwiches ahead of time and maintain a small inventory on the counter so that customers can select items and pay the cashier. Some customers will still ask for special combinations of ingredients, but this prewrapped service method should accommodate most orders and increase the mean service rate to 2 per minute.

If the capacity—that is, the mean service rate—remains at 1 per minute, then from equations 17.10 and 17.11

$$P_0 = \frac{1 - \lambda/\mu}{1 - (\lambda/\mu)^{N+1}} = \frac{1 - (0.75/1)}{1 - (0.75/1)^5} = \frac{0.250}{0.7627} = 0.328$$

$$P_4 = P_0 \left(\frac{\lambda}{\mu}\right)^4 = 0.328(0.75)^4 = 0.328(0.316) = 0.104$$

Sally will miss about 10.4 percent of the potential customers. With $\lambda = 45$ customers per hour and each customer spending an average of $3, she is missing $3(0.104)(45) = \$14.04$ each hour.

If the service rate is increased to 2 customers per minute and customers accept the prewrapped sandwiches and continue to arrive at the previous rate, then

$$P_0 = \frac{1 - (0.75/2)}{1 - (0.75/2)^5} = \frac{0.625}{0.9926} = 0.630$$

$$P_4 = 0.630 \left(\frac{0.75}{2}\right)^4 = 0.630(0.0198) = 0.0125$$

With the increased service rate, Sally would lose only 1.25 percent of her potential business because of balking customers. The loss would be reduced to $3(0.0125) \times 45$ customers per hour = \$1.69 per hour. This change should increase revenue by $\$14.04 - \$1.69$, or \$12.35 per hour. Sally is implementing the new service method in two of her shops.

tions. Consequently, simulation is sometimes used to solve queue problems as well as other types of problems. Simulation is discussed in Supplement H at the end of this chapter. We continue our discussion of scheduling nonfactory operations in Chapter 18, which deals with project scheduling.

SUMMARY

When service operations attempt to schedule for efficient utilization of resources, they face some challenges that do not confront the typical manufacturing operations. Service operations often have more contact with customers than do manufacturing operations, and most service operations cannot hold their output in inventory as many manufacturing operations can.

Customer contact tends to reduce the degree to which a service operation can standardize its service. When customers are present, they can issue special requests and directions while the service is being provided. Some productive capacity can be lost in trying to foster good customer relations. Services can improve the efficiency of their operations by reducing customer contact or by offering only a limited set of choices for the customer. Some services separate their front offices, where customer contact occurs, from their back office operations, where efficiency can be emphasized. When the service is performed on some surrogate for the customer (the equivalent of in-process inventory), jobs can be delayed, batched, or resequenced to achieve better use of resources.

Most service operations, however, cannot hold a ready supply of their "product." These operations have to deal with nonuniform demand in ways that often are different from those available to manufacturers. One strategy of some service companies is to try to smooth the demand pattern so it will be more uniform. They may maintain a fixed schedule (as do airlines or bus lines); they may work on an appointment basis (as do dentists), so that capacity is used when it becomes available; or they may offer economic incentives to try to shift some demand to nonpeak periods (as do telephone companies).

Operations that cannot use inventory and cannot shift demand to fit their capacity may try to vary their capacity so that it more closely conforms to demand. Some services use part-time employees; others maintain a group of versatile employees who serve as floating staff to be moved to the departments where demand is heavy. Some operations subcontract work to persons or companies who furnish personnel and equipment for short-term use. A further option is to provide an alternative form of service, such as drive-through or carry-out service at a fast food restaurant.

Random arrival patterns and random service times make it almost impossible to schedule so that service capacity is fully utilized without having long waiting lines at times. Waiting-line or queuing theory can be used to analyze some capacity options. Formulas provide estimates of the probability that a specified number of units will be waiting for service. These equations can be used under the appropriate conditions to determine how much service capacity and how much waiting space will probably be needed.

KEY TERMS

Service concept	Floating capacity or floating staff	Multiple phase
Service package	Waiting-line or queuing theory	Arrival rate
Customer involvement or contact	Single channel	Queue discipline
Front office	Single phase	Service time
Back office	Multiple channel	Service rate
By appointment only		Utilization factor
Off-peak demand		Truncated queue

DEMONSTRATION PROBLEM

Problem
A hospital's emergency room has one physician on duty full time. Emergency patients arrive according to a Poisson distribution with a mean rate of 2.4 per hour. The physician can provide emergency treatment until another physician arrives for approximately 3.0 patients per hour. The distribution of the physician's time per case is approximately a negative exponential.

(a) On average, how much of the physician's time is utilized in providing emergency care?

(b) How long, on average, would an emergency patient wait for the physician?

(c) If the hospital increased the emergency room staff by one more physician per shift (a two-channel system), what would be the physicians' utilization in delivery of emergency care?

(d) With two physicians available, how long will the average patient wait for a physician? (Begin with L_s from Figure 17.6.)

(e) How long, on average, would a patient wait to see the physician in a system for which the physician and assistants represent a single-channel queue with a mean service rate of 6 patients per hour and the mean arrival rate remains 2.4 per hour?

(f) Since the mean arrival and service rates in part *d* are the same as those used in part *e*, why is the mean wait in part *d* shorter than the mean wait in part *e*?

Solution

$\lambda = 2.4$; $\mu = 3$.

(a) $\rho = 2.4/3 = 0.80$, so the physician should be utilized 80 percent of the time.

(b) The mean wait before seeing the physician would be

$$W_q = \frac{\lambda}{\mu(\mu - \lambda)} = \frac{2.4}{3(3 - 2.4)} = \frac{2.4}{1.8} = 1.333 \text{ hours or 80 minutes}$$

(c) $\rho = 2.4/2(3) = 0.40$, or 40 percent utilization.

(d) L_s (read from graph in Figure 17.6) is 0.95.

$$L_q = L_s - \frac{\lambda}{\mu} = 0.95 - 0.8 = 0.15$$

$$W_q = \frac{L_q}{\lambda} = \frac{0.15}{2.4} = 0.0625 \text{ hour, or 3.75 minutes}$$

(e) W_q (single-channel) $= \frac{\lambda}{\mu(\mu - \lambda)} = \frac{2.4}{6(6 - 2.4)} = 0.111 \text{ hour} = 6.67 \text{ minutes}$

(f) Even though the mean service rate is the same in both cases, the two-channel system can treat 2 patients simultaneously, so that in many cases no queue will form. This system will have a shorter queue when one does form. Notice, however, that the mean service time is 20 minutes for the two-channel system and only 10 minutes for the single-channel system. Thus, patients in the two-channel system will begin being treated earlier, but will complete their treatment later, on average, than patients in the single-channel system.

DISCUSSION QUESTIONS

1. What are two major ways in which service operations differ from manufacturing operations which make a difference in the way services can be scheduled to try to achieve good utilization of their resources?

2. How can some service operations try to shape demand to fit their capacity more closely?

3. How can some service operations try to tailor their capacity to conform more closely to a nonuniform demand pattern?

4. How can service operations utilize the equivalent of in-process inventory even though they cannot maintain an inventory of finished services?

5. Why might a versatile work force be desirable, even though such employees must be paid more than persons who are not so versatile?

6. Why are waiting lines or queues often desirable to some degree?

7. Briefly describe some examples of queuing situations.

8. How does waiting-line theory relate to capacity decisions? How can the theory of multi-channel queues be related to capacity decisions? How might truncated queues be related to a capacity decision?

PROBLEMS

1. Vehicles arrive at Speedy Oil and Lube, a single-channel service facility, at a mean rate of 5.62 per hour. The service takes an average of 7.2 minutes per vehicle with the current equipment, staffing level, and operating procedures. The interarrival times and service times are distributed according to a negative exponential distribution.
   a. What is the utilization of the facility?
   b. What is the average length of the line waiting to get into the service area?
   c. What is the probability that more than 2 vehicles will be in the system?

2. The owner of Speedy Oil and Lube does not have room to expand the facility to more than one channel, but he can purchase a vacuum evacuator to drain oil and other equipment that will reduce the mean service time to 6 minutes. Make the same computations as in problem 1 to see if this new equipment will significantly change the system's performance.

3. The owner of Speedy Oil and Lube thinks that the mean service time with the new equipment can be reduced to 5 minutes by relocating equipment and supplies and training the staff in simplified, standardized procedures. Using this service time, recompute the values you found in problems 1 and 2, and then compare the results.

4. A small branch bank has a single drive-in window. The customer arrival rate is Poisson-distributed with a mean of 14 customers per hour. Service times are exponentially distributed with a mean of 3 minutes per customer.
   a. Compute the utilization of the window and the teller who services it.
   b. How long does the average customer who uses the window spend waiting and being served?
   c. What is the average number of vehicles in the line (including the one being served)?

5. a. With regard to the drive-in window in problem 4, what is the probability of more than 5 vehicles in the system?
   b. If teller operations were improved so that they required an average of 2.8 minutes per customer, what would be the probability of more than 5 vehicles in the system?

6. Assume that the bank in problem 4 has room in its drive for only 5 cars (including the one being served) and that arrivals who appear will not wait if the drive is full.
   a. Find P_0.
   b. Compare this with P_0 computed above for the situation in which there is sufficient room that no customers are turned away.
   c. Compute the probability that the queue will be full.
   d. How many customers per hour will be turned away from the drive-in window?

7. The Armstrong Wholesale Grocery Company, discussed in the chapter as an application of a single-channel queue, is considering the option of adding a second loading dock. The arrival rate for trucks is 3 per hour, and the service rate for a dock will be 4 per hour. Both the arrival rate and the service rate follow Poisson distributions. The

cost of an idle truck is $40 per hour. The labor cost to run the second dock is $12 per hour for each employee, and 2 employees will be required. Compare the costs of labor and idle trucks for a single dock with the costs if 2 docks are operated.

8. Sea Lanes Shipping Services Ltd. operates docks at Tocopilla, Chile, and provides ships to transport ore for the San Carlos Copper Mine nearby. Currently, only 1 dock is used for loading ore ships. Ore transport ships that are to be loaded arrive at the port at an average rate of 5.0 ships per week (7 days). The loading time per ship is distributed according to a negative exponential distribution with a mean of 1 day per ship.

   a. What is the mean number of ships waiting to be loaded?
   b. What is the mean time a ship spends in the system?
   c. If the cost of an idle day for each ship is $4,500 and the cost of providing ore-loading docks is $900 per day for each dock, how many docks, if any, should the company add? (Use Figure 17.6.)

9. The mines discussed in problem 8 have steadily gained sales in several countries and are shipping a larger volume of ore. Sea Lanes Shipping Services Ltd. has started using larger ships that require 1.25 days to load, but the average rate at which these ships arrive at the dock remains at 5.0 ships per week. The cost per idle day for these ships is $5,500 and the cost to operate each dock remains at $900 per day. Determine the number of docks the company should operate in order to minimize the sum of the ship delay and dock operating expenses. (Use Figure 17.6.)

10. Users of a photocopy machine in a local office arrive according to a Poisson distribution and wait until they obtain the copies they desire. The mean arrival rate is 10 users per hour. The service times are exponentially distributed, with a mean service rate of 16 users per hour.

    a. What is the utilization of the equipment?
    b. Find the expected number of users in the line.
    c. Find the expected number of users in the system.
    d. What is the cost per 8-hour day for detaining persons to use the copier if the average user's time is estimated to be worth $11 per hour?

11. How much expense for employees' time would be saved by the company in problem 10 if the copy machine were replaced by a faster one that provided a mean service rate of 22 per hour?

12. On the basis of a traffic count, it is estimated that the number of vehicles using an automatic car wash at a particular location will average 11 per hour. A Poisson distribution is assumed. The owner of the property is considering construction of a car wash and is considering two types of equipment. The first type of equipment is a spray wand that the customer holds and directs while standing outside the vehicle. The service rate for this type of equipment is distributed according to a Poisson distribution with a mean rate of 12 cars per hour for each stall. The second type of equipment is automatically controlled, with a series of spray nozzles that revolve around the car while the driver remains inside. The service rate for this equipment is constant, with a capacity of 12 cars per hour for each stall. The potential car wash owner feels that with an arrival rate of 11 and a service rate of 12, there will be an average of about 1 car in the system even if the capacity is large enough that customers will not have to wait in a queue.

    a. If manually controlled equipment is selected, what is the minimum number of stalls that should be constructed to achieve about 1 car in the system under steady-state conditions?
    b. If the automatic equipment is selected, what is the minimum number of stalls that should be built to achieve about 1 car in the system under steady-state conditions?
    c. What other factors do you think should be considered in the equipment selection decision?

BIBLIOGRAPHY

Albrecht, Karl, and Ron Zemke. *Service America: Doing Business in the New Economy.* Homewood, Ill.: Dow Jones-Irwin, 1985.

Bowen, David E., Richard B. Chase, Thomas G. Cummings, and Associates. *Service Management Effectiveness: Balancing Strategy, Organization and Human Resources, Operations, and Marketing.* San Francisco: Jossey-Bass, 1990.

Chase, Richard B. "Where Does the Customer Fit in a Service Operation?" *Harvard Business Review,* November–December 1978, pp. 137–142.

Collier, David A. *Service Management: Operating Decisions.* Englewood Cliffs, N.J.: Prentice-Hall, 1987.

Czepiel, J., M. Solomon, and Carol Suprenant. *The Service Encounter.* Lexington, Mass.: D. C. Heath, 1984.

Desatnick, Robert L. *Managing to Keep the Customer: How to Achieve and Maintain Superior Customer Service throughout the Organization.* San Francisco: Jossey-Bass, 1988.

Firnstahl, Timothy W. "My Employees Are My Service Guarantee." *Harvard Business Review,* July–August 1989, pp. 28–31, 34.

Fitzsimmons, James A., and Mona Fitzsimmons. *Service Management for Competitive Advantage.* New York: McGraw-Hill, 1994.

Fromm, Bill, and Len Schlesinger. *The Real Heroes of Business: And Not a CEO among Them.* New York: Currency Doubleday, 1993.

Heskett, James L. *Managing in the Service Economy.* Boston: Harvard Business School Press, 1986.

————, **W. Earl Sasser, Jr., and Christopher W. L. Hart.** *Service Breakthroughs. Changing the Rules of the Game.* New York: Free Press, 1990.

Horne, David A., John P. McDonald, and David L. Williams. "Consumer Perceptions of Service Dimensions: Implications for Marketing Strategy." In *Creativity in Services Marketing: What's New, What Works, and What's Developing,* pp. 35–39. Chicago: American Marketing Association, 1986.

Huete, Louis M. "A Matrix for Linking Service Contents with Delivery Options." In *Proceedings of the 1987 Annual Meeting,* pp. 903–905. Atlanta: Decisions Sciences Institute, 1987.

Mabert, Vincent A., and Michael J. Showalter. *Cases in Operations Management.* Plano, Tex.: Business Publications, 1984.

————, **and Charles A. Watts.** "A Simulation Analysis of Tour-Shift Construction Procedures." *Management Science,* May 1982, pp. 520–532.

Sasser, W. Earl, R. Paul Olsen, and D. Daryl Wycoff. *Management of Service Organizations—Text, Cases, and Readings.* Boston: Allyn and Bacon, 1978.

Schmenner, Roger W. "How Can Service Businesses Survive and Prosper?" *Sloan Management Review 27,* no. 3 (Spring 1986): 21–32.

Voss, C., C. Armstead, B. Johnston, and B. Morris. *Operations Management in Service Industries and the Public Sector.* Chichester, England: Wiley, 1985.

Zeithaml, Valarie A., A. Parasuraman, and Leonard L. Berry. *Delivering Quality Service: Balancing Customer Perceptions and Expectations.* New York: Free Press, 1990.

SIMULATION

imulation is more than a single technique because a broad variety of models and techniques can be employed in simulation studies. It is an approach to problem solving. *Simulation* is the process of experimentation with a model of some real system or situation in order to gain understanding of or solve a problem in the real world. Expressed another way, simulation is a means of gaining artificial experience through the use of a model that gives the appearance or effect of reality. The model is used to generate synthetic data that depict the real system's performance. The model is advanced through time to see what can be expected to occur in the real system under the conditions set for the simulated trial. A simulation model is usually applied to evaluate alternative actions and determine which action probably would be most effective in the real situation.

Because many aspects of the real world might be studied and a model can be anything that is used to represent some part of reality, the potential types and applications of simulation are almost endless. The phenomenon of interest can be a continuous variable, such as the path of a missile in flight, or it can be discrete, such as the number of patrons seated in a fast food restaurant. A simulation model might be physical, as when real water is made to flow through a small-scale replica of a geographical area to study flood control problems, or the model might be a set of mathematical equations that describe the behavior of some characteristics of the real system as a function of the conditions that might occur. Simple simulations can be performed manually, but most utilize a computer. If analog computers are used, certain voltages or amperages in the computer can be used to represent the values of continuous variables in the real system. Usually digital computers are used, and the values of real variables are stored as numerical data. Since the types of simulations that seem most useful in operations management and that are most frequently discussed in the operations management literature are discrete simulations performed on digital computers, the simulations illustrated in this supplement use digital values for the variables.

ADVANTAGES OF SIMULATION

Simulation can be used for seemingly intractable problems, ones that are too difficult or complex to solve mathematically. Analytical solutions to some issues may not be achievable. Analytical models of the system may not be available, or the model may be so complex as to defy attempts to arrive at the optimal solution. Trial-and-error simulations may, however, lead to a near-optimal solution.

Simulation can be a valuable training tool. Through it we can gain a better understanding of the system's performance than we could achieve by merely solving an equation for the optimal value. An optimization formula may apply only under *steady-state conditions,* but because the actual environment for a system may vary over time, it is often the *non-steady-state conditions* that bear investigating. A bank, for example, might have very high customer arrival rates at certain periods of the day, such as lunchtime and just before closing time, which would increase the need for tellers at the counter during these parts of the day.

Simulation permits study of a system under controlled conditions. A model is not subject to the *Hawthorne effect,* whereby people's behavior is modified because they are being studied. The investigator can select the variables to be changed and the extent to which they are changed. Results can be obtained for various combinations of internal operation policies and environmental conditions that might not occur in the real environment within a reasonable time. Simulation can then project conditions that might occur in the future so that a company can prepare for them.

Simulation may be less expensive and involve less risk to people, property, or a business than actual experimentation. It is often less expensive to change a replica than to change some aspects of the real world. If some alternative led to failure or serious damage to the real system, it would be expensive or even impossible to restore the original conditions so that another alternative could be tried. If actual customers or employees are lost, they may never return to give you a second chance.

Simulation can expand or compress time to provide a more-detailed review of certain events. Data from several years' performance can be simulated, and the effects of alternatives can be compared without the delay and the distortions that can occur when one relies on people's long-term memory to recall what outcome resulted from a particular set of conditions. Simulation has also been successfully used to slow down chemical or physical phenomena that occur in only a fraction of a second, so that more details can be observed.

LIMITATIONS AND CAUTIONS

A simulation model is a formalized set of assumptions about how the real system behaves. To be workable, the model must give a sufficiently reliable picture of the system that it is assumed to represent. There are obvious dangers in using decisions based on faulty assumptions—whether those assumptions

are a simulation model, intuitive mental impressions, or a mathematical optimization model. Simulation models can hide many critical assumptions. It is advisable to document assumptions so that persons who are familiar with the real system can evaluate the *face validity* of the model—that is, the appropriateness of the assumptions and the logic of the model.

Simulation does not optimize; it just shows that what the model says would result if a certain alternative were tried under a particular set of conditions. Simulation studies do not guarantee that the best solution will be found. Even with an accurate or valid model there is a danger that the investigator will not try the alternatives that would provide the greatest benefit.

Even if simulation did lead to the best alternative, there might be times when the benefit-cost ratio of a simulation study would make simulation inadvisable. Simulation studies can be very expensive. Development and analysis of a simulation study may require extensive field research, which is time-consuming and expensive. Ideally, there should be a reasonable assurance that the potential benefits of a study will justify the expense, and sufficient funds should be available to conduct a proper study before a simulation study is initiated.

METHODOLOGY FOR SIMULATION

A simulation study involves several stages of activities. The stages that are most likely to occur are shown schematically in Figure H.1 and are discussed in the following material. Some stages may be repeated if subsequent stages reveal the need for further consideration in a prior stage.

1. Define the Problem

If you know what you are looking for, you are more likely to find it. The objectives of the study should be defined.

2. Analyze Costs and Benefits

Since a simulation study can be very expensive, it is advisable to review the probable costs and possible benefits of such a study before proceeding too far. Some solution method other than simulation might be quicker or less expensive to use. The remaining steps should be taken if a simulation study is found to be desirable.

Figure H.1 Likely Activities in Simulation

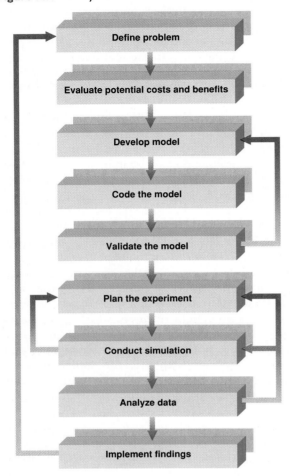

Define problem

Evaluate potential costs and benefits

Develop model

Code the model

Validate the model

Plan the experiment

Conduct simulation

Analyze data

Implement findings

3. Abstract the Real System into a Model

Define the boundaries of the system to be modeled. The system will contain certain *entities,* or components, which are objects of interest in the system. A customer who enters a bank might be an entity.

Each entity can have *attributes,* which are properties of the entity. An attribute of a bank customer might be the type of business he or she will transact. The types of *activities* that occur in the system (such as a customer making a bank deposit) should be defined. The activities can cause some change in the state of the system and can affect several interrelated components.

In the development of a simulation model, symbols or objects are chosen to represent the relevant components of the system, and interactions between

components are expressed in some logical, perhaps mathematical, form. The result should be a reasonably close representation of the real system, yet be simple enough to understand and manipulate. Only in this way can the state of the real system be predicted under dynamic conditions. A conflict arises because of the opposing desires to simplify the model yet achieve a good approximation of the real system.

Several approximations can be used to simplify the model. Sometimes two or more components can be combined to reduce the number of components in the system. The mathematical relationships between components can be approximated by less complex functions. For example, within the range over which the variable will be studied, a linear function might be used as a reasonable approximation of the actual relationship, which is mathematically more complex. Sometimes deterministic relationships are used to simplify *stochastic parts of a model* (parts with values that experience random variation). The model builder must determine where simplifications can be made without losing important details in the real system.

4. Code the Model

For computer simulation, the model must be expressed in language that is acceptable to the computer. Several higher-order simulation languages, such as GPSS, DYNAMO, and SIMSCRIPT, have been developed for this purpose. Use of a special language can save time, and programs in these languages are more flexible. Simulation languages also provide a standardized terminology for conceptualizing and communicating about systems. The advantage of flexibility provided by a general simulation language may, however, make the computer run time more expensive.

Interactive simulation packages, designed for simulation of manufacturing applications, are available to simplify this step. Several packages of this sort are for microcomputers, and they can significantly reduce the cost of many simulation studies. Such packages are discussed later in the supplement.

5. Validate the Model

Unless the model gives results that are adequate approximations of what would occur in the real system, simulation can lead to the wrong answers. *Validation* is achieving a sufficient level of confidence that the model does provide an adequate representation of reality.

There is no single test to prove that a model is 100 percent valid. Face validity can be established by asking people who are familiar with the real system to evaluate the assumptions and results of the model. *Statistical comparisons* of the outputs of the model and the real system under identical inputs can also be made to test the model's accuracy. Goodness-of-fit tests, such as the chi-square or the Kolmogorov-Smirnov test, can be used to compare a distribution of values from the simulation to one from the actual system.

6. Plan the Experiment

The objective of an investigation is usually to learn something about the performance of the real system. Good experimental design should provide a strategy for gathering evidence that will allow inferences to be drawn about the behavior of certain variables. Experiments can provide a measure of the variability of the process to guide decisions about sample sizes and replications required to achieve the desired confidence intervals. Studies often involve sensitivity analysis in which certain parameters are systematically varied over a range of values to determine the extent to which these changes affect the response. The ideal is to obtain the desired information with no more experimentation than is necessary.

7. Conduct the Study and Collect Data

The types of data to be collected depend on the objectives of the study and the types of analyses to be conducted. During the experimental design phase, the investigators must decide what data should be collected and how much detail is needed. It could be expensive to repeat part of the simulation runs because insufficient data were kept. The model should be programmed so that it collects and summarizes the data needed to analyze the experiment. The model is then stepped through time with parameters set at the desired values, and data are recorded. Parameters may be varied one at a time or in various combinations to gain data from the model. Good experimental design may permit the effect of individual parameters to be determined even though two or more are changed at the same time.

8. Analyze Data and Draw Conclusions

The design of an experiment and the type of analyses that will be performed are related. One should design the experiment with analysis in mind. Tests of statistical significance and confidence intervals can sometimes be constructed to draw inferences from the simulation data. It is advisable to recognize the variability of results that can occur even under conditions that are more closely controlled than the real system can be controlled.

9. Document and Implement the Findings

The value of a simulation model does not end after the first application. True validation of a model occurs over time if actual results are like those that the simulation model predicted. A model can become even more valuable after it has been validated by a comparison of its data with actual data. Models that have potential for future use should be documented to record their features, assumptions, and operating procedures so that they can be employed correctly in the future.

The real payoff from a simulation study is that it prevents errors or leads to improved actions in the real system. Although executives usually do not design and construct simulation models, those executives who will decide whether to use simulation results should be involved in the early stages when objectives are defined, and they should be kept abreast of assumptions and findings during the study. These executives are more likely to understand and have confidence in the model and consequently are more likely to use simulation data.

MONTE CARLO SIMULATION

Monte Carlo simulation involves the use of some chance process to determine the value assigned to a probabilistic variable during a run of the simulation. For example, if a book is as likely to be checked out of a library as it is to be on the shelf, one could flip a coin to determine which of these two states will be assumed to exist during a simulated call by a library patron. If the probability is 0.30 that the book is not available, then "out" could be printed on three slips of paper and "available"

AN EXAMPLE OF MONTE CARLO SIMULATION

The Mid-American Grain Company plans to locate a small depot in Iowa to receive and store the grain brought in from local farms by truck before it is shipped out by rail. To determine the capacity required in the facility and to plan how many railcars to schedule to the depot, the company must know how much grain is likely to arrive during each day of the harvest season. The company wants to simulate the distribution of grain received each day based on a discrete distribution of the number of trucks that arrive each day and a continuous probability distribution of the load in each truck. A flow diagram of the simulation model for this study is shown in Figure H.2.

The Monte Carlo technique is used to select values for the number of trucks that arrive each hour and to select the amount of grain in each truck. The probability is 0.10 that one truck will arrive, 0.60 that two trucks will arrive, and 0.30 that three trucks will arrive during an hour of a typical harvest day. These data are displayed in a less-than-cumulative probability distribution as shown in Figure H.3. The increase in height of the graph at each possible number of trucks is proportional to the probability that this particular number of trucks will arrive during the hour. A two-digit random number is selected to represent a value of the cumulative probability, and the value of the simulation variable that corresponds to this cumulative probability is assumed to have occurred. If the random number is 00 through 09, the value of *one truck* is assumed to occur during the hour to be simulated. If a random number from 10 through 69 occurs, *two trucks* are assumed; if a random number from 70 through 99 occurs, *three trucks* are assumed. This procedure causes the relative frequencies to occur randomly in the proper ratios, if the random numbers are uniformly distributed. The value of *two trucks* should occur six times as often as *one truck* and twice as often as *three trucks*. The random number 47 was generated, so it was assumed that two trucks arrived during the first hour, as shown in Figure H.3.

The next question that must be answered is: How much grain was in each truck? The quantity of grain on a truck can vary continuously between 50 and 350 bushels. A cumulative probability distribution for the amount of grain in a truck is shown in Figure H.4. Notice that the curve is steeper between 250 and 300 bushels, so truckloads in this range are more likely to occur. A first random number of 38 was generated, so it was assumed that the first truck delivered 230 bushels. A second random number of 67 was generated, so it was assumed that the second truck delivered 280 bushels of grain. Thus during the first simulated hour the depot received a total of 510 bushels of grain.

Figure H.2 Flow Diagram for Simulation of Daily Grain Accumulation

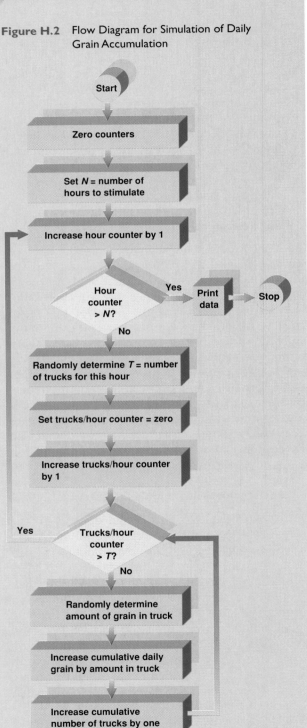

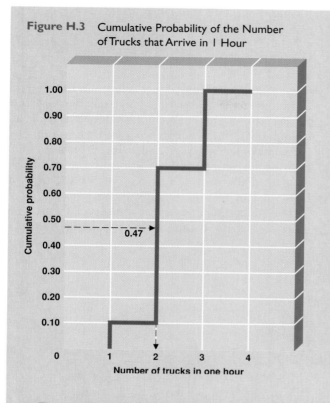

Figure H.3 Cumulative Probability of the Number of Trucks that Arrive in 1 Hour

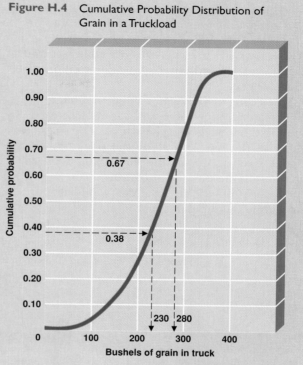

Figure H.4 Cumulative Probability Distribution of Grain in a Truckload

The process outlined in the flowchart of Figure H.2 is continued until the number of hours the depot will be operated during a day, say 10, has been simulated. This provides an estimate of the amount of grain received during 1 day. A sizable sample of 50 or more

days of operation might be simulated to produce the distribution of possible daily receipts of grain. The distribution of grain receipts per day could then be used in planning requirements for operating the depot.

printed on seven slips, and one of these slips could be randomly selected. Some other chance process such as spinning a roulette wheel or rolling dice could be used to set values for a variable. A more common method of selecting a value for a variable, particularly during computer simulation, involves the use of a random number table or a random number generator. A cumulative probability distribution is used to convert the random number to a value of the variable. The Mid-American Grain Company application illustrates the use of random numbers to determine the values of both discrete and continuous variables in a simulation.

The simulation procedure described in the application could be programmed on a computer to reduce the tedious repetition of many trials. When a computer is used, points along the cumulative distri-

bution can be stored in memory, and the computer can be programmed to generate values of the random number and translate them into values of a simulation variable. The computer could also be programmed to assist in data collection and analysis by collecting statistics from the simulation runs and carrying out various analyses. Obviously, a simulation study could require a large amount of programming time if special-purpose simulation languages such as GPSS, MAP/1, SIMSCRIPT, Q GERT, SLAM, SIMAN, and GEMS were not available.

Several new simulation packages run on microcomputers. These packages are interactive and menu-driven, so that the user does not have to write a simulation program. The packages provide the user with a graphic picture of the model as it is developed. The user selects optional blocks from the menu to represent real-world entities and positions them on the screen, using cursor keys or perhaps a mouse or touchscreen. Characteristics of the blocks are entered to describe the system to be simulated. Packages are currently available to simulate manufacturing, and other applications will probably be developed.

When the models are run, computer graphics show material movement and the state of each element in the model. The packages can be run at slow speed so the user can study the operation of the modeled system during the simulation. Some packages permit the user to stop during a run and revise the model "on the fly." Summary information on throughput, equipment utilization, WIP levels, pro-

cessing times, and so forth is accumulated during a run and is displayed after a run is completed. Packages of this general type include EXCELL, MODEL-MASTER, SIMFACTORY, WITNESS, and PC-MODEL.

GPSS (general purpose system simulator) is a commonly used simulation language that is easily applied to queuing situations. Figure H.5 is an example of a simple GPSS program used to simulate bank customers arriving and being served at a single drive-in teller window. Some of the summary data normally provided as part of a GPSS output from the run are also included in the figure.

The function statement at the top of Figure H.5 describes for the computer the probability distribu-

Figure H.5   Example of GPSS Program and Output

```
1        FUNCTION    RN1     G24
0        0           .1      .104    .2      .222
.3       .355        .4      .509    .5      .69
.6       .915        .7      1.2     .75     1.38
.8       1.6         .84     1.83    .88     2.12
.9       2.3         .92     2.52    .94     2.81
.95      2.99        .96     3.2     .97     3.5
.98      3.9         .99     4.6     .995    5.3
.998     6.2         .999    7       .9998   8
*
*        MODEL SEGMENT 1
*
1        GENERATE    400     FN1
2        QUEUE       1
3        SEIZE       1
4        DEPART      1
5        ADVANCE     300     FN1
6        RELEASE     1
7        TERMINATE
*
*        MODEL SEGMENT 2
*
8        GENERATE    48000
9        TERMINATE   1
*
```

QUEUE	MAXIMUM CONTENTS	AVERAGE CONTENTS	TOTAL ENTRIES	ZERO ENTRIES	PERCENT ZEROS
TELLQ	9	1.275	113	34	30.0

$AVERAGE TIME/TRANS = AVERAGE TIME/TRANS EXCLUDING ZERO ENTRIES

AVERAGE TIME/TRANS	$AVERAGE TIME/TRANS
541.610	774.708

FACILITY	AVERAGE UTILIZATION	NUMBER ENTRIES	AVERAGE TIME/TRAN	SEIZING TRANS. NO.
TELLER	.725	113	308.256	5

Table H.1

RESULTS OF SIMULATED TELLER QUEUES UNDER VARYING DEMAND CONDITIONS

MEAN INTERARRIVAL TIME	NO. OF TELLERS	MAXIMUM CONTENT OF ANY LINE	MEAN LENGTH OF LINES	MEMBERS SERVED (TOTAL)	MEMBERS NOT WAITING (PERCENT)	MEAN WAITING TIME FOR ALL MEMBERS (MIN)	MEAN WAITING TIME FOR THOSE WHO HAD TO WAIT (MIN)	MEAN TRANSACTION TIME (MIN)
Superlight (1.5 min)	5*	1	0.04	1,643	91.9	0.29	3.57	3.41
	4*	2	0.14	1,600	77.1	0.82	3.58	3.38
	3*	4	0.52	1,606	50.7	2.32	4.71	3.29
	2*	61	35.40	1,590	0.3	106.90	107.20	3.24
Light (0.93 min)	6*	2	0.09	2,618	85.0	0.49	3.26	3.22
	5*	5	0.29	2,565	69.0	1.33	4.30	3.28
	4	17	4.14	2,652	17.0	14.97	18.05	3.36
	3	74	43.10	. . .	2.1	112.50	114.90	3.22
Medium (0.70 min)	7*	3	0.20	3,474	76.3	0.97	4.09	3.37
	6*	5	0.54	3,498	56.4	2.22	5.09	3.31
	5	17	6.82	3,437	6.1	23.81	25.38	3.44
	4	55	27.00	. . .	2.8	72.58	74.69	3.34
Heavy (0.48 min)	9*	3	0.25	5,053	71.6	1.08	3.83	3.33
	8*	5	0.90	5,124	41.5	3.36	5.74	3.33
	7	37	22.45	5,145	1.7	73.30	74.58	3.40
Very heavy (0.34 min)	11*	3	0.67	7,141	44.9	2.48	4.51	3.34
	10	13	6.21	7,142	4.7	20.87	21.92	3.35

*Designates conditions that meet management's acceptable waiting criteria.
Source: George Overstreet, Khris McAlister, and James Dilworth, "A Study in Waiting Line Patterns," *Credit Union Executive,* Autumn 1979, p. 14. Reprinted by permission of Credit Union National Association, Inc.

tion that should be used when function 1 (that is, FN1) is called. It states that 24 points on a continuous distribution follow, and the coordinates along the curve are then shown. Nine blocks are shown in the model segment of the program.

Block 1 generates customers with interarrival times equal to 4 minutes times a random value for FN1. This simulation is conducted with time units equal to 0.01 minute, so 4 minutes appears as 400 time units. Block 2 places the customers in the queue (queue 1), where they will remain until the teller (facility 1) is available. When the teller is available, block 3 causes the teller to be occupied with a new customer and simultaneously block 4 causes this customer to depart queue 1.

Block 5 says the customer can advance after a service time equal to 3 minutes multiplied by a value randomly selected from FN1. Block 6 then releases facility 1 (the teller), and block 7 "terminates" the customer (takes the customer out of the simulation).

Segment 2 of the program tells the computer to simulate 480 minutes and terminate the simulation run. The program automatically calls for a printout of the type of data shown below the simulation model. Obviously it is much easier to write a program such as the one shown in Figure H.5 than to write one from scratch in a language such as FORTRAN.

Simulation is often used to study more-complex situations and provide data under a variety of circumstances. Consider a bank, savings and loan association, or credit union with numerous teller stations. The customer arrival rate will probably vary during the day and from day to day. Management may want to study various conditions to determine the preferred staffing levels under particular demand levels. Table H.1 provides information from such a study in a credit union. Numerous other applications of simulation studies are possible, and some are mentioned in the following section.

APPLICATIONS OF SIMULATION

Applications of simulation extend to agriculture, government, military activities, education, sports, engineering and scientific research, the social sciences, and business functions other than operations.[1] Simulation has been used in corporate planning to consider broad business issues involving all functional areas. Applications of simulation in the operations function cover a broad variety of issues in both manufacturing and nonmanufacturing settings. Several applications are mentioned below to illustrate the versatility of simulation methodology and some types of applications in which simulation might be beneficial. These applications are illustrative and only begin to show some of the uses of simulation.

Simulation is often the tool selected for the analysis of queuing situations because of the complexity of many queuing problems and because analysts frequently want data for non-steady-state conditions. A wide variety of situations can be formulated as queuing problems. Assembly-line balancing problems and conveyor system design studies can be thought of as a problem of a series of queues that feed each other. Work-in-process inventory, or backlogs, can be considered as objects waiting in queues. Simulation can be used to evaluate proposed changes in routings, equipment additions or deletions, and various scheduling or sequencing methods.

Determination of capacity, in terms of personnel and equipment, can be viewed in many situations as adjustments to service rates so that queues will probably remain within acceptable limits. Studies of materials-handling systems are quite similar, but the focus is on the volume that flows between processes and the queue capacity that must be provided at each location where movement of items may be delayed.

Simulation has been used to estimate the operating characteristics of new production technology and facility arrangements. One study examined the design of a multimillion-dollar modernization of an assembly plant by GM of Canada. The study, centered on the use of automatic guided vehicles (AGVs) in conjunction with robotics and other automation, found the expected throughput for various numbers of AGVs.[2] Other studies have investigated technology and such arrangements as manufacturing cells, flexible manufacturing systems (FMSs), flexible assembly systems, and production lines. Facility arrangements and production technology were discussed in Part II, where we dealt with the design of operations systems. The relevant point here is that simulation can be used to evaluate potential designs before the firm begins construction and purchases equipment, which is very expensive and difficult to modify.

Because job shops are so complex and challenging, much of the simulation research on manufacturing systems has involved job shop simulation. A job shop is a series of work centers with queues in front of them. The flow patterns between work centers may have dynamic variation. Simulation studies can be used to determine the proper capacity for each work center, but more often the studies seek to identify a dispatching rule that will optimize the operation according to some criterion. It is unlikely, in the author's view, that one rule will be best for all sets of problems that arise in dispatching.

Maintenance operations are often viewed as queuing problems, with the breakdown of a machine considered an arrival that waits in queue until it is repaired. The distribution of times to make repairs is considered as service times. The machine down time is studied to evaluate the effects of changes in the number of maintenance workers or in the way priorities are assigned to jobs that are waiting, or the effects of other decisions.

Many of the nonmanufacturing simulations described in the literature involve service scheduling and personnel deployment. A large percentage of these simulations are concerned with health care. Simulation has been used to predict the number of nurses needed in each type of unit within a hospital. It has been used to determine the optimal mix of an obstetrical anesthesia team and dental care delivery teams. The effects of patient scheduling procedures have been studied.

Materials handling in a hospital has been studied through simulation. One system that was studied

---

[1] See, for example, A. Thesen, H. Grant, and W. D. Kelton, eds., *1987 Winter Simulation Conference Proceedings* (San Diego: Society for Computer Simulation, 1987).

[2] James H. Bookbinder and Terrence R. Kotwa, "Modeling an AGV Automobile Body-Framing System," *Interfaces 17*, no. 6 (November–December 1987): 41–50.

consisted of a series of rectangular buggies that traveled on a conveyor to all parts of the hospital, transporting drugs, meals, linens, trash, and so on. The simulation study was done before the actual conveyor was installed to evaluate different configurations of design in order to avoid bottlenecks, delays, or shortages and to keep costs at reasonable levels.

Simulation has also been used in the study of other service problems, such as financial investments, traffic flow, telecommunications and satellite communications systems, and taxi fleets. One non-manufacturing application described a simulation of the New York Bulk Mail Center.[3] Loads of more than 150,000 sacks of bulk mail and 500,000 parcels per day were simulated. Entities included in the system were trucks, docks, parcel sorters, sack sorters, parcel conveyor containers, and sacks of mail. Three levels of volume were considered: an average level, a

Christmas-season level (about 25 percent higher than the average), and a peak-day level (about 50 percent higher than the average). The purpose of the study was to provide suggestions for the design of the actual facility and to predict how the system would perform under various loads, with and without certain equipment malfunctions. The simulation showed the percentage of time that equipment was utilized, how much overtime was required to process the specified level of mail, and what queues or delays occurred. The simulation also provided useful operational information about the probable effects of scheduling decisions and resource allocations.

Simulation is well suited to analysis of the inventory levels at various locations in a large-scale distribution system. Various stocking policies, such as the location of safety stock and the quantities to be ordered, can be simulated. The cost of transferring items between locations and other options can also be evaluated. Still more examples could be mentioned, but the ones that have already been described show the versatility of simulation.

---

[3]Orlino C. Baldonado, "Computer Simulation of Mail Flow through the New York Bulk Mail Center," in *Progress in Simulation,* vol. 3, *Record of Proceedings, 6th Annual Simulation Symposium,* Joseph G. Sowa, John A. Bolan, and Ronald Newmaster, eds. (Tampa, 1973), pp. 165–183.

SUMMARY

This supplement has provided an overview of simulation, primarily in the context of operations. Some advantages and limitations of simulation were reviewed.

A simulation study can involve at least nine stages, some of which may be repeated. These are defining the problem, justifying the cost of the study, abstracting the model, coding the model, validating the model, planning a simulation experiment, conducting the study and collecting data, analyzing the data, and documenting and implementing the study.

Monte Carlo simulation was reviewed and illustrated. The Monte Carlo technique is frequently used to generate random values of variables with the probabilities considered to exist in the real system. The technique frequently involves using a cumulative probability distribution for the variable of interest and some random number generator to select values from the distribution of possible values. Monte Carlo simulation often is very useful in analysis of operations. Several applications of simulation in manufacturing and service settings were described to show the breadth of its applicability.

KEY TERMS

Simulation	Face validity	Stochastic parts of a model
Steady-state conditions	Entities	Validation
Non-steady-state conditions	Attributes	Statistical comparisons
Hawthorne effect	Activities	Monte Carlo simulation

DISCUSSION QUESTIONS

1. Define simulation.
2. Outline the steps that might be involved in a simulation study.
3. Briefly describe five possible advantages of simulation.
4. Briefly describe four types of situations in manufacturing operations that can be studied by means of simulation.
5. Briefly describe four types of situations in nonmanufacturing operations that can be studied by means of simulation.
6. Why is there no guarantee that a simulation study will determine an optimal solution to a problem or an optimal set of conditions for the system being studied?
7. Discuss some of the trade-offs that must be considered in deciding how detailed and realistic to make a simulation model.
8. In a simulation study, how can the investigator determine when enough observations have probably been made with a particular set of values for the model's parameters?
9. Briefly describe the procedure used in Monte Carlo simulation to select simulated values of a discrete random variable with the same probabilities that were observed in the actual system.
10. Is great proficiency in computer programming necessary for the use of computer simulation? Why or why not?

PROBLEMS

1. a. Compute the expected value for the number of trucks that arrive in 1 hour at the Mid-American Grain Company presented as an application within the supplement. Use the formula

$$\mu = \Sigma[X \cdot P(X)]$$

   b. Obtain 20 two-digit random numbers by reading the first two digits in each of the first 20 rows of Appendix IV. Use Figure H.3 to convert these random numbers to 20 values of the number of trucks that arrive per hour. What is the mean of these values?
   c. By what percentage does the value in part *b* differ from the value in part *a?*
2. The time (rounded to the nearest 10 minutes) between customer arrivals at a small appliance repair center is distributed as follows:

TIME	PROBABILITY
10	0.10
20	0.15
30	0.25
40	0.20
50	0.15
60	0.10
70	0.05

   a. Calculate the mean of this distribution by

$$\mu = \Sigma[X \cdot P(X)]$$

   b. Construct a less-than-or-equal cumulative probability distribution suitable for use in Monte Carlo simulation.
   c. Make a table showing the range of two-digit random numbers that would result in the use of each of the seven time values.

3. Appendix IV contains five major columns of random numbers, each of which contains four two-digit columns. Use the first two digits on the left in the middle major column. Begin at the top of the column of random numbers, and translate them to service times by use of the probability distribution constructed in problem 2*b*. Each time an observation is obtained, compute the mean of all observations thus far. Continue taking observations until 5 consecutive values of the estimated mean remain within ±2 percent of the true mean calculated in problem 2*a*.
   a. How many random observations were required to meet this criterion?
   b. Is there a danger from reaching a conclusion regarding steady-state conditions of a system based on only a few runs of a simulation model?

4. Use values from the cumulative Poisson distribution with $\lambda = 2$ as provided in Appendix III. From these values, construct a table for use with random numbers as the technique for generating random observations. Use the first 25 three-digit random numbers found in the right-hand three digits of the middle major column in Appendix IV to obtain 25 random observations of the variable.
   a. What is the mean of these 25 observations?
   b. By what percentage does this mean differ from the $\lambda = 2$ for the original distribution?

5. Repeat the procedure for problem 4, using the last 25 three-digit random numbers in the column used for problem 4.
   a. What is the mean of these observations?
   b. By what percentage does the mean of the observations differ from $\lambda = 2$ for the original distribution?
   c. Combine the means from problem 4 and this problem to get a mean based on 50 observations. By what percentage does this mean differ from the original $\lambda = 2$?

6. a. Perform a simulation to determine the amount of grain received in an 8-hour day by the Mid-American Grain Company (presented as an application in this supplement). Use the cumulative probability distributions presented in Figures H.3 and H.4, and select consecutive two-digit random numbers starting any place you select in the random number table.
   b. Compare your results with those of your classmates, and construct a frequency distribution of the daily amounts that were obtained by the class.

7. A distribution center supplies three company outlets. The probability distributions for weekly demand at the three outlets are given below.
   a. Simulate the demand at the distribution center for each week of a 20-week period, and calculate the mean weekly demand. From Appendix IV, use the top 20 numbers in the left-hand column of two-digit random numbers for the first outlet, the column next to it for the second outlet, and so on.
   b. Construct a table showing the frequencies of different levels of total weekly demand at the distribution center.
   c. Compute the mean weekly demand at the distribution center.

WEEKLY DEMAND	PROBABILITY	WEEKLY DEMAND	PROBABILITY	WEEKLY DEMAND	PROBABILITY
Outlet 1		Outlet 2		Outlet 3	
60	0.20	90	0.15	50	0.15
70	0.40	100	0.35	60	0.35
80	0.30	110	0.30	70	0.35
90	0.10	120	0.15	80	0.15
		130	0.05		

8. **a.** Compute the mean demand at each outlet and sum them. Compare this mean to the mean obtained in problem 7.

   b. Construct a cumulative probability distribution for weekly demand at the distribution center. If the lead time to restock the distribution center is 1 week, how much stock should be on hand at the beginning of the week to provide a 90 percent service level?

9. Suppose that the lead time for the distribution center in problem 8 can be 1, 2, or 3 weeks with these probabilities:

LEAD TIME (WEEKS)	PROBABILITY
1	0.35
2	0.40
3	0.25

   a. Simulate the amount of demand that occurs at the distribution center for 20 lead times by using the weekly demand distribution constructed in problem 8 and the information above. Use the two-digit column at the left of Appendix IV, starting at the top, to generate the length of the lead time. Use the two-digit column at the right of Appendix IV to select weekly demand values from the cumulative probability distribution developed in problem 8.

   b. What amount of product should be on hand at the beginning of a lead time to provide a probability of 0.90 that stock will not run out?

10. Customers arrive at a small appliance repair shop with interarrival times given by the distribution in problem 2. A customer is there when the shop opens, and new customers are accepted for 7½ hours. The appliances are repaired while the customer waits, with a constant service time of 30 minutes. The shop will remain open until all appliances are repaired. Use the leftmost two digits in the middle major column of Appendix IV, beginning at the top of the column, to obtain the interarrival times for a day of operation.

    a. Determine the idle time and percent utilization of the service capacity.

    b. Determine the maximum length of the queue and the average time each customer spends waiting in the queue.

    c. Compute the mean time waiting in the queue for just those customers who had to wait.

11. A two-stage assembly line is balanced with the expected time at each station equal to 4 minutes. Assume that the time at each station has a probability of 0.30 that 3 minutes will be required for the operation and a 0.30 probability that 5 minutes will be required for the operation.

    a. Simulate the passage of 20 objects through these two stages of the line. Start at the top of the left major column of the random number table in Appendix IV. Use the two left-hand digits to determine the time on the first station and the two right-hand digits to determine the time at the second station. When the run is begun, there is a job at each station. The first job on the first station will become the second job on the second station.

    b. Determine the idle time and length of the queue at the second work station.

BIBLIOGRAPHY

Banks, Jerry, and John S. Carson II. *Discrete-Event System Simulation.* Englewood Cliffs, N.J.: Prentice-Hall, 1984.

Christy, David P., and Hugh J. Watson. "The Application of Simulation: A Survey of Industry Practice." *Interfaces 13,* no. 5 (October 1983): 47–52.

Henning, Kathleen. *Simulation in Manufacturing.* New York: McGraw-Hill, 1993.

Hillier, Frederick S., and Gerald J. Lieberman. *Introduction to Operations Research.* Oakland, Calif.: Holden-Day, 1986.

Law, Averill M., and W. David Kelton. *Simulation Modeling and Analysis.* 2d ed. New York: McGraw-Hill, 1991.

Lee, Sang M., Laurence J. Moore, and Bernard W. Taylor. *Management Science.* 2d ed. Dubuque, Iowa: William C. Brown, 1985.

Schelasin, Roland E. A., and John L. Mauer. "Creating Flexible Simulation Models." *IIE Solutions,* May 1995, pp. 50–55.

Schriber, Thomas J. *An Introduction to Simulation Using GPSSH.* New York: Wiley, 1991.

Thesen, Arne, Hank Grant, and W. David Kelton, eds. *1987 Winter Simulation Conference Proceedings.* San Diego: Society for Computer Simulation, 1987.

Watson, Hugh. *Computer Simulation in Business.* New York: Wiley, 1981.

SCHEDULING AND CONTROLLING PROJECTS

A *project* is an organized endeavor to accomplish a specified nonroutine or low-volume task. Although projects are not repetitive, they take significant amounts of time to complete and are large scale or complex enough to be recognized and managed as separate undertakings. Generally the amount of time that an individual or a work center is involved in a project is greater than that involved in a typical manufacturing or service assignment. An operations person may work only with other operations people on a project that pertains to operations, or the same person may work with a team of people from various functions who are assigned to study and solve a problem or to perform some other task.

Here are some examples of projects:

Selecting a software package

Developing a new office plan or layout

Implementing a new computer system

Introducing a new product

Producing an airplane, missile, or large machine

Opening a new store

Constructing a bridge, dam, highway, or building

Relocating an office or a factory

Performing major maintenance or repair

Starting up a new manufacturing or service facility

Instituting a reorganization

PROJECT MANAGEMENT

Management of a project differs in several ways from management of a typical business. The objective of a project team is to accomplish its assigned mission and disband. Few businesses aim to perform just one job and then cease to exist. Since a project is intended to have a finite life, employees are seldom hired with the intent of building a career with the project. Instead, a project team is pulled together on an ad hoc basis from among persons who normally have assignments in other parts of the organization. Persons may be assigned to work full time with the project until its completion; or they may work only part of their time, such as 2 days a week, on the project and work the rest of their time in their usual jobs or on other projects. A project may involve a short-term task that lasts only a matter of days, or it may run for years. After the project's completion, the project team members are normally assigned back to their regular jobs, to other jobs in the organization, or to other projects.

Project Life Cycle

A project passes through a life cycle that may vary with the size and complexity of the project and the style established by the organization. The titles of the various phases may differ from organization to organization, but typically a project will pass through the following phases. There is a *concept phase*, during which the organization realizes that a project may be needed or is requested to propose a plan to perform a project for some customer. There is an initial *planning* or *feasibility phase*, during which the project manager (and perhaps staff if the project is complex) plans the project to a level of detail sufficient for initial scheduling and budgeting. If the project is approved, it will enter a more-detailed planning phase, an *organization phase*, an *execution phase*, and a *termination phase*.

Sometimes a work breakdown structure is developed during the planning phase of a project. A *work breakdown structure (WBS)*, a document similar to a bill of materials, divides the total work into major work packages to be accomplished. These work packages are divided into major elements, and the major elements are further subdivided to develop a list of all work items that must be accomplished to complete the project. The WBS helps to define the work to be performed and provides a frame-

HOW PROJECT MANAGEMENT CAN HELP ADD VALUE FOR CUSTOMERS

Good scheduling and control of projects enables the projects to achieve the customer's objectives on time with efficient use of resources. Such accomplishments give more-dependable customer service and keep costs no higher than necessary. Good project management provides flexibility because it keeps track of project activities so the project team can better respond to changes in plans that may occur.

work for budgeting. It also serves as a framework by which schedule and cost performance can be compared to plans and budgets as the project advances. Table 18.1 shows an abbreviated WBS for an orbital space laboratory vehicle.

The detailed project definition, such as the WBS, is examined during the organization phase of the project to determine the skills necessary to achieve the project goals. Personnel and other resources to accomplish the project are then made available for all or a portion of the project's duration through temporary assignments from other parts of the organization or perhaps by leasing resources or subcontracting portions of the project.

Organization

A variety of organizational structures are used by enterprises to perform project work. The way in which a project is organized may depend on the proportion of the company's work that is performed by projects, the scope and duration of the project, the capabilities of the available personnel, the preferences of the decision makers, and perhaps numerous other factors. Consider the following four options, which range from no special organization to a totally separate project organization.

FUNCTIONAL ORGANIZATION Many companies are organized as a hierarchy with functional departments that specialize in a particular type of work, such as engineering and sales. These functional departments often are broken into smaller units that focus on special areas within the function. Upper management may divide a project into work tasks and assign them to the appropriate functional units. The project is then budgeted and managed through the normal management hierarchy.

Table 18.1
**WORK BREAKDOWN STRUCTURE—
ORBITING SPACE STATION PROJECT**

1.0	Command module
2.0	Laboratory module
3.0	Launch propulsion system
3.1	Fuel supply system
3.1.1	Fuel tank assembly
3.1.1.1	Fuel tank casing
3.1.1.2	Fuel tank insulation
4.0	Guidance system

PROJECT COORDINATION   A project may be handled through the organization as described above, except someone is appointed to coordinate the project. The project is still funded through the normal organization, and the functional managers retain responsibility and authority for their portion of the project work. The coordinator meets with the functional managers, provides focus and impetus for the project, and may report its status to higher management.

PROJECT MATRIX   In a *matrix organization* a project manager is responsible for completion of the project and often is assigned a budget. The project manager essentially contracts with the functional managers for completion of specified parts of the project. The functional managers assign work to employees and coordinate work within their areas. The project manager coordinates project efforts across the functional units.

PROJECT TEAM   A particularly significant project (the development of a new product, such as Chrysler's Neon, or a new venture) that will have a long duration and require the full time efforts of a group may be run by a project team. Personnel are assigned full time to the project and are physically located with other team members. The project has its own management structure and budget, as though it were a separate division of the company.

A survey indicated that its respondents, whose backgrounds were primarily in project management, felt that projects were more successful when the project managers were given strong roles, as in the latter two alternatives.[1] Companies that are frequently involved in a series of projects and occasionally shift personnel among projects often elect to use a project matrix organization, which provides the flexibility to assign employees to one or more projects. Each project is the responsibility of a project manager.

Project personnel maintain a permanent reporting relationship that connects vertically to the supervisor who directs the discipline within which they work. At the same time, each person assigned to a project has a horizontal reporting relationship to the manager of a particular project, who coordinates his or her participation in that project. Pay and career advancement within the organization are developed within a particular discipline even though a person is assigned from time to time to different projects. At times this dual reporting relationship can give rise to personnel problems. Figure 18.1 shows an organization chart for a matrix organization. Regardless of the structure, a project will usually use parts of the company's administrative support. There may be no need to duplicate existing services in procurement, legal, configuration management, personnel administration, logistics, or some other support functions. The availability of microcomputers and software for project management may make it feasible to have separate computer support for managing the project.

The Role of a Project Manager

The project manager's job is important and challenging. The manager is responsible for getting work performed but often has no direct, formal authority over most of the people who perform the work. The project manager must often rely on

---

[1]David H. Gobeli and Erik W. Larson, "Relative Effectiveness of Different Project Structures," *Project Management Journal,* June 1987, p. 84.

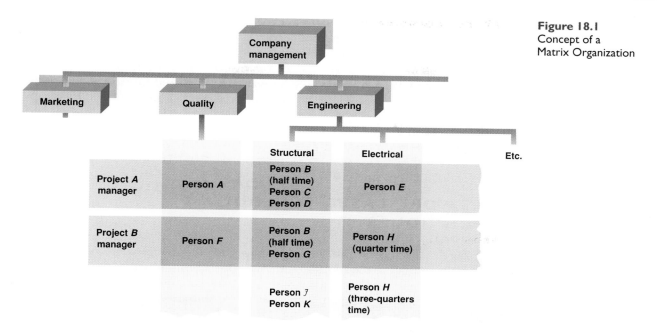

Figure 18.1
Concept of a
Matrix Organization

broader knowledge of the project and skills at negotiation and persuasion to influence participants. A project manager may have the assistance of a staff if the project is large.

The Project Management Institute identifies six basic functions that project management must address:

1. Manage the project's *scope* to define the goals and work to be done, in sufficient detail to facilitate understanding and correct performance by participants.

2. Manage the *human resources* involved in the project.

3. Manage *communications* to see that the appropriate parties are informed and have sufficient information to keep the project coordinated.

4. Manage *time* by planning and meeting a schedule.

5. Manage *quality* so that the project's results are satisfactory.

6. Manage *costs* so that the project is performed at the minimum practical cost and within budget, if possible.

Managing a project can be a complex and challenging assignment. Since projects are one-of-a-kind endeavors, there may be little in the way of experience, normal working relationships, or established procedures to guide participants. A project manager may have to coordinate many diverse efforts and activities to achieve the project goals. Persons from various disciplines and various parts of the organization who have never worked together may be assigned to the project for differing spans of time. Subcontractors who are unfamiliar with the organization may be brought in to carry out major portions of the project. The project may involve thousands of interrelated activities performed by persons employed by any one of several different subcontractors or by the sponsoring organization.

For these and other reasons, it is important that the project leaders have an effective means of identifying and communicating the planned activities and the ways in which they are to be interrelated. An effective scheduling and monitoring method is absolutely essential to management of a large project. Network scheduling methods such as PERT and CPM have proven to be highly effective and valuable tools during both the planning and the execution phases of projects. The remainder of the chapter is devoted to a discussion of network scheduling methods, in order to show the value of these methods and to provide some understanding of the unique features of project management.

NETWORK-BASED SCHEDULING TECHNIQUES

The biggest advance in project scheduling since the development of the Gantt chart in 1917 was made between 1956 and 1958. During this period, two new scheduling techniques were developed that have much in common, although they were developed independently. These techniques are the *program evaluation and review technique (PERT)* and the *critical path method (CPM)*. Both are based on the use of a network or graphical model to depict the work tasks being scheduled. Both were designed to schedule long-duration projects that were to be performed only once or in low volume. Computer programs are available for both PERT and CPM. Computers are helpful in developing timely information about large projects, particularly those that are to be updated or revised several times before completion.

CPM was developed by E. I. du Pont de Nemours & Company in conjunction with the Remington Rand Corporation. Du Pont desired a technique that would help them improve the scheduling of construction and extensive maintenance shutdowns of its production facilities. Most activities to be scheduled with this technique were similar to previously performed construction and maintenance, so the length of time the tasks were expected to require was treated as though it were a deterministic (known) number.

PERT was developed under the auspices of the U.S. Navy's Special Projects Office, working with representatives of Lockheed and Booz, Allen & Hamilton. The technique was developed to assist in managing the development of the Polaris missile-submarine system. This project required the coordination of more than 3,000 individual contractors, suppliers, and agencies—an immense management and scheduling challenge. Since many of the activities involved in this project had never been performed before, the time they might require was uncertain and consequently was treated as a probabilistic variable.

The major basic difference that remains between PERT and CPM is PERT's capability of dealing with probability estimates for activity times. CPM originally included a more-detailed analysis of time-cost trade-offs, but this function can be performed with either CPM or PERT. Other differences in network conventions and vocabulary existed in the early years, but the use of the techniques has become so broad that many of these minor distinctions have disappeared. This section outlines some advantages of network scheduling techniques and the basic steps involved in their use. Some networking fundamentals are presented, and simple examples are provided. The solutions are developed by manual calculations, but computers are often used with larger problems.

Some Advantages of Network Scheduling

Network-based scheduling techniques can be beneficial in many ways if they are properly used. Like all other scheduling techniques, however, they are not panaceas or substitutes for good management judgment. Since scheduling is an attempt to plan future work, the required work times are estimates. No scheduling technique will overcome the problems of poor time estimates for the work tasks. Scheduling can help plan work, but the accuracy of plans and schedules depends on the accuracy of the time estimates used in their development. Knowledgeable people and/or reliable techniques should be used to provide the time estimates.

Assuming that the estimates for a network scheduling method are as good as those for other scheduling methods, the network techniques may offer some advantages:

1. They lead to planning a project to the selected level of detail so that all parts of the project and their intended order of accomplishment are known.

2. They provide a fairly accurate estimate of the length of time it will take to complete the project and the activities that must be kept on time to meet the schedule.

3. They provide a graphical picture and standardized vocabulary to aid in understanding work assignments and communicating among people involved in the project.

4. They provide a means to track progress on a project (that is, show where work is with respect to the plan).

5. They identify and focus attention on potentially troublesome activities to facilitate management by exception.

6. They provide a means of estimating the time and cost impact of changes in the project plan at any stage.

STEPS IN USING NETWORK TECHNIQUES

Three major steps are involved in the use of network scheduling:

1. Plan the project.
   a. Analyze the project by determining all the individual *activities* (sometimes called tasks, jobs, or operations) that must be performed to complete it.
   b. Show the planned sequence of these activities on a *network* (a graph where arrows and circles represent the relationships among project activities).

2. Schedule the project.
   a. Estimate how long it will take to perform each activity.
   b. Perform computations to locate the critical path (the longest time chain of sequential activities, which determines the duration of the project). This step also provides other information that is useful in scheduling.
   c. Use this information to develop a more economical and efficient schedule, if one is indicated.

3. Monitor the project.
   a. Use the plan and schedule to control and monitor progress.
   b. Revise and update the schedule throughout execution of the project so that the schedule represents the current plans and status of progress.

PRECEDENCE RELATIONSHIPS

Some activities cannot be performed until other activities have been completed. This type of requirement establishes a technical *precedence relationship.* There may sometimes be options as to the way activities may be performed, but management's prerogatives or differences in costs lead to a particular planned sequence of activities. Other activities may be performed independently. Task independence and precedence relationships should be incorporated into the plan and indicated on the project network.

Network Conventions

A network is a graph using circles and arrows to represent the planned relationships among the activities required to complete a project. Either of two conventions can be used to develop a network. One uses circles to represent the project activities, with arrows linking them together to show the sequence in which they are to be performed. This is called the *activity-on-node (AON) convention,* or precedence notation. An alternative is to show the activities as arrows and use circles to connect predecessor and successor activities. This method is called the *activity-on-arrow (AOA) convention.* With this convention, the circles or nodes represent *events,* which are points in time at which activities begin or end. An event consumes no resources, whereas an activity consumes time and other resources.

A network is drawn after all activities and their relationships have been defined. There is no proven best approach to the identification of activities. Some people start with what they believe to be logically the first activity and proceed in what they believe to be chronological order; others may start with the last activity and work backward; still others list activities in random sequence. After the activities are identified, one may ask:

1. Which activity must immediately precede this one?

2. Which activity must immediately follow this one?

3. Can this activity be accomplished without dependence on some other activity?

The activity that must be performed just before a particular activity is its *predecessor activity;* the one that follows is its *successor activity.*

Methods of showing various relationships among activities are illustrated in Figure 18.2. An activity in the AOA convention is often identified by numbers indicating the starting and ending events. This identification system is called *i–j* notation (*i* represents the number of the starting event, and *j* represents the number of the ending event). This notation makes it necessary for every activity to have a unique *i–j* pair. A *dummy activity* (indicated by a dashed arrow) consumes no time or other resources but is used merely to indicate a precedence relationship. A dummy activity has been used in Figure 18.2*g* to keep activities *B* and *C* from having the same starting and ending nodes. With the activity-on-arrow convention, dummy activities also may be needed in other instances to indicate precedence relationships, as in Figure 18.2*f.* Activities in the AON convention can be identified by a single number or letter, and there is no need for dummy activities when this convention is used. Generally the AON convention is easier to learn because it consistently uses arrows only to indicate precedence. In contrast, some arrows (solid) are activities, and other arrows (dashed) indicate precedence requirements when the AOA convention is used.

**Activity-on-node convention
(precedence notation)**

**Activity-on-arrow convention
($i - j$ notation)**

Figure 18.2
AON and AOA
Methods of Indicating
Activity Relationships
on Network Diagrams

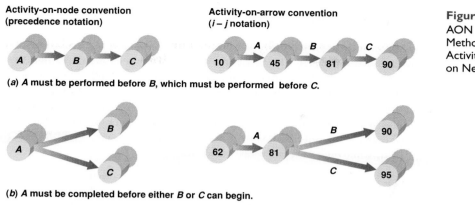

(a) *A* must be performed before *B*, which must be performed before *C*.

(b) *A* must be completed before either *B* or *C* can begin.

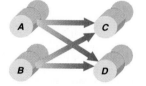
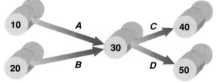

(c) Both *A* and *B* must be completed before *C* can begin.

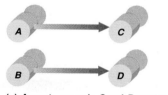
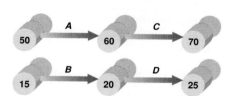

(d) Both *A* and *B* must precede both *C* and *D*.

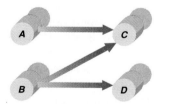
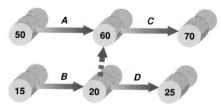

(e) *A* must precede *C* and *B* must precede *D*, but the *A–C* path is independent of the *B–D* path.

(f) *A* and *B* must precede *C* and *B* must precede *D*, but *A* is independent of *D*.

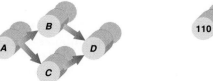
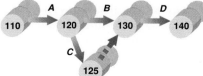

(g) *A* must precede both *B* and *C*. Both *B* and *C* must precede *D*.

SCHEDULING

The network is a graphical representation of the interrelationships among all activities in the project. Developing the network forces detailed planning of the project and provides a valuable communication tool. After the activities have been identified and the network has been drawn, the next step is to assign expected time durations to the activities. The expected duration depends on the planned crew size, work method, equipment, and working hours. A particular level of resources must be assumed to be available when the work is to be performed. Either of the following conditions may exist when the estimates are made:

1. The person who is in charge of an activity or activities assumes that some customary and reasonable level of resources will be used and specifies an expected duration for the activity. Some completion date is thus determined. This approach is in keeping with the theory of CPM.

2. In some actual applications, a completion time or milestone date is specified, and the estimated amount of resources is adjusted so that the duration will be less than or equal to the desired amount of time.

Critical Path

A path is a chain of sequential activities beginning at the project's start and ending at its completion. Several or many paths may exist through the network. Work may proceed on many independent paths concurrently, but of course work can proceed on an activity only after all the necessary predecessor activities in its path have been completed. All the activities, hence all the paths, must be completed before the project is finished. The path through the network that has the longest expected elapsed time is expected to determine the completion date of the project and is called the *critical path*. Often activities that are not on the critical path can be delayed without causing a delay in the completion of the project.

Float or Slack

The total float for an activity, usually referred to as simply *float* or *slack,* is the amount of time that the start of the activity can be delayed beyond its earliest possible starting time without delaying the project completion, if that activity and the other activities take their estimated durations. Float gives some indication of the criticalness of an activity. An activity with little float stands a good chance of delaying the project and should be carefully monitored.

Sometimes, after calculating the float for activities in a network, you will notice that several adjoining activities have the same amount of float. This float is shared by all the activities along this chain. If one of these activities is delayed, the float for other activities in the chain will be reduced by the amount of the delay.

Another type of float is sometimes calculated. *Free float* is the amount of time that an activity can be delayed without delaying the early start of a successor activity. To find free float, we subtract the early finish of an activity from the early start times for all its succeeding activities and take the smallest of these amounts. This type of float is seldom used and is not discussed further.

Float allows some flexibility in scheduling activities. An activity can be intentionally delayed if the delay will result in a more-uniform work load or provide some other advantage. Some amount of float should be retained if possible, because float is like insurance. In days of uncertain material deliveries, possible strikes, delayed drawing approvals, and so on, it is wise to have a time cushion if it can be afforded.

More than one activity may require the same resources and may be planned to occur at the same time. Networking and scheduling data provided by the scheduling method will reveal such conflicts so that readjustments can be planned. To determine the times at which various activities can occur, it is necessary to calculate the earliest date at which each activity can be performed and how much each activity can be delayed without interfering with the project's scheduled completion (i.e., its slack).

CALCULATING FLOAT OR SLACK   Total float (TF), which we refer to simply as float or slack, can be ascertained by either of the following equations:

$$TF = LS - ES \qquad\qquad [18.1]$$

or

$$TF = LF - EF$$

where ES = early start time—the earliest time an activity can be started if its predecessors take the amount of time they are expected to take
  EF = early finish time—the time an activity will be completed if it starts on its ES and takes its expected time

$$EF = ES + t \qquad\qquad [18.2]$$

where LF = late finish time—the latest date an activity can be finished without delaying the project if its successors take the expected amount of time
  LS = late start time—the latest date an activity can start without delaying the project

$$LS = LF - t \qquad\qquad [18.3]$$

where t = duration of the activity under consideration

The process of calculating ES, EF, LF, and LS requires both a forward pass and a backward pass of calculations through the network.

Forward Pass

The early start and early finish for each activity are found by calculations performed in sequence from left to right in the network. This series of calculations is called the *forward pass.* First we assign a project day, usually 0, to the start of the first activity, to represent the ES for that activity. Then we obtain the ES and EF for each activity by making a forward pass through the network, from left to right. The duration of an activity is added to its ES to obtain its EF. The ES of an activity is set equal to the EF of its predecessor if there is only one. If an activity has more than one predecessor, its ES is equal to the latest EF of its predecessors. For example, if the early start for activity M in Figure 18.3 is day 10, its early finish is day 15. If the early start for activity R is day 12, its early finish is day 18. Even though one of its predecessors (activity M) is completed on day 15, activity P cannot begin until day 18, when the latest of all its predecessors is finished. The forward pass is continued until we reach the right-hand side of the network. At this point we have the EF of the final activity, which is the earliest the project can be completed (if the activities take the time that was estimated and are performed in the sequence indicated in the network).

Figure 18.3
Portion of an Activity-
on-Node Network

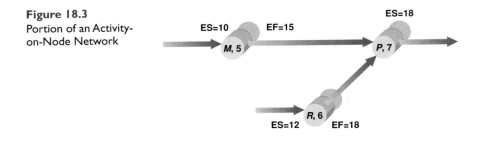

Backward Pass

The LF and LS dates are calculated by means of a *backward pass* from right to left through the network. The LF of the last activity is usually set equal to the EF of the project. Starting with the last activity, subtract the activity duration from LF to obtain LS. The LF for an activity is set equal to the LS for its successor if there is only one. It is set equal to the earliest or smallest LS of all successors if there is more than one successor.

Find efficiency

Example of Scheduling Calculations

Suppose that we are going to construct a small warehouse with an office. The structure will be used to store batteries and will have a large transformer system placed in the overhead truss or attic area of the warehouse. This equipment cannot be installed until the steel roof frame is in place but must be installed before the roof is on. The roof is to extend down over the top of the exterior masonry wall and cannot be installed until the wall is completed. Suppose, too, that the company has decided that it will not put asphalt paving around the warehouse until the fence has been erected around it and the exterior wall of the warehouse has been completed.

An AON network showing the project plan is provided in Figure 18.4. The expected time in days for each activity is shown in each node. The early start and finish times, found by working from left to right, are indicated above each activity.

The early start date for each activity is equal to the early finish of its predecessor when there is only one predecessor. Notice that activities *I*, *J*, and *M* have more than one predecessor. Such activities are called "merge activities" because paths merge at them. They cannot start until all their predecessors have been completed. According to this plan, activity *I* cannot begin until day 21, even though the fence activity (activity *D*) could be completed as early as day 6. Remember, the ES of a merge activity is the latest EF of all its predecessors.

Notice that the early finish for the total project is day 30. This time represents 30 workdays. Additions for weekends, holidays, or other nonwork days (such as days of bad weather) must be allowed to convert the workday numbers to calendar dates for the planned occurrence of the activities. Many computer programs used for PERT and CPM have provisions to convert project days to calendar dates automatically.

The backward pass through the network is based on some latest allowable finish date for the total project. If the expected completion time found in the forward pass is acceptable, the latest finish (LF) for the last activity is set equal to this early finish time. We assume that day 30 is an acceptable finish date and set the LF for activity *M* equal to 30. The estimated duration of each activity is subtracted from its late finish date to find its late start date. If the latest we can finish activity *M* is day 30 and it

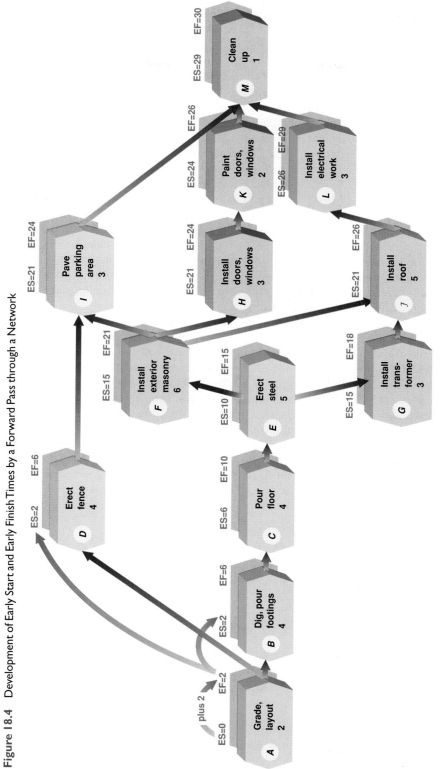

Figure 18.4 Development of Early Start and Early Finish Times by a Forward Pass through a Network

takes 1 day to perform activity *M*, then the latest we can start this activity is day 29. The predecessors for activity *M* must therefore be completed by day 29 if activity *M* is to start on day 29, so their LF is 29. The late start and late finish dates for all the activities are calculated by continuing this procedure from right to left in the network.

An activity that has more than one successor is called a "burst activity" because the network spreads in multiple directions after it. The procedure for finding the LF of a burst activity in the backward pass is the reverse of the logic used at a merge activity during the forward pass. The latest time at which a burst activity can be completed without delaying the project is the earliest of all the late starts for its successors. If the burst activity is not finished by that time, it will delay one of its successors beyond its LS. The network for the warehouse project is shown again in Figure 18.5 with the LS and LF dates indicated below each activity.

The slack or float for each activity can be calculated after the ES, EF, LS, and LF dates have been obtained. Float or slack is the amount of time that an activity can be delayed without delaying the completion of the project if all the other activities require the estimated amount of time. Float, then, is calculated by subtracting ES from LS or EF from LF. The float for each activity is shown in Table 18.2.

The path of activities from the start to the end of the network with the minimum and identical float is the critical path. This sequence of activities determines the completion date of the entire project and requires careful attention to keep the project from being completed late. The critical path is marked with red arrows in Figure 18.5. In this example all activities on the critical path have zero float. Activities on the critical path and perhaps other paths can have a negative float if the project is behind schedule. For example, if the LF for the project had been set at day 28, all activities on the critical path would have −2 for their float. This means that the early finish for each activity would be 2 days later than the time by which it must be completed to keep the project on schedule. In such a situation the duration of the critical path would have to be reduced a total of 2 days to complete the project on schedule. Also all other activities would have had 2 days' less float than was found previously. Alternatively, the critical path may have positive float if the project is ahead of schedule. But the critical path has the least float of any, hence the name *critical* path.

Table 18.2
CALCULATION OF FLOAT

ACTIVITY	LS–ES	LF–EF	FLOAT
A	0–0	2–2	0
B	2–2	6–6	0
C	6–6	10–10	0
D	22–2	26–6	20
E	10–10	15–15	0
F	15–15	21–21	0
G	18–15	21–18	3
H	24–21	27–24	3
I	26–21	29–24	5
J	21–21	26–26	0
K	27–24	29–26	3
L	26–26	29–29	0
M	29–29	30–30	0

Figure 18.5 Determination of Late Finish and Late Start Times by a Backward Pass

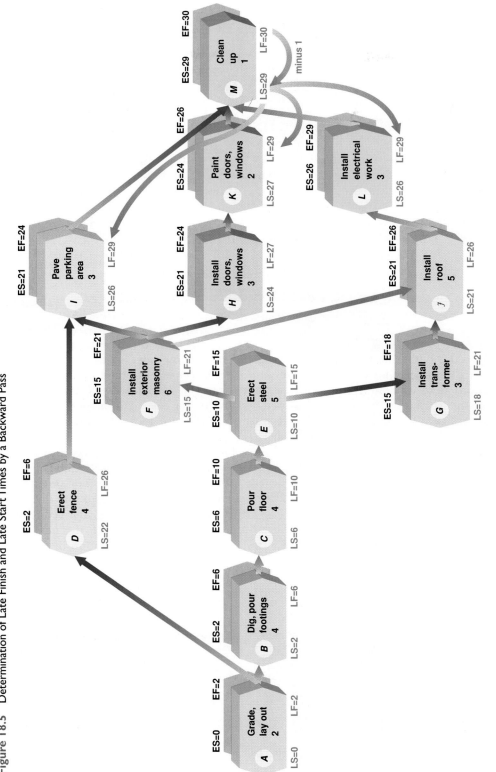

Activities that are not on the critical path usually can be delayed without delaying the project. Notice that adjacent activities along a path segment, such as activities *H* and *K,* have the same amount of float. This float is shared by all the activities between the point where the path leaves one path and the point where it joins some other path. If one activity in such a segment is delayed, it uses some of the float that is available to the other activities along the path segment.

SHIFTING AND ADJUSTING RESOURCES

Working overtime on all activities to expedite a project may involve needless expense. Expediting activities that have considerable float will not change the completion date for the project. A wiser use of resources would be to expedite only the activities on the critical path. The duration of a project can sometimes be reduced by shifting resources (people, equipment, or money) from activities that have excess float to critical activities that constrain the project's completion.

Time-Cost Trade-offs (Crashing the Project)

One feature that frequently is discussed in descriptions of CPM is an analysis of time-cost trade-offs that may reduce the total cost of a project or reduce its duration with a minimum cost increase. This analysis, sometimes called *crashing the project,* can be performed with PERT also. Time-cost trade-offs focus on the critical path because it is this path that determines the project's completion date. It was mentioned earlier that the availability of a certain amount of resources was assumed when activity durations were estimated. Additional resources may be used to reduce the duration of many activities. The relationship between the direct cost of an activity and its duration typically follows the general form shown in Figure 18.6. The direct costs will be increased if the activity is expedited.

Examination of the time-cost curves for the activities on the critical path may reveal the best combination of activities where additional resources can be applied to reduce the project's duration with the least increase in cost. The slope of each activity's cost curve may be different at the currently estimated duration of the activity. The least expensive reduction in the critical path is obtained by first reducing the activity whose cost curve has the least slope, then the activity with the next greater slope, and so on. Suppose that we want to reduce a project's duration by 3 days. We

Figure 18.6
Relationship Between
Cost and Duration of
an Activity

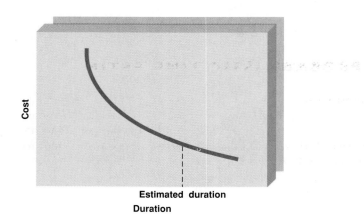

Cost

Estimated duration

Duration

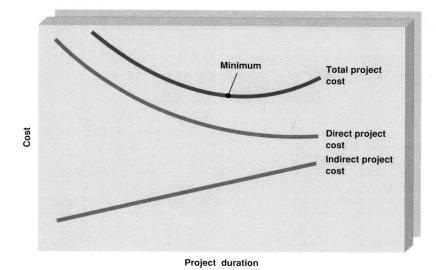

have three combinations to examine, without considering fractional day reductions of some activities:

1. Reduce one activity by 3 days.

2. Reduce one activity by 2 days and another by 1 day.

3. Reduce three activities by 1 day each.

Considerable analysis may be required to select the best combination of activities to expedite and to determine just how much each should be expedited, especially if the network contains a large number of activities. The problem becomes extremely complex when a reduction of perhaps 10, 15, or more days is desired.

It is sometimes possible to reduce the total cost of a project by reducing its duration. Overhead cost associated with the project may be a fixed amount per day. If the cost of reducing the project's duration by a day is less than the daily overhead cost, then the reduction in duration will reduce the total cost. This is not true, of course, if the overhead expenses continue after the project is terminated. This type of relationship between a project's duration and its costs is shown in Figure 18.7. Time-cost trade-offs may be of particular interest when a company has an incentive clause in its contract or a penalty clause specifying that its profit will be reduced if the project is completed later than some specified date.

PERT: USING PROBABILISTIC TIME ESTIMATES

The previous discussion of CPM has treated each estimated activity duration as though it were a deterministic quantity. PERT has the capability of treating the activity times as though they were probabilistic numbers. Hence PERT is best suited to situations in which there is a great deal of uncertainty or information is insufficient to specify the activity durations accurately. Each activity time is treated as though it were a random number that comes from a beta probability distribution. The parameters of the beta distribution can be found from three time estimates, described on page 717 and illustrated in Figure 18.8.

OPERATIONS MANAGEMENT IN ACTION

PROJECT MANAGEMENT: SANTA MONICA FREEWAY RECONSTRUCTION

As a noteworthy example of project management and incentive contracting consider the reconstruction of the Santa Monica Freeway in Los Angeles after the Northridge earthquake of January 17, 1994. The quake knocked down several bridges and overpasses and closed major highways including part of the Santa Monica Freeway section of I-10 which is considered the busiest freeway in the nation. It was estimated that Los Angeles and the surrounding communities would lose about $1 million in extra delivery and commuting time each day the freeway was closed. Design of the new overpasses was begun the day of the earthquake. The California Department of Transportation wrote a contract for the reconstruction of a half-mile section of the freeway including two overpasses. Under conventional construction procedures the work would have taken about 1 year. The contract, however, called for the work to be completed within 140 days and provided for a $200,000 per day bonus for every day the project was completed early and a $200,000 liquidated damages penalty for every day the project was late.

The contractor, C. C. Myers of Rancho Cordova, California, staffed the project with extra employees— 228 carpenters, laborers, and equipment operators where about 65 would normally have been employed and 134 ironworkers where it typically would have employed about 15. Premium rates were paid for workers and materials on the project and work was conducted 24 hours a day. Supplier support was established to deliver concrete on short notice throughout the day and night. Extra equipment was provided to the job site so there would be no delays. Inspectors and engineers were on the site or on call to ensure that quality standards were met. It was assumed that all the extra costs were less than the $200,000 bonus earned for each day saved.

The freeway was opened April 11, 1994, which was 66 days after Myers started and 74 days ahead of the contract date. The contractor earned a bonus of $14.8 million in addition to the original contract price for the work, which was only a little more than the amount of the bonus.

In January 1994, an earthquake seriously damaged the Santa Monica Freeway. Demolition of the damaged sections was the first step to rebuilding.

Richard Mackson/FPG, International

Ulf Wallin/The Image Bank

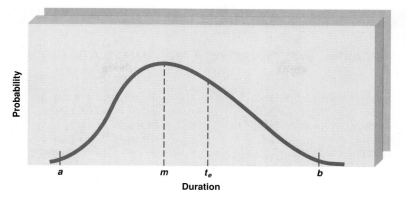

Figure 18.8
Probability Distribution
for an Activity Duration

Optimistic Time

The *optimistic time (a)* is the amount of time that an activity will take if everything goes well. The probability that the activity will take less than this amount of time is 0.01.

Pessimistic Time

The *pessimistic time (b)* is the amount of time that the activity will take if everything goes poorly. The probability that the activity will exceed this duration is 0.01.

Most Likely Time

The *most likely time (m)* is the time that the estimator thinks an activity will probably take. If the activity could be performed many times under the same conditions (no learning), this is the time that would occur most often.

The expected duration of an activity is t_e, the mean of the beta distribution that is defined by the three time estimates. The mean is found by taking a weighted average of the three estimates, using equation 18.4:

$$t_e = \frac{a + 4m + b}{6}$$ [18.4]

The standard deviation of the distribution is assumed to be one-sixth its range. The variance of distribution is given by equation 18.5:

$$\sigma^2 = \left(\frac{b - a}{6} \right)^2$$ [18.5]

After the t_e for each activity is found by equation 18.4, the critical path and slack or float can be determined by the same logic and calculations used with CPM in the previous section. That is, PERT can be performed by the use of AON (activity-on-node) notation. PERT originally used AOA notation, however, and this notation is most frequently seen in introductory discussions of PERT. The earliest an event (end of an arrow) can be reached is T_E and it is found by a forward pass. The latest allowable time an event can be reached if the project is to remain on schedule is T_L, and it is found by a backward pass through the network. For each event T_E and T_L provide the same information that was obtained with CPM.

THE USE OF AOA NOTATION AND PROBABILITY IN PERT

The Ajax Leasing Company has employed the services of Buzzwords Unlimited, a computer software company, to develop an information system to keep leasing and maintenance records on its fleet of cars and trucks. Two Ajax employees and members of the Buzzword staff have formed a project team. A PERT network (using i–j notation and activities on the arrows) for the project is shown in Figure 18.9. Notice that a dummy activity is used to indicate that module II cannot be tested until module I and the input/output program are coded. But module I and the input/output program can be tested without module II. The optimistic time, most likely time, and pessimistic time for each activity, as estimated by the members of the project team, are shown in Table 18.3. Equation 18.4 was used to calculate the expected time t_e from these time estimates; t_e is shown in the rightmost column of Table 18.3.

The network is shown again in Figure 18.10 with the t_e values indicated above each arrow. The same calculations used in the CPM example were performed during a forward pass through the network to calculate the early start and early finish times for each activity. Since a node represents both the end of one activity and the start of another, it is necessary to write the early time for the event only once. This T_E represents both the early finish time for the predecessor and the early start time for the successor at the node. The expected time required to complete the project was determined to be 32.33 weeks.

A backward pass was then performed, and the T_L for each node was determined. The slack, or float, at each node was found by $T_L - T_E$. The slack is indicated below each node of the network shown in Figure 18.10. The critical path connecting the series of nodes with zero slack was determined and is indicated by the series of color arrows through the network in Figure 18.10.

Ajax assumed that the duration of the total project would be determined by the path found to be the critical path in this initial analysis. This assumption is sometimes made if a project does not contain several paths, some of which have only small amounts of slack. The expected completion date for the critical path (that is, the project) T_E (CP) is 32.33 weeks, which represents the sum of the activity times for all activities on the critical path. The central limit theorem states that the sum (or mean) of independent random variables approaches a normal distribution as the number of random variables is increased. Since the expected duration of the critical path is the sum of several activity durations (which are random variables), the expected duration of the critical path is assumed to be normally distributed. Under the assumption that the critical path will determine the completion of the project, the probability that the project will take longer than the expected duration (that is, the mean of a normal distribution) is assumed to be 0.5. The probability that the project will take less than T_E(CP) is also 0.5.

Figure 18.9 PERT Network for Ajax Software Project

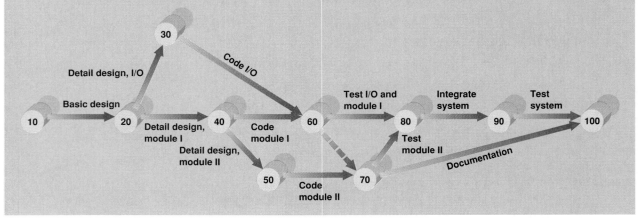

Table 18.3
CALCULATION OF t_e FOR THE ACTIVITIES IN THE AJAX PROJECT

i–j NOTATION	ACTIVITY DESCRIPTION	OPTIMISTIC TIME (WEEK *a*)	MOST LIKELY TIME (WEEK *m*)	PESSIMISTIC TIME (WEEK *b*)	$t_e = \dfrac{a + 4m + b}{6}$
10–20	Basic design	2	3	5	$^{19}\!/_6 = 3.17$
20–30	Detail design, input/output	3	4	6	$^{25}\!/_6 = 4.17$
30–60	Code I/O	6	8	11	$^{49}\!/_6 = 8.17$
20–40	Detail design, module I	5	6	9	$^{38}\!/_6 = 6.33$
40–60	Code module I	6	8	10	$^{48}\!/_6 = 8.00$
40–50	Detail design, module II	4	5	6	$^{30}\!/_6 = 5.00$
50–70	Code module II	5	6	9	$^{38}\!/_6 = 6.33$
60–80	Test I/O and module I	2	3	4	$^{18}\!/_6 = 3.00$
60–70	Dummy	0	0	0	$^{0}\!/_6 = 0.00$
70–80	Test module II	1	3	5	$^{18}\!/_6 = 3.00$
80–90	Integrate system	4	5	8	$^{32}\!/_6 = 5.33$
90–100	Test system	2	3	5	$^{19}\!/_6 = 3.17$
70–100	Documentation	5	9	11	$^{52}\!/_6 = 8.67$

The variance of the distribution of possible project durations is assumed to be the variance of the duration of the critical path. The variance of the total critical path is the sum of the variances of all the activities along its route (as long as the durations are considered independent random variables). Therefore the standard deviation for the duration of the critical path or the project is assumed to be determined by equation 18.6:

$$\sigma_{CP} = \sqrt{\sum_{i=1}^{k} = \sigma_i^2} \qquad [18.6]$$

where σ_{CP} = standard deviation of the duration of the critical path (that is, the project)

σ_i^2 = variance of the *i*th activity on the critical path

k = number of activities on the critical path

Figure 18.10   Network Calculations for Ajax Project, Showing Critical Path

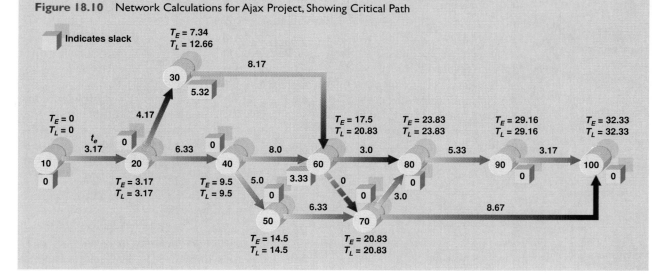

To find the probability that a project will be completed in no more than a given duration D, we must find the probability that a standardized normal variable Z will take on a value less than or equal to Z_D given by the transformation equation 18.7:

$$Z_D = \frac{D - T_E(CP)}{\sigma_{CP}} \qquad [18.7]$$

where Z_D = calculated value of a standardized normal variable
D = duration of the project that we want the probability of meeting
$T_E(CP)$ = expected completion time for critical path
σ_{CP} = assumed standard deviation of the project duration (that is, of the critical path)

Ajax Leasing wants the software package completed in less than 34 weeks, so we will determine the probability that this duration will be achieved. The variances of the activities on the critical path are determined and summed in Table 18.4. The sum of the rightmost column, 86/36 or 2.39 weeks, represents the assumed variance of the critical path, that is, the variance of the distribution for the project's duration.

The standard deviation of the project duration is σ_{CP} = $\sqrt{2.39}$ = 1.55 weeks. The probability that the project will be completed in less than 34 weeks can be determined now that σ_{CP} has been estimated.

Table 18.4
CALCULATION OF THE CRITICAL PATH VARIANCE

ACTIVITY	OPTIMISTIC TIME a	PESSIMISTIC TIME b	$\dfrac{b-a}{6}$	$\left(\dfrac{b-a}{6}\right)^2$
10–20	2	5	3/6	9/36
20–40	5	9	4/6	16/36
40–50	4	6	2/6	4/36
50–70	5	9	4/6	16/36
70–80	1	5	4/6	16/36
80–90	4	8	4/6	16/36
90–100	2	5	3/6	9/36

$$86/36 = \sum_{i=1}^{k} \sigma_i^2$$

$P(D \leq 34 \text{ weeks}) = P(Z \leq Z_D)$

$$Z_D = \frac{D - T_E(CP)}{\sigma_{CP}} = \frac{34 - 32.33}{1.55} = 1.08$$

Reference to a standardized normal probability table (Appendix I) shows that

$P(Z \leq 1.08) = 0.86$

so the probability is assumed to be about 0.86 that the company will complete the project within 34 weeks.

A Caution Regarding Probabilities

The probability statements developed in the application are based solely on the critical path. These probabilities do not take into account the probability that some initially noncritical path will be delayed by more than the amount of slack in it. Consequently the probabilities regarding the project's completion are somewhat optimistic. To be theoretically correct, we should consider all paths. The probability that the project will be completed by a specified date is the probability that all paths will be completed by that date. Each path has its own variance and distribution of completion times, so we can compute the probability that it will be completed by the specified date. The probability that all paths will be completed by this date is the product of the probabilities for all the paths. Of course, all the calculations assume that the estimator actually described the correct probability distributions by providing the correct a, m, and b for the activities.

Simulation of Project Duration

Conventional analysis of a PERT network focuses on finding the critical path and then analyzing its effect on the project's completion. The probability that some other path may be delayed by more than the amount of slack in it is not included in the conventional approach. Finding the probabilities for all paths in a large network is tedious, particularly if several possible dates are considered.

Simulation, taking all paths into account, can be used to develop estimates of the project's completion. Approximations of the probability distributions for each activity's duration are estimated in order to perform PERT. These distributions or more-detailed empirical estimates may be used to represent the likelihood that an activity will require various amounts of time. One time from the distribution of possible durations of each activity is randomly selected. The times for all the activities within a path are totaled, and the durations for the paths are compared to see which path was the longest and how much time it required. Sometimes some other path might take longer than the path that was originally designated the critical path.

The procedure of sampling times and determining the longest path and its duration is continued for many trials. Upon completion of the simulation, one can compute the likelihood that a particular path will be critical and can develop a probability distribution for the project's duration. The relative frequency with which a particular path was the longest indicates the likelihood that this path will determine the project's completion date. The relative frequency of various durations, no matter which path was longest, indicates the likelihood of completing the project within a particular time. A computer is used to simulate any project of a realistic size because many repetitions are required. A short supplement (Supplement H) on simulation is included between Chapter 17 and this chapter.

MONITORING PROJECTS WITH NETWORK TECHNIQUES

Some users of network scheduling techniques have said that networks would greatly improve project management even if they were thrown away as soon as they were developed, because of the detailed planning needed to develop them. This statement may be true, but there is further value to the method. Few, if any, projects go as planned, no matter how carefully the plan has been developed. A network that is kept updated shows where a project is off schedule before it gets too far off. Updating and reviewing the networks or computer reports that represent information obtained from the networks provide management with current information. Continued revision and use of a network technique keep management up to date on current and predicted project status.

The types of calculations done in planning a project may be repeated using actual times for completed activities and the most recent time estimates for the remaining activities. Revised plans may be included in the network if necessary. Current estimates of the slack or float for each path can be obtained to highlight the need for management attention. Sometimes a "rolling wave" of more-detailed planning is used to plan ahead as work progresses on a lengthy project.

THE USE OF COMPUTERS IN PROJECT MANAGEMENT

Project networks may contain thousands of activities and may represent work that spans several years. Such a network would cover the walls of a sizable room. Drawing the network would require so much time that it could not be kept up to date with the project's progress, and it would continually have to be redrawn. Computers are highly useful to support project management, particularly for large projects. A computer can store, update, and selectively retrieve data about a project and can drive printers or plotters to give valuable plans and status reports. Actual start dates, completion dates, costs, and other information can be recorded as the project progresses. The actual status can be compared to the baseline plan so that the impact of any deviations can be assessed and new plans formulated, if necessary.

The computer can provide a rolling wave of detailed information as the project progresses. It may be valuable to sort activities in order of increasing slack, to identify the most critical activities in the project. The activities may be sorted to retrieve all activities with early start dates within a specified horizon, to find where available resources may be utilized. The activities may be sorted to show all late start dates within a set horizon, to see what work must be started within that time to keep the project on schedule. Activities may be sorted by a particular type of work for capacity planning or for subcontracting. Detailed subnetworks of the project may be printed to assist subcontractors in coordinating their parts of the project. Computers can be applied in numerous other ways to assist in project management.

Dozens of software packages are available for support of project management. Many of these packages are for use with microcomputers. Such packages have broadly varying capabilities and sell for prices that range from about $100 to several thousand dollars. Some will handle thousands of activities and have the ability to link multiple projects. The programs can provide graphics for networks, Gantt charts, and a variety of reports. Some will schedule to level resources and can interface with mainframes, spreadsheets, and data base packages. Most packages can provide reports and networks on dot-matrix printers, and some can support plotter output. Harvard Project Manager®, MacProject®, Primavera®, Project Planner®, Time Line®, QUICKNET®, and SuperProject Expert® are only a few of the available packages for microcomputers. Some of the more recent packages such as Microsoft Project for Windows®, Time Line®, and Project Scheduler 4® incorporate graphical user interfaces to provide new features. For example, Microsoft Project for Windows® allows the user to increase or decrease the duration of an activity by stretching or shrinking the bar that represents the activity on the Gantt chart screen. A pop-up box on the screen indicates the date to which the activity has been changed. Tasks can be moved on the PERT chart screen and dependencies can be drawn by use of a mouse.

Figures 18.11, 18.12, and 18.13 show examples from SuperProject Plus® (registered trademark of Computer Associates International, Inc.) to illustrate some of the capabilities of a microcomputer package. One of the first steps in using such a package is to indicate on a project calendar which days are holidays and weekend days in the months during which the project will run. Then, with menus and the keyboard, the user constructs each project task on the screen and designates how the tasks are to be linked. The resource required to accomplish the task is also indicated. The result is a network that can be scanned on the screen or printed, as in Figure 18.11. The availability and cost of resources can be entered into table templates, as in Figure 18.12.

The program can be directed to prepare schedules according to the activity durations specified on the network, or it can level resources (forward-schedule so resources are not used more than their normal work hours). After the start and finish dates have been determined for each task, the program can be directed to display the schedule on a time-scaled Gantt chart, as in Figure 18.13. The planned start and finish dates can be shown as one line for each task on the Gantt chart. Actual start and finish dates and costs can be entered for each task as the project progresses. The

Figure 18.11 A Network

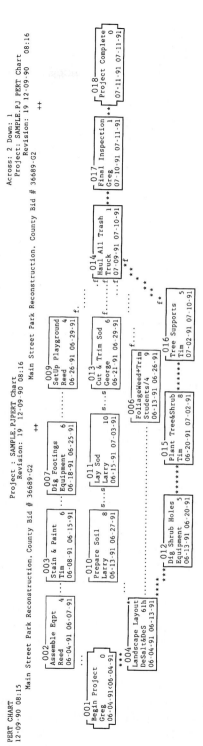

Figure 18.12
Table of Resource Details

```
Resource Details                                                  Project: SAMPLE.PJ
12-09-90  08:19                                                     Revision    19
             Main Street Park Reconstruction, County Bid # 36689-G2                 +
```

Rsrc Name:Students/4	High School Students, Pool of 4 workers at $5 per hour	
	Defaults	Totals
Work Code: Costs: End Total Overscheduled: 122 Rate Multi:1.50 Calendar Variance: 0 No. Units: 4 Sun Mon Tue Wed Thu Fri Sat Workday 0 8 8 8 8 8 0	Hours: 8 Fixed: 5.00 Rate: 5.00 Priority: 50 Allocation: 8x	Var: 2785.00 Fix: 100.00 Tot: 2885.00 Act: 0.00 Hrs: 496 Act: 0

ID	Task	Pr	Hrs	Allc	Un	Ovr	Act	Dur	Start	Finish	
006	FoliageWeed+Trim	50	144	8x	2	0	0	9	06-13-91	06-26-91	
015	Plant Tree&Shrub	50	256	8x	4	58	0	8	06-20-91	07-02-91	C
009	SetUp Playground	50	64	8x	2	64	0	4	06-26-91	06-29-91	
014	Haul All Trash	50	32	8x	4	0	0	1	07-09-91	07-10-91	C

actual durations can be displayed on the Gantt chart as a second line for each task. Maintenance of these baseline data allows the actual data to be compared to them, providing a picture of any schedule slippage. A cost table maintains the actual costs that have been reported. Other features and capabilities are available in this package and in many others of this type.

```
Task Gantt                                                    Project: SAMPLE. PJ
12-09-90      08:09                                               Revision: 19
                 Main Street Park Reconstruction. County Bid # 36689-G2
                                                                              +
┌──────────────────────────────────────────────────────────────────────────────┐
│ 1 Days Per Symbol   Jun 91  Jun    Jun    Jun    Jul    Jul    Jul    Jul    J │
│ ID   Task Name      04      11     18     25     02     09     16     23     3  │
│                                                                                │
│ 001  Begin Project  M....   .....  .....  .....  .. ..  .....  .....  .....  . │
│        Task Scheduled .....  .....  .....  .....  .. ..  .....  .....  .....  . │
│ 002  Assemble Eqpt  ▓▓▓▓ »  »»»»»»  .....  .....  .. ..  .....  .....  .....  . │
│        Task Scheduled .....  .....  .....  .....  .. ..  .....  .....  .....  . │
│ 003  Stain & Paint  ....▓   ▓▓▓▓   »»»»»»»  »».....  .....  .....  .....  .....  . │
│        Task Scheduled .....  .....  .....  .....  .. ..  .....  .....  .....  . │
│ 004  Landscape Layout ▓▓▓▓▓  ▓▓▓.  .....  .....  .. ..  .....  .....  .....  . │
│        Task Scheduled .....  .....  .....  .....  .. ..  .....  .....  .....  . │
│ 006  Foliage Weed+Trim .....  .. ▓  ▓▓▓▓  ▓▓▓>>>  >> >>  >....  .....  .....  . │
│        Task Scheduled .....  .....  .....  .....  .. ..  .....  .....  .....  . │
│ 007  Dig Footings   .....   .....  ▓▓▓▓  ▓>»»»»»  » »» ..  .....  .....  .....  . │
│        Task Scheduled .....  .....  .....  .....  .. ..  .....  .....  .....  . │
│ 009  SetUp Playground .....  .....  .....  .▓▓▓  >> >>  >>....  .....  .....  . │
│        Task Scheduled .....  .....  .....  .....  .. ..  .....  .....  .....  . │
│ 010  Prepare Soil   .....   .. ▓   ▓▓▓▓  ▓▓▓>>>  >>> ..  .....  .....  .....  . │
│        Task Scheduled .....  .....  .....  .....  .. ..  .....  .....  .....  . │
│ 011  Lay Sod        .....   ....▓  ▓▓▓▓  .....  ▓▓: >>>  >>>»».. .....  .....  . │
│        Task Scheduled .....  .....  .....  .....  .. ..  .....  .....  .....  . │
│ 012  Dig Shrub Holes .....  .. ▓▓  ▓▓▓.  .....  .. ..  .....  .....  .....  . │
│        Task Scheduled .....  .....  .....  .....  .. ..  .....  .....  .....  . │
│ 013  Cut & Trim Sod  .....  .....  ...▓  ▓▓▓▓  >> >>  >>....  .....  .....  . │
│        Task Scheduled .....  .....  .....  .....  .. ..  .....  .....  .....  . │
│ 014  Haul All Trash  .....  .....  .....  .....  .. ..  ▓▓▓.  .....  .....  . │
│        Task Scheduled .....  .....  .....  .....  .. ..  .....  .....  .....  . │
│ 015  Plant Tree&Shrub .....  .....  .▓▓▓  ▓▓▓▓  ▓.. ..  .....  .....  .....  . │
│        Task Scheduled .....  .....  .....  .....  .. ..  .....  .....  .....  . │
│ 016  Tree Supports  .....   .....  .....  .....  ▓▓ ▓▓  ▓▓...  .....  .....  . │
│        Task Scheduled .....  .....  .....  .....  .. ..  .....  .....  .....  . │
│ 017  Final Inspection .....  .....  .....  .....  .. ..  .▓▓..  .....  .....  . │
│        Task Scheduled .....  .....  .....  .....  .. ..  .....  .....  .....  . │
│ 018  Project Complete .....  .....  .....  .....  .. ..  ..M..  .....  .....  . │
│        Task Scheduled .....  .....  .....  .....  .. ..  .....  .....  .....  . │
│                                                                                │
└──────────────────────────────────────────────────────────────────────────────┘

 ▓▓ non crit     m  milestone     »»»» float/delay    ▓▓ fin delay      ━━ unassigned
 ▓▓ crit         M  crit milest   >>> free float       ▓▓ crit fin delay ━━ crit unass
```

Figure 18.13
A Gantt Chart for
a Project

SUMMARY

A project is a complex, often large-scale undertaking that is unique or nonroutine for the performing organization. Management of a project can present unique challenges because of various factors. The project may span several years. The type of work may not have been done previously by the organization. The project may require the efforts of diverse groups, and those groups may be involved in only a part of the project, so there is a lack of continuity to develop skills, understanding, and working relationships that would make coordination simpler.

It is imperative to have an effective means of defining and communicating the work requirements and sequencing involved in a project. Sometimes a work breakdown structure (WBS) is used to identify all elements of the work to be performed. Network-based scheduling techniques such as PERT and CPM have proven to be very effective tools for both planning and controlling projects.

The major difference between PERT and CPM is that PERT incorporates probabilities into the estimates of activity times and of project completion times, whereas CPM does not. PERT and CPM have numerous advantages. They entail detailed planning of projects, and they provide estimates of completion dates that are as accurate as can be developed from a given level of accuracy in the input data. They furnish a graphical picture of work assignments and their interrelationships and a uniform vocabulary for communicating about them. Both PERT and CPM identify the critical path, the series of activities that are most likely to delay a project. Both techniques provide an effective means of comparing actual performance to the plan, so that the need for corrective action can be readily recognized and the appropriate corrective action can be planned.

The procedure for using one of the network techniques begins in the planning stage—with identifying all activities that must be performed and the sequence in which they must be performed. A network is constructed to show graphically the sequence of all activities in the project. Either the activity-on-arrow or the activity-on-node convention is used throughout the entire network.

The second major step is scheduling the project. Time estimates must be made for the duration of each activity. A forward pass, from left to right through the network, provides the earliest possible time for completion of each activity. A backward pass, from right to left through the network, provides the latest time that an activity can be completed without delaying the project. The difference between these times is the slack or float—the time that an activity can be delayed beyond its earliest starting time without delaying completion of the project. This information can be used to rearrange the planned use of resources so that either resources are more wisely used or the project can be completed earlier.

The third major step in using PERT or CPM is to monitor the project as work progresses and to update the network. If the actual work deviates from the plan, management can decide what action would be appropriate—to redeploy resources to get the project back on schedule or to revise the schedule. Network techniques provide useful information to assist in planning actions that seem most appropriate.

CPM is sometimes associated with time-cost trade-offs to determine the lowest-cost way to expedite completion of a project. The original time estimates are based on an assumed crew size, amount of equipment, and length of workday. The incremental cost for saving one, two, three, or more units of time, such as days, can be estimated for each activity on the critical path. These estimates can be used to find the lowest-cost way to reduce the duration of the critical path by the desired amount of time.

The expected completion time provided by PERT is assumed to be the mean of a normal distribution of possible project durations. The probability of completing the project in less than some specified time can be found by converting the time to a z value and finding the probability that z will be less than or equal to that value. In some instances, simulation is used to take into account the possible duration of the critical path and of other paths.

KEY TERMS

Project
Concept phase
Planning or feasibility
 phase
Organization phase
Execution phase
Termination phase
Work breakdown structure
 (WBS)
Matrix organization
Program evaluation and
 review technique
 (PERT)

Critical path method
 (CPM)
Activities
Network
Precedence relationship
Activity-on-node (AON)
 convention
Activity-on-arrow (AOA)
 convention
Events
Predecessor activity
Successor activity

Dummy activity
Critical path
Float or slack
Free float
Forward pass
Backward pass
Crashing the project
Optimistic time
Pessimistic time
Most likely time

DEMONSTRATION PROBLEM

Problem

Shown below is an AOA network for a small project. The three time estimates, in weeks, for each activity are shown on each arrow.

(a) Compute the expected time for each activity.

(b) Find the expected duration of the project.

(c) Find the slack at the nodes that are not on the critical path.

(d) Compute the standard deviation of the critical path.

(e) Using the standard deviation of the critical path as the standard deviation of the project's duration, compute the probability of completing the project in 35 weeks or less.

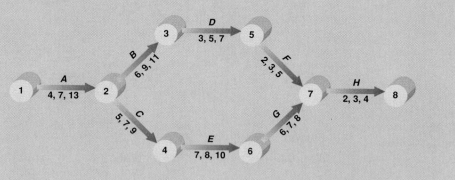

Solution

(a) The expected time for each activity is indicated in column 5 of the table shown at the top of page 728. These times are used to compute the T_E or the earliest expected time for reaching each event (circle) in the network.

(b) The expected completion time for the project is found to be 32.67 weeks, which is the T_E at the last node or event, which represents completion of activity H.

(1) ACTIVITY	(2) OPTIMISTIC TIME a	(3) MOST LIKELY TIME m	(4) PESSIMISTIC TIME b	(5) t_e $(a + 4m + b)/6$	(6)* ACTIVITY VARIANCE $[(b - a/6)]^2$
A	4	7	13	7.50	2.25
B	6	9	11	8.83	
C	5	7	9	7.00	0.44
D	3	5	7	5.00	
E	7	8	10	8.17	0.25
F	2	3	5	3.17	
G	6	7	8	7.00	0.11
H	2	3	4	3.00	$\underline{0.11}$
					$\overline{3.16}$

*Critical path activities only.

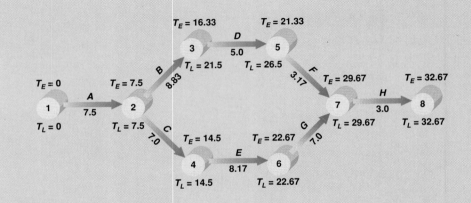

(c) The nodes with nonzero slack are nodes 3 and 5, which have 5.17 weeks' slack, so the critical path is *A-C-E-G-H*. The slack is found by calculating the T_L values in the network by a backward pass through the network. Where they are not equal, T_E is subtracted from T_L, and the result is equal to the slack at that node.

(d) The standard deviation of the critical path is found by summing the numbers in column 6 for every activity on the critical path (*A-C-E-G-H*) and taking the square root of this sum:

$$\sigma^2_{CP} = (2.25 + 0.44 + 0.25 + 0.11 + 0.11) = 3.16$$

$$\sigma_{CP} = \sqrt{3.16} = 1.778$$

(e) $P(D \le 35 \text{ weeks}) =$

$$P\left(Z \le \frac{35 - 32.67}{1.778}\right) = P(Z \le 1.31)$$

Appendix I shows this probability to be 0.9049.

DISCUSSION QUESTIONS

1. Why is it particularly advantageous to have a standardized vocabulary and scheduling technique in a company that uses project management to accomplish many of its jobs?
2. How does a project differ from a job that is processed through a job shop or a service facility?
3. **a.** What is a work breakdown structure (WBS)?
   b. Why is a WBS useful?
4. What is the major difference between PERT and CPM?
5. What is free float?
6. What is the theoretical basis for assuming that the duration of a project can be represented by a normal probability distribution?
7. Why does analysis of only the critical path present an optimistic estimate of the probability that the project will be completed within a given time?
8. Why might simulation provide an estimate of the probability of completing a project by a given time that is different from an estimate based solely on the critical path?

PROBLEMS

1. Given below are the precedence relationships among the activities required to perform a project. Construct an AON network for the project.

ACTIVITY	MUST PRECEDE
A	E, G, L
B, C, K	H
L	D
E	D, F
G	K
D	B
F	C, K

2. Develop an AOA network for the project of problem 1.
3. Given the following durations for the activities of the project in problem 1 find the critical path, the project duration, and the float for each activity.

ACTIVITY	DURATION (DAYS)	ACTIVITY	DURATION (DAYS)
A	6	F	16
B	12	G	5
C	12	H	6
D	8	K	7
E	12	L	11

4. Given the following durations of and the precedence relationships among the activities required to complete a project:
   a. Construct an AON network for the project.
   b. Determine the critical path for the project.
   c. Calculate the completion time.
   d. Determine the slack for the activities not on the critical path.

ACTIVITY	DURATION (WEEKS)	PREDECESSOR(S)
A	4	
B	5	A
C	5	A
D	6	B, C
E	7	B
F	9	A
G	5	E
H	6	D, I
I	5	F
J	5	G, H

5. Given below are the durations of and the precedence relationships among the activities required to complete a project.
   a. Construct an AON network for the project.
   b. Calculate the completion time for the project.
   c. Determine the critical path for the project.
   d. Determine the slack for each activity not on the critical path.

ACTIVITY	DURATION (WEEKS)	PREDECESSOR(S)
A	2	C, F
B	8	H, I
C	8	D
D	6	None (start)
E	4	B, J
F	3	D
G	7	C
H	4	C
I	3	G
J	5	A

6. A CPM diagram is shown below with the estimated times in weeks.
   a. Find the critical path.
   b. Find the expected completion date.
   c. Develop a table showing the slack for each activity.

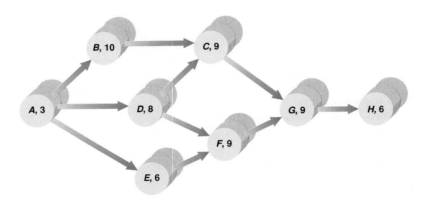

7. For the project shown in the network shown below:
   a. Find the expected project duration.
   b. Find the critical path.
   c. Find the slack at each activity.

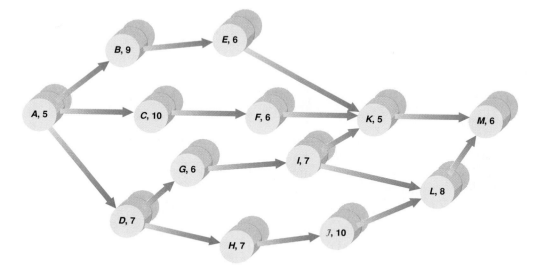

8. The CPM network below represents a project with the times estimated in weeks.
   a. What is the expected project duration?
   b. What is the critical path?
   c. Find the ES, EF, LS, LF, and float at each activity.

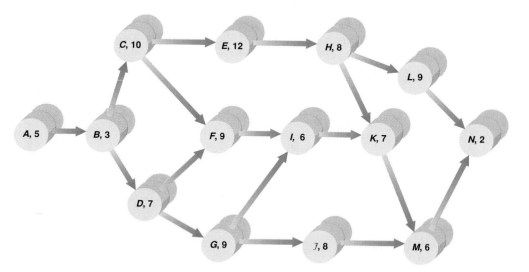

9. Shown at the top of page 732 is an AON network for a PERT schedule on a project.
   The three time estimates, in weeks, for each activity are given in the table below.
   a. Compute t_e for each activity.
   b. Determine the expected completion time for the project.
   c. What is the critical path?
   d. Give the expected slack for each activity that is not on the critical path.

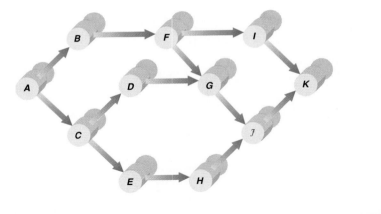

ACTIVITY	a	m	b	ACTIVITY	a	m	b
A	4	6	8	G	6	8	10
B	3	5	7	H	5	7	9
C	4	5	8	I	3	8	13
D	3	5	7	J	6	7	8
E	5	6	7	K	1	2	3
F	6	8	11				

10. Shown below is a network showing the sequence of activities that must be performed to complete a contract. The estimated duration for each task, without expediting, is indicated on the network. Because of the revenue generation ability of this project, the customer has offered an incentive contract that will pay a $600 bonus for each day that the project is completed ahead of 162 days. The table at the top of page 733 indicates the cost to expedite each activity by 1, 2, or 3 days.

   a. Find the critical path and the normal duration.

   b. Determine which activities should be expedited and by what amount they should be expedited so that the net bonus minus expediting costs will be maximized.

   c. How much net bonus will be earned?

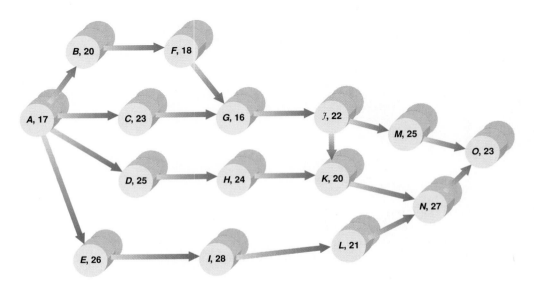

JOB	Incremental Cost to Reduce Activity Duration		
	FIRST DAY	SECOND DAY	THIRD DAY
A	500	650	800
B	90	200	500
C	80	200	500
D	100	300	600
E	70	180	275
F	200	450	700
G	250	500	900
H	1,000	1,200	1,500
I	400	600	800
J	200	400	700
K	250	600	1,000
L	90	300	600
M	300	450	700
N	200	400	700
O	400	800	1,400

11. Shown at the top of page 734 is a network showing the sequence of activities that must be performed to complete a project. The estimated duration in days of each activity, without expediting, is indicated in each node. The following table shows the cost to reduce the duration of each activity by 1 day, the additional cost to reduce the activity a second day, and the additional cost required to reduce an activity a third day, if feasible.

   a. Find the duration of the project if no activity is expedited.
   b. Find the critical path of the project.
   c. Find the lowest possible cost way to reduce the duration of the project by a total of four days.

ACTIVITY	Incremental Cost to Reduce Activity Duration (Dollars)		
	FIRST DAY	SECOND DAY	THIRD DAY
H	40	70	125
K	50	90	200
L	180	275	400
M	220	280	375
P	150	190	*
R	50	100	125
S	60	140	200
T	75	110	190
U	40	60	80
V	50	80	125
W	170	240	350
X	150	180	310
Y	60	100	275
Z	40	150	*

*not feasible

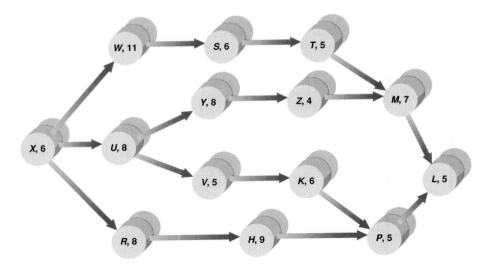

12. A PERT diagram is shown below with the optimistic, most likely, and pessimistic times, in days, shown above each arrow.
    a. Find t_e for each activity.
    b. Find the slack for each event and find the critical path.
    c. What is the expected completion time?
    d. What is the probability that the critical path will be completed in 45 days or less?

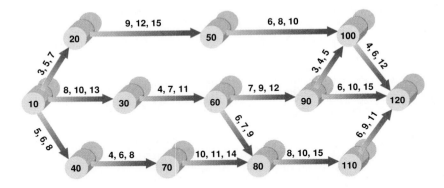

13. A PERT network for a project is shown at the top of page 735.
    a. Find the expected duration of each activity.
    b. Find the expected duration of the critical path.
    c. Find the critical path.
    d. Find the slack at each node.

14. With regard to problem 13:
    a. Find the standard deviation of the critical path.
    b. What is the probability of completing the critical path in 2 days less than the expected duration?

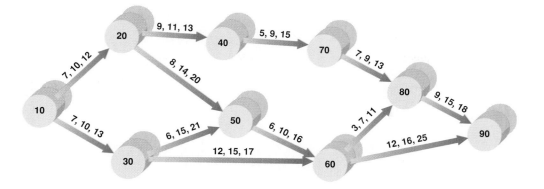

BIBLIOGRAPHY

Burke, Rory. *Project Management: Planning and Control.* New York: Wiley, 1993.

Cleland, David I. *Project Management: Strategic Design and Implementation.* 2d ed. New York: McGraw-Hill, 1994.

Davis, E. W., ed. *Project Management Techniques, Applications, and Managerial Issues.* 2d ed. Norcross, Ga.: Industrial Engineering and Management Press, 1983.

Dreger, J. Brian. *Project Management: Effective Scheduling.* New York: Van Nostrand Reinhold, 1992.

Fersko-Weiss, Henry. "Low-Cost Project Management: Seven Lender $700." *P C Magazine,* September 11, 1990, pp. 331–333, 338, 339, 342, 344, 347–349, 352, 354, 357, 358, 360, 363.

Gobeli, David H., and Erik W. Larson. "Relative Effectiveness of Different Project Structures." *Project Management Journal 18,* no. 2 (June 1987): 81–85.

Hillier, Frederick S. *Introduction to Operations Research.* New York: McGraw:Hill, 1990.

Kerzner, Harold. *Project Management: A Systems Approach to Planning, Scheduling, and Controlling.* 4th ed. New York: Van Nostrand Reinhold, 1992.

Levine, Harvey A. *Project Management Using Microcomputers.* Berkeley, Calif.: Osborne McGraw-Hill, 1986.

Meredith, Jack R., and Samuel J. Mantel, Jr. *Project Management: A Managerial Approach.* 2d ed. New York: Wiley, 1989.

Moder, Joseph J., Cecil R. Phillips, and Edward W. Davis. *Project Management with CPM, PERT, and Precedence Diagramming.* 3d ed. New York: Van Nostrand Reinhold, 1983.

Posner, Barry Z. "What It Takes to Be a Good Project Manager." *Project Management Journal 18,* no. 1 (March 1987): 51–54.

"Project Management Software Survey." *PMNETwork,* May 1994, pp. 33–48.

Rosenberg, Marcy. "The Craft of Project Management." *Business Computer Systems,* September 1985, pp. 48–66.

Schultz, Randall L., Dennis P. Slevin, and Jeffrey K. Pinto. "Strategy and Tactics in a Process Model of Project Implementation." *Interfaces 17,* no. 3 (May–June 1987): 34–46.

APPENDICES

APPENDIX 1

CUMULATIVE PROBABILITIES OF THE NORMAL DISTRIBUTION
(Areas under the Standardized Normal Curve from $-\infty$ to Z)

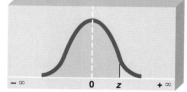

Z	0.00	0.01	0.02	0.03	0.04	0.05	0.06	0.07	0.08	0.09
0.0	0.5000	0.5040	0.5080	0.5120	0.5160	0.5199	0.5239	0.5279	0.5319	0.5359
0.1	0.5389	0.5438	0.5478	0.5517	0.5557	0.5596	0.5636	0.5675	0.5714	0.5753
0.2	0.5793	0.5832	0.5871	0.5910	0.5948	0.5987	0.6026	0.6064	0.6103	0.6141
0.3	0.6179	0.6217	0.6255	0.6293	0.6331	0.6368	0.6406	0.6443	0.6480	0.6517
0.4	0.6554	0.6591	0.6628	0.6664	0.6700	0.6736	0.6772	0.6808	0.6844	0.6879
0.5	0.6915	0.6950	0.6985	0.7019	0.7054	0.7088	0.7123	0.7157	0.7190	0.7224
0.6	0.7257	0.7291	0.7324	0.7357	0.7389	0.7422	0.7454	0.7486	0.7517	0.7549
0.7	0.7580	0.7611	0.7642	0.7673	0.7704	0.7734	0.7764	0.7794	0.7823	0.7852
0.8	0.7881	0.7910	0.7939	0.7967	0.7995	0.8023	0.8051	0.8078	0.8106	0.8133
0.9	0.8159	0.8186	0.8212	0.8238	0.8264	0.8289	0.8315	0.8340	0.8365	0.8389
1.0	0.8413	0.8438	0.8461	0.8485	0.8508	0.8531	0.8554	0.8577	0.8599	0.8621
1.1	0.8643	0.8665	0.8686	0.8708	0.8729	0.8749	0.8770	0.8790	0.8810	0.8830
1.2	0.8849	0.8869	0.8888	0.8907	0.8925	0.8944	0.8962	0.8980	0.8997	0.9015
1.3	0.9032	0.9049	0.9066	0.9082	0.9099	0.9115	0.9131	0.9147	0.9162	0.9177
1.4	0.9192	0.9207	0.9222	0.9236	0.9251	0.9265	0.9279	0.9292	0.9306	0.9319
1.5	0.9332	0.9345	0.9357	0.9370	0.9382	0.9394	0.9406	0.9418	0.9429	0.9441
1.6	0.9452	0.9463	0.9474	0.9484	0.9495	0.9505	0.9515	0.9525	0.9535	0.9545
1.7	0.9554	0.9564	0.9573	0.9582	0.9591	0.9599	0.9608	0.9616	0.9625	0.9633
1.8	0.9641	0.9649	0.9656	0.9664	0.9671	0.9678	0.9686	0.9693	0.9699	0.9706
1.9	0.9713	0.9719	0.9726	0.9732	0.9738	0.9744	0.9750	0.9756	0.9761	0.9767
2.0	0.9772	0.9778	0.9783	0.9788	0.9793	0.9798	0.9803	0.9808	0.9812	0.9817
2.1	0.9821	0.9826	0.9830	0.9834	0.9838	0.9842	0.9846	0.9850	0.9854	0.9857
2.2	0.9861	0.9864	0.9868	0.9871	0.9875	0.9878	0.9881	0.9884	0.9887	0.9890
2.3	0.9893	0.9896	0.9898	0.9901	0.9904	0.9906	0.9909	0.9911	0.9913	0.9916
2.4	0.9918	0.9920	0.9922	0.9925	0.9927	0.9929	0.9931	0.9932	0.9934	0.9936
2.5	0.9938	0.9940	0.9941	0.9943	0.9945	0.9946	0.9948	0.9949	0.9951	0.9952
2.6	0.9953	0.9955	0.9956	0.9957	0.9959	0.9960	0.9961	0.9962	0.9963	0.9964
2.7	0.9965	0.9966	0.9967	0.9968	0.9969	0.9970	0.9971	0.9972	0.9973	0.9974
2.8	0.9974	0.9975	0.9976	0.9977	0.9977	0.9978	0.9979	0.9979	0.9980	0.9981
2.9	0.9981	0.9982	0.9982	0.9983	0.9984	0.9984	0.9985	0.9985	0.9986	0.9986
3.0	0.9987	0.9987	0.9987	0.9988	0.9988	0.9989	0.9989	0.9989	0.9990	0.9990
3.1	0.9990	0.9991	0.9991	0.9991	0.9992	0.9992	0.9992	0.9992	0.9993	0.9993
3.2	0.9993	0.9993	0.9994	0.9994	0.9994	0.9994	0.9994	0.9995	0.9995	0.9995
3.3	0.9995	0.9995	0.9995	0.9996	0.9996	0.9996	0.9996	0.9996	0.9996	0.9997
3.4	0.9997	0.9997	0.9997	0.9997	0.9997	0.9997	0.9997	0.9997	0.9997	0.9998

APPENDIX II

LEARNING CURVE TABLES

95%

UNIT NUMBER	TIME FOR UNIT	CUMULATIVE TOTAL TIME FOR ALL UNITS	CUMULATIVE AVERAGE TIME OVER ALL UNITS
1	1.0000	1.0000	1.0000
2	0.9500	1.9500	0.9750
4	0.9025	3.7744	0.9436
5	0.8877	4.6621	0.9324
7	0.8659	6.4039	0.9148
10	0.8433	8.9545	0.8954
15	0.8184	13.0921	0.8728
20	0.8012	17.1302	0.8565
25	0.7880	21.0955	0.8438
30	0.7775	25.0032	0.8334
40	0.7611	32.6838	0.8171
50	0.7486	40.2239	0.8045
70	0.7302	54.9924	0.7856
100	0.7112	76.5864	0.7659
200	0.6756	145.6929	0.7285
300	0.6557	212.1772	0.7073
400	0.6419	277.0121	0.6925
500	0.6314	340.6472	0.6813
700	0.6158	465.2648	0.6647
1,000	0.5998	647.4463	0.6474
1,500	0.5821	942.5870	0.6284
2,000	0.5698	1,230.3796	0.6152
2,500	0.5605	1,512.8486	0.6051
3,000	0.5530	1,791.1396	0.5970
3,500	0.5467	2,066.0035	0.5903
4,000	0.5413	2,337.9672	0.5845
5,000	0.5325	2,874.4123	0.5749

90%

UNIT NUMBER	TIME FOR UNIT	CUMULATIVE TOTAL TIME FOR ALL UNITS	CUMULATIVE AVERAGE TIME OVER ALL UNITS
1	1.0000	1.0000	1.0000
2	0.9000	1.9000	0.9500
4	0.8100	3.5562	0.8891
5	0.7830	4.3391	0.8678
7	0.7438	5.8447	0.8350
10	0.7047	7.9945	0.7994
15	0.6626	11.3837	0.7589
20	0.6342	14.6078	0.7304
25	0.6131	17.7132	0.7085
30	0.5963	20.7269	0.6909
40	0.5708	26.5427	0.6636
50	0.5518	32.1420	0.6428
70	0.5243	42.8706	0.6124
100	0.4966	58.1410	0.5814
200	0.4469	104.9641	0.5248
300	0.4202	148.2040	0.4940
400	0.4022	189.2678	0.4732
500	0.3889	228.7851	0.4576
700	0.3694	304.4757	0.4350
1,000	0.3499	412.1718	0.4122
1,500	0.3290	581.4952	0.3877
2,000	0.3149	742.2854	0.3711
2,500	0.3044	897.0392	0.3588
3,000	0.2961	1,047.0770	0.3490
3,500	0.2893	1,193.3681	0.3410
4,000	0.2834	1,336.5057	0.3341
5,000	0.2740	1,614.6705	0.3229

85%

UNIT NUMBER	TIME FOR UNIT	CUMULATIVE TOTAL TIME FOR ALL UNITS	CUMULATIVE AVERAGE TIME OVER ALL UNITS
1	1.0000	1.0000	1.0000
2	0.8500	1.8500	0.9250
4	0.7225	3.3454	0.8364
5	0.6857	4.0310	0.8062
7	0.6337	5.3217	0.7602
10	0.5828	7.1161	0.7116
15	0.5300	9.8611	0.6574
20	0.4954	12.4023	0.6201
25	0.4701	14.8007	0.5920
30	0.4505	17.0907	0.5697
40	0.4211	21.4252	0.5356
50	0.3996	25.5131	0.5103
70	0.3693	33.1664	0.4738
100	0.3397	43.7539	0.4375
200	0.2887	74.7885	0.3739
300	0.2625	102.2301	0.3408
400	0.2454	127.5690	0.3189
500	0.2329	151.4504	0.3029
700	0.2152	196.1344	0.2802
1,000	0.1980	257.9180	0.2579
1,500	0.1800	352.0333	0.2347
2,000	0.1683	438.9276	0.2195
2,500	0.1597	520.8187	0.2083
3,000	0.1530	598.9313	0.1996
3,500	0.1476	674.0355	0.1926
4,000	0.1430	746.6567	0.1867
5,000	0.1357	885.8752	0.1772

UNIT NUMBER	TIME FOR UNIT	CUMULATIVE TOTAL TIME FOR ALL UNITS	CUMULATIVE AVERAGE TIME OVER ALL UNITS
1	1.0000	1.0000	1.0000
2	0.8000	1.8000	0.9000
4	0.6400	3.1421	0.7855
5	0.5956	3.7378	0.7475
7	0.5345	4.8340	0.6906
10	0.4765	6.3154	0.6315
15	0.4182	8.5105	0.5674
20	0.3812	10.4849	0.5242
25	0.3548	12.3086	0.4923
30	0.3346	14.0199	0.4673
40	0.3050	17.1935	0.4298
50	0.2838	20.1217	0.4024
70	0.2547	25.4708	0.3639
100	0.2271	32.6508	0.3265
200	0.1816	52.7200	0.2636
300	0.1594	69.6634	0.2322
400	0.1453	84.8487	0.2121
500	0.1352	98.8472	0.1977
700	0.1214	124.3984	0.1777
1,000	0.1082	158.6709	0.1587
1,500	0.0950	209.1580	0.1394
2,000	0.0866	254.3996	0.1272
2,500	0.0806	296.1018	0.1184
3,000	0.0760	355.1843	0.1117
3,500	0.0723	372.2146	0.1063
4,000	0.0692	407.5742	0.1019
5,000	0.0644	474.3001	0.0949

UNIT NUMBER	TIME FOR UNIT	CUMULATIVE TOTAL TIME FOR ALL UNITS	CUMULATIVE AVERAGE TIME OVER ALL UNITS
1	1.0000	1.0000	1.0000
2	0.7500	1.7500	0.8750
4	0.5625	2.9463	0.7366
5	0.5127	3.4591	0.6918
7	0.4459	4.3837	0.6258
10	0.3846	5.5886	0.5589
15	0.3250	7.3190	0.4879
20	0.2884	8.8284	0.4414
25	0.2629	10.1907	0.4076
30	0.2437	11.4458	0.3815
40	0.2163	13.7232	0.3531
50	0.1972	15.7761	0.3155
70	0.1715	19.4296	0.2776
100	0.1479	24.1786	0.2418
200	0.1109	36.8007	0.1840
300	0.0937	46.9427	0.1565
400	0.0832	55.7577	0.1394
500	0.0758	63.6753	0.1274
700	0.0659	77.7693	0.1111
1,000	0.0569	96.0728	0.0961
1,500	0.0481	122.0917	0.0814
2,000	0.0427	144.6762	0.0723
2,500	0.0389	165.0079	0.0660
3,000	0.0360	183.7078	0.0612
3,500	0.0338	201.1512	0.0575
4,000	0.0320	217.5865	0.0544
5,000	0.0292	247.5119	0.0495

APPENDIX III

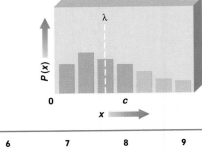

CUMULATIVE POISSON PROBABILITIES $P(x \leq c \mid \lambda) = \sum\limits_{x=0}^{x=c} \dfrac{\lambda^x e^{-\lambda}}{x!}$

λ OR np'	0	1	2	3	4	5	6	7	8	9
0.02	0.980	1.000								
0.04	0.961	0.999	1.000							
0.06	0.942	0.998	1.000							
0.08	0.923	0.997	1.000							
0.10	0.905	0.995	1.000							
0.15	0.861	0.990	0.999	1.000						
0.20	0.819	0.982	0.999	1.000						
0.25	0.779	0.974	0.998	1.000						
0.30	0.741	0.963	0.996	1.000						
0.35	0.705	0.951	0.994	1.000						
0.40	0.670	0.938	0.992	0.999	1.000					
0.45	0.638	0.925	0.989	0.999	1.000					
0.50	0.607	0.910	0.986	0.998	1.000					
0.55	0.577	0.894	0.982	0.998	1.000					
0.60	0.549	0.878	0.977	0.997	1.000					
0.65	0.522	0.861	0.972	0.996	0.999	1.000				
0.70	0.497	0.844	0.966	0.994	0.999	1.000				
0.75	0.472	0.827	0.959	0.993	0.999	1.000				
0.80	0.449	0.809	0.953	0.991	0.999	1.000				
0.85	0.427	0.791	0.945	0.989	0.998	1.000				
0.90	0.407	0.772	0.937	0.987	0.998	1.000				
0.95	0.387	0.754	0.929	0.984	0.997	1.000				
1.00	0.368	0.736	0.920	0.981	0.996	0.999	1.000			
1.10	0.333	0.699	0.900	0.974	0.995	0.999	1.000			
1.20	0.301	0.663	0.879	0.966	0.992	0.998	1.000			
1.30	0.273	0.627	0.857	0.957	0.989	0.998	1.000			
1.40	0.247	0.592	0.833	0.946	0.986	0.997	0.999	1.000		
1.50	0.223	0.558	0.809	0.934	0.981	0.996	0.999	1.000		
1.60	0.202	0.525	0.783	0.921	0.976	0.994	0.999	1.000		
1.70	0.183	0.493	0.757	0.907	0.970	0.992	0.998	1.000		
1.80	0.165	0.463	0.731	0.891	0.964	0.990	0.997	0.999	1.000	
1.90	0.150	0.434	0.704	0.875	0.956	0.987	0.997	0.999	1.000	
2.00	0.135	0.406	0.677	0.857	0.947	0.983	0.995	0.999	1.000	

Appendix III (continued)

λ OR np \ c	0	1	2	3	4	5	6	7	8	9
2.2	0.111	0.355	0.623	0.819	0.928	0.975	0.993	0.998	1.000	
2.4	0.091	0.308	0.570	0.779	0.904	0.964	0.988	0.997	0.999	1.000
2.6	0.074	0.267	0.518	0.736	0.877	0.951	0.983	0.995	0.999	1.000
2.8	0.061	0.231	0.469	0.692	0.848	0.935	0.976	0.992	0.998	0.999
3.0	0.050	0.199	0.423	0.647	0.815	0.916	0.966	0.988	0.996	0.999
3.2	0.041	0.171	0.380	0.603	0.781	0.895	0.955	0.983	0.994	0.998
3.4	0.033	0.147	0.340	0.558	0.744	0.871	0.942	0.977	0.992	0.997
3.6	0.027	0.126	0.303	0.515	0.706	0.844	0.927	0.969	0.988	0.996
3.8	0.022	0.107	0.269	0.473	0.668	0.816	0.909	0.960	0.984	0.994
4.0	0.018	0.092	0.238	0.433	0.629	0.785	0.889	0.949	0.979	0.992
4.2	0.015	0.078	0.210	0.395	0.590	0.753	0.867	0.936	0.972	0.989
4.4	0.012	0.066	0.185	0.359	0.551	0.720	0.844	0.921	0.964	0.985
4.6	0.010	0.056	0.163	0.326	0.513	0.686	0.818	0.905	0.955	0.980
4.8	0.008	0.048	0.143	0.294	0.476	0.651	0.791	0.887	0.944	0.975
5.0	0.007	0.040	0.125	0.265	0.440	0.616	0.762	0.867	0.932	0.968
5.2	0.006	0.034	0.109	0.238	0.406	0.581	0.732	0.845	0.918	0.960
5.4	0.005	0.029	0.095	0.213	0.373	0.546	0.702	0.822	0.903	0.951
5.6	0.004	0.024	0.082	0.191	0.342	0.512	0.670	0.797	0.886	0.941
5.8	0.003	0.021	0.072	0.170	0.313	0.478	0.638	0.771	0.867	0.929
6.0	0.002	0.017	0.062	0.151	0.285	0.446	0.606	0.744	0.847	0.916

	10	11	12	13	14	15	16
2.8	1.000						
3.0	1.000						
3.2	1.000						
3.4	0.999	1.000					
3.6	0.999	1.000					
3.8	0.998	0.999	1.000				
4.0	0.997	0.999	1.000				
4.2	0.996	0.999	1.000				
4.4	0.994	0.998	0.999	1.000			
4.6	0.992	0.997	0.999	1.000			
4.8	0.990	0.996	0.999	1.000			
5.0	0.986	0.995	0.998	0.999	1.000		
5.2	0.982	0.993	0.997	0.999	1.000		
5.4	0.977	0.990	0.996	0.999	1.000		
5.6	0.972	0.988	0.995	0.998	0.999	1.000	
5.8	0.965	0.984	0.993	0.997	0.999	1.000	
6.0	0.957	0.980	0.991	0.996	0.999	0.999	1.000

Appendix III (continued)

λ OR np'	0	1	2	3	4	5	6	7	8	9
6.2	0.002	0.015	0.054	0.134	0.259	0.414	0.574	0.716	0.826	0.902
6.4	0.002	0.012	0.046	0.119	0.235	0.384	0.542	0.687	0.803	0.886
6.6	0.001	0.010	0.040	0.105	0.213	0.355	0.511	0.658	0.780	0.869
6.8	0.001	0.009	0.034	0.093	0.192	0.327	0.480	0.628	0.755	0.850
7.0	0.001	0.007	0.030	0.082	0.173	0.301	0.450	0.599	0.729	0.830
7.2	0.001	0.006	0.025	0.072	0.156	0.276	0.420	0.569	0.703	0.810
7.4	0.001	0.005	0.022	0.063	0.140	0.253	0.392	0.539	0.676	0.788
7.6	0.001	0.004	0.019	0.055	0.125	0.231	0.365	0.510	0.648	0.765
7.8	0.000	0.004	0.016	0.048	0.112	0.210	0.338	0.481	0.620	0.741
8.0	0.000	0.003	0.014	0.042	0.100	0.191	0.313	0.453	0.593	0.717
8.5	0.000	0.002	0.009	0.030	0.074	0.150	0.256	0.386	0.523	0.653
9.0	0.000	0.001	0.006	0.021	0.055	0.116	0.207	0.324	0.456	0.587
9.5	0.000	0.001	0.004	0.015	0.040	0.089	0.165	0.269	0.392	0.522
10.0	0.000	0.000	0.003	0.010	0.029	0.067	0.130	0.220	0.333	0.458

	10	11	12	13	14	15	16	17	18	19
6.2	0.949	0.975	0.989	0.995	0.998	0.999	1.000			
6.4	0.939	0.969	0.986	0.994	0.997	0.999	1.000			
6.6	0.927	0.963	0.982	0.992	0.997	0.999	0.999	1.000		
6.8	0.915	0.955	0.978	0.990	0.996	0.998	0.999	1.000		
7.0	0.901	0.947	0.973	0.987	0.996	0.998	0.999	1.000		
7.2	0.887	0.937	0.967	0.984	0.993	0.997	0.999	0.999	1.000	
7.4	0.871	0.926	0.961	0.980	0.991	0.996	0.998	0.999	1.000	
7.6	0.854	0.915	0.954	0.976	0.989	0.995	0.998	0.999	1.000	
7.8	0.835	0.902	0.945	0.971	0.986	0.993	0.997	0.999	1.000	
8.0	0.816	0.888	0.936	0.966	0.983	0.992	0.996	0.998	0.999	1.000
8.5	0.763	0.849	0.909	0.949	0.973	0.986	0.993	0.997	0.999	0.999
9.0	0.706	0.803	0.876	0.926	0.959	0.978	0.989	0.995	0.998	0.999
9.5	0.645	0.752	0.836	0.898	0.940	0.967	0.982	0.991	0.996	0.998
10.0	0.583	0.697	0.792	0.864	0.917	0.951	0.973	0.986	0.993	0.997

	20	21	22
8.5	1.000		
9.0	1.000		
9.5	0.999	1.000	
10.0	0.998	0.999	1.000

Appendix III (continued)

λ OR np′	0	1	2	3	4	5	6	7	8	9
10.5	0.000	0.000	0.002	0.007	0.021	0.050	0.102	0.179	0.279	0.397
11.0	0.000	0.000	0.001	0.005	0.015	0.038	0.079	0.143	0.232	0.341
11.5	0.000	0.000	0.001	0.003	0.011	0.028	0.060	0.114	0.191	0.289
12.0	0.000	0.000	0.001	0.002	0.008	0.020	0.046	0.090	0.155	0.242
12.5	0.000	0.000	0.000	0.002	0.005	0.015	0.035	0.070	0.125	0.201
13.0	0.000	0.000	0.000	0.001	0.004	0.011	0.026	0.054	0.100	0.166
13.5	0.000	0.000	0.000	0.001	0.003	0.008	0.019	0.041	0.079	0.135
14.0	0.000	0.000	0.000	0.000	0.002	0.006	0.014	0.032	0.062	0.109
14.5	0.000	0.000	0.000	0.000	0.001	0.004	0.010	0.024	0.048	0.088
15.0	0.000	0.000	0.000	0.000	0.001	0.003	0.008	0.018	0.037	0.070

	10	11	12	13	14	15	16	17	18	19
10.5	0.521	0.639	0.742	0.825	0.888	0.932	0.960	0.978	0.988	0.994
11.0	0.460	0.579	0.689	0.781	0.854	0.907	0.944	0.968	0.982	0.991
11.5	0.402	0.520	0.633	0.733	0.815	0.878	0.924	0.954	0.974	0.986
12.0	0.347	0.462	0.576	0.682	0.772	0.844	0.899	0.937	0.963	0.979
12.5	0.297	0.406	0.519	0.628	0.725	0.806	0.869	0.916	0.948	0.969
13.0	0.252	0.353	0.463	0.573	0.675	0.764	0.835	0.890	0.930	0.957
13.5	0.211	0.304	0.409	0.518	0.623	0.718	0.798	0.861	0.908	0.942
14.0	0.176	0.260	0.358	0.464	0.570	0.669	0.756	0.827	0.883	0.923
14.5	0.145	0.220	0.311	0.413	0.518	0.619	0.711	0.790	0.853	0.901
15.0	0.118	0.185	0.268	0.363	0.466	0.568	0.664	0.749	0.819	0.875

	20	21	22	23	24	25	26	27	28	29
10.5	0.997	0.999	0.999	1.000						
11.0	0.995	0.998	0.999	1.000						
11.5	0.992	0.996	0.998	0.999	1.000					
12.0	0.988	0.994	0.997	0.999	0.999	1.000				
12.5	0.983	0.991	0.995	0.998	0.999	0.999	1.000			
13.0	0.975	0.986	0.992	0.996	0.998	0.999	1.000			
13.5	0.965	0.980	0.989	0.994	0.997	0.998	0.999	1.000		
14.0	0.952	0.971	0.983	0.991	0.995	0.997	0.999	0.999	1.000	
14.5	0.936	0.960	0.976	0.986	0.992	0.996	0.998	0.999	0.999	1.000
15.0	0.917	0.947	0.967	0.981	0.989	0.994	0.997	0.998	0.999	1.000

Appendix III (continued)

λ OR np \ c	4	5	6	7	8	9	10	11	12	13
16	0.000	0.001	0.004	0.010	0.022	0.043	0.077	0.127	0.193	0.275
17	0.000	0.001	0.002	0.005	0.013	0.026	0.049	0.085	0.135	0.201
18	0.000	0.000	0.001	0.003	0.007	0.015	0.030	0.055	0.092	0.143
19	0.000	0.000	0.001	0.002	0.004	0.009	0.018	0.035	0.061	0.098
20	0.000	0.000	0.000	0.001	0.002	0.005	0.011	0.021	0.039	0.066
21	0.000	0.000	0.000	0.000	0.001	0.003	0.006	0.013	0.025	0.043
22	0.000	0.000	0.000	0.000	0.001	0.002	0.004	0.008	0.015	0.028
23	0.000	0.000	0.000	0.000	0.000	0.001	0.002	0.004	0.009	0.017
24	0.000	0.000	0.000	0.000	0.000	0.000	0.001	0.003	0.005	0.011
25	0.000	0.000	0.000	0.000	0.000	0.000	0.001	0.001	0.003	0.006

	14	15	16	17	18	19	20	21	22	23
16	0.368	0.467	0.566	0.659	0.742	0.812	0.868	0.911	0.942	0.963
17	0.281	0.371	0.468	0.564	0.655	0.736	0.805	0.861	0.905	0.937
18	0.208	0.287	0.375	0.469	0.562	0.651	0.731	0.799	0.855	0.899
19	0.150	0.215	0.292	0.378	0.469	0.561	0.647	0.725	0.793	0.849
20	0.105	0.157	0.221	0.297	0.381	0.470	0.559	0.644	0.721	0.787
21	0.072	0.111	0.163	0.227	0.302	0.384	0.471	0.558	0.640	0.716
22	0.048	0.077	0.117	0.169	0.232	0.306	0.387	0.472	0.556	0.637
23	0.031	0.052	0.082	0.123	0.175	0.238	0.310	0.389	0.472	0.555
24	0.020	0.034	0.056	0.087	0.128	0.180	0.243	0.314	0.392	0.473
25	0.012	0.022	0.038	0.060	0.092	0.134	0.185	0.247	0.318	0.394

	24	25	26	27	28	29	30	31	32	33
16	0.978	0.987	0.993	0.996	0.998	0.999	0.999	1.000		
17	0.959	0.975	0.985	0.991	0.995	0.997	0.999	0.999	1.000	
18	0.932	0.955	0.972	0.983	0.990	0.994	0.997	0.998	0.999	1.000
19	0.893	0.927	0.951	0.969	0.980	0.988	0.993	0.996	0.998	0.999
20	0.843	0.888	0.922	0.948	0.966	0.978	0.987	0.992	0.995	0.997
21	0.782	0.838	0.883	0.917	0.944	0.963	0.976	0.985	0.991	0.994
22	0.712	0.777	0.832	0.877	0.913	0.940	0.959	0.973	0.983	0.989
23	0.635	0.708	0.772	0.827	0.873	0.908	0.936	0.956	0.971	0.981
24	0.554	0.632	0.704	0.768	0.823	0.868	0.904	0.932	0.953	0.969
25	0.473	0.553	0.629	0.700	0.763	0.818	0.863	0.900	0.929	0.950

	34	35	36	37	38	39	40	41	42	43
19	0.999	1.000								
20	0.999	0.999	1.000							
21	0.997	0.998	0.999	0.999	1.000					
22	0.994	0.996	0.998	0.999	0.999	1.000				
23	0.988	0.993	0.996	0.997	0.999	0.999	1.000			
24	0.979	0.987	0.992	0.995	0.997	0.998	0.999	0.999	1.000	
25	0.966	0.978	0.985	0.991	0.994	0.997	0.998	0.999	0.999	1.000

RANDOM DIGITS

52 01 77 67	75 24 63 38	49 35 24 94	21 81 65 44	29 27 49 45
80 50 54 31	64 05 18 81	54 99 76 54	38 55 37 63	82 29 16 65
45 29 96 34	26 89 80 93	96 31 53 07	28 60 26 55	08 03 36 06
68 54 02 00	45 42 72 68	80 80 83 91	40 05 64 18	43 62 76 59
59 46 73 48	01 39 09 22	05 88 52 36	38 21 45 98	17 17 68 33
48 11 76 74	87 37 92 52	17 90 05 97	08 92 00 48	19 92 91 70
12 43 56 35	20 11 74 52	23 46 14 06	05 08 23 41	40 30 97 32
35 09 98 17	01 75 87 53	56 54 14 30	22 20 64 13	62 38 85 79
91 62 68 03	19 47 60 72	15 51 49 38	70 72 58 15	49 12 56 24
89 32 05 05	36 16 81 08	86 43 19 94	20 73 17 90	27 38 84 35
35 44 13 18	45 24 02 84	08 62 48 26	58 26 05 27	50 07 39 98
37 54 87 30	41 94 15 09	18 51 62 32	21 15 94 66	77 56 78 51
94 62 46 11	96 38 27 07	95 10 04 06	92 74 59 73	71 17 78 17
00 38 75 95	71 96 12 82	75 24 91 40	70 14 66 70	60 91 10 62
77 93 89 19	98 14 50 65	63 33 25 37	52 28 25 62	47 83 41 13
80 81 45 17	77 55 73 22	02 94 39 02	49 91 45 23	68 47 92 76
36 04 09 03	80 99 33 71	17 84 56 11	33 69 45 98	26 94 03 68
88 46 12 33	52 07 98 48	66 44 98 83	10 48 19 49	85 15 74 79
15 02 00 99	31 24 96 47	32 47 79 28	55 07 37 42	11 10 00 20
01 84 87 69	87 63 79 19	07 49 41 38	60 64 93 29	16 50 53 44
09 73 25 33	60 97 09 34	10 94 05 58	19 69 04 46	26 45 74 77
54 20 48 05	29 40 52 42	72 56 82 48	47 44 52 66	95 27 07 99
42 26 89 53	18 47 54 06	74 67 00 78	55 72 85 73	67 89 75 43
01 90 25 29	90 36 47 64	76 66 79 51	48 11 62 13	97 34 40 87
80 79 99 70	93 78 56 13	82 60 89 28	52 37 83 17	73 20 88 98
06 57 47 17	73 03 95 71	04 77 69 74	65 33 71 24	76 52 01 35
06 01 08 05	21 11 57 82	31 82 23 74	23 28 72 95	64 89 47 42
26 97 76 02	45 52 16 42	23 60 02 10	90 10 33 93	19 64 50 93
57 33 21 35	76 62 11 39	93 68 72 03	78 56 52 01	09 37 67 07
79 64 57 53	96 29 77 88	42 75 67 88	70 61 74 29	80 15 73 61
99 90 88 96	94 75 08 99	16 28 35 54	85 39 41 18	34 07 27 68
43 54 85 81	53 14 03 33	29 73 41 35	97 11 89 63	45 57 18 24
15 12 33 87	57 60 04 08	97 92 65 75	84 96 28 52	02 05 16 56
86 10 25 91	96 64 48 94	86 07 46 97	20 82 66 95	05 32 54 70
01 02 46 74	43 65 17 70	21 95 25 63	05 01 45 11	03 52 96 47
79 01 71 19	65 39 45 95	92 43 37 29	80 95 90 91	67 35 48 76
33 51 29 69	82 39 61 01	36 78 38 48	20 63 61 04	80 52 40 37
38 17 15 39	91 19 04 25	62 24 44 31	15 95 33 47	20 90 25 60
29 53 68 70	03 07 11 20	86 84 87 67	88 67 67 43	31 13 11 65
58 40 44 01	26 25 22 96	93 59 14 16	98 95 11 68	03 23 66 53
39 09 47 34	61 96 27 93	86 25 10 25	65 81 33 98	69 73 61 70
88 69 51 19	54 69 28 23	11 96 38 96	86 79 90 94	30 34 26 14
25 01 62 52	77 97 45 00	35 13 54 62	73 05 38 52	66 57 48 18
74 85 22 05	13 02 12 48	60 94 97 00	28 46 82 87	55 35 75 48
05 45 56 14	93 91 08 36	28 14 40 77	60 93 52 03	80 83 42 82
52 52 75 80	86 74 31 71	56 70 70 07	14 90 56 86	17 46 85 09
56 12 71 92	18 74 39 24	95 66 00 00	39 80 82 77	17 72 70 80
09 97 33 34	66 67 43 68	41 92 15 85	06 28 89 80	77 40 27 72
32 30 75 75	59 04 79 00	66 79 45 43	86 50 75 84	66 25 22 91
10 51 82 16	01 54 03 54	88 88 15 53	87 51 76 49	14 22 56 85

APPENDIX V

Factors for Constructing Control Charts

Table I
FACTORS FOR ESTIMATING σ FROM $\bar{R}$

Estimate of $\sigma' = R/d_2$

NUMBER OF OBSERVATIONS IN SUBGROUPS n	FACTOR FOR ESTIMATE FROM $\bar{R}$ $d_2 = \bar{R} \backslash \sigma'$	NUMBER OF OBSERVATIONS IN SUBGROUPS n	FACTOR FOR ESTIMATE FROM $\bar{R}$ $d_2 = \bar{R} \backslash \sigma'$	NUMBER OF OBSERVATIONS IN SUBGROUPS n	FACTOR FOR ESTIMATE FROM $\bar{R}$ $d_2 = \bar{R} \backslash \sigma'$
		11	3.173	21	3.778
2	1.128	12	3.258	22	3.819
3	1.693	13	3.336	23	3.858
4	2.059	14	3.407	24	3.895
5	2.326	15	3.472	25	3.931
6	2.534	16	3.532	30	4.086
7	2.704	17	3.588	35	4.213
8	2.847	18	3.640	40	4.322
9	2.970	19	3.689	45	4.415
10	3.078	20	3.735	50	4.498

Table 2
FACTORS FOR DETERMINING FROM R THE 3-SIGMA CONTROL LIMITS FOR $\bar{X}$ AND R CHARTS

NUMBER OF OBSERVATIONS IN SUBGROUPS n	FACTOR FOR $\bar{X}$ CHART A_2	Factor for R Chart LOWER CONTROL LIMIT D_3	Factor for R Chart UPPER CONTROL LIMIT D_4
2	1.88	0.00	3.27
3	1.02	0.00	2.57
4	0.73	0.00	2.28
5	0.58	0.00	2.11
6	0.48	0.00	2.00
7	0.42	0.08	1.92
8	0.37	0.14	1.86
9	0.34	0.18	1.82
10	0.31	0.22	1.78
11	0.29	0.26	1.74
12	0.27	0.28	1.72
13	0.25	0.31	1.69
14	0.24	0.33	1.67
15	0.22	0.35	1.65
16	0.21	0.36	1.64
17	0.20	0.38	1.62
18	0.19	0.39	1.61
19	0.19	0.40	1.60
20	0.18	0.41	1.59

Upper control limit for $\bar{X} = \text{UCL}_{\bar{X}} = \bar{\bar{X}} + A_2\bar{R}$

Lower control limit for $\bar{X} = \text{LCL}_{\bar{X}} = \bar{\bar{X}} - A_2\bar{R}$

(If aimed-at or a standard value $\bar{X}'$ is used rather than $\bar{\bar{X}}$ as the central line on the control chart, $\bar{X}'$ should be substituted for $\bar{\bar{X}}$ in the preceding formulas.)

Upper control limit for $R = \text{UCL}_R = D_4\bar{R}$

Lower control limit for $R = \text{LCL}_R = D_3\bar{R}$

All factors in Table 2 are based on the normal probability distribution.

INDEX